Emmins on
Criminal Procedure

Emmins on Criminal Procedure

Ninth Edition

John Sprack, BA, LLB, Barrister

Full-time Chairman of Employment Tribunals;
formerly Reader, Inns of Court School of Law

OXFORD
UNIVERSITY PRESS

OXFORD

UNIVERSITY PRESS

Great Clarendon Street, Oxford OX2 6DP

Oxford University Press is a department of the University of Oxford.
It furthers the University's objective of excellence in research, scholarship,
and education by publishing worldwide in

Oxford New York

Auckland Bangkok Buenos Aires Cape Town Chennai
Dar es Salaam Delhi Hong Kong Istanbul Karachi Kolkata
Kuala Lumpur Madrid Melbourne Mexico City Mumbai Nairobi
São Paulo Shanghai Singapore Taipei Tokyo Toronto

and an associated company in Berlin

Oxford is a registered trade mark of Oxford University Press
in the UK and certain other countries

Published in the United States
by Oxford University Press Inc., New York

First edition published by Blackstone Press 1981

© Christopher J. Emmins and John Sprack 2002

The moral rights of the author have been asserted
Database right Oxford University Press (maker)

Ninth Edition first published 2002

Crown copyright material is reproduced with the permission of
Her Majesty's Stationery Office

British Library Cataloguing in Publication Data

Data available

Library of Congress Cataloging in Publication Data

Data available

ISBN 0-19-925350-1

3 5 7 9 10 8 6 4

Typeset by Style Photosetting Limited, Mayfield, East Sussex
Printed in Great Britain
on acid-free paper by
Antony Rowe Ltd, Chippenham

Contents — Summary

PART 4   SENTENCING

PART 5   APPEALS AND ANCILLARY MATTERS

Contents

PART 3   TRIAL ON INDICTMENT

PART 5   APPEALS AND ANCILLARY MATTERS

Preface

The new edition of *Emmins on Criminal Procedure* takes in a substantial number of changes which have been made, both legislatively and judicially, over the past couple of years. The most important of those changes are those which have resulted from what is loosely termed the incorporation of the European Convention on Human Rights into domestic law. This development has had impact throughout the field of criminal procedure. In particular, its jurisprudence has visibly affected the way in which the Court of Appeal undertakes its duties — putting emphasis on the fairness of the trial below, as well as the safety of the conviction. It has also caused us to look again at the way in which the decisions of the court of first instance should be for bias — reinstating the notion that it is not only actual bias, but its appearance which can affect justice. In addition, the law relating to disclosure and public interest immunity has been subject to the scrutiny of Strasbourg. The case of *Rowe and Davis v UK* (see Chapter 26) in its various manifestations, European and domestic, is particularly instructive in demonstrating the interplay between the European Court of Human Rights and the Court of Appeal, and showing the potential for injustice generated by our current law on disclosure.

During the time the new edition was in preparation, Sir Robin Auld released his sweeping review of the criminal justice system (see Appendix 8). Its proposals are both controversial and important, attracting admiration and anxiety in equal measure. They are likely to set the agenda for the debate about change in criminal procedure for the next few years, and the results may well affect the next edition of this work radically.

Meanwhile, two relatively recent creations — the Criminal Cases Review Commission and Panel the Sentencing Advisory Panel — have played an important part in promoting transparency and rationality in the criminal justice system.

At the other end of the spectrum of importance were a number of changes in sentencing terminology which reflected spin rather than substance, but added greatly to the burden of the jobbing author.

Not long before I embarked on this edition of the book, I retired from teaching at the Inns of Court School of Law, and began a new career late in life. I would like to thank all my colleagues at the ICSL (now proudly incorporated into City University), who have provided ideas, encouragement and stimulation for the production of this and previous editions. Finally, my thanks are due to the generations of students who have kept me and my colleagues on our toes over the years, and who are now no doubt performing the same service for the various tribunals before which they appear.

John Sprack
Ashford, Kent
2 July 2002

Preface to the First Edition

In writing this book I have tried to avoid the two main pitfalls which are present in many of the more traditional books on procedure. On the one hand there are those so filled with detail that it is almost impossible for the reader to keep sight of the main outlines of the subject. On the other hand it is tempting, for the sake of clarity, to deal with the main elements of court procedure only, but in so doing, omit many points which are necessary detail for the serious student of the subject.

I believe that this book steers a middle course between these two extremes and I am grateful to my publishers who have presented the book in such a way as to highlight the more important parts of the text. Matters of detail or interest, not essential to a broad understanding of the subject, have been printed in small type, slightly indented from the remainder of the text. The reader may therefore make use of the book at either of two levels. He may gain an overall view of the subject just by reading those parts of the book which are in large type; or he may acquire more detailed knowledge through reading in addition the paragraphs in small type. I have also used examples of the documents most commonly used in connection with criminal procedure either at the appropriate point in the text or in an imaginary Brief to Counsel on the case of John Smith. This further ensures that the book fully justifies its title as *A Practical Approach* to Criminal Procedure.

My thanks are due to my colleague at the Inns of Court School of Law, Miss Lynn Slater, BA, LLM, who has not only prepared the case and statute indexes, but also read the book as it was in the course of composition and made many invaluable suggestions for its improvement. My thanks also go to my publishers for their kindness and helpfulness, and, above all, to my parents for their unstinted support during the time the pages which follow were being written.

Walthamstow
17 September 1981

Table of Cases

Table of Statutes

Table of Statutory Rules and Orders and Statutory Instruments

PART 1   INTRODUCTION

1   Setting the Scene

Criminal trials in England and Wales take one of two forms. They are either trials on indictment or summary trials. Trial in the youth court, which might at first sight appear to be a third distinct form of trial, is in fact a special form of summary trial. Parts 2 and 3 of this book will deal in detail with, respectively, summary trial and trial on indictment. The following two Paragraphs will give an indication of the salient characteristics of the two methods of trial.

1.1   TRIAL ON INDICTMENT

Trial on indictment is the method used for trying the more serious offences. The trial takes place before judge and jury in the Crown Court. The name 'trial on indictment' originates from the formal written statement of charges, and it is to the 'counts' contained in this indictment that the accused pleads 'Guilty' or 'Not guilty' at the beginning of his trial.

The trial is presided over by a paid professional judge, who is or was a practising barrister or solicitor. The judge controls the course of the trial, adjudicates on all matters of the admissibility of evidence, and is the sole arbiter of matters of law in the case.

Matters of fact are decided by the jury, which consists of lay men and women, drawn at random from a broad cross-section of the community, who are summoned for a period usually of two weeks. It is by no means unusual for this to be their only experience of the judicial system. They must accept and apply the law as it is explained to them by the judge in his summing-up at the end of the case, but they alone decide questions of fact. Should the judge, when summing-up, comment on the weight of the evidence or indicate what facts he thinks have been proved thereby, the jury may — and indeed, should — ignore the judge's views entirely unless they happen to coincide with their own. Having heard the evidence, the speeches of counsel and the judge's summing-up, it is then the duty of the jury to bring in the verdict. Thus the general principle may be stated that at trial on indictment, 'the law is for the judge, and the facts are for the jury'.

1.2   SUMMARY TRIAL

Summary trial takes place in the magistrates' courts. At the commencement of the trial the accused pleads guilty or not guilty to a charge contained in a document called an information. The case is heard and determined by magistrates (also known as justices of the peace) who are the judges of both law and fact. The great majority of magistrates are lay men and women, but since most magistrates serve as such for many years, and will normally sit in court at least twice a month, they become familiar with summary proceedings and are not 'complete amateurs' like the average juror. In practice, too, magistrates tend to be drawn from a narrower social and age range than jurors (for details on appointment of magistrates see Chapter 5). A minority of magistrates are district judges, i.e., full-time, paid magistrates appointed from amongst barristers and solicitors of at least seven years' standing. One major difference between district judges and lay magistrates is that the former may, and normally do, sit alone to try cases, whereas at least two lay magistrates are required to try a case, and it is normal for them to sit in benches of three. Magistrates are entitled to seek advice from their clerk on matters of law, admissibility of evidence and procedure, but the decision on these matters remains solely for the magistrates. Clerks are qualified lawyers (for details on appointment see Chapter 5), and, in addition to their duties in advising magistrates, they play an important role in the smooth functioning of the court, both in court (e.g., putting the information to the accused) and behind the scenes (e.g., working on the issue of summonses). The merits and demerits of trial on indictment as opposed to summary trial are much debated. Some of the arguments are mentioned in Chapter 7.

1.3 CLASSES OF OFFENCES

For purposes of mode of trial, offences are divided into three major classes, namely: those triable only on indictment, those triable only summarily, and those triable either way. Chapter 7 explains in detail how to decide into which class a particular offence falls, but the broad principle is that the most serious offences (e.g., murder, manslaughter, robbery, rape, incest and causing grievous bodily harm with intent to do so) are triable only on indictment. Offences of medium gravity, especially those whose gravity varies greatly depending upon the facts of the particular case, are triable either way (e.g. theft, handling stolen goods, obtaining property by deception, most forms of burglary, non-aggravated criminal damage, assault occasioning actual bodily harm, unlawful wounding and indecent assault). The least grave offences are triable only summarily. Most of them are very trivial and are not even punishable with imprisonment. They do, however, include some relatively serious matters such as assaulting a police officer in the execution of his duty, interfering with a motor vehicle, drink-driving offences, using threatening words or behaviour, taking a motor vehicle without the owner's consent and driving while disqualified. Finally, it should be noted that special rules govern the trial of juveniles (i.e. those under 18). The effect of these rules is that many offences which are triable only on indictment or triable either way in the case of an adult must be tried summarily in a youth court if the accused is under 18.

Linked to the three-fold classification of offences described above is a simpler division between 'indictable offences' and 'summary offences'. Those terms are defined by Schedule 1 to the Interpretation Act 1978 as follows:

(a) 'Indictable offence' means an offence which, if committed by an adult, is triable on indictment, whether it is exclusively so triable or triable either way;

(b) 'Summary offence' means an offence which, if committed by an adult, is triable only summarily.

Also, the Interpretation Act, defines, not surprisingly, 'offence triable either way' as an offence which in the case of an adult, may be tried either on indictment or summarily.

Section 40 of the Criminal Justice Act 1988 created a sub-class of offences which, although normally triable only summarily, may be tried on indictment if linked to another offence which is going to be so tried (see Paragraph 7.5). As a result, the 1988 Act adds a rider to the definition, which makes it clear that an offence falling within this sub-class remains a summary offence.

The major point to note from the above definitions is that, when the term 'indictable offence' is used in a statute without further qualification, it encompasses not only offences that must be tried on indictment but also the numerous offences which, depending on the circumstances, may either be tried on indictment or tried summarily. Except when s 40 of the CJA 1988 (see above) applies, a summary offence can never be tried on indictment. By contrast, a great many indictable offences are tried summarily.

2 Preliminaries to Court Appearance

This Chapter aims to deal with what happens to a suspect between his initially being questioned by a police officer about an offence and his making his first court appearance. The subject is a wide-ranging one, involving evidence and constitutional law as well as procedure proper. The aim is to give an overall impression of what happens to a suspect, concentrating especially on police procedure and practice. For those aspects of the subject which are more properly the province of constitutional law or evidence (e.g. powers of arrest and search or the exclusion of inadmissible confessions), the reader is referred for details to *Blackstone's Criminal Practice,* especially sections D1 and F17.

2.1 'PACE' AND CODES OF PRACTICE

For most of the areas of law dealt with in this Chapter, the prime source of authority is the Police and Criminal Evidence Act 1984 and the Codes of Practice promulgated under s 67 thereof.

2.1.1 PACE

The Police and Criminal Evidence Act 1984, generally known as 'PACE', was passed as a result of the wide-ranging report of the Royal Commission on Criminal Procedure (the Philips Commission). To a large measure, the Act reflects the recommendations of the Report, although inevitably the Government departed from the Commission on points of detail. It has brought about a sea-change in several significant aspects of police procedure. Parts of the legislation were completely new (e.g., those sections dealing with the periods of time for which a suspect may be held at a police station without being charged); other parts built upon the pre-existing statute and common law (e.g., the provisions as to powers of arrest). Thus, to understand the Act, it is sometimes necessary to know a little of what preceded it. The Act is supplemented by the Codes of Practice, the importance of which is explained in the next Paragraph.

2.1.2 Codes of Practice

The provisions of PACE are principally concerned with police powers — e.g., to stop and search a member of the public, to search premises in order to find evidence of crime, to arrest a suspect, to detain him at the police station and to question him both before and after arrest. However, an Act would become unwieldy if it tried to do more than lay down a framework for the exercise of such powers. Detailed advice and regulations to cover even a representative sample of the vast range of different problems encountered by the police in the course of their investigations cannot be put into primary legislation. On the other hand, such detailed rules are desirable so that the police and public will know with reasonable certainty how an investigation ought to be conducted and what their respective rights and duties are. The solution adopted by PACE was to empower the Home Secretary to issue Codes of Practice covering certain aspects of police powers and procedure. The Codes are something of a constitutional oddity in that they are not statutory instruments (i.e., they have no legislative effect), but they were brought into operation by a statutory instrument, namely an order made by the Home Secretary which had to be approved by a resolution of each House of Parliament (see PACE, s 67(1)–(7)). Before the order was approved, draft Codes were laid before Parliament. There are five Codes presently in operation, entitled as follows: Code A (Code of Practice for the Exercise by Police Officers of Statutory Powers of Stop and Search), Code B (Code of Practice for the Searching of Premises by Police Officers and the Seizure of Property found by Police Officers on Persons or Premises), Code C (Code of Practice for the Detention, Treatment and Questioning of Persons by Police Officers), Code D (Code of Practice for the Identification of Persons by Police Officers) and Code E (Code of Practice on Tape Recording). They will hereafter be called, respectively, the 'Stop and Search Code', the 'Search of Premises Code', the 'Detention, Treatment and Questioning Code', the 'Identification Code' and the 'Tape Recording Code'. The Codes are published by and are obtainable from HMSO. Copies are kept at police stations, and are made available to detained suspects on request. Code C is the most important, and a reference simply to 'the Code' should be understood as referring to Code C.

The Codes are seen by the Home Office as a concise guide to the proper conduct of criminal investigations. Each Code commences with a paragraph which says that it must be 'readily available at all police stations for consultation by police officers, detained persons and members of the public'. Some of the material is a repetition in less formal language of what is also in PACE itself. Other parts of the Codes are an amplification and explanation of the Act, while yet other parts deal with subjects not directly covered by the primary legislation (e.g., the cautioning of suspects and the holding of identification parades). Any breach of a provision of a Code is not of itself a criminal offence or civil wrong, although in both civil and criminal proceedings the courts are obliged to take into account any provision of a Code which appears to be relevant to a question arising in the proceedings (s 67(10) and (11)). Thus, if evidence against an accused was obtained through breach of a Code, that is a matter which the defence can pray in aid when objecting to the admissibility of the evidence.

The Codes of Practice had no precise equivalent in the pre-1986 law. They are, however, roughly related to the Judges' Rules. Those were rules of practice, formulated by the judges for the guidance of police officers. They dealt with the cautioning of suspects (Rule II), the charging of suspects (Rule III), the taking of written statements under caution (Rule IV), and the showing of statements made by others to persons who had already been charged (Rule V). In addition, there was a Preamble which affirmed certain general principles relating to the questioning of suspects, whilst appended to the Rules were administrative directions (e.g., about giving refreshment to suspects at the police station) which were issued by the Home Office without the direct approval of the judiciary. Evidence obtained through breach of the Judges' Rules, notably confessions, might be excluded at the discretion of the trial judge. In practice, it was rare for that to happen, although a departure from the Rules provided a useful additional ground for the defence to rely upon when their basic argument was that the accused's confession was inadmissible because it had been made involuntarily as a result of police oppression.

2.1.3 Enforcing PACE and the Codes

The proper conduct of criminal investigations is not ensured merely by carefully defining police powers and offering wise guidance on how they should be exercised. It is essential that the police both stay within the powers given to them by PACE and observe the provisions of the Codes of Practice. This obvious truth was not lost upon the Philips Commission. They considered two basic methods of ensuring that such of their proposals as found favour with the legislature would be obeyed by the police. These were (a) to rely on the police to discipline themselves through bringing disciplinary charges against officers who breached PACE or the Codes, and (b) to enable the courts to exclude evidence which had been obtained illegally or unfairly. The Commission came down firmly on the side of the first method, almost to the exclusion of the second. They did not think that the rules on admissibility of evidence at criminal trials should be used as an indirect means of controlling the way the police gather evidence. The one exception to this was in respect of confessions obtained through actual or threatened violence which the Commission wanted automatically excluded so as to mark society's absolute disapproval of the use of force against suspects. Otherwise, they saw the recording of when and why police powers were exercised and the threat of disciplinary charges in cases of apparent excess as the best means of controlling police conduct. The original Police and Criminal Evidence Bill followed the Commission's recommendations, but at a late stage of the progress of the second Bill through Parliament Lord Scarman proposed an amendment which would have placed on the courts a duty to exclude illegally obtained evidence. The Government responded by bringing forward an amendment of its own, which was enacted as s 78 of PACE. As a result, there are now five main sanctions to discourage contravention of the Act and the Codes:

(a) If the contravention amounts to a criminal offence, the officer can be prosecuted in the normal way. For example, the carrying out of an unlawful search of premises might entail damage to the premises and hence a charge of criminal damage, or a prosecution for assault might result from either the effecting of an unlawful arrest or the use of violence to obtain a confession. In other words, being a member of the police confers no immunity against the operation of the criminal law. If the Crown Prosecution Service (CPS) are reluctant to prosecute, it is open to the victim to begin proceedings privately. The disadvantage with criminal proceedings is that proving a case beyond reasonable doubt against a police officer is difficult, especially if there is no independent evidence of what occurred, and anyway a successful prosecution will not directly benefit the victim.

(b) If the contravention of the Act or Codes amounts to a civil tort (e.g., assault, false imprisonment or malicious prosecution), the victim can sue the officers responsible. He may also join as a co-defendant the Chief Officer of Police for the force concerned, who is vicariously liable for the tortious conduct of his officers in the performance or purported performance of their duties. Any damages awarded against the Chief Officer will be paid out of the police fund. Subject to having the necessary evidence, this provides the victim with an effective remedy, although he may be discouraged from bringing a claim by the prospect of paying heavy costs if he loses.

(c) Whether or not it is also against the criminal or civil law, any contravention of a Code of Practice may be a disciplinary offence, covered by the police discipline regulations. The penalty can be as severe as dismissal from the force.

(d)   A contravention of PACE or the Codes (or any other illegal or unfair conduct) may result in the evidence which was thereby obtained being ruled inadmissible. This is the effect of s 78 of PACE, which provides that the court may exclude evidence on which the prosecution proposes to rely if 'having regard to all the circumstances, *including the circumstances in which the evidence was obtained*, the admission of the evidence would have such an adverse effect on the fairness of the proceedings that the court ought not to admit it'. Prior to the passing of PACE, the appellate courts wavered in their attitude to whether a judge was entitled to exclude evidence because of irregularities at the evidence-gathering stage. It was usually said that he did have such a discretion, although it ought to be exercised only in exceptional cases (see for example, *Kuruma v R* [1955] AC 197 and *Jeffrey v Black* [1978] 1 QB 490). Somewhat surprisingly, the House of Lords then ruled in *Sang* [1980] AC 402 that the discretion existed only in respect of a confession or analogous evidence coming from the accused himself. Thus, for example, a judge was not entitled to exclude evidence of incriminating articles found as a result of an illegal search. Section 78 clearly gives the court a discretion to exclude *any* illegally or unfairly obtained evidence whatever its nature or source, including evidence gathered in breach of a Code of Practice. The existence of that discretion has been confirmed by the Court of Appeal. For example, in *Quinn* [1990] Crim LR 581, Lord Lane CJ said:

> The function of the judge is . . . *to protect the fairness of the proceedings*, and normally proceedings are fair if a jury hears *all* relevant evidence which either side wishes to place before it, but proceedings may become unfair if, for example, one side is allowed to adduce relevant evidence which, for one reason or another, the other side cannot properly challenge or meet, or where there has been an abuse of process, e.g. because evidence has been obtained in deliberate breach of procedures laid down in an official code of practice.

(e)   If a contravention of PACE or the Codes leads to the accused making a confession, the contravention may, depending on its precise nature, either be sufficient of itself to make the confession inadmissible or be a contributory factor which — taken in conjunction with other circumstances — will have the same result. Thus, the general rule discussed in (d) is reinforced and extended in the particular case of irregularities leading to confessions (see Paragraph 2.5.1 for details).

In relation to both (d) and (e) above, judges at first instance and the Court of Appeal have, since the passing of PACE, shown a readiness to exercise the discretion in favour of the defence (see Paragraphs 2.5.3 and 2.5.5 in particular). This contrasts with the attitude which prevailed in the days of the Judges' Rules (see above).

2.2   COMMENCING A PROSECUTION: THE TWO BASIC METHODS

There are two basic methods of commencing a prosecution. One is for the police to arrest the suspect without a warrant; take him to the police station, and then (probably after a period of questioning at the station) formally charge him with the offence. The other is for the prosecutor to lay an information before a magistrate or a magistrates' clerk, alleging that the accused has committed the offence specified in the information. On the basis of the information, a summons is issued and served on the accused. The summons requires the accused to attend at the magistrates' court on a specified day to answer the allegation. There is nothing to prevent an accused being summoned in respect of an allegation of murder, but in general arrest and charge is considered appropriate in the more serious cases, laying an information and summons in the less serious ones.

Commencing a prosecution with a charge is an option available only to the police. The police, other prosecuting agencies and private individuals may all make use of summonses. Where the police prosecute by summons, they will almost certainly have first talked to the suspect about the offence and warned him that he might be prosecuted. There are a number of variations on the two basic procedures. For example, a private citizen may arrest a suspect without warrant and then hand him over to the police with a view to their preferring a charge. Or the police sometimes arrest a person, take him to the station, and then decide that the case is more conveniently dealt with by way of summons. They therefore release him without charge, informing him that consideration is still being given to the question of prosecuting him. Yet another possibility is for a magistrate before whom an information has been laid on oath to issue a warrant for the arrest of the person named in the information. This is much less likely than the issue of a summons because, if the allegation is serious enough to justify the issue of a warrant by a magistrate, the probability is that it will carry a power of arrest without warrant, thus rendering application for a warrant superfluous. A warrant for arrest might, however, be of value where the offence suspected does not carry a power of arrest, but serving a summons on the accused would be impracticable (e.g., because he is of no fixed abode).[1] The issue of a summons or warrant for arrest is known as the 'issue of process'.

2.3   ARREST WITHOUT WARRANT AND CHARGE

The pre-court stages in a police prosecution by way of arrest and charge are described in the Paragraphs below.

2.3.1   The arrest

The main power of arrest without warrant is contained in s 24 of PACE, which provides that a police officer may arrest any person whom he has reasonable grounds to suspect of having committed, committing or being about to commit an arrestable offence (s 24(6) and (7)). The section gives slightly less extensive powers to private citizens, who may arrest on reasonable suspicion that a person is committing an arrestable offence, but have no power to arrest on the basis that an offence is about to be committed and, if they arrest on reasonable suspicion that the arrestee has committed an arrestable offence, must show, in order to justify their actions, that somebody (not necessarily the arrestee) actually committed the offence suspected (s 24(4) and (5) and see also *Walters v W.H. Smith and Son Ltd* [1914] 1 KB 595 which established at common law the aforementioned limitation on the private citizen's powers of arrest). An arrestable offence is one punishable with five years' imprisonment or more (s 24(1)), plus a few specific offences mentioned in s 24(2) that do not carry five years but are none the less classified as arrestable (e.g., taking a motor vehicle without the owner's consent, certain sexual offences, and certain customs offences). PACE also preserves a number of powers of arrest granted to police officers by other legislation

---

[1]   In this situation the police do now have a power to arrest without warrant as a result of s 25 of PACE (see Paragraph 2.3.1), but the power is not enjoyed by other prosecuting agencies or private prosecutors.

— e.g., to arrest a person who has or is thought likely not to comply with the conditions of his bail (Bail Act 1976, s 7), or who is using violence to secure entry into any premises (Criminal Law Act 1977, s 6). Section 46A of PACE gives the police power to arrest an accused who fails to answer police bail. As regards non-arrestable offences in general, s 25 of PACE introduced a new power which allows the police (but not private citizens) to arrest on reasonable suspicion that such an offence has been or is being committed by the arrestee, but only if one of a number of *general arrest conditions* is satisfied. These conditions include (i) the arrestee refusing to give his name and address or giving details the correctness of which the officer reasonably doubts, and (ii) the officer reasonably believing that an arrest is necessary to prevent the arrestee harming himself or others, damaging property, committing an offence against public decency or obstructing the highway.

The legislation on powers of arrest repeatedly refers to the arrester reasonably suspecting the arrestee of committing or having committed an offence. Lord Devlin in *Hussien v Chong Fook Kam* [1970] AC 942 at p. 948 described suspicion as 'a state of conjecture or surmise where proof is lacking [which arises] at or near the starting point of an investigation'. It may be contrasted with a mere intuitive hunch based on no ground that could be rationally evaluated by a third party. In deciding whether he has grounds to arrest, an officer may take into consideration information which could not be used at any subsequent prosecution (e.g., knowledge that the arrestee has convictions for roughly similar offences, or an underworld 'tip-off that he committed the offence). Thus, an arrest is very often made while there is still insufficient evidence to charge the suspect with any offence, for a charge is not appropriate until the police have evidence admissible in court on the basis of which a conviction would be more likely than not. The mere fact that a police officer would be entitled to arrest somebody does not, of course, mean that he definitely ought to go ahead and do so. He should consider, as a matter of discretion, whether an arrest is really necessary or desirable, or whether the matter could better be dealt with by talking to the suspect and then reporting him with a view to any subsequent proceedings being taken by way of summons. The officer is, however, entitled to take into consideration the fact that, by arresting the suspect, he gains the advantage of being able to question him at the police station where he may, perhaps, be more likely to confess than in the security of his own home (see *Holgate-Mohammed v Duke* [1983] AC 437). Provided the officer acted in good faith, it is most unlikely that a civil action for wrongful arrest could ever be maintained against him on the basis that, although he had power to arrest the claimant, he should in his discretion have refrained from exercising the power.

Serious arrestable offence
As well as defining arrestable and non-arrestable offences, PACE distinguishes between *serious arrestable offences* and non-serious ones. The distinction has no direct relevance to powers of arrest, but it is important in the context of the period for which an arrestee may subsequently be detained at the police station and his rights while there (see Paragraphs 2.3.5 and 2.5.3 especially). A semi-definition of 'serious' is contained in s 116 and Schedule 5. Certain offences are always serious regardless of their individual facts and circumstances. The main ones are murder, manslaughter, rape, intercourse with a girl under 13, buggery with a person under 16, certain firearms and drug trafficking offences and causing death by dangerous driving. An arrestable offence which is not automatically serious (and these will include the commonest offences of violence and dishonesty) is to be regarded as serious only if it did have or was intended or was likely to have any of the following consequences: serious harm to the State or public order; or serious interference with the administration of

justice; *or* the death of or serious injury to any person; *or* substantial financial gain to any person; *or* serious financial loss to any person. This last is judged by the effect of the loss on the person sustaining it so that a series of petty thefts from victims on low income may come within the definition.

Some indication of what the courts will regard as serious arrestable offences emerges from *McIvor* [1987] Crim LR 409, where Sir Frederick Lawton LJ, sitting at first instance, held that a conspiracy to steal dogs from the kennels of a hunt which resulted in the loss of 28 dogs valued at £880 was not a serious offence in that there was no serious financial loss to the relatively prosperous hunt.

2.3.2   Action on and after arrest

The arrest is effected *either* by using a form of words that makes it clear to the arrestee that he is no longer free to come and go as he chooses, or by physically seizing or touching his person and telling him as soon as practicable thereafter that he is under arrest: *Alderson v Booth* [1969] 2 QB 216 and PACE, s 28(1). The arrestee must also be told the reason for the arrest, even if it is obvious: s 28(3) and (4). The reason given need not, however, be in precise technical language (*Abbassy v Metropolitan Police Commissioner* [1990] 1 WLR 385). If a reason for arrest is given that is inadequate in law (e.g., because the offence mentioned does not carry a power of arrest), the fact that the arrester had other suspicions which would have justified him in detaining the suspect does not validate the arrest: *Christie v Leachinsky* [1947] AC 573.

Often an arrest follows some conversation between the officer and a suspect during which the officer asks questions with a view to establishing whether an arrest is in fact called for. In such cases, the officer ought to have cautioned the suspect immediately he had grounds to suspect him of an offence (see para 10.1 of the Code and Paragraph 2.5.2). The caution was formerly to the effect that the suspect did not have to say anything unless he wished to do so, but anything he said may be given in evidence. The Criminal Justice and Public Order Act 1994, s 34, which provides that in certain circumstances the court may draw inferences from the accused's silence, necessitated a radical change in the nature of the caution. The caution now reads:

> You do not have to say anything. But it may harm your defence if you do not mention when questioned something which you later rely on in court. Anything you do say may be given in evidence.

If no caution was administered before arrest, it must be given upon arrest (unless rendered impracticable by the arrestee's behaviour) (the Code, para 10.3).

Once the arrest has been made, the arrestee should be taken to the police station forthwith, unless there are investigations which it is reasonable to carry out immediately in his presence at a place other than the station: s 30(1) and (10). The reason for insisting that, in general, the officer and his suspect go straight to the police station is that the various procedures prescribed by the Act and the Code to protect suspects can only operate effectively at a station. 'Taking the scenic route' there thus creates an opportunity for improper pressure to be brought on the arrestee but evidence obtained in such circumstances is now likely to be excluded under s 78 of PACE. The exception to the rule reflects the common law (see *Dallison v Caffery* [1965] 1 QB 348 where taking the arrestee first to his home — which was searched with his permission — and then to his place of work to check out an alibi was held to be a justifiable detour on the way to the station).

2.3.3 Initial action at the station

Upon arrival at the police station the arresting officers and their arrestee report to the *custody officer* (who is often called the custody sergeant). He is an officer of at least the rank of sergeant who must be unconnected with the investigation (see PACE, s 36 for details of appointment, etc. of custody officers). His role is to ensure that, while the arrestee (henceforward referred to as the 'detainee') is in detention at the police station, he is properly treated in accordance with the Codes of Practice and the Act: s 39(1). Since the custody officer is not personally involved in the enquiry, he can take a more detached view of proceedings than the investigating officers and will not be tempted to bend the rules in the way the latter might. Should there be a conflict between him and a more senior investigating officer as to how the detainee should be dealt with (e.g. should he be released or detained for further questioning?), the dispute must be referred to the station superintendent: PACE, s 39(6). Otherwise the custody officer always has the last word in such matters.

At the outset of his time at the police station the detainee must be told by the custody officer of his rights to free, independent and private legal advice, to have somebody named by him informed of his arrest and to read the Codes of Practice (para 3.1 of the Code). In addition he should be given a written notice repeating those rights and also setting out the words of the caution. Next the custody officer should open a *custody record*. This, as the name implies, is a standard-form document recording the essential details of what happens to the detainee at the station. He is entitled to a copy on request, and such a copy may well prove useful to his lawyers in, for example, seeking to exclude a confession made at the station. Amongst the items that should go into the record are: the reason why the arrestee is being detained; an acknowledgement, signed by him, that he has received the written statement of his rights; an indication (again signed) of whether he wants legal advice; a list of his property together with a list of anything that is taken from him; details of all visits he receives; the times at which meals are served to him; the time and place of any caution; the times at which he is handed over to the investigating officers for questioning; the time of his being charged and anything he says in response, and any complaints made by him about improper treatment. Other matters to be recorded will be mentioned in the course of the succeeding Paragraphs. Section 2 of the Code deals with the custody record.

One of the first things to go into the custody record is a list of the property which the detainee brought with him to the police station: s 54(1). In order to ascertain what property he has, the custody officer may order that he be *searched:* s 54(6). In addition, there is a general discretion to seize and retain anything found as a result of the search, save that clothing and personal effects may be seized only if *either* the custody officer believes that the detainee might use them to injure himself or others, to damage property, to interfere with evidence or to assist in an escape, *or* there are reasonable grounds for believing that they might be evidence of an offence: s 54(3) and (4). A search should not be regarded as the automatic result of being taken to the police station under arrest, but the custody officer will usually order at least a perfunctory turning out of the pockets. If it seems justified by the circumstances, however, he may order anything up to a full strip search, but not an intimate body search (see Paragraph 2.6.3). Property taken from the detainee should be restored to him on his release from the station unless it is required for use as evidence.

2.3.4 Consideration of the evidence

Once the initial formalities are completed, the custody officer has to consider the evidence against the detainee: PACE, s 37(1). If it appears that he should never have been arrested in the first place, he will order his immediate release. Otherwise, the question is whether there is already enough evidence to charge him with an offence — i.e. evidence on which a conviction is more likely than not. If there is, the custody officer should require the investigating officers to choose between preferring a charge (which would be the usual course to adopt) and releasing the detainee without charge. The latter course might be taken when, for the kind of discretionary reasons discussed in Chapter 4, the police feel that it is not in the public interest to commence a prosecution even though the evidence amply warrants it. A half-way house is to utilise the power given to the police by s 47(3)(b) of PACE to bail the detainee on condition he return to the station on a stated day. During the interim, a decision can be taken as to the desirability of a prosecution, and, if need be, the detainee can be charged when he answers to his bail. Alternatively, the detainee can be released unconditionally from the police station, with a warning that consideration will be given to the question of whether to prosecute him. Proceedings may then be commenced by information and summons (see Paragraph 4.1). Once a suspect has been charged, he may not, in general, be asked any further questions about the offence (see Paragraph 2.5.2). It follows that a decision by the custody officer as to whether there is enough evidence to charge a detainee effectively prevents the investigating officers interrogating him at the police station, since he then either has to be charged (with the effect on questioning just noted) or has to be released.

If, however, there is sufficient material to justify the arrest but not enough evidence to found a charge, the custody officer may sanction *detention without charge,* provided he has reasonable grounds for believing such detention to be necessary:

(i)   to secure or preserve evidence relating to the offence for which the detainee is under arrest, *or*
(ii) to obtain such evidence by questioning him.

Thus, s 37(2) sanctions detention without charge for questioning at the discretion of the custody officer. The custody officer's reasons should be entered in the custody record and also given to the detainee orally: s 37(4) and (5).

2.3.5   Detention without charge

Sections 40–44 of PACE set out a complicated timetable for detention without charge, only an outline of which will be attempted here. The timetable represents a compromise between the principled argument that any statement a suspect makes against his own interests should be totally voluntary, and the pragmatic view that — unless some pressure is brought to bear through skilled questioning in the hostile environment of a police station — hardly anybody would ever confess, with dire consequences for the criminal justice system. The main stages in detention without charge are as follows:

(i)   *Within six hours.*   Within six hours of the custody officer's decision to allow detention without charge, a *review officer* must consider whether it is still proper so to hold the detainee. Essentially he goes through the same sequence of questions as did the custody sergeant, asking whether there is by now enough evidence to charge the detainee and, if not, whether further detention without charge is justified on either of the two grounds mentioned in s 37(2) (see Paragraph 2.3.4 for s 37(2)). The review officer must be of at least the rank of inspector and, like the custody officer, may not be directly involved in the investigation.

He should give the detainee and/or his legal representative an opportunity to make representations about the validity of continued detention. If the decision goes against the detainee, the reasons for it must be given to him orally and also entered in the custody record.

(ii) *Within fifteen hours.* Within nine hours of the holding of the first one, a second review must be held. Thereafter reviews are required at no more than nine-hourly intervals. This applies even if detention without charge has been authorised by the station superintendent and/or magistrates under (iii)–(v) below. It also applies if the detainee has been charged but still not released, although at that stage the custody officer himself can act as reviewing officer.

(iii) *Within twenty-four hours.* Within twenty-four hours a detainee must be released or charged unless his continued detention without charge has been authorised by the *station superintendent*. The twenty-four hours runs from the 'relevant time' — i.e., the time the detainee arrived at the station or (if he initially attended voluntarily but was arrested at the station — see Paragraph 2.3.9), the time he was told he was no longer free to leave.[2] In order to authorise continued detention, the superintendent must be satisfied that at least one of the matters of which the detainee is suspected is a serious arrestable offence. In other words, detainees suspected only of non-serious matters can never be held for more than a day without charge. Assuming there is suspicion of a serious arrestable offence, the superintendent must have reasonable grounds for believing that (a) one or other of the grounds for detention without charge mentioned in s 37(2) still applies, and (b) the investigation is being conducted diligently and expeditiously. Again there are provisions for allowing the detainee or his solicitor to make representations and for noting the reasons for continued detention in the custody record. If the detainee has not yet exercised his rights to consult a solicitor and/or have somebody informed of his arrest, the superintendent must remind him of the rights and decide whether he should be permitted to exercise them. Subject to one exception, the station superintendent cannot authorise detention without charge for a period extending beyond thirty-six hours from the relevant time.

(iv) *Within thirty-six hours.* Within thirty-six hours of the relevant time, the detainee must be released or charged unless a magistrates' court has issued a *warrant of further detention*. An application for such a warrant must be made by a police officer on oath, and must be supported by a written information giving the nature of the offence for which the detainee was arrested and the evidence justifying the arrest, the inquiries which have been or are going to be made, and the reason why the inquiries require the continued detention of the detainee. The hearing is in camera before at least two magistrates. The detainee is entitled to free legal representation. In order to grant a warrant, the magistrates must be satisfied:

(a) that the detainee is being held for a serious arrestable offence;

(b) that his continued detention is necessary to secure or preserve evidence of the offence or to obtain such evidence by questioning him; and

(c) that the investigation is being conducted diligently and expeditiously.

Those are, in fact, the same matters as the station superintendent had to be satisfied about in order to allow detention beyond twenty-four hours. If a warrant is granted, it may be for

---

[2] There are more complex rules, e.g., where a person sought in one police area arrives at a station in another area: see *Blackstone's Criminal Practice*, D1.29.

a period not exceeding thirty-six hours. The Magistrates' Association have indicated that, within reason, their members are prepared to consider applications for warrants of further detention on any day and outside normal court hours. However, should it not be possible for a court to sit at the time the thirty-six hour period expires, the police may hold the detainee for a further six hours, although they then run the risk of having the warrant refused if they acted unreasonably in not applying for a warrant earlier. It would, it is submitted, be unreasonable to hold a detainee for forty-two hours without charge if — although a court could not sit at literally the moment the thirty-six hours expired — one was sitting at the thirty-fifth hour.

(v) *After seventy-two hours.*   Although the period specified in a warrant of further detention is limited to thirty-six hours, the magistrates may subsequently extend the period. Precisely the same rules apply to an application for extension as apply to the original application for a warrant. Although more than one extension may be made, the extended period must not be such as to expire more than ninety-six hours from the relevant time.

(vi) *After ninety-six hours.*   It follows from (v) above that the maximum period a detainee can be held without charge is ninety-six hours running from the relevant time. At the end of that period he must either be released or charged.

As mentioned in Paragraph 2.3.3, the custody officer has the primary responsibility for ensuring that a person in police detention is properly treated in accordance with PACE and the Codes. Paras 8.1 to 8.12 of the Code are headed 'Conditions of Detention' and deal with matters such as the state of the cells; the visiting of the detainee at no more than hourly intervals; the provision of food (two light meals and one main meal per day); the provision of exercise if practicable and access to toilet and washing facilities. If the investigating officers wish to question the detainee, they must persuade the custody officer to release him into their custody (see para 12.1 of the Code). If he agrees to do so, they become responsible for the detainee's treatment, and must report on how they have discharged that responsibility when they return him to the custody officer's charge: PACE, s 39(2) and (3). The rules governing the questioning of a suspect in detention are considered in Paragraph 2.5.2.

2.3.6   Charging the detainee

As soon as the investigating officers consider that there is enough evidence for a successful prosecution, and that the detainee has said all that he wishes to say about the offence, they must take him before the custody officer, who is then responsible for deciding whether to charge him. Assuming that the custody officer decides to charge him, the procedure outlined in paras 16.1 to 16.3 of the Code has to be followed. The detainee is cautioned in terms identical to those laid out in Paragraph 2.3.2. The charge is then written down on the charge sheet and read over to him. Any reply he makes is recorded, and he is supplied with a written notice repeating the charge and caution, and also stating the name of the officer in the case and the case's police reference number. Once a detainee or other suspect has been charged, it is more appropriate to refer to him as 'the accused'. The wording of a charge is the same or similar to the wording of an information (see Paragraph 9.3). Indeed, a copy of the charge sheet is delivered to the magistrates' court at which the accused will be appearing and is traditionally treated as the information to which he will be asked to plead guilty or not guilty should there be a summary trial.

2.3.7 Can persons who are not police officers commence prosecutions by way of charge?

Before PACE 1984, non-police officers who had effected a citizen's arrest would take the suspect to the police station, and ask for a charge to be preferred. The individual might then be asked to sign the charge sheet. This would indicate that, from then on, he (rather than the police) would be responsible for a (private) prosecution. The legality of this procedure was called into question in *Ealing Justices ex p Dixon* [1990] 2 QB 91. There, the standing of the private prosecutor was successfully challenged at the magistrates' court, and the proceedings were dismissed. The private prosecutor applied for judicial review, but the Divisional Court upheld the magistrates. The prosecution had been commenced by the police. That being so, only the CPS could conduct it: Prosecution of Offences Act 1985, s 3(2). They could authorise an agent to prosecute but had not done so.

Ex p Dixon was, however, expressly disapproved in *Stafford Justices ex parte Customs and Excise Commissioners* [1991] 2 QB 339. In that case, L was arrested without warrant. She was subsequently charged under the Drug Trafficking Offences Act 1986, s 24(1)(a). The charge was drafted by a customs officer, who took her to a police station where the custody officer formally charged her. At the subsequent old-style committal, it was submitted that the justices had no jurisdiction to commit since Customs and Excise had no standing to prosecute (relying on *Ex p Dixon*). The justices dismissed the case. They based their decision on the Prosecution of Offences Act 1985, s 3(2)(a), which states that it is the duty of the Director of Public Prosecutions to take over the conduct of all criminal proceedings (other than proceedings specified by order of the Attorney-General) which have been 'instituted on behalf of a police force'. The justices ruled that this prosecution had been instituted on behalf of a police force, so that only the Crown Prosecution Service (on behalf of the Director of Public Prosecutions) could conduct the case. The Commissioners of Customs and Excise sought judicial review and a declaration that they could prosecute under the Drug Trafficking Offences Act 1986, notwithstanding that a police officer had charged the accused. The Divisional Court granted the applications, holding that *Ex p Dixon* had been wrongly decided. The reasoning in *Stafford Justices* was followed in *Croydon Justices ex p Holmberg* (1993) 157 JP 277, where it was held that seeking police assistance did not turn proceedings brought by a local authority into proceedings brought on behalf of a police force.

2.3.8 Release or detention after charge

Once a detainee has been charged with an offence, the custody officer must order his release from the station unless either:

(a)   the detainee has refused to give his name and address; *or*
(b)   there are reasonable grounds for the custody officer to believe any of the following:
   (i)   the name and address furnished are not genuine; or
   (ii)   the detainee will not answer bail; or
   (iii)   (where the offence charged is imprisonable) his detention is necessary to prevent him committing a further offence; or
   (iv)   (where the offence charged is non-imprisonable) his detention is necessary to prevent him causing injury to another or loss of or damage to property; or
   (v)   his detention is necessary to prevent him from interfering with the administration of justice or the investigation of an offence; or

(vi) his detention is necessary for his own protection (PACE, s 38(1), as amended by CJPOA 1994, s 28).

Should the custody officer decide further to detain a charged detainee, and it is intended that the proceedings against him shall be in the local magistrates' court, he must be brought before the court 'as soon as is practicable', and in any event not later than its first scheduled sitting after the charge: PACE, s 46(2). If no sitting is arranged for the day after the day of the charge, the clerk of court must be notified that the police have a detainee who ought to come before the court, and the clerk then arranges for a special sitting: s 46(3) and (6)–(8). This does not apply if the day after charge is a Sunday. Since most courts have scheduled sittings for each weekday, the broad effect of s 46 is that a detainee must be brought before the court on the day after he is charged (special Saturday sittings being arranged for those charged on Friday), save that a detainee charged on Saturday may be held over until the following Monday. If the police wish the proceedings to be in a magistrates' court other than the local one, the detainee is moved to a police station near to the other court, and the time-restrictions in s 46 take effect from the moment of arrival at the second station.

Most detainees are bailed once they have been charged, if only because of lack of space to keep them at the station. One condition of bail is that they attend at the appropriate magistrates' court on a certain day to answer the charge that has been preferred against them. Usually the day named will be only a very short time ahead, but there is a growing practice to grant 'extended bail' — i.e., to allow something like a fortnight to elapse between bail from the station and the first court appearance, during which time the accused may consult solicitors and apply for legal aid.

2.3.9 'Helping police with their enquiries'

So far this account of the procedure for arrest without warrant and charge has proceeded on the assumption that there are just two classes of person for these purposes, namely those who have been arrested and may therefore be detained at the station for the periods prescribed by PACE, and those who are not under arrest. As a matter of pure law, that assumption is entirely correct. It always was so at common law and it has been confirmed by s 29 of PACE. In real life, though, there is a third category of suspect, namely those who are 'helping police with their enquiries'. Such a person has not formally been arrested — the police have merely invited him to come to the station where he may be questioned more conveniently, and he has agreed to their request. Rightly or wrongly, though, the suspect probably thinks that, if he does not voluntarily accompany the police, they will simply arrest him. At the station, he may well feel under as much pressure and be as much in need of protection as an arrestee. Therefore, to protect this category of suspect, para 10.2 of the Code states that, when he is initially cautioned at the police station (or other premises, which presumably would include his home), he must be told that he is not under arrest and is not obliged to remain with the officer. Moreover, if he does choose to remain, he may obtain legal advice. Should the police decide that somebody who has come to the station voluntarily ought to be arrested, they simply inform him that he is no longer free to leave. The timetable for detention without charge then runs from the moment of their so informing him.

2.3.10 Unco-operative detainees

Several parts of the arrest and charge procedure depend on the arrestee/detainee affording the police officers at least a minimum degree of cooperation. It would obviously be absurd if the police were to be blamed for not complying with the provisions of PACE and the Codes if the only reason for their not doing so was the recalcitrance of the subject of their attentions. Accordingly, s 28 (which deals with the information to be given to a person on arrest) only places upon the arrester a duty to tell the arrestee the grounds of the arrest 'as soon as is practicable', which means that if the arrestee behaves in such a way that communication with him is impossible he cannot subsequently claim that the arrest was unlawful because he was not immediately informed of the grounds. Similarly, the custody officer's duty to explain to an arrestee why he is authorising his detention (see Paragraph 2.3.4) does not apply if he is incapable of understanding what is said to him, violent or likely to become violent, or in need of urgent medical attention (see PACE, ss 37(6) and 38(5)). Where the proper procedure for keeping the custody record requires the detainee to sign something (e.g., an acknowledgement that he has received the notice setting out his rights at the station) but he refuses to do so, the custody officer should simply record the refusal (see para 2.7 of the Code). Lastly, if the custody officer considers that there is enough evidence to prefer a charge but the detainee is not in a fit state for that to be done (e.g., he is drunk), he may be held until he has recovered: s 37(9). The special provisions which govern the treatment of juveniles and other vulnerable groups are summarised in Paragraph 2.8.

2.4 ISSUE OF PROCESS

Prosecutions which are not begun by the accused being arrested without warrant and charged are begun by the laying of an information and the issue of process — i.e., the issue of a summons or a warrant for arrest. Paragraph 2.4.1 gives an outline of the main stages in a typical police prosecution by way of summons. Various aspects of the procedure are then looked at in more detail in Paragraphs 2.4.2 to 2.4.6.

2.4.1 The main stages

It will be convenient to relate this description of the information and summons procedure to an imaginary prosecution for careless driving. Of course, it must not be thought that summonses are only used in road traffic cases. As already explained, an offence may be prosecuted by summons whatever its nature and however grave. Nevertheless, the typical use of a summons is in respect of minor offences in general and road traffic matters in particular.

(a) *Speaking to the suspect.* PC Smith on foot patrol in Casterbridge High Street sees a car pass him at a speed he estimates at 50 m.p.h. A short distance down the street, the car brakes sharply and pulls partly on to the wrong side of the road to pass vehicles parked on its own side. In doing so, it scrapes the side of a van coming in the opposite direction. The officer hurries to the scene of the accident, and sees from the position of the vehicles and the debris that the van had apparently stayed on its correct side of the road. Having ascertained that neither driver needs medical attention, he establishes the name and address of the car driver, and asks to see his licence and certificate of insurance. What the officer has himself observed is sufficient to give him grounds for suspecting that the car driver (a Mr Speedy) has committed one or more driving offences. The officer must therefore caution him — the obligation to caution a suspect is as applicable to minor cases as it is to serious ones. Having listened to the caution, Speedy says: 'I thought the van was going to pull in and wait for me'. The officer then speaks to the van driver, who claims that he was in no way to blame for the accident and would like to see 'that maniac' (pointing to Speedy) prosecuted.

(b) *Warning of prosecution.* PC Smith considers that the evidence against Speedy is sufficient to justify criminal proceedings. He cannot arrest him because none of the offences of which he suspects him carry a power of arrest. Neither do any of the general arrest conditions (which permit arrest for a non-arrestable offence — see Paragraph 2.3.1) apply to Speedy. Had he refused to give his name or given an unsatisfactory address, he might have been arrested, but the officer has no grounds for doubting the information he has received on those points. So, instead of arresting Speedy, the officer warns him that he will be reported and that consideration will be given to prosecuting him for dangerous driving, careless driving and speeding. It is always good practice for the police to warn a suspect if they are considering proceeding against him by way of summons, but in the case of certain road traffic offences it is a pre-condition of a conviction that the accused was given notice of intended prosecution either orally at the time of the alleged offence or in writing within 14 days (see ss 1 and 2 of the Road Traffic Act 1988). Speedy is then allowed to go on his way and the officer returns to the police station.

(c) *Decision to prosecute.* PC Smith makes a report of the incident to the police process department. As well as the report, they have a written statement from the van driver, who says he is willing to testify against Speedy. In the light of the evidence and the factors discussed in Chapter 4, they decide whether to prosecute or to deal with the matter in some other way (e.g., sending Speedy a written caution). Their view is that there is clear evidence of carelessness, but that dangerous driving would be difficult to establish and that a prosecution for speeding would fail because the only evidence of Speedy having been over the limit is PC Smith's uncorroborated opinion. They also feel that Speedy's driving was too bad to be glossed over with a caution. Therefore, the decision is to prosecute for careless driving.[3]

(d) *Preparing an information.* Next an information is prepared. A busy police station will deal with literally thousands of prosecutions by way of summons during the course of a year. If they laid oral informations in each case (i.e., went to the local magistrates' court and told a magistrate on oath what the accused did), the work of both the court and the station would grind to a halt. So, the standard procedure is to use a written information. This may be based on a form for informations given in the Magistrates' Courts (Forms) Rules 1981 (SI 1981 No 553 — see page 23 for an example). The essential matters which it must contain are the name and address of the accused; the name, number and station of the reporting officer, and brief particulars of the offence alleged (see Paragraph 9.3 for the wording of an information). It should be signed by the informant. Omitting the formal parts, the information against Speedy might be as follows:

Date: 1 August 2002.
Accused: James Arthur SPEEDY
Address: 10 The Esplanade, SANDITON, Hardyshire.
Alleged offence: On the 28th day of July 2002 did drive a motor vehicle, namely a Vauxhall Cavalier motor car registration number F999 XYZ, on a road, namely the High Street, Casterbridge, without due care and attention, contrary to s 3 of the Road Traffic Act 1988.
The information of: John Smith PC 50B.
Address: Casterbridge Police Station, Law Street, CASTERBRIDGE.

Police forces vary as to whose signature appears on an information — sometimes it is that of the officer who reported the offence; sometimes it is the rubber-stamped signature of a

---

[3] In particularly important or complex cases, they might seek the advice of the CPS. In a simple case such as this, however, the CPS would become involved only at a late stage.

senior officer or of the chief officer of the force. In strict theory, whoever signs the information is the prosecutor, but the courts take the realistic view that where the prosecution is brought by the police it does not matter which individual officer puts his name to it. Thus, in *Hawkins v Bepey* [1980] 1 WLR 419 the death of the nominal informant between the dismissal of the information and the commencement of an appeal by case stated did not affect the right of the police force of which he had been a member to take the case to the Divisional Court.

In the case of a prosecution initiated by the police, the information should be signed by an individual officer. In *Rubin v DPP* [1990] 2 QB 80, an information against R for speeding was preferred by 'The Thames Valley Police'. The Divisional Court held that the Thames Valley Constabulary could not be regarded as the prosecutor. The defect did not, however, nullify the proceedings. There was no injustice, since R could easily have ascertained who the real prosecutor was by enquiring of the police force which constable had laid the information.

On the other hand, where authority is given by statute only to specified persons to sign the information, the right person must sign it or else the information will be invalid. In *Norwich Justices ex p Texas Homecare Ltd* [1991] Crim LR 555, informations were laid against TH alleging unlawful Sunday trading. They were signed by the senior environmental health officer, who had no authority to initiate proceedings under the Shops Act 1950. When this was discovered, the informations were amended to show the deputy director of administration as informant. The justices allowed these informations to stand, and TH was convicted. The Divisional Court quashed their decision. The information was the basis of jurisdiction. It was invalid, and not curable by amendment because of the statutory requirements as to the initiation of proceedings.

(e) *Laying the information.* The written information is delivered to the appropriate magistrates' court, probably the court for the petty sessional area in which the offence occurred. The information against Speedy will just be one of a bundle sent by the prosecutions department of Casterbridge police to the Casterbridge magistrates' court. Together with the information, the police will send several copies of a corresponding summons which they expect one of the magistrates or a magistrates' clerk to issue on the basis of the information. The information is treated as having been laid as soon as it is received in the clerk's office at the magistrates' court: *Manchester Stipendiary Magistrate ex p Hill* [1983] 1 AC 328. This is important because of the rule that an information for a summary matter must be laid within six months of commission of the offence (Magistrates' Courts Act 1980, s 127, and see Paragraph 9.3). Provided the information is received in the office within the six months, it does not matter that nobody considers it until after that time.

(f) *Issuing a summons.* The information is put before a magistrate or magistrates' clerk — more probably the latter. He checks that it is prima facie a valid information. If it is, he issues a summons by signing the draft summonses which the police have delivered with the information. Or he may simply affix his signature with a rubber stamp, or even — provided he has actually considered the information — authorise an assistant in the clerk's office to use the rubber stamp (see *Brentford Justices ex p Catlin* [1975] QB 455). The court keeps the information and a copy of the summons — the remaining copies are returned to the police. In theory, the magistrate or clerk issuing a summons should consider each information judicially to ensure that the issue of process is justified. In practice, at least where police prosecutions are concerned, the examination of informations is perfunctory in the extreme. The summons sets out the information against the accused and also states the date on which he is to attend court to answer it.

(g) *Serving the summons.*   The court and/or the police serve the summons on the accused. In the case of Speedy, the court will probably first send it to him by ordinary post. If that fails to elicit a response, they will try a recorded delivery letter, and, should that be returned undelivered, the police will be asked to attempt personal service. As well as being sent the summons, Speedy is likely, for an offence such as careless driving, to be given a brief statement of the facts and a notice explaining how he can plead guilty by post. In any event, he will be asked to indicate if he intends to plead not guilty, and advised that, if he does, he should not attend court on the date stated in the summons but wait until he has been notified of a day when there will be time for a contested hearing. If he does not plead guilty by post and fails to attend court on the day fixed by the summons (or later day notified to him), the case may be proved in his absence (see Paragraph 9.5.1). This is subject to the prosecution being able to prove due service of the summons and of any adjournment notices. Having convicted him in his absence, the magistrates would then have to adjourn before sentence for Speedy to attend court and produce his licence. At this stage — though not before — they could issue a warrant for his arrest (see Paragraph 9.5.3). If Speedy does attend court in answer to the summons, the information will be put to him, and the trial proceeds.

2.4.2 Jurisdiction to issue a summons

Subject to certain territorial limitations on their jurisdiction (see below), magistrates and magistrates' clerks have power to issue a summons upon an information being laid before them: Magistrates' Courts Act 1980, s 1 and Justices' Clerks Rules 1970 (SI 1970 No 231). The power is not shared by assistants working in the clerk's office, even if they are qualified to sit as clerks in court: *Gateshead Justices ex p Tesco Stores Ltd* [1981] QB 470. Assistant clerks may, however, assist administratively by, for example, 'rubber-stamping' the magistrate's or clerk's signature onto a summons once he has taken the decision that it should be issued.

Section 1 of the Magistrates' Courts Act places territorial limits upon a magistrate's jurisdiction to issue a summons. The restrictions apply equally to magistrates' clerks. The general effect of the section is that:

(a) If the offence alleged in the information is summary, the magistrate may issue a summons only if the offence alleged in the information occurred in the county for which he acts. This is subject to (c) and (d) below.

(b) If the offence alleged is indictable, he may issue a summons if the offence occurred in the county, or the accused is believed to be or to live in the county, or (c) below applies.

(c) Whether the offence alleged is indictable or summary and irrespective of where it occurred, a summons may be issued if it is desirable for the accused to be tried jointly with or in the same place as somebody already being proceeded against within the county (e.g. if a thief is to appear before a magistrates' court for the county, a summons can be issued against the handler of the goods stolen, even if he lives outside the county and received the goods outside the county).

(d) If the information alleges a summary offence, and the accused is already being tried for an offence (indictable or summary) by a magistrates' court within the county, a summons may be issued even if the offence alleged in the information allegedly occurred outside the county so that (a) above does not apply.

The summons must require the accused to appear before a magistrates' court for the county for which the magistrate issuing the summons acts. That court will have jurisdiction to try the offence concerned if it is summary or to hold committal proceedings if it is indictable (see Paragraph 9.2).

Section 1 of the Magistrates' Courts Act (jurisdiction to issue process) and s 2 (jurisdiction to try an offence or inquire into it as examining justices) thus complement each other.

Although a magistrate always has jurisdiction to issue a summons in respect of an offence occurring within his county, even if it took place outside the petty sessional division to which he is assigned, it is normal to lay an information before a magistrate or clerk of the division which was the venue of the offence, and the summons will require the accused to appear before the court for that division.

2.4.3 Laying an information

Issue of a summons depends upon an information first being laid before a magistrate or a magistrates' clerk. An information may be laid orally or in writing. The laying of a written information has been sufficiently described under subheadings (d) and (e) of Paragraph 2.4.1. As explained there, the police and other prosecuting agencies almost invariably use written informations to save both themselves and the courts a great deal of time. Further, where an accused has been charged, it is usual for the charge sheet to be used as the information (see Paragraph 2.3.6). However, a private prosecutor might well choose to lay his information orally. In essence, he tells either an individual magistrate, or a magistrates' clerk or a bench of magistrates sitting as an 'applications court' the nature of the allegation and the name and address of the accused. The substance of his information is taken down in writing and put into the appropriate terminology. He may be asked to sign it, and the magistrate or clerk will also sign that the information was taken before him. The information may, but need not be, substantiated on oath. The advantage of doing so is that it enables the magistrate before whom it is laid to issue a warrant for the arrest of the accused, which he cannot do if the informant has merely made an unsworn allegation. Only magistrates (not magistrates' clerks) can take informations on oath. On page 23 is an example of the way a magistrate might take a sworn information. It is based upon a form given in the Magistrates' Courts (Forms) Rules 1981 (SI 1981 No 553).

2.4.4 The decision to issue a summons

The decision to issue a summons is a judicial, not an administrative one — that is why it cannot be delegated to an official in the clerk's office, however well qualified he might be. The magistrate or clerk must look at each information laid before him, and ask himself whether it justifies a summons: *Gateshead Justices ex p Tesco Stores Ltd* [1981] QB 470. He must not issue a summons if either:

(a) the offence alleged in the information is unknown to law; or
(b) the information was laid out of time; or
(c) any consent necessary to the bringing of a prosecution has not been obtained; or
(d) he lacks jurisdiction in the matter because the offence was committed outside the county etc.

Of course, in most cases none of these impediments to the issue of a summons will apply. Nevertheless, there is still a residual discretion not to issue a summons if the prosecution appears frivolous or vexatious (see *Bros* (1901) 66 JP 54 — proposed prosecution of a Jew for Sunday trading) or if the evidence is clearly inadequate (*Mead* (1916) 80 JP 382) or even if the prosecutor has been inexplicably slow in laying the information (*Clerk to the Medway Justices ex p DHSS* [1986] Crim LR 686). However, it is not in general the duty of the magistrate/clerk to enter upon a preliminary survey of the evidence, and in the case of a police prosecution he is likely to assume that it is neither frivolous nor unsupported by evidence. Indeed, much as the Divisional Court might deplore it, there is reason to suppose that the issue of a summons is often more or less automatic. As the Philips Report said — 'Where a summons is applied for by the police or other recognised prosecution agencies no consideration is given as to whether or not a summons should be issued'. The Commission did, however, find a different attitude prevailing towards private prosecutors, with the magistrate or clerk in such cases seeking to 'ensure the propriety of the prosecution and the technical correctness of the information'. That might involve asking the informant to outline the evidence he has available, or even giving the proposed defendant an opportunity to attend and argue against issue of a summons (see *West London Metropolitan Stipendiary Magistrate ex p Klahn* [1979] 1 WLR 933 for an example of that happening).

INFORMATION (M.C. Act 1980, s 1; M.C. Rules 1981, r 41)
CASTERBRIDGE Magistrates' Court (Court Code 1234)

Date: 12th February 2002

Accused: John David DOE

Address: 1, Port Bredy Road,
CASTERBRIDGE,
Hardyshire

Alleged offence: On the 11th day of February 2002 John David DOE did assault and beat Richard Rose contrary to Common Law.

The information
of: Richard Roger ROE

Address: 3, Port Bredy Road,   Telephone No.
CASTERBRIDGE,
Hardyshire

who upon oath states that the accused committed the offence of which particulars are given above.

Taken and sworn before me

John Justice
Justice of the Peace

The importance of the decision to issue a summons — and hence the importance of each application being looked at judicially — was explained by Donaldson LJ in *Gateshead Justices ex p Tesco Stores Ltd* [1981] QB 470:

> Not all prosecutions are brought by experienced and responsible prosecuting authorities. And even in the case of such authorities, the requirement that a justice of the peace or a clerk to the justices . . . shall take personal responsibility for the propriety of taking so serious a step as to require the attendance of a citizen before a criminal court is a constitutional safeguard of fundamental importance.

Nevertheless, the House of Lords decision in *Manchester Stipendiary Magistrate ex p Hill* [1983] 1 AC 328 revealed how flimsy the 'constitutional safeguard' of which Donaldson LJ spoke really is. H appeared before the magistrates in answer to a summons stamped with the signature of the justices' clerk. It later transpired that the clerk had never seen the papers, and the decision to issue a summons had been taken solely by an assistant clerk, in direct contravention of everything that had been said in *Gateshead Justices ex p Tesco Stores Ltd.* Even so, H's conviction was upheld. The information was laid in time because it had been delivered to the court office within six months of the offence — therefore, there was no breach of s 127 of the Magistrates' Courts Act 1980. The fact that the summons issued on the basis of the information was invalid was irrelevant, since the purpose of a summons is not to found jurisdiction but merely to ensure that the accused attends court. If he does so, and if the case is otherwise one with which the court is empowered to deal, the bench may proceed with the hearing whatever defects there are in the summons. The position might be different if the defence appreciate the defects at the time and object, but even that is doubtful. In any event, it is most unlikely that a defendant will query the validity of a court document which apparently bears the signature of a magistrate or a magistrates' clerk. The same reasoning applies whenever there is an irregularity in the procedure leading to the accused appearing in court (e.g., he is arrested without warrant when there was no power of arrest). His actually appearing before court and saying nothing is taken to have waived any objection he might have made to how he was got there. In *Horseferry Road Magistrates' Court ex p Bennett* [1993] 3 WLR 90, the House of Lords showed that there were limits to the extent to which the magistrates' court should be expected to ignore the history of the accused's production before it. B had been forcibly brought back to the UK in disregard of proper extradition procedures. Their lordships held that, where the police, prosecution or other executive authorities in this country had been a knowing party to such irregularity, the courts should stay the prosecution as an abuse of process (see Paragraph 9.4 for abuse of process).

2.4.5 Contents and service of a summons

A summons should contain the following details:

(a)   the name and address of the accused;
(b)   the address of the court before which he is to appear;

SUMMONS (M.C. Act 1980 s 1: M.C. Rules 1981 r 98)
CASTERBRIDGE Magistrates' Court (Court Code 1234)

To the accused: Mr. John David DOE   Ref Number MN 0220 (P)
of: 1 Port Bredy Road
                  CASTERBRIDGE
                  Hardyshire

                  You are hereby summoned to appear
                  on 26.3.2002   at 10.00 a.m.

                  before the Magistrates' Court
                  at 50 Egdon Street, CASTERBRIDGE
                  to answer to the following information laid
                  today   that you

Alleged Offence: on 1st February 2002 at Bridge Lane, Casterbridge did
                  wilfully obstruct Richard Roe a constable of the Hardyshire
                  Police Force in the execution of his duty.

                  Contrary to Section 89(2) of the Police Act 1996

Informant   Police Inspector 30 (B) Brown
Address   Casterbridge Police Station
Date   28 February 2002

                                                    John Clerk
                                                    Justices' Clerk

PLEASE READ THE IMPORTANT NOTICE OVERLEAF
Complete and sign the tear off acknowledgement slip below and return it to the Clerk
of the Court forthwith. The correct postage must be paid.

(c)   the day on and time at which he is to appear;

(d)   the contents of the information or informations he is to answer; and

(e)   the name and address of the informant (in the case of a police information the address of the police station will be given).

The summons must be signed by the magistrate or clerk who issued it, or, if it was issued by a magistrate, it may state his name and be authenticated by the clerk's signature: Magistrates' Courts Rules 1981, r 98. To save magistrates and clerks the tedium of signing hundreds of summonses, the practice has grown up of rubber-stamping the relevant signature onto the summons. Provided the magistrate or clerk has personally sanctioned the issue of the summons, the manual task of affixing the signature may be carried out by assistants in the clerk's office: *Brentford Justices ex p Catlin* [1975] QB 455. An example of a summons appears above.

Once the summons has been issued and signed it must be served on the accused. That may be effected *(inter alia)* by delivering it personally to him or posting it to his last known or usual address: Magistrates' Courts Rules 1981, r 99. However, a magistrates' court may not treat service by post as proved unless *either* they are satisfied that the summons came to the knowledge of the accused, *or* the summons was issued in respect of a summary offence and it was sent by registered letter or recorded delivery service. As indicated in Paragraph 2.4.1, the usual sequence of events is to send the summons by ordinary post, then (if there is no response from the accused) to send it by recorded delivery, and finally, if the Post Office cannot get anyone to sign for it, to ask the police to try to effect personal service by going to the address where the accused is believed to reside.

The options open to the magistrates if the accused fails to appear in answer to a summons for a summary offence are set out in Paragraph 9.5.1. They can either adjourn and notify him of the new hearing date, or they can issue a warrant for his arrest, or they can proceed in his absence. The latter two options are dependent upon proof of service of the summons; the middle option is also dependent upon the information being substantiated on oath and the offence being imprisonable. If the summons is for an indictable offence, the magistrates cannot proceed with committal proceedings or with proceedings to determine the mode of trial unless the accused is personally present or (in limited circumstances) is absent but represented by counsel or solicitor (see MCA, ss 4(3) and (4) and 18(2) which deal with the need for the accused to be present for committal proceedings and mode-of-trial proceedings, and draw no distinction between prosecutions begun by summons and prosecutions begun by arrest and charge). Thus, the magistrates' only options upon failure to appear in response to a summons for an indictable offence are to adjourn with or without the issue of a warrant for arrest.[4]

2.4.6   Issue of a warrant for arrest

Where a magistrate has jurisdiction to issue a summons in respect of the offence alleged in an information laid before him, he may, instead of issuing a summons, issue a warrant for the arrest of the accused provided:

(a)   the information is in writing and substantiated on oath, and

---

[4] But note that, if the accused appeared for proceedings to determine the mode of trial and agreed to the matter being dealt with summarily, the trial may then proceed in his absence if he fails to attend on any date to which it was adjourned after the mode-of-trial determination.

(b)   either the accused is a juvenile, or his address cannot be sufficiently established for a summons to be served on him, or the offence alleged in the information is punishable with imprisonment: MCA, s 1(3) and (4).

Proviso (a) above will be satisfied if the informant signs a written information, hands it to a magistrate, and then confirms on oath before the magistrate that the allegation in the information is true to the best of his belief. Since a magistrates' clerk cannot receive a sworn information, he has no jurisdiction to issue a warrant for arrest.

An example of a warrant for arrest is shown on page 28. It is a document commanding the constables of the police force for the area in which it is issued to arrest the accused and bring him before the magistrates' court named in it. It must contain particulars of the offence alleged in the information which led to its being issued, and must be signed by the magistrate who issued it. Any constable of the police force named in a warrant may execute the warrant (i.e. arrest the accused) anywhere in England and Wales. In addition, a constable of another force may execute the warrant within the area policed by his force: MCA, s 125(2). Reasonable force may be used in making the arrest (Criminal Law Act 1967, s 3), and force may also be used to enter premises where the accused is known to be: *Launock v Brown* (1819) 2 B & Ald 592. Although the officer effecting the arrest need not have the warrant in his possession at the time of doing so, he must, on demand, show it to the accused as soon as practicable: MCA, s 125(3). Following the arrest the accused must, unless the warrant was backed for bail, be brought forthwith before the magistrates' court named in the warrant. The magistrates may then release him on bail or remand him in custody.

As a compromise between issuing a summons and issuing an unconditional warrant for arrest, a magistrate may issue a warrant but endorse it with a direction that, having been arrested, the accused shall be released on bail subject to a duty to appear at the magistrates' court at a time specified in the endorsement: MCA, s 117. This is known as 'backing the warrant for bail'. The bail may be made subject to conditions — e.g. providing sureties or reporting to the police station at specified intervals or living at a certain address. If the accused cannot comply with those conditions (e.g. he is unable to find a surety), he is brought before the magistrates who will either vary the terms of bail or remand him in custody. Whenever a magistrate or a magistrates' court has jurisdiction to issue a warrant for arrest, it may be backed for bail. The power is particularly useful when an accused fails to appear in answer to a summons or fails to answer to his bail, but the magistrates feel that this is due to inadvertence rather than design. The shock of being arrested should ensure that he attends for the adjourned hearing, while the endorsement for bail saves him from an unnecessary period of custody.

WARRANT OF ARREST IN FIRST INSTANCE (Bail Act 1976, s 3,
M.C. Act 1980 ss 1, 3, 14, 117; M.C. Rules 1981, rr 95, 96)

COURT CODE 1234

CASTERBRIDGE MAGISTRATES' COURT

Date: 28th February 2002

Accused: John David DOE

Address: 1, Port Bredy Road
                       CASTERBRIDGE

Alleged offence: On 1st February 2002 at Bridge Land, Casterbridge did
                       wilfully obstruct Richard Roe a constable of the Hardyshire
                       Police Force in the execution of his duty contrary to 89(2)
                       of the Police Act 1996.

                       Information having been laid before me (on oath) by Richard
                       Roe on 28th February 2002
                       that the accused committed the above offence

Direction: You, the constables of the Hardyshire Police Force are
                       hereby required to arrest the accused and to bring the
                       accused before the Magistrates' Court at 50 Egdon Street,
                       Casterbridge immediately (unless the accused is released on
                       bail as directed below).

Bail: On arrest, after complying with the condition(s) specified in
                       Schedule I hereto, the accused shall be released on bail,
                       subject to the condition(s) specified in Schedule II hereto,
                       and with a duty to surrender to the custody of the above
                       magistrates' court on 26th March 2002 at 10.00 a.m.

                                              John Justice
                                              Justice of the Peace

Schedule I

Conditions to be complied with before release on bail

1. To provide 2 suret(y)(ies) in the sum of £200 (each) to
secure the accused's surrender to custody at the time and
place appointed.

2.

Schedule II

Conditions to be complied with after release on bail

1. To report to Casterbridge Police Station daily between
6 and 7pm.

It is rare for proceedings to commence with the laying of an information and the issue of a warrant for arrest. Apart from the statutory limitations on the issue of warrants for arrest, there is a general principle that a warrant ought not to be issued when a summons would be equally effectual: *O'Brien v Brabner* (1885) 49 JPN 227. Provided the accused's address is sufficiently well established for a summons to be served on him, there is no reason on the face of it why he should not appear at court to answer a charge of a minor nature. If the charge is more serious, it will almost certainly carry a power of arrest without warrant, so obtaining a warrant would be superfluous.

2.5 POLICE QUESTIONING OF A SUSPECT

A major part of the evidence at most criminal trials concerns the answers the accused made in interview with the police and any written statement he may have signed under caution.

2.5.1 The overall framework

Until 1986, police questioning of suspects was conducted within the framework of the common law on involuntary confessions and the rules of practice for police officers set out in the Judges' Rules (see Paragraph 2.1.2 for a brief description of the Rules). Essentially, police officers investigating crime were required to caution the suspect that he need not say anything at a fairly early stage of the investigation; to charge him as soon as they had sufficient evidence to bring the case before court; and thereafter not to question him further save in very limited circumstances. The Judges' Rules have been replaced by the Detention, Treatment and Questioning Code of Practice. The Code, although developing from the Judges' Rules, is far more detailed than they ever were. The description of the questioning of suspects which follows is based upon the Code. It should, however, be remembered that the police must conform not only with the Code directed specifically at them but also with the general law of evidence on involuntary confessions. That is now contained in s 76(2) of PACE, which states that an alleged confession must be excluded (albeit that it appears to be true) if *either* it was obtained by oppression, *or* it was obtained as a result of words or conduct which — given the circumstances then obtaining — were likely to render unreliable any confession the suspect might make in consequence thereof. Oppression is statutorily defined to include any actual or threatened violence (s 76(8)), but otherwise it is restricted to really serious and deliberate abuse of power by a person in authority (see Lord Lane CJ's judgment in *Fulling* [1987] QB 426). It is rare for a court to conclude that police officers have been guilty of oppressive conduct as explained in *Fulling*. However, police questioning which is carried out after repeated denials or refusals may become oppressive (*Paris* (1992) 97 Cr App R 99) with the result that the confession is invalidated. As to the second limb of s 76(2), the court has to consider whether any confession made *by the particular suspect* is, having regard to the words or conduct that induced it, likely to be unreliable, and questioning that might be perfectly acceptable as regards the general run of suspects may none the less cast a doubt on the reliability of admissions made by an especially nervous or inexperienced questionee. For details about inadmissible confessions, the reader is referred to *Blackstone's Criminal Practice,* section F17 in particular. As already explained in Paragraph 2.1.3, breaches of the Code of Practice may lead to a confession being excluded *either* because, with other factors, they lead to the conclusion that any confession the accused might have made is likely to be unreliable, *or* because the judge exercises the discretion given him by s 78 of PACE to exclude unfairly obtained evidence.

2.5.2 The conduct of questioning by the police

The Detention, Treatment and Questioning Code controls the conduct of police questioning. One of the Code's main purposes is to ensure as far as possible that interrogations are conducted in such a way that the defence will not subsequently be able to claim with any plausibility that the accused's confession was obtained by oppression or in breach of the reliability principle. Another purpose is to facilitate the accurate recording of what an interviewee says. In considering the main provisions of the Code, it is helpful to divide the questioning process into a number of stages:

(a) *Gathering information.* The Code states that 'all citizens have a duty to help police officers to prevent crime and discover offenders' (see note 1B). Consequently, an officer is entitled to question any person from whom he thinks useful information can be obtained. Even if the person concerned states that he is unwilling to answer, that does not affect the officer's entitlement to put the questions. The duty to help the police is, however, merely a civic and moral one. There is no legally enforceable obligation to answer their questions (see *Rice v Connelly* [1966] 2 QB 414). False answers might, of course, lead to prosecution for wasting police time or even for assisting an offender. Also, if someone who is ultimately charged with an offence failed or refused to answer a question put to him by an officer at the information-gathering stage, it is possible that his silence might be evidence against him. At common law, the failure by A to deny an allegation put to him by B can be interpreted as an acceptance by A that the allegation is true provided a reasonable man who knew the allegation to be untrue would be expected to deny it (see *Bessela v Stern* (1877) 2 CPD 265). This general principle applies in the context of the police questioning a member of the public who has not yet been cautioned (see below for the effect of the caution). However, a denial of an untrue allegation put by a police officer can only reasonably be expected if the member of the public and the officer are on equal terms. Normally, they will not be (see *Chandler* [1976] 1 WLR 585, which suggested that the presence of the questionee's solicitor redresses any inequality which might otherwise exist, and which cited a local dignitary being questioned by a very junior constable about an allegation of corruption as an example of police officer and member of the public being on even terms notwithstanding the absence of a solicitor). Even if the officer and questionee are on equal terms, silence by the latter may not be taken as a direct admission of involvement in the offence to which the questions relate. The silence is at highest an admission of any facts posited by the question put, and those facts may in turn be evidence tending to show the questionee's guilt. The intellectual process of asking (i) did the questionee's silence amount to an acceptance by him of the facts alleged in the officer's question, and (ii) if so, do those facts establish or tend to establish his guilt of an offence charged, must not be concertinaed into the single process of asking whether the silence indicates guilt.

(b) *The cautioning stage.* A person whom there are grounds to suspect of an offence must be cautioned before any questions about it are put to him for the purpose of obtaining evidence which may be given to a court in a prosecution (see para 10.1 of the Code). If it is the person's unsatisfactory answers to previous questions which have provided grounds for suspicion, he must be cautioned before any further questions are put. The terms of the caution are set out in the Code, para 10.4:

> You do not have to say anything. But it may harm your defence if you do not mention when questioned something which you later rely on in court. Anything you do say may be given in evidence.

Minor deviations from the formula do not matter, provided that the general sense is preserved. This form of the caution was introduced as a result of s 34 of the Criminal Justice and Public Order Act 1994, which permits certain inferences to be drawn at trial where the accused has failed to mention after caution any fact which he relies on in his defence (for an analysis, see *Criminal Evidence and Procedure: the Statutory Framework* by Seabrooke and Sprack (Blackstone Press 1999, p. 83); and see also *Argent* [1997] 2 Cr App R 27). There are, in addition, special warnings laid down in paras 10.5A and 10.5B of the Code which must be administered where s 36 and/or s 37 of the 1994 Act apply (a suspect's refusal to answer questions about objects, marks or substances found on him, or about his presence at the place where he was arrested). For an inference to be drawn from the suspect's failure or refusal satisfactorily to answer a question on one of these matters, the interviewing officer must first tell him the offence which is being investigated, the fact which the suspect is being asked to account for, the officer's belief that this fact is connected to the suspect's participation in the offence, the power of the court to draw an inference from a failure or refusal to account for the fact, and that a record of the interview may later be given in evidence at trial (see Seabrooke and Sprack, p. 87).

The obligation to caution does not arise until there are grounds to suspect the interviewee of an offence (see above). Suspicion has been described as 'a state of conjecture or surmise where proof is lacking'. The grounds for conjecture do not have to be matters which the officer could or would want to put before a court as evidence (e.g., they might be his knowledge of the suspect's criminal record or something he has been told by an underworld informer). Thus, para 10.1 requires a caution to be given at a very early stage of the investigative process — an earlier stage, in fact, than was required by the Judges' Rules prior to 1986. However, no caution is needed if the officer's purpose in questioning is other than to obtain evidence which might be used in the prosecution of the interviewee — e.g., if he is seeking to establish the latter's identity or the ownership of a vehicle.

Para. 10.3 of the Code supplements para 10.1 by providing that an arrestee must be cautioned upon his arrest, unless either that has been done immediately before in pursuance of para 10.1 or his conduct makes the administering of a caution impracticable. When there is a break in the questioning of a cautioned suspect, the officer must ensure on its resumption that the suspect is aware that he is still under caution. If there is any doubt, the caution should be given again in full (para 10.5). This is because the officer may have to satisfy the court that the suspect understood he was still under caution when the interview resumed (note 10A). A suspect who attends voluntarily at a police station must, on being cautioned (or, if he was cautioned before going to the police station, on being reminded of the caution), be informed also that he is not under arrest, need not stay with the officer and has a right to free legal advice (paras 10.2 and 3.15).

(c)   *Questioning away from the police station.*   One of the aims of the Code is to reduce the frequency of allegations that the suspect was 'verballed' prior to arrival at the police station, e.g., in the police car on the way to the station via the 'scenic route'. Para. 11.1 states that, once a suspect has been arrested he must not usually be interviewed about the offence until he is at the station (and hence subject to the protection of the custody regime there). The prohibition on interviews outside the station is relaxed only where the consequent delay is likely to lead to interference with evidence, harm to other persons, the alerting of other suspects or hindrance to the recovery of illegally obtained property.

The restriction applies only to interviews, and the definition of 'interview' in para 11.1A of the Code is:

An interview is the questioning of a person regarding his involvement or suspected involvement in a criminal offence or offences which, by virtue of para 10.1 of Code C, is required to be carried out under caution. Procedures undertaken under section 7 of the Road Traffic Act 1988 do not constitute interviewing for the purpose of this code.

(Section 7 of the 1988 Act deals with the provision of specimens of breath, blood or urine by those suspected of drink-driving offences.)

(d) *Questioning at the police station.* Para. 11.3 of the Code states that no officer may seek to elicit answers by the use of oppression. It then deals more particularly with what an officer may tell a suspect who takes the initiative by asking what plans the police have for him (see below). Interrogation at the police station is covered in paras 12.1 to 12.13. Such questioning may occur either when a person has attended voluntarily to 'help police with their inquiries' (see Paragraph 2.3.9), or when a suspect has been arrested, taken to the station and detained without charge on the authority of the custody officer (see Paragraphs 2.3.4 and 2.3.5). In the latter case, the questioning will inevitably be under caution because of the rule that a person must be cautioned on arrest if not before. In the former case, the probability is that the police officers will already suspect the interviewee of an offence, and therefore should caution him, but that will not necessarily be so. Much of paras 11 and 12 are directly related to detainees, rather than those who are merely helping with enquiries. However, 'those there voluntarily to assist with an investigation should be treated with no less consideration' than is given to detainees (note 1A).

When an investigating officer wishes to interview a detainee, he must first obtain the custody officer's permission in the sense that the detainee has to be 'delivered' from the custody officer's custody into that of the investigating officer (para 12.1). In any 24-hour period, he should be given at least eight hours continuous rest from questioning, normally at night (para 12.2). However, the rest period may be interrupted if there are good reasons for doing so (e.g., the need to obtain quick answers so as to prevent harm to other persons or serious damage to property). If practicable, questioning should take place in an interview room, which is adequately heated, lit and ventilated (para 12.4). The detainee must be allowed to sit (para 12.5). At the beginning of the interview, the interviewing officers must identify themselves by name and rank (para 12.6). Breaks in an interview should occur at approximately two-hour intervals and at regular mealtimes subject to the discretion to delay on reasonable grounds (e.g., risk of harm to others or serious damage to property) (para 12.7). Any complaints by the detainee must be recorded and reported to the custody officer (para 12.8). If the detainee asks what will happen if he stays silent or answers questions or signs a written statement, the officers may tell him the action they propose to take in any of those events (para 11.3). But they may not give this information unless they have first been directly asked. In any event, they must be careful not to phrase their answers in such a way that the admissibility of any subsequent confession could be challenged by suggesting that what the police said makes it likely to be unreliable. However, para 11.3 seems to sanction an officer telling a detainee in response to a question that, for example, once he has made a statement he will be charged and then, in all probability, released on bail. (Contrast the pre-1986 position as established by *Zaveckas* [1970] 1 WLR 516 which was that any promise of bail, even in response to a question from the suspect, made a confession inadmissible.) The maximum periods for which a suspect may be detained for questioning without being charged have already been considered in Paragraph 2.3.5.

(e) *The charging stage.* Immediately a police officer questioning a suspect believes that a prosecution should be brought against him and that there is enough evidence for the prosecution to succeed, he must ask him if he has anything further to say and (if he has nothing more to say) stop questioning him (para 11.4). The evidence against the suspect is then considered by the custody officer, who either supervises the making of a charge or, if it is a case where the police in their discretion decide that it is better not to prosecute, releases the suspect without charge.[5] The terms of para 11.4 (see above), combined with the 'realistic prospect of conviction' test laid down in the Code for Crown Prosecutors (see Paragraph 4.3.1), suggest that the correct time for a charge is as soon as the police have evidence on the basis of which a prosecution would be more likely than not to succeed. Applied rigidly, however, such an approach to charging would have inconvenient results, bearing in mind that after an accused has been charged he cannot normally be further questioned about the offence. For example, if a housebreaker is arrested climbing out of a window with his pockets full of the householder's jewellery, the evidence of his being caught in the act would be ample to sustain a successful prosecution for burglary. It could therefore be argued that he ought not to be asked any questions about the offence but should be charged immediately upon his arrival at the station. That, however, would hardly be fair to the housebreaker himself, in that he should be given an opportunity to make a statement, in which he might frankly admit his guilt, express contrition and thus hope to secure a lighter sentence. Nor would it be fair to the police, who understandably like to complete their case with admissions from the suspect, however strong the rest of the evidence may be. So, the Code should be understood as requiring a suspect to be charged (or released) as soon as the police (i) have evidence making his conviction more likely than not, and (ii) have had a reasonable opportunity to question him with a view to his making a statement about the offence. Point (ii) is reflected in the wording of para 16.1 of the Code. What is impermissible is delaying a charge when there is the evidence for it and the suspect has made it plain that he has said all he intends to say. In such cases, the only purpose of delay would be the improper one of breaking down the suspect by continued detention without charge, hoping that he will eventually confess and thus make a conviction not merely the probable but the almost certain outcome of a prosecution. The procedure for charging has already been described in Paragraph 2.3.6. It will be recalled that the caution must again be given when charging.

(f) *The post-charge stage.* Once a person has been charged he may not, as a general rule, be asked any further questions about the offence. The exceptions are when (i) the questions are necessary to prevent or minimise harm or loss to others, *or* (ii) they are necessary to clear up an ambiguity in a previous answer or statement, *or* (iii) it is in the interests of justice that he should be given the opportunity of commenting on information which has come to light since he was charged (para 16.5). If the police wish him to look at a statement made by some other person (e.g., another suspect who has implicated him), a copy of the statement should be handed to him but no reply or comment is to be invited (para 16.4). Both before asking post-charge questions and before giving the chargee a copy of another's statement, the police must caution him.

The above has been written on the assumption that the offence under investigation is a fairly serious one, which the police would choose to prosecute by way of arrest and charge.

---

[5] As explained in the description of the arrest and charge procedure, the custody officer plays the crucial role in determining whether there is enough evidence for a charge. If the investigating officers make an arrest away from the police station, the custody officer must determine as soon as practicable after the arrestee's arrival there whether the evidence justifies a charge in respect of the offence for which he was arrested: PACE, s 37(1) and (10). If it is while a detainee is being questioned at the station that the investigating officers reach the conclusion that there is the evidence for a prosecution, they must without delay bring him before the custody officer (para 16.1 of the Code).

If it is a trivial matter more appropriately prosecuted by summons, the rules on cautioning still apply and again the officer should not ask any more questions once he has the evidence to prosecute. But, there is unlikely to be any questioning at the station and, instead of being charged, the suspect is told that he may be prosecuted. Once he has been told that, the rules on further questioning are the same as apply after a charge.

2.5.3   Right to consult a solicitor

Suspects questioned by the police are frequently at a disadvantage in that they have little or no knowledge of the law or police powers. Thus, although cautioned, they do not appreciate the arguments for and against staying silent, or realise that, by answering, they may supply the police with vital admissions without which there would not even be a case to answer or the possibility of a prosecution. Similarly, a detainee at the police station is naturally anxious to be released as soon as possible. If he does not know for how long the police can lawfully hold him, he may in desperation give the investigating officers the answers he thinks they want in the hope that they will then bail him, not realising that they would in any event be obliged to let him go (or charge him) after 24 or at most 96 hours. To redress the inequality between suspect and police and ensure that the former understands his rights, PACE provides that, save in very limited and well-defined circumstances, he must be allowed to consult a solicitor. Moreover, having been consulted, the solicitor is then in a position to check that any interrogation is conducted fairly and in accordance with the Code. This is one of the most significant changes made by the Act because, although the preamble to the old Judges' Rules had stated that a suspect should be allowed a solicitor at all stages of an investigation, the 'right' was subject to the massive exception that exercise of it would not 'unreasonably delay or hinder the processes of investigation or the administration of justice'. The vagueness of the exception gave the police in practice virtual *carte blanche* to keep the suspect incommunicado. The position is very different under PACE.

Section 58(1) of PACE provides that a person arrested and held in custody at a police station (a detainee) shall be entitled, if he so requests, to consult an independent solicitor privately at any time free of charge. He must be told of this right by the custody officer when he arrives at the station (para 3.1 of the Code), and should be invited to sign the custody record to indicate whether — at that stage — he wants legal advice (para 3.5). Indeed, any request to see a solicitor, whenever made, should be noted in the custody record: s 58(2). Once a request has been made, the detainee must be allowed to consult a solicitor as soon as practicable unless (i) he is suspected of a serious arrestable offence (see Paragraph 2.3.1), and (ii) delay is authorised by an officer of at least the rank of superintendent: s 58(6). Moreover, the senior officer may authorise delay if, and only if, he has reasonable grounds for believing that immediate consultation with a solicitor would have any of the following consequences:

(i)   interference with or harm to evidence connected with a serious arrestable offence, or interference with or physical injury to other persons; *or*

(ii)   the alerting of other persons suspected of having committed a serious arrestable offence; *or*

(iii)   hindrance to the recovery of the proceeds of a serious arrestable offence (s 58(8)).

It is clear that the suspect must not be refused access to a solicitor merely because the police fear that the solicitor will advise the suspect not to answer questions (*Alladice* (1988) 87 Cr App R 380, and Code C, annexe B, para 3). In *Samuel* [1988] 1 WLR 920, the Court of

Appeal gave guidance on the circumstances in which delay could be authorised. The essential facts were that S was arrested on 6 August 1986 on suspicion of armed robbery from a building society and arrived at the police station at 2 p.m. He first asked to see a solicitor at 8 p.m. during a second interview with investigating officers when the questioning turned to masks and other items discovered in a search of his home. That request and subsequent requests were refused. S was then interviewed a further three times without having had the benefit of legal advice, the last interview being at around 5.30 p.m. on 7 August 1986 when he at last confessed to the robbery. Prior to that he had already confessed to and been charged with two unconnected burglaries. Throughout the afternoon of the 7th, Mr W, a highly respected local solicitor, had been unavailingly seeking access to S. The trial judge was invited to exercise his discretion under s 78 of the Act and exclude the confession on the basis that there had been a breach of s 58 (and also of the Code). In the Court of Appeal, Hodgson J said that the senior officer authorising delay in access must have a subjective belief that, in the event of immediate consultation with a solicitor, one or other of the three harmful consequences mentioned in s 58(8) 'will very probably happen'. That in turn implies a belief that the solicitor would either deliberately interfere with evidence, warn other suspects etc. or would inadvertently do so. As to the first possibility (i.e., deliberate misconduct by the legal adviser), the number of occasions on which fear of it could be genuinely advanced would be rare, and would have to relate to the particular solicitor whom the detainee wished to consult, not to solicitors in general. As to the inadvertent disclosures (e.g., through the solicitor passing on a coded message), that implies a naivety on the part of the solicitor and a sophistication on the part of the detainee which is most unlikely to occur in practice. The task of satisfying the court that a senior officer delaying access genuinely and reasonably believed such a disclosure might occur would be a 'formidable one'. In S's case, the superintendent might just have been entitled to authorise delay when S first asked for a solicitor (since at that stage he did not know who the solicitor would be), but once it was appreciated that it would be the highly respected Mr W, any possible justification for his decision was removed. Accordingly, there had been a clear breach of s 58.

The rights may also be delayed where the officer reasonably believes their exercise will hinder recovery of the suspect's share of proceeds in drug trafficking offences, or offences covered by confiscation orders under part VI of the Criminal Justice Act 1988 (Code C, annex B, para 2).

The detainee must be told why he is being refused access to a solicitor, and that reason must be entered on the custody record: s 58(9). As soon as the reason ceases to exist, access must be allowed: s 58(11). It must in any event be allowed once the detainee has been held for 36 hours, which is the stage at which the police have to go before a magistrates' court to obtain a warrant for further detention if they want to hold and question the detainee further: s 58(5).

Section 58 does not in terms say that the police cannot interview a detainee until he has consulted a solicitor — it merely says that, unless delay has been duly authorised by a senior officer, they must not actively prevent consultation taking place. This raises the question of how feasible it is for the average detainee actually to get a solicitor to come to the station to advise him. Since 1986, a duty solicitor scheme has been organised, the purpose of which is to ensure that any detainee who wants advice can have it quickly. Briefly, the scheme is that local solicitors make themselves available on a rota basis to go to the police station when called. If a detainee indicates that he wants legal advice (and he does not have his own solicitor who is willing to come), the police telephone a special number which puts them in touch with an agency which in turn contacts the appropriate duty solicitor. The costs of his attendance are paid out of the legal aid fund, and the scheme operates on a round-the-clock basis.

The statutory rights contained in s 58 have been buttressed by the provisions of the Code. Para. 6 deals in detail with the right to legal advice. In summary, the Code lays down certain rules which relate to all situations other than those to which exceptions (i) to (iii) above apply, or where the suspect is detained under the Prevention of Terrorism (Temporary Provisions) Act 1989. In summary, these rules of general application are:

(a)   Detainees must be informed of their right to communicate privately with a solicitor, and that independent legal advice is available free of charge from the duty solicitor (para 6.1).

(b)   A poster advertising the right should be displayed prominently in the charge room (para 6.3).

(c)   No police officer should do or say anything with the intention of dissuading a detainee from obtaining legal advice (para 6.4).

(d)   When a solicitor arrives at the station to see the suspect (presumably at the invitation of a friend or relative), then the suspect must be informed of the solicitor's arrival and asked if he would like to see him. This is so even if he has earlier declined legal advice (para 6.15).

(e)   Where the suspect is allowed access to legal advice, he must be allowed to have his solicitor present for interview once the latter is present at the station, or on his way, or easily contactable by telephone (para 6.8).

(f)   If the solicitor requested is on his way to the station or about to set off, an interview should not normally be started until he arrives (note 6A).

(g)   Where the solicitor was asked to attend the station by someone else, the detainee must be informed of his arrival and asked to sign the custody record to signify whether or not he wishes to see the solicitor (annexe B, para 3).

(h)   The solicitor may be required to leave the interview only if his conduct stops the officer from properly questioning the suspect, e.g., by answering questions for his client. He can, however, challenge improper questions or advise his client not to answer certain questions (para 6.9 and note 6D).

Quite apart from the cases where consequences (i) to (iii) above apply, there are two limited sets of circumstances where a suspect can be interviewed without a solicitor despite his request for legal advice. The first is if the solicitor cannot be contacted or refuses to attend, and the suspect refuses to make use of any duty solicitor scheme. The second is if the suspect changes his mind about wanting legal advice, and agrees in writing or on tape to being interviewed without a solicitor. In each of these sets of circumstances, authority for the interview to proceed must be received from an officer of the rank of inspector or above (para 6.6).

The rules in the Code apply to 'solicitors', but the term is defined so as to include trainee solicitors, duty solicitor representatives, and accredited representatives on the register maintained by the Legal Aid Board. Where a solicitor sends a non-accredited representative to provide advice to the suspect, the police have greater powers to refuse access. The representative must still be admitted unless an officer of the rank of inspector or above considers admission 'will hinder the investigation of crime and directs otherwise' (para 6.12). The officer is advised to have regard to whether the representative's identity and status have been satisfactorily established, and whether he is of suitable character to provide legal advice (e.g., a criminal record of any recency and/or substance is likely to prove a bar). If the representative is allowed access, then he is in much the same position as a solicitor (para 6.12). If access is refused, the solicitor and the suspect must be told and the custody record noted (para 6.14). (The revised provisions of the Code in relation to non-accredited representatives have been based in part upon *Chief Constable of Avon & Somerset ex p Robinson* [1989] 1 WLR 793.)

The suspect is entitled to be notified of his right to free legal advice on arrival at the police station (para 3.1). In addition, he must be reminded of the right prior to each interview, including the restart of an interview (para 11.2). Further, the review officer must, when reviewing the suspect's detention in police custody, remind him of his right (para 15.3). In *Beycan* [1990] Crim LR 185, the trial judge held that there had been a failure properly to inform B of his rights when taken to the station, but that those breaches were cured when he was offered a solicitor at the outset of the challenged interview. The Court of Appeal held, bearing in mind that B was a Turkish Cypriot with no previous experience of the police, that this offer did not cure the previous breaches.

The right is to *private* consultation and communication with the solicitor (s 58 and Code C, para 6.1). The interview must take place outside the hearing of third persons. In particular, it must not be capable of being overheard by a police officer (*Brennan v United Kingdom* (2001) *The Times*, 22 October 2001, applying Art 6(3) of the European Convention on Human Rights).

Although s 58 itself is silent as to the consequences of non-compliance with it, the courts have been robust in their attitude to denials of the right given by the section. The leading case is *Samuel*, the facts of which are set out above. Once the Court of Appeal had decided that there had been a clear breach of s 58, the prosecution's contention that breach of the section should lead to exclusion of a confession only in cases of police 'impropriety' was unhesitatingly rejected. The court did not, however, hold that the trial judge definitely ought to have excluded the confession — merely that, in the circumstances, he had a discretion to do so under s 78 of PACE and had failed to take into consideration the major factor relevant to the exercise of that discretion, namely that the superintendent had had no good reason for preventing S consulting Mr W. The case thus stops short of saying that breach of s 58 will definitely, or even probably, deprive the prosecution of the evidence obtained thereby. Where, however, the police do permit consultation with a solicitor but deliberately trick him into believing that their evidence against his client is stronger than it is, the deceit practised on the officer of the court ought to lead to any subsequent confession being excluded (see *Mason* [1987] 1 WLR 139).

Walsh (1989) 91 Cr App R 161 puts forward three propositions which clarify the way in which the Court of Appeal is likely to deal with substantial breaches of the Code insofar as they relate to access to legal advice. First, if there were significant and substantial breaches of s 58 of the Code, prima facie the necessary standard of fairness had not been met. Second, the court must nonetheless (under s 78 of PACE) consider whether the effect would be so adverse that justice required the exclusion of the evidence. Third, breaches which were inherently serious could not be rendered insubstantial by the good faith of the officers.

2.5.4 Other rights at the police station

PACE and the Code give detainees at a police station two further rights in addition to the right to consult a solicitor. The first is simply a right to consult the Codes themselves. Each of the five Codes begins with a paragraph stating that it must be 'readily available at all police stations for consultation by police officers, *detained persons* and members of the public'. The second right is contained in s 56 of the Act. It is the right to have one relative, friend or other person likely to take an interest in one's welfare informed of the fact of one's arrest and of the station where one is being held. This is sometimes loosely referred to as the right to a phone call, although in fact the detainee himself is not entitled to make the call — it is the police who have the duty of passing on the information to the person named by the detainee. Exercise of the right may be delayed in the same circumstances as exercise of the right to consult a solicitor may be delayed. To some extent the rights dovetail with each other in that the person informed of the detainee's arrest may well choose to contact a solicitor on his behalf, irrespective of whether the detainee himself has asked for the duty solicitor to come to the station. Over and above the basic right contained in s 56, a detainee is allowed to make a phone call and/or write letters, but any such communication (unless it is with a solicitor) is liable to be listened to or read by the police (see paras 5.6 and 5.7 of the Code). Again, it is subject to delay in the same way as the right to consult a solicitor (see Paragraph 2.5.3).

2.5.5   Recording what the suspect says

The rules discussed so far about cautioning a suspect, about the periods for which and conditions in which he may be questioned, and about access to legal advice are all designed to ensure that what he says to the police, whether or not it amounts to an admission, is reliable. It is equally important, though, to ensure that the record of anything he may say is reliable. Previously, the police used simply to note an interviewee's answers to questions in their pocket books after the interview had concluded. He was not asked to sign the note. The result was that trials were disfigured by endless arguments over what was or was not said in interview, the accused complaining that he had been 'verballed' by the police. The Detention, Treatment and Questioning Code has introduced rules that have attempted to address these problems (see paras 11.5 to 11.13 and 12.8 to 12.13).

The system now is that any interview with a suspect, whether it takes place at the station or not, must be accurately recorded by the police. Moreover, if the interview is at the station, it must be recorded (i.e. noted down) *contemporaneously* on forms specially provided for the purpose or in the officer's pocket book (para 11.5). Subject to the possibility of tape recording (see below), the only exceptions to contemporaneous noting are if the investigating officer considers it would not be practicable or if it would interfere with the conduct of the interview. At the end of the interview, the suspect should be invited to read the record through (or have it read to him), and be asked to sign it to indicate that it is accurate. If he refuses to sign, a senior officer is told what has happened and certifies to that effect on the record. The record should be signed by the suspect, and may subsequently be used as an exhibit at his trial, either as containing admissions or as being consistent with his defence and therefore of assistance to him. Where the interview record is not made contemporaneously, the reason must be recorded in the officer's pocket book (para 11.9), and the record must be made as soon as practicable after the completion of the interview (para 11.7).

Failure to comply with the above rules may lead to evidence of the suspect's answers being excluded at trial. In *Delaney* (1988) 88 Cr App R 338, the Court of Appeal held that failure to compile a contemporaneous record of the bulk of a 90 minute interview with D was a 'flagrant breach' of the Code. Although the breach did not automatically render evidence of the confession D eventually made inadmissible, in the circumstances of the particular case admission was unfair because, had the whole interview been properly recorded, facts might well have emerged to show that the confession was inadmissible as a matter of law under s 76. In *Canale* (1990) 91 Cr App R 1, the Court of Appeal quashed C's conviction because the trial judge should have acted under s 78 to exclude admissions which had not been contemporaneously recorded. In so doing, their lordships stated that 'the importance of the rules relating to contemporaneous noting of interviews could not be over-emphasised'. Their purpose was to ensure accurate records of suspects' remarks and to protect the police. In *Keenan* [1990] 2 QB 54, the Court of Appeal said that the 'verballing' provisions of the Code should be 'strictly complied with' and that the courts would not be slow to exclude evidence obtained following 'substantial breaches' of the Code.

The obvious alternative to written records of interviews is to tape record them. A detailed Code of Practice now governs the procedure for recording interviews (Code E), and the *Practice Direction (Crime: Tape Recording Police Interviews)* [1989] 1 WLR 631 deals with their use in court, and the provision of summaries or transcripts. According to Code E, para 3.1, tape-recording is to be used at police stations:

(a)   for suspects cautioned in respect of an indictable offence (including an offence triable either way);

(b)   for further questions put to a suspect after charge (note that this can only be done in exceptional circumstances — see Paragraph 2.5.2); or

(c)   for an interview taking place after a suspect has been shown a statement by, or an interview with, another person (e.g., an alleged accomplice).

The usual system is that the interview is taped on a double-deck machine, with two tapes being used and a time-coding device to deter subsequent tampering. After the interview, one tape is sealed and kept as a potential exhibit. The other tape is used as a working copy. From it, the officers prepare a summary of the interview, the defence being given a copy. Upon request, they are also entitled to a copy of the tape itself and can thus check the accuracy of the summary. If, there is a dispute, a transcript of the tape may be ordered, which can then be used as an administrative convenience at the trial. The tape itself will also be produced and, if necessary, played to the jury, while the interviewing officers should be called to identify who spoke the words on the tape and to deal with any suggestion that it has subsequently been falsified. Whether the audio-typist's transcript should also be read to the jury and/or given to them when they retire is a matter for the trial judge's discretion — the actual evidence is the tape itself, not the transcript (see Paragraph 19.1.1 for details).

A final possibility, which has largely died out as a result of contemporaneous interview notes and tape recording, is for a suspect to write or dictate a statement under caution. The statement is headed by the rubric, signed by the suspect — 'I make this statement of my own free will. I understand that I need not say anything unless I wish to do so and that what I say may be given in evidence.' There then follows the body of the statement, and it is signed again at the foot. Statements under caution are dealt with in annexe D to the Code.

2.6   POWERS OF SEARCH

Police powers to search for evidence divide into three main types, namely powers to search the persons of members of the public who are merely under suspicion, powers to search premises and powers to search the person and/or premises of an arrestee.

2.6.1   Powers of stop and search

Sections 1 to 3 of PACE provide the police with a general power to detain a member of the
public without arresting him for the purpose of carrying out a search of his person. Although
the Stop and Search Code, Code A, indicates that it governs the power to search a person
without first arresting him, past police practice in the use of similar powers has been to stop
and search where their suspicions about the proposed subject are too vague to amount to
reasonable grounds for an arrest. The object of the search is to dispel or confirm those vague
suspicions. In the latter event, an arrest will no doubt follow.

A police officer may search a person or vehicle if he has reasonable grounds for
suspecting that he will find stolen or prohibited articles: PACE, s 1(2) and (3). 'Prohibited
articles' comprise (a) offensive weapons and (b) articles made or intended by the persons
carrying them for use in connection with burglary, theft, taking vehicles or obtaining
property by deception: s 1(7) to (9). Paras 1.6, 1.6A, 1.7, 1.7A and 1.7AA of the Stop and
Search Code give quite full guidance on what amounts to reasonable suspicion justifying a
stop and search. The main point is that there must be a concrete basis in fact for the
suspicion, as opposed to a mere 'hunch' or instinct. Such a basis may be found in the nature
of the property which the member of the public is seen or thought to be carrying, coupled
with facts such as the time and place and his general behaviour. But para 1.7 states:

> Subject to the provision in paragraph 1.7AA below, reasonable suspicion can never be
> supported on the basis of personal factors alone without supporting intelligence or
> information. For example, a person's colour, age, hairstyle or manner of dress, or the fact
> that he is known to have a previous conviction for possession of an unlawful article,
> cannot be used alone or in combination with each other as the sole basis on which to
> search that person. Nor may it be founded on the basis of stereotyped images of certain
> persons or groups as more likely to be committing offences.

(Paragraph 1.7AA deals with the wearing of distinctive clothing to indicate gang membership.)

The power to stop and search may be exercised only in a place to which the public have
access: s 1(1). Broadly speaking, this means any public place; any place to which the public
(or a section thereof) have access by permission whether with or without payment, and any
place to which the public do in fact have 'regular access' even though they might not be
entitled to go there. Within the last-mentioned category are car-parks, forecourts, the
common parts of blocks of flats and even private yards or gardens adjoining the road.
However, a person may not be stopped and searched in his own garden or yard; nor may
somebody who is there by his permission. But, if a stranger jumps over the garden fence to
hide behind a hedge, the police have power to search him where he is. The period for which
a person may be detained by virtue of the s 1 power is that necessary to carry out the search
either at the place where he was stopped or nearby: s 2(8). The most that the officer carrying
out the search can require the subject to do in public is to remove an outer coat, jacket or
gloves: s 2(9)(a). However, there is nothing to stop the officer taking the subject to a nearby
van or police station where a more thorough examination can take place out of the public
view (para 3.5). Reasonable force may be used both for purposes of detaining the person to
be searched and then for actually searching him, but it should be employed as a last resort
where the subject is not willing to cooperate (para 3.2). Every effort should be made to spare
the subject embarrassment, and not to extend the search beyond what is strictly necessary
(e.g., if the officer thought he saw the subject slipping a knife into his pocket, the search

ought to be confined to that pocket, assuming there was no opportunity to transfer whatever it was the officer saw to somewhere else about the subject's person). Before commencing the search, the officer must tell the subject his name and the name of the police station to which he is attached; the object of the proposed search; the grounds on which it is being made, and the right of the subject to have a copy of the record of the search: s 2(2) and (3). If the officer is not in uniform, he must produce his warrant card (para 2.5 of the Code). The officer may also ask some preliminary questions. The subject is not obliged to answer, nor is the officer entitled to detain him for the purpose of asking questions — it is a power to stop and search, not a power to stop and question. However, if answers are forthcoming, they may dispel the suspicions which led to the original decision to stop, and thus avoid the need for a search (see s 2(1)). Although a vehicle may be stopped in order to search it, this may only be done by a constable in uniform: s 2(9)(b). Where an unattended vehicle is searched, a notice must be left on it, stating what has happened and giving the information about the officer's name etc. which would have been given to the driver in person had he been there: s 2(6).

The powers to stop and search contained in ss 1 to 3 of PACE are among the most controversial of its provisions. There is, plainly, room for abuse, in that individuals or groups could be harrassed by over-enthusiastic use of the powers. This is acknowledged in guidance given by the Stop and Search Code. The Code says that the powers are to be employed 'responsibly' and that misuse could 'lead to mistrust of the police by the community' (Notes for Guidance 1AA). The Philips Commission's answer to such anxieties was to require the police to make adequate records of when and why they exercise the stop and search power. This is dealt with in s 3 of PACE. The record is to be made on the spot or as soon as is practicable after the carrying out of the search. It must give the name of the officer concerned and, if known, that of the subject, otherwise a description of him. The object, grounds, date, time and place of the search are all to be specified, together with what was found and details of any injury to a person or damage to property apparently caused. The subject is entitled, on request made within 12 months, to a copy of the record: s 3(7) and (9). That might assist him, for example, in suing the police if the search appears to have been unjustified or in making a complaint about their conduct.

The Criminal Justice and Public Order Act 1994, s 60, introduced a new police power to stop vehicles or pedestrians and search for offensive weapons or dangerous instruments. The power can be exercised only in a particular locality where written authorisation has been signed by a police officer of the rank of superintendent or above. If no more senior officer is available, an inspector may sign the authority. In any event, authority may be issued only where serious violence may occur. It is then valid for up to 24 hours, but can be extended for a further six hours. Once authority has been issued under s 60, it gives a constable the right to make such search as he sees fit 'whether or not he has any grounds for suspecting that the person or vehicle is carrying weapons or articles of that kind': s 60(5). This is in stark contrast to the exercise of the power under s 1 of PACE, which is restricted to cases where the officer has 'reasonable grounds for suspecting that he will find stolen or prohibited articles'.

There are also powers:

(a)   to stop and search vehicles which could be used in acts of terrorism (Prevention of Terrorism (Temporary Provisions) Act 1989, s 13A);
(b)   to stop and search pedestrians for articles which could be used for acts of terrorism (Prevention of Terrorism (Temporary Provisions) Act 1989, s 13B);

(c)   to search for controlled drugs under the Misuse of Drugs Act 1971, s 23;

(d)   to search for firearms under the Firearms Act 1968, s 47.

2.6.2   Powers to search premises

Prior to PACE, a wide variety of statutory provisions gave the police power to enter premises and search for evidence relating to a criminal offence. Usually, a warrant had to be obtained from a magistrate to authorise the search. In other cases it could be authorised by a senior police officer. However, there were some strange lacunae in the law, the best known of which was that there was no power to enter premises to search for evidence of murder (see *Ghani v Jones* [1970] 1 QB 693). Sections 8 to 14 of PACE are designed to fill these lacunae. Most of the pre-existing powers to authorise searches are retained, so the Act supplements the earlier law, rather than changing it. Sections 15 to 22 contain general provisions relating to the obtaining and executing of search warrants both under PACE and under any other legislation.

Section 8 of PACE provides that a magistrate may issue a warrant authorising a police officer to enter and search premises if there are reasonable grounds for believing that:

(a)   a *serious arrestable offence* has been committed; and

(b)   there is material on the premises in question which is likely to be both of *substantial value* to the investigation of the offence, and ultimately admissible as evidence should there be a prosecution; and

(c)   the aforementioned does not consist of or include *legally privileged* items, *excluded material or special procedure material*; and

(d)   it is either not practicable to obtain permission to enter the premises without a warrant (e.g., because the person entitled to grant permission would refuse it or cannot be contacted) or the purpose of the search would be frustrated (e.g., by destruction of the evidence) if the officers arriving to make it could not insist upon immediate entry.

In short, the offence suspected must be serious; the evidence likely to be found must be cogent, and the alternatives to entering with a warrant must be unsatisfactory. The three categories of material mentioned in (c) above and the special provisions relating to them are described below.

Of the still effective pre-1986 legislation dealing with the issue of search warrants by far the most important is s 26(1) of the Theft Act 1968. This provides that a magistrate who has reasonable cause to believe that a person has 'in his custody or possession or on his premises any stolen goods' may 'grant [a police officer] a warrant to search for and seize the same'. 'Stolen goods' are defined so as to include those obtained by deception or blackmail. There is an overlap between s 8 of PACE and s 26 of the Theft Act in that the stolen goods might be evidence of a serious arrestable offence, but s 26 — unlike s 8 — will apply even if the offence to which the goods relate is not a serious one. Moreover, under s 26, there is no express requirement that the magistrate must be satisfied that gaining entry otherwise than by a warrant would be unsatisfactory or impracticable. Thus, in cases where it seems on the face of it that a warrant could be granted under either section, it will be simpler to make the application under s 26 of the Theft Act. Other provisions giving magistrates power to issue search warrants include s 6(1) of the Criminal Damage Act 1971 (search for anything which has been or is intended for use in damaging property); ss 7 and 24 of the Forgery and Counterfeiting Act 1981 (search for false instruments or counterfeit notes or coins and for anything used to make the same); s 46 of the Firearms Act 1968 (search for firearms and ammunition); s 23(3) of the Misuse of Drugs Act 1971 (search for controlled drugs), and s 3 of the Obscene Publications Act 1959 (search for obscene articles kept for publication for gain). There are also a few situations in which a warrant may be issued to search premises for people rather than things (see, for example, Sch 2 to the Immigration Act 1971 which deals with searches for a person suspected of being liable to deportation). Of the pre-1986 provisions which enabled a senior police officer to bypass the need for a warrant by giving his junior officers written authority to enter and search, the most important (s 26(2) of the Theft Act which related to a superintendent authorising a search for stolen goods) has been repealed by PACE. However, senior officers still have power *inter alia* to authorise in an emergency a search of premises for evidence of offences under PACE, (s 9(2).

The proposal in the Police and Criminal Evidence Bill that there should be a general power to issue warrants to search for evidence of serious arrestable offences caused great concern to various groups of professional and business people, who felt that their relationships with clients would be jeopardised if they could be forced to surrender to the police documents or other material that had been entrusted to them in confidence. In deference to these concerns, the Act was eventually passed with complicated safeguards to protect the following three classes of material:

(i) *Items subject to legal privilege* (s. 10).   These are essentially any communications between a legal adviser and his client; communications between a legal adviser or the client and a third party made in contemplation of legal proceedings; and items enclosed with such communications (provided they are lawfully in the possession of whoever has them and are not, for example, stolen). The concept of documents which attract legal professional privilege is, of course, familiar in evidence and civil procedure, and s 10 should be regarded as a statutory adoption of the common law definition (see dicta in *Central Criminal Court ex p Francis and Francis* [1989] AC 346). Again following the common law, s 10(2) provides that items held with the purpose of furthering a criminal purpose cannot enjoy legal privilege. This applies even if the person actually in possession of the items (e.g., the solicitor of a person being investigated by the police) was entirely unaware of anything improper (*Ex p Francis and Francis,* in which case files held by the respondent solicitors concerning a client's business transactions were not items subject to legal privilege because it was contended that the transactions were a means by which the client 'laundered' and distributed the proceeds of drug trafficking). Where the police seek material which is prima facie covered by legal privilege, it will be rare for the judge to issue a blanket order granting a search warrant in respect of wide categories of documents held by a firm of solicitors. In certain circumstances, however, such an order may be proper. Hence, in *Leeds Crown Court ex p Switalski* [1991] Crim LR 559, the Divisional Court upheld the circuit judge in granting such a blanket order where the firm in question were subjects of an enquiry into fraud on the legal aid fund and conspiracy to pervert the course of justice.

(ii) *Excluded material* (ss 11–12).   This consists of 'personal records' held in confidence by the person who created them. Personal records are defined as medical records, records of spiritual counselling and files kept on their clients by social workers, probation officers and the like. Thus, the category of excluded material is a narrow one.

(iii) *Special procedure material* (s 14).   This is a rather wider category than excluded material, covering anything that a person acquired in the course of his trade, business or employment, and which he holds subject to an express or implied undertaking to keep it confidential. It also covers 'journalistic material' (unless it was acquired and has always been held in confidence, in which case it comes within the category of excluded material).

The scheme of the Act is that legally privileged items are totally protected from seizure under a search warrant. Access to excluded material or special procedure material may be obtained, if at all, only by application to a circuit judge, not through a warrant issued by a magistrate or authorisation given by a senior police officer: s 9(1). Any pre-PACE enactment authorising a search for legally privileged items, excluded material or special procedure material ceases to that extent to have effect: s 9(2). The procedure for obtaining excluded or special procedure material is contained in Sch 1 to PACE. Essentially, a police officer must apply to a circuit judge for an order that the person in possession of the material (the respondent) shall, within a week or longer period specified by the judge, hand the material over to the police or allow them to take copies of it. Notice of the application must be given to the respondent, and should specify the documents or other material sought (see *Central Criminal Court ex p Adegbesan and others* [1986] 1 WLR 1293). The defendant, on the other hand, has no right to be made a party to, or be given notice of, the application. The applicant must tell the judge of anything known which might weigh against making the order (*Lewes Crown Court ex p Hill* (1990) 93 Cr App R 60). If the material is excluded material, a production order may be made only if, prior to the enactment of s 9(2) of PACE, a warrant to search for the material could have been issued under provisions such as s 26(1) of the Theft Act. If it is special procedure material, the judge may make an order if he considers that what is sought would be of substantial value in the investigation of a serious arrestable offence; that other methods of obtaining access to the material would clearly not succeed, and that it is in the public interest to make the order. Deciding where the 'public interest' lies will involve balancing the benefits to be gained from the successful investigation of a serious crime against the harm done by damaging confidential relationships. Having been served with notice of intention to apply for a production order, the respondent is under a duty not to hide, destroy, damage, etc. the subject matter of the proposed order. Where the police think that he cannot be trusted not to do those things, they may apply without notice for a search warrant, which the judge may grant if he considers that (i) he would be entitled to make a production order, but (ii) an application on notice for such an order would indeed have entailed undue risks to the preservation of the evidence. Failure to comply with a production order is contempt of court, and may sometimes also result in the issue of a search warrant.

The scheme of the legislation means that it can never be right for a magistrate to issue a s 8 warrant to search for documents which are prima facie legally privileged. If they turn out to be privileged, they will be covered by s 10. If they are excluded from the scope of legal privilege because of a criminal purpose, they are pushed into the ambit of special procedure material. Hence s 14 would come into play, and application must be made to a judge, not a magistrate.

If a party is aggrieved by the decision of the judge, it is not appropriate to apply to him to rescind his order. The proper course is to apply to the Divisional Court for judicial review (*Liverpool Crown Court ex p Wimpey plc* [1991] Crim LR 635).

Sections 15 and 16 of PACE and the Search of Premises Code contain numerous detailed safeguards relating to the obtaining and execution of search warrants. For example, the application for a warrant should be made *ex p* without notice, for the obvious reason that, if notice were given, the items sought might vanish. The application should be supported by a written information, specifying *inter alia* the premises to be searched, the items it is hoped to find, and how those items relate to the investigation on which the police are engaged. The officer should attend and be prepared to answer questions on oath — e.g. as to the general nature of the information which leads him to want to search the premises, although he should not be expected to reveal the name of an individual informant.

When executing the warrant, the police should have it with them to show to the occupier of the premises. Normally they should seek his permission to enter, but they need not do so if that might frustrate the object of the search or endanger the officers. A warrant should not be used as an excuse to ransack the entire premises — i.e. the police should look in those places where the items they are authorised by the warrant to search for are most likely to be. If, however, they come across other items which appear to be the proceeds or evidence of crime, they may seize them, even though they are not mentioned in the warrant (s 19). The officer conducting the search must endorse the warrant with a statement of whether the property mentioned therein and/or anything else was found. Anything taken by the police may be retained 'for so long as is necessary in all the circumstances' (s 22) — e.g. until after the trial at which the item is to be used as evidence. A record of what has been seized must be given to the occupier of the premises, who then has certain limited rights to see, photograph and take copies of the items concerned.

2.6.3   Searches arising out of arrests

The following are the main powers of search connected with the exercise of a power of arrest:

(a)   *Search of person on arrest.*   An officer who arrests a suspect otherwise than at the police station may search him if he has reasonable grounds to suspect that he has anything which might *either* be used for purposes of an escape *or* might be evidence of an offence (not necessarily the offence for which the arrest was made): PACE, s 32(2)(a). This merely reflects the common law (see *Dillon v O'Brien and Davis* (1887) 16 Cox CC 245). Anything found which comes within the two stated categories may be seized and retained by the officer. The search should not extend beyond what is reasonably required to discover whether the arrestee has anything on him which might be so seized: s 32(3). He may not, in any event, be required to remove any clothing in public, other than an outer coat, jacket or gloves: s 32(4).

(b)   *Search of arrestee at police station.*   One of the custody officer's initial duties in respect of an arrestee brought to the police station is to record what he has with him. For this purpose, he may and normally would authorise a search. The extent of the search is in the custody officer's discretion. It may extend to a strip search, in which case it must be carried out by an officer of the same sex. Nobody of the opposite sex (other than a doctor or nurse) may be present. Nor may anybody whose presence is unnecessary (see Annex A to the Detention, Treatment and Questioning Code, which defines a strip search as one involving more than the removal of the outer clothing). Searches at the police station are dealt with in s 54 of PACE. For further details, see Paragraph 2.3.3.

(c)   *Intimate searches.*   A strip search is not necessarily an intimate search as defined by PACE. The latter is 'a search which consists of the physical examination of a person's body orifices other than the mouth': s 65 and Code C, annexe A, para 1. Clearly, such searches should be subject to strict controls because they might be used to humiliate or intimidate the subject. If inexpertly carried out, they could cause physical harm. So, the custody officer, although entitled to order a strip search under s 54 to ascertain what an arrestee has with him, may not sanction an intimate search: s 54(7). Section 55 deals with intimate searches. They must be authorised by an officer of at least the rank of superintendent, but only if he reasonably believes that an arrestee in detention at the station has concealed on him *either* anything which he could and might use to cause physical injury to himself or others while in police detention or at court, *or* a Class A drug which, prior to his arrest, he had in his possession for purposes of supply or illegal exportation. Class A drugs are the 'hard drugs' (cocaine, heroin etc. but not cannabis). If the superintendent believes that the detainee might have, say, heroin concealed in his body but that he is simply a user (not a supplier or exporter) of the drug, an intimate search should not be authorised. Neither should it be authorised if the object of the search might be found by other means (e.g., by waiting for it to be passed through the natural bodily functions). A search *must* be carried out by a doctor or nurse at a hospital or doctor's surgery, not at the police station. If possible, a search for items capable of causing injury should also be by a doctor or nurse, although they may be asked to come to the station for the purpose rather than the detainee having to be taken to hospital. However, in an emergency the senior officer may authorise another officer to make the search (e.g., if the police doctor called to the station refuses to search without the detainee's consent and that consent is not forthcoming, or if it is likely to be a long time before the doctor arrives).

(d) *Search of premises where arrested.* Section 17 of PACE, which is basically a codification of the common law, provides *inter alia* that a police officer may enter and search premises in order to execute a warrant for arrest or to make an arrest without warrant for an arrestable offence. He must have reasonable grounds for believing that the person he seeks is on the premises. Reasonable force may be used to effect an entry. The power to search given by s 17 is limited in the sense that the officer may only do whatever is reasonably required to ascertain whether his quarry is on the premises — he is not entitled to search for evidence. However, s 32(2)(b) supplements s 17 by empowering the police to search premises in which an arrestee was at the time of or immediately before his arrest for evidence relating to the offence in respect of which the arrest was made. The subsection applies even if the arrest was for a non-arrestable offence. If, in making a search under either s 17 or s 32(2)(b), the officer discovers evidence of other offences he may seize that too (see s 19 of PACE).

(e) *Search of arrestee's home etc.* The premises searched under s 17 or s 32(2)(b) could be the arrestee's own home, but that will not necessarily be so. For many years, the police assumed that, if they arrested a person away from his home, they had the same right to search it as if he had been arrested there. This was confirmed in *Jeffrey v Black* [1978] 1 QB 490, subject to the important qualification that the property which the police hoped to find as a result of the search had to have some connection with the matter for which the arrestee had been detained. The reasoning in *Jeffrey v Black* was doubted by the Lord Chief Justice in *McLorie v Oxford* [1982] QB 1290, a case which suggested that, unless the arrest happened to take place at the arrestee's home, there was no power to search it against his will without a warrant. Section 18 of PACE broadly speaking restores the position to what it was before *McLorie v Oxford,* but with certain additional safeguards for the arrestee. The section enables an officer of at least the rank of inspector to give written authorisation for 'any premises occupied or controlled by a person under arrest for an arrestable offence' to be searched by the investigating officers. In addition to a search of the arrestee's home, a search of his shop or other business premises might be authorised. Authorisation may only be given if the inspector reasonably suspects that there is evidence on the premises relating either to the offence in respect of which the arrest was made, or to another connected or similar arrestable offence. The facts of *Jeffrey v Black* provide a good example of when authorisation for a search would *not* be justified. Cannabis was found in B's lodgings when they were searched without his consent following his arrest for stealing a sandwich from a public house. The Divisional Court held that the search was unlawful because the officers could have had no reason to suppose that it would yield evidence relating either to the theft for which B was under arrest, or to other 'sandwich thefts', or even to other offences of dishonesty. Precisely the same reasoning would apply under s 18. Having authorised a search, the inspector should note his reasons and the nature of the evidence sought in the arrestee's custody record. The only situation in which a s 18 search may be made without prior authorisation is when the arresting officer decides that it is appropriate to delay taking the arrestee to the station so that they can go together to the premises in question, with a view to carrying out the search in the arrestee's presence (see s 30(10)). The officer should then inform the inspector as soon as practicable of what has occurred.

Finally, three general points about police searches remain to be made. First, in cases where the police do not have the power to carry out a search against the will of the occupier of the premises concerned, they may, of course, ask him for his consent. Paras 4.1 to 4.3 of the Search of Premises Code deal with what the occupier should be told when his permission for a search is sought and also provide that any consent should be given in writing if practicable. Secondly, where any provision of PACE gives the police power to perform a certain act and does not make that power dependent upon the consent of the person affected by it, reasonable force may be used in the exercise of the power: PACE, s 117. Thus, reasonable force may be used *inter alia* to effect an arrest under ss 24 or 25, to enter premises to effect an arrest under s 17, to search an arrestee both upon arrest and at the police station under ss 32 and 54, to make an intimate search under s 55 and to enter and search an arrestee's premises under s 18. Lastly, evidence discovered as a result of unlawful searches may well be admissible at an accused's trial, irrespective of whether he or some third party was the victim of the illegality. As explained at the beginning of the Chapter, there is merely a discretion to exclude unlawfully obtained evidence if its effect on the fairness of the proceedings would be so marked that it ought not to be admitted (see s 78). There clearly is a discretion under s 78 of PACE to exclude the fruits of an illegal search (see, for example, *Wright* [1994] Crim LR 55). But the courts have traditionally been slow to disallow evidence on this basis, and the Court of Appeal will be reluctant to interfere with the trial judge's discretion (*Christou* [1992] QB 979).

2.7 EVIDENCE OF IDENTITY

The methods by which the police gather evidence to establish that their suspect was indeed the person who committed the *actus reus* of the offence in question are too many and various for a comprehensive survey. However, two particular ones call for comment, since they are dealt with in PACE and the Codes. They are identification parade evidence and fingerprint evidence.

2.7.1 Identification parades etc.

The simplest means of identifying the accused as the person who perpetrated or took part with others in the perpetration of the *actus reus* of the offence charged is to call an eye-witness of the crime, and ask him whether the person he saw committing the offence is present in court. The witness will almost certainly say, 'Yes, there he is, standing in the dock'. Such evidence is, however, far from satisfactory. A witness knows perfectly well that whoever is in the dock is the man the police believe committed the offence. He is therefore likely to identify him, not because of the resemblance between him and whoever he saw committing the offence, but simply because he is where he is — i.e., in the dock. Therefore, unless there has been some prior identification of the accused by the witness (e.g., at an identification parade), the courts will not normally permit a 'dock identification'. This general principle may be departed from if the accused refused to go on a parade, or if it was not practicable to hold one because the witness did not recover from the injuries he received through the alleged offence until shortly before the trial, or the accused was of such unusual looks that not enough people even roughly resembling him could be found to go on a parade with him (see *John* [1973] Crim LR 113, *Caird* (1970) 54 Cr App R 499, and *Hunter* [1969] Crim LR 262). However, the basic rule is that, if there is any possibility of a dispute arising at a suspect's future trial about his being the person who was seen in a certain place or committing certain acts, the police should give him the chance of standing on an identification parade at which the witness(es) can try to pick him out. If he is not given that option, any evidence of identity from the witnesses will probably be ruled inadmissible. (For a two year period commencing 1 April 2002, the rules relating to the type of visual identification procedure which applies have been altered (see the end of this Paragraph). However, the basic principle remains that a regulated pre-trial identification procedure is required).

The procedure relating to identification, including the holding of parades, is contained in Code D, which is referred to as 'the Code' in the remainder of this Paragraph. Para. 2.0 states that a written record should be made of the description of a suspect first given by a potential witness. The aim is to ensure that it is clear whether the witness's description is a good 'fit' for the actual appearance of the suspect. This record may form part of a witness statement, or may be in the form of an immediate record, such as a police control room log. (Note 2A makes it clear that as a general rule a police officer who is a witness is subject to the same principles and procedures as a civilian witness.) The written record must be made available to the suspect or his solicitor as soon as practicable and, if available, before any identification parade takes place (para 2.0 and annexe A). Where a potential witness is shown photographs of possible suspects, the officer supervising the showing of the photographs must ensure that the first description is recorded before the photographs are shown (annexe D).

Code D, para 2.3, requires a parade to be held in any case involving disputed identification evidence if either the suspect asks for one or the officer in charge of the case considers that it would be useful and the suspect consents. The suspect's right to demand a parade is subject to its being practicable to hold one and to the possibility that the investigating officer may order a group or video identification (see below) as more satisfactory than a parade (paras 2.4, 2.7 and 2.10). The arrangements are in the hands of an officer in uniform of at least the rank of inspector, who must not be involved in the investigation of the offence (para 2.2). He is referred to as 'the identification officer'. None of the investigating officers may share in the arranging or conducting of the parade. Before it takes place, the identification officer must explain to the suspect its purpose, the procedure for holding it (including his right to have a friend or solicitor present), the fact that he may refuse to take part, and the consequences of his so refusing (para 2.15). A written notice containing this information is then given to the suspect, after which he is invited to sign a copy of the notice to indicate whether he is or is not willing to take part in the parade (para 2.16).

The actual conduct of the parade is prescribed by annexe A to the Code. The main points are that:

(a) The parade may be held either in an ordinary room or in a room with a one-way screen which will permit the witnesses to see the parade without themselves being seen. The idea of one-way screens is an innovation of the Code. Since the suspect will not himself be able to tell whether he has been picked out by the witness, a screen can be used only if he has a friend or solicitor present or the parade is videoed. If a parade involves a prison inmate, he may be brought to the police station for it if there are no security problems. Otherwise it may be held in the prison, under normal parade rules insofar as that is practicable.

(b)   The parade is to consist of at least eight persons in addition to the suspect, who should as far as possible resemble him in 'age, height, general appearance and position in life'. Normally only one suspect should be put on a parade, but if there are two suspects of roughly similar appearance they may be paraded together with at least 12 non-suspects. Each position where the members of the parade will stand is numbered, this being a second innovation of the Code.

(c)   Immediately before the parade the identification officer reminds the suspect of what will happen and cautions him. He then asks him whether he has any objections to the arrangements — e.g., the suspect might say that there is too great a difference between his appearance and the appearances of the others making up the parade for it to be fair. Where he has a friend or solicitor present, the suspect may consult him. If there are objections to the arrangements, all reasonable steps should be taken to remove them. The suspect is entitled to choose his own position on the line-up.

(d)   Prior to inspecting the parade, the witnesses should not speak to each other about the case, or see the suspect or any other parade members. They should not see or be reminded of any photograph or description of the suspect, or other indication of his identity. Nor should they be allowed to overhear anything said by a witness who has already made his inspection. It is the responsibility of the identification officer to ensure that none of these things occur. Immediately before going into the room, the witness should be told by the identification officer that the person he saw may or may not be on the parade, and that if he cannot make a positive identification he should say so. The witness is then asked to look at each member of the parade at least twice, taking as much time as he wishes. Once he has done so, the identification officer asks him whether 'the person he saw on an earlier relevant occasion' is there. The witness should make any identification by indicating the number of the person he has picked out (previously he pointed him out, or touched him on the shoulder, but many timid witnesses found that a nerve-wracking experience). The witness may ask any parade member to speak or adopt a particular posture, but he should first try to make an identification on the basis of appearance alone.

(e)   If there are two or more witnesses, they must each view the parade separately, and the suspect should be allowed to change his position on the line after each witness.

(f)   If a witness makes an identification after the parade has ended, the suspect should be informed and consideration should be given to allowing the witness a second chance to identify the suspect.

(g)   At the end of the parade, the identification officer must ask the suspect whether he has any comments to make about it. A written record of how it was conducted is made on the appropriate forms. A colour photograph or video film is taken of the line-up, a copy of which has to be supplied to the suspect or his solicitor on request.

As an alternative to an identification parade, arrangements may be made for the witness to see the suspect in a group. This *group identification* should be done if the suspect refuses or fails to attend an identification parade, or if the investigating officer considers that it would be more satisfactory than a conventional parade (para 2.7). It is dependent upon it being practicable to make the necessary arrangements (e.g., if the group identification takes place outside the station and the suspect is in police detention, there will have to be adequate precautions against an escape). The suspect's consent for a group identification should be sought but, if it is refused, the identification officer has a discretion to proceed with it. A group identification may be arranged covertly where the suspect has refused to co-operate or failed to attend. As far as possible, a group identification should follow the principles and procedure for a parade (see above). If he considers it the most satisfactory course of action, the identification officer may show the witness *a video film* of a suspect (para 2.10). As with a group identification, the suspect's consent should be sought, but the identification officer has a discretion to proceed anyway. The principles and procedures for a video film identification are laid down in annexe B to Code D. If he refuses to take part in a parade, a group identification, or a video film identification, a *confrontation* may be arranged between him and the witness (para 2.13). This is not dependent upon consent, although a solicitor or friend must be present on the suspect's behalf unless that would cause unreasonable delay. Each witness in turn confronts the suspect, and is asked by the identification officer, 'Is this the person?'

From a tactical viewpoint, there are arguments both for and against agreeing to a parade. If one is picked out, that will seem much more convincing to a jury than if the witness merely made his identification at a confrontation. On the other hand, even if one is guilty, there is a fair chance that when the parade is held the witness will be so overcome with nerves or so uncertain of himself that he will fail to make the identification. Moreover, the penalty for refusing to be paraded is that it will seem to the jury that one had something to hide. Even in cases where there has been a successful identification parade, the judge in his summing-up must remind the jury of the caution with which all identification evidence must be approached (see *Turnbull* [1977] QB 224). Any irregularities in the parade should be mentioned. Indeed, they might even lead to the judge withdrawing the case from the jury on the grounds that the identification evidence is weak and there is no supporting evidence.

As is well known, the police keep a 'rogues' gallery' of pictures of convicted criminals. If the officers investigating a crime do not have information which would justify them arresting a particular suspect but there are eye witnesses to what happened, they may show those witnesses photographs from the rogues' gallery (Code D, annexe D). A witness looking at photographs should be given as much privacy as possible, and not be allowed to communicate with other witnesses. He should be shown at least 12 photographs at a time, being told that the person he is looking for may or may not be amongst those photographed. No prompting or guidance is permissible. If the police already have suspicions of a certain person (but nothing to justify an arrest), they should ensure that his picture is shown with pictures of others who as far as possible resemble him. Once a positive identification has been made from photographs, then — unless it was plainly wrong — neither the witness making the identification nor any other witness should be shown further pictures, but they should be asked to attend an identification parade. The defence should be told if a witness who attended an identification parade had previously been shown photographs (or an Identikit likeness) of the suspect. Defence counsel could then argue that an identification at the parade should be discounted because the witness was picking out the person whose photograph he had seen, rather than picking out the person he saw committing the offence. Unfortunately, this inevitably reveals to the jury that the accused has previous convictions, for otherwise the police would not have a photograph of him.

For a period of two years from 1 April 2002, the hierarchy of visual identification procedures outlined above is altered. Article 2 of the Police and Criminal Evidence Act (Codes of Practice) (Temporary Modifications to Code D) Order, SI 2002 No 615, modifies Code D. The officer in charge of the case has a free choice between a video identification and an identification parade. A group identification may be offered initially if the officer considers it more satisfactory and that it is practicable. Otherwise it should be offered only if video identification or an identification parade are refused or are impracticable. If none of these are practicable, the identification officer has discretion to arrange for covert video or group identification to take place. A confrontation remains the last resort.

2.7.2 Fingerprints

The National Identification Bureau at Scotland Yard keeps records of convictions and the fingerprints of those convicted. Broadly speaking, only offences punishable with imprisonment are 'recordable offences', conviction for which will result in the offender's fingerprints being added to the national collection if they are not already there. Section 61 of PACE and paras 3.1 to 3.8 of Code D deal with the taking of fingerprints. The police are always at liberty to fingerprint somebody with his consent (e.g., the occupiers of burgled premises might be asked for their prints so as to distinguish them from any left behind by the burglars). Consent given at the police station should be in writing: PACE, s 61(2). Fingerprinting of detainees at police stations otherwise than by consent is allowed if an officer of at least the rank of superintendent authorises it on the grounds that it will tend to confirm or disprove the detainee's involvement in the offence of which he is suspected: s 61(3)(b) and (4). The authorisation should be in writing or confirmed in writing as soon as practicable: s 61(5). The reasons should be explained to the detainee and noted on his custody record: s 61(7) and (8). The superintendent's authorisation may be given even if the offence suspected is non-recordable. Once a detainee has been charged, his prints may be taken without his consent and without authorisation, provided the offence concerned is a recordable one: s 61(3)(b). And, having been convicted of a recordable offence, an offender is again liable to fingerprinting, and again no authorisation from a senior officer is required: s 61(6). Thus, if it did not seem necessary to fingerprint the offender when he was charged with a recordable offence, his prints may be taken from him at court immediately after he is found guilty. Whenever there is a right to fingerprint without the subject's consent, reasonable force may be used to accomplish the task if he does not co-operate. Fingerprints taken from a non-suspect or from a suspect who is cleared of the offence must be destroyed as soon as is practicable after the conclusion of the proceedings. He is entitled to be present when they are destroyed (see PACE, s 64).

Section 61 represents a significant change from the pre-1986 law, under which a suspect's fingerprints could be taken against his will only if the police obtained an order from the magistrates permitting that to be done. PACE also deals with the taking of other samples from a suspect which are of potential use for forensic purposes. *Intimate samples* (e.g., blood, urine, semen, saliva) may only be taken from someone in police detention if (a) the taking has been authorised by an officer of at least the rank of superintendent (inspector, once the Criminal Justice and Police Act 2001 comes into force), and (b) the detainee gives his written consent. The senior officer's authorisation is dependent upon his reasonably believing that the sample will tend to disprove or confirm the detainee's involvement in a recordable offence (this includes all imprisonable offences, and a few non-imprisonable ones). If the detainee refuses consent, inferences can be drawn from that refusal in subsequent proceedings: s 62(10). When asked for his consent, the detainee must be warned of the possible evidential consequences of refusing it. *Non-intimate samples* (e.g., hair other than pubic hair, scrapings from under a nail, footprints, saliva) may be taken with the written consent of the person concerned whatever the nature of the offence under consideration and without the authorisation of a senior officer. Since there is no statutory provision allowing the prosecution to adduce evidence of refusal of a non-intimate sample, the person concerned is not under the same pressure to give the sample as he is when intimate samples are requested. However, in the case of non-intimate samples, a senior officer can authorise their being taken against the suspect's will, provided a recordable offence is suspected, and the officer reasonably believes that the sample will assist in proving or disproving the case against the suspect. An intimate sample, other than one of urine, must be taken by a doctor (or registered nurse, once the Criminal Justice and Police Act 2001 comes into force). There are no express requirements about the taking of non-intimate samples. Sections 62 and 63 deal respectively with intimate samples and non-intimate ones. Section 62 contains a saving subsection making it clear that it does not affect the provisions of the drink-driving laws relating to samples of blood or urine.

In addition, by PACE, s 63(3A), a non-intimate sample can be taken without consent where the person has been charged with a recordable offence or told he will be reported for one, and he has not given a non-intimate sample suitable for analysis. A similar power exists where an offender has been convicted of a recordable offence (s 63(3B)) or acquitted on grounds of insanity or found unfit to plead (s 63(3C)).

2.8 SPECIAL GROUPS

So far police powers and procedures have been considered on the assumption that the suspect is an adult of normal intelligence and with all his faculties. Some extra protections for the suspect are necessary if he is a juvenile or a member of another vulnerable group. At the other end of the scale, those arrested for terrorist offences are denied some of the rights that other suspects have.

2.8.1 Juveniles

The various powers of arrest without warrant described in Paragraph 2.3.1 may be exercised in respect of a juvenile just as they may be exercised in respect of an adult — the relevant legislation, in particular ss 24 and 25 of PACE, makes no mention of the age of the arrestee. Similarly, the powers of a magistrate to issue a warrant for arrest (e.g., under ss 1 and 13 of the MCA) are in no way restricted by the accused's youth. In practice, of course, both a police officer and a magistrate considering, respectively, the making of an arrest without warrant and the issuing of a warrant will bear in mind the undesirability of taking a youngster to the police station, and might refrain from exercising their powers when, in an equivalent case involving an adult, they would unhesitatingly do so. Any person who arrests a juvenile must take all reasonable steps to inform his parents of what has occurred: s 34 of the Children and Young Persons Act 1933.

Having arrived under arrest at the police station, a juvenile's continued detention there depends, just like an adult's, on whether the custody officer considers there is enough evidence to charge him and whether — if there is not — detention without charge is necessary to secure or preserve evidence relating to the offence suspected or to obtain such evidence by questioning him. One major difference, however, between an adult and a juvenile is that, if a juvenile is charged and not released, the custody officer must arrange for him to be taken into the care of the local authority and detained by them until he can be brought before the juvenile court: PACE, s 38(6). This does not apply — i.e., the juvenile can be kept in detention at the police station — if the custody officer certifies that it is impracticable to make the necessary arrangements with the local authority. Nor does it apply if the juvenile is aged 12 or over, no secure accommodation is available, and the officer certifies that keeping him in such other local authority accommodation as is available would not be adequate to protect the public from serious harm from him. Neither before nor after charge should a juvenile be put in a police cell unless that is the only secure accommodation available and he could not safely be left in a non-secure room (para 8.8 of the Detention, Treatment and Questioning Code).

The questioning of juveniles is dealt with in paras 11.14 to 11.16 of the Code. Save in exceptional circumstances (see below), a juvenile should not be interviewed or asked to provide a statement unless an 'appropriate adult' is also present. This applies whether or not the juvenile is himself suspected of an offence. An appropriate adult is defined as either his parent/guardian or a social worker or (in default of either of those) some other responsible adult unconnected with the police. Note 1C points out that a parent or guardian will *not* be the appropriate adult if he is the victim, a witness or a suspected accomplice, or has received admissions. Similarly, where a child in care admits the offence to a social worker, another social worker should be the appropriate adult. Further, if juvenile and parent are 'estranged', and the juvenile objects, then the parent should not be called as the appropriate adult (following *DPP v Blake* [1989] 1 WLR 432). The appropriate adult's role, according to para 11.16 of the Code, is not merely to act as an observer, but also to advise the juvenile and, if necessary, to 'facilitate communication with him'. A decision to exercise the right under s 58 to consult a solicitor may be taken on the juvenile's behalf by the appropriate adult. The reasons for taking extra care in questioning juveniles are fairly obvious, but the Code reminds investigating officers of them. They are that, without necessarily meaning to do so, juveniles are particularly prone to give information which is 'unreliable, misleading or [falsely] self-incriminating'. Even so, in an emergency, it may be necessary to question a juvenile without the safeguard of an appropriate adult being present. This may only be done if an officer of at least the rank of superintendent considers that delay will lead to physical harm to other people or harm to evidence connected with an offence, or alert other suspects not yet arrested for the offence, or hinder the recovery of property obtained from an offence (see para 11.1 and annexe C to the Detention, Treatment and Questioning Code). What if the police cannot obtain an appropriate adult from one of the above categories, and an interview cannot be justified on these emergency grounds? The juvenile cannot then be interviewed, and must be charged or released (para 11.14).

Reference has been made to a juvenile being charged. However, the more appropriate course usually is to release him from the station without charging him, so that the police and the other interested agencies can consider at their leisure whether it is an appropriate case for prosecution or can better be dealt with by way of a caution (see Paragraph 4.2.1 for the practice of giving a formal caution). Should the eventual decision be to prosecute, it will probably be easier to obtain a summons rather than have the juvenile come back to the station to be charged.

A juvenile suspect may not be put on an identification parade unless his parent consents. If he is a young person (i.e., has attained the age of 14), his own consent is required as well. Either the parent or some other appropriate adult must be present at the holding of the parade (see paras 1.11 to 1.14 of the Identification Code).

2.8.2 The mentally handicapped

For purposes of the Codes, the mentally handicapped are broadly defined to include not only those with a specific mental illness but also those whose low intelligence etc. make them incapable of understanding the significance of questions put to them by an officer and/or the significance of their replies. Moreover, if the officer has a suspicion or is told in good faith that somebody is mentally handicapped, he should treat him as such. Broadly speaking, the mentally handicapped are regarded as a vulnerable group and are equated with juveniles. Thus, like juveniles, they should normally have an appropriate adult present when they are questioned. Furthermore, if a mentally handicapped accused is prosecuted substantially on the basis of a confession which he made in the absence of an appropriate adult, the judge must warn the jury of the special need for caution before convicting: PACE, s 77. It might seem surprising that Parliament thought it necessary to have a specific provision to that effect — surely, any judge in the circumstances predicated by s 77 would be expected to emphasise the unsatisfactory nature of the prosecution evidence without being told to do so by statute. In *Lamont* [1989] Crim LR 813, however, L was charged with the attempted murder of his baby. He was mentally subnormal, with an IQ of 73 and a reading age of eight. He confessed after 18 hours at the police station. He was very emotional in interview and cried. There was no other adult present. The judge allowed the confession in. He omitted any direction along the lines of s 77 and stated that the absence of the appropriate adult from the interview was of little importance. The Court of Appeal quashed the conviction, commenting adversely on both the failure to give a direction under s 77 and the statement about the absence of an appropriate adult. The 'appropriate adult' in respect of a mentally handicapped person is *either* a relative, guardian or other person responsible for his welfare, *or* a person who has had experience in dealing with mental problems (e.g., a specialist social worker), *or* (in default of either of the above) any other responsible adult unconnected with the police. This is slightly different from the definition of appropriate adult *vis-à-vis* a juvenile. As regards identification parades, although an appropriate adult must be present both when the mentally handicapped person gives his consent to standing on one and when it is held, there is no requirement that the appropriate adult should himself agree to the holding of the parade.

> A person who appears to be deaf may not be interviewed in the absence of an interpreter (i.e., somebody who can communicate with him by sign language) unless he agrees or a senior officer considers that waiting for an interpreter would involve the risk of injury to third persons or serious damage to property. When an interpreter is present, he should take a note of the interview for possible future use if he is called as a witness at the interviewee's trial. The services of an interpreter will also be needed if the interviewee has difficulty in speaking English. Again the interpreter should take a note of the interview. He should also take down in the relevant foreign language any written statement the suspect wishes to make, the statement then being signed by the suspect. An official English translation is made in due course. Interpreters are provided at the public expense.

2.8.3   Suspected terrorists

Section 14 of the Prevention of Terrorism (Temporary Provisions) Act 1989 gives a power to arrest without warrant persons suspected of acts of terrorism or of being members of a proscribed organisation (i.e., the IRA and INLA). 'Terrorism' is defined as the 'use of violence for political ends'. A person arrested under s 14 may be detained by right of the arrest for up to *48 hours*. He may then be held for up to a further *five days* on the authority of the Home Secretary. The provisions of PACE about the authorisation for and maximum periods of police detention do not apply (see s 51(b)). However, ss 56 and 58 of the Act (right to have somebody informed of the arrest and right to consult with a solicitor) do apply to this group of suspects, though with significant modifications. Exercise of the right may be delayed for up to 48 hours (not up to 36 hours), and the grounds for authorising delay are wider. They include the fear that exercise of his rights by the suspect would interfere with the gathering of information about terrorism or, by alerting other persons, would make it more difficult to arrest them or prevent further terrorist actions by them. Furthermore, a very senior officer (a commander or assistant chief constable) may give a direction that, if the suspect wishes to exercise his s 58 right, the consultation with a solicitor must be in the sight and hearing of a police officer. The observing officer must be of at least the rank of inspector, unconnected with the investigation and in uniform. Clearly, the suspect may not feel at liberty to talk openly about the case if a police officer is listening to what he says. On the other hand, from a suspected terrorist's viewpoint, s 58 represents an improvement on the pre-1986 position when he had no right whatsoever to consult a solicitor until after he had been charged.

There is no power of arrest under s 14 of the Prevention of Terrorism (Temporary Provisions) Act 1989 if the suspect's acts of terrorism were connected solely with the affairs of the UK, excluding Northern Ireland, although he could almost certainly be arrested under s 24 of PACE. The significance of a terrorist being arrested under the latter rather than the former section is that his rights at the police station will be exactly the same as the rights of any other person detained for a serious arrestable offence — e.g., he will have to be released after 24 hours unless a senior officer authorises continued detention; he will have to be taken before magistrates after 36 hours, and he will have to be released or charged after, at the very most, 96 hours.

3　Prosecutors

The English constitutional system has traditionally avoided a centralised ministry of justice on the continental model. Responsibility for investigating crime, commencing prosecutions and presenting the case at court has been shared amongst a large number of different agencies. In October 1986, however, a major change was made to the system by the introduction of the Crown Prosecution Service (the CPS). Although the Service is still far short of a Justice Ministry, it has assumed a dominant role in the prosecution (but not the investigation) of crime. This Chapter will summarise the roles of the police, the CPS, other prosecuting authorities and the private individual in the prosecution process. The subject is complex, but, for purposes of understanding criminal procedure in court, it is only necessary to deal with it in outline.

3.1　THE POLICE

The great majority of the prosecutions in England and Wales are commenced by the police in the sense that the accused is either charged at a police station or an information is laid against him by a police officer in the course of his duty (see Paragraph 4.1 for explanation of charging and laying an information). Prior to commencing a prosecution, the police will, of course, have been responsible for investigating and obtaining evidence about the alleged offence. Under the pre-Crown Prosecution Service system, they were also responsible for the presentation of the case at court in the sense that they employed solicitors who appeared for the prosecution in the magistrates' court and instructed counsel for the Crown Court. Most police forces had salaried 'in-house' solicitors' departments. A minority simply instructed firms of solicitors in private practice. Either way, the police had the last word on, for example, the charges which should be proceeded with as the relationship between them and their solicitors was, in the final analysis, one of client and lawyer. Since October 1986, the police have been stripped of their responsibility for actually prosecuting crime. Once the accused has been charged or an information laid the papers go to the local branch office of the CPS which takes over the prosecution (see Paragraph 3.2). The police and CPS obviously need to act in close cooperation, since it will be necessary for police officers to attend court as witnesses, to warn private witnesses as to when they will be required, and to gather any further evidence that the CPS wants. However, the CPS is independent of the police, not their agent in prosecuting offences.

In common speech, one refers to 'the police' as if they were a unified force. In fact, however, there are a number of separate police forces, each acting within its own geographical area. Each force has a chief officer, called the 'Commissioner' in the City of

London and Metropolitan forces, the 'Chief Constable' in other forces. The chief officer is answerable for the general efficiency of his force to a police authority made up of local authority members and magistrates from the areas served by the force, save that the Home Secretary is the police authority for the two London forces. It is generally accepted that the police authority should not interfere in operational matters — i.e., the day-today running of the force. In particular, they should not interfere with the police discretion on whether or not to commence prosecutions, either by seeking to influence general policy on the kinds of cases in which prosecutions are appropriate or by ordering a prosecution in a particular case. Such decisions are for the chief officer and his men, not the police authority. Even the courts lack power to intervene, save in extreme cases where a policy adopted by the chief officer amounts to a dereliction of his duty to uphold the law. As Lord Denning put it in *Metropolitan Police Commissioner ex p Blackburn (No 1)* [1968] 2 QB 118:

> I hold it to be the duty of the Commissioner of the Police of the Metropolis, as it is of every chief constable, to enforce the law of the land . . . . He must decide whether or not suspected persons are to be prosecuted . . . . But [in this] he is not the servant of anyone, save of the law itself. No Minister of the Crown can tell him that he must or must not prosecute this man or that one. Nor can any police authority tell him so. The responsibility for law enforcement lies on him. He is answerable to the law and to the law alone.

Thus, police policy on prosecuting suspects can only be challenged in the unlikely event of the chief officer laying down a manifestly unreasonable policy, such as never commencing proceedings for theft if the amount involved is under £100. If that were to happen, any person with sufficient locus standi could apply for an order of mandamus to compel the chief officer to fulfil his duty of enforcing the law. The considerations taken into account in deciding whether or not to prosecute are discussed in Chapter 4.

3.2   THE CROWN PROSECUTION SERVICE

The Crown Prosecution Service was created by s 1 of the Prosecution of Offences Act 1985. It consists of the Director of Public Prosecutions, who is its head; the Chief Crown Prosecutors, each of whom is responsible to the Director for supervising the operation of the service in a particular area, and some 6000 other staff (including Crown Prosecutors and non-legally qualified support staff) who are appointed by the DPP with Treasury approval (see s 1(1) of the 1985 Act).

3.2.1   The Director of Public Prosecutions

The office of Director of Public Prosecutions was created in 1879. For over a century, despite the all-embracing nature of the title, the DPP's role in the prosecution system was relatively limited. However, the Prosecution of Offences Act 1985 transformed the position by requiring the DPP to take over the conduct of *all* criminal proceedings instituted by the police (s 3(2)(a)). Section 3(2) lists the duties of the DPP. The major ones are as follows:

(i)   to take over the conduct of all criminal proceedings commenced by the police;[1]

---

[1] There is a small exception to this in that the Attorney-General may specify categories of police prosecutions which the DPP need not take over. A number of minor road traffic offences have been so specified.

(ii)   to commence proceedings himself in any case where that appears appropriate (e.g. because of its importance or difficulty);

(iii)   to take over the conduct of all proceedings under s 3 of the Obscene Publications Act 1959 for the forfeiture of obscene articles;

(iv)   to give advice to police forces on all matters relating to criminal offences;

(v)   to appear for the prosecution, if so directed by the court, on appeals from the Crown Court to the Court of Appeal, from the Court of Appeal to the House of Lords and from the High Court to the House of Lords;

(vi)   to discharge any other functions assigned to him by the Attorney-General.

In addition, s 6(2) enables the DPP to take over any prosecution begun by a person or authority other than the police, while miscellaneous legislation other than the 1985 Act imposes further duties on him (e.g., consenting to the institution of certain types of prosecution).

The DPP is appointed by and acts under the general 'superintendence' of the Attorney-General (ss 2 and 3(1) and see Paragraph 3.4 for the role of the Attorney). Since the DPP is responsible to the Attorney and the Attorney is responsible to Parliament, there is an indirect sense in which the DPP can be called to account by Parliament for the way she discharges her functions. Before the 1985 Act, the DPP had a fairly small department of lawyers and other staff. However, the massive extension of duties entailed in assuming responsibility for all police prosecutions meant that the old DPP's department would no longer be remotely adequate. Hence, the Crown Prosecution Service was brought into being.

3.2.2   Structure of the Crown Prosecution Service

Below the DPP at the head of the Crown Prosecution Service are *Chief Crown Prosecutors,* each of whom is responsible for the operation of the CPS in a particular geographical area (see Prosecution of Offences Act 1985, s 1(1)(b)). Within each of the 42 areas there are one or more local branches, each of which is responsible for handling prosecutions at a group of magistrates' courts. The personnel at a branch office will consist of CPS lawyers, known as *Crown Prosecutors,* plus non-legally qualified executive officers and general support staff. The office will be headed by a *Branch Crown Prosecutor* and the area by a *Chief Crown Prosecutor.* All Crown Prosecutors must be designated as such by the DPP, and must be either barristers or solicitors (s 1(3)). They have 'all the powers of the Director as to the institution and conduct of proceedings' (s 1(6)). In particular, they may authorise the commencement of proceedings in those cases where the DPP's consent to a prosecution is required (s 1(7)). Although a Crown Prosecutor must exercise his powers under the direction of the Director, it is not necessary for him to obtain specific authority for every action he takes on the DPP's behalf. The point is well-illustrated by *Liverpool Crown Court ex p Bray* [1987] Crim LR 51 where it was held that an application by a Crown Prosecutor for a voluntary bill of indictment[2] had been made 'by or on behalf of' the DPP and therefore, according to the relevant rules of court, did not require an affidavit in support, even though the Crown Prosecutor had acted entirely on his own initiative. Watkins LJ described the defence contention that s 1(6) of the Prosecution of Offences Act conferred powers on

---

[2]   Applications to a High Court judge for his consent to the preferment of an indictment against an accused are occasionally used by the prosecution as an alternative to the usual procedure (for details, see Paragraph 12.6).

Crown Prosecutors only when they acted on the DPP's express instructions as 'absurd'. It follows that, when legislation such as the Prosecution of Offences Act gives powers to or imposes duties upon the DPP, it is more realistic to read the enactment as empowering or burdening the CPS.[3]

Crown Prosecutors, whether they are barristers or solicitors, have the same rights of audience as practising solicitors without the right of audience in the higher courts (s 4). In other words, they may appear in magistrates' courts but not in the Crown Court except in limited circumstances. The original intention when the Crown Prosecution Service was being planned was that the bulk of the advocacy required to be done on its behalf in the magistrates' courts would be undertaken by internal staff — i.e., Crown Prosecutors. In practice, difficulty in recruiting staff and the sheer volume of work have meant that some of the advocacy is still delegated to solicitors or barristers in private practice who act as agents for the CPS (see Paragraph 3.2.3). As to representation of the CPS at the Crown Court (e.g., for trials on indictment), that has to be by barristers briefed by the CPS since, as already stated, even Crown Prosecutors who are barristers do not have rights of audience in the higher courts.

Details of the way the CPS functions are a matter of internal administration and beyond the scope of this book. However, in broad outline, the system is that, once a person has been charged by the police or an information has been laid against him, the papers in the case are sent to the appropriate branch office of the CPS. There the evidence is reviewed by a CPS lawyer who decides whether or not the charges are justified. If he considers that no prosecution should have been brought, then he has power to discontinue the proceedings (see Paragraph 3.2.5). If he considers that additional or alternative charges are needed, he can have them put to the accused when he appears in court. The great majority of cases, even serious and/or complex ones, will be handled throughout at branch office level. The more difficult the case, however, the more likely it is that the branch Crown Prosecutors will liaise and seek advice from lawyers at the area office and/or refer the case to the CPS headquarters staff. A handful of offences must always be referred to headquarters (e.g. those where the Attorney-General's consent to a prosecution is required; large scale drugs and immigration conspiracies, and most prosecutions of police officers). On the other hand, even murder and rape are handled at branch office level unless it is thought there that exceptional factors require the file to be sent higher. Besides taking direct responsibility for a small minority of prosecutions as described above, CPS headquarters staff formulate general prosecutions policy, conduct relevant research, and generally support the area and offices of the Service. However, the offices are permitted a considerable degree of autonomy so that, although the CPS is a national service with certain operational guidelines laid down at national level, each office develops its own particular approach to prosecuting in a way that reflects local conditions.

Perhaps the single most important feature to notice about the CPS is that it does not investigate crime and it does not, in general, initiate prosecutions. Its role begins once the

---

[3] It is important to note, however, that the DPP's power to delegate the conduct of proceedings is a power to delegate to Crown Prosecutors, not a power to delegate to non-legally trained executive support staff. Thus, in *DPP ex p Association of First Division Civil Servants* (1988) 138 NLJ 158, the Divisional Court held that a scheme whereby non-lawyers in the CPS would have screened the papers relating to summary offences to see whether a prosecution was prima facie justified, and would have referred the case to a Crown Prosecutor only if they thought the proceedings ought to be discontinued, was ultra vires because it effectively delegated to persons other than Crown Prosecutors decisions on the discontinuance and/or conduct of proceedings.

police have charged or laid an information against a suspect. Then it is for a CPS lawyer to say whether the case should continue and, if the answer is 'yes', to conduct the proceedings by representing the prosecution in the magistrates' court (or employing an agent to do so) and briefing counsel for the Crown Court. In taking decisions about a case, the CPS lawyer will obviously liaise closely with the police but he should be independent of them and, in the last resort, must act on his own view of what should be done, not on the police's.

3.2.3   Agents

The DPP (i.e., Crown Prosecutors acting on her behalf) may assign the conduct of cases to barristers or solicitors in private practice (Prosecution of Offences Act 1985, s 5). Any agent thus acting for the CPS has the powers of a Crown Prosecutor but must exercise those powers in accordance with any instructions given him by an actual Crown Prosecutor. The usual system is for a CPS agent to be engaged for a day (or perhaps a morning or afternoon) in a particular magistrates' court. He then handles all the CPS cases appearing in the list for that day, the files having (hopefully) been sent to him the day before. The position of an agent in the magistrates' court is subtly different from that of counsel briefed to appear for the prosecution in the Crown Court. Whereas the latter has the final word about how the case should be conducted, the former is, at least in theory, obliged to abide by the wishes of the CPS. Thus, agents are normally forbidden to drop cases except with the authority of a CPS lawyer, whereas counsel in the Crown Court may — and indeed should — exercise his own judgment on whether there is sufficient evidence to proceed and/ or whether a proposed set of pleas would be an acceptable way of disposing of the case.

3.2.4   Taking over prosecutions

The commencement of prosecutions is not, of course, the exclusive prerogative of the police. Indeed, in strict constitutional theory, the police are merely paid to do what any private citizen or organisation may do as a matter of civic duty. Paragraph 3.3 mentions some of the organisations, other than the police and CPS, which are commonly involved in prosecuting crime. On occasions, however, the institution of a prosecution by a private individual or non-police body may be considered against the public interest. Alternatively, the prosecution may be considered so much in the public interest that it ought to be handled by the state rather than the individual. To cater for such situations, s 6(2) gives the DPP (which, in practice, of course means the CPS) an unfettered discretion to take over the conduct of any non-police prosecution. Having taken over a prosecution, the CPS may carry it to its conclusion or discontinue it as it sees fit.

3.2.5   Discontinuing prosecutions

A major reason for creating the CPS was to provide an independent check on whether police prosecutions were justified and, if not, to halt them at an early stage. To help the CPS fulfil this role, s 23 of the Prosecution of Offences Act provides that, where the CPS has the conduct of proceedings for an offence, they may give notice to the clerk of the magistrates' court that they do not want them to continue (s 23(3)). The notice must be given before the prosecution start calling their evidence for purposes of a summary trial or, if there is going to be a trial on indictment, before the accused is actually committed for trial (s 23(2)).

In the case of an indictable-only offence 'sent' for trial in the Crown Court, the prosecution may serve the notice at any time before the indictment is preferred. The CPS must include in the notice their reasons for discontinuing (s 23(5)). The effect of the notice is automatically to halt the proceedings, although the accused is not technically acquitted so it would be possible to commence fresh proceedings at a later date if, for example, further evidence came to light (s 23(9)). However, the accused must be served with a copy of the notice of discontinuance (though not the reasons for discontinuing), and he may insist on the prosecution going ahead (s 23(7)). The great majority of accused persons will be only too happy to receive a notice of discontinuance, but very occasionally an individual may want his day in court either to proclaim publicly that the charges against him were totally unfounded or to preclude any possibility of a fresh prosecution by obtaining a formal acquittal (once someone has been acquitted, he may not again be prosecuted for the same offence).

The number of cases discontinued by the CPS in the magistrates' courts is quite substantial: 12 per cent of all completed cases in the year 1998/9.

Quite apart from serving notice of discontinuance, the CPS can always in effect ensure that a prosecution does not go ahead by offering no evidence at court. If there is no prosecution evidence, the court has no option but to acquit. The CPS would seem to have an unfettered discretion to offer no evidence in the magistrates' court (dicta in *Canterbury and St Augustine Justices ex p Klisiak* [1982] QB 398). For the position in the Crown Court see Paragraph 16.6.

3.2.6 Other powers of the DPP in connection with the CPS

The Prosecution of Offences Act places upon the DPP (and also the Attorney-General) a number of powers and duties in relation to the CPS in addition to those already mentioned above:

(i)   By s 8 the Attorney-General may make regulations requiring the police to inform the DPP whenever there is a prima facie case that offences falling into certain defined categories have been committed within their police area. This is a re-enactment of provisions contained in earlier Prosecution of Offences Acts. The list of reportable offences was formerly quite long, but it was greatly reduced in 1985 and now only includes a few highly important or politically sensitive types of crime (e.g., large-scale drugs offences, large-scale conspiracy to contravene immigration laws, criminal libel and obscenity cases). By and large, the DPP and the CPS do not need to know that there is evidence of an offence unless and until the police act upon that evidence and charge somebody. If a charge is preferred, the papers have to go to the CPS in any event, as described above. However, in the few categories of offence still covered by the regulations, it is presumably thought that the police should not be left to decide by themselves whether to bring charges. Therefore, the DPP has to be informed as soon as there is prima facie evidence which might justify a prosecution, and she can then advise on how to proceed.

(ii)   By s 9, the DPP has to make an annual report to the Attorney-General dealing with how she has discharged her functions in the preceding 12 months. The AG is required to lay the report before Parliament. Also, the report is published and obtainable from HMSO. In addition, the Attorney may request the DPP to report to him on any other matters.

(iii)   By s 10, the DPP is required to issue a Code for Crown Prosecutors, giving guidance on (a) when a prosecution should be discontinued; (b) charging policy in general, and (c) the factors which make an offence triable either way suitable for summary trial or, as the case may be, trial on indictment. The current code is considered in Paragraph 4.3.

3.3   OTHER PROSECUTORS

The 25 per cent or so of prosecutions not commenced by the police are brought by a wide variety of prosecutors. For example, the Inland Revenue prosecute for tax offences; Customs and Excise for VAT offences and also for illegal import or export of drugs; the Department of Social Security for fraudulent benefit claims, and local authorities for breach of food and health regulations. Big stores used to prosecute for shoplifting offences but the almost invariable practice now is to hand such cases over to the police and CPS. The Criminal Justice Act 1987 created a new investigative and prosecuting authority, namely the Serious Frauds Office. This was done in response to fears about the increase in major fraud. The Office consists of a small number of specialists in anti-fraud work. As well as lawyers, there are accountants and investigators. The function of the SFO is to assume responsibility for the investigation and prosecution of a small minority of extremely serious suspected frauds (perhaps less than 100 a year). The Office works in conjunction with the police fraud squads, directing them to relevant lines of inquiry. It also has extensive powers to compel those who might have information about a fraud under investigation to answer questions and/or supply documentary evidence. Unlike the CPS, the SFO both investigates suspected major fraud and then, if the evidence is forthcoming, commences and conducts the prosecution.

As will be apparent, most non-police prosecutions are commenced by a government or quasi-governmental authority. However, a minority are still brought by individuals acting in a purely private capacity. Thus, it is not unusual for trouble between neighbours to result in the parties cross-summoning each other for assault. Occasionally, too, an individual will feel so outraged at the decision of the police not to prosecute that he will take the initiative and commence proceedings himself. A famous example was the case of *Whitehouse v Lemon* [1979] AC 617 where Mrs Mary Whitehouse successfully prosecuted the defendants for blasphemous libel, that being the first recorded prosecution for the offence since 1922. More recently, the parents of a young man who had died through injecting a certain drug both gathered the evidence and then initiated proceedings for manslaughter against a person who had assisted their son in making the injection. The DPP had originally advised the police against any action, and he only took over the prosecution after there had been a committal for trial. The ultimate result was a conviction for manslaughter.

Section 6 of the Prosecution of Offences Act 1985 gives the DPP a discretionary power to take over the conduct of any non-police prosecution. He may then, again at his discretion, either continue the prosecution in the normal way, or discontinue the proceedings under s 23, or simply offer no evidence. Provided he is not acting completely unreasonably, his conduct in taking over a prosecution and then discontinuing it will not be open to judicial review by the High Court. In *DPP ex p Duckenfield* [2000] 1 WLR 55, the Divisional Court considered the basis upon which the DPP ought to take over private prosecutions in order to stop them. It was held that the DPP acted quite properly in not adopting the same test for stopping a prosecution as for starting one. The policy of the DPP was that he would only intervene to stop a private prosecution on evidential grounds where there was clearly no case to answer, and the Divisional Court made it clear that such a policy was in accordance with s 6(1) of the 1985 Act. It follows that, provided there is evidence to support a private prosecution, the DPP will not intervene to stop it, even though he would not have commenced proceedings himself.

3.4 THE LAW OFFICERS OF THE CROWN

A discussion of prosecuting authorities would be incomplete without mention of the Law Officers of the Crown — i.e., the Attorney-General and the Solicitor General. The Attorney-General is a barrister member of the Government who, inter alia, advises his government colleagues on questions of law; takes proceedings for contempt of court (e.g., against newspapers for breach of the sub judice rules), and seeks injunctions against public bodies which have acted unlawfully. In the realm of criminal procedure, as already mentioned, he supervises the work of the DPP, and thus is accountable to Parliament for the operation of the Crown Prosecution Service. There are also certain categories of prosecution which may only be commenced with the Attorney's consent (see Paragraph 4.4.4). A further power of the Attorney is to enter a *nolle prosequi,* the effect of which is to halt a trial on indictment. The power is completely discretionary but is normally used only on compassionate grounds where an accused has become seriously ill during the course of his trial. Alternatively, the Attorney could take over the conduct of the prosecution and offer no evidence, although this power now seems superfluous in view of the DPP's similar power.

The second Law Officer of the Crown is the Solicitor General. He is a kind of deputy Attorney-General who may discharge the latter's functions when authorised to do so or when the Attorney is absent or sick (Law Officers Act 1944, s 1).

4 The Decision to Prosecute

The chapter is mainly concerned with the considerations taken into account by the police and the Crown Prosecution Service in deciding respectively whether they should commence a prosecution and whether they should discontinue a prosecution already begun. First, however, it is necessary to describe briefly the way in which criminal proceedings commence. A more detailed account will be found in Chapter 2.

4.1 METHODS OF COMMENCING A PROSECUTION

There are two main methods of commencing a prosecution. One, which is open to the police, other prosecuting authorities and private citizens alike, is to *lay an information* before a magistrate. If the information appears prima facie correct, the magistrate will then issue a *summons* requiring the accused to appear before the magistrates' court to answer the allegation contained in the information.

The second way of commencing a prosecution is used only by the police, and it is to *charge* a suspect with an offence at the police station. Laying an information, charging a suspect and procedures for arrest and questioning at the police station are considered in detail in Chapter 2.

While there is no hard and fast rule as to when proceeding by way of a charge is appropriate rather than proceeding by information and summons, the police generally use a summons for less serious offences, especially summary ones, whereas most prosecutions for indictable offences are commenced by charging at the police station. The decision on whether or not to charge would normally be taken by the arresting and investigating officers, perhaps after consultation with their superiors and/or the CPS. Where proceedings are by way of summons, the suspect is usually spoken to by the police away from the station (e.g., at his home or at the scene of a road traffic offence), and is told that he will be reported for consideration for prosecution. The officer's report then goes before the police prosecutions department who decide whether to proceed further. Whereas the decision on whether to prosecute an adult is essentially taken by the police alone, other agencies, such as social services and the local education authority, may be involved in any decision to prosecute a juvenile.

4.2 ALTERNATIVES TO PROSECUTION

Apart from the obvious alternative of doing absolutely nothing, there are two alternatives to a prosecution which, depending on the nature of the suspected offence, the police might consider. They are (i) administering a formal caution, and (ii) issuing a fixed penalty notice.

4.2.1 Cautions

The police have a discretion to issue a formal caution. This practice was initially developed as a means of keeping juveniles out of the machinery of the criminal justice system. It can now only be used for adults, in view of the system of reprimands and warnings introduced for juveniles by the Crime and Disorder Act 1998. A caution is normally administered in the police station by an officer of the rank of inspector or above. Although a caution does not rank as a conviction, records are kept of them for at least five years and they may be cited in court as evidence of the offender's character should he subsequently be convicted of an offence. Cautioning practice is dealt with by a Home Office Circular on the subject (18/1994), which incorporates revised National Standards for Cautioning.

The Crime and Disorder Act 1998 introduced major changes to the system of alternatives to prosecution in the case of juveniles, abolishing the formal caution and replacing it with a scheme of reprimands and warnings. Details of this new scheme are set out in Paragraph 4.2.2.

The major conditions for issuing a caution are, first, that the evidence should be strong enough to justify a prosecution (see Paragraph 4.3.1). Cautioning should not be used as a way of saving the police's face when they do not really have a case that would stand up in court. Secondly, the offender must admit the offence. If he does not, the police are thrown back on the stark choice between prosecuting and doing nothing. This aspect of the cautioning system is perhaps open to criticism in that it can unfairly pressurise a suspect into admitting something he has not done so as to avoid all risk of a prosecution.

Where these conditions are satisfied, consideration must then be given to whether a caution is in the public interest. Home Office Circular 18/1994 and the National Standards for Cautioning make the following points about the factors in making this decision:

(a) The police should take into account the public interest principles in the Code for Crown Prosecutors (see Paragraph 4.3.2).

(b) Cautions should not be used for offences which are triable on indictment only, other than in the most exceptional circumstances.

(c) Other offences may also be too serious for a caution. In deciding on this, factors to be considered include, for example, the harm resulting from the offence, whether it was racially motivated, whether it involved a breach of trust, and whether it was carried out in an organised way.

(d) The victim's view of the offence, and whether a caution is appropriate, should be sought and considered, but is not conclusive.

(e) Only in the following circumstances should an offender be cautioned for the second time:

(i)   where the subsequent offence is trivial; or

(ii) where there has been a sufficient lapse of time since the first caution to suggest that it had some effect.

(f) There should be a presumption in favour of cautioning rather than prosecuting certain categories of offender, such as the elderly, and those who suffer from mental illness or impairment or a severe physical illness. Membership of these groups does not, of course, afford absolute protection against prosecution.

(g) The offender's attitude to the offence must be considered — in particular the wilfulness with which it was committed, and his subsequent attitude. An apology and/or an offer to put matters right may support the use of a caution.

(h)   Each offender must be separately considered, even in the case of a group offence. Different disposals may be justified in the light of different degrees of involvement and personal circumstances.

The police may in some cases issue an oral warning (sometimes misleadingly referred to as 'an informal caution'). Such a warning has no official status, and may not be cited in subsequent court proceedings, whereas a formal caution may be.

The police decision whether to caution or not is closely related to the CPS decision whether to prosecute or not (see Paragraph 4.3). In *Chief Constable of Kent ex p L; R v DPP ex p B* [1993] 1 All ER 756, the Divisional Court considered the availability of judicial review in relation to the question of whether a juvenile should be cautioned or prosecuted. It was held that any judicial review could only lie against the body which had 'the last and decisive word, the CPS' (Watkins LJ at p. 767), and not the police. Watkins LJ went on to say:

> I have come to the conclusion that, in respect of juveniles, the discretion of the CPS to continue or discontinue criminal proceedings is reviewable by this court but only where it can be demonstrated that the decision was made regardless of or clearly contrary to a settled policy of the Director of Public Prosecutions evolved in the public interest, for example the policy of cautioning juveniles. . . . But I envisage that it will be only rarely that a defendant could succeed in showing that a decision was fatally flawed in such a manner as that.

4.2.2   Reprimands and warnings

The policy of cautioning, as an alternative to prosecution, has been radically altered as far as juveniles are concerned by the Crime and Disorder Act 1998. Sections 65 and 66 of the CDA have replaced cautions for juveniles with a new scheme of reprimands and warnings. The aim is to set out a series of stages, under which the juvenile may expect to be reprimanded for a first offence, warned for a second, and prosecuted for a third.

A juvenile suspect who has not previously been reprimanded or warned may be reprimanded, provided that certain conditions are met. Those conditions are set out in s 65(1) of the CDA, and may be summarised as follows:

(a)   a police officer must have evidence that the juvenile has committed an offence;
(b)   the officer must consider that there would be a realistic prospect of conviction;
(c)   the juvenile must admit the offence to the officer;
(d)   the juvenile must not previously have been convicted of any offence; and
(e)   the officer must be satisfied that it would not be in the public interest for the suspect to be prosecuted.

As can be seen, the fact that the suspect must not previously have been reprimanded or warned means that a second reprimand is ruled out. In addition, a prior conviction for any offence, no matter how trivial or unrelated to the one under consideration, shuts out the prospect of a warning or reprimand.

The officer must decide whether there would be sufficient evidence, and a realistic prospect of conviction, if the suspect were to be prosecuted. The officer has also to decide that it would not be in the public interest to prosecute the suspect. These questions are also posed by the CPS in deciding whether a prosecution should proceed (see Paragraphs 4.3.1 and 4.3.2).

4.2.3 Fixed penalty notices

Fixed penalty notices require merely a brief mention as they are relevant only to certain road traffic offences, and are not significant as regards the overall structure of the criminal justice system. Parking tickets are the fixed penalty notices with which the public are perhaps most familiar. However, Part III of the Transport Act 1982 extended the fixed penalty system from parking infringements (where, of course, the great bulk of the enforcement is done by traffic wardens) to some of the commonest non-parking offences, including a few which carry endorsement of the driving licence as part of the penalty (see now, the Road Traffic Offenders Act 1988, Sch 3). Thus, notices can now be given for, *inter alia*, speeding, going through a red light, failing to stop when required to do so by a constable, breach of the construction and use regulations regarding the condition of a vehicle, breach of pedestrian crossing regulations, not wearing a seat-belt and not wearing a crash helmet. As regards these non-parking matters, a notice may only be issued by a police officer in uniform. Essentially, the officer stops the motorist and points out the offence. If he decides to give the motorist the option of paying a fixed penalty, he issues a ticket which will give brief particulars of the offence and the name and address of the clerk of the magistrates' court to which payment of the penalty should be made. If the offence is endorsable, the motorist must either surrender his licence at the time or hand it in to a police station of his choice within seven days. Once a notice has been issued there is a 'suspended enforcement period' of 21 days during which the motorist should either pay the penalty or give notice himself requesting a hearing. If he pays the penalty, that is the end of the matter, save that, if the offence is endorsable, his licence will be sent to the fixed penalty clerk (justices' clerk for the area) for endorsement of penalty points (see Paragraph 23.16 for penalty points etc.). If a hearing is requested, the police are told and then have to decide whether they should proceed by summons in the normal way. Should the motorist neither pay the penalty nor give notice requesting a hearing, he becomes liable for a sum equal to the fixed penalty plus one half of that penalty, which can then be enforced as if it were a fine. If the fixed penalty offence is not a moving traffic offence, the notice does not have to be given to the motorist but can be affixed to the vehicle. This is, of course, what usually happens in respect of parking offences.

The advantage of the fixed penalty system to the police and courts is that the consequences for the motorist are virtually the same as if he had gone through the prosecution system in the normal way, but court time is saved in that there is no hearing. There is merely the administrative task of collecting the fixed penalty and sending the licence to Swansea to be endorsed. To tempt the motorist to cooperate with the procedure, the fixed penalties are pitched deliberately low. But, it is a matter for the police officer's discretion whether he issues a fixed penalty notice or takes alternative action (or takes no action at all). To take the example of speeding on a motorway, a motorist who was only a little over the limit (say 80 mph) will almost certainly be given a notice. If the speed was somewhat higher but still not really bad (say 90 mph), the police might choose to proceed by summons while giving the motorist the option of pleading guilty by post (see Chapter 9). This means that there is a prosecution and the fine is fixed by the magistrates, but the motorist need not attend court and can explain any mitigation he has in a letter. In bad cases (say 100 mph or more), however, where the court might consider disqualification, the motorist is simply summoned and would prima facie be expected to attend court and explain his conduct. The practice of police forces varies considerably as to the circumstances in which they are content to issue a fixed penalty notice rather than prosecuting in the normal way.

4.3   FACTORS TO CONSIDER IN DECIDING WHETHER TO PROSECUTE

As was explained in Chapter 3, taking the decision on whether to prosecute is, as far as police prosecutions are concerned, a two-stage process. First, the police themselves decide whether to initiate proceedings by, as appropriate, charging the suspect or laying an information. Secondly, if the police decision is for prosecution, the papers go to a branch office of the CPS where a lawyer reviews the case and may discontinue the proceedings if he considers that the police were wrong to start them.

As regards the approach of CPS lawyers when reviewing papers with a view to discontinuance, guidance for them is contained in the Code for Crown Prosecutors that the DPP issues under s 10 of the Prosecution of Offences Act 1985 (see Paragraph 3.2.6). For their part, the police are encouraged to follow the criteria laid down in the Code, for example when deciding whether to caution or prosecute an offender (see Home Office Circular 18/1994, National Standards for Cautioning, para 3).

4.3.1   Sufficiency of evidence

The first essential precondition for the commencement of a prosecution is the availability of sufficient evidence. The approach for Crown Prosecutors is laid down in paras 5.1 to 5.3 of their Code. They must be satisfied that there is enough evidence for a 'realistic prospect of conviction' in respect of each charge against each defendant. In their consideration, they must take into account the likely defence case. The test of a 'realistic prospect of conviction' is objective. The question is: Would a jury or a bench of magistrates, properly directed in accordance with the law, be more likely than not to convict the defendant of the charge alleged? In attempting to answer this question, the Crown Prosecutor should consider whether there is sufficient evidence, whether it can be used, and whether it is reliable. Hence, the Prosecutor should consider:

(a)   The likelihood that evidence will be excluded by the court, e.g., because of an impropriety in the way that it was gathered, or because of the rule against hearsay. If a piece of evidence may be excluded, is there enough other evidence?

(b)   The reliability of the evidence, e.g., whether identification evidence is likely to be excluded on the basis of the guidelines in *Turnbull* [1977] QB 224.

Using this approach, a legally trained and relatively detached Crown Prosecutor may well take a different view of the strength of the case from that taken by the investigating officers who commenced the proceedings. It is submitted that such an approach is in accordance with the interests of justice and efficiency. It is wrong that someone should be punished if he is innocent, and prosecution often involves serious consequences for the person accused. It is at the least a source of inconvenience and worry, and it may well entail considerable expense. In some cases, the very fact that the accused has been prosecuted may lead to a stigma, with the suspicion that there is 'no smoke without fire'. In addition to these ethical considerations, there are questions of resources. It is a waste of time and money for the various parts of the criminal justice system to deal with a case which is going to result in an acquittal. It was largely to weed out weak cases, in fact, that the CPS was set up. (For a perceptive analysis of this and other ethical questions in the criminal justice system, see A. Ashworth, *The Criminal Process* (Oxford University Press, 1998, especially Chapter 6).)

4.3.2 Public interest factors

Lord Shawcross, the former Attorney-General, in a House of Commons debate of 1951, stated that:

> It has never been the rule of this Country — I hope it never will be — that suspected criminal offences must automatically be the subject of prosecution. Indeed, the very first regulations under which the Director of Public Prosecutions worked provided that he should prosecute 'wherever it appears that the offence or the circumstances of its commission are of such a character that a prosecution in respect thereof is required in the public interest'.

In other words, the availability of sufficient evidence should not automatically result in a prosecution. Before bringing a case to court, first the police and then the CPS must consider, as a matter of discretion whether a prosecution is really in the public interest. If it is not, the suspect should either have no action taken against him or be 'let off' with a caution. The approach adopted by the Code for Crown Prosecutors in calculating the public interest is to list first the factors which tend towards a decision to prosecute, and then those factors which militate against bringing a prosecution. The aim is that once the factors in each list have been considered, it can be decided whether the prosecution is in the public interest or not. The factors favouring the commencement of a prosecution are listed in para 6.4 of the Code:

(a) a conviction is likely to result in a significant sentence;

(b) a weapon was used or violence was threatened during the commission of the offence;

(c) the offence was committed against a person serving the public (for example, a police or prison officer, or a nurse);

(d) the defendant was in a position of authority or trust;

(e) the evidence shows that the defendant was a ringleader or an organiser of the offence;

(f) there is evidence that the offence was premeditated;

(g) there is evidence that the offence was carried out by a group;

(h) the victim of the offence was vulnerable, has been put in considerable fear, or suffered personal attack, damage or disturbance;

(i) the offence was motivated by any form of discrimination against the victim's ethnic or national origin, sex, religious beliefs, political views or sexual preference;

(j) there is a marked difference between the actual or mental ages of the defendant and the victim, or there is any element of corruption;

(k) the defendant's previous convictions or cautions are relevant to the present offence;

(l) the defendant is alleged to have committed the offence whilst under an order of the court;

(m) there are grounds for believing that the offence is likely to be continued or repeated, for example, by a history of recurring conduct; or

(n) the offence, although not serious in itself, is widespread in the area where it was committed.

The factors which tend against a prosecution are set out in para 6.5 as follows:

(a) the court is likely to impose a very small or nominal penalty;

(b) the defendant has already been sentenced and conviction for this offence would be unlikely to add to his sentence;

(c) the offence was committed as a result of a genuine mistake or misunderstanding (these factors must be balanced against the seriousness of the offence);

(d) the loss or harm can be described as minor and was the result of a single incident, particularly if it was caused by a misjudgment;

(e) there has been a long delay between the offence taking place and the date of the trial, unless:

   (i)   the offence is serious;

   (ii)   the delay has been caused in part by the defendant;

   (iii) the offence has only recently come to light; or

   (iv)   the complexity of the offence has meant that there has been a long investigation;

(f) a prosecution is likely to have a very bad effect on the victim's physical or mental health, always bearing in mind the seriousness of the offence;

(g) the defendant is elderly or is, or was at the time of the offence, suffering from significant mental or physical ill health, unless the offence is serious or there is a real possibility that it may be repeated (the CPS, where necessary, applies Home Office guidelines about how to deal with mentally disordered offenders and Crown Prosecutors must balance the desirability of diverting a defendant who is suffering from significant mental or physical ill health with the need to safeguard the general public);

(h) the defendant has put right the loss or harm that was caused (but defendants must not avoid prosecution simply because they can pay compensation); or

(i) details may be made public that could harm sources of information, international relations or national security.

The Code then makes the obvious point in para 6.6 that the decision on the public interest is not simply a matter of adding up the number of factors on each side. The Crown Prosecutor must decide how important each factor is in the case under consideration, and go on to make an overall assessment. In doing so, the interests of the victim must be very carefully considered, even though the CPS act in the interests of the public as a whole rather than any particular individual (paras 6.7 and 6.8).

There are particular considerations in deciding whether to proceed with the trial of a juvenile, as 'the stigma of a conviction can cause very serious harm to the prospects of a youth offender or a young adult'. Although young offenders can sometimes be dealt with outside the court system, Crown Prosecutors are told that they should not decline to prosecute simply because of the defendant's age. The seriousness of the offence and previous behaviour may make prosecution necessary (para 6.9).

Clearly, the most common alternative to a prosecution, in the case of an adult, is a formal caution. The Code states that Crown Prosecutors should apply the same guidelines as the police in deciding whether a caution is appropriate (see Paragraph 4.2.1 above). The caution will, however, be administered by the police rather than the CPS. The Crown Prosecutor should therefore inform the police when deciding that a caution is more suitable than a prosecution (para 6.12).

In addition to the decision whether to prosecute or not, there is also the question of the appropriate offence to charge. A series of Charging Standards has now been agreed by the police and the CPS. Their purpose 'is to make sure that the most appropriate charge is selected at the earliest opportunity'. The fact that the standards have been agreed between the police and CPS will lead, it is hoped, to a reduction in the need to amend charges. So far, standards have been published in relation to:

(a) offences against the person (this is reprinted as Appendix 1);
(b) driving offences;
(c) public order offences.

Generally, each set of charging standards attempts to reflect the basic principles of the Code for Crown Prosecutors, as applied to the offences in question.

4.4 SPECIAL FACTORS RELEVANT TO THE DECISION TO PROSECUTE

Whether there is sufficient evidence and, if so, whether there are none the less discretionary reasons for not prosecuting are questions which fall to be considered whenever criminal proceedings are proposed. In a minority of cases, however, a potential prosecutor will also have to answer the following questions:

4.4.1 Do the English courts have jurisdiction?

The jurisdiction of the English courts is essentially territorial. In other words, they accept jurisdiction over offences committed in England or Wales irrespective of the nationality of the accused, but, generally speaking, they refuse jurisdiction over offences committed abroad even if the accused is a British subject. There are, however, several examples of 'foreign' offences being triable in England if the accused is a British subject, and very occasional examples of such offences being triable here irrespective of the accused's nationality. In this context, 'abroad' should be understood to mean outside England and Wales, and 'British subject' includes not only citizens of the United Kingdom but also, for example, citizens of Commonwealth countries: British Nationality Act 1981, s 51.

The main exceptions to the general rule that the English courts only try offences committed in England or Wales are:

(a) Offences of murder, manslaughter, bigamy or perjury are triable in England wherever committed, provided the accused is a British subject: Offences against the Person Act 1861, ss 9 and 57, and Perjury Act 1911, s 8. The same applies to offences under the Official Secrets Acts (see s 10 of the 1911 Act).

By virtue of the War Crimes Act 1991, s 1, proceedings for murder may be brought in United Kingdom courts against anyone who was, on 8 March 1990 or later, a British citizen or resident in the United Kingdom, if the offence was committed during the Second World War in Germany or a place under German occupation and the offence violated the laws and customs of war.

(b)   *Any* offence committed by a British subject abroad is triable here if, at the time of the offence, he was a servant of the Crown, and was acting (or purporting to act) in the course of his employment: Criminal Justice Act 1948, s 31.

(c)   *Any* offence committed abroad is triable here if, at the time of the offence or within the three months preceding it, the accused was a member of the crew of a British merchant ship: Merchant Shipping Act 1995, s 282. It is not clear whether s 282 is meant to apply only to British crew members or also to foreigners who join British ships.

(d)   By s 4 of the Suppression of Terrorism Act 1978, the English courts may try both British subjects and foreigners for terrorist offences committed in any country which is a party to the European Convention on the Suppression of Terrorism 1977. However, unless the courts would have jurisdiction apart from s 4, prosecutions may only be brought with the consent of the Attorney-General, and in most cases extraditing the accused to the country where the offence occurred might seem preferable to sanctioning proceedings here.

(e)   Offences committed on a British ship on the high seas are triable here whether or not the accused is a British subject: Merchant Shipping Act 1995, s 281. The same applies to offences committed on any ship (British or foreign) within British territorial waters: Territorial Waters Jurisdiction Act 1878, s 2. In effect, British ships on the high seas and British territorial waters are treated as an extension of England and Wales. In addition, offences committed by a British subject on a foreign ship to which he did not belong are triable in England: Merchant Shipping Act 1995, s 281. Thus, British passengers on a Danish vessel who committed acts of criminal damage were rightly tried in England because they could not be said to 'belong' to the Danish ship: *Kelly* [1982] AC 665.

(f)   Offences committed on board British-controlled aircraft while they are in flight are triable here even if the plane was outside United Kingdom airspace at the relevant time: Civil Aviation Act 1982, s 92.

(g)   Piracy and aircraft hijacking are triable here wherever they occurred, and whatever the nationality of the ship, aircraft or accused involved. Piracy is an ancient example of an offence against the law of nations, and hijacking is dealt with in s 1 of the Aviation Security Act 1982.

(h)   The Sexual Offences (Conspiracy and Incitement) Act 1996 confers jurisdiction on British courts over certain specified offences of conspiracy or incitement to commit sexual acts against infants (aged under 16) abroad, where such acts constitute offences in the foreign country concerned. For details of the offences listed, and the conditions which must be met before jurisdiction is conferred, see *Blackstone's Criminal Practice*, D1.81.

(i)   The Sex Offenders Act 1997 confers jurisdiction on British courts over certain sexual offences against infants (aged under 16) committed abroad, where the act in question constitutes an offence in the country in which it is committed, and also in this country. The statute, together with the Sexual Offences (Conspiracy and Incitement) Act 1996, is aimed at 'sex tourism', and attempts to penalise the exploitation of children for sexual purposes, wherever it occurs. Details of the offences involved and the procedural conditions are dealt with in *Blackstone's Criminal Practice*, D1.81 and D1.82.

(j)   The Criminal Justice (Terrorism and Conspiracy) Act 1998 confers jurisdiction on the English courts to try conspiracies to commit offences abroad, subject to certain conditions. The conspiracy must be to commit an act which would be an offence both in this country, and in the foreign state in question. In addition, certain qualifying conditions must be met. The provisions are not confined to terrorism, but apply to all criminal offences. Details can be found in *Blackstone's Criminal Practice*, D1.74.

A number of offences of fraud and dishonesty are now dealt with under rules contained in the Criminal Justice Act 1993, ss 1 to 4 and 6. Among the most important of these offences are theft, obtaining property by deception, false accounting, blackmail, handling stolen goods and forgery. If any act or omission, proof of which is required for conviction of the offence in question, occurs in England or Wales, the offence is triable in our courts (Criminal Justice Act 1993, s 2(1)) (see *Blackstone's Criminal Practice*, D1.76 to D1.79).

4.4.2 Is the offender entitled to immunity?

A second special question the prosecutor may have to consider is whether the accused is entitled to immunity. The Queen is immune from criminal jurisdiction. The same applies to foreign sovereigns or heads of state, together with their families and private servants: State Immunity Act 1978, s 20. Diplomatic agents, members of the administrative and technical staff of a diplomatic mission and the families of such agents or staff are similarly immune: Diplomatic Privileges Act 1964, s 2(1). Members of the service staff of a diplomatic mission have immunity in respect of acts performed in the course of their duties, and some consular officials also enjoy a limited immunity: Consular Relations Act 1968. Immunity may always be waived by the state sending the diplomat, etc., but unless there has been an express waiver a conviction obtained against a person entitled to immunity will be quashed. The above rules are subject to some modification where the person claiming immunity is a citizen of, or permanently resident in, the United Kingdom.

Although the phrase is not usually employed in the context, children under ten are also immune from prosecution. This follows from it being conclusively presumed that no child under that age can be guilty of any offence: Children and Young Persons Act 1933, s 50, as amended.

4.4.3 Can the prosecution be commenced in time?

The fact that an offence is stale is, as explained in Paragraph 4.3.2, a reason for deciding, as a matter of discretion, not to prosecute. In addition, there are some statutory provisions which, as a matter of law, require proceedings to be commenced within a certain time-limit. Examples are set out in table 4.1.

Table 4.1

Enactment	*Offences*	*Time-limit*
Magistrates' Courts Act 1980, s 127	All summary offences	6 months from commission of the offence
Schedule 2 to the Sexual Offences Act 1956, para 10	Unlawful sexual intercourse with a girl under 16, contrary to s 6 of the 1956 Act	12 months from commission of the offence

Enactment	Offences	Time-limit
Sexual Offences Act s 7	Gross indecency between men and buggery where no assault is involved and the 'victim' is not under 16	12 months from commission of the offence
Trade Descriptions Act 1968, s 19(1)	All indictable offences under the 1968 Act	3 years from commission of the offence or one year from its discovery, whichever is the earlier
Customs and Excise Management Act 1979, s 146A	All indictable offences under the Customs and Excise Acts	20 years from commission of the offence

Of the above provisions, the only one of general importance is s 127 of the Magistrates' Courts Act 1980, which lays down the blanket rule that an information for a summary offence must be laid within six months of its commission. The obvious purpose of the rule is to ensure that summary matters, being relatively trivial, are tried quickly before memory of what occurred has faded from the minds of the witnesses. Prosecutions for indictable offences may, in general, be commenced at any time, although some exceptions to that rule are noted in the Table. The time-limit (or lack of time-limit) for an indictable offence is unaffected by the fact that the offence is triable either way and the accused has elected summary trial.

Finally, in connection with time limits, it should be noted that the courts do have a very limited discretion to halt proceedings if they consider that, although no statutory limit has been breached, delay in bringing the case to court is such as to amount to an abuse of proper process. For details, see Paragraphs 9.4, 12.1.4 and 18.1.4.

4.4.4 Is any consent required?

The consent of, in some cases, the Attorney-General and, in other cases, the Director of Public Prosecutions is a pre-condition of the bringing of prosecutions for certain offences. Although there is no clearly defined practice, Parliament tends to stipulate the Attorney's consent (or fiat) where prosecution for an offence might raise considerations of public policy, national security or relations with other countries. The DPP's consent is required in areas where a rigid application of the letter of the law is likely to be oppressive to the individual or offensive to public opinion. As regards the DPP's consent, it can be given on his behalf by a Crown Prosecutor (see Prosecution of Offences Act 1985, s 1(7) and Paragraph 3.2.2). Thus, what is now required is, effectively, the consent of the CPS rather than the consent of the DPP personally. Since all police prosecutions require the retrospective consent of the CPS in the sense that it takes over the conduct of the proceedings and may discontinue them if they so wish, it could be argued that the requirement of a prior consent should be limited to private prosecutions. However, when passing the legislation creating the CPS, Parliament chose not to interfere with the existing statutory provisions governing consents, presumably thinking that in certain sensitive areas proceedings should not even be allowed to start unless they have been sanctioned by the authorities. The level at which consent to a proposed prosecution is given is a matter of internal CPS administration. As regards some offences requiring consent, the papers must always be sent to CPS headquarters where, presumably, they are considered either by the DPP personally or a very senior CPS lawyer. In other cases the question of consent can be handled at local level. Papers in a case requiring the Attorney's consent are automatically sent to CPS headquarters for transmission to the Attorney.

Examples of the Attorney's consent being necessary for a prosecution are:

(a)   offences of bribery under the Public Bodies Corrupt Practices Act 1889 and the Prevention of Corruption Act 1906 (s 4 of the 1889 Act and s 2 of the 1906 Act);

(b)   offences under the Official Secrets Act 1911 (s 8 of the Act);

(c)   offences of stirring up racial hatred, possessing racially inflammatory material, etc. contrary to Part III of the Public Order Act 1986 (s 27 of the Act);

(d)   offences of belonging to a proscribed organisation and other offences under the Prevention of Terrorism (Temporary Provisions) Act 1989 (s 19 of the Act), and

(e)   offences under the Explosive Substances Act 1883 (s 7 of the Act).

The DPP's consent is necessary for prosecutions for:

(a)   offences of theft or criminal damage where the property in question belongs to the spouse of the accused (s 30(4) of the Theft Act 1968);

(b)   offences of assisting offenders and wasting police time contrary to ss 4(4) and 5(3) of the Criminal Law Act 1967;

(c)   homosexual offences where either or both of the parties are under 21 (s 8 of the Sexual Offences Act 1967);

(d)   offences of incest (Sch 2 to the Sexual Offences Act 1956);

(e)   offences of aiding and abetting suicide (s 2 of the Suicide Act 1961); and

(f)   riot contrary to s 1 of the Public Order Act 1986 (s 7 of the Act).

The necessity for the Attorney's or DPP's consent to prosecution does not prevent a suspect being arrested, charged at the police station and thereafter remanded by a court (in custody or on bail) prior to consent having been obtained (Prosecution of Offences Act 1985, s 25). However, it is submitted that no effective stage in the proceedings (such as determination of mode of trial or committal) should be embarked upon until the consent is forthcoming, and the prosecutor should in any event use his best endeavours to obtain a decision from the Attorney or, as the case may be, DPP as soon as possible. In *Whale* [1991] Crim LR 692, it was held that the consent of the Attorney-General, as required under the Explosive Substances Act 1883, could be obtained validly up to the time that the defendant appeared in court for the purpose of committal. It should be noted, however, that a magistrate will not issue a summons in respect of an offence requiring consent to prosecution unless satisfied that consent has been granted (see *Gateshead Justices ex p Tesco Stores Ltd* [1981] QB 470). It follows that non-police prosecutors (who, or course, do not have the option of proceeding by way of charge but are forced to use a summons) must apply for consent before taking any steps whatsoever against their suspect.

5   Magistrates and their Courts

The office of justice of the peace, or magistrate, is an ancient one first mentioned in 1264. As early as 1361 the Justices of the Peace Act provided for the appointment in each county of 'one lord and three or four of the most worthy in the county with some learned in the law' whose duty it would be to 'pursue, arrest . . . and chastise' offenders and rioters, and take surety of good behaviour 'towards the King and his people' from those who were not 'of good fame'. The magistrates retain their original function of assisting in the keeping of the peace, and, to further that end, can still bind a person over to keep the peace or be of good behaviour even though no offence has been proved against him.

Over the centuries the work of the magistrates widened in scope. By the eighteenth century they had extensive judicial and administrative powers. Administratively, they were responsible for, *inter alia,* the licensing of ale houses, the appointment of overseers of the poor and surveyors of highways, the levying of rates in their counties, and the transaction of important county business. Judicially, they not only tried minor cases summarily but, at quarter sessions, benches of two to nine magistrates presided over trials by jury. Only the most serious of indictable offences were excluded from the jurisdiction of quarter sessions and reserved for the assize courts. However, in the late nineteenth and early twentieth centuries the magistrates' powers were reduced. Their administrative functions were transferred to elected local authorities, although traces of the old system can still be seen in, for example, the work of the licensing justices who control the granting of licences to sell alcohol. Their judicial functions were not expressly reduced, but the introduction of a rule that at quarter sessions the bench must always have a legally qualified chairman (usually the sort of person who today would be appointed a circuit judge or recorder) meant that lay magistrates had much less influence than formerly. The role of the magistrates at quarter sessions is reflected today in the requirement that two of them be present at appeals in the Crown Court: Supreme Court Act 1981, s 74 and see Paragraph 13.3.

Although the powers of magistrates are not as great as they were, they still play a very important part in the administration of the criminal law. In summary, their work is as follows:

(a)   They can issue either a warrant for the arrest of a person against whom an offence is alleged or a summons requiring him to attend at a magistrates' court to answer the allegation (see Chapter 2). In practice, this does not form a major part of their work as proceedings against a person for a serious offence normally begin with an arrest without warrant by a police officer, while the issuing of a summons, which is the appropriate way to commence proceedings in less serious cases, can be and usually is done by a magistrates' clerk rather than the magistrate himself.

(b)   They sit as examining justices for the hearing of committal proceedings (see Chapter 12).

(c)   They try cases summarily in the adult magistrates' courts (see Chapter 9).

(d)   They try in the youth courts cases brought against those under 18. Only magistrates who have been appointed by their colleagues to the youth court panel are eligible to sit in the youth court (see Chapter 10).

(e)   They have a minor role to play in the work of the Crown Court (see Paragraph 13.3).

In addition, magistrates have a wide-ranging civil jurisdiction. For example, they make maintenance orders as between the parties to a marriage and custody orders in respect of the children of the family; they rule upon the paternity of children in affiliation proceedings; they put children into care on grounds such as neglect or ill-treatment of the child; the licensing justices, as already mentioned, grant licences to sell alcohol; Betting Licensing Committees perform a similar function in granting permits to bookmakers and licensing premises for gaming — in short, the administration of justice in England and Wales depends to a greater extent than many people realise on the work of the magistrates.

5.1   LAY MAGISTRATES

There are about 30,000 active lay magistrates in England and Wales. Lay magistrates are so called because their work is unpaid, although they can claim allowances for travelling, subsistence and loss of earnings: Justices of the Peace Act 1997, s 10. Most lay magistrates are also 'lay' in the sense that they have no legal qualifications, but there is no bar to lawyers or, indeed, holders of high judicial office becoming magistrates. Academic lawyers may find work as lay magistrates a suitable way in which to serve the community.

5.1.1   Appointment of lay magistrates

Lay magistrates are appointed by the Lord Chancellor 'on behalf and in the name of Her Majesty': Justices of the Peace Act 1997, s 5. Appointments are made each year to replace magistrates who die or whose names are placed on the supplemental list (see Paragraph 5.1.3), or to cope with an increase in the amount of work to be done. It is said that the number of suitable candidates for appointment considerably exceeds the vacancies to be filled. In deciding whom to appoint, the Lord Chancellor is principally concerned that the appointee will, by character and ability, be suited for the work of a magistrate, and that he will be recognised by his fellows as being so suited. The major statutory limitation on eligiblity for appointment is a residential one (see Paragraph 5.3) but certain categories of persons will not, in practice, be considered (e.g., those aged 60 or over, members of the armed forces or the police and those with convictions for serious crime). Although political affiliations are ignored in deciding whether a person is suited to be a magistrate, many magistrates are or were involved in local politics. Magistrates in a particular area should not be heavily weighted in favour of one party. As well as trying to maintain a political balance, the Lord Chancellor tries to maintain a balance between the sexes (in fact, there are roughly three male to every two female magistrates), and to introduce younger people in their thirties or early forties to the magistracy. Criticism of the approach to appointing magistrates is usually based on an assertion that magistrates do not represent a sufficiently broad cross-section of the local community. Too often, it is said, they are drawn from what, for want of a better term, may be described as the upper social classes. Further, adverse comment is frequently made about the under-representation of ethnic minorities among magistrates. A high proportion of the magistracy comprises people who have retired from full-time employment, and those falling within this category are in addition able to sit more frequently than those who are in work. The magistracy is balanced according to gender, by contrast with the overwhelmingly male ranks of professional judges. There have been concerns, however, about the extent to which members of ethnic minorities are adequately represented. It appears that in 2000 about 2 per cent of magistrates were black, and about 2 per cent of Asian origin — figures which were beginning to approach the proportions in the population at large (see the Auld Report, p. 119).

5.1.2   Training and court attendance of lay magistrates

Before appointment magistrates undertake to complete, within one year of appointment, a course of basic instruction in the duties which they will be carrying out. It is the responsibility of Magistrates' Courts Committees (see Paragraph 5.3) to administer training schemes for the areas for which they are responsible. The aim of the training is to impress upon the new magistrate the necessity of acting judicially, to give him a grounding in law and evidence which will enable him to follow intelligently the types of case he will normally encounter, to inform him of the nature of the sentences he will be able to pass, and to help him understand the role of others who work in the courts (e.g., the clerk, court staff and legal representatives). The training should include, in addition to formal lecturing, visits to courts and penal institutions, and group discussions of the problems magistrates frequently face.

Magistrates are expected to sit in court at least 26 times during a year. No doubt, the frequency with which they actually do sit varies greatly, but the average attendance is around 40 times a year. The significance of this is that through their initial training and through their regular attendance at court, often over many years, magistrates become knowledgeable about the work of their courts. Although the adjective 'lay' is used to describe them, they are far from being ignorant of the ways of the law. This was recognised by Lord Bridge of Harwich in a handsome tribute which he paid to magistrates in the course of giving the House of Lords' judgment in *Re McC (A Minor)* [1985] AC 528. He was discussing, *obiter dicta,* the rule that a judge of a court of record is not liable civilly for wrongs he may do when exercising his jurisdiction, even if he acts in bad faith, whereas in earlier centuries magistrates acting *intra vires* were held liable for acts done maliciously and without reasonable or probable cause. His Lordship doubted whether this still applied because the rule:

> had its origins in society's view of the justice, reflected in Shakespeare's plays, as an ignorant buffoon. How long this view persisted and how long there was any justification for it, I am not a good enough legal or social historian to say. But it clearly has no application in today's world either to stipendiary magistrates or to lay benches. The former are competent professional judges, the latter citizens from all walks of life chosen for their intelligence and integrity, required to undergo some training before they sit and advised by legally qualified clerks. They give unstinting voluntary service to the community and conduct the major part of the criminal business of the courts. Without them the system of criminal justice in this country would grind to a halt.

No doubt many lawyers, not to mention defendants, would regard Lord Bridge's compliments as exaggerated, but it remains true — as his Lordship said — that the modern magistrate is far removed from the buffoon of Shakespeare's day.

5.1.3 Removal and 'retirement' of magistrates

Lay magistrates can be removed from office by the Lord Chancellor: Justices of the Peace Act 1997, s 5. This is only appropriate in extreme cases where for instance the magistrate has been convicted of serious crime. If a magistrate is infirm or it is expedient for any other reason that he should cease to exercise judicial functions, or if he fails to attend court as often as he ought, the Lord Chancellor can order that his name be placed on the supplemental list: Justices of the Peace Act 1997, s 7. A magistrate on the supplemental list retains the status of justice of the peace but the only powers he can exercise are trivial ones in connection with the witnessing of documents — he cannot sit in court or even issue a summons or warrant. At the age of 70 (75 in the case of one who holds or has held high judicial office) a magistrate is automatically placed on the supplemental list. In effect, therefore, lay magistrates retire at the age of 70.

5.2 DISTRICT JUDGES (MAGISTRATES' COURT)

District judges (magistrates' courts) are professional salaried members of the judiciary who were until recently known as stipendiary magistrates. They are appointed by the Queen upon the recommendation of the Lord Chancellor from among barristers and solicitors of at least seven years' standing: Justices of the Peace Act 1997. There are about 105 of them, supported by some 150 deputy district judges, who sit part-time as a precursor to full-time appointment. Although district judges are assigned to a particular centre or magistrates' courts committee area, they may be required to sit anywhere as the work demands. About half of the full-time appointees sit in London, and half in the provinces. A district judge may be removed from office by the Lord Chancellor for inability or misbehaviour. Otherwise he can continue in office until the retirement age, which is 70 (subject to the Lord Chancellor's power to extend for a limited period).

A district judge can try a case sitting alone, whereas at least two magistrates must sit together for the purposes of a summary trial (see Chapter 10 for the position in the youth court). This fact, together with his legal knowledge and experience, enables the district judge to be significantly faster than lay magistrates, who need to confer among themselves and take the advice of their clerk. The district judge is characteristically more interventionist than a lay bench, and there is some evidence that the typical district judge sentences more heavily, and is more likely to remand in custody than the lay magistracy (Auld Report, p. 95). There is some controversy over the respective roles of the professional district judge and the lay magistrates. Supporters of the lay magistracy rely upon the wide experience of life which they bring to the bench, and the greater chance that a decision reached by several people will be more considered, and consequently fairer, because of the interaction between the members of the bench. Those favouring a greater role for the district judges focus upon their greater speed and efficiency in dealing with a day's list, and their ability to take hold of longer and more complex cases.

Apart from the power of the district judge to sit alone, there is at present no rigid distinction between their powers and those of the lay magistracy. However, district judges tend to be allocated cases involving complex points of law or evidence, long and/or inter-linked cases, those involving considerations of public safety, public interest immunity applications and extradition cases.

5.3   ORGANISATION OF THE COURTS

The appointment of justices of the peace under the Justices of the Peace Act 1361 (see beginning of the Chapter) was on the basis of one lord and three or four worthy men being appointed for each county. Today a magistrate is appointed to act for a commission area not a county, but the change is one of nomenclature as, outside London, there is a commission area for each county whether metropolitan or non-metropolitan. In London there are six commission areas, namely the City of London, the inner London area, the north-east, south-east and south-west London areas, and the Middlesex area: Justices of the Peace Act 1997, ss 1–2. Henceforward, the commission areas will be referred to as counties. Unless the Lord Chancellor otherwise directs, a magistrate must live in or within 15 miles of the county for which he acts: Justices of the Peace Act 1997, s 6. Generally speaking, magistrates only have jurisdiction to try a summary offence if it was allegedly committed within the county for which they act (see Chapter 9).

The counties are subdivided into petty sessional divisions, with a magistrates' court in each division. Although a magistrate can sit in any of the courts for his county, he is assigned to the bench for the division in which he lives or works, and normally would only sit in the court for that division. Where proceedings are begun against a magistrate in his own petty sessional division it is convenient to have magistrates from another area deal with the case, so as to avoid the embarrassment of the accused magistrate being tried by his colleagues on the bench. The Lord Chancellor decides in which courts district judges shall sit.

> Each year the magistrates for a petty sessional division must elect by secret ballot a chairman and one or more deputy chairmen: Justices of the Peace Act 1997, s 22. If a chairman or deputy chairman so elected is present at a sitting of the magistrates' court he is entitled to preside over the proceedings. His powers are no greater than those of his colleagues with him in court but he speaks for the bench in that, for example, he announces the court's decisions. If none of the elected chairmen are present, the longest-serving magistrate acts as chairman subject to any established rule or custom of the bench. An elected chairman does not have the right to preside when sitting with a district judge, or when sitting in the youth court. The procedure for electing chairmen is set out in the Justices (Size and Chairmanship of the Bench) Rules 1990 (SI 1990 No 1554).
>
> Sections 27 and 29 of the 1997 Act provide for a magistrates' courts committee to be set up in each county, metropolitan district and outer London borough, with one for the inner London area and another for the City of London. Each committee is composed of magistrates from the area in question, and must appoint a justices' chief executive, who shall administer the magistrates' courts in the area. The justices' chief executive has an administrative role, and need not be qualified to be appointed as a justices' clerk (Access to Justice Act 1999, ss 87 and 88).

5.4   MAGISTRATES' CLERKS

One or more magistrates' clerks may be appointed for each petty sessional division: Justices of the Peace Act 1997, s 42. The appointments are made by the relevant magistrates' courts committee from amongst barristers and solicitors who are either of at least five years' standing or have worked for at least five years as assistant to a magistrates' clerk (s 26). The duties of the magistrates' clerk are such that he could not, in a busy court, carry them out unaided. The magistrates' courts committee may, therefore, after consultation with the clerk, employ staff to assist him. The assistants to the magistrates' clerk need not be, but often are, legally qualified.

The nature of the work done by the magistrates' clerk and his assistants is described in later Chapters. Briefly, they play a major part in the behind the scenes administration of the court (e.g., issuing summonses and processing legal aid applications), and, in court, they advise the magistrates on the law. The primary duty of the justices' clerk is to his bench or benches, as a legal adviser, and in that role he is not accountable to the justices' chief executive: Justices of the Peace Act 1997, s 48). However, he may also exercise certain *administrative* functions on behalf of the justices' chief executive, who is his 'line manager' for that purpose.

6   Bail and Remands

The principal subject-matter of this Chapter is bail, which may be defined as the release of a person subject to a duty to surrender to custody at an appointed time and place. The time when a person bailed is to surrender to custody may be fixed when bail is granted or, in the case of a person sent on bail to the Crown Court for trial or sentence, it may be notified to him subsequently. The place where he is to surrender is either a court or a police station, usually the former. The granting of bail in criminal proceedings is governed by the Bail Act 1976.

6.1   REMANDS AND ADJOURNMENTS

The power of courts (especially magistrates' courts) to remand an accused person is closely bound up with the power to grant bail. A remand occurs when a court adjourns a case and either bails the accused for the period of the adjournment or commits him to custody to be brought before the court on the adjournment date. As the above implies, remands are either on bail or in custody, by contrast with a simple adjournment, which does not entail the same restrictions. A magistrates' court has a general discretion to adjourn a case at any stage prior to or during committal proceedings or summary trial (see Magistrates' Courts Act 1980, ss 5 and 10). It also has power to adjourn after summary conviction for the preparation of reports.

In fact, it is rare for a case of any gravity or complexity to be totally disposed of on the occasion of the accused's first appearance. Either the prosecution will need time to prepare statements for committal, or serve advance information, or ensure that their witnesses are present for summary trial; or the accused will want an adjournment to apply for legal aid, see a solicitor and generally put his case in order. The only type of case likely to need only one appearance is where the accused pleads guilty to a relatively minor offence and the court does not consider it needs reports before passing sentence.

Assuming the magistrates do have to adjourn, they are always entitled to remand the accused. However, if the offence is summary and it is an adjournment prior to trial, they have a discretion simply to adjourn without remanding. Similarly, if the offence is triable either way and the accused has not been remanded before and appears in answer to a summons (as opposed to having been charged and bailed from the police station), there is a discretion not to remand upon adjourning. In all other cases (e.g., offences triable only on indictment, those triable either way where the prosecution was commenced by way of charge, and all adjournments after conviction for reports), the magistrates must remand —

i.e. grant the accused bail or remand him in custody. The difference between, on the one hand, simply adjourning and, on the other, adjourning and granting bail is that, in the former case, no adverse consequences flow from the accused failing to appear on the adjournment date, save that the offence will very likely be proved against him in his absence, whereas in the latter case he is under a duty to appear and commits an offence by not doing so. Normally, magistrates only adjourn without remanding in trivial cases, especially road traffic matters. The next Paragraph deals especially with the periods for which magistrates may remand an accused; the remainder of the Chapter deals with bail.

6.1.1 Periods of remand

Subject to what follows, when magistrates remand an accused in custody prior to committal proceedings or summary trial, the period of the remand must not exceed eight clear days: MCA, s 128(6). Usually it is simpler to make the adjournment and remand for a week, rather than using the full period allowed. The limitation on remands in custody is inconvenient when a period of several weeks or months is bound to elapse before the committal or summary trial can take place. Again, subject to what follows, the accused has to be brought before the court each week, even though the virtually foregone conclusion of his appearance is that he will be remanded in custody for another week. The pointlessness of his appearing in the dock just to be told that his case is further adjourned until such and such a date is accentuated by the fact that, since the decision of the Divisional Court in *Nottingham Justices ex p Davies* [1981] QB 38, the defence have basically only been allowed one, or at most two, fully argued bail applications. Once they have exhausted those applications, they can only re-open the question of bail if fresh considerations have arisen which were not placed before the bench that originally refused bail. Obviously, if the defence are prevented from arguing for bail, the remand hearing turns into a charade. The decision in *Ex p Davies* has been statutorily confirmed by the insertion in 1988 of Pt IIA in Sch 1 to the Bail Act 1976 (see Paragraph 6.5.1).

In recognition of the unsatisfactoriness of successive remands in custody and the necessity for the accused's presence at each remand, the Criminal Justice Act 1982 introduced several new subsections into s 128 of the MCA, the basic effect of which is to allow the accused to consent to being remanded in custody for up to a 28 days without attending court. The system is that, on the first or any subsequent occasion when magistrates propose to adjourn prior to committal or summary trial and remand the accused in custody, they must, if he is legally represented in court, inform him of the possibility of further remands being made in his absence. If, and only if, he consents, they may then remand him thrice without his being brought to court. On the fourth occasion he must attend whether he wishes or not. The possibility of custodial remand in absence does not arise if the accused is unrepresented or if he is a juvenile. There are also detailed provisions about his initially agreeing to a remand in absence and then withdrawing his consent, and about his ceasing to be legally represented whilst on remand. Two main points to notice, however, are that (under the provisions now being discussed) the accused can insist on being produced for each remand hearing, however much the court and the advocates hint that it is a total waste of time, and — even if there is consent to not being produced — the case has to be listed and mentioned each week, just so that the magistrates may formally remand in custody again.

Although probably the bulk of defendants who will have to be remanded in custody for substantial periods do sooner or later agree to remands in absence, the Government apparently came to think that, given the pressures under which the prison service is currently working, it was unsatisfactory to burden the service with the task of bringing remandees to court when no useful purpose could possibly be served by that being done. Accordingly the Criminal Justice Act 1988 inserted a new section (s 128A) into the Magistrates' Courts Act which allows a magistrates' court to remand an accused in custody for up to 28 clear days, whether or not he consents. Since 1991, it has been available in all petty sessions areas. It enables a magistrates' court, once it has set a date for the next stage of the proceedings to take place, to remand an accused in custody for a period ending on that date, or for a period of 28 clear days, whichever is the less. Importantly, it does not apply on the occasion of a first remand in custody but only if at a second or any subsequent remand the court again decides to refuse bail. Section 128A thus dovetails with the statutory provisions about argued bail applications, because the defence has a right to make an argued bail application both on the occasion of the accused's first appearance in connection with the charge and (if bail is then refused) at the next hearing. Thus, it is only when the ration of argued applications has been used up that the court may remand in custody for up to 28 days. If they are considering an extended remand under s 128A, magistrates should have regard to the total period of time the accused would spend in custody if they were so to remand him (see para 9B, added to Pt 1 of Sch 1 to the Bail Act 1976).

Where magistrates remand an accused after conviction for the purpose of preparing reports on him, the period of the remand must not exceed three weeks if it is in custody; four weeks if it is on bail: MCA, ss 10(3) and 30(1). Remands on bail prior to summary trial or committal proceedings may be for any convenient period. There is also a power in addition to the new s 128A to remand in custody for up to 28 days if the accused is already serving a custodial sentence for some other offence (see MCA, s 131(1)).

6.2   OCCASIONS ON WHICH A PERSON MAY BE GRANTED BAIL

The occasions on which a court or magistrate or police officer is faced with the decision to grant or refuse bail are as follows:

(a)   During the arrest and charge procedure at the police station, the question of bail can arise either as a result of the police charging the arrestee or as a result of their deciding that he should be released from the station without being charged. In the last resort, the decision on whether or not the arrestee should be bailed rests with the custody officer, although he will no doubt be much influenced by the views of the investigating officers. For details, see Paragraph 2.3.8 and ss 37 and 38 of the Police and Criminal Evidence Act 1984.

(b)   A magistrate issuing a warrant for the arrest of the person named in a written information which has been laid before him and substantiated on oath should consider whether to endorse the warrant for bail: MCA, s 117 — see Paragraph 2.4.6. Similarly, a magistrates' court or the Crown Court on issuing a warrant may back it for bail: s 117 and Supreme Court Act 1981, s 81(4).

(c)   A magistrates' court has jurisdiction to grant bail when:

(i)   it remands an accused for the period of an adjournment prior to committal proceedings or summary trial: MCA, ss 5, 10(4) and 18(4) — see the preceding Paragraph; or

(ii)   it remands an offender after conviction for the period of an adjournment for reports under MCA, ss 10(3) or 30 — see Paragraph 9.8; or

(iii)   it commits an accused to the Crown Court for trial on indictment or for sentence (MCA, ss 6(3) and 38 which provide respectively that committals for trial and sentence may be in custody or on bail); or

(iv)   a person in custody is appealing to the Crown Court or the Divisional Court against one of its (the magistrates' court's) decisions: MCA, s 113 — see Paragraphs 25.1.2 and 25.2.2.

The maximum periods for remands in custody prior to committal proceedings or summary trial have been explained in Paragraph 6.1.1. A remand for preparation of reports following summary conviction may be for a maximum of three or four weeks depending on whether the offender is or is not in custody (see MCA, ss 10(3) and 30). Committals for trial or sentence in custody will be for whatever period may elapse until the case can be heard in the Crown Court. Because that period will certainly be one of several weeks and may extend to several months, the decision to grant or refuse bail on committal is a particularly important one.

(d)   The Crown Court has jurisdiction to grant bail when:

(i)   a magistrates' court has remanded an accused in custody and has issued a certificate to the effect that it heard full argument before taking the decision to refuse bail (see Paragraph 6.5.3 for details); or

(ii)   a person has been committed to it for trial or sentence in custody or is appealing to it against conviction or sentence by the magistrates; or

(iii)   a person is appealing from it by case stated to the Divisional Court or is seeking judicial review of its decision; or

(iv)   the appropriate Crown Court judge has certified that a case is fit for appeal to the Court of Appeal against conviction or sentence (see also Paragraph 24.2.1).

The above powers to grant bail are contained in s 81(1) of the Supreme Court Act 1981 as amended. The Crown Court also has inherent jurisdiction to grant bail during the course of a trial on indictment and for the period of an adjournment for reports following conviction. If the accused was on bail prior to the commencement of the trial and surrenders to custody at the appointed time, it is normal practice to renew his bail for any overnight adjournments. Bail may be withdrawn, however, where there is a real danger that he might abscond (e.g. because the case is going badly for him), or interfere with witnesses or jurors. When a custodial sentence would be the likely result of conviction and the prosecution case seems strong, bail is often withdrawn once the judge has commenced his summing-up. *Practice Direction (Crime: Bail during Trial)* [1974] 1 WLR 770 deals with the principles governing bail during the course of a trial.

(e)   The High Court has jurisdiction to grant bail when:

(i)   a magistrates' court withholds bail: Criminal Justice Act 1967, s 22; or

(ii)   a person is applying to it for *certiorari* to quash a magistrates' court's decision: Criminal Justice Act 1948, s 37; or

(iii)   a person is appealing to it by way of case stated from the Crown Court, or is applying to it for *certiorari* to quash a Crown Court decision: s 37 of the 1948 Act.

There is also jurisdiction to vary any conditions of bail imposed by a magistrates' court. The High Court's jurisdiction to grant or vary the terms of bail is exercised by a judge in chambers.

(f)   The Criminal Division of the Court of Appeal has jurisdiction to grant bail both to a person appealing to it against conviction or sentence in the Crown Court, and to a person who, after an unsuccessful appeal to it, is further appealing to the House of Lords: Criminal Appeal Act 1968, ss 19 and 36 — see Paragraphs 24.6.7 and 24.9. The power of the Court of Appeal to grant bail is one of the powers exercisable by a single judge.

6.3   PRINCIPLES ON WHICH THE DECISION TO GRANT OR REFUSE BAIL IS TAKEN

Section 4 of the Bail Act 1976 gives to an accused person what may usefully, if slightly inaccurately, be described as a right to bail. The section does not apply at all stages of the criminal process, and, even if it does apply, the accused may be refused bail if the circumstances of his case fall within one of a number of sets of circumstances defined in Schedule 1 to the Act. Where the accused is charged with an offence punishable with imprisonment, the circumstances mentioned in Schedule 1 as justifying the refusal of bail are just those circumstances in which, prior to the passing of the Act, judges and magistrates would, as a matter of practice, have tended to remand or commit in custody. Nevertheless, the right to bail is of value to an accused because it emphasises that it is for the prosecution to show a good reason why bail should be withheld, not for the defence to plead for bail as a favour to which the accused is not prima facie entitled.

There is a group of defendants who may be granted bail only if there are 'wholly exceptional circumstances which justify it'. This is the category covered by s 25 of the Criminal Justice and Public Order Act 1994. That provision covers any person charged with murder, attempted murder, manslaughter, rape or attempted rape, if he has previously been convicted in the United Kingdom of one of those offences, or of culpable homicide. Where the prior conviction was manslaughter or culpable homicide, however, the provision applies only if the sentence imposed on that occasion was imprisonment or long-term detention. The current offence with which the accused is charged does not need to be the same as that for which he was convicted previously. The restriction on bail for accused in this category applies also on appeal against conviction.

It follows that defendants prohibited from bail by s 25 of the 1994 Act are excluded from the presumptive right to bail conferred by s 4 of the Bail Act 1976.

6.3.1   Occasions on which there is a 'right to bail'

Section 4 provides that a person to whom it applies 'shall be granted bail except as provided in Schedule 1'. The section applies whenever a person accused of an offence appears or is brought before a magistrates' court or the Crown Court in the course of or in connection with proceedings for the offence. Thus, at his first court appearance before the magistrates and at all subsequent appearances before the magistrates or the Crown Court up to the occasion on which he is convicted or acquitted, the accused has a right to bail. Even following conviction, he still has a right to bail if his case is adjourned for reports prior to sentencing. He can also rely on the right to bail if, during these stages of the proceedings, he applies to the High Court or the Crown Court for bail following a refusal of bail by the magistrates. There is no right to bail when:

(a)   the custody officer is considering bailing an arrestee from the police station after he has been charged; or

(b)   the magistrates, having summarily convicted an offender, commit him to the Crown Court for sentence; or

(c)   a person who has been convicted and sentenced, whether by the magistrates or in the Crown Court, is appealing against conviction or sentence.

Of course, in all three of the above cases the police officer or court has power to grant bail, but there is no statutory presumption in its favour by virtue of s 4. In case (a), s 38(1) of the PACE gives the accused something very similar to the Bail Act 'right to bail'. The subsection provides that a person who has been charged *shall* be released from the police station (either on bail or unconditionally) unless the custody officer reasonably fears that that would have one or more of a number of undesirable consequences (e.g., the arrestee absconding or interfering with witnesses — Paragraph 2.3.8).

6.3.2 Refusing bail for a defendant charged with an imprisonable offence

Schedule 1 to the Bail Act 1976 sets out the circumstances in which a person to whom s 4 applies (i.e., a person with a right to bail) may be refused bail. Schedule 1 refers to a person with a right to bail as 'the defendant'.

Part I of Sch 1 applies when the defendant stands accused or convicted of at least one offence punishable with imprisonment. He need not be granted bail if:

(a)   the court is satisfied that there are substantial grounds for believing that, if released on bail, he would:

(i)   fail to surrender to custody; or

(ii)   commit an offence while on bail; or

(iii)   interfere with witnesses or otherwise obstruct the course of justice whether in relation to himself or some other person; or

(b)   the offence with which he is charged is indictable-only, or triable-either-way, and he was already on bail at the time of the charged offence; or

(c)   the court is satisfied that he should be kept in custody for his own protection or, if he is a juvenile, for his own welfare; or

(d)   he is already serving a custodial sentence; or

(e)   the court is satisfied that lack of time since the commencement of the proceedings has made it impracticable to obtain the information needed to decide properly the questions raised in (a) to (c) above; or

(f)   he has already been bailed during the course of the proceedings, and has been arrested under s 7 of the Act (arrest of absconders etc. — see Paragraph 6.7.1).

The above reasons for refusing bail are listed in paras 2 to 6 of Pt I of Sch 1. The one most commonly relied upon is that set out in (a). It will be noticed that the wording of the reason is very precise. The court must be 'satisfied that there are substantial grounds for believing' that, if bail were granted, one or other of the undesirable consequences specified would ensue. A subjective belief that that is what would happen is not enough if it is based on flimsy or irrational grounds. On the other hand, the prosecution are not required to prove beyond reasonable doubt that the defendant would jump bail etc., or even to produce formal evidence to that effect. The question for the court is essentially a speculative one, not amenable to proof according to the rules by which disputed issues are normally resolved in a court of law. Thus, a prosecutor objecting to bail may state his opinion that it would lead to the accused absconding, or he may even, with a view to showing that there is a risk of interference with witnesses, recount to the court what a police officer has been told by a potential witness of threats the latter has received (*Re Moles* [1981] Crim LR 170). This was confirmed by *Mansfield Justices ex p Sharkey* [1985] QB 613, where the Divisional Court accepted counsel's proposition that 'a bail application is an informal inquiry and no strict rules of evidence are to be applied'. However, para 9 of Pt I of Sch 1 does give the courts some guidance on how this informal inquiry should be approached by listing a number of considerations to be taken into account; para 9 only applies when the objection to bail is one of those presently being discussed — i.e., that the defendant would abscond, commit further offences or interfere with witnesses.

First, there is 'the nature and seriousness of the offence and the probable method of dealing with the defendant for it'. The more serious the charge the more likely it is that he will abscond because he will realise that conviction would result in a lengthy prison sentence. Secondly, the 'character, antecedents, associations and community ties' of the defendant are relevant. Under the heading of 'community ties' the court will be assessing how much the defendant has to lose by absconding. If he is a married man with a family living in his own house, he is less likely to abscond than a teenager with a room in a hostel. However, a person should not be refused bail simply because he is living in the latter type of accommodation — it is merely one factor which goes to indicate a lack of roots in the local community and therefore a greater risk of jumping bail (see Home Office Circular, No 155 of 1975). The defendant's character and previous convictions are important in two ways. They may show that he is untrustworthy, and they may also show that, even though the offence charged is not intrinsically in the first rank of gravity, he is likely if convicted to receive a custodial sentence because, for example, he will be in breach of a suspended sentence. Thirdly, the court may look at the defendant's past record for answering bail and/or committing offences while on bail. If he has previously been bailed and has not abused the trust placed in him, that is some reason for saying that he can be trusted on bail on the present occasion. Lastly, the court should consider the strength of the prosecution case — the weaker the evidence seems, the stronger is the argument for bail. Unfortunately, the strength or weakness of the case will probably not emerge until the committal proceedings stage, by which time the defendant may have spent a considerable period in custody. The list of relevant considerations in para 9 is not intended as an exhaustive one. One obviously important factor not mentioned in the paragraph is whether the defence can put forward sureties.

Reason (b) for refusing bail was added to the list by s 26 of the Criminal Justice and Public Order Act 1994. It covers the position of the offender who is alleged to have committed a further offence while on bail. An accused who is in due course found guilty of that further offence can expect a harsher sentence as a result (see CJA 1991, s 29, and Paragraph 21.2). But his bail prospects will also be affected. The court still has a discretion whether to grant him bail or not. In exercising that discretion, however, they need not regard him as having the right to bail (provided that the offence for which he was already on bail was indictable-only or triable-either-way). As a result, the refusal of bail will be easier, for in cases where there is a right to bail there must be substantial grounds for believing that one of the exceptions applies before bail can be withheld. In this context, 'substantial' means more than a subjective perception (*Ex p Sharkey* at p. 625).

The other justifications in Sch 1 for refusing to bail a defendant with a right to bail call for little comment. Keeping somebody in custody for his own protection might be necessary where the offence charged has raised a great deal of local anger, as where it is alleged that the defendant sexually assaulted a number of young children. If the defendant is a juvenile, bail can be refused in his own best interests even though he would not be physically endangered through being released (e.g., if he has run away from home, remanding him into the care of the local authority may be preferable to leaving him to fend for himself). Where the defendant is already serving a custodial sentence which will last until well after his next court appearance on the present charge, there is little point in going through the motions of considering a bail application. Lack of information on which to base a proper decision about bail is a problem when the defendant makes his first court appearance before the magistrates after being arrested without warrant, charged at the police station and thereafter kept in police detention. He may not have been able to consult with a solicitor or to arrange for one to be at court to make a bail application for him. Although the duty solicitor will no doubt be asked to assist, there will be little time for him to be given proper instructions (e.g., as to who might be prepared to stand surety). From the police viewpoint, they may not have been able to check on matters such as the defendant's address, identity and previous convictions. The magistrates are therefore allowed to 'play safe' by remanding in custody for a week or so, at the end of which the arguments for and against bail can be properly presented on both sides. Lastly, if the defendant has already been bailed in connection with the present proceedings against him and has had to be arrested for absconding or otherwise failing to comply with the conditions of his bail, the court is entitled to say the legal equivalent of 'once bitten twice shy' and refuse to set him at liberty again.

At the stage of an adjournment for reports following the defendant's conviction, there is one additional possible reason for refusing bail, namely that the court believes it will not be practicable to complete the report without the defendant being in custody. For example, the court may have ordered medical reports, but the mental condition of the defendant may make it obvious that he will not voluntarily attend at a hospital so as to be examined. The court should therefore remand him in custody (or it may now have the additional option of remanding him to a mental hospital — see Paragraph 9.8).

6.3.3 Refusing bail for a defendant charged with a non-imprisonable offence

Part II of Sch 1 applies when none of the offences of which the defendant stands accused or convicted is punishable with imprisonment. He need not be granted bail if reasons (b), (c) or (e) for refusing to grant bail to a defendant accused of an imprisonable offence apply in his case (i.e., he should be kept in custody for his own protection, he is already serving a custodial sentence, or he has been bailed in the course of the proceedings and arrested under s 7). There is no general power to refuse bail on the grounds that he might abscond, but, if he failed to surrender to custody after being bailed in previous criminal proceedings and the court therefore believes that, if now granted bail, he would again fail to surrender, bail may be refused. It is very rare for a court to refuse bail if the offences are non-imprisonable.

6.3.4 Custody time-limits

Under a s 22 of the Prosecution of Offences Act 1985, there are regulations which lay down custody time-limits (i.e., maximum periods during which the accused can be kept in custody). The regulations were originally in force in certain areas only, but have now been extended to all parts of the country. They fix the following maximum periods for which an accused may be held:

   (a) 70 days between his first appearance in the magistrates' court and committal proceedings;

   (b) 70 days between first appearance and summary trial for an offence which is triable either way (reduced to 56 days if the decision for summary trial is taken within 56 days); and

   (c) 56 days between first appearance and trial for a summary offence;

(d)   112 days between committal for trial and arraignment;

(e)   182 days between the date sent for trial under s 51 of the Crime and Disorder Act 1998 (indictable-only offences), and the start of trial.

Special rules apply to the accused's right to bail when the prosecution fails to comply with a custody time-limit. When the limit has expired, the exceptions to the right to bail listed in Sch 1 to the Bail Act 1976 no longer apply (reg 8 of the Prosecution of Offences (Custody Time-Limits) Regulations 1987: SI 1987 No 299). The effect is to give the accused an absolute right to bail. Further, the court is prevented, when bailing an accused entitled to bail by reason of the expiry of a custody time-limit, from imposing a requirement of a surety or deposit of security or any other condition which must be complied with *before* release on bail. It may impose a condition such as a curfew, or a condition of residence or reporting, which has to be complied with *after* release. The prosecution can, of course, avoid these consequences by ensuring that the case is dealt with quickly, so as to avoid the expiry of the custody time-limit. Failing that, it can apply for an extension of the time-limit.

The application for an extension must be made before the custody time limit expires. In considering whether to grant an extension, the criteria laid down in s 22(3) of the Prosecution of Offences Act 1985 are applied. The court must be satisfied:

(a)   that the need for the extension is due to:

(i)   the illness or absence of the accused, a necessary witness, a judge or a magistrate;

(ii)   the ordering by the court of separate trials in the case of two or more accused or two or more offences; or

(iii)   some other good or sufficient cause; and

(b)   that the Crown has acted with all due expedition.

(For a detailed analysis of the case law on custody time limits, see *Blackstone's Criminal Practice*, D10.4.)

6.4   REQUIREMENTS IMPOSED WHEN GRANTING BAIL

A defendant may be granted bail unconditionally, in which case he is not required to provide sureties before being released and, having been released, the only obligation he is under is that of surrendering to custody at the appointed place and time. Alternatively, s 3 of the Bail Act allows the police or the courts to attach requirements to a grant of bail.

The most common of the requirements attached to bail is that of providing one or more sureties. Both the police when bailing an arrestee from the station and the courts may require sureties, but they should only do so if it is necessary to ensure that the defendant surrenders to custody (see s 3(4)). A surety is a person who undertakes to pay the court a specified sum of money in the event of the defendant failing to surrender to custody as he ought. The undertaking into which the surety enters is called a recognisance. If the defendant absconds the surety may be ordered to pay part or all of the sum in which he stood surety. This is known as forfeiting or estreating the recognisance. A surety whose recognisance has been estreated is dealt with as if he had been fined, so if he fails to pay the sum forfeited a means inquiry is held and, ultimately, he could be committed to prison. The possibly serious consequences of being a surety mean that no person proffered as a surety should be accepted as such unless he apparently has the means to satisfy his potential liability under the recognisance. On granting bail, the police officer or court fixes the number and amount of the sureties which will be required, and the defendant must remain in custody until suitable sureties in the stated sums have entered into their recognisances. If the sureties are not forthcoming the defendant, at his next appearance before the court or on an application to a High Court judge in chambers, may argue that the requirement for sureties should be varied or dispensed with all together.

Note that a surety for an adult accused is responsible only for ensuring that the accused attends court. He is not obliged to ensure that other conditions of bail (e.g., not to commit further offences) are met. Some magistrates' courts have been in the practice of asking for 'sureties for good behaviour'. There is no power to do this under the Bail Act 1976, so they attempt to remedy the deficiency by using their general powers to bind over under the Justices of the Peace Act 1361 and the Justices of the Peace Act 1968. There are two problems with this practice:

(a)   Binding over to keep the peace is only of relevance where the court fears repetition, for example, of an offence of violence. It can hardly be properly invoked in relation, say, to an offence of dishonesty.

(b)   A court requiring a surety for good behaviour appears to be contravening the Bail Act 1976, s 3(3)(c) of which provides: 'Except as provided *by this section* . . . no other requirement shall be imposed [on the accused] as a condition of bail' (emphasis added).

The position as far as sureties for juveniles is concerned is different. By s 3(7) of the Bail Act 1976, where the accused is a juvenile and his parent or guardian stands surety for him, the court may require that surety to ensure that the juvenile complies with any condition of bail imposed by virtue of s 6. Hence, the court can quite properly require the parent or guardian to be a surety for good behaviour. The recognisance under s 3(7) is, however, limited to £50.

A requirement for sureties does not involve the sureties or the defendant himself paying money to the court as a pre-condition of his release on bail. The position is different, however, where the court requires that the defendant supply security for his surrender to custody (s 3(5)). Giving security means that the defendant or somebody on his behalf deposits money or other property with the court, which will be forfeited if he absconds.

Instead of or in addition to imposing a requirement for sureties or, where appropriate, a requirement for the giving of security, a court may require the defendant to comply with such other conditions as appear necessary to ensure that he does not abscond, commit offences while on bail or interfere with witnesses: (s 3(6)(a) to (c)). A condition may also be imposed to ensure that the defendant attends an interview with his legal representative (s 3(6)(e)). By virtue of s 3(6), the defendant may be required, for example, to report to the police station once a week or even once a day, to surrender his passport, to live at a certain address (e.g. his home address or, if he is of no fixed abode, a bail hostel run by the probation service), to report any change of address, or to be indoors by a certain time each night. Negatively, he could be ordered not to contact potential prosecution witnesses or not to go within a certain distance of where the victim of the alleged offence lives. More controversially, in *Mansfield Justices ex p Sharkey* [1985] QB 613, a number of miners from Yorkshire involved in the strike of 1984–5 were required as a condition of bail not to picket otherwise than at their own pits, which were solidly for the strike anyway. They were awaiting trial on threatening behaviour charges, the alleged offences having occurred when they were taking part in the mass picketing of working pits in the East Midlands. The Divisional Court upheld the requirements on the basis that the defendants would otherwise have returned to the picket lines which, given that the picketing was 'by intimidation and threat' (per the Lord Chief Justice at p. 627), might have resulted in their committing further offences. *Ex p Sharkey* was of interest not only for its political implications and the impact it had on the course of the miners' strike, but also for the Lord Chief Justice's comments on how probable the commission of further offences must appear if that is to be used as a justification for imposing conditions of bail. The court must perceive a real, as opposed to a fanciful, risk of unconditional bail resulting in offences being committed while on bail, but it need not have the 'substantial grounds' for its belief which it would have to have if it were minded to refuse bail completely for the same reason. Thus, the justices were entitled to impose the conditions even though the defendants were of previous good character and the only grounds for supposing they would commit offences if allowed to picket again was the justices' local knowledge of how the picketing was in general being conducted. The implication of Lord Lane's judgment was that those grounds would not have been substantial enough for a total refusal of bail.

Ex p Sharkey was a case where the accused were charged with an imprisonable offence. In *Bournemouth Magistrates' Court ex p Cross* (1989) 89 Cr App R 90, the point at issue was whether conditions could be imposed on bail for non-imprisonable offences. C was a hunt protester who was arrested for an offence under s 5 of the Public Order Act 1986 (non-imprisonable). He was bailed on condition he did not attend another hunt meeting before his next court appearance. He was arrested for alleged breach of this condition, and remanded in custody by the magistrates. On application for judicial review, the Divisional Court held that the condition had been validly imposed. The justices had been of the view that it was necessary to prevent the commission of further offences, and they were entitled to impose it by s 3(6) of the Bail Act 1976.

> When a convicted defendant is remanded on bail for the preparation of reports on his physical or mental condition prior to sentencing the Crown Court may and a magistrates' court must require him to make himself available for the necessary medical examinations (see Bail Act 1976, s 3(6), and s 30(2) of the Magistrates' Courts Act 1980). When a juvenile has conditions attached to his bail, his parents (provided they consent) may be required to secure his compliance with the conditions, on pain of forfeiting a recognisance of not more than £50 (Bail Act 1976, s 3(7)). Otherwise sureties have no responsibility for ensuring that the defendant complies with any conditions of bail, other than the basic one of surrendering to custody at the appropriate time.

6.5 PROCEDURE AT AN APPLICATION FOR BAIL IN A MAGISTRATES' COURT

Most bail applications are made in the magistrates' courts. Essentially the procedure is that the court asks defence counsel or solicitor whether there is an application for bail and the Crown Prosecutor (or agent representing the CPS) whether there are any objections. Strictly speaking, the granting or withholding of bail is always a matter for the court, not for tacit agreement between the parties, but obviously if a bail application is unopposed the court is unlikely to raise objections, whereas if no application is made it will need little convincing that there are sufficient reasons for remanding in custody. Assuming, however, that there is an opposed bail application, the CPS representative outlines his objections. It is rare for the police officer in the case actually to attend court, but he should have completed a form contained in the CPS file stating why (in his view) bail is undesirable. Reasons commonly given are that the gravity of the offence charged and/or the accused's previous record make it likely that he will receive a custodial sentence if convicted; that he is currently appearing in other courts for other matters and that the present offences were committed while on bail; that he has past convictions for failing to appear after being granted bail; and that he knows the chief prosecution witnesses and, if at liberty, would be in a position to influence them. A list of previous convictions may be handed into the court and commented on in general terms but it is not normally read out in full (see *Dyson* (1943) 29 Cr App R 104). Following the prosecution objections to bail, the defence representative makes a speech countering those objections as best he can. He may, for example, stress that the accused has a permanent address and strong community ties and so is unlikely to abscond, even though the charges are serious. If there are sureties available, it is sometimes helpful to call them so that the bench can appreciate the quality of the persons who are prepared to put money at risk on behalf of the accused. The more impressive the surety, the more likely it is that bail will be granted. On the other side of the argument, while it is unusual for a police officer to be called by the prosecution at the outset, the court may occasionally ask that a responsible investigating officer attend to elucidate the nature and strength of the case against the accused and — if one of the objections to bail is that enquiries are still being undertaken which may result in more serious charges against the accused or others — to explain the nature of those enquiries in general terms. Having heard the arguments for and against bail, and having considered the evidence of any witnesses called, the magistrates announce their decision.

Bail hearings have been much criticised for what is perceived as their cursory nature. One study of two busy London magistrates' courts put the average length of bail proceedings at six minutes, leading to a recommendation from Lord Justice Auld that 'magistrates and judges in all courts should take more time to consider matters of bail' (Auld Report, pp. 428–430).

In addition, the form taken by hearings related to bail has been questioned in the light of the Human Rights Act 1998, and the safeguards contained in Art 6 of the European Convention on Human Rights. The question may be posed in this way: to what extent should the safeguards in Art 6 apply in reviews of pre-trial detention guaranteed by Art 5 (see Paragraph 26.2.5 for the terms of the Articles). The question was examined in *DPP v Havering* [2001] 1 WLR 805. In that case, the need for formal evidence and procedures was rejected, in favour of a focus upon the quality of the material, with the accused given a right to cross-examine if oral evidence is presented.

Whenever magistrates (or any court) refuse bail to an accused with a prima facie right to bail, they must state the reasons for their so doing (see Paragraph 6.5.3 for details). In addition, para 9A was inserted into Pt I of Sch 1 to the Bail Act by the Criminal Justice Act 1988, requiring a court which grants bail to an accused charged with certain offences to give reasons and cause those reasons to be entered into the record of the court proceeding. The offences to which para 9A applies are murder, manslaughter, rape and attempts to commit the same. The duty to state reasons where one of these grave offences is alleged is distinct from the restrictions on the grant of bail for a person who is charged with such an offence and has a previous conviction for a similar crime (see Paragraph 6.3).

6.5.1 Successive bail applications

The rule that a remand in custody prior to committal proceedings or summary trial could not exceed eight clear days led in the past to defendants using each weekly appearance before the magistrates to renew a bail application. The same arguments for bail that had been presented at perhaps numerous previous hearings would be re-presented, the magistrates would listen with as much patience as they could muster, and the result would almost inevitably be a further remand in custody. Eventually the courts devised a way of preventing these time-consuming charades. In *Nottingham Justices ex p Davies* [1981] QB 38 the Divisional Court held that a decision by one bench of magistrates that bail should be refused was a finding to which *res judicata* or something akin to it applied, and the defence could not therefore re-open the question of bail unless they had some fresh argument to put forward which had not been before the magistrates who originally remanded in custody. Most courts interpreted this decision fairly liberally so as to allow the accused two bail applications, one on his first appearance after being arrested without warrant and charged, and a second when, perhaps a week later, the defence solicitors had had more time to consider the case, find potential sureties and generally marshal the arguments for bail. A minority of courts took a stricter view, restricting the defence to one argued application, even if that application had been hurriedly presented by the duty solicitor after an overnight charge. The Criminal Justice Act 1988 confirmed and clarified the decision in *Ex parte Davies* by inserting a new part (Pt IIA) into Sch 1 to the Bail Act.

First, Pt IIA states that it is the court's duty, having refused bail, to consider at each subsequent hearing while the accused remains in custody whether the decision ought to be reversed (para 1). But there is an element of unreality about this statement of principle because paras 2 and 3 then provide that, although the accused at the first hearing after that at which the court decided not to grant him bail may as of right 'support an application for bail with any argument as to fact or law whether or not he has advanced that argument previously', at subsequent hearings 'the court need not . . . hear arguments which it has heard previously'. Of course, although it is not expressly stated in Pt IIA of Sch 1, the accused may on his first appearance support a bail application with any relevant argument. Thus, the new statutory provisions effectively confirm the more liberal interpretation of *Ex p Davies*. The defence (perhaps through the duty solicitor) may argue for bail on the occasion when the accused is first brought before the magistrates in custody by the police, secure in the knowledge that — should their arguments fail — a second argued application may be presented a week later. However, should that second application also fail, any further argued application will be at the court's discretion unless the defence can point to some fresh argument (whether of fact or law) that has not previously been aired. (*Ex p Davies* similarly gave an accused the right to an extra argued application if some fresh 'circumstance or consideration' had arisen since the earlier refusal/s.) In *Blyth Juvenile Court ex p G* [1991] Crim LR 693, the Divisional Court gave consideration to the question of what constitutes a fresh argument such as to trigger off the right to make a further bail application. The situation was that G, aged 11, was charged with the murder of the 18-month-old child whom she was baby-sitting. She was remanded into the care of the local authority for the protection of her own welfare, and it was ordered that she be held in secure accommodation. Various unsuccessful bail applications were made on her behalf, but an appeal against the secure accommodation order was successful. The justices were asked to hear a further bail application on her behalf, and refused on the ground that there were no changed circumstances. The fresh arguments put forward on G's behalf were that the passage of time had meant that feelings against her no longer ran so high; that there had been a change from secure to non-secure accommodation; that the move to some 46 miles from her home meant it was difficult for her mother to visit her; and that G had been assaulted by three other inmates. The Divisional Court allowed the application, and directed the justices to hear a further application for bail. The necessary change in circumstances need not be major, and it was sufficient in this case.

Once the defence have used up their argued applications, further remand hearings become meaningless exercises. Although in theory the magistrates consider whether a remand in custody is necessary, in fact the decision is a foregone conclusion, and the 'hearing' consists in the chairman saying that the case of Z is adjourned to such and such a date, he being remanded in custody. In recognition of the pointlessness of the accused being present to hear the above take place, Parliament amended the Magistrates' Courts Act 1980 first to allow three successive remands in custody to take place in the accused's absence provided he consents and then to allow remands in custody for up to 28 days whether or not he consents so long as he has already been remanded in custody once (see Paragraph 6.1.1).

What is the position if the accused consents to being remanded in his absence? In *Dover & East Kent Justices ex p Dean* [1992] Crim LR 33, D made no bail application on his first appearance, and consented to be remanded in his absence for three weeks. He appeared before the justices at the end of the three-week period, and wished to make a bail application. The justices decided that the hearing at which he had the right to do so was the first date on which he was remanded in his absence. Not surprisingly, the Divisional Court held that D had a right to make a bail application when he came before the justices at the end of the period of remand by consent.

6.5.2 Taking sureties

If the magistrates grant bail subject to the provision of sureties, and the necessary sureties are present at court, they may enter into their undertakings before the magistrates. Section 8(2) of the Bail Act 1976 provides that, in considering the suitability of a proposed surety, regard may be had to his financial resources, character and previous convictions, and connection with the defendant (e.g. is he a relative, friend, neighbour etc?). Before he formally agrees to be a surety, it is normal practice to explain to him the nature of his obligations and the possible consequences to him of the defendant absconding. He is also asked whether he is worth the sum involved after all his debts are paid. If the sureties are not at court when bail is granted, they may enter into their recognisances subsequently before a magistrate, magistrates' clerk, police officer not below the rank of inspector, or (if the defendant has already been taken to a prison or remand centre) the governor of that establishment. Until they have done so, the defendant must remain in custody. If a surety attempts to enter into a recognisance before one of the persons mentioned above, but he declines to take the recognisance because he considers the surety unsuitable, the surety may apply to the court to take the recognisance.

To avoid the inconvenience to the sureties of their having to enter into recognisances every time the defendant's case is adjourned, the magistrates may make the sureties continuous. This means that on the occasion when bail is first granted the surety undertakes to pay the specified sum if the defendant fails to appear on any of the occasions to which his case is adjourned. If the offence charged is indictable the recognisance may be further extended to secure the defendant's appearance before the Crown Court should he be committed for trial: MCA, s 128(4).

Similar provisions to those described above apply when the Crown Court, Divisional Court or Court of Appeal grants bail subject to sureties. Continuous bail is particularly useful where, following the defendant's surrender to custody on the first day of his trial on indictment, he is granted bail for the overnight adjournments. If bail is made continuous the sureties only need to be present to enter into their recognisances on the occasion of the first adjournment: Criminal Justice Administration Act 1914, s 19.

6.5.3 Recording and giving reasons for decisions on bail

Section 5 of the Bail Act 1976 sets out some administrative procedures which must be followed when decisions on bail are taken. They are that:

(a) Whenever bail is granted (whether by a court or by the police) and whenever a court withholds bail from a defendant with a right to bail under s 4, a *record* must be made of the decision. A copy of the record should be given to the defendant on request.

(b)   When a magistrates' court or the Crown Court withholds bail from a defendant with a right to bail (or grants bail but subject to conditions), it must give *reasons* for its decision. The reasons should be such as to help the defendant decide whether it is worth making an application for bail to another court (see Paragraph 6.6). A note must be made of the reasons and a copy given to the defendant (unless the decision was taken by the Crown Court and the defendant is represented by counsel or solicitor who does not request a copy). As a result of the Criminal Justice Act 1988 it is now also necessary for the court to give its reasons for granting bail to defendants charged with certain offences (see Paragraph 6.5).

(c)   If a magistrates' court withholds bail from an unrepresented defendant, they must tell him of his right to make a bail application to the High Court and/or the Crown Court.

(d)   If a magistrates' court remands a defendant in custody after a fully argued bail application, they must *issue a* certificate confirming that they did hear argument. Where it was not the first or second argued bail application, the certificate must state the change in circumstances which persuaded the court to listen to renewed argument. A copy of the certificate must be given to the defendant. Its significance will emerge in Paragraph 6.6. However, no certificate is required if the defendant was committed for trial or sentence in custody or had an application for bail pending determination of an appeal from the magistrates turned down.

6.5.4   Variations in the conditions of bail etc.

Where a court has granted bail either the prosecution or the defence may apply to it for a variation in the conditions of bail, or, if bail was granted unconditionally, the prosecution may apply for conditions to be imposed: Bail Act 1976, s 3(8). If the defendant has been committed on bail to the Crown Court for trial or sentence, an application for variation may be made to either the Crown Court or the magistrates' court. Should the court decide to vary or impose conditions a record must be made of its decision. If the defendant has a right to bail, reasons for the decision are required, and the defendant is entitled to a copy of the note of the reasons: s 5.

A magistrates' court which has remanded a defendant on bail to appear before it on a certain date may, if it is convenient, appoint a later date for the defendant to appear and amend the recognisances of any sureties accordingly: MCA, s 129(3). This power to 'enlarge bail' is useful if, for example, the court will not have time to deal with the defendant's case on the day originally fixed. Where a defendant who has been remanded in custody or on bail cannot be brought or appear before the magistrates on the day appointed because of illness or accident, the magistrates may further remand him in his absence, and a remand in custody may exceed eight clear days: MCA, s 129(1).

6.5.5   Reviewing bail on new information

What if the court grants bail, and information later comes to light which throws light on the correctness of that decision? Under s 5B of the Bail Act 1976 (inserted by the Criminal Justice and Public Order Act 1994), the court may then reconsider the whole question of bail on the application of the prosecution. This power is only available if the offence is indictable-only or triable-either-way. The application must be based on information not available to the court (or to the police officer) who made the grant of bail which is now under review. If invoked, it enables the court to vary bail conditions, impose conditions for the first time, or remand in custody. The application can be heard in the defendant's absence, provided he has been notified of the prosecution's application for review. At the time of writing, it is not known how the courts will apply these new and potentially far-reaching provisions. In what circumstances will the prosecution be able to claim that there is new information on which to base a review? What if the prosecution on the earlier occasion omitted (for whatever reason) to supply the court with the missing information? Some clue as to the intention of Parliament is provided by Mr Maclean, the Home Office minister, who said, when explaining the provision in the standing committee, '. . . there may be other occasions in which, through negligence, the prosecution has made a mistake and it might not be appropriate to withdraw someone's bail because of another mistake in the system' (*Hansard*, HC, Standing Committee B, 27 January 1994, col. 336). It is submitted, in accordance with this perspective, that information is 'available to the court' even if it was not introduced by the prosecution on the earlier occasion. It will undoubtedly lead to a justified sense of grievance if the prosecution (with all the resources at their command) are able to obtain a second bite at the custody cherry by neglecting to place information before the magistrates.

6.6 APPLICATIONS TO THE CROWN COURT AND HIGH COURT CONCERNING BAIL

Whenever a magistrates' court withholds bail or grants bail subject to conditions the defendant may make an application to the High Court, which has jurisdiction to grant bail or vary the conditions of bail as the case may be: Criminal Justice Act 1967, s 22. The Crown Court may grant bail to a defendant refused it by the magistrates if either:

(a)   they remanded the defendant in custody (whether prior to committal proceedings or summary trial or after summary conviction and before sentence), and heard a fully argued bail application before deciding on the remand in custody; or

(b)   they committed the defendant in custody to the Crown Court for trial or sentence; or

(c)   they convicted him summarily, imposed a custodial sentence and refused to bail him pending determination of his appeal to the Crown Court: Supreme Court Act 1981, s 81, as amended by the Criminal Justice Act 1982.

Thus, in most cases a defendant whose bail application to the magistrates fails will have the option of making a further application either to the Crown Court or the High Court — indeed there is nothing to stop him applying to both. So that there will be no disputes as to whether there has been an argued bail application, the magistrates must issue a certificate stating, if it be the case, that they refused bail after hearing argument (see Paragraph 6.5.3). From a defendant's viewpoint, applications to the Crown Court for bail have considerable advantages over applications to the High Court. Note, however, that the Crown Court's power to intervene in the decision of the magistrates is limited to cases where bail has been refused. A High Court judge, by contrast, can vary the terms of bail which magistrates have made conditional.

6.6.1   Applications to the High Court for bail

An application to the High Court for bail is made to a judge in chambers. The procedure is set out in Ord 79, r 9 of the Rules of the Supreme Court 1965. It is to be followed both when an application is made under s 22 of the 1967 Act after magistrates have refused bail, and when the High Court has jurisdiction under s 37 of the Criminal Justice Act 1948 to grant bail to a person who has applied to the Crown Court to state a case or who is applying for *certiorari* to quash a Crown Court or a magistrates' court decision (see Paragraph 6.2).

The application is made by summons. The summons must be served on the prosecutor at least 24 hours before the hearing date, and must be supported by an affidavit setting out the grounds of the application. The summons calls upon the respondents to the application (i.e. the prosecution) to show cause why the defendant should not be granted bail or, if the defendant has been granted bail, to show cause why the conditions of bail should not be varied. If the application fails the defendant is not allowed to make a fresh application to another High Court judge or to the Divisional Court (Ord 79, r 9(12)), nor is there any provision made for an appeal to the House of Lords. If bail is granted subject to sureties being provided, the sureties may enter into their recognisances before any of the persons who may take a surety following a grant of bail by a magistrates' court (see Paragraph 6.5.2).

A defendant who is not legally represented will have great difficulty in swearing an affidavit and arranging for a summons to be served on the prosecutor. Since representation under the Criminal Defence Service is not available for applications to a judge in chambers for bail, a method has had to be devised to enable impecunious defendants to have their applications heard. The procedure they must adopt is laid down by paragraphs 4 and 5 of Ord 79, r 9. Paragraph 4 states that a defendant who is in custody and desires to apply for bail, but is unable through lack of means to instruct a solicitor, may give written notice to the judge in chambers that he wishes the Official Solicitor to act for him for purposes of a bail application. If the judge, in his discretion, accedes to the defendant's request, the Official Solicitor makes the arrangements necessary for the proper presentation of the application. Having assigned the Official Solicitor to act for the defendant, the judge may, if he thinks fit, dispense with the requirements of serving a summons on the prosecutor and filing an affidavit in support. This will enable what seems to be on the face of it, a meritorious application to be brought before the judge with a minimum of delay. Although the Official Solicitor prepares the papers, he does not attend the hearing. This particular procedure is, perhaps in consequence, not much used by defendants.

6.6.2 Applications to the Crown Court for bail

A defendant refused bail by the magistrates is usually able to make a further application to the Crown Court (see above). The advantage of applying to the Crown Court, rather than going to a High Court judge in chambers, is that if, as will usually be the case, the defendant has been granted legal representation for the proceedings as a whole (or even if he was just granted it for the purpose of making a bail application to the magistrates) it will cover a Crown Court bail application. The application, which may be heard in chambers, is normally listed for hearing by a circuit judge or recorder. If an unsuccessful application for bail has already been made to a High Court judge in chambers, the Crown Court should be informed of that fact (Crown Court Rules 1982 (SI 1982 No 1109), r 20), but it still has jurisdiction to hear the application: *Reading Crown Court ex p Malik* [1981] QB 451. Conversely, a judge in chambers may grant bail notwithstanding a prior application to the Crown Court. In other words, the jurisdictions of the High Court and Crown Court in relation to bail are distinct and independent of each other.

The procedure for applying to the Crown Court for bail is to serve written notice on the prosecutor of intention to make the application. The notice must be served at least 24 hours before the application. The prosecutor must then do one of three things. He may either notify the appropriate officer of the Crown Court and the defendant that he wishes to be represented at the hearing of the application, or he may give notice that he does not oppose the application, or he may give to the appropriate officer, for the consideration of the Crown Court, a written statement of his reasons for opposing the application. A copy of the written statement must be sent to the defendant. Although he may be given leave to attend the hearing of the application, the defendant has no right to be present. If bail is granted subject to the provision of sureties, they may enter into their recognisances before an appropriate officer of the Crown Court or before any of the persons who may take a surety following a grant of bail by magistrates (see Paragraph 6.5.2).

The above procedure is not applicable where a bail application is made during the course of the Crown Court proceedings (e.g. for bail during the period of an overnight adjournment). Such applications are made without notice to the judge trying the case. As a matter of practice, counsel waits for the jury to leave court before making the application.

6.6.3   Prosecution appeals against bail

The Bail (Amendment) Act 1993 confers upon the prosecution the right to appeal to the Crown Court against a decision by magistrates to grant bail. The right is limited to cases where:

(a)   the defendant is charged with or convicted of an offence which is (or would be in the case of an adult) punishable by a term of imprisonment of five years or more or an offence of taking a conveyance without authority or aggravated vehicle-taking; and

(b)   the prosecution is conducted by the CPS, or by a person falling within a class prescribed by statutory instrument; and

(c)   the prosecution made representations against bail before it was granted.

The 1993 Act lays down procedural requirements with which the prosecution must comply in order to exercise their right. They must give oral notice of appeal at the conclusion of the proceedings in which bail was granted, and before the defendant is released from custody. This notice must be confirmed in writing within two hours after proceedings end; otherwise the appeal is deemed to be disposed of. Pending appeal, the magistrates must remand the defendant in custody. The Crown Court, for its part, must hear the appeal within 48 hours (excluding weekends and public holidays). The appeal takes place by way of rehearing in the usual way and the judge may then remand the defendant in custody or grant bail with or without conditions.

This right to appeal against the grant of bail is distinct from the review of bail at the instance of the prosecution (see Paragraph 6.5.5). It is triggered off immediately after the magistrates have decided to grant bail (whereas the power to review may take place some considerable time thereafter). The conditions for the exercise of the right to appeal are also somewhat different. Crucially, moreover, where the procedure under the Bail (Amendment) Act 1993 is used, the accused is kept in custody until the appeal is heard (whereas with the review procedure the accused will typically be at large).

In view of the somewhat Draconian nature of its powers under the Bail (Amendment) Act 1993, the CPS has issued guidance to Crown Prosecutors on its use. The CPS states that the number of appeals should be small. Wherever possible, approval should be sought in advance from a Crown Prosecutor of at least four years' experience. The factors relevant in eciding whether to appeal include risk to victims (particularly where weapons are involved), the lack of established identity or any community ties (especially in cases where terrorism or drug trafficking is alleged), and a strong indication that the defendant may abscond. In the first three months of the Act's operation, there were 50 such appeals by the CPS over the whole of England and Wales, of which 34 succeeded.

6.7   CONSEQUENCES OF A DEFENDANT ABSCONDING

If a defendant who has been granted bail fails to surrender to custody at the appointed time and place, three questions arise for the court's consideration. There is the immediate question of how to secure the defendant's attendance before the court, and there are the further questions of how to deal with him for his breach of bail and how to deal with any sureties for breach of their recognisances.

Prior to discussing these questions, it is necessary to consider just what is meant by 'failing to surrender to custody'. According to *DPP v Richards* [1988] QB 701, it means complying with whatever procedure the court prescribes for those answering to their bail. If the court operates a procedure whereby persons bailed are required to report to an usher, and are then allowed to wait in the court precincts until their case is called, a person who so reports has surrendered to custody. If he then goes away before the court calls his case, he has not absconded within the meaning of s 6 of the Bail Act 1976. (Note, however, that in these circumstances the court is entitled to issue a warrant under s 7(2) of the Act — see Paragraph 6.7.1.)

6.7.1   Powers in respect of an absconder

Section 7(1) of the Bail Act 1976 provides that if a defendant has been bailed to appear before a court and fails to do so, the court before which he should have appeared may issue a warrant for his arrest. This is known as a bench warrant. Although it could be endorsed for bail, it is unlikely that the court would want to take the risk of the defendant again absconding.

In the circumstances which arose in *DPP v Richards* [1988] QB 701, s 7(2) can be invoked. This provides that, where a person on bail absents himself at any time after he has surrendered to custody but before the court is ready to hear the case, then the court may issue a warrant for his arrest. Where a person was arrested without warrant and bailed by the police to appear back at the police station, s 7 does not apply, but should the person fail to answer to his bail, the police will have power to arrest him without warrant.

In order to prevent possible breaches of bail, a police officer may arrest without warrant a defendant whom he reasonably believes is unlikely to surrender to custody: s 7(3). The power only applies if the defendant was bailed to surrender to the custody of a court. A police officer also has power to arrest a defendant whom he reasonably suspects of having broken, or reasonably believes will break, a condition of his bail. Thus, if it was a condition of bail that the defendant report to a police station, and he fails to report, he may forthwith be arrested without warrant. Similarly, if a surety notifies the police in writing that the defendant is unlikely to surrender to custody and that he (the surety) therefore wishes to be relieved of his obligations, the defendant may be arrested. A defendant who is arrested for suspected or anticipated breach of bail must be brought before a magistrate as soon as practicable and, in any event, within 24 hours of arrest (unless he was to have surrendered to custody within 24 hours in which case he is brought before the appropriate court). If the magistrate is of the opinion that the defendant has broken or is likely to break any condition of his bail, or is not likely to surrender to custody, he may remand him in or commit him to custody, or impose more stringent conditions of bail. Otherwise, he must release him on bail on the same conditions, if any, as were originally imposed.

In addition, s 46A of PACE (as inserted by the Criminal Justice and Public Order Act 1994, s 29) gives the police power to arrest anyone who has been bailed to return to the police station and fails to do so (s 7 of the Bail Act does not apply in these circumstances).

6.7.2   The offence of absconding

Until 1976 the normal practice was to require an accused to enter into a recognisance to secure his own attendance at court on the date to which he had been bailed. If he failed to appear, he — like any sureties he had been required to provide — could and probably would be ordered to forfeit his recognisance. However, s 3(2) of the Bail Act provided that an accused might no longer be bailed 'on his own recognisance', although he could, of course, still be required to provide sureties. At the same time, in order to ensure that 'jumping bail' would involve adverse consequences for the accused himself as well as for any sureties, the Act created a new offence of *absconding*. Section 6(1) provides that:

if a person who has been released on bail in criminal proceedings fails without reasonable cause to surrender to custody he shall be guilty of an offence.

Similarly, an offence is committed if, having had reasonable cause for not surrendering at the time he should have done, the accused then fails to surrender as soon thereafter as is reasonably practicable (s 6(2)). An offence may be committed under s 6 even though the accused is acquitted of the offences that formed the subject matter of the proceedings in respect of which bail was granted. Moreover, it is always for him to prove, on a balance of probabilities, that he had reasonable cause for not surrendering when he ought.

Section 6 prescribes three methods by which an accused may be prosecuted and sentenced for an offence of absconding. First, he may be tried summarily for the offence and sentenced by the magistrates to up to three months' imprisonment and/or a £5,000 fine. Although the Act appears to contemplate summary trial as a possibility even when the offence consisted in failure to surrender to the custody of the Crown Court, judicial interpretation of s 6 has subsequently decreed that magistrates should deal only with failure to attend at their own court (see the paragraphs in small print below).

Secondly, following summary conviction for a s 6 offence, the magistrates may commit the offender to the Crown Court to be sentenced if *either:*

(i)   they consider their own powers of punishment to be inadequate; *or*

(ii)   they are committing the offender for trial in respect of an indictable offence and they consider it preferable that the Crown Court should sentence him both for the absconding and (should he be convicted) the other offence.

The Crown Court's powers of sentence upon such a committal are 12 months' imprisonment and/or an unlimited fine.

Thirdly, failure to answer bail at the Crown Court can and should be dealt with by that court as if it were a criminal contempt. This means that the Crown Court judge 'tries' the accused without empanelling a jury. The enquiry is semi-informal with the judge adopting whatever rules of procedure or evidence appear to him appropriate for giving the accused a fair hearing. If convicted, the accused is liable to the same penalties as if he had been committed for sentence for the offence following summary conviction (see above).

Whether an alleged offence of absconding is tried summarily or dealt with as if it were a criminal contempt, the only issue likely to be in dispute is whether the accused had reasonable cause for failure to surrender. The actual non-appearance can be established from the court records which are virtually incontrovertible.

The nature of the offence of absconding and the correct procedure for dealing with it were analysed in some depth by Watkins LJ in *Schiavo v Anderton* [1987] QB 20. Some minor clarifications of the judgment are contained in *Practice Direction (Bail: Failure to Surrender)* [1987] 1 WLR 79. The effect of the judgment and Direction are summarised in the following propositions, which apply to bail granted by a court, rather than police bail.

(i)   The offence of absconding is *sui generis* in the sense that it is neither summary nor triable either way, and the normal rules about commencing prosecutions by the laying of an information do not apply. It follows that it may be tried summarily however long after the event the proceedings begin. Section 127 of the Magistrates' Courts Act, which normally requires an information for a summary offence to be laid within six months, is irrelevant.

(ii) The offence should *invariably* be tried in the court at which the substantive proceedings in respect of which bail was granted have been or are to be heard. Thus, if an accused was remanded on bail prior to committal proceedings or summary trial, any alleged failure to answer to bail should be heard by the magistrates as the substantive proceedings (i.e. the committal or trial) are in their court. If, on the other hand, there was a committal for trial on bail, the Crown Court is obliged to deal with non-appearance as a criminal contempt. Contrary to earlier suggestions by Roskill LJ in *Harbax Singh* [1979] QB 319, it would never be right for the Crown Court to remit such a case to the magistrates for summary trial. The rule that magistrates should try summarily allegations of failing to appear before their court is, of course, without prejudice to their power to convict and then commit for sentence in the circumstances already described.

(iii) Since absconding is 'tantamount to the defiance of a court order', it is normally more appropriate for the court to initiate proceedings on its own motion without waiting for any formal information or charge to be preferred. However, the court should not act except upon the invitation of the prosecutor, who should consider whether proceedings are necessary or desirable in the light of factors such as the seriousness of the failure to appear and any explanations advanced by the accused. In magistrates' courts, the prosecution normally indicate that they wish the court to proceed by causing an allegation of failing to appear to be added to the court register, the charge being put to the accused for the first time in court by the clerk.

(iv) According to the *Practice Direction*, alleged abscondings should be tried immediately after the disposal of the substantive proceedings in respect of which the accused was bailed. However, that indication should perhaps be understood as relating primarily to cases where the accused denies the offence. If he admits it, it is often more convenient to sentence him forthwith, adjourning the substantive proceedings to another day. The court will also have to consider whether bail can again be granted. Although an admitted s 6 offence is a powerful reason for withdrawing bail, the accused often has an excuse for not appearing which, although not sufficient to provide him with a defence to the charge, does at least indicate that he was not deliberately running away (e.g. he might say that he forgot the date on which he should have come to court and surrendered voluntarily at a later stage). In such cases, the court can often be persuaded to continue bail, perhaps with more stringent conditions attached.

(v) If the accused denies absconding, the prosecution should conduct the proceedings and call the evidence in the normal way, notwithstanding that the proceedings are, in a sense, initiated by the court (see (iii) above). But, since proof of the actual failure to surrender to custody will come from the court's own records, the role of the prosecution representatives is likely to be confined to cross-examining the accused about any reason for non-appearance which he puts forward.

As far as police bail is concerned, the failure to surrender cannot be said to be in defiance of a court order. There is therefore no compelling reason for the court to act of its own motion, and any failure to surrender should be dealt with by charging the accused or laying an information. Hence, failure to commence proceedings in six months will render them void (*Murphy v DPP* [1990] 1 WLR 601).

6.7.3   Estreating a surety's recognisance

Where bail was granted subject to a surety being provided, and the defendant absconds, the court before which he was due to appear must:

(a)   order that the recognisance of the surety be estreated (i.e., that he has to pay the sum in which he stood surety); and

(b)   issue a summons to the surety requiring him to appear before the court to show cause why he should not be ordered to pay the sum promised

(MCA, s 120, as amended by the Crime and Disorder Act, s 55). The court should then consider the means of the surety, and the extent to which he was to blame for the defendant absconding — e.g., did he, on first having reason to suspect that the defendant would abscond, give written notice to the police and ask to be relieved of his obligations as a surety? Failure to consider these matters may lead to the quashing of a decision by magistrates to forfeit a recognisance: *Southampton Justices ex p Green* [1976] QB 11. However, the presumption is that the defendant's absconding will lead to the surety having to pay the whole sum in which he stood surety. As it was put in *Horseferry Road Magistrates' Court ex p Pearson* [1976] 2 All ER 264:

> The surety has seriously entered into a serious obligation and ought to pay the amount which he or she has promised unless there are circumstances in the case, relating either to means or culpability, which make it fair and just to pay a smaller sum.

The above principles have been confirmed in numerous more recent cases, including *Uxbridge Justices ex p Heward-Mills* [1983] 1 WLR 56 and *Warwick Crown Court ex p Smalley* [1987] 1 WLR 237. *York Crown Court ex p Coleman and How* [1987] Crim LR 761 provides an example of the kind of exceptional case in which it is unfair to forfeit the whole recognisance. C and H stood surety for C's son who had been committed for trial at York Crown Court. They telephoned him at regular intervals to remind him of the trial; they arranged for other relatives to accompany him to court on the actual day; and they received a message that he had arrived. Unfortunately, the case could not commence until the afternoon and, during the wait, the accused's nerve broke and he absconded. The Divisional Court held that C and H had done everything they practically could to secure proper surrender to custody and so should not have lost the entire amount of their recognisances. However, May LJ stressed what had earlier been said by McCullough J in *Ex p Heward-Mills* (supra), namely that 'the burden of satisfying the court that the full sum should not be forfeited rests on the surety *and is a heavy one*'.

The point was underlined in *Maidstone Crown Court ex p Lever* (1994) *The Times*, 7 November 1994, where the remarks of Lord Widgery CJ in *Southampton Justices ex p Corker* (1976) 120 SJ 214 were quoted with approval:

> The real pull of bail . . . is that it may cause the offender to attend his trial rather than subject his nearest and dearest who had gone surety for him to pain and discomfort.

The surety's obligation is extinguished once the defendant surrenders to the court. After such surrender, the surety is no longer at any risk of being estreated (unless, of course, the surety is renewed). In *Central Criminal Court ex p Guney* [1996] AC 616, the House of Lords held that, where a defendant was formally arraigned, the arraignment amounted to a surrender to the custody of the court, so as to extinguish the liability of the surety. Neither the agreement of the parties nor the order of the judge could deprive arraignment of its legal effect.

6.8 DETENTION OF A DEFENDANT WHEN BAIL IS REFUSED

The arrangements for detaining a defendant who is refused bail are as follows:

(a) If he has attained the age of 21, he is committed to prison.
(b) If he is aged 17 to 20 inclusive he is committed to a remand centre, provided that one is available 'for the reception from the court of persons of his class or description':

Criminal Justice Act 1948, s 27. If a remand centre is not available he is committed to prison.

(c) If he is under 17 he is committed to the care of a local authority: Children and Young Persons Act 1969, s 23. However, where the juvenile is a male aged 15 or over, then he may be remanded to a remand centre or prison on the ground of need to protect the public, if he:

(i) is charged with offences which for an adult would be punishable with 14 years' imprisonment;

(ii) is charged with a violent or sexual offence; or

(iii) has a history of absconding or of offending while on bail.

(d) By the Crime and Disorder Act 1998, ss 97 and 98, courts have additional powers to remand children between 12 and 14, and girls of 15 or 16, to local authority secure accommodation. For qualifying juveniles, there is a clear order of priority when the decision is made as to the remand institution. It should be to a local authority secure accommodation, and failing that, to a remand centre, with remand to a prison as the last resort.

When a magistrates' court has power to remand a defendant in custody it may instead commit him to police detention for a period not exceeding three days (24 hours in the case of a juvenile: Children and Young Persons Act 1969, s 23(14)), provided that is necessary for the purpose of inquiries into offences other than the one charged: MCA 1980, s 128(7). As soon as the inquiries have been completed the defendant must be brought back before the magistrates, who will either bail him or, more probably, remand him in custody to prison or remand centre. Whilst in police detention, he is entitled to the same safeguards as is an ordinary arrestee (e.g., there must be periodic reviews of the propriety of continuing to detain him). Presumably, if the offences to which the inquiries relate are not serious arrestable ones, he should be charged or brought back before the magistrates within 24 hours, since an ordinary arrestee suspected of a non-serious offence would have to be released or charged within that period (see Paragraph 2.3). However, s 128 is not clear on the point.

7   Mode of Trial

7.1   CLASSIFICATION OF OFFENCES

An offence is either summary or indictable (see Paragraph 1.3). An indictable offence is one for which an adult either must or may be tried on indictment; a summary offence is one which must be tried summarily: Interpretation Act 1978, Sch 1.[1] As the definition of indictable offence implies, some are only triable on indictment and some may be tried either on indictment or summarily. The latter are known as offences triable either way.

7.1.1   Summary offences

Summary offences are all statutory. The statute creating a summary offence shows that it is summary by specifying a maximum penalty which may be imposed on summary conviction without specifying a second greater penalty for offenders convicted on indictment. For example, s 89(1) of the Police Act 1996, as amended, provides that:

> any person who assaults a constable in the execution of his duty . . . shall be guilty of an offence and liable on *summary* conviction to imprisonment for a term not exceeding six months or to a fine not exceeding the amount at level 5 on the standard scale, or to both.

Since s 89(1) does not mention a penalty imposable following conviction on indictment, the offence of assaulting a constable in the execution of his duty is summary.

A vast number of minor and occasionally not so minor offences are summary. They include dropping litter, not paying the TV licence fee, offences under the Food and Drugs Act 1955 (e.g., selling food that is unfit for human consumption), offences under the Factories Act 1961 (e.g., not maintaining machinery in a safe condition), travelling on the railway without a ticket and almost all road traffic offences (e.g., careless driving, speeding, going through red lights, defective brakes, tyres, etc., failing to report an accident, no insurance and many more). Among the most serious summary offences are using threatening words or behaviour contrary to s 4 of the Public Order Act 1986, drink/driving offences contrary to ss 4 to 7 of the Road Traffic Act 1988, interference with a motor vehicle contrary to s 9 of the Criminal Attempts Act 1981, and assaulting a constable in the execution of his

---

[1] Unless it is one of the summary offences specified in s 40 of the Criminal Justice Act 1988, in which case it may be tried on indictment if it is linked with an indictable offence (see Paragraph 7.5).

duty. In addition, ss 37 and 39 of the Criminal Justice Act 1988 made summary three offences which were formerly triable either way, namely taking a motor vehicle without the owner's consent, driving while disqualified and common assault. All the offences mentioned in the last two sentences carry six months' imprisonment, except motor vehicle interference which carries only three.

7.1.2　Indictable offences

All common law offences (e.g., murder, manslaughter and conspiracy to defraud or corrupt public morals) are indictable. Statutory offences are indictable if the statute creating the offence specifies a penalty to be imposed following conviction on indictment. For example, the Theft Act 1968 shows that robbery is an indictable offence by providing, in s 8(2), that 'a person guilty of robbery . . . shall on *conviction on indictment* be liable to imprisonment for life'. Where a statute creating an offence provides for two separate penalties, one to be imposed on summary conviction and the other on conviction on indictment, the offence created is indictable but triable either way. An example is dangerous driving which is punishable on summary conviction with six months' imprisonment and a £5,000 fine and punishable on conviction on indictment with two years' imprisonment and an unlimited fine. It should be noted, however, that many offences are triable either way even though the statute creating them does not itself provide for a penalty on summary conviction (see below). Theft, for example, may be tried summarily, but there is no indication to that effect in s 7 of the Theft Act.

7.1.3　Offences triable either way

Offences triable either way fall into two groups. They are either, like dangerous driving, made triable either way by the statute creating them, or they are included in Sch 1 to the Magistrates' Courts Act 1980, s 17 of which provides that 'the offences listed in Schedule 1 . . . shall be triable either way'.

　As one would expect, the most serious offences are triable only on indictment. Offences triable either way tend to be those which, although serious enough to be indictable, are never, even at worst, very grave (e.g. dangerous driving or making off without payment contrary to s 3 of the Theft Act 1978), and those which vary greatly in gravity depending upon the facts of the particular case (e.g. criminal damage or theft). The table below lists some of the most common indictable offences according to whether they are triable only on indictment or triable either way.

Nature of offence	Triable only on indictment	Triable either way
Offences against the person	Murder, manslaughter, child destruction, attempt to procure abortion, causing grievous bodily harm with intent to do so.	Inflicting grievous bodily harm, unlawful wounding, assault occasioning actual bodily harm, assault with intent to resist arrest.
Sexual offences	Rape, intercourse with girl under 13, buggery, incest.	Unlawful sexual intercourse with girl under 16, indecency between men, indecent assault, living on the earnings of prostitution

Nature of offence	Triable only on indictment	Triable either way
Offences under the Theft Acts 1968 and 1978	Robbery, aggravated burglary, blackmail, assault with intent to rob, burglary comprising the commission of or intention to commit an offence triable only on indictment (e.g. entry as a trespasser with intent to rape), burglary in a dwelling if any person therein was subjected to violence or the threat of it.	All offences under the Acts apart from those which are triable only on indictment and taking a motor vehicle or pedal cycle which are summary. They include theft, handling stolen goods, obtaining property by deception, most forms of burglary, going equipped, obtaining services by deception, evading liability by deception, making off without payment.
Criminal damage	Damage or arson charged under s 1(2) of the Criminal Damage Act 1971 (offence committed with intent to endanger life or being reckless as to the endangering of life).	Criminal damage offences where no intent etc. to endanger life is alleged.
Road traffic offences	Causing death by dangerous driving.	Dangerous driving.
Miscellaneous offences	Perjury in judicial proceedings contrary to s 1 of the Perjury Act 1911; attempt to pervert the course of justice; collecting, communicating etc. information intended to be useful to an enemy contrary to s 1 of the Official Secrets Act 1911; possessing firearm with intent to endanger life, using firearm to resist arrest, and carrying firearm to commit indictable offence; riot contrary to s 1 of the Public Order Act 1986; assisting an offender contrary to s 4 of the Criminal Law Act 1967 if the person assisted's offence was triable only on indictment.	Making false statements on oath otherwise than in a judicial proceeding and making certain other false statements or declarations contrary to ss 2–6 of the Perjury Act 1911; communicating, using etc, information entrusted in confidence to a person holding office under the Crown contrary to s 2 of the Official Secrets Act 1911; carrying a loaded firearm in a public place, shortening a shotgun, and having an offensive weapon in a public place; violent disorder, affray and stirring up racial hatred contrary to ss 2, 3 and 18 of the Public Order Act 1986; all offences under the Forgery and Counterfeiting Act 1981 (e.g., forgery, using a forged instrument, counterfeiting, passing a counterfeit note or coin, having equipment for counterfeiting); all offences of possessing, supplying, cultivating etc. controlled drugs contrary to the Misuse of Drugs Act 1971 (apart from a few minor ones which are summary); assisting an offender contrary to s 4 of the Criminal Law Act 1967 if the person assisted's offence was triable either way.

Attempts and incitement to commit offences triable either way are themselves triable either way, but conspiracy is only triable on indictment.

Leaving aside road traffic offences and minor summary offences carrying no real social stigma, the offences which occur most frequently are triable either way. Therefore, how one decides the mode of trial for these offences is a question of major importance.

7.2 ADVANCE INFORMATION

The accused plays an important part in determining the mode of trial process, with the right to elect Crown Court trial for an offence which is triable either way. In order to exercise that election on an informed basis, it is necessary that the accused should be aware of the evidence which the prosecution relies upon. One of the reasons why this awareness is important is that the prosecution is obliged to reveal information about its evidence prior to committal for trial in the the Crown Court. If the accused does not know the strength of the prosecution case, there will be a temptation to elect Crown Court trial, in order to discover it. As a result, rules were introduced in 1985 to allow the defence the right to a measure of advance information about the prosecution case. It is important to distinguish this right to advance information (which is set out in the remainder of this Paragraph) from the rules relating to disclosure of unused information by the prosecution (which are detailed in Chapter 8). We are here dealing with information about evidence which the prosecution *intend* to call. The prosecution's duty of disclosure relates to evidence which they do *not intend* to call.

The Magistrates' Courts (Advance Information) Rules 1985 (SI 1985 No 601) provide that, if the accused is charged with an offence triable either way, the prosecution must upon request provide the defence *either* with copies of the prosecution witnesses' written statements *or* with a summary of the facts and matters about which evidence will be adduced during the course of the prosecution case (r 4). A request for advance information should be made before the proceedings to determine the mode of trial (see Paragraph 7.3) and should be complied with as soon as practicable. Knowledge of the prosecution case is intended to assist the defence in deciding where the case should be dealt with, and to remove the temptation (which formerly existed) to elect trial on indictment as a tactical ploy to get a sight of the prosecution evidence, after which the court was asked to allow the election to be withdrawn. So that the accused will know of his rights, a notice explaining the advance information rules has to be given to him as soon as possible after he has been charged with/summoned for an either-way matter (r 3). In addition, the magistrates must satisfy themselves that the accused is aware that he can request advance information before they go on to consider mode of trial (r 6). The only situation where the prosecution may properly refuse such a request is if they fear that complying with it might lead to the intimidation of witnesses or other attempts to interfere with the course of justice (r 5). Except when r 5 applies, failure to comply with such a request will necessitate the adjournment of the proceedings (unless the court is satisfied that the defence will not be prejudiced by the non-compliance).

Advance information has become a familiar part of magistrates' court's procedure with surprising rapidity. The usual practice upon an accused charged with an either way offence making his first appearance is to adjourn for a fortnight so that 'AI' can be served and considered by the defence. Mode of trial can then be dealt with at the next hearing. There are, however, many variations upon the usual practice. For example, the prosecution sometimes have the information ready to serve at court upon the first appearance; in other cases, the defence forgo their rights either because the accused is determined to be tried on indictment and it is therefore quicker to proceed straight to committal, or, conversely, because the case is very simple (e.g., petty shoplifting) and he wants it disposed of as soon as possible by means of a guilty plea.

What the prosecution give by way of advance information varies considerably from one branch office of the CPS to another. Some serve typed copies of the prosecution witnesses' statements, which are virtually the same as would be served for purposes of a committal under s 6(2) of the Magistrates' Courts Act 1980; others give photocopies of handwritten statements and of the police officers' notebooks; yet others serve a copy of the summary of the case that is sent to the CPS by the police, together with copies of the notes of any interview with the accused at the police station. Where the defence consider the advance information to be inadequate, they can apply to the justices to rectify the situation. The justices have no power under the Magistrates' Courts (Advance Information) Rules 1985 to order that the prosecution provide further information, but they can have recourse to their power to adjourn under the Magistrates' Courts Act 1980, s 10, if they agree that the information has been inadequate (*Dunmow Justices ex p Nash* (1993) *The Times*, 17 May 1993).

The Advance Information Rules apply only to either-way offences. As regards summary offences, the defence still have no legal right to know the prosecution case prior to trial although defence solicitors frequently request it. Of course, some summary offences both carry imprisonment and are quite likely in practice to be dealt with by a custodial sentence (e.g. assaulting a police officer, taking a motor vehicle without the owner's consent and driving while disqualified). Guidelines issued by the Attorney-General in November 2000 therefore now require advance provision to the defence of all proposed prosecution evidence 'in sufficient time' to allow proper consideration of it before it is called (*Attorney-General's Guidelines. Disclosure of Information in Criminal Proceedings*, para 43). This is likely to ensure that the hearing concentrates upon the issues, and that the court's time is not wasted while the defence representative obtains instructions from the accused. It also appears to be within the spirit of the prosecutor's general duty not to 'attempt to obtain a conviction by all means at his command' nor to 'regard himself as appearing for a party' (see the Code of Conduct of the Bar, annexe F, standards applicable to criminal cases, para 11.1).

In *Stratford Justices ex p Imbert* [1999] 2 Cr App R 276, the Divisional Court considered whether this lack of a legal obligation upon the prosecution is a violation of Article 6(3)(a) of the European Convention on Human Rights (ECHR) 'to be informed promptly . . . and in detail, of the nature and cause of the accusation against him . . .'. The Divisional Court held that it was not, although their lordships recognised that their decision was clearly obiter.

It is submitted that the absence of advance information might in certain circumstances be a violation of Article 6(3)(b), which lays down the right 'to have adequate time and facilities for his defence', as well as a violation of Article 6(3)(a). In order that the trial should be fair, it is necessary that the defence should be able to consider the prosecution evidence, and prepare upon the basis of knowledge rather than guesswork. Sometimes the nature of that evidence will be predictable, and the defence advocate will be able to respond with the necessary agility of thought. But in other instances, the defence may be ambushed by an unexpected line of evidence. Overall, it may be that what is generally recognised as good practice (the provision of the statements of prosecution witnesses in summary trials) should also be regarded as part of the rights provided by the European Convention on Human Rights.

7.3   DETERMINING MODE OF TRIAL

The procedure for determining whether an adult charged with an offence triable either way shall be tried on indictment or summarily is contained in ss 18–21 and 23 of the Magistrates' Courts Act 1980. It must be carried out before any evidence is called for purposes of committal proceedings or summary trial: s 18(2). It may take place before a single magistrate (s 18(5)), but it is more usual for the court to consist of at least two lay justices (or, of course, a stipendiary). Depending on the outcome of the procedure, the court may, upon its completion, have to adjourn either for preparation of the prosecution statements for committal to the Crown Court or for the attendance of witnesses for a summary trial. If, however, the accused pleads guilty, the magistrates may be able to proceed to sentence forthwith. The following are the main steps in the procedure for determining mode of trial:

(a)   The clerk to the justices reads the charge to the accused;

(b)   The clerk then explains that the accused may indicate whether he would plead guilty if the case proceeded to trial. The clerk should further explain that, if the accused pleads guilty, the proceedings will be treated as a summary trial at which a guilty plea has been tendered. The clerk must also explain that the accused will be committed to the Crown Court for sentence if the magistrates regard their powers of punishment as inadequate.

(c)   The clerk asks the accused if he pleads guilty or not guilty.

Steps (a) to (c), taken together, constitute the 'plea before venue' procedure. If the accused has indicated a plea of guilty, then the court proceeds as if he had pleaded guilty at summary trial. If, on the other hand, the accused indicated a plea of not guilty, then the court proceeds to determine the mode of trial, as follows:

(i)   First the prosecution and then the defence are given the opportunity to make representations as to whether trial on indictment or summary trial would be the more suitable method of trial: s 19(2)(b). The factors relevant to that question, to which the prosecution or defence might refer in their representations, are indicated in (ii) below.

(ii)   The magistrates consider which of the two methods of trial is the more suitable. They must bear in mind the representations, if any, made by the prosecution and defence, and they must have regard to the nature of the case, whether the circumstances make the offence one of serious character, whether the punishment which a magistrates' court would have power to inflict for it would be adequate, and any other circumstances which make the case more suitable for one method of trial rather than the other: s 19(3).

(iii)   If the magistrates consider that the offence is more suitable for summary trial, the court clerk tells the accused that the magistrates have taken that view. He then informs him that he may, if he consents, be tried by the magistrates, but that if he wishes he can choose to be tried by a jury instead. However, if he is tried by the magistrates and found guilty and if the magistrates consider that greater punishment should be imposed than they have power to inflict, they may send him to the Crown Court to be sentenced. The clerk then puts the accused to his election — he asks 'Do you wish to be tried by this court or do you wish to be tried by a jury?' If, and only if, the accused consents, the magistrates proceed to summary trial with the accused pleading guilty or not guilty to the charge against him. If the accused does not consent to summary trial, committal proceedings must be held: s 20.

(iv)   If the magistrates consider that trial on indictment is more appropriate, the accused is told of their decision, and the case will be sent to the Crown Court: s 21.

The essence of the procedure laid down in ss 18–21 is that there can be a summary trial for an offence triable either way only if both the magistrates and the accused agree to it. Of the matters mentioned in s 19(3) to which the magistrates must pay regard in considering the more suitable method of trial by far the most important is whether, in the event of a conviction, they would be able to inflict adequate punishment. In brief, the maximum penalties they can impose are: six months' imprisonment and/or a fine of £5,000 for any one offence triable either way; for two or more such offences, an aggregate prison term of 12 months and/or fines of £5,000 per offence. In deciding whether those powers would be sufficient to deal with the accused should he be convicted, the magistrates will look first at what the wording of the charge itself reveals about the gravity of the offence. For example, a charge of theft will list the items stolen; that will give a rough idea of the value involved in the offence, which, in turn, is a very rough guide to the appropriate level of penalty. Other charges are worded less informatively. Thus, a charge of unlawful wounding will not specify whether the victim suffered merely a slight graze or a deep stab-wound. In such cases, the magistrates should seek extra information from the parties (especially the prosecution) about the nature of the allegations. Of course, the parties may volunteer such information unasked in the representations they make about the more suitable method of trial. Magistrates should also be aware that a charge which, on the face of it, seems fairly minor may be rendered far more serious by the circumstances surrounding the offence (e.g., a charge of theft of £100 seems prima facie well within the magistrates' proper jurisdiction, but if the offence was committed by an employee stealing in the course of his employment, the aggravating element of a breach of trust might make the matter more suitable for the Crown Court). It is open to the prosecution to mention any such aggravating features to the magistrates — indeed, they might properly be criticised for failing to do so. One aggravating feature of which the magistrates must, however, remain unaware is the bad character of the accused. Where he has previous convictions, that must *not* be revealed to the court at the stage of determining the mode of trial: *Colchester Justices ex p North East Essex Building Co Ltd* [1977] 1 WLR 1109. Thus, the question the magistrates have to answer may be reduced to this: assuming the accused to be of good character, and bearing in mind what we know about the gravity of the offence from (a) the wording of the charge and (b) any additional information about the prosecution case and the circumstances of the crime given to us in the course of the parties' representations, would six months' imprisonment and a £5,000 fine be a sufficiently severe punishment should we agree to summary trial and convict? If the answer to that question is no, the magistrates ought to opt for Crown Court trial, however strongly one or both parties may argue in favour of summary trial. If the answer is yes, then summary trial will normally be the more suitable method, but occasionally other factors (e.g., the potential complexity of the legal issues involved or the fact that the accused is a well-known public figure who would suffer greatly from conviction even for a minor crime) may still tip the scales in favour of trial on indictment.

The decision which the magistrates make has an important bearing on the efficient administration of justice. If they accept jurisdiction in respect of a case which really ought to go to the Crown Court, then, because of the limits on their powers, there is a danger that the sentence passed will be inadequate. On the other hand, if they err on the side of caution by committing too many cases to the Crown Court, it will lead to delays, both in the cases referred, and in the others with which the Crown Court has to deal. The potential extent of the problem is considerable. In the year 1998/9, of the cases which went to the Crown Court for trial, some 49 per cent went on the magistrates' direction, 30 per cent were indictable only, and 21 per cent went on the accused's election: (*Annual Report of the Crown*

Prosecution Service, HMSO). The proportion sent on the magistrates' direction has been increasing over the past few years. Further, an influential Home Office study has shown that, in the sample analysed, in some 60 per cent of the cases committed by magistrates to the Crown Court for trial, the sentence eventually imposed by the Crown Court would have been within the powers of the magistrates.

Guidance was issued to magistrates in the *Practice Note (Mode of Trial: Guidelines)* [1990] 1 WLR 1439.

A revised version was issued by the Criminal Justice Consultative Council in the form of a booklet in January 1995, with a commendatory foreword by the Lord Chief Justice. The Guidelines spell out certain points of principle as follows:

(a) the court should never make its decision on the grounds of convenience or expedition;

(b) the court should assume for the purpose of deciding mode of trial that the prosecution version of the facts is correct;

(c) the fact that the offences are alleged to be specimens is a relevant consideration; the fact that the defendant will be asking for other offences to be taken into consideration, if convicted, is not;

(d) where cases involve complex questions of fact or difficult questions of law, the court should consider Crown Court trial;

(e) where two or more defendants are jointly charged with an offence each has an individual right to elect his mode of trial;

(f) in general, except where otherwise stated, either-way offences should be tried summarily unless the court considers that the particular case has one or more of the features set out in its guidance on specific offences *and* that its sentencing powers are insufficient;

(g) the court should also consider its powers to commit an offender for sentence under s 38 of the Magistrates' Courts Act 1980 (see Chapter 11) if information emerges during the course of the hearing which leads them to conclude that the offence is so serious, or the offender such a risk to the public, that their powers of sentence are inadequate.

It then goes on to enumerate certain of the common either-way offences, and to indicate the factors which will make them more appropriate for the Crown Court. In view of the importance of the Guidelines, they are reproduced in full as Appendix 2. As an example, however, it is instructive to see the way in which burglary of a dwelling-house ('domestic burglary') is dealt with. In general, state the Guidelines, cases should be tried summarily unless the court considers that one or more of the following features is present *and* that its powers of sentencing are inadequate:

(1) Entry in the daytime when the occupier (or another) is present.

(2) Entry at night of a house which is normally occupied, whether or not the occupier (or another) is present.

(3) The offence is alleged to be one of a series of similar offences.

(4) When soiling, ransacking, damage or vandalism occurs.

(5) The offence has professional hallmarks.

(6) The unrecovered property is of high value (defined by the Guidelines so as to mean £10,000 or more).

This advice is in stark contrast to the long-standing practice of certain magistrates' courts (at least before the original Guidelines were issued) of committing all 'domestic' burglaries to the Crown Court.

Point (e) above deals with the problem which arises where two or more accused are jointly charged and one (or more) wants summary trial, while the other(s) want trial on indictment. Frequently co-defendants differ in their intentions in this way, with one wanting summary trial (usually prior to pleading guilty) and the other seeking jury trial with a view to contesting the matter fully. In this situation, are the magistrates entitled, when deciding whether to accept jurisdiction, to take into account the fact that, in respect of one accused at least, the case will have to go to the Crown Court? In *Brentwood Justices ex p Nicholls* [1992] 1 AC 1, the House of Lords held, in effect, that, in these circumstances, the court should not be influenced by the fact that one of the accused was electing Crown Court trial. Hence, they should proceed to try summarily the accused who elected summary trial, and should hold committal proceedings in respect of the accused who elected trial on indictment. The reason is that s 20(3) gives the right of election as to mode of trial to each accused individually, and not to all accused collectively. Point (e) above reflects this decision.

Except as mentioned below, the prosecution cannot insist upon trial on indictment. Their views on the appropriate method of trial are, however, given great weight by the magistrates, who may feel that the police are the people in the best position to know how serious the alleged offence is. Therefore, if the prosecution are content with summary trial, and the defence indicate that the accused wishes to opt for summary trial, the magistrates may, in practice, agree without enquiring minutely into whether their sentencing powers will be adequate. Conversely, if the prosecution wish to go for trial on indictment, the defence may have a difficult task in persuading the magistrates that the matter is suitable for them to deal with. Moreover, if the prosecution is being carried on by the Attorney-General, Solicitor General or Director of Public Prosecutions, and he applies for trial on indictment, the magistrates *must* comply with his wishes and hold committal proceedings: s 19(4). This is subject to the proviso that the DPP may make such an application only if he has the consent of the AG: s 19(5). There would have to be something very unusual about a case for the DPP to think it right to bother the Attorney with a request that he (the DPP) be allowed to make a binding application for trial on indictment.

Where the prosecution are aggrieved by the magistrates' decision to try the defendant summarily, it is open to them to seek judicial review of that decision in the Divisional Court. They will have an uphill struggle, since the Divisional Court will refuse an application for certiorari unless the magistrates' decision is so wrong that no reasonable bench could have arrived at it (*McLean ex p Metropolitan Police Commissioner* [1975] Crim LR 289). Occasionally, however, the Divisional Court will overrule the magistrates, as they did in *Northampton Magistrates' Court ex p Commissioners of Customs and Excise* [1994] Crim LR 598. In that case, the defendant was charged with a VAT fraud causing loss of over £193,000. The Divisional Court held that the decision to try him summarily measured up to the yardstick which they had to apply in deciding whether to overrule it, in that it was 'truly astonishing'. The unrecovered property was of very high value, the offence was of a serious character, and in the absence of mitigating features a sentence of more than six months could be expected. The Divisional Court allowed the application, and remitted the case to the magistrates to deal with as examining justices.

In the majority of cases the procedure for determining the mode of trial will not take nearly as long to carry out as it has taken to describe. The prosecution representative — be he a Crown

Prosecutor, agent for the CPS or lawyer instructed by a private prosecutor — is asked whether the prosecution desire summary trial. If he says that they do, the defence counsel or solicitor is invited to comment. He may indicate that the accused also wants the case dealt with summarily. If so, the magistrates will probably agree to summary trial without more ado. Should the charge seem more serious than is normally tried summarily, they may enquire further into how grave the case really is before accepting jurisdiction (e.g. they may ask whether all the property allegedly stolen has been recovered, or whether the victim of an assault has suffered any permanent injury, or whether the accused abused a position of trust in order to commit the offence). Immediately the magistrates have said that they consider summary trial appropriate, the clerk informs the accused of his right to be tried by a jury etc. (see stage (d) of the procedure), and the accused elects summary trial.

Where the prosecution ask for summary trial, but the defence wish the case to go for trial on indictment, there is little point in counsel or solicitor making lengthy representations to show that the case is one fit for the Crown Court, as it cannot in any event be tried by the magistrates unless the accused consents. Accordingly, counsel or solicitor may make no representations, the magistrates say that they consider summary trial appropriate, and the clerk proceeds to put the accused to his election. Having asked for summary trial, the prosecution cannot be criticised for having inflicted on the public the extra expense of a judge and jury trial. The only situations in which determining the mode of trial is likely to lead to any real argument are where the prosecution say that trial on indictment is appropriate but the defence are anxious that the case stay in the magistrates' court, and where both prosecution and defence are content with summary trial but the magistrates have doubts about the adequacy of their sentencing powers.

7.3.1   Failure to comply with the procedure

The magistrates' jurisdiction to deal with offences triable either way derives solely from ss 18–20 of the Magistrates' Courts Act 1980. Therefore, if the procedure set out in those sections is not strictly complied with but the court nevertheless proceeds to try an accused for an offence triable either way, the magistrates act in excess of jurisdiction, and any conviction they pronounce is liable to be quashed by an order of *certiorari*: *Kent Justices ex p Machin* [1952] 2 QB 355. In *Machin,* the justices — purporting to act under legislation then in force which was similar in effect to the present ss 18–20 — convicted M of larceny and obtaining credit by fraud, and committed him to Quarter Sessions to be sentenced. M's solicitor had said to the magistrates, 'My client wishes you to deal with the case', so there was no doubt that M wanted summary trial. However, the clerk had failed to warn him of the possibility of his being committed for sentence, and for that reason the High Court held that both the conviction and the subsequent committal were nullities which had to be quashed. Almost certainly, M would have been told by his solicitor of the risk of a committal for sentence, but that did not absolve the court from its duty to follow the statutory procedure to the letter. As Lord Goddard CJ put it:

> The justices took upon themselves, although with the consent of the prisoner, to try offences without a strict compliance with the provisions of the Act which alone allows an indictable offence to be dealt with summarily. It was a very venial offence in the magistrates, but the prisoner is entitled to take advantage of it, and therefore the committal and the convictions were bad.

It is interesting that no objection was taken to the fact that consent to summary trial was expressed by M's solicitor not by M himself. Normally, however, the accused is asked to state personally in which court he wishes to be tried.

Lord Goddard's uncompromising insistence on the need to follow the statutory procedure was echoed by Donaldson LJ in *Horseferry Road Justices ex p Constable* [1981] Crim LR

504, a case where failure to ask C for his representations as to the more appropriate method of trial meant that his original election for summary trial was not binding on him, even though one might have thought that — as he then wanted summary trial — any representations he might have made would only have reinforced the magistrates' opinion that the case was fit for them to deal with. There has also been one instance of non-compliance with the procedure leading to the quashing of a summary *acquittal* (see *Cardiff Magistrates' Court ex p Cardiff City Council* (1987) *The Times*, 24 February 1987).

7.3.2 Presence of the accused

The accused should normally be present for proceedings under ss 18–21 to determine the mode of trial. His presence can be dispensed with, however, in certain circumstances. The court can proceed in his absence if his disorderly conduct makes it impracticable to continue the proceedings in his presence: s 18(3). It can also proceed in his absence if there is a good reason for so doing, and he is represented by counsel or solicitor who states that he (the accused) consents to the proceedings being conducted without him: s 23(1). The 'good reasons' for proceeding without the accused are not limited to reasons of health, but might include the accused having an important prior engagement for the day in question. If the magistrates consider that summary trial is more appropriate, the accused's consent to their dealing with the case can be signified by counsel or solicitor on his behalf. The magistrates could then deal with the case immediately (e.g. if the defence representative has been further authorised to enter a guilty plea) or adjourn to give the accused an opportunity to attend.

7.3.3 Changing the original decisions

The decision in favour of summary trial or, as the case may be, trial on indictment is not irreversible. If the original decision is for summary trial, the court may, at any stage before the close of the prosecution evidence, discontinue the trial and hold committal proceedings instead: MCA, s 25(2). The evident purpose of the subsection is to allow the magistrates to revise their original affirmative opinion as to the adequacy of their sentencing powers in the light of extra information about the offence emerging during the course of the prosecution case. Once the prosecution have closed their case, the full gravity of what the accused allegedly did will have been revealed, and the magistrates are from that point irretrievably committed to a summary trial. Although s 25(2) does not expressly say so, it applies only when the accused pleads not guilty. This is implied in its referring to the conclusion of the prosecution evidence, since it is only when the accused denies the offence that there will be any such evidence: *Dudley Justices ex p Gillard* [1986] AC 442. Thus, if the accused agrees to summary trial and pleads guilty, the magistrates are precluded from switching to committal proceedings even if some further development in the case makes them wish they could. A further consequence of the wording of s 25(2) is that, even where the accused has pleaded not guilty to an either-way offence, the magistrates must usually wait until they have actually heard some evidence before withdrawing their acceptance of jurisdiction. The point is illustrated by *St Helens Magistrates' Court ex p Critchley* [1988] Crim LR 311 where, after C had elected summary trial on two charges and pleaded not guilty, he was further charged with five more offences arising out of the same series of events, and the magistrates at the resumed hearing forthwith decided that he should go to the Crown Court on all seven matters. The High Court held that their decision as regards the original two charges was ultra vires since it was only s 25(2) that gave them power to decide to send the case to the Crown Court, and that subsection required them to commence the summary trial. In certain circumstances, however, the power to switch to committal proceedings may commence before the court has begun to hear evidence (e.g., where it has heard submissions on a point of law which has a direct and immediate bearing upon the process of determining the accused's guilt or innocence, such as the availability or otherwise of the defence of insanity in the magistrates' court: *Horseferry Road Magistrates' Court ex p K* [1996] 3 WLR 68).

Where the original decision is for trial on indictment, the magistrates may decide that the charge is not as grave as they at first thought, and give the accused the opportunity of having it tried summarily: s 25(3). They must first ask the prosecution and defence for their views on the proposed change, and — if he has not already done so — the clerk must explain to the accused the possibility of his being committed for sentence. Any switch to summary trial is, of course, dependent upon the accused's consent. It is also dependent upon the prosecution's consent in those limited cases where they would at the outset have been able to insist on trial on indictment. The magistrates' court can only change its decision from trial on indictment to summary trial *after* it has begun the committal proceedings. In *Liverpool Justices ex p Crown Prosecution Service, Liverpool* (1989) 90 Cr App R 261, D was charged with reckless driving and a number of other offences. The justices decided on trial on indictment. At a later hearing, a differently constituted bench heard an application from D's solicitor for summary trial. The application was made before committal proceedings began. The justices acceded to the request and accepted pleas of guilty to all matters charged. The prosecution applied for judicial review of their decision, on the ground that they had no jurisdiction to change the mode of trial. The Divisional Court held that there was no power to vary the decision for trial on indictment except that contained in the Magistrates' Courts Act 1980, s 25. Since D's submissions had been made before the justices began committal proceedings, the provisions of s 25(3) had not been complied with. Thus the decision to change to summary trial was a nullity. The case was remitted to the magistrates to continue the committal proceedings, bearing in mind that D's admission of guilt in open court was a compelling reason for changing to summary trial.

A probably unintended consequence of the wording of s 25(3) is that, if the only charge against the accused is one triable only on indictment (e.g., wounding with intent to cause grievous bodily harm contrary to s 18 of the Offences against the Person Act 1861) but the magistrates decide on a submission that there is a case to answer only in respect of an offence triable either way (e.g. unlawful wounding contrary to s 20 of the 1861 Act), they may not hold a summary trial in respect of the latter offence however much they and the parties might desire them to do so: *Cambridgeshire Justices ex p Fraser* [1984] 1 WLR 1391.

The magistrates have a discretion to allow an accused who has elected summary trial to withdraw his election. The question most often arises when he is initially unrepresented, agrees to summary trial at that stage, and then obtains legal advice during an adjournment prior to the hearing of the case. The central factor in the magistrates' decision should be the accused's state of mind at the time of his election. 'Did he properly understand the nature and significance of the choice which was put to him?' (see McCullough J's judgment in *Birmingham Justices ex p Hodgson* [1985] QB 1131). Whether one intends to plead guilty or not guilty always has a major influence on where one would prefer to be tried (see Paragraph 7.6). Therefore, if the accused elects summary trial and pleads guilty under the misapprehension that he has no defence to the charge, but he is subsequently advised that he might have a defence, and the magistrates in consequence allow the plea of guilty to be withdrawn, then it follows almost automatically that they should also allow the election for summary trial to be withdrawn (see *Ex p Hodgson* and especially Watkins LJ's judgment in *West London Metropolitan Stipendiary Magistrate ex p Keane* (1985) *The Times,* 9 March 1985). Where the accused has intended to plead not guilty throughout, but claims that his original willingness to be tried summarily was due to his not realising the seriousness of the charge and/or the advantages of trial on indictment from a defendant's point of view, the exercise of the magistrates' discretion will depend upon matters such as the accused's age, intelligence and apparent understanding of court proceedings. These criteria were applied in *Highbury Corner Metropolitan Stipendiary Magistrate ex p Weekes* [1985] QB 1147. W (aged 17) was arrested on a Saturday evening on a charge of unlawful wounding. He was bailed to attend at the magistrates' court on the Monday morning, and did so in company only with his mother. He had not had any opportunity to obtain legal advice, nor had he ever been in a magistrates' court before. Upon his agreeing to summary trial and pleading not guilty, the case was adjourned. At a subsequent unsuccessful application for the election to be withdrawn, it was conceded that W had not even understood what the Crown Court was, so obviously he could not have appreciated 'the nature and significance' of the choice between modes of trial that he was making. The High Court accordingly held that the magistrate had erred in refusing the defence application. The magistrate's mistake perhaps arose from his view that 'this court can grapple with the difficulties in this case'. No doubt it could have done, but that was not a consideration relevant to the application with which he was dealing. Even in a case eminently suitable for summary trial, the accused has the right to be tried on indictment if the offence charged is indictable, and he should not be deprived of that right by an election made at a time when he does not really know what he is doing. McCullough J's judgment in *Weekes* shows that he was unhappy that the question of method of trial had been dealt with on a first appearance by a young and unrepresented accused. However, His Lordship was not prepared to lay down any general principle to the effect that the court should always wait until the accused has had the opportunity of applying for legal aid and obtaining advice before putting him to his election.

> The power that magistrates have to switch from summary trial or to allow an accused to withdraw his consent to summary trial should not be confused with the power to commit for sentence, described in Chapter 11. Committal for sentence occurs where the accused pleads or is found guilty by the magistrates and they then consider that their powers of punishment are insufficient. The Crown Court's only function is then to sentence the offender. In the event of the case being sent for trial in the Crown Court, on the other hand, there is no completed summary trial and questions of guilt or innocence are determined in the Crown Court. Moreover, as already explained, s 25(2) only applies where the accused pleads not guilty, whereas powers to commit for sentence are in no way dependent on the plea.

7.3.4 Adjusting the charges

As explained in Paragraph 7.3, the prosecution, for all practical purposes, have no direct veto on an offence triable either way being tried summarily. Conversely, they cannot prevent the accused insisting on trial on indictment. Indirectly, however, they can control the mode of trial through the almost unfettered discretion they enjoy in relation to charging a suspect. Thus, if they choose to regard the conduct alleged as giving rise only to a summary offence, the accused cannot ask to be charged with something triable either way. Since either-way offences are generally more serious than summary offences, it might be thought inconceivable that anybody would prefer to be charged with the former rather than the latter. In practice, however, there is an overlap between the most serious summary matters and the least serious either-way ones, so that, in certain situations where the facts alleged would fit either, the sentence an offender will actually receive (as opposed to the legal maximum theoretically imposable) is likely to be the same whether he is convicted of the summary offence or the either-way alternative. The prosecution can then ensure that he is tried in the magistrates' court by the simple expedient of charging only the former. (As to the reason why the prosecution might wish to avoid jury trial, see Paragraph 7.6.)

The further question arises of whether the prosecution can have the best of both worlds by first charging an either-way offence and then, if the accused elects trial on indictment, reducing the charge to one that is summary only. The answer, basically, is 'yes, they can, as a matter of strict law'. In *Canterbury & St Augustine Justices ex p Klisiak* [1982] QB 398 four defendants were charged with assault occasioning actual bodily harm plus a variety of minor public order offences, all arising out of disturbances on the seafront one Bank Holiday. They elected trial on indictment for the assault and the remaining charges (being summary) were adjourned *sine die*. During an adjournment prior to committal proceedings, further charges of assaulting a police officer in the execution of his duty (a summary offence) were preferred. Subsequently, no evidence was offered at what would have been the committal proceedings for 'ABH', but a date was fixed for summary trial of both the public order charges and the assault on police. The Divisional Court held that the prosecution was entitled to choose what offence to charge. The court could not prevent them from acting in this way, unless it resulted in blatant injustice.

The principles in *Ex p Klisiak* do not apply to the reverse situation where the prosecution feel aggrieved by the magistrates' decision to accept jurisdiction in respect of an either-way charge. Thus, in *Brooks* [1985] Crim LR 385, where B was convicted of causing grievous bodily harm to his lover's husband by striking him over the head with a hammer, the Court of Appeal heavily criticised the prosecution for adding the GBH charge (which is triable only on indictment) after the magistrates had held that the original either-way charge of unlawful wounding was suitable for summary trial. Given the timing of the additional charge, it looked very much like a refusal to accept the ruling of the bench. Largely because of the procedural irregularity, their lordships reduced B's sentence from 15 to 9 months.

Whatever the strictly legal position may be with regard to the adjustment of charges, CPS prosecutors are now put under ethical constraints by the Code for Crown Prosecutors. Para. 7.3 of the Code addresses the fundamental issue raised by the cases discussed above when it states: 'Crown Prosecutors should not change the charge simply because of the decision made by the court or the defendant about where the case will be heard'. The introduction of charging standards provides further limits within which the discretion of the prosecution will in practice be exercised (see Paragraph 4.3.2 and Appendix 1).

7.4 THE SPECIAL PROCEDURE FOR CRIMINAL DAMAGE CHARGES

The Criminal Law Act 1977 contained many provisions, now repealed and re-enacted in the Magistrates' Courts Act 1980, for simplifying the law on the mode of trial of offences, and also for redistributing the work of the criminal courts so that a greater proportion of cases would be heard in the magistrates' courts than had been so previously. Offences such as driving with excess alcohol in the blood and assaulting a police constable in the execution of his duty, which had formerly been triable either way, became summary, and offences ranging from bigamy to failing to provide one's apprentice with sufficient food, which had before been triable only on indictment, became triable either way. However, the most controversial proposal for shifting work to the magistrates only reached the statute book in an attenuated form. The Criminal Law Bill contained provisions which would have made minor offences of theft, obtaining property by deception and criminal damage triable only summarily, but the outcry at this restriction on the right to jury trial was such that only the provisions in respect of criminal damage offences became law. The present legislation is contained in the Magistrates' Courts Act 1980, s 22.

If the accused is charged with criminal damage contrary to the Criminal Damage Act 1971, s 1(1), or an attempt to commit such an offence, then, unless the offence involved damage or attempted damage by fire, the magistrates must proceed as follows:

(a) They consider, having regard to any representations made by the prosecution or defence, the value involved in the offence — i.e. the cost, in a case where property was allegedly destroyed or damaged beyond repair, of replacing the property, or, in other cases, the cost of repair. 'Representations' normally entail merely arguments and assertions of fact by counsel, perhaps accompanied by the production of documents such as a bill for repairs that have been carried out on the damaged property. There is no need to call evidence at this point (see *Canterbury & St Augustine Justices ex p Klisiak* [1982] QB 398).

(b) In *R (on the application of Abbott) v Colchester Magistrates' Court* [2001] Crim LR 564, the Divisional Court made it clear that the value on which the magistrates must focus is the value of the damage to the property itself. They should not concern themselves with any consequential losses which might have been sustained as a result of the damage.

(c) If the value involved is clearly £5,000 or less, the magistrates proceed as if the offence were triable only summarily. They do not follow the procedure in ss 19 to 21 of MCA (see Paragraph 7.3), and the accused has no right to a trial on indictment.

(d) If the value involved is clearly over £5,000, the charge is dealt with like any other offence triable either way. The magistrates hear any representations as to the more suitable mode of trial, and, if they consider that summary trial is appropriate, the clerk asks the accused if he consents to the magistrates dealing with the case.

(e) Where the case is tried summarily under (b) above, the maximum sentence the magistrates can impose is three months imprisonment or a £2,500 fine: Magistrates' Courts Act 1980, s 33. They cannot commit for sentence to the Crown Court under s 38 of the 1980 Act, although, in appropriate circumstances, they could exercise one of the other primary powers of committal mentioned in Paragraph 11.3.

(f) Where the case is tried summarily under (c) above, the maximum sentence is that which can be imposed for any other of the offences triable either way listed in Sch 1 to the 1980 Act — i.e. six months imprisonment and a £5,000 fine. In addition, the magistrates may commit for sentence under s 38.

(g) If the magistrates are not sure whether the value involved is more or less than £5,000, the clerk asks the accused if he consents to summary trial. If he does so and is convicted, the maximum penalty is as in (d) above and, again, he cannot be committed for sentence under s 38. The clerk explains the maximum penalty to the accused before asking for his consent to summary trial. If he does not want to be tried summarily, the normal ss 19–21 procedure for determining the mode of trial comes into operation.

Where an accused is charged on the same occasion with two or more offences of criminal damage that appear to the court to form a series of the same or similar character, the relevant consideration in determining mode of trial is the *aggregate* value involved in all the offences — i.e. if the aggregate is more than £5,000 the accused retains his right to jury trial even though the value of each individual offence is less than that amount (see Magistrates' Courts Act 1980, s 22(11) which was inserted by s 38 of the Criminal Justice Act 1988).

Prior to the amendment made by the CJA 1988, there was an arbitrary rule that, if the accused faced a series of criminal damage charges, he was entitled to elect Crown Court trial however small the values (see, for example, *St Helens Justices ex p McClorie* [1983] 1 WLR 1332 where magistrates were compelled to hold committal proceedings in respect of (i) damaging a padlock in breaking into a yard, and (ii) damaging a watch belonging to a police officer trying to arrest the accused for being in the yard, the total aggregate value involved being a mere £20). The figure at or beneath which the special procedure applies has increased massively in real terms over the years. When it was introduced in 1977, it was £200. It was then increased to £400 in 1984, £2,000 in 1988 and £5,000 in 1994. It is rare for an accused to do more than £5,000 worth of damage (other than by arson, which is excluded from the procedure anyway). The great majority of criminal damage charges have therefore been excluded from the ambit of jury trial.

It should be noted that even where the special procedure applies and the value involved in the offence is £5,000 or less, s 22(2) merely requires the *magistrates* to proceed as if the offence charged were triable only summarily — it does not provide that the offence shall be deemed to be summary for all purposes. (*Considine* (1980) 70 Cr App R 239.)

It is submitted that an accused in a case such as *Considine* (where the charge was criminal damage valued at £34) would be entitled to advance information from the prosecution (see Paragraph 7.2 for details of advance information). This is so since the entitlement to advance information is triggered off by the nature of the offence. The offence is criminal damage, and it is triable either way, notwithstanding that the magistrates are obliged to deal with it summarily in certain circumstances.

7.5 LINKED SUMMARY AND INDICTABLE CHARGES

Subject to what is explained in this Paragraph, a fundamental principle of classification of offences is that summary offences must be tried in a magistrates' court. The only way the Crown Court can become involved in dealing with a summary matter (other than on appeal) is if the accused has pleaded or been found guilty in the lower court and is then committed for sentence under s 56 of the Criminal Justice Act 1967. Until the passing of the Criminal Justice Act 1988 there were no exceptions to the above principle. However, ss 40 and 41 of that Act introduce two new procedures, one of which enables a limited range of summary offences actually to be tried on indictment and the other of which allows the accused, having been convicted on indictment of an either-way offence, to be sentenced at the same time for a summary offence to which he enters a guilty plea. But, both these procedures apply only if the accused is charged with an indictable offence and a linked summary matter. It remains true that a summary charge standing by itself must always and without exception be tried summarily.

Since the use of s 40 and/or 41 is dependent on the accused having been sent to the Crown Court for trial on an indictable charge, it makes more sense to deal with this topic in detail later (see Paragraph 12.9).

7.6 TRIAL ON INDICTMENT OR SUMMARY TRIAL?

Where the accused has a choice of trial on indictment by judge and jury, or summary trial by magistrates, the following points should be borne in mind as to the advantages and disadvantages of each method.

Summary trial is less expensive and less time-consuming than trial on indictment. If the accused elects to be tried by the magistrates and is found guilty, any order to pay some of the prosecution's costs or contribute towards his own legal aid costs will almost certainly reflect the fact that he has chosen the less costly form of trial. In addition, the sentence itself may well be less severe than if he had been tried at the Crown Court. If he cannot be committed for sentence (see Chapter 11), the punishment will not of course, exceed six months' imprisonment and a £5,000 fine (twelve months if convicted of two or more offences triable either way). Even if the magistrates have power to commit for sentence, they may well deal with the offender themselves in cases where, had he been convicted on indictment, the Crown Court judge would have passed a sentence in excess of that which the magistrates may pass. As a result of the plea before venue procedure, of course, a defendant who intends to plead guilty will be dealt with in any event by the magistrates' court (subject to the possibility of committal for sentence — see Chapter 11). However, the constraints upon sentencing powers in the magistrates' court will be borne in mind by the astute legal adviser who is aware that the defendant will plead not guilty, but knows there is a chance that he will nevertheless be convicted.

However, the general view is that trial by a jury offers a better prospect of an acquittal. Three reasons may be advanced in support of this view. First, at a trial on indictment, the defence know exactly what evidence the prosecution propose to adduce because that will have been disclosed by the committal proceedings and any notices of additional evidence. Although the Magistrates' Courts (Advance Information) Rules 1985 (see Paragraph 7.2) now provide for advance information of the prosecution case whenever the offence charged is triable either way, the rules do not in terms require the prosecution to give the defence copies of the statements made by prosecution witnesses — it is sufficient to provide 'a summary of the facts and matters about which the prosecutor proposes to adduce evidence in the proceedings'. Thus, knowledge of evidence prior to summary trial may still not be as satisfactory from the defence point of view as the information which they enjoy prior to trial on indictment. Secondly, as explained in Paragraph 9.7.2, it is difficult to object effectively to inadmissible evidence at summary trials, because the magistrates learn what the evidence is in the course of ruling on its admissibility, and are inevitably influenced even by material which they ultimately decide should be excluded. At a trial on indictment, the judge decides whether evidence is admissible in the absence of the jury. Finally, it is suggested that jurors are more likely to believe the accused than are magistrates, especially in cases where there is a conflict between police evidence and defence evidence. Some would say that this is because magistrates are less gullible than juries, others that through often sitting in court magistrates become 'case-hardened' and suspend their critical faculties in relation to police evidence. Whatever the reason, statistics appear to support professional opinion on this point. In the year 1998/9, 43 per cent of Crown Court trials ended in acquittal and 57 per cent in conviction. In the magistrates' court, by contrast, only 26 per cent of defendants were acquitted whereas 74 per cent were found guilty after trial.

8 Disclosure

One crucial feature of the criminal trial in England and Wales has always been the duty of the prosecution to disclose the evidence which is at its disposal to the defence. The rationale for this duty is the disparity of resources between the Crown on the one hand (with its access to the investigative facilities of the police and specialist services such as those of forensic scientists), and the individual accused of an offence on the other hand. In an effort to ensure a fair trial for the accused, and to achieve 'equality of arms' as far as possible between the Crown and the accused, there developed a common law duty owed by the prosecution to the defence. This duty had two aspects:

(a)   The obligation to notify the defence of the evidence upon which the prosecution intend to rely. This can conveniently be referred to as the 'duty to provide advance information'. As far as trial on indictment is concerned, this is met in part by the papers served upon the defence prior to committal to the Crown Court, or after a case is sent to the Crown Court under the indictable-only procedure (see Chapter 12). Any further evidence which the prosecution later decide to adduce as part of their case must be brought to the defence's attention by way of a notice of additional evidence (see Paragraph 18.3.3). The duty in respect of summary trial is less comprehensive, and is dealt with in Paragraph 7.2.

(b)   The duty to make available to the defence any material of relevance to the case upon which they do *not* intend to rely — 'unused material'. It is upon this aspect of the prosecution's obligations (known as the 'duty of disclosure') that most of the remainder of this Chapter concentrates, but it will also deal with the duty placed upon the defence to make disclosure of the case upon which it will rely at trial.

Although the prosecution duty of disclosure was evolved by the judges at common law, in an effort to ensure a fair trial for the accused, it has now been made subject to the statutory regime set out in the Criminal Procedure and Investigations Act 1996 (CPIA), as supplemented by a Code of Practice issued under that Act. The disclosure provisions of the CPIA came into effect on 1 April 1997. Their application is set out in s 1(3), which states that part I (containing the disclosure provisions) applies in relation to alleged offences into which no criminal investigation has begun before the appointed day (1 April 1997). 'Criminal investigation' is defined in s 1(4) as 'an investigation which police officers or other persons have a duty to conduct with a view to it being ascertained (a) whether a person should be charged with an offence, or (b) whether a person charged with an offence is guilty of it'. The Act is supplemented by the Code of Practice and a series of rules and regulations which came into effect on the same day (on the statutory rules as to disclosure, see Sprack,

The Criminal Procedure and Investigations Act 1996: (1) The Duty of Disclosure [1997] Crim LR 308; and Leng and Taylor, *Blackstone's Guide to the Criminal Procedure and Investigations Act 1996,* Chapters 1 and 2).

The scheme of the legislation is as follows:

(a)   There is a statutory duty upon the police officer investigating an offence to record and retain information and material gathered or generated during the investigation (see Paragraph 8.1).

(b)   The prosecution should, in what the CPIA terms 'primary prosecution disclosure', inform the defence of certain categories of that material which they *do not* intend to use at trial — as stated, there are separate obligations to inform the defence of material which they *do* intend to use (see Paragraph 8.2).

(c)   The defence then have a duty to inform the prosecution of the case which they intend to present at trial (see Paragraph 8.3).

(d)   Disclosure by the defence triggers off a duty on the part of the prosecution to present further material to the defence — 'secondary prosecution disclosure' (Paragraph 8.4).

The legislation makes provision for applications to be made to the court in certain circumstances where there is a dispute about whether the prosecution should disclose certain material (see Paragraph 8.5); and there are sanctions laid down for defence failure to disclose, or disclosure which is false or inconsistent (Paragraph 8.8).

The cases to which this legislative scheme applies are laid down in s 1. In brief, it is compulsory in relation to cases sent to the Crown Court to be tried on indictment. It may also apply on a voluntary basis to any summary trial, including those in the youth court, whether the charges in question are summary, triable either way, or even (in the case of the youth court) indictable only (see Paragraph 8.9 for the application of the statutory provisions to summary trial).

8.1   THE INVESTIGATOR'S DUTY

Section 23 of the CPIA requires the Secretary of State to prepare a Code of Practice which will govern investigations carried out by police officers. By s 26, those other than police officers (e.g., customs officers and trading standards officers) charged with the duty of conducting criminal investigations must have regard to the Code's provisions.

The Code of Practice (which is reproduced as Appendix 3) makes the investigator responsible for ensuring that any information relevant to the investigation is recorded and retained, whether it is gathered in the course of the investigation (e.g., documents seized in the course of searching premises) or generated by the investigation (e.g., interview records). Where there is any doubt about the relevance of material, the investigator should retain it. The duty to retain material includes in particular the following categories:

(a)   crime reports, including crime report forms, relevant parts of incident report books and police officers' notebooks;

(b)   final versions of witness statements;

(c)   draft versions of witness statements where their content differs from the final version;

(d)   interview records (written or taped);

(e)   expert reports and schedules;
(f)   any material casting doubt upon the reliability of a confession;
(g)   any material casting doubt on the reliability of a witness.

But the duty to retain material does not extend to items purely ancillary to that in the above categories which possess no independent significance, such as duplicate copies of documents. The material must be retained at least until criminal proceedings are concluded. Where the accused has been convicted, the material must be retained for at least six months after conviction, or until he is released from custody (whichever is the later).

Where the investigator believes that the person charged with an offence is likely to plead not guilty at a summary trial, or that the offence will be tried in the Crown Court, he or she must prepare a schedule listing material which has been retained and which does not form part of the case against the accused. If the investigator has obtained any sensitive material, this should be listed in a separate schedule. Sensitive material is material which the investigator believes it is not in the public interest to disclose. The Code gives a number of examples, which range from material relating to national security to material given in confidence, and include material relating to informants, under-cover police officers, premises used for police surveillance, techniques used in the detection of crime, and material relating to a child witness generated, e.g., by a local authority social services department (see Paragraph 8.7).

The investigator should draw the prosecutor's attention to any material which might undermine the prosecution case. The disclosure officer (defined as the person responsible for examining the records created during the investigation and criminal proceedings and disclosing material as required to the prosecutor or the accused) must certify that to the best of his knowledge and belief the duties imposed under the Code have been complied with.

After the defence have complied with their duty of disclosure (see Paragraph 8.3), the investigator must look again at the material retained, and draw the prosecutor's attention to any material which might reasonably be expected to assist the defence disclosed. Again the disclosure officer must certify compliance with the duties imposed by the Code. If the investigator comes into possession of any new material after complying with the duties described above, then this must be treated in the same way.

If the prosecutor so requests, the investigator must disclose to the accused:

(a)   material which might undermine the prosecution case;
(b)   where the accused has given the prosecutor a defence statement (see Paragraph 8.3), material which might reasonably be expected to assist the defence which the accused has disclosed;
(c)   any material which the court orders be disclosed.

The statute has therefore placed the police disclosure officer at the centre of the obligation to disclose material in the possession of the prosecution. This role is controversial, and the way in which it is carried out has led to fierce criticism by the legal profession. As was noted in a major study carried out for the Home Office, most police forces regard the training which they receive on disclosure as inadequate — its average length is less than one day. Officers frequently provide to prosecutors documentation which is late, inaccurate or incomplete. Frequently, prosecutors disagree with the assessment of disclosure officers as to whether material should be disclosed or not (Auld Report, pp. 449–451, relying in part on Plotnikoff and Woolfson, *A Fair Balance? Evaluation of the Operation of Disclosure Law*, Home Office 2001).

8.2 PRIMARY PROSECUTION DISCLOSURE

Section 3 of the CPIA requires the prosecutor to disclose previously undisclosed material to the accused if, in the prosecutor's opinion, 'it might undermine the case for the prosecution against the accused'. The test is a subjective one, in that it is based on the opinion of the prosecutor (compare the objective test for secondary prosecution disclosure laid down in s 7(2): 'material which . . . might be reasonably expected to assist the accused's defence as disclosed by the defence statement', dealt with in Paragraph 8.4). If there is no such material, then the accused must be given a written statement to that effect. Prosecution material includes material which the prosecutor possesses or has been allowed to inspect under the provisions of the Code (see Paragraph 8.1). It may be disclosed either by giving it to the defence, or allowing them to inspect it at a reasonable time and place. This step is called 'primary prosecution disclosure', and it must be carried out as soon as reasonably practicable (s 13). In due course, the duty will have to be carried out within a time limit which will be laid down by statutory instrument (s 12). Material must not, however, be disclosed under this provision if a court has concluded that it is not in the public interest that it be disclosed, (s 3(6), dealt with in Paragraph 8.7). By s 4, if the prosecutor has been given a document indicating any non-sensitive material which has not been given to the accused, that document must be given to the accused at the same time as primary prosecution disclosure takes place.

It will be the prosecutor who will judge, then, whether material should be disclosed to the defence. On what basis will that judgement be exercised? The common law position prior to the CPIA was encapsulated in the test laid down in *Keane* [1994] 1 WLR 746, which held that material fell to be disclosed (unless subject to immunity) if it could:

> be seen on a sensible appraisal by the prosecution: (a) to be relevant or possibly relevant to an issue in the case; (b) to raise or possibly raise a new issue whose existence is not apparent from the evidence the prosecution proposes to use; (c) to hold out a real (as opposed to a fanciful) prospect of providing a lead on evidence which goes to (a) or (b).

When the government introduced the new statutory disclosure scheme contained in the CPIA they aimed, by the use of the word 'undermine', to narrow the test of relevance as defined in *Keane* (*Hansard*, Lords, 18 December 1995, cols 1436–47; and see Leng and Taylor, *Blackstone's Criminal Procedure and Investigations Act 1996*, pp. 13–14). Parliamentary attempts by amendment to incorporate the relevance test as laid down in that case were resisted. Nevertheless, it was also made clear during the passage of the Bill that material which might undermine the prosecution case would include more than evidence which was *fatal* to the prosecution case. The test was, for example, described as follows by the Home Office Minister, Mr David McLean:

> The test for primary disclosure is designed to ensure that the prosecutor discloses at the first stage material that, generally speaking, has an adverse effect on the strength of the prosecution case. It is not confined to material raising a fundamental question about the prosecution. . . . The disclosure scheme is aimed at undisclosed material that might help the accused, notwithstanding the fact that there is enough evidence to provide a realistic prospect of conviction (*Hansard*, House of Commons Standing Committee B, 14 May 1996, col 34).

One category of material which 'might undermine' the prosecution case is notification of the previous convictions of prosecution witnesses. In *Vasiliou* [2000] Crim LR 845, the Court of Appeal held that the appellant's conviction had been rendered unsafe because the prosecution had failed to reveal the previous convictions of their witnesses. This had meant that the appellant was deprived of the chance to challenge those witnesses as to their character. Lack of knowledge had resulted in the appellant being unable to pursue a different strategy at trial from that which had been taken. The conviction was quashed and a retrial ordered.

8.3 DEFENCE DISCLOSURE

By s 5, once primary prosecution disclosure has taken place, and the case is committed to the Crown Court, the accused must give a defence statement to the prosecutor and the court. The defence statement is a written statement setting out in general terms the nature of the defence and the matters on which the accused takes issue with the prosecution, with reasons.

If the defence statement discloses an alibi, particulars of alibi must be given, including the name and address of any alibi witness, or information which might be of use in finding the witness if his or her name or address is not known. This provision replaces s 11 of the Criminal Justice Act 1967, which is abolished by s 74 of the CPIA, although a similar definition of alibi evidence is adopted — 'evidence tending to show that by reason of the presence of the accused at a particular place or in a particular area at a particular time he was not, or was unlikely to have been, at the place where the offence is alleged to have been committed at the time of its alleged commission' (see Paragraph 18.5.3 for examples of the way in which this definition has been applied).

The duty which the CPIA places upon the defence is a novel one as, with certain limited exceptions such as the revelation of a defence of alibi discussed in the preceding paragraph, there has historically been no obligation for the defence to reveal their case in advance of trial. The argument against placing the defence under such a duty has traditionally been that it erodes two fundamental principles: that the prosecution have the burden of proof, and that the accused is entitled to protection against self-incrimination. As soon as any pressure is placed on the accused to reveal his defence, so the argument runs, then he may in effect be conscripted to help fill in the gaps in the prosecution case against him. Notwithstanding these arguments, the CPIA introduced the duty of defence disclosure. It does place the defence lawyers in a difficult tactical quandary. They must weigh up the advantages and drawbacks of a detailed defence statement. An appropriate degree of detail can trigger off the release of further prosecution material (see Paragraph 8.4), whereas non-disclosure can result in the drawing of inferences potentially unfavourable to the defendant (see Paragraph 8.8). On the other hand, if the defence are bound by a detailed statement which later proves to be inaccurate, there is the danger of adverse inferences being drawn for that reason.

A tight time-limit for defence disclosure has been laid down by regulations which come into effect at the same time as the statutory provisions (see the Criminal Procedure and Investigations Act 1996 (Defence Disclosure Time Limits) Regulations 1997: SI 1997 No 684). The defence statement must be served within 14 days of the prosecution's compliance (or purported compliance) with the duty of primary disclosure (reg 2). Whilst the defence may apply for an extension, specifying their belief, on reasonable grounds, that it is not possible to meet the deadline, the application must be made before the deadline expires (reg 3). The court may grant an extension 'entirely at [its] discretion', and may order further extensions on the same basis. The rules of court (the Crown Court (Criminal Procedure and

Investigations Act 1996) (Disclosure) Rules 1997 (SI 1997 No 698), r 8; and the Magistrates' Court (Criminal Procedure and Investigations Act 1996) (Disclosure) Rules 1997 (SI 1997 No 703), r 8), which also came into force at the same time as the statutory provisions, envisage the application being heard *at least* 14 days after it has been received, to give the prosecutor an opportunity to make representations on whether an extension should be granted. It is therefore envisaged that the defence will have to make application before the deadline expires, but will not be aware of the fate of the application until after its expiry.

It should be stressed that the duty of disclosure imposed on the defence is of a different kind from what is normally meant when one talks about 'the prosecution duty of disclosure'. The prosecution duty is to disclose *unused material*, i.e., material which they do not intend to introduce at trial. As far as defence disclosure is concerned, the duty is to reveal the case which *will* be presented at trial. There is no obligation on the *defence,* either at common law or under the new statutory scheme, to reveal material which is *not* to be used at trial.

While that much is clear, it is less certain just how detailed the defence statement needs to be. Does it have to provide the prosecution with an account of the evidence which will be produced at trial? Should it include the lines upon which it is intended to cross-examine prosecution witnesses? The question is an important one, because of the inference which the court may draw if the defence statement is inconsistent with the defence which is run at trial.

In addressing this question, one needs to consider what the defence will have received by the time their duty to serve a defence statement is triggered off, and what they will not have received. The prosecution must have served the committal papers, or their equivalent in cases sent to the Crown Court under the indictable-only procedure or by notice of transfer or voluntary bill of indictment (see Chapter 12 for an account of the process of committal for trial and the alternative procedures). The prosecution must also have complied, or purported to comply, with the duty to make primary disclosure (s 5(1)(b)). What the prosecution will not have done is to serve a statement of the way in which they intend to put the case. The prosecution case, in this latter sense, consists of the inferences and conclusions to be drawn from the evidence upon which it relies. Whilst in some cases the evidence relied on by the prosecution will be self-explanatory, in others it may be impossible for the defence to say in what way they take issue with the prosecution case, or the reasons (see the contribution of Lord Ackner during the debate on the Bill: *Hansard,* Lords, 18 December 1995, cols 1458–9).

In interpreting the intended scope of the defence statement, the remarks of the Solicitor-General in dealing with what is now s 5(6) are apposite. He said: 'There is no suggestion that in giving the reason [why it takes issue with the prosecution], detail of the evidence to support that reason should be given'. In particular, he stated that 'the fear that this might require the defence to set out its oral cross-examination is not well founded. That is not intended at all' (*Hansard*, House of Commons Committee, 16 May 1996, cols 66–69). If one takes this statement of intent, along with the context of what might reasonably be required of the defence at a stage when they may not be clear about the way in which the prosecution put their case, then it would seem reasonable for the courts to take a relatively relaxed view as to what the defence statement should contain.

Where the accused does serve a defence statement under s 5, another important question arises: Should the prosecution be allowed to put it in evidence as part of their case? Such a course of action might prove tempting where the prosecution case is a weak one. Say, for example, that the accused is charged with assault. The defence statement states that the accused acted in self-defence. During the course of the jury trial, the prosecution are unable to prove that the accused struck a blow. The way would be clear for a successful submission of no case to answer (see Paragraph 18.4 for details of the submission of no case to answer). Can the prosecution adduce the defence statement in evidence, so as to frustrate such a submission?

It is submitted that to allow such a course of action would be a serious derogation from the privilege against self-incrimination, and the principle that the burden of proof should rest upon the prosecution throughout. The Royal Commission on Criminal Justice (chaired by Lord Runciman), which suggested a form of defence disclosure, recommended that the prosecution should *not* be allowed to adduce as part of its case matters disclosed by the defence. Such a limitation was, they said significantly, 'more consistent with the principle that the burden of proof should lie upon the prosecution' (Report of the Royal Commission on Criminal Justice, Cm 2263, para 62).

There is no specific authority in the statute for such a course of action, and the prosecution would have to clear two hurdles in order to be able to use the defence statement:

(a)   they would have to show that the statement was the defendant's; and
(b)   they would have to establish an evidential route for its admission.

In the normal course of events, where the defence statement is prepared and issued by the defendant's solicitors, the prosecution would need to show that it was issued with the defendant's authority so as to be, in effect, his statement. The position at common law, however, is that in criminal cases a client is not bound by statements written by his or her solicitor in the absence of proof of specific instructions (*Downer* (1880) 43 LT 445). Agency may be inferred from the circumstances, as it was in *Turner* (1975) 61 Cr App R 67, where a barrister made an admission in court on behalf of his client and in the client's presence. The circumstances may of course be such that an inference of agency cannot be drawn. In *Evans* [1981] Crim LR 699, it was held that agency could not be inferred from the fact that the admission was made by the accused's solicitor's clerk. Further, any inference of agency can be challenged by admissible evidence. In *Turner,* for example, the barrister who had purported to make the admission gave evidence that he had exceeded his authority in doing so, and the accused's statement was ruled inadmissible. The evidence used to support or refute the allegation that the admission was made with the accused's authority must in itself be admissible. In *Evans,* evidence by the solicitor's clerk that he acted with the accused's authority was held to be inadmissible hearsay.

In the absence of statutory authority, then, evidence would be required to establish that the defence statement under s 5 was issued with the accused's authority, before it could properly be said to be the *defendant's* statement. The Act contains no such authority. The issue was dealt with differently in the provisions relating to alibi evidence contained in the CJA 1967, which are repealed by the CPIA. In s 11(5) of the CJA 1967, there was a deeming provision: 'Any notice purporting to be given under this section on behalf of the defendant by his solicitor shall, unless the contrary is proved, be deemed to be given with the authority of the defendant'. In *Rossborough* (1985) 81 Cr App R 141, it was held that a notice of alibi could be proved by the prosecution as part of its case. The case may be distinguished, however, because of the deeming provision contained in the 1967 Act, which has no counterpart in the disclosure provisions of the CPIA.

Assuming that the prosecution are able to clear the hurdle of establishing the accused's authority for the s 5 statement, so that it is the defendant's statement, it is still an out-of-court statement, and they must then establish its admissibility notwithstanding its hearsay nature. One way of doing so would be to show that it was a confession. According to s 82(1) of PACE, a confession is 'any statement wholly or partly adverse to the person who made it'. In *Sat-Bhambra* (1988) 88 Cr App R 55, the Court of Appeal held that the definition was restricted to statements adverse *when made.* Hence a statement which is exculpatory when made but which later proves adverse (e.g., a false alibi) is not a confession. This would seem to exclude many defence statements made under the new disclosure scheme from falling within the definition of a confession, and hence prevent their admissibility under this route. Insofar as the defence statement makes any concession relating to the case which the prosecution have to prove, it would seem (technically) to be a confession, i.e. a statement which is partially adverse to the maker. Moreover, it would be a confession which is not caught by s 76(2) of PACE.

Even if *Sat-Bhambra* applies and the defence statement is not adverse when made, the prosecutor determined to put it in evidence could sometimes argue that it is original evidence of the defendant's state of mind (e.g., a lie).

Once the s 5 statement is established as the defendant's statement, it is clear that there are several evidential routes to admissibility. It is doubtful whether this was an intended (or an expected) consequence of defence disclosure. If the prosecution attempt to adduce the defence statement in evidence as part of their case, they may be expected to face the prospect that the judge will exercise a discretion under s 78 of PACE to exclude it on the basis that 'it would have such an adverse effect on the fairness of proceedings that the court ought not to admit it'.

8.4 SECONDARY PROSECUTION DISCLOSURE

Once the defence have served a statement, the prosecutor must disclose to the accused any previously undisclosed prosecution material 'which might be reasonably expected to assist the accused's defence as disclosed by the defence statement (s 7). If there is no such material, the prosecutor must give to the accused a statement to that effect. This obligation on the part of the prosecutor is complemented by the duty which the Code (para 8.2) places on the investigator, who is required to look again at the material retained, and draw the prosecutor's attention to any material which might reasonably be expected to assist the defence as disclosed in the defence statement. This process is termed 'secondary prosecution disclosure', and must be carried out within a time-limit to be laid down by statutory instrument or (until such a limit is set) as soon as reasonably practicable (s 13(7)). The methods of disclosure are identical to those set out in respect of primary prosecution disclosure, and the process is subject to the same exception in respect of material which the court orders should not be disclosed because it would not be in the public interest to do so (s 7(5)), or where material has been intercepted under the Interception of Communications Act 1985 (s 7(6)). The test for secondary disclosure is an objective one ('any prosecution material which might be reasonably expected . . .') and is subject to challenge by the accused and review by the court (see Paragraph 8.5).

8.5 APPLICATIONS TO THE COURT

The prosecutor may make application to the court that material should not be disclosed, either at the primary or the secondary stage, on the basis that it is not in the public interest to disclose it. For its part, the defence can under s 8 apply to the court for an order that the prosecutor should disclose material. This applies to material held or inspected by the prosecutor (s 8(3)), but also to any material which the disclosure officer must either supply to the prosecutor, or allow the prosecutor to inspect if requested (s 8(4)). Such an application may only be made, however, after the defence have served a defence statement (s 8(1)). In practice, the defence may find it difficult to mount a successful challenge to prosecution disclosure. First, the scope of any such challenge is limited to matters which were raised in the defence statement. The failure to include matters in a defence statement may not, of course, mean that the defence in question is invalid, let alone that the accused is inevitably guilty. What about the case of the defendant who is mentally ill, too drunk to remember events with any clarity, or prone to confess to crimes which he has not committed? (Judith Ward is perhaps the most memorable instance of a victim of a miscarriage of justice falling into the latter category: see *Ward* [1993] 1 WLR 619.) The restricted scope of secondary disclosure therefore necessarily limits the ability to claim that it is defective. Second, there is the problem of identifying the material which has not been disclosed. In doing this, the defence will be reliant on the good faith and efficiency of the investigator, who is charged with bringing to the prosecutor's attention the material which ought to form the basis of secondary disclosure. The investigation will in most cases be long closed, and the case passed over to the Crown Prosecution Service, so that any incentive to ferret out relevant material will be negligible. The investigator will almost inevitably have formed a firm view of the accused's guilt, and will be sceptical (at any rate at a sub-conscious level) about whether any material really does assist the defence. And the investigator is unlikely to have the legal skills (let alone the defence perspective) to be able to identify material which an advocate could turn to advantage at trial. Third, the defence will -have to satisfy the court that it has 'reasonable cause to believe':

    (a)   that 'there is prosecution material which might be reasonably expected to assist' the defence as notified; and
    (b)   that the material has not been disclosed to the accused.

The operation of s 8 is crucial to the whole disclosure scheme, for it provides the means whereby the court can monitor its operation. It is therefore important, if there is to be some corrective to the disparity of resources between prosecution and defence, that the courts should recognise the practical difficulties faced by the defence in mounting a successful challenge to what is suspected to be inadequate disclosure, and reflect that recognition in deciding upon applications for review. It is submitted that an order for disclosure should follow where there is a reasonable chance that it might assist the defence.

8.6 CONTINUOUS REVIEW

The prosecutor remains under a continuing duty to review questions of disclosure (s 9). If he at any time before the accused is acquitted or convicted forms the opinion that there is material which might undermine the prosecution case (s 9(2)), or be reasonably expected to assist the accused's defence (s 9(5)), then it must be disclosed to the accused as soon as reasonably practicable (provided that the court has not ruled against disclosure in respect of that material). This duty of continuous review would come into play, for example, where a prosecution witness gives evidence which is materially inconsistent with a statement made earlier to the police. If the defence are unaware of the statement, prosecuting counsel should disclose it to his opposite number so that he can use it in cross-examination to discredit the witness' testimony (*Clarke* (1931) 22 Cr App R 58 — although the case was many years before the CPIA, it is submitted that the principle still holds).

For its part, the court must keep under review the question of whether it is still not in the public interest to disclose material affected by its order (s 15).

8.7 PUBLIC INTEREST IMMUNITY

The prosecution duty of disclosure, whether at the primary or secondary stage, is subject to immunity where the public interest so dictates. There will be some cases where the prosecution take the view that the material should be withheld, for example, because it is so sensitive that it is subject to public interest immunity. This would be the case if the material disclosed the identity of an informer (*Marks v Beyfus* (1890) 25 QBD 494). The obvious reason for the rule is to prevent retaliation against informers, and the fear that revelation of their identity would lead to the drying up of sources of information for the police. *Marks v Beyfus* made it clear, however, that the rule may be departed from if the judge is of the opinion that the informer's name should be disclosed in order to show the defendant's innocence. The rule about police informers has been extended to observation posts used by the police (*Rankine* [1986] QB 861). The reasoning is that those members of the public who make premises available for the police to observe suspected criminals might be subject to retaliation in the same way that informers are.

Even if the Crown believes that the unused materials should be immune from disclosure, at common law that did not end the matter. The case of *Ward* [1993] 1 WLR 619 makes it clear that it is for the court, and not the prosecution, to make the final decision as to whether immunity from disclosure should be granted. Judith Ward had been convicted of multiple murder and explosives offences. The prosecution failed to disclose material relevant to her alleged confessions and certain scientific evidence. The Court of Appeal held that, if the prosecution claimed that they were entitled to withhold material documents on the basis of public interest immunity, the court must be asked to rule on the legitimacy of their claim. If the prosecution were not prepared to have the issue determined by a court, they would have to abandon the case.

Although the CPIA generally disapplies the rules of common law in relation to the prosecution duty of disclosure (s 21(1)), it preserves 'the rules of common law as to whether disclosure is in the public interest' (s 21(2)).

Public interest immunity (PII) is a thread which runs through the provisions of the CPIA. By s 3(6), primary disclosure is made subject to PII. Section 7(5) performs a similar function with regard to secondary disclosure. Section 8(5) prohibits the court from ordering disclosure where it would be contrary to the public interest. Section 9(8) places a similar limitation on the prosecution's continuing duty of review.

In addition, the Code of Practice has bearing on the question of PII, in that it compels the disclosure officer to 'list on a sensitive schedule any material which he believes it is not in the public interest to disclose, and the reason for that belief' (para 6.12). The Code gives examples of such sensitive material, which include material:

(a) relating to national security;
(b) given in confidence;
(c) relating to the identity or activities of informants or under-cover police officers;
(d) revealing the location of premises used for police surveillance;
(e) revealing surveillance techniques and other methods of detecting crime;
(f) relating to a child or young person and generated e.g. by a local authority social services department.

Crucially, inclusion on a 'sensitive' schedule is in no way conclusive of the question whether disclosure is in the public interest. That question is quite clearly one to be answered by the court, both in terms of the statutory provisions referred to above, and the common law rules which the statute preserves. The principle in *Ward* [1993] 1 WLR 619 therefore remains intact: the court, rather than the prosecutor (let alone the investigator) is the final arbiter as to whether disclosure can be avoided on the basis of PII. Further, it is clear that the categories of 'sensitive material' as spelt out in the Code are wider than the types of material which the courts have been prepared to shield behind public interest immunity. The Code gives as an example of sensitive material, 'material given in confidence'. But the fact that material has been given in confidence is not sufficient of itself to ensure that it attracts public interest immunity, so as to enable the prosecution to avoid disclosing it. It is submitted that the courts will be alive to the dangers of a category such as this. If 'sensitivity' was sufficient to attract PII, then all that a police officer would have to do in order to ensure non-disclosure would be to state that material would be treated in confidence, and such an assurance could be given even if it was not sought by the informant.

There may be certain circumstances in which the prosecution want to make an application for non-disclosure, but believe that revealing the arguments in favour of PII (or even the fact that they are making the application) would 'let the cat out of the bag', e.g., by revealing the existence of an informer and hence allowing the defendant to guess who that informant might be. The Crown Court (Criminal Procedure and Investigations Act 1996) (Disclosure) Rules 1997 and the Magistrates' Courts (Criminal Procedure and Investigations Act 1996) (Disclosure) Rules 1997 follow the procedure set out in *Davis* [1993] 1 WLR 613 governing the circumstances in which the defence must be informed of applications made for non-disclosure. The hearing can be either *inter partes* or *ex parte*, and notified to the defence or not notified, depending on the type of application made by the prosecutor. The problem with an *ex p* hearing is, of course, that there is no opportunity for the defence to argue in favour of disclosure. The court will hear only arguments from the prosecution. As a result, the *ex p* procedure was challenged in the European Court of Human Rights in *Rowe and Davis v UK* (2000) 30 EHRR 1.

The applicants, Rowe and Davis, were tried (together with Johnson) in February 1990 for murder, assault occasioning grievous bodily harm and three counts of robbery. Their appeal came before the Court of Appeal in October 1992. At the first hearing, counsel for the prosecution handed a document to the court, which was not shown to defence counsel, seeking a ruling on disclosure. He informed the court that the contents were sensitive, and that he should either be heard *ex parte* or, if *inter partes,* only on an undertaking by defence counsel not to disclose what took place to their solicitors or clients. At that hearing, defence counsel indicated that they could not conscientiously give such an undertaking, and the prosecution in effect argued *ex parte* for non-disclosure. The Court of Appeal in its judgment:

(a)   stated that the procedure relating to material in the prosecution's possession which they sought to avoid disclosing had been changed by *Ward* [1993] 1 WLR 619 — it was now for the court, not the prosecution, to decide whether disclosure should be made;
(b)   set out the procedural guidelines to be followed in such cases, as mentioned above;
(c)   refused to order disclosure.

At the hearing of the substantive appeal, the convictions of Rowe and Davis, and their co-defendant Johnson, were upheld.

In due course, the case was referred to the Criminal Cases Review Commission (see Paragraph 24.8), which investigated the case in the period 1997–1999. The investigation revealed that one of the leading prosecution witnesses was a long-standing police informant, who had approached the police and told them that the applicants Rowe and Davis were responsible for the crimes in question. He had received a reward of £10,300 and immunity from prosecution in relation to his admitted participation in the offences. He had never identified Johnson as one of the offenders. These facts had not previously been disclosed to the defence on grounds of public interest immunity. The CCRC commented that 'if the jury had been aware of this then the credibility of [the prosecution witnesses] might have been assessed in a more critical manner'. The case of the applicants and Johnson was referred back to the Court of Appeal, where their appeal was eventually upheld.

Meanwhile, the applicants sought a ruling from the European Court of Human Rights that their trial violated Art 6(1) and (3)(a) and (b) of the European Convention on Human Rights (see Paragraph 26.2.5 for the terms of those Articles).

At the hearing before the European Court of Human Rights, the applicants argued that the procedure at their trial, whereby the prosecution withheld evidence from the defence without consulting the judge, violated Art 6. This defect was not rectified by the *ex parte* procedure before the Court of Appeal, which gave the defence no opportunity to put forward arguments on disclosure. It was argued on behalf of the applicants that the exclusion of the accused from this procedure should have been counterbalanced by the introduction of a special independent counsel who could argue the relevance of the undisclosed evidence, test the strength of the prosecution claim to public interest immunity, and safeguard against the risk of judicial error or bias. A special counsel procedure has now been introduced in the UK in respect of fair employment cases in Northern Ireland, certain immigration appeals, complaints relating to the interception of electronic communications, and cases where the trial judge prohibits an accused from cross-examining in person the complainant in a sexual offence.

The following points emerge from the decision of the full European Court of Human Rights:

(a)   The right to a fair trial means that the prosecution authorities should disclose to the defence all material evidence in their possession for and against the accused.

(b)   The duty of disclosure is not absolute, and 'in any criminal proceedings there may be competing interests, such as national security or the need to protect witnesses at risk of reprisals or keep secret police methods of investigation which must be weighed against the rights of the accused'.

(c)   Only such measures restricting the rights of the defence to disclosure as are strictly necessary are permissible under Art 6(1).

(d)   Any difficulties caused to the defence by a limitation on its rights must be sufficiently counterbalanced by the procedure followed by the court.

(e)   The pre-*Ward* procedure, whereby the prosecution could decide to withhold relevant evidence without notifying the judge, was in violation of Art 6(1).

(f)   The procedure adopted by the Court of Appeal in relation to disclosure did not remedy the unfair procedure adopted at trial. It was *ex parte* and the Court of Appeal was therefore reliant upon prosecution counsel and transcripts of the trial for an understanding of the possible relevance of the undisclosed material. In any event, if the trial judge had received the material, he could have monitored the importance of the undisclosed evidence at a stage when it could have affected the course of the trial. Further, the Court of Appeal, in considering the evidence *ex post facto* may have been unconsciously influenced by the jury's verdict of guilty into underestimating the significance of the undisclosed evidence.

The applicants did not therefore get a fair trial. The case could be contrasted with that of *Edwards v UK* (1992) 15 EHRR 417. In *Edwards*, appeal proceedings were able to remedy defects in the trial because, by the time of the appeal the defence had received most of the missing information, and was able to argue in detail about the impact of the new material upon the tests for disclosure laid down in the CPIA 1996, since the trial took place at a time when the (pre-*Ward*) common law rules were in place. It is worth noting, however, that the reasoning on points (a) and (c) above points towards the wider test of materiality under *Keane* [1994] 1 WLR 747, rather than the more limited duties under the 1996 Act. Further, the requirement as far as secondary disclosure under the 1996 Act is concerned, that it is confined to previously undisclosed prosecution material 'which might be reasonably expected to assist the accused's defence as disclosed by the defence statement' (s 7(2)(a) of the CPIA 1996) does not sit easily with point (c).

The European Court's decision casts doubt upon the ability of the Court of Appeal to remedy defective disclosure at trial. What it does not do, however, is to give a clear indication as to the fairness of *ex parte* procedure, in so far as that procedure is adopted at first instance (now embodied in the Crown Court (Criminal Procedure and Investigations Act 1996) (Disclosure) Rules 1997). It would seem that the special independent counsel procedure which was put forward in argument for the applicants is likely to be canvassed again in this context, given its adoption in a number of other areas, and the reasoning of the Court in point (d) above.

8.8   SANCTIONS RELATING TO DEFENCE DISCLOSURE

Integral to the scheme of the disclosure provisions is the notion that, if the defence fail to make disclosure, the prosecution's obligation to make secondary disclosure (which is of material which may reasonably be expected to assist the defence advanced in the defence statement) will not be triggered off.

Section 11 lays down additional sanctions to which the defence will be liable if they are deficient in their duty of disclosure. They apply if the defence:

    (a)   fail to make disclosure;
    (b)   make disclosure after the deadline laid down by statutory instrument;
    (c)   set out inconsistent defences in their statement;
    (d)   put forward a defence at trial which is different from the defence statement;
    (e)   at trial adduce evidence of alibi without having given particulars of alibi in the statement;
    (f)   at trial call an alibi witness without having given details of that witness in the statement.

If any of these conditions apply then deficiencies in the defence's disclosure may be commented on by the court (or by a party with the court's leave); and the court or the jury may draw inferences from the accused's failure to disclose properly. In deciding what to do where the accused has put forward different defences, however, the court is to have regard to the extent of the difference and whether there is any justification for it. Further, an accused may not be convicted solely on the basis of an inference drawn under s 11.

In a trial on indictment, where the judge decides to allow the jury to draw an inference, this may trigger off the need for a direction in accordance with *Lucas* [1981] QB 720 (see

Burge [1996] 1 Cr App R 163 as to the circumstances in which a *Lucas* direction ought to be given). The judge would need to direct the jury to consider whether the defence statement constituted a deliberate lie, on a material issue, which was due to the realisation of guilt and the fear of the truth. As far as the final point is concerned, the admonition in *Lucas* that a lie did not equate with guilt, but might originate from a variety of causes, including the wish to bolster a just cause, is perhaps particularly apposite in the case of a defence statement which makes exaggerated claims. It is difficult to predict what inference could be drawn where the accused might have lied in order to gain a tactical advantage, let alone where the accused alleges that the falsehood originates in faulty legal advice, or an administrative error on the part of his solicitor.

In *Wheeler* [2000] All ER (D) 914, the Court of Appeal gave important guidance on the consequences where there is inconsistent defence disclosure. The defendant was charged with knowingly importing cocaine from Jamaica. He had been arrested at Gatwick when 'swallower' packages of the drug were found in his briefcase. Four further packages were found in the room where he was detained, and a further 17 packages were later excreted from his body. When interviewed he said that he did not know how many of the packages he had swallowed. He had brought them into the country out of desperation because he was being threatened by drug suppliers, to whom he owed money.

The issue at trial was whether he knew that he had been carrying the drugs. He gave evidence that he had been given the drugs to swallow at the airport in Jamaica, but had later vomited, and thought that he had vomited all the packages. He stated that he was not aware that any drugs remained in his stomach when he was stopped at Gatwick, and did not realise that he had drugs with him until the customs officers had found the drugs in his luggage. That version of events was at odds with the defence statement served by his solicitors prior to the trial, which indicated that he was aware that he was carrying drugs, but had done so under duress. When that statement was put to the defendant in cross-examination, he said that the statement was a mistake. Prosecuting counsel then suggested that he had knowingly lied about his defence. In summing up, the judge mentioned that the defendant had said that his defence statement was mistaken, but gave no specific direction to the jury about the inconsistency between it and the defendant's evidence. The defendant was convicted, and appealed. It was the appellant's case, and was accepted by his solicitors, that the defence statement did not reflect his instructions, and had not been approved by him.

The appeal was allowed. In cases where there was a conflict between the defence statement and the defendant's evidence at trial, the judge ought to give the jury a specific direction on how to approach that inconsistency. The defendant's credibility had been crucial to his case, and the conviction was unsafe in all the circumstances. A retrial was ordered.

The court made it clear that it was undesirable for solicitors to serve a defence statement without obtaining the defendant's signature as acknowledgement of its accuracy.

It seems right that the Court of Appeal should insist on clear guidance to the jury in cases where there is apparent inconsistency between the defence statement and the case run by the defence at trial. The judge needs first to make a decision as to whether the jury should be permitted to draw an inference from the inconsistency, in accordance with s 11(3)(b) of the CPIA 1996. Even where it is likely that the defendant has lied, either in the defence statement or in his evidence, then there should be a direction in accordance with *Lucas* [1981] QB 720. In the instant case, it seems that the fault did in fact lie with the solicitors in any event. The Court of Appeal made the point that it would have been wise for the judge to have accepted that, given that the conduct of the defence at trial was in accordance with the version of events given in interview.

8.9 SUMMARY TRIAL

The account in the preceding paragraphs relates to trial on indictment. As far as summary trial is concerned, the CPIA partially incorporates such proceedings into the statutory disclosure scheme, by virtue of s 1(1). The prosecution's duty of primary disclosure applies whenever the accused pleads not guilty and the court proceeds to summary trial. Once the prosecutor has complied (or purported to comply) with that duty, the accused *may* give the prosecutor and the court a defence statement (s 6). If he does so, that triggers off secondary disclosure. It also means that the court may allow comment or draw inferences from disclosure which is late, defective or inconsistent, in much the same circumstances as it may do so in a jury trial (s 11(2)). These sanctions for the defence apply also to the notification of alibi evidence (which until the CPIA has had no formal role in summary proceedings). The voluntary regime applies to summary trial, whether it is of a summary or an either-way offence or even (in the case of a juvenile) of an indictable-only offence (s 1(1)).

There are several points which call for comment. The first is that, under common law, the prosecution has a duty of disclosure in summary trial. Thus, for example, successful applications for judicial review have resulted from prosecution failure to reveal the existence of a potential witness (*Leyland Justices ex p Hawthorn* [1979] QB 283) and failure to disclose a previous inconsistent statement by a prosecution witness (*Liverpool Crown Court ex p Roberts* [1986] Crim LR 622). Because the duty is founded on what the courts have perceived to be necessary on the basis of natural justice, there is no reason to think that it does not extend to matters which would assist the defence, as well as those which undermine the prosecution, if indeed a clear distinction can be drawn between the two categories of material (as the Act attempts to do in relation to primary and secondary disclosure). The CPIA, however, purports to disapply 'the rules of common law which relate to the disclosure of material by the prosecutor' (s 21(1)). Does this mean that a defendant who does not volunteer to join the disclosure scheme applicable to summary trial is thereby shut out from the common law rights, with the result that he will have no rights to further disclosure either at common law or under statute? Leng and Taylor (*op cit* p. 12) suggest not, arguing that, while common law rules can be abolished, the principles which gave rise to them remain intact, and will fill any vacuum which statute creates with rules which will be very similar to those which were abolished. If that is right, then the defence will have the right to secondary disclosure in summary trials, without having to accept the adverse consequences of opting for defence disclosure and the adverse inferences which can be drawn if it is faulty.

Few defendants have in any event volunteered to enter the scheme. The chance that there may be some material available on secondary disclosure which the prosecution have failed to provide as part of primary disclosure must be weighed against the imposing list of sanctions available if the defence trip up in their defence statement. It is probable that most defence lawyers see the balance of advantage as lying in remaining firmly outside the statutory scheme where that is an available option.

The question of public interest immunity (PII) in summary trial is dealt with in s 14.

Where the court has made an order that material should not be disclosed because it is not in the public interest, the accused may apply at any time for the ruling to be reviewed. Section 14 does not impose upon the court an obligation to keep under continuous review any decision not to disclose on PII grounds in summary trial, however, despite the fact that s 15 does impose such an obligation upon the Crown Court in respect of trial on indictment. The difference would appear to stem from the dual role of the magistrates as triers of both fact and law, which was encountered in *South Worcester Magistrates' Court ex p Lilley* [1995] 1 WLR 1595 (and see the commentary at [1995] Crim LR 954). The problem is that, when the magistrates (in their role as triers of law) conduct a review of documents for which PII is claimed, it may appear to prejudice them in their role as triers of fact; the problem is compounded when the review is conducted *ex parte*, in the absence of the defendant and the defence lawyer. As a result, a new bench may be needed to try the case, after the old bench rules against disclosure. If that new bench were under a duty of continuous review, it would mean that it would be impossible ever to recruit a bench proof against the contamination which results from looking at the material. Hence the onus is put on the defendant to make the application, presumably inhibited by knowledge of the consequences.

8.10 THIRD PARTY DISCLOSURE

Sometimes the information which the accused needs for his defence will be in the hands of someone other than the prosecution — a 'third party' as far as the criminal case is concerned. This would be so, for example, if an alleged victim in a child abuse case had files which were in the possession of the local authority, and which the accused alleged were relevant. In such a case, the local authority would be likely to oppose disclosure in any event, on the basis of public interest immunity. But how could the accused apply for disclosure?

In some cases, the documents would have come into the possession of the police, and possibly the prosecution as well, in the course of the investigation. If so, the documents in question must be retained by the police, and fall within the CPIA disclosure regime (Code, para 5.1).

If the material remains in the hands of the third party, then the accused is obviously entitled to request it. If the third party is not prepared to hand it over, the procedure available to the accused (or anyone else seeking disclosure from a third party, but it is usually the accused who is in this position) is laid down by s 2(1) of the Criminal Procedure (Attendance of Witnesses) Act 1965, as far as Crown Court trial is concerned (for the position in the magistrates' court, see Paragraph 9.7.2). The procedure involves seeking a witness summons to compel the third party to attend with the document(s) to give evidence, and/or to produce the document(s) in advance. The person seeking the witness summons must satisfy the court that the third party:

(a) is likely to be able to give or produce material evidence in the case; and

(b) will not voluntarily attend or produce the evidence.

The application will usually be heard on notice to the person to whom the summons is directed (the third party), who may appear or be represented at the hearing. The application should be supported by an affidavit, setting out the charges, identifying the evidence or document sought, stating the grounds for believing that the third party is able to give or produce it, and the grounds for believing that it is material. At the hearing, the third party would be able to argue, for example, that there is no evidence held, or that it is not material, or that it should not be disclosed on grounds of public interest immunity (PII).

In *Brushett* [2001] Crim LR 471, the Court of Appeal considered a case where disclosure of reports held by social services departments was sought by the accused in a case of alleged sexual abuse of children. Their lordships characterised the principles governing disclosure by third parties as 'narrower' than those where the prosecution held such material. They indicated that disclosure should nevertheless be granted, for example, where there had been false accusations by the subject of the report in the past, or where there had been sexual activity with another adult.

9 Course of a Summary Trial

Subject to a limited exception introduced by the Criminal Justice Act 1988 (see Paragraph 7.5), all summary offences are tried in a magistrates' court. Offences which are indictable but triable either way (see Paragraph 1.3) are tried in a magistrates' court if, essentially, both the magistrates and the accused agree. Because the most commonly committed offences (e.g. those under the Road Traffic Act 1988) are summary, and because many accused charged with a triable either way matter elect, if given the option, to stay in the lower court, over 95 per cent of criminal cases are disposed of by the magistrates. The course of a summary trial is the same whether the offence charged is summary or triable either way. In the latter case, however, the procedure set out in the Magistrates' Courts Act 1980, ss 19–22 for determining the mode of trial must be complied with before the start of the hearing (see Chapter 7).

The conduct of a summary trial is governed principally by the Magistrates' Courts Act 1980 (MCA). Where a pre-1981 case is quoted as being relevant to the interpretation or application of a section of the 1980 Act it is a case on the equivalent earlier legislation. Notice also that the terms 'summary trial', 'trial on information' and 'trial by the magistrates' may be used interchangeably.

9.1 JURISDICTION OF A MAGISTRATES' COURT

A magistrates' court has jurisdiction to try an offence triable either way wherever it was allegedly committed: MCA, s 2(3) and (4). This is subject (a) to its being an offence in respect of which the English courts claim jurisdiction (see Paragraph 4.4.1), and (b) to the accused consenting to summary trial following the procedure for determining the mode of trial described in Chapter 7. Assuming those two conditions are met, the magistrates' jurisdiction simply depends upon the accused appearing or being brought before their court. An accused will come to court either in answer to a summons, or in answer to his bail, or in the custody of the police or of the prison authorities (see Chapter 6 for details). Even if the accused's attendance is secured by unlawful means (e.g., through the execution of a wrongfully issued warrant for arrest) the magistrates' jurisdiction is unaffected, at least if no objection is made at the time to the illegality: *Hughes* (1879) 4 QBD 614. In most cases, the prosecutor — who, in effect, takes the initial decision as to which court the proceedings shall be held in — will opt to have the accused come before the magistrates' court for the petty sessional division where the offence allegedly occurred.

Generally speaking, a magistrates' court has jurisdiction to try a summary offence only if it was allegedly committed within the county for which it acts: MCA, s 2(1). Counties are subdivided into petty sessional divisions, with a court for each division (see Paragraph 5.3), but it is not essential for jurisdictional purposes that the offence occurred within the division — it is enough that it occurred within the county. It follows that, in order to avoid several courts having to sit at weekends, a number of neighbouring courts in a county may arrange between them that suspects arrested on a Friday who have to be brought to court by the police on Saturday should all come before one particular court, which court may then remand them to appear on a weekday at the court for the division where the offence occurred: *Avon Magistrates' Court's Committee ex p Bath Law Society* [1988] QB 409. In addition, magistrates may try a summary offence committed outside their county if *either* (a) their court is already trying the accused for some other offence (MCA, s 2(6)), *or* (b) it is in the interests of justice that the accused be tried jointly with or in the same place as another person who is being proceeded against in their court (MCA, ss 1(2)(b) and 2(2)).

The advantage of restricting the magistrates' jurisdiction over summary offences basically to those committed in the locality for which they act is that local knowledge may assist in the determination of some cases (e.g., knowledge of the road where a road traffic offence allegedly occurred). The disadvantage from the accused's point of view is that contesting a charge against him may involve a long journey to court. For example, if the accused lives in Newcastle and, while on his annual holiday in Devon, allegedly commits an offence of driving without due care and attention, the case would have to be heard in a Devon magistrates' court. Assuming that the accused has returned home before the hearing date, he has the unattractive options of pleading guilty by post, being found guilty in his absence, or making a long journey to contest the charge.

> The rather complicated provisions about a magistrates' court's jurisdiction to try summary offences may be made clearer by an illustration. John Smith is driving his car in Loamshire, and Paul Brown is his passenger. Smith goes through a red traffic light. He is seen by a police officer who follows him in his police car, waiting for an opportunity to stop him. Smith's journey takes him across the county boundary into Clayshire, at which stage he realises he is being followed and accelerates rapidly, breaking the speed limit. He then decides that running away will only make matters worse, and pulls in to the side of the road. While the police officer is speaking to Smith, Brown becomes agitated and, despite the officer's request that he be silent, repeatedly interrupts the conversation and jogs the officer's arm as he tries to write in his notebook. All three possible offences (failure to comply with traffic directions and speeding against Smith, and obstructing a police constable in the execution of his duty against Brown) are summary. Even though only one of them took place in Loamshire, the Loamshire magistrates have jurisdiction to try all three. The offence of going through a red light occurred in Loamshire, so s 2(1) applies. Since they are trying Smith for that offence, the Loamshire magistrates also have jurisdiction to try him for speeding in Clayshire: s 2(6). As Brown's offence of obstructing the police officer is linked with Smith's offences, a magistrate for Loamshire can issue a summons requiring Brown to appear before the Loamshire court, s 1(2)(b), and, upon his appearing, that court can try the case: s 2(2).
>
> To avoid meritless disputes on whether an offence was committed in one county or another s 3 provides that offences committed within 500 yards of a county border and offences begun in one county and completed in another may be treated as having been committed in either of the counties concerned. Similarly, an offence committed against a person who or property which, at the time of the offence, was in a vehicle engaged on a journey through two or more counties can be dealt with in a court for any of the counties.

9.2 THE BENCH

'A magistrates' court shall not try an information summarily . . . except when composed of at least 2 justices . . .' MCA, s 121(1). The maximum number who may sit is three (r 3 of the Justices of the Peace (Size and Chairmanship of Bench) Rules 1995: SI 1995 No 971).

Usually the bench consists of three in order to avoid the risk of being equally divided as to the verdict. Except in the youth court, a district judge may and normally does sit alone: Justices of the Peace Act 1997, s 14. Where, exceptionally, a district judge sits with lay justices, he acts as their chairman. The chairman of an all lay bench will be one of the chairmen chosen at the annual elections held by the bench (see Paragraph 5.3), unless none is present in which case it will simply be the most senior magistrate.

During the course of a trial, the bench has a discretion to hear representations in chambers, i.e., in private: *Nottingham Magistrates' Court ex p K* (1996) 160 JP 201. However, the discretion must be exercised with even greater caution than applies to the equivalent procedure when seeing a judge in a trial on indictment (for the details of which, see Paragraph 18.1.3). All parties should be made aware of the hearing and be represented in chambers (except where there is an issue of public interest immunity to be heard on an *ex p* basis: see Paragraph 8.7). A contemporaneous note of proceedings should be taken, normally by the clerk, so as to have a record in the event of any future dispute.

A magistrate is disqualified from adjudicating in a particular case if *either* he has any direct pecuniary interest (however small) in the outcome *or* he has a non-pecuniary interest substantial enough to lead to a real danger of bias (*Gough* [1993] AC 646). This is one aspect of the rule of natural justice that 'nobody shall be a judge in his own cause'. The rule applies equally to civil and criminal cases, and to the Crown Court and Court of Appeal as well as to the magistrates' courts. However, it is of special importance in the context of summary proceedings as magistrates, by reason of the local nature of their jurisdiction, are far more likely to have an interest in a case than, say, a High Court judge sitting in the Crown Court. The strictness of the rule against a judge or magistrate having a pecuniary interest in the matter before the court is illustrated by the old case of *Dimes v Grand Junction Canal* (1852) 3 HL Cas 759, where decrees granted by the then Lord Chancellor in favour of a canal company were set aside when it was discovered that he owned shares therein. Nobody could seriously have suspected that the Lord Chancellor would be swayed by the thought that his shares might have risen marginally in value were he to hold in favour of the company, but even that minimal pecuniary interest disqualified him from hearing the case. As regards non-pecuniary interests, the rule is slightly less strict in that an interest does not disqualify if it is so slight that there is no 'real danger' of bias. Until recently there were grounds for thinking that a different test applied to the magistrates' court from that in force in the Crown Court (where the 'real danger' test had been authoritatively endorsed by the House of Lords). In the magistrates' court, it was thought for some time that the test was whether a fair-minded person sitting in court and knowing the relevant facts would have a reasonable suspicion that a fair trial would not be possible with the magistrate sitting (*Liverpool City Justices ex p Topping* [1983] 1 WLR 119). The matter was resolved in *Gough* by the House of Lords. The test is: Is there a real danger of bias? It follows that *Ex p Topping* no longer represents the law. The same test applies in all cases of apparent bias, whether concerned with justices, with members of other inferior tribunals, or with jurors, or with arbitrators (for application of the test to jury trial, see Paragraph 17.6.2).

In *Altrincham Justices ex p Pennington* [1975] 1 QB 549 a conviction for delivering less than the contracted weight of carrots to two state schools was quashed by the High Court because the chairman of the convicting magistrates was a co-opted member of the county council's education committee and thus had a general interest in the good running of local schools. By contrast, in *Camborne Justices ex p Pearce* [1955] 1 QB 41, a magistrates' clerk was held to be under no duty to withdraw from a case where a trader was being proceeded against by the local authority under food and drugs legislation since, even though the clerk was a local councillor, he was not a member of the health committee that had advised the prosecution.[1]

It quite often happens that a magistrate realises (perhaps after the case has started) that he knows a witness or a party, or is aware of information detrimental to the accused. In such cases, the test of whether the magistrate should sit or continue to sit is again that postulated in *Gough*. Where the charge sheets informing the magistrates of the day's business indicate that an accused is appearing in court for several unconnected matters, and he then pleads not guilty to the first charge, the knowledge that there are other charges may be sufficient to disqualify the bench from hearing the not guilty plea, but it will depend on the facts of the individual case. Thus, in *Ex p Topping* the charge sheets showed that T was appearing to be sentenced for one offence and had also been charged with a second offence. The High Court held that the magistrates should not have tried T's not guilty plea to the second matter. On the other hand, in *Weston-super-Mare Justices ex p Shaw* [1987] QB 640, where S was listed as appearing on seven charges, one of wasting police time and the remainder arising out of a quite separate 'escapade' with a motor cycle, the bench were entitled to try the first information (to which S pleaded not guilty) even though they knew of the six other allegations (which he ultimately admitted after being convicted of the first). Perhaps the vital distinction between the two cases is that in *Ex p Topping* the magistrates knew that T had already been convicted by their court of something else, whereas in *Ex p Shaw* they merely knew that S faced several charges. As a matter of administration, the clerk's office at a magistrates' court usually tries to prevent the occurrence of problems such as arose in *Ex p Topping* and *Ex p Shaw* by concealing from the magistrates due to try an accused for one offence any other charge sheets relating to unconnected offences. After the trial of the not guilty plea, the bench can be given the additional charge sheets. If the accused pleads guilty to them, he can be sentenced both for those offences and (if he was convicted) for the offence he denied. If he pleads not guilty, the magistrates would probably be well advised to avoid any suspicion of unfairness, and would therefore adjourn for a hearing by different magistrates. Ultimately, though, it is a matter for the justices' discretion, applying the *Gough* test.

Decided cases also deal with the position of a magistrate who happens to know that the accused has previous convictions (e.g. because he was a member of the court which previously convicted and sentenced him). It has been stated that it is desirable that the magistrate should withdraw but there is no rule of law to that effect: *McElligott ex p Gallagher* [1972] Crim LR 332. Indeed, in the case of a recidivist offender from a small community, it might be difficult to find a magistrate who does not know that the accused is, so to speak, a regular client. In *Downham Market Magistrates' Court ex p Nudd* [1989] RTR 169, N was convicted of various motoring offences, including failure to provide a specimen of breath. A month before, the chairman of the convicting magistrates had imposed a suspended sentence on him for threatening to kill his wife, and had seen his record, which included a conviction for drink-driving. He applied to have his conviction quashed. The Divisional Court accepted that the justices would sometimes be called on to deal with defendants whom they had dealt with before. This was inevitable where the bench was small (Downham Market's was 11 strong at the time). In view of the fact that N's

---

[1] Section 66 of the Justices of the Peace Act 1997 provides that magistrates who are members of local authorities shall not adjudicate in proceedings brought by or against their authority. However, the section does not apply to co-opted members of local authority committees or to magistrates' clerks, so the statutory proviso was irrelevant to the decisions in *Ex p Pennington* and *Ex p Pearce*.

solicitor had sent a letter to the clerk well before the hearing, however, he should have considered whether it was in the interests of justice for the chairman to sit. The convictions were quashed. Where knowledge about previous convictions has been gained as a result of adjudicating upon a bail application by the accused in the same proceedings, there is an absolute statutory rule that the magistrate must not sit for a summary trial: MCA, s 42.

Failure by a magistrate to withdraw from a case if he has a disqualifying interest will render any decision the court arrives at liable to be quashed through an application for judicial review.

> The rule that magistrates must not sit if they have a disqualifying interest entails the corollary that their names should not unnecessarily be kept secret — otherwise it may be impossible for the parties, the press or the public at large to discover that somebody was on the bench who ought not to have been. For that reason, and also on account of general considerations of the desirability of open justice, it was held in *Felixstowe Justices ex p Leigh* [1987] QB 582 that the respondent justices' practice of withholding their names from the press and even the parties was unlawful. While it may not be practicable to print the names of the adjudicating magistrates on the court lists for the day, any bona fide enquirer ought to be able to ascertain from a court clerk who they are or were. If the clerk reasonably thinks that the information is wanted for improper purposes (e.g. to threaten or harass the magistrate), he has a discretion to withhold it.

9.3 THE INFORMATION

The information plays a dual role in criminal procedure. It is the charge to which the accused pleads guilty or not guilty at the beginning of a summary trial, and also, at a much earlier stage of the proceedings, it is the justification for the issue of a summons in a case where the accused's first appearance before the magistrates is secured by that means. This Paragraph is concerned with the information's first-mentioned role, but to put the discussion into context it is necessary to recapitulate on how the information comes into being (see also Paragraphs 2.4.3 and 4.1).

An information originates in one of three ways. Either the prosecutor puts his allegation against the accused into writing, signs it and delivers it to the magistrates' court; or he goes before a magistrate or a magistrates' clerk, makes his allegation orally, and relies on the magistrate or clerk to take it down in writing in the correct form; or, if it is a police prosecution, the allegation may be written down on a charge sheet at the police station and read over to the accused. In the first case the prosecution is commenced by means of a written information, in the second case it is commenced by an oral information, and in the third case it is commenced by a charge, the charge sheet being treated as an information and delivered to the magistrates' court. Thus, whichever way an information originates, the prosecutor is responsible for its contents, save that if it is laid orally the magistrate or clerk before whom it is laid will no doubt ensure, when he takes it down in writing, that it is properly particularised (see (b) below). Also, the contents of the information are made known to the accused at a very early stage of the proceedings. If he is charged at the police station, that involves reading the charge (i.e., the information) to him, and giving him a copy of it. If a written or oral information is laid before a magistrate and a summons is issued requiring the accused to attend at the magistrates' court, the summons must be served on him and the information is set out in the summons.

The following rules about informations are of special relevance to the conduct of a summary trial:

(a)   An information may be likened to a count in an indictment. Like a count it must not charge more than one offence, although two or more separate criminal acts may be alleged in one information if the accused's conduct comprised a single activity (see *Jemmison v Priddle* [1972] 1 QB 489 and *Horrix v Malam* [1984] RTR 112 where the High Court approved single informations for, respectively, shooting two deer one after the other, and for careless driving on three different roads, the driving complained of being divided into two incidents separated by about ten minutes in time and two miles in distance and observed by two different police officers). An information which includes allegations in the alternative is valid if it is alleging different ways of committing what, on a true construction of the relevant statutory provision, is a single offence. It is invalid if it is alleging two different offences in the alternative, even if those offences are created by a single provision (see *Thompson v Knights* [1947] KB 336, where a conviction on an information for driving under the influence of drink *or* drugs contrary to what is now s 4 of the Road Traffic Act 1988 was upheld because the section creates one offence of driving when unfit which can be committed either in a drunken or a drugged condition. Contrast *Surrey Justices ex p Witherick* [1932] 1 KB 450 in which an information for driving without due care and attention or without reasonable consideration contrary to what is now s 3 of the Road Traffic Act 1988 was held invalid since under s 3 there are two separate offences, one of careless driving and a second of driving without reasonable consideration). Although the above principles are relatively easy to state, applying them to informations seems to cause even more difficulty than applying them to counts in an indictment. The High Court is asked surprisingly frequently to quash a summary conviction on the ground that the information was bad for duplicity, and in such cases their Lordships tend to draw distinctions which are so fine as to be almost invisible. Thus, in *Bristol Crown Court ex p Willets* [1985] Crim LR 219 it was held that a single information for possessing for publication for gain five different obscene video tapes contrary to s 2(1) of the Obscene Publications Act 1959 was valid since it alleged a single activity — there was no need to have a separate information for each tape. In *Ward* [1988] Crim LR 57, on the other hand, an information for possessing by way of trade 15 videotaped films in breach of copyright contrary to s 24(1) of the Copyright Act 1956 was held duplicitous. In both cases, the articles wrongfully in the accused's possession were found as a result of a single search of his premises, so it is difficult to see why in the one case the conduct amounted to a single activity and in the other it did not. Trying to reconcile all the decisions in this area of procedure is a fruitless task.

An information which is bad for duplicity can, however, be rescued even after the trial has commenced. Rule 12 of the Magistrates' Courts Rules 1981 (as amended in 1993) provides that, if the fact that the information charges more than one offence is spotted at any stage in the trial, the court shall call on the prosecutor to elect on which offence he desires the court to proceed. The other offences are then struck out, and the court proceeds to try the information afresh. Failing an election by the prosecution, the information will be dismissed. Where the accused requests an adjournment to deal with the amended information, the court must grant his request if it appears he has been unfairly prejudiced.

(b)   The contents of an information are similar to the contents of a count. Using, as far as possible, non-technical language, it must give reasonable particulars of the nature of the charge, but it need not state every element of the offence alleged. Where the offence is statutory it must refer to the statute and section contravened. It is not necessary, however, to allege specifically that the accused falls outside the ambit of any defence provided by the statute creating the offence (see r 6 of the Indictment Rules 1971 for a similar rule in relation to counts in an indictment). The main difference between an information and a count is that the former, unlike the latter, is not split into a Statement of Offence and Particulars of Offence. Below are three examples of informations:

John Smith on the 1st day of January 2002 did assault Richard Brown, a constable of the county of Barsetshire, in the execution of his duty contrary to s 89(1) of the Police Act 1996.

John Smith on the 1st day of January 2002 interfered with a motor vehicle, namely a Ford Sierra number H123 ABC, with intent to steal the said motor vehicle or take it for his own use without lawful authority or steal property within the said motor vehicle, contrary to s 9(1) of the Criminal Attempts Act 1981.

John Smith on the 1st day of January 2002 drove a motor vehicle, namely a Rolls-Royce number H100 CJE, on a road, namely Acacia Avenue, London W30, without due care and attention, contrary to s 3 of the Road Traffic Act 1988.

Rule 100 of the Magistrates' Courts Rules 1981 (SI 1981 No 552) governs the drafting of informations. Precedents are to be found in Oke's *Magisterial Formulist* and Stone's *Justices' Manual* (both Butterworths).

(c)   Two or more accused may be charged in one information with having committed an offence jointly. If so, they will nearly always be tried together, irrespective of their wishes in the matter.

(d)   Where there are two or more informations against one accused or where two or more accused are charged in separate informations, the magistrates may try the informations together if none of the parties objects. Should there be an objection (albeit only from one of several accused) there must be separate trials, unless the magistrates decide that the informations are so related to each other by time or other factors that the interests of justice will best be served by a single hearing. The interests of justice include the convenient presentation of the prosecution case as well as the minimising of any risk of injustice to the accused (see *Re Clayton* [1983] 2 AC 473, which abolished the previous inconvenient rule that a single trial of separate informations was always conditional upon all the parties agreeing, however unreasonable any objection might appear to be). Where magistrates hear submissions as to whether several informations against one accused should be tried together, and they decide against that course, they will further have to consider whether, in the light of the principles set out in *Gough* [1993] AC 646 (see Paragraph 9.2), it is appropriate for them to deal with any part of the case. They may well decide that, knowing that the accused faces other charges, there is a real danger of bias if they accept jurisdiction even in respect of one matter. They would therefore have to adjourn for all the informations to be heard in sequence by differently constituted benches.

(e)   The court may not try an information for a *summary* offence unless it was laid within six months of the offence being committed: MCA, s 127. The rule does not apply to summary trials of either-way offences, which may take place at any time, subject only to the few exceptional cases in which the statute creating an indictable offence lays down a time-limit for commencing prosecutions (see Paragraph 4.4.3). Such time-limits apply regardless of whether the proposed mode of trial would be summary or on indictment. The purpose of s 127 was succinctly expressed by May J in *Newcastle upon Tyne Justices ex p Bryce (Contractors) Ltd* [1976] 1 WLR 517, where he said that the section existed:

To ensure that summary offences are charged and tried as soon as reasonably possible after their alleged commission, so that the recollection of witnesses may still be reasonably clear, and so that there shall be no unnecessary delay in the disposal by magistrates' courts of the summary offences brought before them to be tried.

It could be argued that those considerations apply equally to summary trial of either-way offences, but Parliament no doubt considered that the graver nature of either-way offences and the fact that witnesses are likely to remember such crimes more vividly than they remember trivial summary infractions made it undesirable to extend s 127 beyond summary offences. Where the aims of the section are indirectly thwarted by tardiness between the laying of an information and the bringing of the case to court the magistrates have a discretion to prevent the prosecution calling their evidence (see Paragraph 9.4). It has even been held that there is a discretion not to issue a summons if the information, although technically within time, has been laid tardily and no explanation for the delay is given (see *Clerk to the Medway Justices ex p DHSS* [1986] Crim LR 686 where the High Court refused to order the clerk to issue a summons against X for fraud on the DHSS, the relevant facts being that, although the information was laid within the period of 12 months prescribed by s 147(3) of the Social Security Act 1973, officials of the Department had simply sat on the papers relating to X for about four months before bothering to ask for a summons).

Since the information must be laid within six months of the commission of the offence, it is necessary to pinpoint:

(i)   the date on which the offence was committed; and

(ii) the date when the information is laid.

As far as (i) is concerned, the case of *Lawrence v Ministry of Agriculture Fisheries and Food* (1992) *The Times*, 26 February 1992 illustrates the problem which may occasionally arise. L was charged with making a false statement to obtain a farm capital grant. He completed the form on 6 December 1989, it was received by the appropriate office on 15 December, and the information was laid on 12 June 1990. The justices held that the information was laid in time. On appeal, the Divisional Court upheld their decision: the offence was committed when the statement was made, and it was made when the person to whom it was made received it.

As to (ii), the question of when an information is laid arose in *Kennet Justices ex p Humphrey* [1993] Crim LR 787. H and W were charged with affray; W also faced a charge of reckless driving. The CPS decided to reduce the charges to breach of the peace and driving without due care, and wrote to the clerk to the justices to that effect, attaching copies of the reduced charges. The letter arrived at the magistrates' court within six months of the date of the alleged offences. H and W did not appear in court until after the six months had expired. The original charges were then dismissed, and the new ones preferred. H and W objected that the new informations had not been laid within six months. The Divisional Court disagreed, and dismissed their appeal. Section 127 of the MCA merely imposed a time-limit for the laying of informations — not for the first appearance of a defendant to answer a charge. The informations were laid when the prosecution informed the clerk by letter of the intention to charge H and W at a later date.

(f)   The magistrates have a discretion to allow, at any stage of the hearing, an amendment to the information. In addition, MCA, s 123 provides that defects in the form or substance of an information and variations between the allegations in it and the evidence adduced by the prosecution at the trial are not grounds for objecting to the information. Where, however, the accused has been misled by a variance between the information and the prosecution evidence he must, on application, be granted an adjournment.

Section 123 is so widely worded that, if read literally, it would enable the prosecution to support a conviction however grossly inadequate or misleading the information was. In fact, numerous cases have given a restricted meaning to the section. The cases establish that where the defect in the information, or variation between it and the evidence, is trivial, so that the accused is not prejudiced or misled by it, any conviction upon the information will stand even though the information is not amended. Mis-spellings of the accused's name or of place names provide examples of such trivial errors. In *Sandwell Justices ex p West Midland Passenger Transport Board* [1979] Crim LR 56 a variation between the evidence (that the Board had put on the road a bus with a defective rear off side tyre) and the information (which alleged that the defective tyre was the rear near side one) was stated by the High Court to be so slight that, even in the absence of the amendment which was in fact made, the conviction would have stood. The Board had always been aware of which tyre was the subject of complaint, and, indeed, brought it to court for examination. The position of the tyre on the bus was a matter of no consequence.

Where the variation between the information and the evidence is substantial, the prosecution should apply for an amendment. If they allow the amendment, the magistrates should consider whether the accused has been misled by the original information, and, if he has, they must grant him an adjournment. Failure to obtain an amendment, or failure by the magistrates to allow the accused an adjournment when he is entitled to one, will lead to any conviction being quashed. In *Wright v Nicholson* [1970] 1 WLR 142, for example, the High Court quashed W's conviction for inciting a child to commit an act of gross indecency contrary to the Indecency with Children Act 1960, s 2. The information, which was not amended, alleged that the offence occurred on 17 August 1967. The evidence of the child was vague as to when the incident happened — it could have been any time in August. W, who had called alibi evidence in respect of August 17, was convicted on the basis that he committed the offence some time in August. The information misled W, it was not amended, and it may have caused him grave injustice because, in the absence of an adjournment, he was unable to call alibi evidence for other days in August.

Amendment of the information and, if appropriate, the granting of an adjournment can remedy almost any defect in it. In *Wyllie v CPS* [1989] Crim LR 753, the Divisional Court upheld the bench's decision to allow amendment of an information from failing to supply a specimen of urine to failing to supply blood. The evidence in that case would have been the same regardless of which offence was proceeded with. Further, the Divisional Court found it significant that, faced with the amendment, the defence had not asked for an adjournment. That suggested that they had not been prejudiced. Where, however, the information is laid against the wrong person (e.g. a company secretary and not the company itself) the defect is so fundamental that even an amendment will not assist the prosecution: *City of Oxford Tramway Co. v Sankey* (1890) 54 JP 564. It is sometimes difficult to distinguish between cases where the prosecution have named the wrong accused so that their only possible remedy is to lay a fresh information against the right person (assuming that can still be done timeously) and cases where they have merely misstated the right person's name, a matter which can be cured by amendment and, if necessary, an adjournment. Thus, in *Allan v Wiseman* [1975] RTR 217, the High Court held that magistrates had power to amend an information for speeding so as to name 'Jeffrey Thomas Allan' as the accused, instead of 'Jeffrey Thomas Loach'. The latter name had been put on the information through a clerical error, but the summons issued as a result of the information had been served on Allan and he was never in any doubt that he was the person the police meant to charge. On the other hand, in *Marco (Croydon) Ltd, trading as A & J Bull Containers v Metropolitan Police* [1984] RTR 24 a conviction for leaving an unlighted skip on the road at night was quashed, the fact being that the information had originally named the defendants 'A & J Bull Ltd', a company distinct from Marco although in the same group. The magistrates had regarded the substitution of Marco's name as simply correcting an error in the description of the accused, but the High Court decided that it went beyond that. Bearing in mind that the summons had actually been served on A & J Bull Ltd and that, when defence counsel first appeared in court, he understood his corporate client to be Bull and not Marco, the amendment in truth substituted a different accused for the one originally charged, and thus was beyond the magistrates' powers.

Where an information is laid within the time limit, the magistrates may allow the information to be amended after the expiry of the time limit, provided that:

(i)   the proposed amendment arises out of substantially the same facts as gave rise to the original offence; and

(ii)   the interests of justice favour the amendment (*Scunthorpe Justices ex p M* (1998) *The Times*, 10 March 1998).

Where the relevant statute confers the authority to sign the information upon a specific person, he must sign it or the information will be invalid (see Paragraph 2.4.1 and *Norwich Justices ex p Texas Homecare Ltd* [1991] Crim LR 555).

9.4 DISCRETION NOT TO TRY AN INFORMATION

The magistrates are under a general statutory duty, imposed by MCA, s 9(2), to hear the available evidence first, and then decide whether to convict or acquit. Thus in *Birmingham Justices ex p Lamb* [1983] 1 WLR 339, the High Court criticised magistrates for (in effect) refusing the prosecution a hearing for reasons such as the triviality of the charges; the long period of time which, through no fault of the prosecution, would elapse before the cases could be heard on a contested basis, and the apparent frailty of the prosecution evidence in so far as that could be gauged from what the court had been told during the course of pre-trial remand hearings. McNeill J said:

At the end of the day, the law does not permit cases, on grounds of supposed injustice, to be dismissed out of hand without hearing any evidence. In the magistrates' court, there is no power which enables the justices to dismiss [an information] simply on the basis that it would be 'unjust to let it continue' [or that] 'the continuation of the proceedings would be prejudicial to the defendant'.

It is clear, however, that this statement is too wide in suggesting that magistrates may never dismiss an information without hearing it. A series of cases has made it clear that the general rule is subject to certain exceptions. The first is connected with the statutory rule that an information for a summary offence must be laid within six months of its commission (see MCA, s 127 and Paragraph 9.3(e)). Clearly, the purpose of this provision is to ensure that trials for summary offences, which by and large are trivial matters unlikely to remain for long in the minds of witnesses, shall take place speedily before memories have completely faded. There is, however, no statutory prohibition on the prosecution laying an information just within time, and then — whether by accident or design — being very slow in serving the summons and bringing the case to court. To prevent Parliament's intentions being thus indirectly thwarted, the High Court has recognised that magistrates do have a discretion to acquit without hearing evidence if *either* the prosecution have abused correct court procedure by deliberate delay, *or* their inefficiency has led to extreme delay which might prejudice the accused if the trial were to be allowed to proceed. The first-mentioned type of case is illustrated by *Brentford Justices ex p Wong* [1981] QB 445. Having laid an information just within the six-month period, the police prosecutor then took a further four months to serve the summons on W. Apparently, he laid the information without having decided whether or not to proceed with a prosecution, and it was only after the additional four months that he made up his mind. This amounted to a deliberate abuse of the criminal process, in that an information should be laid with the intention of serving the resultant summons on the accused as soon as reasonably possible. Therefore, the justices were entitled to dismiss the information without a hearing. An example of the second type of case — i.e. inefficiency but no deliberate abuse — is *Oxford City Justices ex p Smith* (1982) 75 Cr App R 200. The offence, driving with excess alcohol in the blood, was allegedly committed during S's last term at university, but, by the time the information was laid, he had gone down. However, he had sensibly given the police both the address of his 'digs' and his home address. Unfortunately, the prosecutions department failed to realise until some two years later that they had the home address, and it was only then that they managed to serve the summons. Since S's recollection of relevant matters might have been affected by a delay for which he was not to blame, the High Court held that the magistrates should not have allowed the prosecution to proceed. The police had been 'inefficient, unobservant or both', and the delay was so long as to be 'unconscionable'.

Furthermore, even in cases where there has not been any significant delay, the prosecution's behaviour may amount to an abuse of process (see Paragraphs 12.1.4 and 18.1.4 for consideration of this topic in the context of committal proceedings and jury trial respectively).

In *Grays Justices ex p Low* [1990] 1 QB 54 the Divisional Court held that, even though the withdrawal of an earlier summons in exchange for L agreeing to be bound over did not enable the defence to rely on autrefois acquit when fresh proceedings were brought for the same offence, the magistrates should have declined to proceed on the second summons because (a) the circumstances of the withdrawal of the first summons had not been brought to the attention of the magistrates issuing the second summons, and (b) that withdrawal, coupled with the bind-over, had involved the concurrence not just of the Crown Prosecution Service but of the first court (which had to decide whether the conditions for a bind-over were met) and L himself (who voluntarily took upon himself the risk of having his recognisance estreated if he offended during the relevant period). Apparent bad faith on the part of the prosecutor has also been held sufficient to justify dismissal without hearing. In *Sherwood v Ross* [1989] Crim LR 576 it was held that private prosecutions for theft, assault and threatening words or behaviour arising out of an incident at the prosecutor's business premises were properly stayed because, after the police had declined to prosecute, a period of six months elapsed during which there was correspondence between the solicitors for the parties mentioning only the possibility of civil proceedings. In all the circumstances, it seemed that the prosecutor had decided to institute criminal proceedings merely as a bargaining counter in the negotations over a civil settlement.

On the other hand, in *Dorchester Justices ex p DPP* [1990] RTR 369, the circumstances fell short of what was necessary for the bench to refuse properly to try the information. In that case, an ambulance driver attended court as a defence witness. He was seen talking to police officers, who were witnesses for the prosecution. The defence solicitor submitted that the police officers' evidence could have been tainted. Without hearing any evidence, the bench dismissed the information. The Crown applied for judicial review. The Divisional Court allowed the application, remitting the case to be heard by a different bench. No decision as to whether testimony would be tainted could be reached properly without hearing evidence.

See also *DPP v Gane* [1991] Crim LR 711; *Milton Keynes Justices ex p DPP* [1991] Crim LR 712. It was made clear in *Crawley Justices ex p DPP* (1991) *The Times,* 5 April 1991, that before dismissing an information as an abuse of process, the justices should hear from both prosecution and defence.

9.5   APPEARANCE OF THE ACCUSED

A major difference between summary trial and trial on indictment is that in the latter case the accused must be present to plead to the indictment, and should normally be in court throughout his trial (see Paragraph 18.5.7). Summary trials, on the other hand, may and often do take place in the accused's absence. Section 12 of the MCA permits the accused to plead guilty by post, ss 11 and 13 set out the options open to the magistrates when an accused, who has not intimated under s 12 that he wishes to plead guilty, fails to appear at the time appointed for trial.

Where the accused does appear in court, he should not be in handcuffs, unless there are reasonable grounds for apprehending violence or an attempt to escape (*Cambridge Justices ex p Peacock* [1993] Crim LR 219).

9.5.1 Proceeding in the accused's absence under s 11

If the accused does not appear at the time and place fixed for summary trial, the magistrates have a discretion to proceed in his absence: s 11(1). If they do so, a plea of not guilty to the information is entered on behalf of the accused, and the prosecution proceed to call their evidence. In the circumstances, they are unlikely to have much difficulty in proving their case, but should the evidence for any reason prove insufficient (e.g. an essential witness fails to give the evidence which was expected of him) the magistrates would be obliged to find the accused not guilty. The position is different where the accused pleads guilty by post under s 12 (see the next Paragraph). If there are several informations against an absent accused, or if several absent accused are charged in separate informations, the magistrates can dispose of the informations together if that is in the interests of justice (see *Re Clayton* [1983] 2 AC 473 and Paragraph 9.3(d)).

It would obviously be unfair to proceed without the accused if he did not know of the proceedings against him. Accordingly, if the proceedings began with the laying of an information and the issue of a summons requiring the accused to appear at court, the magistrates may not begin to try the case without him unless it is proved that the summons was served on him a reasonable time before the hearing date, or he appeared on a previous occasion in answer to the summons when the case was adjourned: s 11(2). A summons can be served by sending it through the post to the accused's last known address. Where that method of service is adopted, and the offence charged is indictable, the prosecution in order to prove service must prove that the summons actually came to the knowledge of the accused. If the offence charged is summary, proof that the summons was sent by registered letter or recorded delivery to the last known address is sufficient proof of service: Magistrates' Courts Rules 1981, r 99. That gives rise to the possibility that the prosecution may be able to prove service when the accused is, in fact, totally unaware of the summons (e.g., because the recorded delivery letter containing it was left with somebody else at the same address, and that person failed to pass it on to the accused). Section 14 accordingly provides that where proceedings commence with the issue of a summons, and the accused is tried in his absence, he may deliver to the magistrates' clerk a statutory declaration to the effect that he did not know of the summons or the proceedings until a date after the trial's commencement. The declaration should normally be delivered within 21 days of the date on which the declarant found out about the proceedings. A timeously delivered declaration makes void the summons and all subsequent proceedings, but the information remains valid so the prosecution can restart the prosecution process.

Where proceedings begin, not with the issue of a summons, but with the accused being arrested, either with or without warrant, the fact of the arrest alerts him to the charge against him. Accordingly, if he is bailed from the police station to appear at the magistrates' court but fails to do so, the magistrates can try him in his absence without any formal proof that he knows of the hearing. In fact, if the offence charged is serious enough to justify an arrest, the magistrates would be unlikely to deal with it without the accused.

Bolton Justices ex p Merna (1991) 155 JP 612 considered the position where the accused is absent, and seeks an adjournment. After M's case had been adjourned on a number of occasions, it was set down for trial, the justices indicating that if he failed to attend, they would proceed in his absence. He did not attend, but provided a medical certificate and a doctor's letter stating that he was suffering from acute anxiety and depression and was not fit to attend court. The justices refused to adjourn, and proceeded to try and convict him. M sought judicial review, which was granted, and the conviction quashed. The Divisional Court said that the magistrates should have exercised their discretion judicially. If an accused claimed to be ill with apparently responsible professional support for his claim, the court should not reject that claim without satisfying itself that it was proper to do so.

Two final points should be noticed about proceeding in the absence of the accused. First, although he can be tried summarily in his absence for an offence triable either way, he must normally be present for the hearing at which it is decided to deal with the case summarily (see Chapter 7). Second, if the magistrates, as often happens, do not try the case on the first occasion it comes into their list but adjourn it to another day, the adjourned hearing cannot proceed unless all parties have had adequate notice of the date to which the case was adjourned: s 10(2).

> Even if the magistrates have power to try the information without the accused they may choose not to do so if for example the offence alleged seems fairly serious. The court ought generally to be more reluctant to try in his absence an offender who is young, has not been placed on bail, and/or has no record of failing to appear on previous occasions (*Dewsbury Magistrates' Court ex p K* (1994) *The Times*, 16 March 1994). If there is apparently a good reason for the accused's non-appearance (e.g. the police officer in the case says that he is in hospital) the magistrates may simply adjourn, and trust that on the date the hearing is to resume the accused will be present. Should there be no satisfactory explanation for his absence, the magistrates will want to issue a warrant for his arrest. Where the accused was on bail and has failed to surrender to custody in answer to his bail, the court can issue a bench warrant: Bail Act 1976, s 7. If he is not on bail but has merely failed to appear in answer to a summons, s 13 provides that a warrant for arrest can only be issued if there is proof of service of the summons, or the case has been adjourned from a previous occasion and the accused appeared on that occasion. In the case of an accused aged 18 or over, there are additional requirements that the information must be substantiated on oath and the offence charged must be punishable with imprisonment, or that the court must propose to impose a disqualification upon the accused. In the case of a juvenile, there is a condition that the information must be substantiated on oath, or that the court proposes to impose a disqualification upon the accused. As to the requirement that the information be substantiated on oath, that involves merely calling a police officer to testify formally that the information is true to the best of his belief.

9.5.2 Pleas of guilty by post

Proceeding in the absence of the accused under MCA, s 11 has at least three disadvantages. The court's time is wasted hearing evidence which nobody is present to challenge, the prosecution witnesses are inconvenienced, and the accused has no opportunity to tell the magistrates about any mitigating circumstances which ought to reduce the penalty imposed upon him. These disadvantages are overcome by the s 12 procedure for pleading guilty by post. The procedure can only be used where the accused is summoned to appear before a magistrates' court to answer an information alleging a summary offence for which the maximum penalty does not exceed three months imprisonment. The procedure is as follows:

(a) The prosecutor serves on the accused, together with the summons, a notice explaining how he can plead guilty by post and what will happen if he does so. A form for the notice is given in the Magistrates' Courts (Forms) Rules 1981 (SI 1981 No 553). In addition, the prosecutor serves a brief statement of the facts of the alleged offence, which may either be on a separate form or printed at the bottom of the summons. The statement of facts is necessary because the accused may admit that he committed the offence alleged in the information set out in the summons but be unwilling to forgo attending court unless he knows what the prosecution will say about the manner in which he committed the offence. In place of a statement of facts, the prosecution may supply witness statement(s).

(b) The prosecutor notifies the magistrates' clerk that the documents referred to in (a) have been served.

(c) The accused, if he so wishes, notifies the clerk in writing that he wants to plead guilty without appearing before the court. With the notification, he can send a statement of any mitigating facts which he would like to be brought to the court's attention.

(d) On the day of the 'hearing', neither the defence nor the prosecution witnesses attend court. All that happens is that the clerk states that a plea of guilty by post has been received; the prosecution representative (or the clerk) recites the brief statement of facts; and the clerk reads out the letter in mitigation. The magistrates may then proceed to sentence. So that an accused pleading guilty by post can know with confidence what will and what will not be said against him, it is a strict rule that the only facts about the offence given to the court are those set out in the brief statement served with the summons.

(e) If, having given notice that he wished to plead guilty, the accused changes his mind, he may notify the clerk in writing that he wants his original notification to be withdrawn. The case is not dealt with under s 12, and the accused is entitled to attend court and plead not guilty in the usual way.

(f) The magistrates always have a discretion not to accept a plea of guilty by post. If the accused's statement of mitigating circumstances should allege facts which, if accepted, would amount to a defence to the charge it would clearly be wrong to proceed on the guilty plea. Instead, the court should adjourn the case. Notice is then given to the accused of the adjournment and the reason for it, and the case proceeds as if no notification of a guilty plea had ever been given.

Prior to the introduction of the Criminal Justice Act 1991, the procedure for pleading guilty by post was restricted to the adult magistrates court. By s 69, that Act extended the procedure to allow 16-year-olds to plead guilty by post, where a summons is issued for them to appear before a youth court. The same restrictions apply as in the adult magistrates' court, i.e., it is limited to summary offences carrying a penalty not exceeding three months' imprisonment. The procedure continues to apply to 17-year-olds, who are now covered by the youth court system.

Section 12 can still apply, by virtue of s 12A, even when the defendant does make an appearance in court. If the defendant has indicated that he wants to plead guilty by post but then appears, the court may with his consent proceed under s 12, just as if he were absent. The court is given a similar power even where the defendant has never notified it of an intention to plead guilty by post. In either event, if the s 12 procedure is used but the defendant is present, the court must give him the option of making a statement in mitigation.

A great many minor summary offences are disposed of through pleas of guilty by post. The procedure is especially well-suited to road traffic offences, as may be seen in the following example. The information laid against John Smith is that 'on the 1st day of January 2000 he drove a motor vehicle on a restricted road called The High Street, Barchester, at a speed exceeding 30 miles per hour contrary to s 89 of the Road Traffic Regulation Act 1984'. The information is set out in the summons served on Smith, but if that was all he was told about the offence he would be ill-advised to plead guilty by post as the speed at which he was driving is highly relevant to the sentence which will be imposed. The brief statement of facts served with the summons solves the problem. The statement may say that Smith drove for half a mile along the High Street at a speed which varied between 38 and 40 mph; that there was no danger to pedestrians or other road-users, and that, when stopped, he said 'Why don't you go and catch some burglars?' Smith may feel that, although not absolutely accurate, the statement of facts is substantially correct. He therefore posts to the magistrates' court a letter containing his guilty plea and a description of any mitigating circumstances (e.g. his speed was not as stated by the prosecution, but only around 33 mph, and he was anxious to get home to his wife as he had received a message that she was unwell). He must also send to the court his driving licence because speeding is an endorsable offence (i.e. particulars of the conviction will be endorsed on the licence — Road Traffic Offenders Act 1988, s 96). When the case is heard, and Smith's letter is read to the magistrates, they will take into account the mitigation he has put forward when fixing the amount of the fine he should pay.

The system of fixed penalty fines for offences such as speeding and jumping the lights (see Paragraph 4.2.3) has to some extent replaced pleas of guilty by post. However, whether or not to deal with a road traffic matter by means of a fixed penalty notice is within the discretion of the police, and officers still frequently opt for proceeding by summons (but with the option of a plea by post) if they consider that a fixed penalty would be inadequate having regard to the speed the vehicle was doing.

9.5.3   Sentencing an offender in his absence

Magistrates may not pass a custodial sentence in the absence of the offender (MCA, s 11(3)). Nor may they disqualify from driving unless *either* the offender is present *or* the case was previously adjourned for him to attend and show cause why he should not be disqualified, notice to that effect having been served on him (s 11(4)). Following conviction in the accused's absence under s 11(1), magistrates may issue a warrant for his arrest provided (i) the offence is punishable with imprisonment or they are considering disqualification, and (ii) they think it undesirable to continue in his absence having regard to the gravity of the offence (s 13(3) and (4)). The obvious reason for issuing a warrant is that they are considering a custodial sentence. If they are merely considering disqualification, they would probably adjourn once and then, should the offender not attend in response to the adjournment notice, issue a warrant. Where the s 12 plea of guilty by post procedure has been adopted, the magistrates may adjourn for the offender to attend before sentencing but they may not issue a warrant on the occasion of the first adjournment (s 13(4)). This is because it would be oppressive to arrest somebody who was initially led to believe that the offence would be dealt with in his absence without giving him the opportunity to attend voluntarily in answer to an adjournment notice.

9.5.4   Non-appearance of the prosecution

If the prosecution fail to appear at the time and place fixed for summary trial, the magistrates have a discretion either to dismiss the information or adjourn the case: MCA, s 15. If the case has been adjourned part-heard from a previous occasion, and the prosecution do not appear for the adjourned hearing, the magistrates have the additional option of proceeding in the absence of the prosecution. The evidence given for the prosecution on the previous occasion will then be the case against the accused, and in meeting that case he has the obvious advantage of not facing any prosecution challenge to his evidence or arguments.

9.6   LEGAL REPRESENTATION

Both barristers and solicitors have the right of audience in the magistrates' courts. The prosecution need not be legally represented so, for example, a private prosecutor alleging an assault by his neighbour could present the case himself. Until the introduction of the

Crown Prosecution Service, it was the practice of the police in the metropolitan area to be 'represented' by the officer in the case who thus figured in the dual role of advocate and witness. Now, however, that the conduct of police prosecutions has been taken over by the CPS, officers have lost their advocacy role. The accused may, of course, defend himself if he so wishes. Where he is not legally aided and the consequences of a conviction are unlikely to be serious, he would be well advised to save money by doing so. The clerk may assist him in presenting his case (e.g., by indicating the sort of questions he should ask in cross-examination), and an unrepresented accused sometimes seems to attract the sympathy of the bench in a way a represented one would not.

It is not the practice for the magistrates to grant persons other than the parties or their counsel or solicitor the right of audience. Occasionally, however, a party may wish to have a friend to sit by him and advise him. Traditionally such a person has been referred to as a '*McKenzie* friend' (after *McKenzie v McKenzie* [1971] P 33) although, as will be seen, that phrase has provoked judicial irritation. The status of this 'friend' was examined by the Court of Appeal in *Leicester City Justices ex p Barrow* [1991] 2 QB 260. The justices refused to allow the applicants to have the assistance of their adviser in court, during proceedings for recovery of the community charge or poll tax. The justices made liability orders against the applicants, who then sought judicial review. Their application was refused by the Divisional Court and they appealed to the Court of Appeal. The Court of Appeal emphasised that what was at issue was a party's right to reasonable assistance. The applicants had wanted their friend to assist them in court by taking notes, quietly making suggestions, and giving advice. A litigant had the right to present his own case and, in doing so, to arm himself with such assistance as he thought necessary, subject to the right of the court to intervene. It was misleading to refer in this context to a '*McKenzie* friend', since that implied a special status and a right akin to a right of audience. The right at issue here was that of a party to the case to arm himself with assistance. He did not have to seek the leave of the court to exercise that right. Nevertheless, the court should be informed of the fact that the party would have his adviser with him. Further, if the assistance was unreasonable in manner or degree, or was provided for an improper purpose or in a way inimical to the administration of justice, the court could restrict him in the use of that assistance. The justices here had erred. Their error created apparent unfairness and the potential for actual unfairness. Their order was quashed.

Where an accused (or, indeed, any party) does not physically attend at a magistrates' court, but he is legally represented for the hearing, he is for most purposes deemed to be present: MCA, s 122(2). Thus, solicitor or counsel for an absent accused may cross-examine the prosecution witnesses, call defence witnesses and, in the event of a conviction, present mitigation on behalf of his client, just as if the latter were present. Further, the presence of the legal representative prevents the issue of a warrant for arrest under s 13 of the MCA (warrant where the accused does not appear for the trial of an information — see Paragraphs 9.5.1 and 9.5.3). However, the deeming provision does not apply if the accused's personal presence is required either by statute or by the terms of his bail: s 122(3). Thus, the accused must normally be at court for committal proceedings and proceedings to determine the mode of trial for an offence triable either way (MCA, ss 4(3) and 18(2)). Also, if he has been bailed to appear and does not do so, a bench warrant may be issued for his arrest and he may subsequently be prosecuted for absconding (see Chapter 6), irrespective of whether he had a lawyer at court. It is not clear whether, in theory at least, magistrates could pass a sentence of imprisonment on an offender merely deemed to be present — in practice, it is very doubtful whether they would want to do so.

9.7 COURSE OF THE TRIAL

The course of a summary trial is, to a large extent, identical to the course of a trial on indictment (described fully in Chapters 16 to 18). The following Paragraphs will concentrate upon such differences as do exist. There is also one general distinction to be borne in mind, namely that the magistrates are judges both of questions of law and of questions of fact, whereas in the Crown Court the professional judge rules on the law and the jury decide the facts. As to the law, however, the magistrates are advised by their clerk (see Paragraph 9.9) and, in practice, usually do what he tells them.

9.7.1 The plea

A summary trial begins with the clerk putting the information to the accused. He must either plead guilty or plead not guilty. The various alternatives to a straightforward guilty or not guilty response, which are available to the defence at trials on indictment, do not apply in summary trials. In particular, it is not open to the accused to plead not guilty as charged but guilty of some other (lesser) offence. However, the prosecution could be invited to have a separate information for the lesser offence, thus allowing the accused to plead guilty to that but not guilty to the original allegation. There is no special procedure for pleading autrefois acquit or autrefois convict (see Paragraph 16.8) at summary trials, but the fact of a previous acquittal or conviction for the offence charged could be raised on an ordinary not guilty plea. Neither can one avoid pleading by claiming that one is unfit to plead, although it may be possible for the magistrates to make a hospital order under s 37(3) of the Mental Health Act 1983 without convicting the accused if there are medical reports showing him to be suffering from certain forms of mental disorder (see Paragraph 9.8).

If the accused stays silent when the information is put to him, a not guilty plea must be entered on his behalf. Where a plea is ambiguous, the magistrates should try to resolve the ambiguity, but, if they cannot, again a not guilty plea should be entered. Ambiguous pleas at summary trials are normally referred to as 'equivocal pleas'. For the extended meaning given to the term 'equivocal plea', and for the consequences of the magistrates proceeding to sentence on a plea which remains equivocal, see Paragraph 25.1.1.

Where the accused unequivocally pleads guilty, the procedure before sentence described in Chapter 20 may commence forthwith. Alternatively, the magistrates may prefer to adjourn for reports. Like a judge at the Crown Court, magistrates have a discretion to allow the accused to withdraw a guilty plea at any stage before sentence is passed (*S (an infant) v Recorder of Manchester* [1971] AC 481; *Bristol Justices ex p Sawyers* [1988] Crim LR 754 and see Paragraph 16.5).

9.7.2 Prosecution case

If the accused pleads not guilty, the prosecution have the right to an opening speech. Unless the case is particularly complicated, their representative tends to keep his remarks short since even lay magistrates are much more experienced at trying cases than jurors and do not need the kind of lengthy preliminary explanations which assist the latter. In, say, a simple road traffic matter, counsel or solicitor may dispense entirely with an opening.

After the opening (if any), the prosecution witnesses are called. The sequence of examination in chief, cross-examination, re-examination and questions from the bench is exactly the same as at a trial on indictment. The prosecution may also make use of s 9 of the Criminal Justice Act 1967 under which written statements may be read as evidence in criminal proceedings if (i) the statement contains a declaration that it is true to the best of the maker's knowledge and belief and he realises the risk of prosecution for wilful misstatements, and (ii) a copy has been served on each of the other parties and none has objected within seven days of service to the statement being read. Should a prosecution witness, in giving evidence, depart significantly from earlier statement/s of which the prosecution are aware, the defence should be informed so that they can use the inconsistencies as a basis for cross-examination (see *Liverpool Crown Court ex p Roberts* [1986] Crim LR 622 where the High Court quashed R's conviction for assaulting a police officer because his defence was that the officer had head-butted him, not vice versa, and the prosecution failed to tell the defence that the officer had earlier told his sergeant that 'he did not know what had happened but there must have been a clash of heads'). See also Paragraphs 8.6 and especially 8.9 on the prosecution duty of disclosure in summary trial.

Where the prosecution have notified the defence that they will be calling a witness, and the defence wish to have the opportunity of cross-examining that witness, the witness should be called by the prosecution even if they do not wish to examine him in chief. They can then tender the witness for cross-examination (*Wellingborough Justices ex p Francois* (1994) JP 813). In any event, ultimately the justices have a power to call a witness not called by either party: *Haringey Justices ex p DPP* [1996] QB 351.

A vexed question in respect of summary trials is how the magistrates should deal with objections to the admissibility of evidence. They are, of course, judges of both law and fact, so — at least in theory — they must rule on whether evidence should be allowed. But, in determining any objection to evidence, they will inevitably discover what the evidence is, and thus be somewhat influenced by it even if they rule it inadmissible. A more narrowly procedural problem is *when* the magistrates should decide if evidence is admissible and whether they are ever obliged to adopt the Crown Court procedure of holding a 'trial within a trial' (see Paragraph 18.3.5). The general principle is that they have an unfettered discretion as to how they deal with objections to evidence. They can rule on the objection as a preliminary point; or they can deal with it immediately before the evidence would otherwise be given in the normal course of the trial; or they can receive the disputed evidence provisionally and then decide to ignore it once all the evidence in the case has been received (see *F v Chief Constable of Kent* [1982] Crim LR 682). It followed from the decision in the last-mentioned case that the defence could not insist upon a trial within a trial even when they claimed that a confession was involuntary. If the accused wanted to testify that he was forced into confessing, he could only do so as part of the general defence case, and that exposed him to cross-examination on all matters relevant to guilt or innocence — i.e. he could not restrict his evidence to the admissibility or otherwise of his confession. The position has, however, been changed by s 76 of the Police and Criminal Evidence Act 1984 which now governs whether confessions are inadmissible as a matter of law. If the defence represent to the bench that a confession was obtained by oppression or in circumstances likely to render it unreliable, the general principle in *F v Chief Constable of Kent* does not apply and the magistrates are obliged forthwith to hold a 'trial within a trial' at which they rule on the confession's admissibility: *Liverpool Crown Court ex p R* [1988] QB 1. Unfortunately, to make matters even more complicated, it has also been held that, where the court is asked to exclude a confession as a matter of discretion (e.g., because the police breached a provision in the Codes which govern their behaviour), the usual rules on objections to evidence in magistrates' courts apply — i.e., it is up to the justices when they make their decision on the objection. The objective is to secure a trial that is fair and just to both parties. The accused will therefore in some cases be given the opportunity to exclude the evidence before giving evidence on the main issues, so as to retain his right to remain silent on the main issues. In most cases, however, the whole of the prosecution case should be heard first, including the disputed evidence, so that regard can be had to 'all the circumstances' as s 78 requires. In making its decision, the court may take account of the extent of the issues raised by the accused's evidence in the trial within a trial. A trial within a trial will be more acceptable if the issues are limited, but is less likely to be appropriate if they will be protracted, and raise questions which will need to be examined in the main trial: *Halawa v Federation Against Copyright Theft* [1995] 1 Cr App R 21. Moreover, the *time* the ruling is made still does not overcome the basic problem that, having realised what the evidence is, the magistrates will not be able to put it out of their minds even if they do exclude it.

If either the prosecution or defence wish to call a witness, but have reason to think that he might not attend court voluntarily, they should apply before trial to a magistrate or a magistrates' clerk for a summons requiring the witness to attend: MCA, s 97. If the summons is not obeyed and there appears to be no just excuse for the disobedience, the magistrates may issue a warrant for the witness's arrest, provided that they are satisfied by evidence on oath that the witness is likely to be able to give material evidence, that he has been served with the summons, and has been paid a reasonable sum to cover the costs of the court attendance. The magistrates may also adjourn the case until the witness is brought to court. In extreme cases, where a magistrate is satisfied by evidence on oath that a summons issued under s 97 is unlikely to be obeyed, he may before trial issue a warrant to arrest the witness. Section 97 may also be used for the issue of a summons where either the prosecution or the defence wants to obtain production of 'a document or thing likely to be material evidence' (see Paragraph 8.10 for the implications in relation to 'third party disclosure').

The power under s 97 is conditional on the magistrate being satisfied that the witness can give or produce material evidence. It cannot be used to conduct a 'fishing expedition', where the applicant just hopes something might turn up if the summons is granted, as opposed to showing that the person summoned actually has or can give material evidence: *Reading Justices ex p Berkshire County Council* [1996] 1 Cr App R 239. Where the document is subject to legal professional privilege which has not been waived, a summons under s 97 should not be issued to compel its production: *Derby Magistrates' Court ex p B* [1996] AC 487, HL.

9.7.3 Submission of no case

At the conclusion of the prosecution evidence, the defence may make a submission of no case to answer. The submission should be upheld if *either* there is no evidence to prove an essential element of the offence charged *or* the prosecution evidence has been so discredited as a result of cross-examination *or* is so manifestly unreliable that no reasonable tribunal could safely convict on it (see *Practice Direction (Submission of No Case)* [1962] 1 WLR 227). Thus, magistrates may take into account on a submission of no case the fact that defence cross-examination has simply led them not to believe the prosecution witnesses, whereas a Crown Court judge at the equivalent stage of a trial on indictment should not be influenced by his personal view of a witness's credibility (see Paragraph 18.4). Although this may seem anomalous, it is explained by magistrates being judges of both fact and law, whereas, at a trial on indictment, law is for the judge and facts for the jury. If a submission of no case is upheld, the accused is found not guilty and discharged. If the justices are provisionally minded to uphold the submission of no case to answer, they should call on the prosecution to address them, to avoid the possibility of injustice: *Barking and Dagenham Justices ex p DPP* (1994) 159 JP 373.

9.7.4 Defence case

Assuming there is a case to answer, the defence may but need not call evidence. Just as at a trial on indictment, the accused is a competent but not compellable witness in his own defence. If the prosecution know of a witness who can give material evidence and they do not themselves propose to call him, they are under a duty to make him available to the defence (see *Leyland Justices ex p Hawthorn* [1979] QB 283 where failure by the prosecution to tell the defence of a witness who would have testified that H's car had stayed on the left-hand side of the road, rather than crossing the centre white line and colliding with the prosecution witness's car, led to H's conviction for careless driving being quashed and see Paragraph 8.9 on disclosure in summary trials). After the defence evidence, defence counsel or solicitor has the right to a closing speech. The prosecution do not have a closing speech as such, although they may reply to any point of law raised by the defence in their closing.

As to closing speeches, the precise position is that the defence have the right to either an opening or a closing speech, and will almost always opt for the latter so as to have the advantage of the last word. Either party can apply to the magistrates to grant them a second speech. This is a matter solely within the court's discretion, but if one party obtains a second speech, the other must be given one as well. A second prosecution speech will be made before the defence closing speech. The above provisions are contained in r 13 of the Magistrates' Courts Rules.

9.7.5 Verdict

A district judge sitting alone normally announces his decision immediately after the defence closing speech. Lay magistrates nearly always retire to consider their verdict. They need not be unanimous. In the event of an even-numbered court being equally divided, the chairman has no casting vote, and it will be necessary to adjourn the case for rehearing by a differently constituted bench: *Redbridge Justices ex p Ram* (1991) 156 JP 203. One major difference between the powers of magistrates and of juries is that the former may not usually return a verdict of guilty of a lesser offence. They must either convict of the offence charged in the information or acquit. This applies even when the offence is triable either way and a jury, on an equivalently worded count in an indictment, could bring in an alternative verdict: *Lawrence v Same* [1968] 2 QB 93. Of course, as already mentioned, the prosecution may avoid the potential inconvenience of this rule by having two separate informations, one for the greater and one for the lesser offence. The magistrates may then choose on which, if either, charge to convict. Also the Road Traffic Offenders Act 1988, s 24, permits the bench, in respect of certain driving offences, to acquit of the offence charged and convict of another specified offence, e.g., where the defendant is charged with dangerous driving, the magistrates may acquit and convict him of careless driving. Further, s 12A(5) of the Theft Act 1968 constitutes another statutory exception to the general rule that magistrates do not have power to convict of a lesser offence. Thus where a defendant is charged with an aggravated offence of taking a vehicle without the owner's consent contrary to s 12A of the

1968 Act, he may be found guilty of the lesser offence of unauthorised taking of a vehicle contrary to s 12 of the Act. The specific authority for such a course of action, which is contained in s 12A(5) and is not confined to trial on indictment, overrides the general principle: *R (on the application of H) v Liverpool City Youth Court* [2001] Crim LR 487.

If, after convicting an accused, the magistrates have second thoughts about the correctness of their decision, they may direct that the case be reheard by different justices: MCA, s 142. The power is not available if the Crown Court or the High Court has determined an appeal in the case. The effect of a direction is that the conviction and any sentence subsequently imposed are nullified. The magistrates who rehear the case may, of course, convict the accused and pass whatever sentence they consider fit.

9.8   POWERS OF SENTENCING AFTER CONVICTION BY THE MAGISTRATES

The powers of the courts when sentencing offenders and the restrictions placed on the imposition of each form of sentence are dealt with in Chapters 22 and 23. This Paragraph chiefly concerns certain additional restrictions which apply when magistrates are sentencing an offender for one or more *summary* offences. Some of the points made are equally relevant to summary sentencing for offences triable either way, but to obtain a full picture of the latter topic it will be necessary to read this Paragraph in conjunction with Paragraph 11.1, which deals in detail with the maximum custodial and financial penalties that magistrates may impose for such offences. In addition, the position as far as the youth court is concerned is somewhat different (see in particular Paragraph 10.5.2).

Section 31(1) of the Magistrates' Courts Act provides that magistrates may not impose imprisonment for more than six months in respect of any one offence. This applies whether the offence is summary or triable either way. Thus, where pre-1980 legislation states that an offence created by it may be punished on summary conviction by imprisonment for a term exceeding six months, it must be understood as providing for a maximum summary penalty of six months: s 31(2). In post-1980 legislation, Parliament may expressly override s 31(1), and give magistrates power to pass a sentence of more than six months for one offence, but, as far as the author is aware, Parliament has not yet chosen to grant such powers. Subject to the above, the statute creating a summary offence sets out the term of imprisonment (if any) and/or fine which may be imposed as a maximum penalty for the offence. As a result of the Criminal Justice Act 1982, the fine will be expressed in terms of a level on a standard scale of fines (see Paragraph 23.13.1). To take a random example, s 9(3) of the Criminal Attempts Act 1981 (as amended by the 1982 Act) provides that a person who commits the offence of interfering with a motor vehicle 'shall be liable on summary conviction to imprisonment for a term not exceeding three months or to a fine of an amount not exceeding level 4 on the standard scale or to both'. Level 4 on the standard scale is at present £2,500, so the maximum penalty for an offence under s 9 of the Criminal Attempts Act is three months' imprisonment and/or a £2,500 fine (see Paragraph 23.13.1 for further detail).

When a court, be it the Crown Court or a magistrates' court, passes a sentence of imprisonment it may make the sentence take effect either after or at the same time as any other sentence of imprisonment which the offender may be serving. In the former case, the sentence is consecutive to the sentence already being served; in the latter case, it is concurrent with it. Similarly, where a court on one occasion sentences an offender to separate terms of imprisonment for two or more offences, the court can order that the terms run consecutively to or concurrently with each other. The magistrates' powers to order consecutive sentences are, however, limited in that if they sentence an offender for two or more summary offences, the aggregate sentence imposed must not exceed six months: MCA, s 133. If, therefore, magistrates convict an offender of three offences of interfering with a motor vehicle, they could sentence him to three terms of three months' imprisonment to run concurrently, or they could sentence him to three terms of two months to run consecutively, but they could not sentence him to three terms of three months to run consecutively. If an offender is convicted of one summary offence and one offence triable either way (e.g. interfering with a motor vehicle and theft of another vehicle) the magistrates are still restricted to an aggregate prison term not exceeding six months, but if they convict of two or more offences triable either way the aggregate term may exceed six months but must not exceed 12 months (see Paragraph 11.1).

There are, of course, many methods of dealing with offenders apart from imprisoning them or fining them. For example, they can be absolutely or conditionally discharged, placed on probation, ordered to attend at an attendance centre, ordered to perform community service or sent to a young offender institution. These sentencing powers and others are at the disposal of the Crown Court and magistrates' courts alike, although the availability of a sentence in any particular case will turn upon matters such as the age of the offender and whether the offence of which he has been convicted is punishable with imprisonment. Again like the Crown Court, magistrates can suspend sentences of imprisonment, but the term suspended must not exceed that which they could have imposed as an immediate sentence. Similarly, the term of any sentence of detention in a young offender institution must be within the maximum prison sentence that would be imposable were the offender aged 21.

Several of the sentences and orders mentioned above are available in the cases of some or all young persons (under the age of 18). Occasionally a young person is tried and found guilty in an adult magistrates' court, not in the youth court. When this happens the adult court's sentencing powers are very restricted, and they usually have to remit the young person to the youth court to be sentenced (see Paragraph 10.5.3 for details).

Having convicted an offender, the magistrates often feel that to sentence him properly they must learn more about him. To that end, they can adjourn for inquiries to be made (e.g. through a probation officer preparing a pre-sentence report), but the adjournment must not be for more than four weeks if the offender is remanded on bail or for more than three weeks if he is remanded in custody: MCA, s 10(3).

Section 10(3) is supplemented by two further sections, namely MCA, s 30, and s 35 of the Mental Health Act 1983. The former section provides that if magistrates trying an accused for an imprisonable offence are (a) satisfied that he 'did the act or made the omission charged' (i.e., committed the *actus reus* of the offence), and (b) are of the opinion that an inquiry should be made into his physical or mental condition to enable them to decide how to deal with him, then they must adjourn for medical reports to be prepared. If the accused is granted bail, attendance at a hospital for the preparation of the reports is made a condition of bail. The maximum period of the adjournment is again three or four weeks, depending on whether the remand is in custody or on bail. Section 35 of the Mental Health Act 1983 applies only if there is evidence from a suitably qualified doctor showing that the accused may be suffering from one or more of certain specified forms of mental disorder. The section enables the court to remand the accused to a hospital for the preparation of fuller reports on his mental condition. This is preferable to remanding him in custody, since incarceration — albeit in a prison hospital — is obviously undesirable for somebody who may be mentally disturbed. It also avoids the risk of absconding or non-cooperation in the preparation of reports which is inherent in a remand on bail.

Although remands under both s 30 of the MCA and s 35 of the Mental Health Act may, and often will, take place after the magistrates have convicted the accused, a conviction is not a pre-condition of such remands. The magistrates may make use of the sections merely upon being satisfied that the accused committed the *actus reus* of the offence. This enables the court to avoid injustices which might otherwise result through an accused at a summary trial not being able to raise the issue of unfitness to plead (see Paragraph 9.7.1). Should it appear that the accused might have mental problems such as to prevent him making a proper defence to the information, the magistrates can cause a not guilty plea to be entered on his behalf. The prosecution then call their evidence, and, if that satisfies the court that the accused committed the *actus reus,* the case may be adjourned under MCA, s 30 or Mental Health Act 1983, s 35, for the preparation of reports. Should those reports indicate that the accused is suffering from either mental illness or severe mental impairment, the magistrates may make a hospital order under s 37(3) of the Mental Health Act 1983 without completing the trial of the information, and without recording a conviction. The effect of the hospital order is that the accused is taken to hospital, and detained there for an initial period of six months, after which his discharge is dependent upon the improvement or otherwise in his mental condition. The procedure described above may be adopted even in cases where the offence charged is triable either way and the accused is too disturbed to give his consent personally to summary trial, provided he is legally represented and counsel or solicitor agrees on his behalf to the magistrates dealing with the case: *Lincoln (Kesteven) Magistrates' Court ex p O'Connor* [1983] 1 WLR 335. For further details about remands under s 35 of the Mental Health Act 1983 and hospital orders, see Paragraph 23.22.

It appears that the common law defence of insanity is available to a defendant in a summary trial where *mens rea* is in issue: *Horseferry Road Magistrates' Court ex p K* [1996] 3 WLR 68.

9.9   ROLE OF THE CLERK

The court clerk plays a major role in the conduct of summary proceedings. He is not necessarily the magistrates' clerk himself, but may be a legal adviser qualified to act as a clerk in court (see Paragraph 5.4). During the course of a hearing, the clerk's tasks include putting the information to the accused; taking a note of the evidence; helping an unrepresented accused in the presentation of his case, and advising the magistrates upon points of law or procedure as they arise. This last is probably his most important function, for, although the magistrates are the judges of both law and fact, lay magistrates do, as a matter of practice, accept their clerk's advice on matters of law. Because of the importance of his advice, it is desirable that when a point of law has to be decided during a hearing (e.g., as to the admissibility of evidence) the clerk should give his advice publicly so that the parties know what he has said. Where a clerk who was not present when legal submissions were made to the court is called by the justices to advise them, it is crucial that he hears those submissions himself, in open court, from the parties or their advocates (*Chichester Justices ex p DPP* [1994] RTR 175). Similarly, if there is a point of law which has not been argued by the parties but which the clerk feels should be brought to the magistrates' attention, he should refer to the point in open court so that the parties have an opportunity of commenting upon the matter. Even if the justices have retired to consider their decision, if their clerk refers to additional cases not cited in argument, they should return to court and invite representations from the advocates on the new cases before finally making their decision (*W v W* (1993) *The Times,* 4 June 1993).

When the magistrates retire to consider their verdict, the clerk may retire with them, but only to advise them on the law and, if they are minded to convict, on their powers of sentencing. Generally speaking, he should not join the magistrates in their retirement unless asked to do so, but, if he realises while they are 'out' that there is a point of law on which they might need assistance and about which they inadvertently failed to advise in open court, he may join them on his own initiative: *Uxbridge Justices ex p Smith* [1985] Crim LR 670. As soon as he has advised on the point of law, he should return to open court. However, in a complicated case, where the issues of fact and law are inextricably intertwined, it may be proper for him to stay with the magistrates for virtually the whole period of their retirement:

Consett Justices ex p Postal Bingo Ltd [1967] 2 QB 9. The essential point is that the clerk should neither interfere with the magistrates' decision on the facts, nor, through retiring with them when there is no good reason for doing so, put himself in a position where he might appear to be interfering with their decision. Thus, in *Stafford Justices ex p Ross* [1962] 1 WLR 456 the High Court quashed R's conviction because, during the trial, the clerk had passed a note to the magistrates in which he suggested that R's defence was implausible. Similarly, in *Guildford Justices ex p Harding* (1981) 145 JP 174 the conviction could not stand because, in a case where the law was absolutely straightforward, the clerk had retired with the magistrates to advise them on the standard of proof. The High Court appeared to regard this reason for wanting the clerk's advice as little better than a pretence.

Practice Direction (Justices: Clerk to Court) [1981] 1 WLR 1163, summarises the functions of the clerk.

10   Trial of Juveniles

A juvenile is normally tried by magistrates in a special form of magistrates' court, known as the 'youth court'. In the circumstances described below, it is either obligatory or possible for a juvenile to be tried on indictment (see Paragraph 10.1) or in the adult magistrates' court (see Paragraph 10.2). In all other cases, he must stay in the youth court, even if the offence charged is one which, if he were an adult, either could or would have to be tried on indictment.

By 'a juvenile' is meant a person who has not attained the age of 18. Juveniles are either children, who have not attained the age of 14, or young persons, who have attained the age of 14 but are not yet 18: Children and Young Persons Act 1969, s 70. For purposes of criminal procedure, children under the age of ten may be ignored as they have not yet reached the age of criminal responsibility. As far as method of trial is concerned, all persons aged 18 and over are treated in exactly the same way, and are referred to in this chapter simply as adults. However, if a person aged 18 to 20 inclusive is convicted of an offence, several methods of dealing with him are open to the courts which are not available in respect of offenders who have attained the age of 21.

Under the Criminal Justice Act 1991, what was the juvenile court was renamed the 'youth court' (s 70). In addition, the jurisdiction of the newly named youth courts was extended to 17-year-olds (s 68). Therefore, under the statutory provisions, adults are individuals aged 18 and over.

10.1   TRIAL OF JUVENILES ON INDICTMENT

Like adult accused, juveniles make their first court appearance before magistrates, even if they are ultimately tried on indictment. If a juvenile is charged by himself or with other juveniles, he will appear in the youth court; if he is charged jointly with an adult, both he and the adult will come before the adult magistrates' court. The decision on whether a juvenile is tried summarily or on indictment is taken by the magistrates, applying the relevant statutory provisions. The juvenile never has the right to elect trial on indictment. Sometimes he must go to the Crown Court, and neither he nor the magistrates have a choice in the matter; sometimes the magistrates have a choice between summary trial and committal proceedings; usually, statute decrees that the trial must be summary. In no case, however, is the juvenile able to choose, although sometimes he or his legal representatives will be asked for their views on which court would be more appropriate.

Section 24(1) of the Magistrates' Courts Act 1980 provides that a juvenile *must* be tried summarily (i.e., in the youth court or in an adult magistrates' court) unless:

(a)   he is charged with an offence of homicide; *or*

(b)   he is charged jointly with an adult who is going to be tried on indictment, and the magistrates consider that it is in the interests of justice to commit them both for trial; *or*

(c)   the magistrates consider that he could properly be sentenced under the Children and Young Persons Act 1933, s 53(2), if he were convicted on indictment, and either

(i)   he is charged with an offence carrying a maximum sentence of 14 years' imprisonment or more, or with indecent assault; or

(ii)   he is a young person (i.e., has attained the age of 14 or more), and is charged with causing death by dangerous driving or causing death by careless driving while under the influence of drink or drugs.

Each of these circumstances for trial on indictment calls for further consideration.

(a)   *Offences of homicide.*   These obviously include murder and manslaughter. Since these offences are triable only on indictment, the magistrates have no discretion as to the method of trial, but must hold committal proceedings and, if there is a case to answer, send the juvenile to the Crown Court.

(b)   *Charged jointly with an adult.*   If two or more accused are charged with having jointly committed an offence, it is, generally speaking, desirable to have them tried together (see Paragraph 14.6.1). But, the question then arises of how there can be a joint trial if an adult and a juvenile are charged with an indictable offence and the adult either must be tried on indictment or rejects the offer of summary trial but the matter is one for which a juvenile would ordinarily have to be tried summarily. To deprive the adult of his fundamental right to jury trial simply because he happens to be jointly charged with a juvenile would be unacceptable. So, Parliament has approached the problem from the opposite direction, and has given the magistrates a discretion to hold committal proceedings in respect of both accused and to send the juvenile for trial with the adult if that is in the interests of justice (MCA, s 24(2)). Usually, 'jointly charged' in this context means charged with the same offence in the same information. Exceptionally, the driver and passenger of a motor vehicle taken without consent should be regarded as jointly charged, even though there is a different information in respect of each of them: *Ex p Allgood* (1994) *The Times*, 25 November 1994. In exercising their discretion, the magistrates should balance the desirability of a joint trial against the undesirability of having youngsters put through the possibly traumatic experience of appearing in the Crown Court. The younger the juvenile and the less serious the offence charged, the more likely it is that the magistrates will decide that the interests of justice do not require the juvenile to be committed for trial. If they do so decide, the adult will go to the Crown Court by himself, and the juvenile will be asked to plead to the charge in the magistrates' court. Should he plead not guilty, the adult court has a discretion (which it will almost certainly exercise) to remit him to the youth court to be tried: MCA, s 29. If he pleads guilty, the adult court should proceed to consider sentence, but their sentencing powers in respect of juveniles are limited (see Paragraph 10.5.3), and, if those powers are not adequate to deal with the case, there will again have to be a remittal to the juvenile court. Where the juvenile is committed for trial with the adult, he may also be committed in respect of any other indictable offence which arose out of circumstances the same as or connected with the circumstances of the joint charge: MCA s 24(2). Thus, if A (aged 18) and J (aged 16) are charged with burglary, and J is charged by himself with using a cheque book stolen in the burglary to obtain property by deception, the likely course of events is that both will appear together in the adult magistrates' court. As regards A, the magistrates will go through the normal procedure to determine the mode of trial. Probably they will give him the option of summary trial, but, if he rejects it, they will have to consider whether committal proceedings are also appropriate in J's case. Since J is nearly an adult, the arguments for sending both accused to the Crown Court are strong. Assuming the prosecution can establish a prima facie case against them both in respect of the burglary, J could also be committed for trial on the deception charge, since that is linked to the joint charge. Should there not be a case to answer against A, the committal proceedings against J will be discontinued; he will be asked to plead to the two charges against him, and, if he pleads not guilty, the magistrates will be able to remit him to the youth court for trial.

(c) *Young persons at risk of a s 53(2) sentence.* When a juvenile is convicted in circumstances falling within the Powers of Criminal Courts (Sentencing) Act 2000, s 91 (see Paragraph 22.10.2 for details), the Crown Court may sentence him to detention in accordance with the Home Secretary's directions for a term not exceeding the maximum prison term imposable in the case of an offender over 21. Sentences under s 91 are only possible if there has been a conviction on indictment. Consequently, magistrates must be enabled to commit for trial where they think that the allegation is grave enough to warrant a sentence of detention, for otherwise the imposition of such a sentence will be precluded by the conviction being in the wrong court. As already mentioned, s 24 of the MCA does give them that power. It should be noted, however, that s 91 detention (as opposed to detention in a young offender institution) is in practice reserved for a small minority of very serious cases. Thus, although burglary of a dwelling and handling carry 14 years' imprisonment, a youth court will almost automatically proceed with summary trial of such a charge unless alerted to the fact that there is something quite exceptional about the circumstances that might warrant a sentence of detention under s 91 were the young person to be found guilty on indictment.

A good example of the exceptional case is *South Hackney Juvenile Court ex p RB and CB* (1983) 77 Cr App R 294. RB (aged 15) and CB (aged 14) were charged, together with six other juveniles, with conspiracy to commit burglaries. They were also charged with having participated in a few specific burglaries, although the total number of burglaries committed by the gang as a whole was 15. In the course of those burglaries some £27,000 worth of property had been stolen. Moreover, the juveniles had planned the offences with care, found places to store the stolen property and had arranged to sell it through a carefully organised distribution network. This set the case apart from the normal run of juvenile crime, and justified the juvenile court's decision to hold committal proceedings. The Divisional Court also held that the procedure adopted by the magistrates before embarking on committal proceedings — namely to hear representations from the prosecution and defence about which method of trial would be more appropriate, but not to consider evidence at that stage about the gravity of the allegations — was the correct one.

From time to time, the appellate courts have issued guidance on how the youth court ought to approach its task of deciding whether to send the young defendant for trial in the Crown Court. In *Fairhurst* (1987) Cr App R 19, the Court of Appeal said that it was not necessary that the crime 'should be one of exceptional gravity' before the magistrates should decline jurisdiction. In *Billam* (1986) 82 Cr App R 347, it was stated that a juvenile charged with rape should always be tried in the Crown Court. The reasoning process which ought to govern the youth court's decision was spelt out in *Inner London Youth Court ex p DPP* [1996] Crim LR 834, where the defendant, aged 15, was charged with causing grievous bodily harm. The prosecution case was that he had grabbed the victim, pushing her into a shop door and thrusting her head through the broken glass, whilst commenting upon how pleased he was with what he had done. The justices ruled that the case was suitable for summary trial. The prosecution, who had argued that the case should be tried on indictment in the Crown Court, appealed. The Divisional Court held that the application should be allowed, and remitted the matter for committal proceedings. Clearly the offence fell within the ambit of what is now s 91 of the Powers of Criminal Courts (Sentencing) Act 2000, since an offence under s 18 is punishable in the case of an adult with a maximum sentence of imprisonment of more than 14 years (the maximum available in the case of an adult is life imprisonment for a s 18 offence). Unless the accused was sent to the Crown Court for trial, the maximum sentence which could be imposed would be 24 months. The proper approach for the magistrates was to consider whether, if the defendant was convicted of the offence, it would be proper for the Crown Court to exercise its powers under s 91, and to sentence the defendant to a term of detention greater than the two years to which its powers would otherwise be limited. If the answer was yes, the magistrates must make it possible for such a sentence to be imposed, and they should have done so in this case. The European Court of Human Rights scrutinised the procedure for the trial of juveniles on indictment in *V v UK* (2000) 30 EHRR 121 dealt with in Paragraph 26.2.5. The analysis above must be read subject to the impact of that case, which will certainly figure in the consideration of any court deciding whether a juvenile should be tried in the Crown Court. It will also affect the statutory position as far as the compulsory trial of juveniles for offences of homicide is concerned.

As with the decision about mode of trial for an adult, so the decision as to how a juvenile should be tried is not irreversible. Having originally decided in favour of trial on indictment, the court may revert to summary trial at any stage of committal proceedings if it decides that the conditions described in sub-paragraphs (b) and (c) above are not after all satisfied (see *Brent Juvenile Court ex p S* (1991) *The Times,* 18 June 1991). Conversely, it may, up until the close of the prosecution evidence, switch from summary trial to committal proceedings (see MCA, s 25(5)–(7)). It has also been held that, where the court at a first hearing considers representations as to whether a juvenile's case should be committed for trial in view of the likelihood of a sentence of detention under s 91 and decides against that course, a differently constituted bench may not — at a subsequent hearing — reverse their colleagues' decision unless some fresh circumstance has arisen that was not before the court on the previous occasion: *Newham Juvenile Court ex p F* [1986] 1 WLR 939. In *R (K) v Leeds Youth Court* (2001) 165 JP 694, the issue was whether a fresh circumstance had arisen so as to enable the magistrates to change their minds about accepting jurisdiction. K (aged 17) was charged with robbery. He entered a not guilty plea before the youth court, once it had accepted jurisdiction. The matter subsequently came back before a differently con-stituted bench of the youth court, and the prosecution submitted that the magistrates should commit to the Crown Court. After hearing a prosecution witness, the justices determined that the trial should be discontinued, so that the matter could be heard in the Crown Court, since their powers of sentencing would be inadequate if K were convicted. K applied for judicial review, arguing that the power to change the mode of trial should only be used where there had been a change of circumstances. The Divisional Court held that the youth court was entitled to keep the trial under review and change its decision if the original decision was no longer appropriate. Circumstances justifying such a decision were likely to vary, but included a change in circumstances, and instances where new material was adduced. There would also be cases, like this one, where as the evidence unfolded, the manner in which it was presented would justify such a decision. Once it became clear to the justices that the oral testimony had put a different perspective on the bare statement of the offences, they had been entitled to exercise their powers under s 25(6). The Divisional Court was saying, in effect, that the manner in which the evidence was presented was enough. Although such an interpretation does not exactly strain the statute, its subjective character might give rise to the suspicion that the real reason why the juvenile is sent to the Crown Court is because of a change of mind, and possibly a change of composition, on the part of the bench. In the light of *V v UK* (2000) 30 EHRR 121 (see Paragraph 26.2.5), however, it is submitted that there ought to be a strong presumption in favour of trying juveniles in the youth court, and that the court's decision to change its mind and send a juvenile to the Crown Court should be firmly based upon fresh material.

> Once the decision that a juvenile should be tried on indictment has been taken, the procedure generally follows the procedure in respect of adults. Just as in the case of an adult, the committal may be with or without consideration of the evidence (MCA, s 24(1)). At the trial on indictment, the juvenile has the same rights as an adult accused (e.g. to challenge jurors), and his defence is conducted in the same way as that of an adult. The court may also order that the media shall not reveal the name, address, school or any other identifying details of the juvenile charged or any juvenile who is a witness in the case: Children and Young Persons Act 1933, s 39. Sentencing of juveniles by the Crown Court is considered in Paragraph 10.5.

In the wake of the European Court of Human Rights judgment in *V v UK*, the Lord Chief Justice issued a *Practice Direction (Crown Court: Trial of children and young persons)* which emphasised that all possible steps should be taken to assist a young defendant to understand and participate in proceedings in the Crown Court (for details see the final points made in Paragraph 26.2.5).

10.2 TRIAL OF JUVENILES IN AN ADULT MAGISTRATES' COURT

By a combination of s 46 of the Children and Young Persons Act 1933 and s 18 of the Children and Young Persons Act 1963, it is provided that a juvenile who is to be tried summarily shall be tried in a youth court unless:

    (a)   he is charged jointly with an adult; or

    (b)   he appears before the magistrates together with an adult and, although (a) above does not apply as the prosecution have chosen to charge them separately, the charge against him is that he aided and abetted commission of the offence alleged against the adult or vice versa; or

    (c)   he appears before the magistrates together with an adult, and the charge against him arises out of circumstances the same as or connected with the circumstances giving rise to the charge against the adult; or

    (d)   the adult magistrates' court began to hear the proceedings against him in the erroneous belief that he was an adult.

Where (a) above applies, the adult magistrates' court *must* try the juvenile unless the adult with whom he is jointly charged pleads guilty and he pleads not guilty, in which case the court may, and probably would, remit him to a youth court to be tried: Magistrates' Court Act 1980, s 29. According to *Ex p Allgood* (1994) *The Times*, 25 November 1994, which was decided in the context of the trial of a juvenile on indictment (see Paragraph 10.1), the driver and passenger of a motor vehicle taken without consent should be regarded as being jointly charged. Where (b) to (d) above apply the adult court merely has a discretion to hear the case if it so wishes.

Section 39 of the Children and Young Persons Act 1933 (orders restricting the reporting of the juvenile's name etc. — see Paragraph 10.1) applies to trials of juveniles in an adult magistrates' court.

The position as far as the attendance of parents or guardians is concerned is governed by s 34A of the Children and Young Persons Act 1933: see Paragraph 10.4.

10.3 TRIAL OF JUVENILES IN A YOUTH COURT

The great majority of charges against juveniles are tried in a special form of magistrates' court, known as a youth court. The magistrates for each petty sessional division must meet together every third year to appoint from amongst their number a panel of magistrates whom they consider particularly suited to dealing with juvenile cases. This is known as the youth court panel, and the magistrates who sit in the youth court for that division must be drawn from the panel: Youth Courts (Constitution) Rules 1954 (SI 1954 No 1711), rr 1 and 11. Where convenient, two or more petty sessional divisions may combine to have a single youth court panel. Also, special rules apply to the composition of youth courts in the Inner London area. A lay magistrate who has attained the age of 65 may not be a member of the panel: r 5. Vacancies occurring in the membership (e.g., through a magistrate dying or attaining the age of 65) may be filled as they arise. A district judge (magistrates' court) is a member of the youth court panel for his area by virtue of his office, even if he is over 65.

Youth courts are differentiated from the ordinary adult courts in the ways described below:

(a)   The general public are excluded from youth courts. Only the parties and their legal representatives, officers of the court (e.g., court ushers), witnesses after they have given their evidence and others directly concerned in the case, probation officers and social workers, and members of the press are allowed in: Children and Young Persons Act 1933, s 47. In addition, the court may especially authorise other persons to be present (e.g., law students). By contrast, proceedings against juveniles in the adult magistrates' courts or Crown Court are normally in open court, although there is power to clear the court whenever a juvenile is called as a witness in relation to an offence against decency or morality: Children and Young Persons Act 1933, s 37.

(b)   The bench of magistrates hearing the case must consist of no more than three magistrates, and must include a man and a woman: Youth Courts (Constitution) Rules 1954, r 12. If, through unforeseen circumstances, the members of the youth court panel available for a sitting of a youth court are all male or all female, they can waive the above rule and form a single-sex court should they not consider it expedient to adjourn. A district judge (magistrates' court), however, may sit alone in the youth court.

(c)   All witnesses in the case, whether juveniles or adults, 'promise before Almighty God to tell the truth, the whole truth' etc. instead of swearing by Almighty God that they will do so. The different form of oath for youth courts was introduced by the Children and Young Persons Act 1963, s 28. It is also used by juveniles giving evidence in other courts. If the magistrates decide that the juvenile committed the offence charged, they do not 'convict' him, but 'record a finding of guilt'. When they deal with him for the offence, they do not 'sentence' him but 'make an order upon a finding of guilt': Children and Young Persons Act 1933, s 59. The same terminology should be employed for juveniles appearing in the adult magistrates' court.

(d)   Where the juvenile is not legally represented the court may permit his parent or guardian to assist him in conducting his defence (e.g., by cross-examining prosecution witnesses on his behalf).

(e)   The media may not report the name or any other identifying details of the juvenile charged or any other juvenile involved in the proceedings: Children and Young Persons Act 1933, s 49. The prohibition may be lifted if the court thinks that to be necessary in order (a) to avoid injustice to the juvenile or (b) to apprehend a juvenile who is unlawfully at large. This power of the court in respect of a juvenile who is unlawfully at large may be exercised only on application from the DPP, in a case where the juvenile is charged with a violent or sexual offence or an offence carrying a maximum sentence of 14 years in prison or more. Thus, in the adult magistrates' courts and in the Crown Court, the juvenile's name etc. may be published unless the court makes an order to the contrary; in the youth court, the position is the opposite.

(f)   In general, the atmosphere in a youth court is more relaxed and less formal than in an adult court. The juvenile charged does not go into a dock, but sits on a chair facing the magistrates, with his parents alongside or behind him. The magistrates are usually seated behind a slightly raised table. They address the juvenile by his first name, and, when making an order upon a finding of guilt, may talk to him in a semi-informal fashion.

10.4   ATTENDANCE OF PARENTS

A juvenile defendant will normally be accompanied by his parents. The youth court (like the adult magistrates' court and the Crown Court) has the power to require the attendance of the juvenile's parents or guardians. It should require such attendance in the case of an accused aged 15 or under, unless satisfied that it would be unreasonable to do so. Where the accused is aged 16 or over, by contrast, the court *may* require a parent's attendance. It should be stressed that any element of choice is that of the court, not the parent, who is obliged to attend in the event that the court so orders.

10.5   SENTENCING POWERS OF THE COURTS DEALING WITH JUVENILES

Depending on matters such as his age, record, whether the offence of which he has been found guilty is punishable with imprisonment and what the reports on him say, a juvenile may be dealt with in the following ways: a sentence of detention under s 91 of the Powers of Criminal Courts (Sentencing) Act 2000 (PCC(S)A); a detention and training order (for those aged 12 to 17); a community rehabilitation order, community punishment order or community rehabilitation and punishment order (16 and 17 year olds only); an attendance centre order; a reparation order; a fine; a supervision order; a hospital order under s 37 of the Mental Health Act 1983; a compensation order; a bind-over; a conditional discharge, or an absolute discharge. It is also possible to order the juvenile's parent or guardian to enter into a recognisance to take proper care of him or to ensure that he complies with the requirements of a community sentence. For driving offences the court may be able to disqualify the juvenile (which in effect postpones the date at which he can lawfully acquire a licence), or order that particulars of the offence be endorsed on any licence which he subsequently obtains.

Section 150 of the PCC(S)A 2000 places the court under a duty to bind over the parents of an offender under the age of 16 if it is satisfied that it will help to prevent him from committing further offences. The court must state its reasons if it does not exercise the power. Where a juvenile offender is aged from 10 to 15 inclusive, and the court imposes a fine, it *must* order his parents to pay the fine (unless this would be unreasonable, or they cannot be found). In the case of juveniles aged 16 or 17, the parents *may* be ordered to pay

(PCC(S)A, s 137). The court must take into account the means of the person whom it orders to pay (whether parent or child), just as it must do when it fines an adult offender. The same rules apply to compensation orders.

The nature of these various sentences, and the general restrictions on their imposition, are described in Chapters 21 to 23. The following Paragraphs deal with whether a sentence may be passed, in appropriate circumstances, by any of the courts having power to deal with juveniles, or by the Crown Court only, or by the Crown Court or a youth court.

10.5.1 The Crown Court

All the sentencing options available in the cases of juveniles are at the disposal of the Crown Court. However, s 8 of the PCC(S)A 2000 provides that, except in cases of homicide, the Crown Court must remit a juvenile convicted on indictment to the youth court to be sentenced, unless satisfied that it would be undesirable to do so. In *Lewis* (1984) 6 Cr App R (S) 44, Lord Lane CJ mentioned some of the reasons which will justify a Crown Court judge in not remitting for sentence. They include the following:

(a) that the judge, having presided over the trial of a not guilty plea by the juvenile, will be better informed about the case than the youth court could hope to be;

(b) that the juvenile and an adult have both been convicted on a joint charge, and sentencing the former in the youth court and the latter in the Crown Court would entail an unacceptable risk of disparity in sentencing; and

(c) that remitting would cause delay, unnecessary duplication of proceedings and unnecessary expense.

The third argument against remitting will apply in almost every case where a juvenile is convicted on indictment, so Lord Lane in effect seems to be saying that, notwithstanding the statutory provisions, juveniles should *not* normally be sent back to the youth court for sentence. His Lordship did, however, give one example of remittal being appropriate, namely where the Crown Court judge cannot sentence forthwith because no reports on the juvenile have been prepared but he realises that he will not be available to pass sentence on the date to which the case will have to be adjourned.

10.5.2 The youth court

The youth court's powers are less extensive than those of the Crown Court in the following ways:

(a) It cannot pass a sentence of detention under s 91 of the PCC(S)A 2000. As explained in Paragraph 10.1, such sentences are only appropriate in a minority of very serious cases.

(b) The maximum fine it may impose is £1,000 in the case of a young person and £250 in the case of a child (Magistrates' Courts Act 1980, s 24(3) and (4) and s 36). However, the court is unlikely in any event to want to fine a youngster a large sum of money.

Prior to 1999, the youth court was restricted to a maximum custodial sentence of six months for a single offence or 12 months for two triable either-way offences. That meant that its custodial powers were less than those of the Crown Court on the committal of a juvenile offender for sentence (24 months). The position was changed with the introduction of the secure training order, replaced in due course by the detention and training order (see Paragraphs 22.10.4 and 22.10.5). The youth court, like the Crown Court, was given the power to pass a secure training order of 24 months in length, later to be replaced by the power to pass a detention and training order of 24 months. As a result, the power to commit certain juveniles to the Crown Court for sentence under s 37 of the Magistrates' Courts Act 1980 was repealed, since it no longer served any real purpose.

10.5.3   The adult magistrates' court

An adult magistrates' court's powers of dealing with a juvenile are very limited. It can fine him, or absolutely or conditionally discharge him, or make an order that his parents enter into a recognisance. It can also make any order which may be combined with a conditional discharge (e.g. disqualification from driving, an order that any subsequently obtained licence be endorsed, or an order ancillary to the sentence proper relating to a matter such as costs or the payment of compensation). If, in the court's opinion, the case cannot properly be dealt with by any of these methods, it must remit the juvenile to the youth court to be sentenced: Children and Young Persons Act 1969, s 7(8).

10.6   AGE LIMIT AND MODE OF TRIAL

The right of a person charged with an indictable offence to be tried on indictment depends crucially upon whether he is under or over 18 (s 68 of the Criminal Justice Act 1991 made his 18th birthday the watershed). If he is under 18, s 24 of the Magistrates' Courts Act 1980 applies, and he will usually be tried in the youth court. Even if he is tried on indictment, it will be because the magistrates decided for one reason or another that summary trial was inappropriate, not because the juvenile elected to go to the Crown Court. On the other hand, if he is 18 or over, he will — depending on whether the offence charged is triable only on indictment or triable either way — either be obliged to stand his trial on indictment or will have the option of doing so. Unfortunately, the MCA does not make it clear whether the relevant consideration is the accused's age when he first appears in court charged with the offence, or his age at some subsequent stage in the procedure. However, case law on the subject, especially the House of Lords decision in *Islington North Juvenile Court ex p Daley* [1983] 1 AC 347, does help to clarify the Act, although there are still some points of doubt. The position seems to be as follows:

(a)   If an accused is under 18 when he first appears in court charged with an indictable offence, but has attained that age by the time mode of trial is to be determined, he must be treated as an adult: *Ex p Daley* (supra). In other words, he is entitled to refuse to plead in the youth court and can elect trial on indictment. Although the point was not directly in issue in *Ex p Daley,* he could not be tried summarily for an offence triable only on indictment in the case of an adult, even if the offence is one which the youth court would have been entitled to deal with had he still been under 18 and he himself does not wish to go to the Crown Court (see *Rotherham Justices ex p Brough* [1991] Crim LR 522, the facts of which are summarised at (g) below). One confusing point about their Lordships' judgment is that, as mentioned above, it refers to the accused's age when mode of trial is determined as the crucial factor. In fact, there is no prescribed procedure in the juvenile court for deciding mode of trial — usually, the bench simply proceeds to summary trial without enquiry of any sort. Perhaps the judgment should be interpreted as meaning that, if a 'juvenile' accused celebrates his 18th birthday before the hearing at which he would otherwise be asked to plead guilty or not guilty to the charge, the clerk (who will be aware of his age from the court papers) should take the initiative and alert the magistrates to the fact that ss 18–21 of the MCA apply, rather than s 24. If the accused then elects trial on indictment (or the charge is triable only on indictment), he will no doubt be remitted to the adult magistrates' court for committal to the Crown Court.

(b)   If the accused was under 18 when he admitted or denied the charge, his being 18 by the time the youth court is ready to hear the case does not give him a right to trial on indictment (see *Lewes Juvenile Court ex p T* (1984) 149 JP 186, where T pleaded not guilty to a triable-either-way matter when 16 — the 'watershed' age being 17 at that time; the case was immediately adjourned through lack of court time, and, although he reached 17 before the date fixed for the hearing, T had to be tried in the juvenile court).

(c)   Conversely, where the youth court has accepted summary jurisdiction before the accused turns 18, it cannot commit him to the Crown Court for trial after his 18th birthday. Again, the material date is that at which mode of trial is determined: *Nottingham Justices ex p Taylor* [1992] QB 557.

(d)   The youth court does, however, have a discretion to transfer a case to the adult court where the defendant turns 18 during the course of proceedings, provided that the discretion is exercised (i) before the start of the trial or (ii) after conviction and before sentence (s 47(1) of the Crime and Disorder Act 1998). What distinguishes this option from the situation described in (c) is that the decision on transfer must take place either before the beginning or at the end of the trial process. It is also clear that it *is* a discretion, and that the youth court may well wish to retain the case, e.g., if the defendant is relatively immature.

(e)   If proceedings are begun against an accused when he is under 18, but he is 18 before they are completed, the youth court may deal with him as if he were still 17: Children and Young Persons Act 1963, s 29. The House of Lords in *Ex p Daley* apparently ignored s 29. Clearly, in the light of the decision in *Daley,* the section cannot be used to deprive an accused of his right to trial on indictment if he is 18 before he is asked to plead. The section will apply, however, where an accused admits guilt or is found guilty in the youth court when 17, but reaches 18 during an adjournment prior to sentencing. The youth court retains the right to sentence him, and could even pass a sentence which is only available in the case of juveniles (e.g., it could make a care order). What is not clear is whether s 29 entitles a youth court to proceed with the trial of an 18-year-old if he was 17 when the proceedings commenced, and is going to be tried summarily because, although he was 18 when the information was put, he either elected for summary trial or had no right to trial on indictment as the offence was summary. Normally, of course, summary trial of an 18-year-old would take place in the adult magistrates' court, but it may be that the accused's age when the proceedings commenced allows the youth court to retain jurisdiction. In practice, the kinds of problems discussed in this Paragraph can be avoided by ensuring that if an accused is approaching 18 the proceedings are expedited, and at least a plea is taken from him while he is under the crucial age.

(f)   The relevant date for sentence is the date of conviction, or in the case of a defendant who pleads guilty, the date when a plea is entered: *Starkey* [1994] Crim LR 380 (see Paragraph 22.10 for details).

(g)   It is implicit in the points discussed above that the age of the accused when he allegedly committed the offence is not the crucial factor. What if the prosecution manipulate the date of the accused's court appearance to ensure that the matter is dealt with by the court of their preference? In *Rotherham Justices ex p Brough* [1991] Crim LR 522, B was aged 16 when he was involved in a 'glassing', and charged under s 18 of the Offences against the Person Act 1861. The CPS ensured that process was issued on the day after his 17th birthday (which was the 'watershed' age at the time), so that, since he was an adult at the time when mode of trial was determined, the matter had to go to the Crown Court. B's solicitor applied to the justices for a stay on the grounds of abuse of process, claiming that the actions of the CPS were a deliberate manipulation of the situation to suit the purposes of the Crown. The bench concluded that the CPS had acted properly and without malice, and committed B to the Crown Court, on the s 18 charge. B applied to the Divisional Court for an order of certiorari, which was refused. Their lordships agreed that the conduct of the CPS was incorrect. They should have preferred the information and allowed matters to take their course. Their lordships concluded, however, that there was no misconduct on the Crown's side. The delay was just under a week. In any event, the youth court would probably have committed B to the Crown Court, so there was no prejudice. Notwithstanding this decision on the facts, however, the Divisional Court was firmly of the view that prosecutors should not manipulate the process in this way, but should allow the youth court to take the decision which the law entrusts to them.

11 Committal for Sentence

Where a defendant is convicted or pleads guilty in the magistrates' court, the magistrates will usually proceed to sentence, in accordance with the procedure detailed in Chapter 20. In doing so, however, they are limited by the restrictions on their powers of punishment. They should, of course, only have agreed to deal with an offence which is triable either way if they considered their powers of punishment adequate (see Paragraph 7.3). However, in a case where the defendant indicates, at the plea before venue procedure, that he intends to plead guilty, then the magistrates will have proceeded to sentence without considering the adequacy of their powers of punishment.

11.1 MAGISTRATES' POWERS

The magistrates' sentencing powers in respect of an offence triable either way are set out in ss 78 and 131 of the Powers of Criminal Courts (Sentencing) Act 2000 (PCC(S)A) and ss 32 and 133 of the Magistrates' Courts Act 1980 (MCA), and are as follows:

(a)   If the offence is one of those listed in Sch 1 to the MCA, the magistrates may fine the offender up to £5,000 and/or pass a sentence of up to six months' imprisonment (s 32(1)). Offences listed in Sch 1 are those for which the offence-creating provision merely specifies a maximum penalty following conviction on indictment, they being made triable either way by MCA, s 17, and Sch 1 (see Paragraph 7.1.3).

(b)   If the offence is made triable either way by the statute creating it, the maximum sentence of imprisonment the magistrates can impose is six months or the maximum laid down in the statute, whichever is the *less* (s 78 of the PCC(S)A — see also Paragraph 9.8). Conversely, the maximum fine is the *greater* of £5,000 or the sum prescribed in the statute. Thus, if a statute creating an either-way offence provides for a maximum penalty of 12 months' imprisonment and/or a fine of £1,000 on summary conviction, the actual maximum that may be imposed is six months and £5,000.

(c)   Where the magistrates sentence an offender for two or more offences triable either way, they may pass sentences of imprisonment for each offence and make the sentences run consecutively to each other (and consecutively to sentences of imprisonment passed in respect of any summary offences of which they have also convicted the offender). The aggregate term of the sentence must not, however, exceed 12 months (s 133(2)). Thus, if magistrates convict an offender of two offences of theft and one of assaulting a police constable in the execution of his duty (i.e., of two offences triable either way and one summary offence), they may sentence him to six months' imprisonment for each offence to run concurrently; or they may sentence him to four months for each offence to run consecutively, but they may not sentence him to six months for each offence to run consecutively. If the offender was convicted of only one offence of theft and one of assaulting a police constable, the aggregate term would be restricted to six months (s 133(1) and see Paragraph 9.8).

Other forms of sentence at the disposal of magistrates (e.g. community sentences) are mentioned in Paragraph 9.8.

What if the accused pleads guilty, or the magistrates agree to summary trial, and on fuller consideration the magistrates believe that their powers of punishment are inadequate? There is an escape route, in the form of committal for sentence to the Crown Court.

11.2   COMMITTAL FOR SENTENCE UNDER THE POWERS OF CRIMINAL COURTS (SENTENCING) ACT 2000, s 3

The most important of the powers to commit for sentence which the magistrates possess is that contained in PCC(S)A, s 3, which reads as follows:

(1)   Subject to subsection (4) below, this section applies where on the summary trial of an offence triable either way a person who is not less than 18 years old is convicted of the offence.

(2)   If the court is of opinion—

(a)   that the offence or the combination of the offence and one or more offences associated with it was so serious that greater punishment should be inflicted for the offence than the court has power to impose; or

(b)   in the case of a violent or sexual offence, that a custodial sentence for a term longer than the court has power to impose is necessary to protect the public from serious harm from him,

the court may, commit the offender in custody or on bail to the Crown Court for sentence in accordance with section 5(1) below.

Section 5(1) essentially provides that, following a committal for sentence under s 3, the Crown Court may deal with the offender as if he had just been convicted on indictment.

From the wording of the statute, it is apparent that there are certain limitations to the power to commit under s 3.

First, the accused must be aged 18 or more at the date of conviction. Although the statute is not explicit on the point, it is arguable that he should be aged 18 at the date when mode of trial was determined, by analogy with the cases where jurisdiction depends on age (see Paragraph 10.6 and the cases cited there, especially *Islington North Juvenile Court ex p Daley* [1983] 1 AC 347).

Secondly, the offender must have been convicted of an offence triable either way. This excludes, in this context, an offence of criminal damage where the value involved is £5,000 or less (for the special procedure on such criminal damage charges, see Paragraph 7.4).

Thirdly, the magistrates must be of the opinion that their powers of punishment are inadequate for one of the two reasons set out in s 3. Either:

(a)   the offence is so serious that greater punishment should be imposed than they are empowered to inflict; or

(b)   in the case of a violent or sexual offence, the protection of the public demands a longer term of custody than they can impose.

The reasons reflect the criteria which the court eventually passing sentence must apply in determining the length of that sentence, and are explained in more detail in that context in Paragraphs 21.2, 21.3 and 22.6.

The PCC(S)A, s 3, allows the magistrates to commit for sentence because of the limitations imposed on their power to impose a fine, as well as those relating to custody: *North Essex Justices ex p Lloyd* [2001] Crim LR 145.

In many cases, the magistrates will be considering sentence in a triable either-way case because the defendant has indicated that he intends to plead guilty during the plea before venue procedure (see Paragraph 7.3). In cases where the defendant indicates a plea of not guilty, however, the bench will have made a positive decision to accept jurisdiction after hearing representations from both prosecution and defence. As far as these latter cases are concerned, the seriousness of the offence, at least, ought to have been revealed at the time when mode of trial was determined. If the magistrates thought the offence was so serious that their powers of punishment were inadequate, they should have sent the matter to the Crown Court for trial. Exceptionally, however, there may be aspects of offence seriousness which emerge only after conviction, and which may lead the magistrates to commit to the Crown Court for sentence. These are:

(a)   where the defendant is revealed as having a record of previous convictions (the PCC(S)A 2000, s 151(1), states that 'the court may take into account any previous convictions of the offender' in determining offence seriousness: see Paragraph 21.2); or

(b)   where the defendant asks for further offences to be taken into consideration (for an explanation of this procedure see Paragraph 20.5) or;

(c)   where there are aggravating features about the offence charged, of which the magistrates were not aware when they accepted jurisdiction.

There has been some controversy about the extent to which the magistrates can, as it were, change their minds about the adequacy of their powers of punishment. That, after all, is what committal for sentence involves (other than in cases where a guilty plea was indicated). On a previous occasion the bench decided to accept jurisdiction. In order to do so, they must have concluded that their powers of punishment were adequate. By committing for sentence, they are now coming to a different conclusion. As far as categories (a) and (b) are concerned, such a change of mind seems quite legitimate. The magistrates are not supposed to know of any previous convictions, or offences which the defendant wants taken into consideration, when they decide on mode of trial.

The difficulty arises over category (c). It has been argued that aggravating features about the offence charged can justify committal for sentence only where the magistrates were not aware of them when they accepted jurisdiction. If they were aware of them, so this line of argument runs, then either they should have refused jurisdiction, or the features are not such as to justify committal for sentence. After all, the offender gave up his right to jury trial in the knowledge that the magistrates had taken the view that their powers of punishment were adequate. For the magistrates to change their minds without new information would be inequitable. This was the conclusion of the Divisional Court in *Manchester Magistrates' Court ex p Kaymanesh* [1994] Crim LR 401. K was charged with offences under the Trade Descriptions Act 1968 and the Fair Trading Act 1973. The magistrates accepted jurisdiction, a date was set for trial and K was convicted two months later. He had no previous convictions and there were no offences to be taken into consideration. The magistrates committed him to the Crown Court for sentence. This was a particularly serious decision for K, as the sentencing options on summary trial did not include custody, whereas those available after trial on indictment (and hence on committal for sentence) did. K sought to have their decision quashed. The Divisional Court held that it was wrong to allow K to be committed for sentence after he had given up his right to jury trial in the knowledge that the magistrates had decided that their powers of punishment were adequate. The magistrates' decision was quashed, Balcombe LJ stating that, if nothing further came to light after the decision to try the case summarily had been made, the magistrates should not normally commit for sentence to the Crown Court.

The court took a different view in *Sheffield Crown Court ex p DPP* (1994) 15 Cr App R (S) 768 and *Dover Justices ex p Pamment* (1994) 15 Cr App R (S) 778. In both of these cases, the Divisional Court held that the power of the magistrates to commit under the predecessor to s 3 was unfettered. Their lordships held that there was nothing unreasonable or illogical about permitting a court to form one view at the stage of deciding on summary trial, and a different view at the stage of deciding to commit for sentence. In *North Sefton Magistrates' Court ex p Marsh* (1994) 159 JP 1, the Divisional Court came down firmly in favour of a broad interpretation of the statute, and stated that *Ex p Kaymanesh* was wrongly decided. The magistrates had 'an open-textured decision' on whether to commit for sentence, which was apparently separate from their decision on mode of trial. However, the Divisional Court in both *Ex p Marsh* and *Ex p Pamment* did stress that magistrates should think carefully when deciding to accept jurisdiction because normally an accused should be able to conclude that, once jurisdiction had been accepted, he would not on the same facts be committed for sentence.

The discretion of the magistrates in relation to committal is, however, subject to a general principle of 'legitimate expectation'. If the defendant has been led to believe, expressly or by implication, that he will be sentenced by the magistrates, then he should not subsequently be committed for sentence, whether by the same or a differently constituted bench: *Nottingham Magistrates' Court ex p Davidson* [2000] 1 Cr App R (S) 167 and *Norwich Magistrates' Court ex p Elliott* [2000] 1 Cr App R (S) 152. The burden is on the defendant who asserts that his expectations were aroused to establish that they were: *Sheffield Magistrates' Court ex p Ojo* [2001] Crim LR 43. The defendant ought to have been warned of the court's power to commit, but the warning may have given the impression that the court is satisfied on the material that it has that the matter should remain in the magistrates' court unless new material emerges. If that is the case, and no such material emerges, then the defendant is entitled to expect that he will not be committed for sentence: *Wirral Magistrates' Court ex p Jermyn* [2001] Crim LR 45.

Magistrates sometimes use the phrase 'all options open' when adjourning for a pre-sentence report, in an effort to avoid arousing the expectations of the defendant. The question whether this includes the option to commit for sentence, or merely the option of a custodial sentence, arose in *Feltham Justices ex p Rees* [2001] Crim LR 47. The Divisional Court held that it must be considered in context. The court echoed the observations in *ex p Elliott* that if the justices had in mind that one of the options which they were considering was committal for sentence, they should specifically say so.

11.2.1 Committal for sentence after the plea before venue procedure

In *Warley Magistrates' Court ex p DPP* [1998] 2 Cr App R 307, the Divisional Court made the following points of guidance for magistrates deciding whether to commit for sentence as a result of the plea before venue procedure:

(a)   In deciding whether their powers of punishment were adequate, they should take into account the discount granted on a plea of guilty.

(b)   Where it was obvious that the gravity of the offence required punishment which would exceed the magistrates' powers, they should commit to the Crown Court without seeking any pre-sentence report or hearing mitigation.

(c)   The defence should, however, be allowed to make a brief submission in opposition to this course of action, and the prosecution should be allowed to reply.

(d)   If there was any dispute as to the facts which triggered off the need for a *Newton* hearing, the magistrates should proceed to hold one if the decision whether to commit for sentence might depend on the outcome of the *Newton* hearing.

(e)   Similarly, a *Newton* hearing should be held if the magistrates considered that, whatever the outcome, their powers of sentencing would be adequate.

(f)   But if they considered that, whatever the outcome, the case would have to be committed for sentence, it was clearly preferable to leave the *Newton* hearing to the Crown Court.

(See Paragraph 20.1 for details of the procedure at a *Newton* hearing.)

11.2.2   Bail on committal for sentence

A committal for sentence under PCC(S)A, s 3, may be in custody or on bail. Traditionally, it was rare for bail to be granted because by committing for sentence the magistrates have indicated that in their view, a relatively severe custodial sentence is called for.

In *Rafferty* [1998] 2 Cr App R (S) 449, the Court of Appeal dealt with the situation where the accused gives, as part of the plea before venue procedure (see Paragraph 7.3), an indication that he will plead guilty, and is then committed to the Crown Court for sentence. Their lordships stated that it would not be usual, in most such cases, to alter the position as regards bail or custody. When a person who had been on bail pleaded guilty at the plea before venue, the usual practice would be to continue bail, even if it was anticipated that a custodial sentence would be imposed by the Crown Court, unless there were good reasons for remanding the accused in custody. By the same token, an accused who had been in custody could expect to remain there if the reasons for remanding in custody were unchanged. *Rafferty* does seem to reflect concern that, unless defendants could expect a reasonable chance of bail after an indication of a guilty plea, they would adopt a tactical not guilty plea in order to postpone the evil moment.

11.2.3   Powers of the Crown Court

When magistrates commit an offender for sentence under PCC(S)A, s 3 they should commit him to the most convenient location of the Crown Court, where the case is normally listed for hearing by a circuit judge or recorder (see para 5 of Part B of *Practice Direction (Crown Court Business: Classification)* [1987] 1 WLR 1671). The professional judge should sit with two magistrates (see Paragraph 13.3). The offender is asked whether he admits that he was convicted by the magistrates and committed by them to the Crown Court for sentence. In the absence of an admission, the prosecution must call evidence to prove those facts (*Barker* [1951] 1 All ER 479), probably the evidence of a police officer who was present at the magistrates, court when the committal for sentence was made. Once the convictions and committal have been admitted or proved, the proceedings before sentence is passed are the same as those which follow a guilty plea on indictment (see Chapter 20).

When sentencing an offender who has been committed to it under s 3, the Crown Court can deal with him as if he had just been convicted of the offence(s) concerned on indictment: PCC(S)A, s 5. The maximum sentence upon a committal for sentence is consequently greater, and often much greater, than that which the magistrates have power to impose. For example, an offender convicted on indictment of theft may be sentenced to seven years' imprisonment and an unlimited fine. If he is convicted of two or more thefts, prison sentences for those offences may be made to run consecutively even if the aggregate term exceeds seven years. An offender who has been committed for sentence under s 3 in respect of offences of theft may be similarly sentenced. On the other hand, had he been sentenced by the magistrates, the maximum for one offence of theft would have been six months' imprisonment and a £5,000 fine, and the maximum prison term for several offences of theft would have been one year. Of course, the Crown Court would not in practice consider passing a sentence anywhere near the maximum it could pass for offences of theft which the magistrates considered suitable for summary trial. However, it is common for the Crown Court upon a committal for sentence to inflict punishment considerably more severe than that which the magistrates could have inflicted.

11.3 OTHER POWERS TO COMMIT FOR SENTENCE

Section 3 of the PCC(S)A 2000 contains the most important but by no means the only power to commit for sentence. Some of the other powers to commit are necessary to deal with cases where, as a result of a summary conviction, the offender is liable to be dealt with by the Crown Court in respect of a matter such as breach of probation or breach of a suspended sentence. Details will be found in Chapters 22 and 23, but it should be noted that magistrates can commit for sentence when:

(a)   they have convicted an offender of an imprisonable offence (indictable or summary) committed during the operational period of a suspended sentence of imprisonment passed by the Crown Court (PCC(S)A, s 120); or

(b)   they have convicted an offender of any offence committed during the period of a probation order or order for conditional discharge made by the Crown Court (PCC(S)A, s 13(5) and Sch 3); or

(c)   they have convicted an offender of an imprisonable offence between the date of his early release and the expiry of the full term of his sentence (PCC(S)A, s 116(3)).

Following a committal in the circumstances mentioned in (a), (b) or (c) above the Crown Court can, respectively: bring the suspended sentence into force; sentence the offender for the offence for which he was put on probation or conditionally discharged; or order that the offender be returned to prison to serve the remainder of his original sentence. The magistrates do not have jurisdiction to do any of those things.

All the powers to commit for sentence mentioned so far are primary powers in the sense that they may be exercised even though the magistrates have no other reason to commit. They are supplemented by a secondary power to commit for sentence contained in s 6 of the PCC(S)A 2000. This provides that, where magistrates have decided to commit for sentence under s 3 or any other of their primary powers, they may also commit the offender to be dealt with by the Crown Court for:

(a)   any offence of which they (the magistrates) have convicted the offender;

(b)   breach of a suspended sentence of imprisonment passed by their court or any other magistrates' court;

(c)   breach of probation or conditional discharge ordered by a magistrates' court, provided (if the order was not made by their court) they have been given permission to deal with the breach (see Paragraph 23.6 for details).

The above is subject to a minor qualification explained in the passage in small print.

When an offender has been committed under s 6, the Crown Court does *not* sentence him as if he had just been convicted on indictment, but it deals with the matter which occasioned the committal in any way the magistrates could have done had they chosen not to commit. Thus, the purpose of s 6 is not to render the offender liable to a more severe punishment, but to enable the Crown Court to deal with all matters outstanding against him in cases where, were it not for the section, the sentencing function would have to be split between the magistrates and the Crown Court. Two examples will show the usefulness of the section. O is summarily convicted of stealing from a Ford Sierra (an offence triable either way) and of interfering with an Austin Montego (a summary matter). Having heard about O's previous convictions, the magistrates decide to commit him under s 3 of the PCC(S)A in respect of the theft. They cannot commit under s 3 for interfering with the Montego, for the section only applies if there has been a conviction for an offence triable either way. Nor do any of the other primary powers of committal apply. However, it will be possible to have the Crown Court deal with both offences by committing the offence of interfering with a motor vehicle under s 6. As a second example of the operation of s 6, consider a case where O is convicted of the summary offence of assaulting a police officer in the execution of his duty. He committed the offence during the operational period of a suspended sentence of imprisonment passed by the Crown Court for an indictable offence of assault occasioning actual bodily harm. Magistrates have no power to bring into effect a suspended sentence passed by the Crown Court (see Paragraph 22.9.4). They may, however commit the offender under s 120 of the PCC(S)A 2000 with a view to the Crown Court doing what they cannot. Section 120 does not, however, entitle them to commit O to be sentenced for the offence which has put him in breach of the suspended sentence, and, since that offence is summary, s 3 is of no assistance. Again, the answer is to commit under s 6.

Section 4 of the PCC(S)A applies to the situation where the magistrates commit an accused for trial for some offences, but also have to deal with him for other related either-way offences to which he has indicated his intention to plead guilty at the plea before venue procedure (see Paragraph 7.3). Offences are related to each other in this context if they can both be tried on the same indictment. The magistrates are given the power by s 4 to commit the accused to the Crown Court for sentence for the related offences, even if they do not meet the criteria laid down in s 3 (offence seriousness or public protection — see Paragraph 11.2). Once the accused reaches the Crown Court, its powers to sentence him depend on whether:

(a)   it convicts him of one or more related offences; or

(b)   the magistrates' court in committing him for sentence under s 4 stated that it also had the power to do so under s 3.

If either of these conditions is fulfilled, the Crown Court can sentence the offender as if he had just been convicted on indictment. If they are not, the court's powers are limited to those of the magistrates.

In the great majority of cases, the offence which gives rise to the magistrates' primary power of committal (the 'relevant offence') will be indictable. If the primary committal is under s 3 of the MCA, that will inevitably be so. But, occasionally, the relevant offence is summary (e.g., when a summary conviction puts the offender in breach of a suspended sentence passed by the Crown Court in dealing with an appeal from the magistrates against conviction or sentence for a summary offence). In such cases, the power to commit under s 6 is more restricted than when the relevant offence is indictable. The magistrates are only able to commit in respect of (a) breach of a magistrates' court suspended sentence, and (b) any imprisonable or endorsable offences of which they have convicted the offender.

12 Committal for Trial, and the Alternatives

Trial on indictment always takes place in the Crown Court. However, most trials on indictment are preceded by preliminary proceedings in a magistrates' court. These proceedings must not be confused with the trial itself.

In certain circumstances, a case can be sent for trial on indictment in the Crown Court without the necessity for any preliminary proceedings in the magistrates' court. This may happen following the preferment of a bill of indictment by a High Court judge (for details see Paragraph 12.6) or the serving of a notice of transfer (see Paragraph 12.7). A major change to the system of committals took place as a result of the implementation of s 51 of the Crime and Disorder Act 1998. This provision lays down that indictable-only offences must be sent directly to the Crown Court, without holding any committal proceedings. It is examined in more detail in Paragraph 12.8.

Where the magistrates *do* have to decide whether an accused should face trial on indictment, that decision usually takes the form of committal proceedings. Historically, the function of committal proceedings has been to decide whether the evidence before the examining justices (as the magistrates are called in such proceedings) raises a prima facie case that the accused has committed an indictable offence. If so, the examining justices commit (i.e., send) the accused to the Crown Court to be tried for that offence. If not, the accused is discharged. By a prima facie case is meant evidence on which a reasonable jury *could* convict the accused. This explains the statement made above that the justices are not, strictly speaking, concerned with whether they would want to convict on the evidence. In many cases, an examining justice might say to himself — 'I do not find the prosecution evidence convincing' — but, unless that evidence is so poor and unconvincing that no reasonable jury could convict on it, he is under a duty to commit the accused for trial. To put the same point yet another way, the standard of proof that the prosecution has to satisfy at committal proceedings is a very low one. For that reason most (though by no means all) committal proceedings end in the accused being sent for trial. (Committal proceedings are dealt with in detail in Paragraphs 12.1 to 12.5.)

The Criminal Justice Act 1987 introduced a new procedure to replace committal in serious fraud cases. This was the notice of transfer system, which reduced delay by eliminating the need to hear oral evidence (see Paragraph 12.7.1). The Criminal Justice Act 1991 extended a similar procedure to cases involving child witnesses. The aim here was to protect children from the trauma of giving evidence at committal (see Paragraph 12.7.2).

The procedures prior to the decision to commit to the Crown Court are described in detail in Chapter 2, but it may be helpful to summarise what occurs in a typical case before that point. The accused is arrested without warrant by a police officer and is taken to a police station. There, he is questioned under caution, and, when the investigating officers consider that they have sufficient evidence, he is charged with the offence. At that stage he is either released on bail under a duty to attend the magistrates' court at a stated time to answer the charge, or he is kept in custody at the police station and brought before the magistrates as soon as reasonably possible. On the occasion of the first court appearance neither prosecution nor defence is likely to have its case prepared, so the matter has to be adjourned. The magistrates either grant the accused bail or remand him in custody. The period of the adjournment is used by the accused to instruct his solicitors and possibly obtain representation from the Criminal Defence Service, and by the prosecution to take all necessary statements and, if the offence is triable either way, to prepare advance information for the defence (see Paragraph 7.2). The time between first court appearance and committal may be as short as a couple of weeks, or as long as several months, depending on the complexity of the case and whether the police have further enquiries to make.

12.1 THE TWO TYPES OF COMMITTAL PROCEEDINGS

Prior to 1967 the examining justices always considered the evidence put forward at committal proceedings so as to decide whether or not there was a prima facie case against the accused on which they should commit for trial. However, this led to waste of the court's time and unnecessary inconvenience for witnesses in cases where the defence conceded that there would have to be a committal. Accordingly, s 1 of the Criminal Justice Act 1967 introduced an alternative procedure by which the examining justices could, in certain circumstances, commit the accused for trial without considering the evidence against him. Section 1 of the 1967 Act was re-enacted in s 6(2) of the Magistrates' Courts Act 1980. Committals with consideration of the evidence are dealt with in s 6(1) of the Magistrates' Courts Act. Most committals then took place under s 6(2), i.e., without consideration of the evidence. Pressure continued during the 1980s and early 1990s for the role of committals to be reduced further. The Royal Commission on Criminal Justice, chaired by Lord Runciman, said in its report (Cm 2263, 1993) that more efficient ways should be found of weeding out the weak cases before they went to trial in the Crown Court. The Commission estimated that some 93 per cent of cases were committed to the Crown Court by the ritualistic formality of a 'paper committal' under MCA, s 6(2). The remaining 7 per cent went up to the Crown Court by way of s 6(1), but the Commission was even less impressed by the operation of this procedure, although for different reasons. The full committal was criticised for the amount of court time which it wasted (including the outdated requirement for the clerk to transcribe the depositions of witnesses), and for the pressure to which witnesses were subjected by being compelled to give their evidence twice over.

As a result of the complaints about the committal system, the government introduced, in the Criminal Justice and Public Order Act 1994, a system called 'transfer for trial', which was purely administrative rather than judicial. The transfer for trial system under the 1994 Act bore only a passing resemblance to the 'notice of transfer' system described in the preceding Paragraph, despite the confusing similarity of terminology. In any event, it was widely perceived by practitioners as a bureaucratic nightmare, and was consigned to oblivion without ever being brought into force. In the Criminal Procedure and Investigations Act 1996, however, the committal system was subjected to radical reform. Crucially, the examining justices now decide whether to commit to the Crown Court on the basis of a series of statements, and without any oral evidence (see Paragraph 12.2).

There are still two types of committal procedure:

(a)   committal where the evidence (consisting entirely of documents) is considered by the bench, and submissions are made by the parties as to whether the accused should be sent to the Crown Court for trial; and

(b)   committal where the accused is committed without consideration of the evidence.

Committals as described in (a) are governed by s 6(1) of the MCA, and are held when the accused has no legal representative acting for him in the case, or his legal representative has requested the court to consider a submission of no case to answer (see Paragraph 12.2.3).

The law on committal proceedings is contained chiefly in the Magistrates' Courts Act 1980 and the Magistrates' Courts Rules 1981 (SI 1981 No 552). In the remainder of this Chapter, the Act and the Rules are denoted by the letters 'MCA' and 'MCR' respectively. Before looking in detail at the two forms of committal proceedings, it will be convenient to consider four topics relevant to both forms.

12.1.1   Jurisdiction of the magistrates

Whereas a magistrates' court's jurisdiction to try an accused for an alleged summary offence is geographically limited to offences committed within the county where the court is situated, its jurisdiction to conduct committal proceedings is subject to no such restrictions. Magistrates have jurisdiction to act as examining justices upon an accused appearing or being brought before them[1] charged with an indictable offence: MCA, s 2(3). Where the offence occurred is irrelevant, save that if it was abroad the general rule is that the English courts will not deal with the matter at all, so obviously no committal proceedings should be held (see Paragraph 4.4.1). But, the effect of s 2(3) is that, if an accused lives in, say, Newcastle and has allegedly committed an indictable offence in Newcastle, he could theoretically be brought before the Plymouth Magistrates' Court for committal proceedings, and that court would be entitled to commit him for trial if the evidence justified it. Subsequently the Crown Court sitting at Plymouth could try the case. Obviously, it is generally speaking inconvenient to have proceedings for an offence committed at one end of the country take place at the other end of the country, so normal practice is to bring an accused charged with an indictable offence before the magistrates' court which acts for the area where the offence allegedly occurred. If there is a case to answer, he would probably then be sent to a nearby location of the Crown Court to stand his trial. Although this Paragraph has referred to magistrates in the plural conducting committal proceedings, one lay magistrate does in fact have jurisdiction to send an accused for trial: MCA, s 4(1). In practice, however, it is usual for two or three to sit.

12.1.2   Presence of the accused and the public

Evidence tendered at committal proceedings must be given in the presence of the accused unless the examining justices consider that his disorderly conduct makes that impracticable, or he cannot be present for health reasons but is legally represented and has consented to evidence being given in his absence: MCA, s 4(3) and (4). As with criminal proceedings in general, the public as well as the accused have a right to attend, although the justices do

---

[1] An accused *appears* before a magistrates' court in answer to a summons or in answer to his bail. He is *brought before* a magistrates' court following his arrest without warrant and detention at the police station for questioning or following a remand in custody to a prison or remand centre.

have a discretion to sit in camera if the ends of justice would not be served by an open court hearing: MCA, s 4(2). If proceedings are open to the public then they are also, of course, open to the press. However, special rules govern the extent to which the media may report committal proceedings (see Paragraph 12.4.1).

12.1.3 Number of accused

Committal proceedings may concern two or more accused persons. This is obviously appropriate where they are charged jointly with committing a single offence. It is also appropriate where the accused persons are charged with separate offences which are linked together in some way so that it is in the interests of justice to have a single set of proceedings: *Camberwell Green Magistrates ex p Christie* [1978] QB 602. Thus if two accused are charged with committing a robbery, a third is charged with stealing the 'get-away car', and a fourth is charged with handling the proceeds of the robbery, the most convenient course of action is to deal with all four in one committal hearing.

12.1.4 Abuse of process: discretion to halt proceedings

Examining justices have a discretion to discharge the accused without hearing the prosecution evidence if there has been delay in bringing the proceedings of such magnitude as to render them an abuse of the court's process. The leading cases are *Derby Crown Court ex p Brooks* (1984) 70 Cr App R 164, *Grays Justices ex p Graham* [1982] QB 1239, *Bow Street Stipendiary Magistrate ex p Director of Public Prosecutions* (1989) 91 Cr App R 283 and *Horseferry Road Magistrates' Court ex p Bennett* [1993] 3 WLR 90. The principle emerging from those decisions is that justices are entitled to discharge the accused without considering the evidence on which committal is sought if *either* the prosecution have deliberately manipulated the normal criminal process so as to take unfair advantage of the accused (e.g., delayed commencing proceedings in the hope that a potential defence witness would die, emigrate or otherwise become unavailable), *or* there has been delay on the part of the prosecution which — although not deliberate — is none the less unjustifiable and is likely to prejudice the accused in the preparation and conduct of his defence (e.g., because potential witnesses will have forgotten the relevant events).

The doctrine of abuse of process is by now well established. It was applied in *Bow Street Stipendiary Magistrate ex p Director of Public Prosecutions* (1989) 91 Cr App R 283. The Divisional Court made it clear that mere delay which gave rise to prejudice and unfairness might by itself amount to an abuse of process. It had to be shown that the delay had produced genuine prejudice and unfairness. In some cases, prejudice would be presumed from substantial delay which the Crown would have to rebut. The Director of Public Prosecutions had applied for judicial review of the magistrate's decision to refuse to commit police officers for trial. It was alleged that the officers concerned had conspired to pervert the course of justice. The prosecutions arose from the Wapping demonstrations on 24 January 1987. Notices of disciplinary proceedings were not served on the officers until 17 December 1987. At the committal on 3 May 1989, magistrate A declined jurisdiction on the ground that it would be an abuse of process to hear the charges. In addition, C, another police officer, applied for judicial review of the decision by magistrate B that his prosecution for assault was not an abuse of process. Again, the allegation arose from events on 24 January 1987. C was said to have assaulted W in the course of arrest. C was not served with a disciplinary notice until 16 February 1988 and the summons was not issued until

January 1989. Magistrate B held that the delay was not an abuse of process and that C should be committed for trial. The Divisional Court refused the application of the Director of Public Prosecutions but granted C's, thus holding in effect that both prosecutions involved delays which were an abuse of process. It was perfectly proper, in the circumstances, to infer prejudice from the mere passage of time. With regard to the allegation of assault against C, such an inference was more easily drawn in the case of a single, brief, but confused event which must depend on the recollections of those involved.

The power of the justices is nevertheless strictly confined, and instances of the discretion not to proceed being exercised in favour of the accused are rare. Thus, in *Ex p Brooks,* the decision of the Divisional Court was that examining justices had been right to consider the evidence and commit even though some five years had elapsed since the date of the offences. Similarly, in *Ex p Graham,* the prosecution were not ready to start committal proceedings in respect of obtaining some £1,600-worth of goods by deception until December 1981, nearly two years after the offences. Had the matters been investigated with reasonable expedition, committal could have taken place in about six months. The officer in charge of the case admitted that the only reason for his not having acted more promptly was the size of his case load and the fact that he had more serious matters to investigate. Nevertheless, an application to the High Court for an order requiring the examining justices not to proceed was refused. The following passage from May LJ's judgment in *Ex p Graham* shows the constraints which the higher courts have tended to put upon the discretion of examining justices:

> We are well aware that there is today a substantial amount of delay and inefficiency in criminal proceedings both before and at trial. This is to be deplored, and all concerned must do their utmost to bring criminal proceedings to trial and to verdict as swiftly and efficiently as possible. But we do not think that this court should create any artificial limitation period for criminal proceedings where it cannot truly be said that the due process of the courts is being used improperly to harass a defendant.

In an appropriate case, however, the doctrine of abuse of process can certainly be invoked in an accused's favour. Thus, in *Telford Justices ex p Badhan* [1991] 2 QB 78, a complaint was made against the applicant in 1988 that he had committed an offence of rape in 1973 or 1974. He appeared before the examining justices in May 1989. It was submitted that the committal should not proceed, since it would be an abuse of process. The justices rejected the submission, and the applicant sought judicial review. In the Divisional Court, the prosecution argued that the doctrine of abuse of process had no application to committal proceedings, and that *Ex p Brooks* and subsequent decisions were *per incuriam.* The Divisional Court allowed the application and granted prohibition. Examining justices had the power to decide that the initiation of the process of committal was an abuse of that process. If their decision was disputed, the complainant could seek judicial review. In the present case, it was for the accused to show on a balance of probabilities that he was prejudiced in his defence. Where the period of delay was long, it was legitimate for the court to infer prejudice. The period in question here was that between the date of the alleged offence and the opening of committal — some 15 or 16 years. The court could infer prejudice and conclude that a fair trial was impossible.

As to the procedure which the examining justices ought to adopt, it is submitted that they should deal with the question prior to the commital proceedings proper. They should consider evidence on the course of proceedings thus far, particularly as to the extent of the delay, the reasons for it, and any prejudice which the defence may suffer as a result. They should hear from both the prosecution and the defence. Thus, in *Clerkenwell Stipendiary Magistrate ex p Bell* [1991] Crim LR 468, the magistrate heard evidence from a police officer explaining that the delay of two and a half years between commission of the offence and committal proceedings was due to B's change of address. He declined to hear evidence from B, and then committed him for trial. The Divisional Court held that this was a breach of natural justice and quashed the committal. Conversely, in *Crawley Justices ex p DPP* (1991) *The Times*, 5 April 1991, the Divisional Court quashed the decision of the justices to dismiss informations because of delay. The bench had not heard from the prosecution, nor enquired fully from the accused as to the facts.

For discussion of the linked question of whether magistrates have a discretion not to proceed with a summary trial (as opposed to committal proceedings) on the grounds of delay, see Paragraph 9.4. Reference may also be made to Paragraph 18.1.4, which deals with the judge's corresponding discretion at a trial on indictment. Further, see Paragraph 6.3.4, which deals with the regulations under the Prosecution of Offences Act 1985 laying down custody time-limits for the completion of early stages of criminal proceedings.

12.2   COMMITTALS WITH CONSIDERATION OF THE EVIDENCE

A committal under MCA, s 6(1) is held whenever:

(a)   the accused (or one of them) has no legal representative acting for him in the case; or

(b)   the legal representative of the accused (or one of them) has requested the court to consider a submission of no case to answer (see Paragraph 12.2.3).

12.2.1   Procedure at a committal with consideration of the evidence

The hallmark of a committal under s 6(1) is that the bench is charged with considering the evidence before deciding whether to send the accused to the Crown Court for trial. Proceedings begin when the accused is called into the dock and has the charges read out to him (but he does not plead since that will not be appropriate until arraignment in the Crown Court). If the prosecution wish to vary the charges (either by adding fresh ones or not proceeding on an original one), that can be explained to the bench. Any additional charge should have been put into writing and handed to the clerk so that he can read it to the accused.

If the prosecution is being conducted by the Crown Prosecution Service, they will be represented by a Crown Prosecutor or an agent. Other prosecutors should instruct a solicitor, who may in turn brief counsel (both solicitors and barristers have the right of audience in magistrates' courts). The accused is, of course, entitled to be legally represented, or he may conduct his own defence.

The procedure is governed by MCR, r 7. The prosecutor is entitled to outline the case and explain any relevant points of law, before tendering the evidence (all of which is written). The evidence may be read through or, with the leave of the court, summarised. The magistrates' court may view any original exhibits and may retain them. No witnesses are called, and no depositions are taken during the course of the committal (such as used to be taken in s 6(1) committals before the changes introduced by the Criminal Procedure and Investigations Act 1996). No evidence can be tendered by the defence. The accused may then make a submission of no case to answer and, if he does so, or the court is minded not to commit for trial, the prosecutor is entitled to respond (see Paragraph 12.2.3 for details about the submission of no case). The court then reaches its decision as to whether to commit the accused for trial in the Crown Court.

12.2.2 Evidence at committal

For evidence to be admissible at committal:

(a) it must be tendered by the prosecutor (the defence is no longer able to adduce evidence at committal); and

(b) it must fall within one of the categories of evidence defined in ss 5B, 5C, 5D and 5E of the MCA.

In most cases, the evidence will be in the form of witness statements under MCA, s 5B. Any such statement may be admitted if it is adduced by the prosecutor and:

(a) It is signed by the maker.

(b) It contains a declaration by the maker that it is true to the best of his knowledge and belief, and that he made it knowing that if it were tendered in evidence he could be prosecuted for wilfully stating in it anything that he knew to be false or did not believe to be true.

(c) The prosecution gives a copy of it to each of the other parties to the committal proceedings before tendering it to the court.

> A statement under s 5B should give the maker's age if under 18. If the maker cannot read, it should be read through to him before he signs it, and should contain a declaration that it was so read. (Note that it is not necessary for any witness to write his statement personally, provided that he reads it through before signing it.) Where the statement refers to another document as an exhibit (e.g. a police officer's statement might refer to signed notes of an interview that he had with the accused at the police station), a copy of the exhibit should be given to each of the other parties. If a witness makes a statement to the police it is normally taken down on a standard form which incorporates the declaration that the statement is true etc. as required by s 5B. Examples of such statements will be found in Appendix 5.

Although the usual route for a statement to be admitted in committal proceedings is by MCA, s 5B, there are other possibilities. Section 5C is an innovation introduced by the Criminal Procedure and Investigations Act 1996. It allows for evidence by way of deposition taken in advance of the committal where a prosecution witness is reluctant to provide a written statement. Such a deposition may be taken under MCA s 97A where a person 'is likely to be able to make on behalf of the prosecutor a written statement containing material evidence' and 'the person will not voluntarily make the statement'. If a magistrate is satisfied of these conditions, then a summons and, if necessary, a warrant can be issued to secure that person's attendance, using the procedure under s 97 (see Paragraph 9.7.2). The procedure does not require a court to be convened for the deposition to be taken, and neither the accused nor his legal advisers need be present, nor even notified that the deposition is being taken. The deposition once taken is admissible by virtue of s 5C in a subsequent committal.

A further route is provided by s 5D, which allows in first-hand hearsay which might be admissible by virtue of s 23 or 24 of the Criminal Justice Act 1988 if the case came to trial.

This covers statements made by persons now dead, unfit to attend trial, abroad and not reasonably expected to attend or who will be kept away from a trial by fear or threat to their safety, as well as evidence contained in business or trade documents. The prosecutor need not prove that the conditions laid down in ss 23 or 24 are satisfied, but must notify the court of his belief that the statement will be admissible. Such belief must be based on reasonable grounds.

Finally, documents which 'prove themselves' or are made admissible by other legislation, such as certificates of conviction or DVLA certificates in road traffic proceedings, are made admissible in committal proceedings by s 5E.

12.2.3   Submission of 'no case to answer'

After the prosecution have read or summarised their written statements, the defence have the opportunity to submit that there is no case to answer: MCR, r 7(5). The question for the examining justices is whether the evidence discloses a prima facie case in respect of any indictable offence. If the answer is 'yes', the proceedings continue as described in the next Paragraph. If the answer is 'no', the accused is discharged — i.e., he is free to leave court unless he is being held in custody for some other matter (see Paragraph 12.2.5 for details of the effect of discharge at committal proceedings). Unless it is obviously ill-founded, the prosecution will be invited to reply to the defence submission.

The test the justices should apply in deciding whether there is a case to answer has already been described in general terms. The *Practice Direction (Submission of No Case)* [1962] 1 WLR 227 handed down by Lord Parker CJ in 1962 stated:

> A submission that there is no case to answer may properly be made and upheld: (a) when there has been no evidence to prove an essential element in the alleged offence; (b) when the evidence adduced by the prosecution has been so discredited as a result of cross-examination or is so manifestly unreliable that no reasonable tribunal could safely convict on it.

The terms of the *Practice Direction* relate to a committal where witnesses give oral evidence — a feature which was abolished by the Criminal Procedure and Investigations Act 1996. Clearly, limb (a) of the test still retains its force — the magistrates should uphold a submission of no case to answer where 'there has been no evidence to prove an essential element in the alleged offence'. On the other hand, that part of the formulation which refers to cross-examination is now irrelevant to committal proceedings, since there are no witnesses, and hence no cross-examination. What about evidence which 'is so manifestly unreliable that no reasonable tribunal could safely convict on it'? Frequently in the criminal process, the issue of reliability or credibility of evidence arises in the context of oral testimony. It is quite possible, however, that written evidence, whether in the form of statements under MCA s 5B or depositions under s 5C, could be judged 'manifestly unreliable' if it is hopelessly contradictory or inherently unlikely. In *Governor of Pentonville Prison ex p Osman (No 4)* [1989] 3 All ER 701, for example, the Divisional Court accepted (in the context of oral evidence) that an examining justice could reject any evidence considered 'worthless' (per Lloyd LJ at p. 721). (See also *Brooks v DPP* [1994] 1 AC 568 at p. 581; and Brownless and Furniss 'Committed to Committals?' [1997] Crim LR 3.) In general, however, it is likely that the bench will be concerned only with evidential sufficiency, and will leave questions of credibility to the Crown Court, where the jury will have a chance to assess the witnesses at first-hand. (For a discussion on submissions of no case to answer in the context of suunmary trial and trial on indictment, see Paragraphs 9.7.3 and 18.4 respectively.)

Finally, it should be noted that the question for the bench is not merely whether there is a case to answer in respect of the charges preferred against the accused at the police station, as supplemented or amended during the course of the hearings. The question is whether *any* indictable offence has been disclosed. Thus, if the accused is charged with murder and the prosecution are seeking committal on that charge, the examining justices could decide that there is no evidence on which a reasonable jury might find that the accused acted with malice aforethought but there is ample evidence of unlawful killing. They would then refuse to commit for murder but allow the proceedings to continue on the basis of manslaughter. The fact that the accused has never been expressly charged with manslaughter is irrelevant. Of course, where two or more offences have been expressly charged (whether in the alternative or cumulatively), the justices can commit on one and refuse to commit on another.

12.2.4   Procedure if submission of no case to answer is rejected

If the submission of no case to answer is rejected (or the defence elect not to make a submission), the charges on which the examining justices find there is a case must be read to the accused: MCR, r 7(7). Where the examining justices decide there is a case in respect of an offence with which the accused has not yet been charged, as when they refuse to commit on a charge of murder but consider that the evidence shows a prima facie case of manslaughter, the new charge must be put down in writing.

The examining justices will formally announce that they are committing the accused to the Crown Court to stand his trial on those charges for which there is sufficient evidence. A particular location of the Crown Court should be specified (see Paragraph 13.2).

12.2.5   Effect of a discharge

Discharge at committal proceedings is not equivalent to an acquittal, and the prosecution may therefore prefer fresh charges for the same offence or offences: *Manchester City Stipendiary Magistrate ex p Snelson* [1977] 1 WLR 911. They may then seek to persuade either the examining justices who originally refused to commit for trial or a differently constituted bench that there is a case to answer. Should the prosecution act improperly or oppressively in making a second attempt to secure a committal for trial, the High Court has power to issue an order prohibiting the continuation of the second set of committal proceedings: *Horsham Justices ex p Reeves* (1981) 75 Cr App R 236n.

In *Ex p Snelson* the second application to examining justices to commit was justified because at the first committal proceedings, the case had not been considered on its merits. Expecting that the examining justices would agree to an application for an adjournment, the prosecution had had literally no evidence available at court on the day fixed for the hearing, so when the adjournment was refused the inevitable result was the discharge of the accused. Thus, there was nothing unfair or oppressive in the prosecution initiating further committal proceedings at which they could ensure that their evidence was available for the examining justices' consideration. In *Ex p Reeves,* on the other hand, the first committal proceedings lasted three days, involved full consideration of the prosecution evidence, but nonetheless ended in the discharge of the accused. In so far as the prosecution case was not effectively presented, that was their own fault because much confusing and irrelevant material had been put before the justices along with the cogent evidence. The second committal proceedings were merely an attempt to repair the damage done by the prosecution's mistakes at the first. Therefore, the High Court held that the prosecution's conduct was an abuse of the process of the court, and ordered that the proceedings be discontinued. As an alternative to a second attempt to have the accused committed for trial, the prosecution can always apply to a High Court judge for a voluntary bill of indictment (see Paragraph 12.6). In the light of *Ex p Reeves* this seems the more appropriate course of action whenever the original decision to discharge the accused was taken after a full hearing on the merits of the case.

12.2.6   Objections to evidence

What if the prosecution seek, at committal proceedings, to introduce evidence which is inadmissible? Specific provision is made for such a situation where part of a written statement is inadmissible. MCR, r 70(5), states that the words 'treated as inadmissible' should be written against the offending part. The commonest basis for objecting to the admissibility of evidence, however, has no application to committal proceedings. As a result of changes introduced by the Criminal Procedure and Investigations Act 1996, ss 76 and 78 of the Police and Criminal Evidence Act 1984 do not apply to committals. This means that the defence cannot, for example, challenge the admissibility of a confession which the accused alleges was obtained by oppression, or in circumstances which render it unreliable. They must wait until the Crown Court before obtaining an opportunity to argue in front of the judge that the confession in question is inadmissible (see Paragraph 18.3.5 for the procedure adopted in the Crown Court).

12.3   COMMITTALS WITHOUT CONSIDERATION OF THE EVIDENCE

The Criminal Justice Act 1967 introduced a procedure by which the defence could agree to the examining justices committing the accused for trial without considering the evidence against him. The legislation is now contained in s 6(2) of the 1980 Act. Most committals take place under the provisions of this subsection.

The accused may be committed for trial without the examining justices considering the evidence against him if:

(a)   the accused (or, if there is more than one accused, each of the accused) has a solicitor acting for him in the case, whether present in court or not, and

(b)   there is no submission from counsel or solicitor for the accused (or any one of the accused) that there is no case to answer.

These conditions for a committal without consideration of the evidence should ensure that an accused is only so committed in cases where, were the examining justices to consider the evidence, they would conclude that there was a case to answer. It is the duty of the accused's solicitor (or counsel instructed by him) to read through the statements and other documents, which should have been served beforehand, and only allow the committal to proceed under s 6(2) if the documents clearly disclose a prima facie case. However, it should be noted that, provided the accused has a solicitor acting for him in the case as a whole, neither that solicitor nor counsel instructed by him need be present in court for the committal itself — the accused himself may inform the examining justices that a committal without consideration of the evidence is acceptable. This was a change effected by s 61 of the Criminal Justice Act 1982, which amended MCA, s 6(2). In practice, however, many solicitors still consider it preferable to arrange for the legal representation of their clients at committal proceedings, even though the evidence is not going to be considered. A number of ancillary matters arise at committal proceedings (e.g., the granting of bail pending the trial on indictment and the extension of legal aid, see Paragraph 12.4.3), and it is always possible that these will give rise to unexpected problems which the accused could not cope with personally. Moreover, many accused persons are genuinely apprehensive about what will happen in court, and are entitled to have their own barrister or solicitor to allay their fears.

Committals without consideration of the evidence are a pure formality, and may take five minutes or less to accomplish. The exact procedure varies from court to court, but the example below is typical of what happens:

(*John Smith*, the accused is brought into the dock.)
Clerk of Court Are you John Smith?
Smith I am.
Clerk You are charged that on the 1st day of January 2000 you robbed Jane Price of a handbag, a cheque card, five keys, a purse and £25 in cash, contrary to section 8 of the Theft Act 1968. You may sit down.
Mr Stryver (Crown Prosecutor) The prosecution are ready for committal. Statements have been served on the defence and I understand from my learned friend that he does not wish the evidence to be considered at this stage.
Mr Bigwig (defence counsel) That is correct.
[Mr Stryver hands to the clerk a bundle of the statements made by prosecution witnesses, plus copy bundles for the magistrates and the Crown Court.)
Clerk I have here statements made by Jane Price, WPC Perkins, DC Potter and Dr Phillips. Mr Bigwig, I should formally ask you whether you wish to submit that the statements do not disclose a case to answer?
Mr Bigwig I do not.
Very well (the clerk turns to the chairman) — I think that completes the formalities.
Chairman Mr Smith, we are committing you to stand trial on this charge of robbery at the Coketown Crown Court. At your trial, any statement or deposition tendered here today may be read in evidence, without oral evidence being given by the person who made it or the opportunity to cross-examine that person, unless you object in writing to the court and the prosecutor within the next 14 days. Is there any application for bail?
Mr Bigwig There is, sir. Mr Smith has been on bail throughout with one surety in the sum of £500. I would ask for that to continue. The surety is his brother and he is at court today.
Mr Stryver No objection.
Chairman Very well. Bail as before; the surety can be taken downstairs.
Mr Bigwig There is one final matter, sir. Mr Smith was granted representation by the Criminal Defence Service for the proceedings in this court. His means have not changed. Might representation be extended to cover the Crown Court proceedings?
Chairman Yes, it is extended . . . . Now, what's the next case on the list?

The explanation for any parts of the above procedure which have not yet been discussed will be found in Paragraph 12.4 which deals with various incidental orders and applications made at committal proceedings.

12.4 OTHER ORDERS AND APPLICATIONS MADE AT COMMITTAL PROCEEDINGS

The following additional matters may, and in some cases must, be considered at committal proceedings whether the latter be with or without consideration of the evidence.

12.4.1   Publicity

Committal proceedings inevitably give a picture of the case which is distorted in favour of the prosecution. At a committal which considers the evidence, as has been explained, the defence is not permitted to cross-examine prosecution witnesses, nor to call evidence of its own. If reports are published of the statements and depositions which were read out or summarised by the prosecutor, only the prosecution case would receive publicity. Even at committals without consideration of the evidence information may be disclosed which is prejudicial to the accused, as when the prosecution object to the accused being granted bail on the ground that he was on bail awaiting trial for another offence when the offence now alleged against him was committed. Thus, if the press, television or radio report in full what occurs at committal proceedings the public could be prejudiced against the accused, and, assuming there is a committal for trial, it is from the public that jurors to try the case will have to be drawn.

For these reasons, s 3 of the Criminal Justice Act 1967 restricted the extent to which the media could lawfully report committal proceedings. The legislation is now contained in MCA, s 8. The media may report essential details of what occurs such as the names, addresses, ages and occupations of the parties and witnesses; the identity of the court; the names of the examining justices, counsel and solicitors; the charges against the accused and those on which he is committed for trial, and the arrangements as to bail and legal aid. Full reporting (e.g., of the evidence given) is allowed only if reporting restrictions are lifted (see below), or after all the accused have been discharged by the examining justices, or, if there is a committal for trial, after the close of the trial on indictment. Contravention of s 8 is a summary offence punishable with a fine of up to £5,000, but the Attorney-General's consent is required for the bringing of a prosecution. The restrictions apply not only to the committal proceedings themselves but also to any prior remand hearings.

Section 8 of MCA 1980 is intended to protect the accused. It follows that if he wants publicity, for example so that witnesses might come forward to support his case, the law should not stop him having it. Therefore, s 8(2) provides that the examining justices *must* lift reporting restrictions if there is only one accused and he makes an application for that to be done. A difficult problem arises if there are two or more accused, and one applies for the restrictions to be lifted, but another objects. Originally the rule was that if any one accused wanted the restrictions lifted they had to be lifted in respect of all the accused joined in the committal proceedings, irrespective of their wishes in the matter. However, the Criminal Justice (Amendment) Act 1981 amended s 8 so that where A1 applies for the lifting of restrictions but A2 objects the examining justices are to accede to the application only if it is in the interests of justice to do so. The onus is on the accused making the application to show that his chances of a fair trial will be prejudiced through lack of publicity. If, for example, he wants publicity only to make a protest at the conduct of the police, who first said they would not charge him but then did, his application should not be granted (see *Leeds Justices ex p Sykes* [1983] 1 WLR 132).

Section 4 of the Contempt of Court Act 1981 (see also Paragraph 18.11) empowers a court to order that media reporting of part or all of a case be postponed if contemporaneous reporting would involve a 'substantial risk of prejudice to the administration of justice' in the case itself or any other pending or imminent proceedings. The powers contained in s 4 are at the disposal of examining justices: *Horsham Justices ex p Farquharson* [1982] QB 762. Thus, even where reporting restrictions have been lifted as a result of an application under MCA, s 8(2), they can in effect be re-imposed, in whole or in part, by an order under s 4 of the 1981 Act. However, a court is unlikely to hold that reporting of committal proceedings involves a risk of prejudice to the administration of justice when the very possibility of their being reported only arises because the accused wants publicity. One situation, though, where s 4 could be useful is when the accused (or one of them) needs a measure of publicity so that, for example, witnesses may be encouraged to come forward, but parts of the prosecution case are of a particularly shocking or sensitive nature and might prejudice the public against him (or another accused). The examining justices could then make an order under MCA, s 8(2) lifting reporting restrictions, and a further order under the Contempt of Court Act postponing publication of the shocking or sensitive material. The Divisional Court has held, however, that examining justices should be slow to make use of their powers in this way (*Beaconsfield Justices ex p Westminster Press Ltd* (1994) *The Times*, 28 June 1994).

12.4.2 Objecting to statements being read at trial

When the Crown Court trial takes place, the prosecution has to adduce evidence before the court to prove the case against the accused. The usual way to place this evidence before the jury is by calling the witness, who then testifies, and is subject to cross-examination. Some of the evidence may be uncontroversial, however, and it would be a waste of time for all concerned if the witness had to attend to give it. The Criminal Procedure and Investigations Act 1996, Sch 2, para 1(2) states that a statement under s 5B of the MCA tendered at committal 'may without further proof be read as evidence on the trial of the accused'. (Identical provisions apply to a deposition taken under s 97A of the MCA.) By para 1(3)(c), if the accused (or one of them) objects to the statement, then it cannot be read. The objection must be given in writing to the prosecutor and the Crown Court within 14 days of committal (MCR, r 8). However, by para 1(4), even where there has been an objection, the court 'may order that the objection shall have no effect if the court considers it to be in the interests of justice so to order', thus allowing the statement to be read.

These provisions replace the old practice of allowing the parties at committal to state whether each witness should be 'fully bound' or 'conditionally bound', with the result that fully bound witnesses were expected to attend and give evidence at the Crown Court, whereas conditionally bound witnesses would only have to attend if notice was subsequently given. Another significant difference in the new procedure for the reading of written evidence is the right of the court to overrule defence objections and decide that a statement may be read even though the defence request that the witness should be there to give evidence and be cross-examined (for further discussion of the effect at the trial itself, see Paragraph 18.3.4).

12.4.3 Bail and legal aid

Having committed the accused for trial on indictment, the examining justices must then decide whether the accused should be allowed bail and whether representation from the Criminal Defence Service should be granted for the proceedings in the Crown Court.

MCA, s 6(3) empowers the court to commit the accused for trial either in custody or on bail. Committal in custody means the accused is detained in prison, or, where he is under 21, a remand centre. Bail means that he is released under a duty to surrender to custody at the Crown Court on the day fixed for the trial. As months may elapse between committal and trial, the decision to grant or withhold bail at this stage is of great importance. Bail is dealt with fully in Chapter 6.

It is also standard practice for the examining justices to be asked to grant representation by the Criminal Defence Service for the proceedings in the Crown Court. If, as is normally the case, the accused was granted representation for the hearings before the magistrates, and if his financial circumstances have not changed, then extending the grant for the Crown Court is almost automatic. Full discussion of this topic may be found in Chapter 27.

12.5 CHALLENGING THE CONDUCT OF COMMITTAL PROCEEDINGS

There is no appeal as such against a decision by examining justices to commit the accused for trial or, as the case may be, discharge him. The prosecution may, however, in effect challenge a decision to discharge by applying to a judge in chambers for a voluntary bill of indictment (see the next Paragraph). Alternatively, they could prefer a fresh charge for the same offence and hope that a second bench of examining justices will find there is a case to answer (see Paragraph 12.2.5).

The higher courts have tended to take the view that the defence have little need of a right of appeal against a committal since, if there was not in fact a case to answer and the prosecution have not supplemented their evidence by the time of trial on indictment, the Crown Court judge will direct the jury to acquit at the end of the prosecution case. Defence lawyers have, however, shown considerable ingenuity in their attempts to have examining justices' decisions reversed by a higher tribunal. Their efforts, which have met with only limited success, are summarised below:

(i) Occasionally the Court of Appeal will quash a conviction on indictment because of errors at the committal stage. But, the appellant will have to show that the proceedings before the examining justices and hence the decision to commit were so flawed as to be total nullities (see for example *Phillips and Quayle* [1939] 1 KB 63).

(ii) Although a trial judge has a discretion to refuse to let the prosecution call their evidence if their doing so would be oppressive or an abuse of process, he is not entitled to exercise that discretion merely on the basis that he considers the accused should not have been committed for trial or had inadmissible evidence tendered against him at the committal proceedings (*Norfolk Quarter Sessions ex p Brunson* [1953] 1 QB 503). In other words, the judge is obliged to let the prosecution call their evidence, although *after* they have done so he may direct the jury to acquit if he considers there is no case to answer (see Paragraph 18.4 for submissions of no case to answer in the Crown Court).

(iii) Judicial review is the means by which the High Court controls the behaviour of inferior tribunals, including magistrates' courts (see Chapter 25). A review will succeed against examining justices who have acted or are threatening to act in excess of jurisdiction. Thus, in *Hatfield Justices ex p Castle* [1981] 1 WLR 217 prohibition was granted to prevent the justices embarking upon committal proceedings in respect of an offence of criminal damage which, by reason of a special statutory provision, they were obliged to deal with as if it were a summary offence. Had the committal gone ahead, the justices would have been exceeding their powers — therefore it was a proper case for the High Court to intervene. But judicial review is not appropriate if the justices have merely erred (or allegedly erred) in exercising a jurisdiction which is rightfully theirs. Thus, defence attempts to have a committal for trial quashed on the basis either that the evidence did not disclose a prima facie case, or that evidence was admitted which the justices should in their discretion have excluded have all failed (see, respectively, *Roscommon Justices ex p Blakeney* [1894] 2 IR 158, and *Highbury Corner Magistrates ex p Boyce* (1984) 79 Cr App R 132). The High Court has also held that applications for judicial review should not be brought while committal proceedings are actually in progress (*Wells Street Stipendiary Magistrate ex p Seillon* [1978] 1 WLR 1002).

(iv) Appeal by way of case stated, which is a means of appealing to the High Court against an erroneous decision of law by a magistrates' court, is only available once there has been a final determination of a case on the part of the magistrates. A decision to commit for trial does not rank as a final determination, and is therefore not appealable by case stated (see *Cragg v Lewes District Council* [1986] Crim LR 800).

12.6 VOLUNTARY BILLS OF INDICTMENT

In the great majority of cases, trials on indictment are preceded by committal proceedings resulting in the accused's committal for trial. There is, however, an alternative to committal proceedings, namely a direction by a High Court judge for the preferment of a voluntary bill of indictment (see Administration of Justice (Miscellaneous Provisions) Act 1933, s 2 as amended). The terminology is explained in Chapter 14, but what it means essentially is that a High Court judge orders that the accused be tried on indictment.

In theory, the prosecution could always avoid the holding of committal proceedings by applying to a High Court judge for a voluntary bill. However, the *Practice Direction (Crime: Voluntary Bills)* [1990] 1 WLR 1633 states that a voluntary bill should be granted 'only where the interests of justice, rather than considerations of administrative convenience require it'. In fact, voluntary bills are only sought if *either* committal proceedings have been held but have resulted in the discharge of the accused or the holding of committal proceedings would for some special reason be undesirable. In the former case, the High Court judge is effectively being asked to rule on whether the examining justices were right to refuse to commit. In *Brooks v DPP of Jamaica* [1994] 1 AC 568, the Privy Council stressed that the decision to prefer a voluntary bill in these circumstances is one to be exercised with great circumspection, treating the magistrates' decision with the utmost respect. An example of committal proceedings being undesirable is provided by *Paling* (1978) 67 Cr App R 299. P was charged with assault on a traffic warden. Before the examining justices he conducted his own defence, but became overexcited and would not sit down when told to do so. A police officer intervened and, for his pains, was assaulted. The examining justices adjourned, leaving the committal proceedings part-heard, and P was further charged with assaulting the police officer. Rather than risk any further outbursts in court, the prosecution successfully applied for a voluntary bill in respect of all matters outstanding against P.

Committal proceedings may also be inconvenient where, after one accused has been committed for trial and an indictment signed against him, a second accused is arrested, the prosecution case against him being that he committed an offence jointly with the first accused. The prosecution will wish to have both accused tried together, but this can only be done if there is a single indictment against them both. Application may be made for a voluntary bill of indictment charging both accused. The indictment outstanding against the first accused will not be proceeded with. It seems that the same result could be achieved simply by holding committal proceedings for the second accused and then drafting an indictment against both (*Groom* [1977] QB 6) but the voluntary bill procedure may be swifter.

The procedure for obtaining a High Court judge's consent to the preferment of a voluntary bill of indictment is set out in the Indictments Procedure Rules 1971. The application must be in writing, signed by the applicant or his solicitor. Unless there have already been unsuccessful committal proceedings, the application should state why it is being made. It should be accompanied by (i) the bill of indictment it is proposed to prefer, and (ii) proofs of evidence from the proposed prosecution witnesses and/or depositions taken and statements tendered at the committal proceedings (assuming there have been any). Save where the prosecutor is the Director of Public Prosecutions, there must also be an affidavit verifying that the statements contained in the application are true to the best of the applicant's knowledge and belief. However, a Crown Prosecutor applying for a voluntary bill on behalf of the DPP is, like the DPP himself, under no obligation to file an affidavit in support (*Liverpool Crown Court ex p Bray* [1987] Crim LR 51). The actual decision on whether there should be a voluntary bill is taken by the judge in chambers. Normally neither the prosecution nor defence attend (i.e. the judge simply reads through the papers and notifies his decision to the parties in writing). The defence do not even have a right to make representations to the judge, although there is a discretion to receive such representations (*Raymond* [1981] QB 910). Oral representations should be allowed only in quite extraordinary circumstances.

12.7 NOTICES OF TRANSFER

The introduction of the notice of transfer system means that in certain limited circumstances the prosecution can, without seeking judicial approval, avoid the need to have the accused committed for trial. The system operates in two very different situations:

(a)   in cases of serious and complex fraud; and
(b)   in certain cases involving child witnesses (as a result of the Criminal Justice Act 1991, s 53).

Although the factual situations in (a) and (b) differ greatly, the procedural consequences are much the same. The notice of transfer system in serious fraud cases is dealt with first in Paragraph 12.7.1, and those features which are peculiar to its use in child witness cases are discussed in Paragraph 12.7.2.

12.7.1   Serious fraud cases

The main reason for giving the prosecution the power to bypass the committal stage in these cases is to reduce delays. It was the report of the Roskill Committee in 1986 which led to the introduction of the notice of transfer system in the Criminal Justice Act 1987 (CJA 1987). One of the primary difficulties highlighted by the report was the very considerable delay in the prosecution of major fraud, resulting from the hearing of oral evidence in the preliminary stages.

The CJA 1987 gives the Director of Public Prosecutions, the Director of the Serious Fraud Office, the Commissioners of Inland Revenue, the Commissioners of Customs and Excise and the Secretary of State the status of 'designated authorities'. A notice of transfer may be given whenever a designated authority is of the opinion that the evidence against an accused charged with an indictable offence is:

(a)   sufficient for him to be committed for trial; and
(b)   'reveals a fraud of such seriousness or complexity that it is appropriate that the management of the case should without delay be taken over by the Crown Court' (CJA 1987, s 4(1)(a) and (b)).

Notice of transfer may be given at any time between the accused being charged and the commencement of committal proceedings. It must be given to the 'magistrates' court in whose jurisdiction the offence has been charged' (s 4(1)(a) and (c)).

The notice must specify the location of the Crown Court at which it is proposed that the trial should take place, and the charges to which it relates (s 5(1) and (2)).

Once served, the effect of a notice of transfer is that the functions of the magistrates' court cease, except in respect of bail, grant of legal representation and witness orders (s 4(1)).

The accused is provided with a measure of protection against being put on trial for offences in respect of which there is inadequate evidence. This is contained in s 6, which enables the accused to apply to the Crown Court for the dismissal of the transferred charges. The application for dismissal must be made within 28 days of the service of the notice of transfer, unless the Crown Court gives leave for late notice. The application itself may be presented and determined either orally or in writing, but an oral application must be preceded by written notice (Criminal Justice Act 1987 (Dismissal of Transferred Charges) Rules 1988 (SI 1988 No 1695), rr 2 and 3).

By s 6(3), oral evidence may be given at an application for dismissal only with the leave of the judge, such leave not to be given unless the interests of justice so require.

A judge determining an application for dismissal must dismiss any of the charges specified in the notice of transfer in respect of which 'it appears to him that the evidence against the applicant would not be sufficient for a jury properly to convict him' (s 6(1)). The corresponding counts in any indictment preferred against the accused must be quashed. The effect of a successful application for dismissal is basically the same as a refusal by examining justices to commit for trial, i.e., the accused is not acquitted but may be re-prosecuted for the same matters. It is provided that any further proceedings on the dismissed charges must be brought by way of a voluntary bill of indictment (s 6(5); see Paragraph 12.6 for the voluntary bill procedure).

12.7.2 Child witnesses

The notice of transfer system has been extended to cases of sexual offences and offences of violence involving child witnesses by s 53 of the Criminal Justice Act 1991. The intention is to protect the child witnesses in question from being compelled to give their evidence at committal with the trauma that almost inevitably involves. Further, the reform aims to bring on the Crown Court trial more speedily by dispensing with committal proceedings altogether. This means both that the recollection of the child witness is likely to be more accurate, and that any therapy to help the child recover from the incident can begin as soon as possible.

In child witness cases, the Director of Public Prosecutions (rather than the list of 'designated authorities' in serious fraud cases) is authorised to serve a notice of transfer, in respect of proceedings for certain offences, and provided that certain conditions are fulfilled. The offences are:

   (a)   an offence which involves an assault on, or injury or a threat of injury to, a person;

   (b)   an offence under s 1 of the Children and Young Persons Act 1933 (cruelty to persons under 16);

   (c)   an offence under the Sexual Offences Act 1956, the Indecency with Children Act 1960, the Sexual Offences Act 1967, s 54 of the Criminal Law Act 1977 or the Protection of Children Act 1978; and

   (d)   attempting or conspiring to commit, or aiding, abetting, counselling, procuring or inciting the commission of an offence within (a), (b) or (c) above.

The conditions of which the DPP must be satisfied are that:

(a)   the evidence of the offence would be sufficient for the accused to be committed for trial;

(b)   a child who is alleged to be the victim or to have witnessed the commission of the offence, will be called as a witness at trial; and

(c)   for the purpose of avoiding any prejudice to the welfare of the child, the case should be taken over and proceeded with without delay by the Crown Court.

According to s 53(6), the meaning of 'child' varies according to the offence with which the accused is charged. For an offence of violence or cruelty (or attempting or conspiring etc. to commit such an offence), it means a person aged under 14. For sexual offences, it means a person under 17. The relevant date for determining the child's age is not laid down in s 53, but the context suggests that it is the date of the notice of transfer. In each case, if a video recording was made of an interview about the offence by the child witness, when he was below the relevant age, then the age limit is increased by a year, to 15 or 18, as the case may be. The contents of a notice and, once served, its effect are much the same as in a serious fraud case (see Paragraph 12.7.1). One notable difference is that, in an application for dismissal, the judge cannot give leave for oral evidence to be adduced from a child witness, as defined above.

Special considerations arise where the defendant is a juvenile and the CPS is considering whether to make use of the transfer for trial procedure. In *T and C* [2001] Crim LR 398, the Court of Appeal stated that the prosecution should not consider using the transfer for trial procedure unless satisfied that a magistrates' court would be likely to find that it should be possible to sentence the defendant under PCC(S)A 2000, s 91 (see Paragraph 10.1). The reason is that the interests of both the juvenile defendant and the young witness are served by a speedy trial. It follows that summary trial is desirable unless there is a need to ensure greater powers of punishment under s 91.

12.8   INDICTABLE-ONLY OFFENCES

A major new route to the Crown Court was opened up as a result of the the procedure set out in s 51 of the Crime and Disorder Act 1998 (CDA). This lays down that offences which can be tried only on indictment, and those related to them, must be sent immediately to the Crown Court from a preliminary hearing in the magistrates' court. These provisions were the subject of an extended pilot scheme. They were implemented nationally in respect of cases where the defendant's first appearance took place on or after 15 January 2001.

Section 51 provides that the magistrates *must* send for trial in the Crown Court, without holding committal proceedings:

(a)   an adult defendant charged with an indictable-only offence, to be tried for that offence;

(b)   an adult defendant sent for trial for an indictable-only offence, to be tried also for any related offence which is triable either way for which he appears at the same time;

(c)   an adult defendant sent for trial for an indictable-only offence, to be tried also for any related summary offence for which he appears at the same time and which is imprisonable or carries disqualification from driving;

(d)   an adult co-defendant appearing on the same occasion charged with a related offence which is triable either way.

In addition, the magistrates *may* send immediately to the Crown Court for trial:

(a)   an adult defendant already sent to the Crown Court for trial for an indictable-only offence, to be tried for a related offence which is triable either way (or summary and imprisonable and carrying disqualification) and which has been charged subsequently;

(b)   an adult co-defendant charged with a related triable either-way offence, who appears subsequently to a defendant sent to the Crown Court for an indictable-only offence;

(c)   a juvenile jointly charged with an adult defendant with an indictable-only offence, where the magistrates consider that it is in the interests of justice for the juvenile to be tried jointly with the adult; and

(d)   a juvenile sent to the Crown Court by virtue of (c), in respect of any related either-way or summary offence (provided it is imprisonable or carries disqualification).

For the purposes of these provisions, an offence triable either way is related to an indictable-only offence if they could be joined in the same indictment. A summary offence is related to an indictable-only offence if it arises out of circumstances which are the same as or connected with those giving rise to it.

12.8.1   Indictable-only offences and the transfer procedure

In cases where the notice of transfer procedure might otherwise be available to the prosecution, the provisions of s 51 of the CDA 1998 take precedence. In a child witness case, where s 53 of the CJA 1991 might have been considered as a route to the Crown Court, if the charge is indictable-only (e.g. rape), or is related to an indictable-only charge, the prosecution is not able to make use of the notice of transfer procedure, and must proceed according to s 51 of the CDA 1998 (see Sch 8, para 93 to the CDA 1998). Similarly, where a serious fraud is charged, the case will be governed by the indictable-only procedure, rather than the provisions of the CJA 1987 (see Sch 8, para 65 to the CDA 1998).

12.8.2   Procedure in the magistrates' court

The accused appears in the magistrates' court for a preliminary hearing. The matter must be dealt with by at least two justices, or a district judge (s 50(1)). The court must send the case *forthwith* to the Crown Court (s 51(1)). This is, however, subject to the magistrates' power to adjourn (s 52(5)), for example where the situation is developing and it may not be necessary to send the case to the Crown Court, or where the defence needs to muster the necessary information for a bail application.

Despite the historical link between the provision of advance information and the decision as to mode of trial, the CPS recommends that a standard package of advance information be served upon the defence for cases falling within the s 51 procedure, preferably prior to the preliminary hearing in the magistrates' court. This includes the charge sheet, any summary of the prosecution case which has been prepared, the key witness statements and a print-out of previous convictions.

12.8.3   Summary only offences sent to the Crown Court under s 51 CDA 1998

A summary only offence may be sent to the Crown Court under the provisions of s 51 of the CDA 1998 if it is related to an indictable-only offence. When it is sent, it will be adjourned by the magistrates in accordance with s 51(9), i.e. no date will be fixed for it to be heard. If it is disposed of in the Crown Court in due course, in accordance with Sch 3, para 6 of the CDA 1998, then the magistrates do not need to deal with it. If it is not disposed of in the Crown Court, then it can, in effect, be remitted to the magistrates to deal with it. The procedure is similar to that under s 41 of the CJA 1988 (see Paragraph 12.9.2).

12.8.4   Appearance in the Crown Court

After the preliminary hearing which sends the defendant to the Crown Court, the magistrates' court will send a notice to the Crown Court. The defendant's first appearance in the Crown Court should then take place within eight days if he is in custody, or within 28 days if he is on bail. The preliminary hearing may be in chambers (Crown Court Rules 1982, r 27(2)(h)).

12.8.5   Service of the prosecution case

The papers comprising the prosecution case must be served upon the defendant, and upon the Crown Court specified in the notice served by the magistrates' court. Service must take place within six weeks of the case being sent to the Crown Court subject to an extension by the judge. It is of course, open to the judge to order a shorter period. The papers take a similar form to the bundle served for committal proceedings and should contain the charges, statements and other evidence, together with a draft indictment, a separate list of any summary charges sent up by virtue of s 51 of the CDA 1998 (unless these can be included in the indictment under s 40 of the CJA 1988) and a schedule of unused material for disclosure purposes.

The bill of indictment must be served within 28 days of service of the prosecution case. It may contain any count which is supported by the evidence contained in the papers served by the prosecution, either in addition to or in substitution for the charges upon which the defendant was sent to the Crown Court by the magistrates' court (Sch 8, para 5, CDA 1998). Any such counts must, however, be capable of being lawfully joined in the same indictment.

12.8.6   Discontinuance of the prosecution case

The prosecution has power to discontinue the case against the defendant not only in the magistrates' court, but also, in the case of offences sent up to the Crown Court by s 51 of the CDA 1998, at any time before the indictment is preferred (Prosecution of Offences Act 1985, s 23A).

12.8.7   Challenges to the prosecution case

The defence is able to challenge the prosecution case under the procedure set out in Sch 3 to the CDA 1998. After the prosecution case has been served, but before arraignment, the defendant may apply to the Crown Court for the charges (or any of them) to be dismissed. The details of the procedure are covered in the Crime and Disorder Act 1998 (Dismissal of Charges Sent) Rules 1998 (SI 1998 No 3048). The application may be made orally (r 2) or in writing (r 3). Where the judge gives leave or so orders, then oral evidence may be given on the application. This may be done only, however, if the judge considers that it is in the interests of justice to do so (Sch 3, para 2(4)). The proceedings are covered by reporting restrictions (para 3) and depositions (para 4) which are broadly equivalent to those which apply to committal proceedings.

At the conclusion of the hearing, the judge must dismiss the charge, and quash any related count in the indictment if it appears to him that the evidence against the applicant would not be sufficient for a jury properly to convict him (Sch 3, para 2).

12.8.8 Effect of dismissal of charges

Where at least one indictable-only charge remains, then the Crown Court can proceed to deal with the indictment in the normal way. Where there are no indictable-only charges left as a result of a successful application for dismissal, however, then the remaining charges must be put on an indictment, which is read to the accused (Sch 3, paras 7 to 15). The Crown Court must then carry out, in respect of each triable either way offence, the plea before venue procedure and, if there is an indication of a not guilty plea or no indication, the mode of trial procedure (see Paragraph 7.2). If, as a result, the case is to be tried summarily, it must be remitted to the magistrates' court. If not, the Crown Court will continue to deal with it. Where the defendant is under the age of 18, the Crown Court will remit the case to the youth court unless:

(a)   the offence ought to be dealt with as a grave crime under the provisions of the PCC(S)A 2000, s 91; or

(b)   there is an either way offence in which the juvenile is charged jointly with an adult, and the Crown Court considers that it is in the interests of justice for them to be tried together.

12.9   LINKED SUMMARY AND INDICTABLE OFFENCES

An offence can be tried in the Crown Court if it is triable on indictment only, or triable either way (for an examination of how offences are classified see Paragraphs 7.1 to 7.1.3). This general rule is, however, subject to an exception, in that a limited category of summary offences can be sent to the Crown Court for trial if linked with an offence properly triable on indictment. This exception was introduced by s 40 of the Criminal Justice Act 1988, and is dealt with in Paragraph 12.9.1. It is convenient to consider here, in addition, the procedure introduced by s 41 of the CJA 1988, by which a summary offence, linked to a triable either-way offence can be sent up to the Crown Court for plea and sentence (see Paragraph 12.9.2).

12.9.1   Trial of summary offence on indictment

Section 40 of the CJA 1988 provides that, if the accused has been sent or committed for trial in respect of an indictable offence and the evidence that was before the committing court discloses also a summary offence, then the prosecution may include in the indictment a count for the latter. There are two further conditions that must be satisfied, namely that:

(i)   the summary charge is *either* founded on the same facts or evidence as the indictable charge *or* forms with it a series of offences of the same or a similar character; and

(ii)   the summary charge is *either* for common assault or assault on a custody officer, taking a motor vehicle without the owner's consent, driving while disqualified or criminal damage falling within the special MCA, s 22 procedure, or it is punishable with imprisonment or disqualification and is specified by the Home Secretary in an order made by statutory instrument.

Points to notice about the s 40 procedure are that, although the evidence of the summary offence must be disclosed on the committal statements for the linked indictable matter, the initiative for putting it in the indictment must come from the prosecution — the magistrates commit for trial only in respect of the indictable charge (contrast the procedure under s 41, see the next Paragraph). Secondly, the legislation expressly includes within the s 40 procedure only certain specified summary offences. Thirdly, the summary offence must be linked with the indictable charge in one or other of the ways specified in s 40. The wording of that part of the section is taken from r 9 of the Indictment Rules, governing joinder of counts in one indictment (see Paragraphs 14.5.1 and 14.5.2). No doubt the section will be interpreted in the same liberal way that the rule has been. Fourthly, no method of challenging the joinder of a count for a summary offence is laid down by s 40. It is submitted, however, that the defence will be entitled to move to quash the count before arraignment if either the joinder is unlawful as falling outside the terms of s 40, or the committal statements do not disclose a case to answer for the offence. Lastly, assuming a count for a summary offence is validly included in an indictment by virtue of s 40, the method of trial will be exactly the same as for an indictable offence — i.e. the summary count will be put to the accused on arraignment together with the indictable count, and, if he pleads not guilty (either to both or even just to the former), a jury will be empanelled to hear the evidence and return a verdict. However, should he be convicted of the summary offence, the Crown Court's powers of sentence are limited to those the magistrates would have had (s 40(2)).

12.9.2   Committal for plea

Section 41 supplements s 40 by providing that magistrates committing for trial for an either-way offence may also commit the accused for any summary offence punishable with imprisonment or disqualification that arises out of circumstances which are the same as or connected with the either-way matter. The summary offence need not actually be disclosed by the evidence tendered at the committal proceedings — it would seem to be sufficient for the prosecution representative simply to explain that, in the course of committing an either-way offence, the accused also allegedly committed a summary one. As regards the summary offence, the magistrates commit neither for trial nor for sentence. What they do is perhaps best described as 'committing for plea', although that term is not used in the section. Thus, the summary offence is not included in the indictment, and is only mentioned in the Crown Court if and when the accused pleads guilty to or is found guilty of the either-way charge(s). At that stage the summary allegation is put to him. If he pleads guilty, the Crown Court judge will sentence him for all matters, thus ensuring that the sentencing function for offences arising out of one incident is not split between the magistrates' court and the Crown Court. The sentence for the summary offence is, of course, limited to that which the magistrates could have imposed. Should the accused deny the offence, the case is remitted to the magistrates for summary trial.

The differences between the s 40 and s 41 procedures have already emerged in the course of the preceding Paragraphs. However, a summary of them may illuminate the two sections. The differences are:

(i)   Section 40 applies only to those offences listed in the section plus any specified by the Home Secretary — s 41 applies to any summary offence punishable with imprisonment or disqualification.

(ii)   The magistrates play no part in the s 40 procedure, the onus being on the prosecution to include a count for a summary offence in the indictment if they consider that to be appropriate. Under s 41, it is the magistrates who must commit the summary offence to the Crown Court.

(iii)   But, under s 41, the summary offence need not actually be disclosed by evidence at the committal proceedings, whereas under s 40 it must.

(iv)   Under s 40, the summary offence must be founded on the same facts or form part of a series with the indictable charge; under s 41, it must arise out of the same or connected circumstances.

(v)   Under s 41, the linked indictable charge must be triable either way (see *Miall* [1992] Crim LR 71), whereas under s 40 it does not matter whether it is triable either way or only on indictment.

(vi)   Section 40 envisages a full trial on indictment for the summary offence; s 41 merely allows the offender to be sentenced for the summary offence if he admits it after being convicted of the offences actually on the indictment.

Committal of a summary offence under s 41 does not preclude the prosecution from putting a count for it in the indictment under s 40 (see s 4(4)). If that is done, the s 41 committal is disregarded and the Crown Court proceeds only under s 40.

PART 3 TRIAL ON INDICTMENT

13 The Crown Court

The Courts Act 1971 created a new criminal court — the Crown Court — to replace the ancient courts of assize and quarter sessions which had formerly dealt with trials on indictment. The Courts Act has now been largely repealed and its provisions incorporated into the Supreme Court Act 1981 ('SCA').

The Crown Court is part of the Supreme Court: SCA, s 1. The main heads of its jurisdiction are as follows:

(i) It has exclusive jurisdiction over trials on indictment: SCA, s 46. In other words, all trials on indictment take place in the Crown Court.

(ii) It deals with offenders who have been committed for sentence by the magistrates' courts. Committal for sentence usually occurs when magistrates summarily convict an offender of an offence triable either way and then decide that their limited powers of punishment are insufficient. They then send him to the Crown Court with a view to a heavier sentence being passed (see Chapter 11).

(iii) It hears appeals from the magistrates' courts against conviction and/or sentence (see Chapter 25).

(iv) It has a miscellaneous jurisdiction in respect of civil matters (e.g., hearing appeals against care orders made by youth courts or decisions of the licensing justices).

13.1 CROWN COURT JUDGES

High Court judges, circuit judges and recorders may all sit as judges of the Crown Court: SCA, s 8(1).

13.1.1 High Court judges

At any one time there may be around 20 High Court judges sitting in the Crown Court. They handle the most serious cases coming before the Court (see Paragraphs 13.1.6 and 13.2 for details of the way work is distributed amongst the various types of Crown Court judge). One would normally expect a High Court judge sitting in the Crown Court to come from the Queen's Bench Division and to have had some experience of criminal work as an advocate. In theory, however, there is nothing to stop a judge of, say, the Chancery Division being asked to sit. It is also possible for a Court of Appeal judge to sit in the Crown Court, but that would only happen in quite extraordinary circumstances.

13.1.2   Circuit judges

The office of circuit judge, like the Crown Court itself, was created by the Courts Act 1971. There are nearly 600 circuit judges, most of whom spend the bulk of their time sitting in the Crown Court. Circuit judges and recorders (see Paragraph 13.1.3) handle most of the routine work of the Crown Court, and the circuit judge in particular may be regarded as the typical Crown Court judge, presiding over some 80 per cent of Crown Court trials. Circuit judges are appointed by the Queen on the recommendation of the Lord Chancellor. It is a full-time appointment which cannot be combined with practice as a barrister or solicitor. On appointment, a circuit judge must have had the right of audience in the Crown or county courts for ten years, or have been a recorder, or have held a full-time post such as a member of an administrative tribunal or a district judge (Courts and Legal Services Act 1990, s 71). Retirement is normally at the age of 70 although the Lord Chancellor may authorise continuance in office until the age of 75. Conversely, the Lord Chancellor could remove a circuit judge from office before normal retiring age on grounds of incapacity or misbehaviour. For appointment, retirement etc. of circuit judges, see the Courts Act 1971, ss 16 to 20 and the Judicial Pensions and Retirements Act 1993, s 26 and Sch 6.

> Circuit judges may and, if possible, should sit in the county courts as well as the Crown Court. One of the suggestions made by Lord Beeching, on whose report the Courts Act was based, was that a reasonable 'mix' of civil work in the county courts and crime in the Crown Court would prevent circuit judges becoming jaded through lack of variety in their work. Accordingly, circuit judges are appointed to serve 'in the Crown Court and county courts': Courts Act 1971, s 16. Obviously, some circuit judges will be predominantly Crown Court judges and others predominantly county court judges, but the intention was that they should not be exclusively one or the other.

13.1.3   Recorders

Like circuit judges, recorders are appointed by the Queen on the recommendation of the Lord Chancellor. Unlike circuit judges, their appointment is a part-time one, and, when not sitting in the Crown Court, they may undertake private practice. The appointment is for a fixed term, during which the recorder agrees to make himself available to sit on a certain number of occasions. Barristers or solicitors of at least ten years' standing are eligible for appointment (Courts Act 1971, s 21). Provisions as to retirement and removal from office are similar to those which apply in the case of circuit judges, save that there is no discretion for the Lord Chancellor to allow a recorder to continue to act until he is 75. There are about 1,400 recorders but only a minority of them will be sitting in the Crown Court at any one time. Recorders deal with some 15 per cent of trials in the Crown Court.

13.1.4   Deputy circuit judges

As a temporary measure, in order to assist the disposal of business in the Crown Court (e.g. when there is a substantial backlog of cases waiting to be heard) the Lord Chancellor may appoint for a fixed period a deputy circuit judge: Courts Act 1971, s 24 as amended by SCA, s 146. For the period of his appointment a deputy circuit judge is in all ways equivalent to a circuit judge. Retired Lord Justices of Appeal, High Court judges and circuit judges are eligible for appointment as deputy circuit judges.

13.1.5   Mode of addressing Crown Court judges

High Court judges, all judges sitting at the Central Criminal Court (the Old Bailey) and any circuit judge holding the office of honorary Recorder of Liverpool, Manchester or Cardiff are addressed in court as 'My Lord' (or 'My Lady'). Except as stated above, circuit judges, recorders and deputy circuit judges are addressed as 'Your Honour'. The court list of cases for hearing in a particular court should refer to a circuit judge as 'His/Her Honour Judge . . .', and to a recorder as 'Mr/Mrs/Miss Recorder . . .' (see *Practice Direction (Judges: Modes of Address)* [1982] 1 WLR 101).

13.1.6   Distribution of work between High Court judges and circuit judges etc.

Practice directions given by the Lord Chief Justice govern the distribution of work between the various types of Crown Court judge. The general principle is that the gravest offences either must or normally will be tried by a High Court judge; less serious cases are assigned to circuit judges or recorders. Only a tiny fraction of the Crown Court's work comes before High Court judges. For details of the Practice Directions, see the next Paragraph.

13.2   ORGANISATION OF THE CROWN COURT

The Crown Court is a single court but it sits in many different locations throughout the country. Thus, strictly speaking, one should refer to the 'Crown Court sitting at Barchester' rather than the 'Barchester Crown Court'. One advantage of being a single court is that the Crown Court sitting anywhere in England or Wales may try any indictable offence over which the English courts have jurisdiction, irrespective of where it was allegedly committed (e.g., the Crown Court sitting at Plymouth can try an offence of, say, theft allegedly committed in Newcastle and vice versa). The jurisdictional disputes which used to arise under the pre-Crown Court system, whereby a conviction might be quashed because the appellant had been tried at Loamshire Quarter Sessions when he should have been tried at Bricktown Assizes, are thus avoided. It is also easier to ensure an even distribution of work between the various locations of the Crown Court. One of the few concessions to tradition made by the Courts Act 1971 was that when the Crown Court sat in the City of London (i.e. at the Old Bailey) it should continue to be known as the Central Criminal Court, not the Crown Court sitting in London. This nomenclature is preserved by s 8(3) of the SCA.

Locations of the Crown Court are classified as first, second or third tier. The first tier locations have facilities not only for Crown Court work but also for High Court civil work. They are attended by High Court judges as well as circuit judges and recorders. Second tier locations have no facilities for civil work but do have the services of at least one High Court judge on a regular basis; third tier locations have neither High Court work nor High Court judges. The various locations, of whatever tier, are grouped on a geographical basis into six circuits (Midland and Oxford, North-Eastern, Northern, South-Eastern, Wales and Chester, and Western). For each circuit there is appointed at least one High Court judge, known as the '*presiding judge*', who has special responsibility for the Crown Court locations within the circuit. In addition, each location has a '*resident judge*'. He is a senior circuit judge who, as the name implies, sits permanently at the location in question. Some of the presiding judge's duties in connection with the distribution of work (see below) may be devolved to the resident judge.

When a magistrates' court commits, sends or transfers an accused for trial it must specify the location of the Crown Court at which the trial is to take place. In selecting the appropriate location, the examining justices are to consider (Magistrates' Courts Act 1980, s 7 and Crime and Disorder Act 1998, s 51(10)):

(a) the convenience of the defence, the prosecution and the witnesses;
(b) the expediting of the trial; and
(c) any direction given by the Lord Chief Justice under s 75 of the SCA.

The SCA, s 75 empowers the Lord Chief Justice, with the concurrence of the Lord Chancellor, to give directions concerning the distribution of business in the Crown Court. Directions are contained in *Practice Direction (Crown Court: Business)* [2001] 1 WLR 1996. It is divided into two parts, one headed '*Classification*' and the second headed '*Allocation of business within the Crown Court*' (hereafter referred to as 'Part A' and 'Part B' respectively). Broadly speaking, their effect is as follows:

Offences are divided into four classes. Class 1 offences, consisting principally of murder and offences contrary to the Official Secrets Act 1911, *must* be tried by a High Court judge, save that murder trials may be released by or on the authority of the presiding judge to an approved circuit judge (i.e., one whom the Lord Chief Justice has approved for trying murder cases). Class 2 offences (principally, manslaughter, abortion, rape and intercourse with a girl under 13) must be tried by a High Court judge unless a particular case is released by or on the authority of the presiding judge for trial by a circuit judge. As regards rape (and any serious sexual offence, whether a Class 2 offence or not), the circuit judge or recorder to whom it is released must be one approved by the Lord Chief Justice. Class 3 offences consist simply of those not in any of the other classes. They may be tried by a High Court judge, circuit judge or recorder in accordance with general or particular directions from the presiding judge. Class 4 offences — the largest group by far — include all offences triable either way, plus robbery and wounding/causing grievous bodily harm with intent. They should not be listed for trial by a High Court judge except with the consent of the judge concerned or the presiding judge. Thus, the presumption is that the great majority of Class 4 offences will be handled by a circuit judge or recorder.

It will be apparent that offences in Classes 1–3 either must or prima facie will be tried by a High Court judge; offences in Class 4 will prima facie be tried by a circuit judge or recorder. Accordingly, para 2 of Part A of the Directions states that, if the offence (or any one of the offences) for which an accused is being committed for trial is in Classes 1–3, the trial should take place at the most convenient location of the Crown Court at which a High Court judge regularly sits (i.e., a first or second tier location). If all the offences are in Class 4, it should simply be the most convenient location. In deciding on the most convenient location (or most convenient location at which a High Court judge regularly sits), the justices should have regard to the location/s which the presiding judge has specified as being those to which their petty sessional division should normally send cases for trial. Thus, the decision on venue is, in practice, taken automatically, each magistrates' court knowing the location to which it is expected to send defendants.

However, the venue selected will not necessarily be that at which the case is tried, since s 76(1) of the SCA provides that the Crown Court itself may give directions varying the place of a trial on indictment. A direction under s 76 may be given by an officer of the Court on his own initiative (e.g., as a matter of administrative convenience to even out the work-load of the various locations, or to facilitate trial by a High Court judge where, exceptionally, a Class 4 offence warrants it but the magistrates have committed to a third tier location). In addition, either the prosecution or defence may apply to the Court for a change of venue. Such applications must be heard by a High Court judge in open court (s 76(4)). The application might be based on the matters specifically mentioned in s 7 of the Magistrates' Courts Act 1980, namely the convenience of the parties and witnesses. Occasionally, other reasons for a change are advanced (e.g., local hostility to the accused making it desirable to have the trial well away from where the offence was allegedly committed, or fear of an escape attempt necessitating a switch to a location which can be securely guarded). An application to vary the location to one where a higher proportion of black people live, in order to obtain a multiracial jury panel, is unlikely to be successful, following the Court of Appeal's judgment in *Ford* [1989] QB 868 (see Paragraph 17.4.4).

13.3 MAGISTRATES AS JUDGES OF THE CROWN COURT

The primary role of magistrates in the judicial system is, of course, to adjudicate in the magistrates' courts. They do, however, have a secondary role to play as judges of the Crown Court. When the Crown Court is dealing with an appeal from a magistrates' court it *must* consist of a 'professional' judge (i.e., a High Court judge, circuit judge or recorder) sitting with not less than two and not more than four lay justices: SCA, s 74(1). In fact, para 5 of Part B of the Lord Chief Justice's directions states that the professional judge should be an experienced circuit judge or recorder, not a High Court judge. Also, r 4 of the Crown Court Rules 1982 (SI 1982 No 1109) provides that the hearing may take place with a professional judge and only one lay justice if insisting upon two would cause unreasonable delay. Furthermore, should any of the magistrates initially comprising the court have to withdraw, the hearing may be completed in his or their absence. Having regard to the availability of magistrates for work in the Crown Court, the Lord Chancellor may give directions that at certain locations the above rules shall be relaxed: SCA, s 74(4). As well as being required to sit for appeals for sentence, lay justices *may* sit with a circuit judge or recorder for any Crown Court proceedings other than those listed for a not guilty plea (para 8 of Part B of the Lord Chief Justice's directions). The idea is that working with a professional judge will broaden the magistrate's experience and assist him when he returns to his local bench.

Whenever magistrates sit in the Crown Court, whether their presence is obligatory or optional, they should play a full part in all decisions of the court: *Orpin* [1975] QB 283. Indeed, in the event of disagreement, decisions are taken by a majority so that, at least in theory, the lay magistrates could overrule the professional judge: SCA, s 73(3). However, should the court be equally divided, the professional judge has a casting vote. Also, on any questions of law that arise, the magistrates must accept the judge's direction. Thus, if the defence contend during an appeal against conviction that a confession by the accused should not be admitted into evidence, the judge will tell his lay colleagues what the law on admissibility of confessions is, but any relevant findings of fact (e.g. as to whether a police officer used threats to obtain the confession) will be for the court as a whole, not just for the judge. At the sentencing stage, it is particularly important for the magistrates not only to contribute to the decision but to be *seen* to contribute. Thus, in *Newby* (1984) 6 Cr App R (S) 148, N was sentenced to 12 months' imprisonment following his plea of guilty to an indictment charging him with handling stolen goods. Although the recorder and the two magistrates who comprised the court which sentenced N apparently talked about the case before coming into open court, and although the recorder passed notes to his colleagues whilst defence counsel was making his plea in mitigation, the recorder announced the sentence immediately the plea in mitigation was concluded. There was no *appearance* of consultation, although there had been consultation in fact. N appealed against sentence, and, in giving the Court of Appeal's decision, Caulfield J said:

> This court would like to emphasise that where a learned judge is sitting with magistrates, not only should he consult his fellow-magistrates by law but he should make sure that the court appreciates that he has consulted. It is not necessary for the court to retire after each particular case. There is nothing wrong in notes being passed between members of the court. But when it comes to the point of sentence having to be given, it is far wiser for the court to show the public that it is a composite court and that each member has a view which is expressed eventually through the chairman or president of the court.

As has been seen, a magistrate, sitting in the Crown Court upon the hearing of an appeal, plays a major role in the proceedings. If the appellant or offender were to find himself in the Crown Court before one of the magistrates who had previously decided against him, he might justifiably feel aggrieved. Rule 5 of the Crown Court Rules provides, therefore, that a magistrate who was involved in the proceedings in the magistrates' court may not be a member of the court for the appeal.

13.4 RIGHTS OF AUDIENCE IN THE CROWN COURT

Barristers, of course, have the right of audience in the Crown Court. In addition, the Courts and Legal Services Act 1990 enacted a statutory scheme for the definition and regulation of rights of audience before the courts. The aim is to preserve all existing rights of audience (see ss 31 and 32), and to set up a framework for the granting of new rights (see s 27). Machinery can thereby be introduced for advocates who are not barristers to obtain rights of audience formerly held only by barristers. What is taking place, in particular, is the extension of rights of audience to certain solicitors, subject to training provided by the Law Society.

Even without the machinery introduced by the Courts and Legal Services Act 1990, however, the Bar's right of audience in the Crown Court has not been exclusive. The Lord Chancellor has issued directions entitling solicitors to 'appear in, conduct, defend and address the court' in appeals and committals for sentence where they, or a member of their firm, represented the accused in the magistrates' court. At some of the remoter locations of the Crown Court (e.g., Caernarvon, Barnstaple, Doncaster and Truro) solicitors have a more general right of audience, being able to appear for the defence at trials on indictment for Class 4 offences.

The accused has the right to defend himself if he so wishes. As far as the prosecution in a trial on indictment is concerned, the position is governed by the Courts and Legal Services Act 1990, s 27(2)(c). This gives the Crown Court a discretion to allow a private individual to conduct a private prosecution before it. Glidewell LJ stated in *Southwark Crown Court ex p Tawfick* (1994) *The Times*, 1 December 1994 that this was a discretion which would only be exercised occasionally, so almost invariably, the prosecution must be legally represented in the Crown Court even if it is a private prosecution.

13.5 THE LAYOUT OF THE CROWN COURT

This chapter has described the legal structure of the Crown Court. It may be useful to conclude with a brief description of the physical appearance of a location of the Crown

Court. Externally, the court buildings vary enormously, from modern glass and concrete structures to ornate Victoriana. Internally, the court rooms themselves also vary, but one may detect a basic pattern. At the front of the court is the raised bench where the judge sits in a throne-like chair beneath the Royal coat-of-arms. Below the judge is the clerk at his desk. Facing the judge, either at the rear or in the middle of the court, is the accused in the partitioned off area known as the dock. In front of the dock are the seats for counsel. To one side of the court is the jury box — twelve seats, usually in two tiered rows of six — and, on the other side, is the witness box from where the witnesses give their evidence. At the back of court, or in a gallery looking down from above, are seats for the public. Special areas in court may also be set aside for probation officers or social workers. A room leading off the court is reserved for the use of the jury, and it is to that room, at the end of the trial, that they retire to consider their verdict.

14   The Indictment

The indictment is the formal document containing a list of the charges against the accused, to which he pleads either guilty or not guilty at the beginning of his trial on indictment. A jury may try only one indictment at a time: *Crane v DPP* [1921] AC 299. The law on drafting indictments is contained principally in the Indictments Act 1915 (IA) and the Indictment Rules 1971 (IR) (SI 1971 No 1253) made under the Act.

On page 212 you will find the form of indictment which might be expected to follow from an imaginary incident involving three young men (David Wilson, John Burton and Paul Green) who, after a football match, attacked two supporters of the opposition team (Barry and Charles Johnson). The police arrived to find Wilson and Burton kicking Barry Johnson as he lay on the ground. This caused sufficient severe bruising to require outpatient hospital treatment. Meanwhile Green was threatening Charles Johnson with a broken milk bottle, with which he had already inflicted a facial wound requiring stitches but not sufficiently serious to leave a subsequent scar.

The indictment illustrates certain fundamental points about indictments which will be discussed in detail later in the Chapter:

(a)   The heading or commencement to the indictment is always in a standard form. At the top is the word 'INDICTMENT', followed by the place of trial and the name of the case. The prosecution is always formally in the name of the Queen. After the name of the case comes the standard phrase 'AB, CD etc. are charged as follows', known as the presentment.

(b)   The offences alleged against the accused are set out in separate counts of the indictment. Each count must allege only one offence.

(c)   Each count is divided into a Statement of Offence and Particulars of Offence. The Statement of Offence gives the name of the offence and, if it is statutory, the statute and section contravened: IR, r 6. If the offence is contrary to common law, that does not have to be expressly stated — e.g., had Barry Johnson died as a result of the kicks he received and had Wilson and Burton been charged with his unlawful killing, the Statement of Offence would simply have read 'manslaughter'.

(d)   The Particulars of Offence give the names of the accused alleged to have committed the offence set out in the count, and the basic details of what they allegedly did (IA, s 3 and IR, r 6).

(e)   Although a count may allege only one offence, an indictment may contain two or more counts against an accused. Paul Green is charged with wounding Charles Johnson (the cut to the cheek) and with having an offensive weapon (the broken milk bottle). Had the injuries to Barry Johnson been more serious the prosecution might have included in the indictment a count for causing grievous bodily harm with intent against Wilson and Burton as well as the count for occasioning actual bodily harm. The jury could then convict on one count or the other depending on whether they thought the evidence established the more serious or the less serious offence. Green can, of course, be convicted on either or both of the counts against him.

No 023210

INDICTMENT

The Crown Court at BARCHESTER

THE QUEEN v DAVID WILSON, JOHN BURTON and PAUL GREEN

DAVID WILSON, JOHN BURTON and PAUL GREEN are CHARGED AS FOLLOWS:—

Count 1   Statement of Offence
Assault occasioning actual bodily harm contrary to s 47 of the Offences against the Person Act 1861.

Particulars of Offence
DAVID WILSON and JOHN BURTON, on the 1st day of January 2002, assaulted Barry Johnson thereby occasioning him actual bodily harm.

Count 2   Statement of Offence
Wounding contrary to s 20 of the Offences against the Person Act 1861.

Particulars of Offence
PAUL GREEN, on the 1st day of January 2002, maliciously wounded Charles Johnson.

Count 3   Statement of Offence
Having an offensive weapon contrary to s 1(1) of the Prevention of Crime Act 1953.

Particulars of Offence
PAUL GREEN, on the 1st day of January 2002, without lawful authority or reasonable excuse had with him in a public place, namely Cathedral Row, Barchester, an offensive weapon, namely a broken milk bottle.

Date 1 March 2002

A. N. Other
Officer of the Crown Court

(f)   Two or more accused may be charged in a single count if the prosecution case is that they acted in concert to commit an offence. Wilson and Burton were both kicking Barry Johnson so it is proper to put them both in one count.

(g)   Two or more accused may be charged in a single indictment even though they are not alleged to have committed any single offence together. Green was not involved in the attack on Barry Johnson, but since his attack on Charles Johnson and the attack by the other two on Barry Johnson were all part of one incident they may all be joined in one indictment.

(h)   The indictment is signed by an officer of the Crown Court.

14.1   PREFERRING THE BILL OF INDICTMENT

An indictment must be signed by an officer of the Crown Court: Administration of Justice (Miscellaneous Provisions) Act 1933, s 2(1). If, through inadvertence, no signature is appended, the 'indictment' is a nullity and any conviction based upon it will be quashed by the Court of Appeal (see *Morais* (1988) 87 Cr App R 9 for an example of that occurring). The officer's signature should appear at the end of the indictment (Indictments (Procedure) Rules 1971 (SI 1971 No 2084), r 4) but the fact that it appears at the beginning does not invalidate the indictment (*Laming* (1989) 90 Cr App R 450). Technically, until the indictment is signed, it is merely a 'bill of indictment'. Bills of indictment are drafted either by counsel or by officers of the Crown Court. In the former case, the bill has to be delivered to the Crown Court to be signed. Such delivery is known as '*preferment of the bill of indictment*'. Where a Crown Court officer does the drafting, the bill is deemed to be preferred as soon as it is drafted (see r 4 of the 1971 Rules).

In an attempt to reduce delays in the criminal process, r 5 of the 1971 Rules provides that a bill of indictment must be preferred within 28 days of committal to the Crown Court. However, the rule does little in practice to expedite trials since it permits an officer of the Crown Court to extend the original 28-day period by 28 days, and further extensions can be granted by a Crown Court judge. An application for extension of time should normally be in writing, and should state why more time is needed. It is preferable, though not essential, to make the application before the permitted time has actually expired. Thus, the r 5 time-limit is an extremely flexible one, but even if the rule is not complied with (i.e., the bill of indictment is preferred outside the 28 day period with no extension of time having been obtained) it has been held that the accused may be validly tried and convicted on the indictment: *Sheerin* (1977) 64 Cr App R 68. In other words, r 5 is directory not mandatory. It states what ought to be done, not what must be done. The distinction between an indictment and a bill of indictment is only relevant in the context of preferment of a bill of indictment, so further references will be simply to drafting an indictment.

Only in a minority of particularly important or complex cases are the papers sent to counsel for an indictment to be drafted. However, in *Newland* [1988] QB 402, the Court of Appeal expressed concern at the quality of some drafting, and stated that, before the indictment is put to the accused at the beginning of the trial, counsel for the prosecution should check that it complies with the Indictment Rules. In other words, it is counsel's responsibility to correct any errors in the Crown Court officer's drafting. Watkins LJ said (at p. 409):

[Drafting of indictments] is undertaken by and large by staff of the Crown Courts in this country. The unfortunate fact is, so we are informed and as we from some experience in this court know, that the defective manner in which indictments are drafted is giving cause for concern . . . .

It is . . . necessary for a restatement to be made upon the question of responsibility for the ultimate presentation of an indictment to the court. It was the responsibility of counsel to ensure that the indictment was in proper form before arraignment. A return to that practice . . . may in our view be a salutary thing for everyone concerned.

At the time when Watkins LJ gave his judgment, the usual practice was for the drafting to be done by Crown Court staff. In CPS prosecutions, the system now is for a CPS lawyer to prepare a schedule (in effect a draft indictment). This is sent to the Crown Court with the committal papers. The Crown Court officer is (in theory) supposed to check that there has been no contravention of the statutory provisions.

14.2 COUNTS WHICH MAY BE INCLUDED IN AN INDICTMENT

The first and most basic question for the person drafting the indictment is: What counts (i.e. charges) should be included in it? If there were committal proceedings, the drafter will have been provided with copies of the documents from them. He will also know on what charges the magistrates' court committed the accused and on what charges, if any, it refused to do so. But, he is not bound by the magistrates' view as to the offences for which there is a case to answer. Subject to the rules on joinder of counts (see below), he may include in the indictment counts for *any* indictable offence that he considers to be disclosed by the evidence before the magistrates' court, whether or not the accused was committed for trial in respect of that offence: Administration of Justice (Miscellaneous Provisions) Act 1933, s 2(2). Thus, where the prosecution evidence is that the accused was found in possession of stolen goods an hour after they were stolen and he has been sent for trial on a charge of theft, the indictment may include counts in the alternative for both theft and handling stolen goods to cover the possibility of the accused saying that he did not steal the goods but merely received them. Again, where the committal is for manslaughter, the indictment could contain a single count for murder and no count for manslaughter if counsel or the Crown Court officer considers that there is sufficient evidence of malice aforethought. That would be possible even if the magistrates' court had been specifically asked to commit on a charge of murder, but had refused and merely committed for manslaughter. The power to include a count for an offence for which the magistrates' court expressly refused to commit should, however, be very sparingly exercised: *Dawson* [1960] 1 WLR 163, quoted with approval in *Kempster* [1989] 1 WLR 1125. The count must in any event be based upon the evidence before the magistrates' court (see Paragraph 14.7.3 for details). In addition, a charge upon which the accused was not sent for trial can only form part of the indictment if it is 'in substitution for or in addition to' a count upon which he *was* sent. Further, any such extra counts must be of a kind that can 'lawfully' be joined in that indictment (proviso (i) to s 2(2) of the Administration of Justice (Miscellaneous Provisions) Act 1933). Thus, in *Lombardi* [1989] 1 WLR 73, L faced two indictments. On the first he was convicted of three forgery offences. On the second there were four bankruptcy offences (unrelated to the forgery counts), upon which the magistrates had not committed him for trial, although there was ample evidence to do so on the committal papers. The judge ruled the second indictment valid, whereupon L pleaded guilty and then appealed. The Court of Appeal held that the second indictment was invalid since the counts in it could not have been joined with the counts in the first indictment without breaching r 9 of the IR (see Paragraph 14.5.2 for the terms of r 9). Consequently, the counts in it were barred by s 2(2)(i) of the 1933 Act. (For the consequences where the indictment is invalid, see Paragrah 14.8.)

14.3 CONTENTS OF THE COUNT

A count consists of a statement of offence, giving the short name of the offence and the statute contravened if it is statutory, followed by particulars of the offence. IA, s 3 provides that the indictment shall contain 'such particulars as may be necessary for giving reasonable information as to the nature of the charge'. IR, r 6 is a little more specific, saying that where the offence is a statutory one, the particulars must disclose the 'essential elements of the offence', save that if the accused would not be 'prejudiced or embarrassed in his defence' by failure to disclose an essential element that element need not be mentioned. Where the accused is entitled to be acquitted if he can bring himself within some exception or proviso, it is not necessary to state in the particulars that he is outside the exception and the proviso. For example, a count alleging the production or supplying or possession of a controlled drug need not state that the accused falls outside those categories of persons who are entitled to produce, supply or possess such drugs under the Misuse of Drugs Act 1971.

The guidance on drafting particulars given by s 3 and r 6 is so vague that the best advice to a person settling an indictment is to look up a precedent for any count he wishes to include. *Blackstone's Criminal Practice* contains specimen counts for all the common indictable offences, and the practitioner can usually follow the form of wording in there with safety. Specimen counts for some offences are set out on pages 224–28, but the following general comments may be helpful:

(a)   The particulars start with the forename and surname of the accused charged in the count. An error in giving the name will not be a good ground of appeal against conviction provided the accused could reasonably be identified from the name stated. Similarly, where any other person is referred to in the particulars, fore-name and surname should be stated but errors will not defeat a conviction.

(b)   The date of the alleged offence is then stated. Surprisingly, a conviction can be upheld even where the prosecution evidence shows that the offence was committed on a day other than that laid in the particulars, although if the change in date would prejudice the accused in his defence (e.g., he has an alibi for the date in the particulars) he should be granted an adjournment. If the exact date of the offence is unknown the particulars may allege that it was on a day unknown between the day before the earliest day on which it could have been committed and the day after the latest day on which it could have been committed. Thus, if property was stolen on 1 January 2002 and found in possession of the accused on 31 January, the count would allege that 'A.B., on a day unknown between the 31st day of December 2001 and the 1st day of February 2002 dishonestly received . . .'

(c)   The elements of the offence are alleged. It is not usually necessary to write out the elements in full. For example, in a count for theft, it is sufficient to allege that 'AB stole a wrist-watch belonging to CD' — one need not allege that 'AB dishonestly appropriated a wrist-watch belonging to CD with the intention of permanently depriving CD of the said wrist-watch.' However, in counts for certain offences such as handling stolen goods a fuller form of particulars is recommended.

(d)   Where property is mentioned in the particulars, the owner should be named in order to identify the property, but the value need not be given. If the owner is unknown the property can be referred to as 'belonging to a person or persons unknown'. If the property relevant to a count is cash, it may be described simply as money without specifying the individual coins and bank-notes (e.g., 'A.B., on . . . . stole a purse and £5.50 in money').

(e)   The place where the offence occurred need not be alleged, unless the definition of the offence requires that it be committed in or with reference to a limited range of places. Thus, a count for dangerous driving must specify the road where it occurred since the offence can only be committed on a road, and a count for burglary must specify the building burgled since the offence necessitates entering a building as a trespasser. Theft, on the other hand, can be committed anywhere so the count need not say from where the property was stolen.

14.4 THE RULE AGAINST DUPLICITY

An indictment may contain several counts, but each count must allege only one offence. If the wording of a count in itself shows that it is alleging two or more offences, the count is said to be 'bad for duplicity', and the defence should bring a motion to quash, i.e. apply to the judge, before the indictment is put to the accused, to quash the count. If the motion succeeds, the accused is not asked to plead to the count (see Paragraph 14.7.3). Should the judge wrongly reject the motion, the accused will have a good ground of appeal against conviction if the jury find him guilty.

A count alleging that 'A.B., on . . . , murdered or unlawfully killed C.D.' is bad for duplicity or duple, since both murder and manslaughter are particularised in one count. Similarly, a count alleging that 'Jane Smith, on 1st January 2002, stole a dress belonging to Spencer Ltd and on 2nd January 2002 stole a coat belonging to Marks Ltd' is duple because the different days and different victims named show that two quite separate thefts are being charged. On the other hand, a count for stealing a coat and dress from Spencer and Marks Ltd on 1st January is perfectly valid. The wording of the count is consistent with the accused having gone into one shop (Spencer and Marks Ltd) on one occasion and stolen two items. Of course, in strict logic it could be argued that there must have been two separate acts of appropriation, one in relation to the coat and the other in relation to the dress. Therefore, assuming the necessary *mens rea* was present, the accused committed two separate thefts which should be charged in separate counts. However, as Lord Diplock said in *DPP v Merriman* [1973] AC 584, 'the rule against duplicity has always been applied in a practical, rather than in a strictly analytical way', and if several items are stolen from one victim on one occasion it is standard practice to have just one count listing all the items. In other words, several criminal acts may be alleged in one count if they were so closely linked together as to form one activity or transaction. Whether there was one or more than one activity is a matter of degree, turning upon the facts of the individual case. In *Wilson* (1979) 69 Cr App R 83 the facts were that W went into a 'Boots' department store, and moved from department to department, taking items from each department. He left the store without paying, and went into 'Debenhams' where he behaved in similar fashion. The indictment against him contained two counts, one listing all the items stolen from 'Boots' and the other the items stolen from 'Debenhams'. The jury found W guilty, and he appealed on the basis that there should have been separate counts in relation to his conduct in each of the departments. The Court of Appeal upheld the convictions. W's acts in each store were not broken into separate activities by his leaving one department and entering another, and therefore two counts — one for each store — were sufficient.

It is unusual for a count to name more than one victim of the offence alleged. Thus, in *Mansfield* [1977] 1 WLR 1102 M's single act of setting fire to a hotel caused the deaths of seven victims, but the prosecution nonetheless elected to have seven separate counts for murder, each count naming one victim. However, there is no rule of law that a count must not name several victims. Thus, in the old case of *Giddins* (1842) Car & M 634, a count for robbing A of one shilling and B of two shillings was held valid, since the prosecution case was that the two acts of robbery had been virtually simultaneous. *Giddins* was referred to with approval by the House of Lords in *DPP v Merriman,* although a similar case today would almost certainly be charged in two counts, as a matter of practice.

Where a count is not bad for duplicity, since its wording is consistent with the accused having only committed one offence, but the prosecution evidence tends to show that his criminal conduct was broken into separate activities, the correct remedy is to apply to the judge to amend the indictment (see Paragraph 14.7.2). The amendment would take the form of splitting the single count into several counts. Failure to amend would be a ground of appeal, but the Court of Appeal might well dismiss the appeal because there had been no miscarriage of justice.

14.4.1 'General deficiency' cases

The rule that separate activities should be charged in separate counts would be inconvenient if strictly applied in the not uncommon type of case where a person is suspected of having stolen cash or property from the same victim on a large number of separate occasions, but it is not possible to specify the precise dates when the thefts occurred or the precise amounts that were stolen (e.g., the prosecution case is that the manager of a shop has been taking small amounts from the till over a lengthy period, but their only evidence of that is that when the takings at the end of the period were compared with the amount of stock which had been sold there was found to be a significant shortfall). Such an allegation is usually referred to as 'theft of a general deficiency'. In such a case it is permissible to allege in the particulars of one count that the accused stole the *aggregate* amount on a day or days unknown during the whole period over which the appropriations must have occurred (see *Tomlin* (1954) 38 Cr App R 82 and *Lawson* (1952) 36 Cr App R 30).

14.4.2 Specimen or sample counts

Where a person is accused of a systematic course of criminal conduct, the prosecution may choose to proceed by way of specimen or sample counts. This might be the case, for example, where dishonesty over a period of time is alleged, or where a series of indecent assaults is alleged in a case of child abuse. In order to keep the indictment to a manageable length, a limited number of sample counts are included. In such a case, the prosecution should provide the defence with a list of all the offences of which those contained in the indictment are samples. If the defendant pleads not guilty, however, care must be taken to ensure that he is not deprived of his right to trial by jury on those offences which do not appear in the indictment. In other words, the judge must not assume that, because the jury has found him guilty of the offences in the indictment, he is also guilty of the other offences of which those in the indictment are samples. The problems which this presents for the judge in passing sentence are discussed in Paragraph 20.1.

14.4.3 Rule 7 of the Indictment Rules

So far, the application of the rule against duplicity may seem to be largely a matter of commonsense and convenience. Rule 7 of the IR unfortunately introduces some hair-splitting technical distinctions. The rule says that, if a section or subsection of a statute has — on its true construction — created a single offence, but has defined one or more elements of the offence in the alternative, then the statutory alternatives may be alleged in the alternative in a single count. Thus, a count for damaging property 'intending to damage it *or* being reckless as to whether the property would be damaged' is valid since s 1 of the Criminal Damage Act 1971 defines the *mens rea* of criminal damage in terms of intent or recklessness. Similarly, a count for being in possession of a controlled drug may allege that the drug was cannabis or cannabis resin: *Best* (1980) 70 Cr App R 21. The problem is that r 7 does *not* permit the alleging of separate offences in the alternative in a single count, even if those offences are created by one section of a statute, and Parliament often fails to make it clear whether it has created one offence which can be committed in different ways or a number of different offences. *Naismith* [1961] 3 All ER 735 illustrates the difficulty that can arise. Section 18 of the Offences against the Person Act 1861 makes it criminal to wound or cause any grievous bodily harm to any person with intent to do some grievous bodily harm or with intent to resist or prevent a lawful arrest. Is the section creating one, two, four or six offences? Ashworth J decided that there are probably two offences — wounding contrary to s 18 and causing grievous bodily harm contrary to s 18 — both of which can be committed with any of the three intents mentioned in the section. Therefore, a count alleging that AB wounded or caused grievous bodily harm to CD would be bad for duplicity, but a count for wounding with intent to cause grievous bodily harm or to resist or prevent a lawful arrest is valid. The case of *Naismith* enables the drafter of a bill of indictment to know how he should word a count under s 18 of the 1861 Act, and how many counts he should have. However, in respect of some other equally common offences there is no decided case, and no means of being certain how many offences Parliament has created. For example, s 12 of the Theft Act 1968 provides that a person who takes a conveyance for his own or another's use without the consent of the owner or other lawful authority, or who drives a conveyance knowing that it has been so taken, or who allows himself to be carried in a conveyance knowing that it has been so taken, commits an offence. It is suggested that the section is creating two offences, namely taking a conveyance without the owner's consent or other lawful authority, and knowingly driving or allowing oneself to be carried in a wrongfully taken conveyance, but until the Court of Appeal are called upon to give a ruling on the question nobody can be sure. It is certainly arguable that s 12 is creating three offences, and it is even arguable that there is only one offence.

14.4.4   Counts for handling stolen goods

Section 22 of the Theft Act 1968 creates a single offence of handling stolen goods: *Griffiths v Freeman* [1970] 1 WLR 659. It can be committed in some 18 different ways, by receiving the goods, or by undertaking or assisting in their retention, removal, disposal or realisation by or for the benefit of another person, or by arranging to do any of those things. Therefore, if the particulars of a handling count merely allege that the accused *handled* certain stolen goods namely . . . knowing or believing the same to be stolen, it is technically correct but it hardly gives the defence a fair indication of how the prosecution intend to present their case. The prosecution ought to 'nail their colours to the mast', and state in the count whether they are alleging receiving or one or more of the other forms of handling. In a case of genuine uncertainty, there should be two counts. The particulars of count one will allege that the accused received the goods, and the particulars of count two that he undertook or assisted in their retention, removal, disposal or realisation by or for the benefit of another person or arranged so to do. The jury can then choose whether to convict on count one (generally regarded as the most serious form of handling) or on count two (see *Nicklin* [1977] 1 WLR 403).

14.5   JOINDER OF COUNTS IN AN INDICTMENT

The circumstances in which several counts against one accused may be put in one indictment are set out in IR, r 9, which says:

Charges for any offences may be joined in the same indictment if those charges are founded on the same facts, or form or are part of a series of offences of the same or a similar character.

The operation of the rule is illustrated by *Mansfield* [1977] 1 WLR 1102, where M was charged in an indictment containing ten counts. Three counts were for arson, alleging that on 12 December 1974 M had started a fire in the Worsley Hotel, Bayswater, and that on 19 December and 28 December 1974 he had started fires in the Piccadilly Hotel in the West End of London. The three offences were a series of the same or a similar character, so counts for them were rightly put in one indictment. The remaining counts were for murder, based on the fact that seven people had died in the Worsley Hotel fire. Since these counts were founded on the same facts as the Worsley Hotel arson count, all ten counts could properly be joined in one indictment.

14.5.1 Charges 'founded on the same facts'

The simplest application of the first limb of r 9 is to be found in cases such as *Mansfield* where a single act by the accused (setting fire to a hotel) gives rise to several offences (arson and seven murders). The rule will also apply where the accused allegedly committed several offences in a continuous course of conduct. Thus, if X robs a bank; drives his 'get-away' car at high speeds in a built up area to shake off pursuit, and then, when finally cornered, struggles with police officers to avoid arrest, he could be charged in one indictment with robbery, dangerous driving and assault with intent to resist arrest. If he carried a shotgun and/or stole the get-away car, further counts could be added for theft and having a firearm to commit an indictable offence. But, substantial contemporaneity is not an essential prerequisite for the application of r 9. If two offences are separated in time, but the later one would not have happened without the prior occurrence of the first, then they may be said to be founded on the same facts: *Barrell and Wilson* (1979) 69 Cr App R 250. In that case, W was indicted for (i) assault and affray at a discotheque and (ii) attempting to pervert the course of justice. The prosecution case was that W, having been committed for trial for the offences of violence, tried to bribe witnesses not to testify against him. That obviously happened several weeks after the incident at the discotheque, but W would have had no cause to offer bribes unless he had faced prosecution for assault. Therefore, the Court of Appeal held that the time-lag did not prevent the charges being founded on the same facts. A simpler example of the same principle is where the accused allegedly used stolen cheques to purchase goods — he can be charged in one indictment with (i) theft or handling of the cheque book and (ii) obtaining property by deception in respect of each individual cheque tendered, regardless of how long elapsed between his getting the cheque book and his first dishonest use of it.

In *Barrell and Wilson*, the jury could — and indeed did — convict W on all the counts against him. A more difficult problem for the courts is whether two counts may be joined in one indictment if the prosecution cases on the counts are mutually destructive of each other — i.e. a verdict of guilty on count 1 would presuppose that the jury were not satisfied that the accused committed count 2 and vice versa. The decisions of the appellate courts on the point are somewhat inconclusive. In brief, it was stated in *Barnes* (1986) 83 Cr App R 38 that charges of (i) perjury at B's brother's trial for wounding M and (ii) wounding M with intent might not have been founded on the same facts within the meaning of r 9, the prosecution case being that either B told the truth at the brother's trial when he testified that he (B) had attacked M and his brother was innocent, or he lied and was ipso facto guilty of perjury. The jury convicted of the latter. The Court of Appeal pointed out that the case was not on all fours with *Barrell and Wilson* because the prosecution were not asking the jury to convict on both counts — on the contrary, their case on count 1 was the very antithesis of their case on count 2. However, their Lordships avoided a definite decision on the validity or otherwise of the indictment by holding that the error — if there was one — had not led to a miscarriage of justice. In *Bellman* (1987) 86 Cr App R 40, on the other hand, B's appeal did succeed. He had been convicted of obtaining money by deception. The indictment included a count both for that and conspiracy to import drugs. According to the prosecution, money had been paid to B by persons who expected him to use it to smuggle drugs into the country. Either B genuinely intended to carry out the plan to smuggle drugs (in which case he was guilty of conspiracy), or he did not (and was guilty of obtaining the money by deception). The Court of Appeal held that the prosecution should have been required to elect on which charge they wished to proceed. In the House of Lords [1989] AC 836, it was conceded that the ground of appeal upheld by the Court of Appeal was wrong. Since there was a prima facie case on each alternative, it was for the jury (not the prosecution or the judge) to determine which (if either) of the alternatives was proved. B's counsel argued instead that it could never be right for mutually contradictory counts to be contained in one indictment. The House of Lords rejected that argument as without authority. Indeed it had long been the practice to include in one indictment counts for stealing and handling the same property, even though a conviction for theft would preclude a conviction for handling and vice versa (see Paragraph 14.5.4). Lord Griffiths in *Bellman* went on, in an *obiter dictum*, to confirm the legality of the joinder in *Barnes*, since the factual origin of both counts was the attack on the victim.

14.5.2 Charges of 'the same or a similar character'

The meaning of this phrase was discussed by the House of Lords in *Ludlow v Metropolitan Police Commissioner* [1971] AC 29. Lord Pearson (their lordships all concurring) said that for two or more offences to form a series or part of a series of the same or a similar character there must be a nexus between them. The nexus must arise from a similarity both in law and in the facts constituting the offences. In *Ludlow*, L was charged in the first count with attempted theft and in the second count with robbery. The element of attempted or actual theft in both counts provided a sufficient similarity in law. The facts of the first count were that L was seen emerging from a window in the private part of a public house in Acton, the jury being asked to draw the inference that he had been disturbed when attempting theft. The facts of the second count were that 16 days later, at another public house in Acton, L paid for a drink and then snatched the money back, punching the barman. The House of Lords held that there was a sufficient similarity between the facts of the two offences to justify the joinder of the counts in one indictment. This might seem a surprising decision, since both offences happening to be committed in public houses appears purely coincidental, and otherwise the only similarity arises from the closeness in time and geographical location of the offences. The lesson to be drawn from *Ludlow* is that only a slight similarity on the facts is necessary to satisfy r 9. Another point confirmed by *Ludlow* is that two offences are sufficient to constitute a series within r 9.

The time between the alleged offences may well be important in determining whether there is a sufficiently close nexus between them. After all, the second limb requires that the charges should be 'part of a series', and use of the word 'series' would seem to imply some limit as to time. Nevertheless, in *Baird* (1993) 97 Cr App R 308, the Court of Appeal held that a count of indecent assault against one young boy was properly joined with a count of indecent assault against another young boy nine years later. Their lordships were influenced by the fact that, although there was no coincidence in time or place, the other factual similarities between the two offences were remarkable.

There was an even wider separation in time in the case of *C* (1993) *The Times*, 4 February 1993. C was charged in the same indictment with the rape of his seven-year-old daughter in 1978, and an attempt to rape her in 1989. Notwithstanding the gap of 11 years, the Court of Appeal held that the counts were properly joined. The fact that the alleged victim was the same in each case, and that the offences were of a broadly similar character, meant that there was sufficient nexus for the second limb of r 9.

The requirements of r 9 are undemanding, but care must be taken not to forget those requirements completely. In *Harward* (1981) 73 Cr App R 168, the indictment against H contained a count for conspiring to use cheque cards to obtain money fraudulently from banks, and a count for handling stereo equipment which was found in H's possession shortly after it had been stolen. H was acquitted on the conspiracy count, but convicted of handling. Quashing the conviction, the Court of Appeal held that joinder of the two counts in one indictment was not justified by r 9, and was therefore unlawful. The offences were not founded on the same facts, and the only point of legal or factual similarity between them was that they both involved dishonesty. But the dishonesty alleged in the conspiracy count related to H's involvement in fraudulent practices, whereas that alleged in the handling count related to his state of mind when he received the relevant goods. Thus, even on the loose interpretation of r 9 adopted in *Ludlow,* there was not a sufficient nexus between the offences for them to form part of a series of the same or a similar character.

In *Williams* [1993] Crim LR 533, W was charged with (1) indecently assaulting a girl of 13 in a London hotel and (2) falsely imprisoning her five days later, by forcing her on to a seat in a train travelling from Stevenage to London. The Court of Appeal held that the two offences were not of a similar character, and had been wrongly joined in the same indictment.

14.5.3 Discretion to order separate trials

If the judge is of the opinion that the accused may be 'prejudiced or embarrassed in his defence' through a single trial of all the counts against him in an indictment, or if for any other reason he considers that separate trials of at least some of the counts is desirable, then he may make an order to that effect: IA, s 5(3). This is commonly referred to as severing the indictment. The power to sever given by s 5(3) is meant to deal with cases where the joinder of counts in one indictment is technically justified (i.e, there is no breach of r 9), but, if the accused were to be tried by a single jury on all counts, there would be a risk of the jurors not considering some of the matters fairly. However, where the indictment is invalid because it contains counts which are neither founded on the same facts nor form part of a series of the same or similar character, the invalidity cannot be cured by a purported exercise of the power to sever: *Newland* [1988] QB 402. In *Newland,* N was indicted for possessing a controlled drug with intent to supply and totally unrelated offences of assault. Prosecuting counsel, realising that the joinder was improper, applied successfully for severance and N thereupon pleaded guilty, but his convictions had to be quashed on appeal as they resulted from an invalid indictment. Watkins LJ stated that the prosecution could have partially rescued the situation by amending the indictment so as to delete either the drugs count or the assault counts — there could then have been a valid conviction on whatever part of the indictment remained (see Paragraph 14.7.2 for amending the indictment). If they wished, the prosecution could then have brought fresh proceedings for the counts that had been deleted out, although that would have entailed either a second committal or a voluntary bill of indictment. But, what neither they nor the judge could do was to treat the indictment as if it had been properly drafted in the first place and then purport to exercise the statutory power to sever valid indictments.

The Indictment

Another way forward for the prosecution, when faced with an indictment which is invalid because of improper joinder, is to adopt the course approved in *Follett* [1989] QB 338. They may, in effect, ignore the invalid indictment and seek leave to prefer fresh, separate indictments out of time. They must then elect on which indictments they wish to proceed. They will obviously choose the replacement indictments. Then (and only then), the judge will be asked to quash the original, invalidly joined indictment.

The correct judicial approach to applications to sever under s 5(3) was explained by the House of Lords in *Ludlow v Metropolitan Police Commissioner* (see Paragraph 14.5.2). The judge is under a duty to direct separate trials only if there is a special feature in the case which would make a joint trial of several counts prejudicial or embarrassing. Examples are cases where the evidence relevant to one count would be difficult to disentangle from the evidence relevant to the other counts, and cases where one of the counts is of a scandalous nature so that if the jury were satisfied that the accused had committed that offence they would be so prejudiced against him that they would convict on the other counts regardless of any lack of proof. The above principles were restated by the Court of Appeal in *McGlinchey* (1984) 74 Cr App R 282 (trial judge held to have exercised his discretion properly in refusing to sever two handling counts, one for receiving stolen photographic equipment on 19 July 1982 and the other for receiving a stolen credit card on or before 2 September 1982). The Court emphasised that, although certain dicta in *DPP v Boardman* (see below) advocate separate trials of counts for sexual offences if they were allegedly committed against different victims and there was no striking similarity between the crimes, those dicta are not intended to apply across the full range of offences. The general rule remains that stated in *Ludlow* — i.e., where joinder of two or more counts is justified under r 9 they should normally be tried together.

The argument for the appellant in *Ludlow* was that the offence of attempted theft was not sufficiently similar to the offence of robbery for the jury to be entitled to consider the evidence on one count when deciding whether the accused committed the offence alleged in the other count (see works on evidence and *DPP v Boardman* [1975] AC 421 on the need for a striking similarity between offences before evidence that the accused committed one offence can be admissible to prove that he committed the other). Therefore, it was argued, L was inevitably prejudiced and embarrassed in his defence on the attempted theft charge through the jury hearing irrelevant accusations about the robbery. The same applied in reverse on the robbery charge. The House of Lords accepted the premise that *Ludlow* was not a 'similar fact evidence' case but rejected the argument founded on that premise. In a simple case, such as *Ludlow*, the jury were quite capable, given a suitable direction from the judge, of ignoring the evidence of the robbery when considering the attempted theft and vice versa. In more complicated cases, however, the difficulty of disentangling the evidence relevant on the various counts might necessitate an order for separate trials. In particular, where a single indictment contains several counts alleging offences of a sexual nature committed against different victims (e.g. indecent assaults on different children) the counts should be tried separately, unless the similarity between the offences is sufficient to bring them within the similar fact evidence rule: see *DPP v Boardman* and *Scarrott* [1978] QB 1016. In *Cannan* (1990) 92 Cr App R 16, however, it was emphasised that the trial judge, even in sexual cases, has a discretion whether to order severance or not. The Court of Appeal would not interfere with that discretion unless it was shown that the judge had failed to exercise it on the usual and proper principles. This approach was endorsed in *Christou* [1996] 2 WLR 620 by the House of Lords.

14.5.4 Alternative counts

Sometimes the evidence available to the prosecution clearly shows that the accused has committed an indictable offence, but precisely what he has done is less obvious. In such cases, the indictment may include counts for *all* the offences that might be proved and the jury can then decide on which (if any) they should convict. The indictment will not expressly say that the counts are in the alternative, but counsel and/or the judge in his summing-up will explain to the jury that they are not being invited to find the accused guilty of everything alleged against him. The precise form of the direction to the jury will depend upon the circumstances of each case. Sometimes they are told to consider Count 1 first and only go on to consider Count 2 if the prosecution have failed to satisfy them on Count 1; in other cases, they are in effect told to decide in a global way whether the accused is guilty of anything and, if he is, to convict of whichever count seems the more appropriate in the light of the evidence. The latter approach is useful where the alternatives are of roughly equal gravity (e.g., theft and handling), and it would be absurd for the jury to acquit of both because they were not sure whether the accused was the original thief or a receiver.

Alternative counts may be included in an indictment when the accused's conduct, depending on his state of mind at the relevant time and/or the consequences of his acts, might make him guilty of one of a number of offences of differing degrees of gravity. Thus, if the accused injured a victim without breaking the skin, he might be indicted for (i) causing grievous bodily harm with intent contrary to s 18 of the Offences against the Person Act 1861; (ii) unlawfully and maliciously inflicting GBH contrary to s 20 of the same Act, and (iii) assault occasioning actual bodily harm contrary to s 47. If satisfied that the injuries amounted to really serious harm and that the accused intended to cause such harm, the jury would convict of (i); if satisfied as to the gravity of the injuries but not as to the accused's intentions, they would convict of (ii); if satisfied merely that the accused had occasioned some actual bodily harm by an assault, they would convict of (iii), and if in doubt as to all of the above, they would simply acquit. The judge would direct them to go through the counts in descending order of gravity.

Another common example of alternative counts is where the accused was allegedly found in possession of stolen goods soon after they were stolen, and the prosecution ask the jury to convict him either of the theft or receiving. Here the alternatives are mutually exclusive as a matter of law, for s 22 of the Theft Act expressly provides that the act of handling must be otherwise than in the course of theft (contrast ss 18 and 20 of the Offences against the Person Act which are alternatives only in the sense that it would be oppressive to find the accused guilty of both when the lesser offence is virtually included in the greater). Despite the fact that theft and handling are thus true alternatives, it has never been doubted that it is appropriate to join them in one indictment on the basis that they are founded on the same facts within the first limb of r 9 of the Indictment Rules (see *Shelton* (1986) 83 Cr App R 379, where Lawton LJ said that the practice of charging theft and handling as alternatives should continue whenever there is a real possibility that the evidence might support one rather than the other). It is also common practice to have two separate handling counts as alternatives to each other, the particulars of one alleging that the accused 'received' stolen goods, and the particulars of the other alleging that he 'undertook their retention, removal, disposal or realisation by or for the benefit of another person'. The jury can then convict either on the first limb of s 22 (which is generally considered the more serious) or on the less serious second limb.

14.6 JOINDER OF DEFENDANTS IN AN INDICTMENT

A count in an indictment may charge two or more defendants with committing a single offence. Further, two or more counts in an indictment may charge different defendants with separate offences even though there is no one count against them all collectively. In order to distinguish conveniently between the singular and the plural, reference will be made in this section to the defendant or defendants, not to the accused.

14.6.1 Joint counts

All parties to a single offence may — and normally will — be charged with it together in a single count. This applies not only to the principal offenders, but also to those who aid, abet, counsel or procure the commission of the offence, for s 8 of the Accessories and Abettors Act 1861 provides that all secondary parties are liable to be 'tried, indicted and punished as a principal offender'. Thus, if A provides information which assists B and C to enter a building as trespassers and steal property, whilst D keeps watch outside, the prosecution could have one count against them for burglary alleging that 'A, B, C and D, having entered a building known as . . . as trespassers, stole therein . . .'. In a sense, the count is inaccurate because A and D did not enter the building. However, should there be a not guilty plea, counsel can easily explain to the jury that A and D were not, so to speak, the actual burglars but may be held liable in law as burglars on the basis that they assisted B and C in their break-in. Moreover, there is no injustice to the defendants, since they will know in advance of trial from the committal proceedings what roles the prosecution allege they respectively played in the offence. If found guilty, the actual sentence the judge passes (as opposed to the maximum which he could theoretically pass) will be related to whether they played a major or a minor role. Although it is convenient to word a count against an aider and abettor as if he were a principal offender, there is nothing to stop the prosecution specifically alleging that he was merely a secondary party. This might be preferable, for example, where the prosecution case is that a woman assisted a man to commit rape. Rather than confuse a jury with a count which apparently attributed the act of rape to a woman, the prosecution could make the statement of offence, 'Aiding and abetting rape contrary to s 1 of the Sexual Offences Act 1956', and the particulars of offence, 'Jane Smith aided and abetted Jack Brown to rape Jill Black'.

The jury are entitled to convict one or more but acquit other defendants named in a joint count. Furthermore, although the prosecution will not include defendants in a joint count unless their evidence suggests that there was a joint enterprise or cooperation between them, it has been held by the House of Lords in *DPP v Merriman* [1973] AC 584 that any or all of them may be convicted on the basis that they committed the offence independently of the others charged in the count.

The judge always has a discretion to order separate trials of defendants who are accused of committing an offence jointly, but there are strong reasons for a single trial which usually outweigh any opposing arguments. In favour of a single trial are the saving of time and convenience to witnesses of only having the evidence given once; the desirability of the jury having a full picture of what occurred which is more likely to be given through a single trial, and the risk of differing verdicts being returned by different juries on virtually identical evidence should there be separate trials. These considerations led the Court of Appeal to state in *Moghal* (1977) 65 Cr App R 56 that separate trials of those joined in a single count should only be ordered in very exceptional cases. However, the decision is essentially one for the judge. Although, in *Moghal,* the Court of Appeal disagreed with the judge's decision to order separate trials, they did not quash the conviction. The judge was exercising a discretion given to him, not to the Court of Appeal, and it could not be said that his decision had led to a miscarriage of justice. If a decision, whether for or against separate trials, is shown to have led to a miscarriage of justice an appeal would be upheld. However, the fact that a joint trial will result in the jury hearing evidence against A, which is inadmissible against B but highly prejudicial to him, does not oblige the judge to accede to an application by B for separate trials (see *Lake* (1977) 64 Cr App R 172, where the judge's refusal of a separate trial for L was upheld even though L's co-defendants had made confessions in L's absence which implicated not only themselves but L also). Similarly, the fact that A and B are going to put forward defences in which they put the entire blame for the offence on each other does not necessitate separate trials: *Grondkowski and Malinowski* [1946] KB 369. Of course, in cases resembling *Lake* and *Grondkowski and Malinowski,* a judge more sympathetic to the problems of the defence would be entitled to order separate trials, but, if no such order is made, an appeal on the basis that there was a single trial is unlikely to succeed. For an exceptional case, in which an appeal on these grounds succeeded, see *O'Boyle* (1990) 92 Cr App R 202. On the facts of that case, the Court of Appeal said that joint trial had prejudiced the appellant, whereas separate trials would have done little or no harm to his co-accused or the prosecution. Accordingly, the trial judge had erred in the exercise of his discretion.

14.6.2 Separate counts

An indictment may include separate counts each naming a different defendant, no defendant being joined with any other defendant in a single count. The circumstances in which this may be done are not closely defined. It is a matter for the practice of the court, but there must be some linking factor between the offences to justify joining their alleged perpetrators in one indictment. The linking factor may be that the defendants were apparently acting in concert although committing separate offences, or that the offences all occurred in one incident (e.g., various assaults during a gang fight), or that they occurred successively (e.g., two witnesses at the same trial committing perjury one after the other). An example of correct joinder is *Assim* [1966] 2 QB 249. Two defendants were charged in a single indictment, one with unlawfully wounding X and the other with assaulting Y occasioning him actual bodily harm. Since their respective acts of violence had separate victims they could not be charged in a single count. The joinder of the separate counts in one indictment was, however, justified as the defendants were the doorman and receptionist at the same night-club, and X and Y were customers who were attempting to leave without paying their bills. The offences were linked by proximity in time and place, and by their apparent motive of discouraging bad payers.

The Theft Act 1968, s 27(1) provides for handlers of stolen property to be charged in one indictment. All persons who at any time handle any portion of the goods stolen in one theft may be jointly indicted and jointly tried. So, if A, in the course of a burglary, steals a watch and a necklace which he sells to B and C respectively, and C sells on the necklace to D — all four can be indicted and tried together. The separate counts of handling against B, C and D are properly put in one indictment because of s 27(1), and the burglary count against A is sufficiently linked with the handling counts to fall within the principle in *Assim.*

Where defendants are joined in one indictment but not charged in a joint count, the judge again has a discretion to order separate trials, even though the single indictment was justified. The arguments for and against splitting the indictment are similar to those rehearsed above in the context of defendants charged in a joint count, but the argument for a single trial is less strong where there is no joint count, as the evidence in the case of one defendant will not be so closely inter-twined with the evidence in the cases of the other defendants. An illustration of the circumstances in which a judge might think it fair to order separate trials is provided by *Johnson* [1995] 2 Cr App R 41. The indictment contained a count alleging that A assaulted B, and another count that C assaulted A. In other words, A was victim and defendant in the same trial. As the Court of Appeal pointed out, this had the effect that, if A gave evidence, counsel for the prosecution could ask him in cross-examination about C. It was inevitably prejudicial to C, especially when the issue was whether C was A's assailant. Their lordships said that separate trials would often (though not always) be preferable in such a situation. The avoidance of the unusual prejudice to C would normally outweigh the inconvenience of calling the same witnesses at two trials.

14.6.3 Overloading indictments

The preceding Paragraphs have shown that the rules governing joinder of counts and joinder of defendants are far from strict, and, if joinder is prima facie within the rules, the Court of Appeal are reluctant to quash a conviction on the ground that the judge, in the exercise of his discretion, refused to sever the indictment. However, their lordships have often warned of the danger of overloading indictments. For example, in *Thorne* (1978) 66 Cr App R 6, no fewer than 14 defendants were tried together on an indictment containing three counts for robbery and numerous related offences such as conspiracy to rob, handling the proceeds of the robberies and attempting to pervert the course of justice in respect of the robbery prosecutions. The trial, involving 27 counsel and 10 firms of solicitors, lasted 111 working days and included a 12-day summing-up from the judge. Although none of the appeals were allowed simply on the basis that the trial had been too long, the Court of Appeal stated that two or three shorter trials would have been far preferable. Such a huge trial placed an unfair burden on judge and jury. Protracted though the trial in *Thorne* was, it is not the longest criminal jury trial in English legal history. That 'ignoble distinction' (as Farquharson LJ put it) belongs to the case of *Kellard* [1995] 2 Cr App R 134. The trial of K and his co-defendants (which was for various offences of fraudulent trading) was spread over 17 months, and the court sat on 252 working days. Even so, the Court of Appeal dismissed the appeal, which had been based in part on the prejudice caused to the appellants by a trial of that length. Their lordships said the correct approach was to consider whether the length of the proceedings created a situation where a fair trial was not possible. Were any of those taking part, especially the jury, unable to discharge their function? Notwithstanding the length of this particular trial, the Court of Appeal found that there was no danger of the jury being confused. But the Court of Appeal stressed that it is the duty of the judge and counsel to ensure that a potentially long trial remained manageable. In *Kellard*, defence counsel had applied for one set of counts to be severed. The judge was sympathetic to the application, but prosecuting counsel said that the evidence on the potentially severable counts was admissible on the counts that remained, and that he would call that evidence. As a result, the judge understandably saw no point in severance, and the trial proceeded. The Court of Appeal said that is was not appropriate for prosecuting counsel to frustrate the judge's purpose in this way. It was in fact prosecuting counsel's duty to review the evidence in a long case and decide how much of it, even though relevant, could be withheld to save time and enable clear presentation.

Similarly, if the accused's conduct on one occasion may possibly make him guilty of several offences, the prosecution should assess what the 'real' offence was and have a count for that, ignoring the other offences which as a matter of strict law are disclosed on the committal statements (see May LJ's comments in *Staton* [1983] Crim LR 190). Of course, where there is genuine uncertainty about what is the more appropriate charge the prosecution will need two or more counts in the alternative — the point being made in *Staton* and in *Thorne* is that the prosecution should not automatically include in an indictment as many counts and as many defendants as are technically justified by the rules. They should consider also whether joinder will make for a fairer and more efficient trial.

14.6.4 The Code for Crown Prosecutors and the indictment

The Code for Crown Prosecutors (issued by the Director of Public Prosecutions — see Paragraph 4.3) contains guidance as to the counts which ought to be included in an indictment (the Code refers to 'charges', which is the generic term, but 'counts' is the more appropriate term when dealing with an indictment). The Code exhorts Crown Prosecutors to 'select charges which (a) reflect the seriousness of the offending; (b) give the court adequate sentencing powers; and (c) enable the case to be presented in a clear and simple way'.

This means that Crown Prosecutors should not continue with more charges than are necessary (para 7.1 of the Code). Further, Crown Prosecutors are told not to include more charges than are necessary just to encourage a defendant to plead guilty to a few. Nor should they include a more serious charge just to encourage the defendant to plead guilty to a lesser charge (para 7.2).

14.7 APPLICATIONS CONCERNING THE INDICTMENT

The following applications may be necessary:

14.7.1 Application to sever the indictment

If the defence considers that two or more counts in the indictment against the accused should be tried separately, or that he should not be tried with the other defendants named in the indictment, application must be made to the judge to sever the indictment. The application is usually made immediately after the pleas to the indictment have been taken. Such applications may be made to the trial judge in a pre-trial hearing, where there is provision for one.

14.7.2 Applications to amend the indictment

If the judge considers that the indictment is defective he must order it to be amended, unless such amendment would cause injustice: IA, s 5(1). The amendment may be ordered before or at any stage during the trial, the defence, if necessary, being given an adjournment to consider the way their position has been affected: s 5(4). Subject always to not causing injustice, *any* defect in an indictment can be remedied by amendment, whether the defect be trivial (e.g., the mis-spelling of a name) or fundamental (e.g., omitting from the particulars an essential element of the offence charged in the count). Amendment is also appropriate where the evidence at the trial differs from the allegations in the particulars, although if such amendments are sought at a late stage, they may well be refused because of potential injustice. For example, in *Gregory* [1972] 1 WLR 991, the Court of Appeal quashed G's conviction on a count for handling a starter-motor because, after all the evidence had been given, the judge deleted from the particulars an allegation that the starter-motor belonged to 'W.A.W.' Much of the evidence had turned on whether a starter-motor, admittedly found in G's possession, was the one that had earlier been stolen from W.A.W. The defence contended that it was not, and that G had legitimately bought the motor from a casual acquaintance whose name he did not know. By deleting the allegation as to ownership the judge altered the whole basis of the prosecution case, and, in effect, invited the jury to convict on the basis that even if G's story were correct, the circumstances of the purchase (at a quarter of the proper price) showed that the motor had been stolen from someone and that G knew it to be stolen. Had the amendment been made before the indictment was put to the accused, with the defence being offered an adjournment, it is unlikely that any appeal could have succeeded.

Amendment may also take the form of inserting new counts in the indictment either in substitution for or in addition to those originally drafted. This may be done after the accused has pleaded to the indictment: *Johal and Ram* [1973] QB 475. Indeed, in *Collison* (1980) 71 Cr App R 249, the Court of Appeal approved the addition of a count when, after the jury had retired to consider their verdict, a difficulty arose concerning whether they could properly return a verdict of guilty of a lesser offence (see Paragraph 19.4). In *Johal* and *Collison* the fresh counts were needed to solve purely technical problems that had arisen on the indictments as originally drafted but they did not alter the nature of the prosecution case. If a count containing a genuinely fresh charge were to be added after the start of the evidence, it would almost certainly cause injustice.

The question may arise whether it is necessary for the amendment to be founded on the evidence disclosed at committal. In *Osieh* [1996] 1 WLR 1260, the Court of Appeal held that it was not necessary (although the amendment in the case in question *was* actually founded upon the committal evidence). As is pointed out by Professor J.C. Smith in 'Adding Counts to an Indictment' [1996] Crim LR 889, dicta in both *Dixon* (1991) 92 Cr App R 43 and *Hall* [1968] 2 QB 788 point to the need for the amendment to be supported by the committal evidence. In any event, the fact that an amendment raises for the first time something which is not foreshadowed in the committal evidence may be reason for refusing leave for an amendment, or allowing the defence an adjournment to cope with the change in direction (per Schiemann LJ in *Osieh*).

Where an amendment appears necessary counsel for the prosecution should apply for it. If he fails to do so, the judge may raise the matter on his own initiative, asking for the views of prosecution and defence.

14.7.3 Motion to quash the indictment

The defence may apply to the judge to quash the indictment. If the application (or motion) succeeds no further proceedings may take place on the indictment. It follows that the appropriate time for moving to quash is before the indictment is put, as success at that stage will mean that the accused does not even have to plead. The judge may, however, entertain an application at a later stage. A motion to quash may also be brought in respect of a single count in an indictment.

Motions to quash are not of great value to the defence for three reasons. First, even after a successful motion, the prosecution are entitled to commence fresh proceedings in respect of the same matters, hoping to avoid the mistake that led to the first indictment or count being quashed. Second, a suitable amendment to the indictment can often prevent the motion to quash from succeeding. Third, the grounds for a successful motion are very limited. Those grounds are that:

(a) the bill of indictment was preferred without authority, or
(b) the wording of the indictment or count reveals a fundamental defect, or

(c) the count is for an offence in respect of which the magistrates did not commit for trial, and no case to answer for that offence is revealed from the committal evidence (or the evidence upon which a notice of transfer or a voluntary bill of indictment is based: see Paragraphs 12.6 and 12.7).

As to (a) above, there is authority to prefer a bill of indictment if either the accused has been committed, or a High Court judge has directed the preferment of a voluntary bill, or the Court of Appeal has ordered a re-trial (see Administration of Justice (Miscellaneous Provisions) Act 1933, s 2). It is almost inconceivable that the prosecution would, in the absence of such authority, even try to prefer a bill. As to (b) it must be stressed that the judge is only entitled to look at the wording of the indictment to see if there is something fundamentally wrong (e.g., a count fails to allege an essential element of the offence charged or is bad for duplicity). Except as described in (c), he may not be asked to consider any inadequacies in the prosecution evidence foreshadowed in the statements. In other words, a motion to quash is not a way of challenging the magistrates' court's decision to commit for trial on a certain charge. If the indictment or count is defectively worded the prosecution may prevent a successful motion to quash simply by applying to amend.

Perhaps the most valuable use of motions to quash is that mentioned in (c) above. If the indictment contains a count alleging an offence for which the magistrates' court did not commit the accused for trial, the defence may invite the judge to read the evidence considered by the magistrates, and, if it does not disclose a case to answer, to quash the count. It is the one situation where, on a motion to quash, the judge considers the evidence: *Jones* (1974) 59 Cr App R 120. It is right that he should do so because either the magistrates' court held that there was not a case to answer for the offence charged in the count, or, at the very least, it was not invited to give a decision on the point.

In examining the evidence considered by the magistrates' court, the judge should ensure that any offence in the indictment, other than one on which the defendant was sent for trial, is founded on the evidence. The evidence contained in the statements need not, however, be conclusive (*Biddis* [1993] Crim LR 392). In *Biddis*, a count of possessing a firearm was added to the charge of robbery on which the defendant had been committed. It was argued on appeal that the committal bundle did not include any evidence to show that the gun could be fired so that it could be a firearm within the meaning of the Firearms Act 1968, s 57(1). The Court of Appeal held that there was evidence that the gun had been loaded, and that this was, in the circumstances of the case, sufficient evidence from which the jury could reasonably have inferred that it was an effective weapon.

14.7.4 Staying the indictment

In addition to the powers referred to above, the court has power to stay (i.e. to postpone proceedings) in relation to an indictment. This is part of its inherent power to regulate the efficient and fair disposal of criminal cases (*Connelly v DPP* [1964] AC 1254 at p. 1346). The court is also able to stay part of an indictment, so that, for example, proceedings continue against one defendant only or in respect of one count only (*Munro* [1993] Crim LR 393).

14.8 APPEALS BASED ON DEFECTIVE INDICTMENTS

An error in the indictment which is not corrected during the trial may provide the accused with a good ground of appeal should he ultimately be convicted. Unfortunately the cases on the subject tend to turn upon technicalities as to the Court of Appeal's powers when determining an appeal. Since detailed consideration of appeals against conviction must wait until Chapter 24, the propositions below are intended to summarise the position with regard to defective indictments without fully explaining the reasoning behind the decisions:

(a)   A significant defect in the drafting of a count — e.g., omission from the Statement of Offence of the statute contravened, or a failure to allege the full particulars of the offence, or a discrepancy between the evidence at trial and the particulars — may amount to a ground for quashing a conviction. Where the mistake is very trivial (e.g., mis-spelling a name) it can be disregarded as being too minor to amount to a good ground of appeal. However, even a serious mistake will not automatically result in a successful appeal. The essential question is whether, in all the circumstances, the error in pleading prejudiced or embarrassed the accused. If it did not, the Court of Appeal will uphold the conviction on the basis that there has been no miscarriage of justice, i.e., it is safe. Lord Bridge in *Ayres* [1984] AC 447 stated the guiding principle thus:

> If the statement and particulars of offence can be seen fairly to relate to and be intended to charge a known and subsisting criminal offence but plead it in terms which are inaccurate, incomplete and otherwise imperfect, then the question whether a conviction on that indictment can properly be affirmed . . . must depend on whether, in all the circumstances, it can be said with confidence that the particular error in the pleading cannot in any way have prejudiced or embarrassed the defendant.

There is a strong tendency for their lordships to hold that there has been no such prejudice. Thus, convictions have been upheld:

(i)   where the particulars of a count for possessing explosives contrary to s 4 of the Explosive Substances Act 1883 failed to allege that the accused *knowingly* had possession of the explosives, knowledge being an essential clement of the offence (*McVitie* (1960) 44 Cr App R 201);

(ii)   where the Statement of Offence in a count for having an offensive weapon in a public place omitted the statute contravened, namely s 1 of the Prevention of Crime Act 1953 (*Nelson* (1977) 65 Cr App R 119); and

(iii)   where the Statement of Offence for an offence contrary to s 5 of the Perjury Act 1911 wrongly described the offence as 'perjury' when it should have been making a false declaration not on oath (*Power* (1977) 66 Cr App R 159);

(iv)   where the particulars of a count of riot contrary to the Public Order Act 1986, s 1(1), charged that the defendant had 'used or threatened' unlawful violence, when the offence required that he should have 'used' unlawful violence (*Jefferson* [1994] 1 All ER 270).

In each of these cases, the court essentially reasoned that, while the indictment was defective, it described an offence known to law (albeit in terms which were inaccurate). Crucially, the accused had not, on the facts, been misled or prejudiced in the conduct of his defence by the error.

(b)   Where, however, the defect consists not merely in the wording of a count but in a fundamental procedural error which renders the whole indictment a nullity, the conviction cannot stand. Examples are where the committal proceedings that purported to justify the preferring of a bill of indictment were themselves invalid (*Phillips and Quayle* [1939] 1 KB 63), and where the so-called indictment was not signed by an officer of the Crown Court (*Morais* (1988) 87 Cr App R 9). In such cases the Court of Appeal is obliged to quash the conviction but it may, in its discretion, order a *venire de novo* (i.e. sanction a fresh prosecution). Further, it is submitted that a conviction on a count which is bad on its face for duplicity can never be upheld because it is impossible to know of which offence the jury intended to find the accused guilty.

(c) Where counts are unlawfully joined in one indictment contrary to r 9 of the IR, the indictment is merely invalid, not a nullity. The prosecution can amend the indictment at trial by deleting one or more of the counts, so that what results is an indictment consisting of counts which are lawfully joined. If they fail to do so, the question arises as to the status of the subsequent proceedings. In *Newland* [1988] QB 402, the Court of Appeal held that the entire indictment must be quashed, so that any proceedings on it were null and void, although a *venire de novo* could be ordered. This decision was, in effect, overruled in *Lockley* [1997] Crim LR 455. In that case, the Court of Appeal held that technical points should not generally nullify the whole indictment, unless there was prejudice to the accused.

14.9 CONSPIRACY COUNTS

Counts for conspiracy have probably caused more drafting problems than counts for any other offence. Three particular points should be noted. First, where the conspiracy alleged is a complicated one the particulars need to be more detailed than is the case with other offences. If the judge considers that the particulars as originally drafted are too brief to give the defence a fair idea of how the prosecution put their case, he may order that further particulars be provided (see *Landy* (1981) 72 Cr App R 237).

Second, the problems arising from the interrelationship of s 1 of the Criminal Law Act 1977 (which created the offence of statutory conspiracy, committed by two or more persons agreeing to a course of conduct that, if carried out, would involve the commission of a substantive offence by one or more of their number) and s 5 of the Act (which preserved the common law offence of conspiracy to defraud) have hopefully been resolved by s 12 of the Criminal Justice Act 1987. This reverses the decision of the House of Lords in *Ayres* [1984] AC 447 by providing that a count for conspiracy to defraud may be laid even though the agreed course of conduct would necessarily have involved a substantive offence such as obtaining property by deception. In straightforward cases, the prosecution will no doubt still find it simpler to charge statutory conspiracy. However, where the alleged fraudulent plan was a complicated one, the commission of an offence may have been but a small part of the overall swindle, and the only way to put the whole picture before a judge and jury will be to charge conspiracy to defraud. The advantage of s 12 is that it gives the drafter of the indictment a discretion as to which count is more appropriate, instead of being obliged to charge statutory conspiracy whenever the agreement alleged involved any substantive offence, however trivial.

Thirdly, the prosecution sometimes include in one indictment a count for (i) conspiracy to commit certain offences, and (ii) counts for actually committing those offences. The practice seems to have originated as a way of bringing before the jury evidence which was admissible on the conspiracy count but was, technically speaking, inadmissible on the substantive counts in the hope that, having heard the evidence, the jury would take it into consideration on all counts. However, in *Jones* (1974) 59 Cr App R 120 the Court of Appeal held that joinder of a conspiracy count with counts for the substantive offences can only be justified if *either* the evidence may turn out to be too weak for convictions on the latter but ample for conviction on the former, *or* a number of counts for minor substantive offences would not truly reflect the gravity of the accused's conduct. Moreover, the trial judge must require the prosecution to justify the joinder and, if they cannot, they must elect on which part of the indictment they wish to proceed.

SPECIMEN COUNTS[1]

1 Murder
                             STATEMENT OF OFFENCE

Murder.

                            PARTICULARS OF OFFENCE

CAIN ADAMSON, on the 1st day of January 2002, murdered Abel Adamson.

2 Manslaughter
                             STATEMENT OF OFFENCE

Manslaughter.

                            PARTICULARS OF OFFENCE

CAIN ADAMSON, on the 1st day of January 2002, unlawfully killed Abel Adamson.

3 Grievous bodily harm with intent
                             STATEMENT OF OFFENCE

Causing grievous bodily harm with intent, contrary to section 18 of the Offences against the Person Act 1861.

                            PARTICULARS OF OFFENCE

PETER PUNCH, on the 1st day of January 2002, caused grievous bodily harm to Judy Punch with intent to do her grievous bodily harm.[2]

4 Unlawful wounding
                             STATEMENT OF OFFENCE

Unlawful wounding, contrary to section 20 of the Offences against the Person Act 1861.

                            PARTICULARS OF OFFENCE

PETER PUNCH, on the 1st day of January 2002, unlawfully and maliciously wounded Judy Punch.[3]

---

[1] Most of the specimen counts are for famous fictional or historical crimes. As the dates of these offences are not known with accuracy, it is imagined that they took place on 1 January 2002. In some cases, it would seem that the accused could successfully plead that the English courts do not have jurisdiction to try him as his offence was committed abroad and he is not a British subject.

[2] An offence contrary to s 18 of the Offences against the Person Act 1861 can be committed by *wounding* with intent to cause grievous bodily harm. If that is the nature of the prosecution case, 'Causing grievous bodily harm' in the Statement of Offence should be changed to 'Wounding', and 'caused grievous bodily harm' in the Particulars of Offence should be changed to 'unlawfully wounded'.

[3] An offence contrary to s 20 of the Offences against the Person Act 1861 can be committed by inflicting grievous bodily harm. If that is the nature of the prosecution case, the references in the count to 'wounding' and 'wounded' should be amended accordingly.

5   Rape

STATEMENT OF OFFENCE

Rape, contrary to section 1(1) of the Sexual Offences Act 1956.

PARTICULARS OF OFFENCE

JOHN SMITH, on the 1st day of January 2002, raped Jane Brown.

6   Robbery

STATEMENT OF OFFENCE

Robbery, contrary to section 8(1) of the Theft Act 1968.

PARTICULARS OF OFFENCE

RICHARD TURPIN, on the 1st day of January 2002, robbed Bess Black of a cloak, a necklace and 100 sovereigns.

7   Theft

STATEMENT OF OFFENCE

Theft, contrary to section 1(1) of the Theft Act 1968.

PARTICULARS OF OFFENCE

BERTRAM WOOSTER, on the 1st day of January 2002, stole a cow-creamer belonging to Watkyn Bassett.

8   Handling
    stolen goods

STATEMENT OF OFFENCE

Handling stolen goods, contrary to section 22(1) of the Theft Act 1968.

PARTICULARS OF OFFENCE

JAMES JEEVES, on a day unknown between the 31st day of December 2001 and the 1st day of February 2002, dishonestly received certain stolen goods, namely a cow-creamer belonging to Watkyn Bassett, knowing or believing the same to be stolen goods.

or

STATEMENT OF OFFENCE

Handling stolen goods, contrary to section 22(1) of the Theft Act 1968.

PARTICULARS OF OFFENCE

JAMES JEEVES, on a day unknown between the 31st day of December 2001 and the 1st day of February 2002, dishonestly undertook or assisted in the retention of certain stolen goods, namely a cow-creamer belonging to Watkyn Bassett, by or for the benefit of Bertram Wooster, knowing or believing the same to be stolen goods. [4]

9   Burglary

STATEMENT OF OFFENCE

Burglary, contrary to section 9(1)(b) of the Theft Act 1968.

PARTICULARS OF OFFENCE

WILLIAM SIKES and TOBY CRACKIT, on the 1st day of January 2002, having entered as trespassers a building known as 1 Dickens Lane, Chertsey, Surrey, stole therein a cashbox and £100 in money.

---

[4] If the prosecution are not sure whether their evidence will show retention of stolen property, or removal of it, or disposal of it or some other form of handling specified in the second limb of s 22 of the Theft Act, they can frame a count with some or all of those forms alleged in the alternative, i.e. 'A.B., on . . . dishonestly undertook or assisted in the retention, removal, disposal or realisation of certain stolen goods . . . by or for the benefit of another, or dishonestly arranged so to do . . .'.

10 Obtaining by
    deception

STATEMENT OF OFFENCE

Obtaining property by deception, contrary to section 15(1) of the Theft Act 1968.

PARTICULARS OF OFFENCE

JACOB ANDERSEN and CHRISTIAN GRIMM, on the 1st day of January 2002, dishonestly obtained from Rex King 100 pieces of gold with the intention of permanently depriving Rex King thereof by deception, namely, by falsely representing that they were entitled to the said gold in payment for a suit of clothes visible only to the eyes of wise people which they had delivered to the said Rex King.

11 Obtaining
    services by
    deception

STATEMENT OF OFFENCE

Obtaining services by deception, contrary to section 1(1) of the Theft Act 1978.

PARTICULARS OF OFFENCE

MICHAEL MAYOR, on the 1st day of January 2002, dishonestly obtained from Peter Piper services, namely the removal of rats from the town of Hamelin, by deception, namely by falsely representing that Peter Piper would be paid 100 guilders for removing the said rats.

12 Making off
    without
    payment

STATEMENT OF OFFENCE

Making off without payment, contrary to section 3(1) of the Theft Act 1978.

PARTICULARS OF OFFENCE

GERALD GOURMET, on the 1st day of January 2002, knowing that payment on the spot for a meal supplied to him at MacWimpey's restaurant, High Street, Burgertown was required of him, dishonestly made off without having paid the amount due or so required and with intent to avoid payment thereof.

13 Going
    equipped

STATEMENT OF OFFENCE

Going equipped for burglary, contrary to section 25(1) of the Theft Act 1968.

PARTICULARS OF OFFENCE

WILLIAM SIKES, on the 1st day of January 2002, not being at his place of abode, had with him articles for use in the course of or in connection with burglary, namely a jemmy, a screwdriver and a torch.[5]

14 Criminal
    damage

STATEMENT OF OFFENCE

Damaging property, contrary to section 1(1) of the Criminal Damage Act 1971.

---

[5] An offence contrary to s 25 of the Theft Act is committed when the offender, not being at his place of abode, has with him articles for use in connection with a burglary, theft or cheat. Depending on the purpose for which the prosecution allege the accused had the articles, the Statement of Offence and Particulars of Offence should be worded accordingly.

PARTICULARS OF OFFENCE

VICTOR VANDAL, on the 1st day of January 2002, without lawful excuse, damaged a statue known as the *Venus de Milo*, having a value of £2 million, belonging to the Louvre Museum, intending to damage such property or being reckless as to whether such property would be damaged.[6]

15 Dangerous driving

STATEMENT OF OFFENCE

Dangerous driving, contrary to section 2 of the Road Traffic Act 1988.

PARTICULARS OF OFFENCE

THOMAS TOAD, on the 1st day of January 2002, drove a mechanically propelled vehicle on a road, namely Willow Avenue, Banktown, Grahamshire, dangerously.

16 Possessing drugs

STATEMENT OF OFFENCE

Possessing a controlled drug, contrary to section 5(2) of the Misuse of Drugs Act 1971.

PARTICULARS OF OFFENCE

THOMAS DE QUINCEY, on the 1st day of January 2002, had in his possession a controlled drug of Class A, namely opium.

17 Perjury

STATEMENT OF OFFENCE

Perjury, contrary to section 1(1) of the Perjury Act 1911.

PARTICULARS OF OFFENCE

TITUS OATES, on the 1st day of January 2002, having been lawfully sworn as a witness in a judicial proceeding, namely the trial of a criminal cause in the Crown Court of one R . . . C . . . for treason, wilfully made a statement material in that proceeding which he knew to be false, namely that he saw the said R . . . C . . . speaking to an agent of the government of France on the 1st day of June 2001.

18 Conspiracy

STATEMENT OF OFFENCE

Conspiracy to murder, contrary to section 1(1) of the Criminal Law Act 1977.

PARTICULARS OF OFFENCE

GUY FAWKES and ROBERT CATESBY, on divers days before the 6th day of November 2002, conspired together and with persons unknown to murder James Stuart and such other persons as would attend the sitting of the House of Commons on the 5th day of November 2002.

---

[6] In a more conventional case of criminal damage, the property is simply identified by reference to the owner, e.g., 'a dress belonging to Jane Smith'. If the property was not merely damaged but destroyed, the count should be worded accordingly.

19   Attempt
STATEMENT OF OFFENCE

Attempted murder, contrary to section 1(1) of the Criminal Attempts Act 1981.

PARTICULARS OF OFFENCE

GUY FAWKES, on the 5th day of November 2002, attempted to murder James Stuart.

15 Pre-Trial Proceedings

In recent years, various reforms have aimed to increase the scope of pre-trial proceedings in the Crown Court. The underlying aim is to enable the judge (preferably the one who will preside at trial but, if that is impossible, one of the other judges who are available at that Crown Court centre) to start the business of managing the trial before it begins. That means that the parties must supply information as to the issues and the way in which they intend to conduct their case; and that the judge must act upon that information by making any orders which seem necessary in order to assist the efficient conduct of the trial.

Perhaps the most important of the issues on which early information is necessary in the interests of efficiency is the intended plea of the defendant. If the defendant decides to plead guilty on the day of the trial, after a court and a judge have been allocated to the case, lawyers have prepared and witnesses have been summoned to attend court, then there is a substantial waste of resources. One aim of pre-trial management is therefore to ensure that the defendant's plea is taken at an early stage before the trial, and the main vehicle for this is provided by the appropriately named plea and directions hearing.

There are other points which need to be canvassed prior to the trial, however, such as the points of law which are likely to arise, and any arguments as to the admissibility of evidence. It is important for the judge to know of these, since they will affect the course of the trial. Further, since points of law and admissibility are decided in the absence of the jury, as many of them as possible should be resolved in advance of the trial, so as to avoid extensive argument after the jury has been empanelled. If the judge ruling on these points is not the eventual trial judge, however, then much of the value of early resolution of the issues can be lost if the parties have an unfettered right to apply for the matter to be decided again (e.g., by the trial judge). As a result, it has been seen as desirable that the decisions taken prior to trial should be binding, at least to an extent, and this need has led to the statutory provisions on pre-trial rulings. In complex or lengthy matters, a more detailed framework of pre-trial proceedings has been thought necessary, and this is contained in the statutory regime which governs preparatory hearings.

This Chapter deals with the main forms of pre-trial proceedings as follows:

(a) plea and directions hearings (Paragraph 15.1);
(b) pre-trial rulings (Paragraph 15.2);
(c) preparatory hearings (Paragraph 15.3).

Paragraph 15.4 summarises the special measures which can be ordered preparatory to trial in order to protect vulnerable witnesses.

15.1 PLEA AND DIRECTIONS HEARINGS

Before a trial on indictment can take place, both parties need to prepare, and the court needs to ensure that any necessary arrangements are made. In 1995, a new procedure was introduced to ensure that steps are taken to prepare cases committed to the Crown Court for trial. The procedure is known as the plea and directions hearing (PDH). PDHs are governed by the *Practice Direction (Crown Court: Plea and Directions Hearings)* [1995] 1 WLR 1318, and apply to all cases other than serious fraud. They may be conducted by a judge other than the one who will preside at trial.

The arrangement is that each magistrates' court should commit the defendant to appear in the Crown Court on a specific date. The purpose of the PDH is to ensure that any steps necessary for trial have been taken, and that the court is provided with sufficient information to fix a trial date. The advocate briefed in the case should appear in the PDH wherever practicable. The defendant(s) should be present unless the court gives leave. Where a defendant intends to plead guilty, the court, prosecution and probation service must be notified as soon as possible.

At the PDH, the defence must supply a full list of the prosecution witnesses whom they require to attend at trial. Both prosecution and defence should submit to the court and the other parties a summary of the issues on which the court's directions are sought, referring to any authorities which are relied on. For cases which are serious, lengthy or complex, a case summary should be prepared by the prosecution for use by the judge at the PDH. At the PDH, arraignment will normally take place (see Paragraph 16.1 for details of the arraignment). If the defendant pleads guilty, the judge should proceed to sentencing whenever possible. Where the defendant pleads not guilty, or his pleas are not acceptable to the prosecution, the parties are expected to inform the court of the following matters (inter alia):

(a)   the issues in the case (including any issues as to the mental or medical condition of the defendant or any witness);

(b)   the number of witnesses whose evidence will be placed before the court;

(c)   any exhibits or schedules;

(d)   the order in which prosecution witnesses are likely to be called;

(e)   any point of law anticipated, any questions of admissibility of evidence, and any authorities relied on;

(f)   any alibi which should already have been disclosed;

(g)   any applications for a child's evidence to be given through live television links or in the form of a pre-recorded interview;

(h)   the estimated length of the trial;

(i)   dates on which witnesses and advocates are available.

Appendix 4 shows a copy of the questionnaire which advocates fill in and hand to the judge at the PDH. The intention is that, armed with this information, the judge will be able to fix a suitable date and make any other appropriate directions. Each of the parties, moreover, will be better fitted to prepare for trial with an indication of the likely issues at trial.

15.2 PRE-TRIAL RULINGS

The plea and directions hearing described in Paragraph 15.1 is now compulsory in all cases except serious fraud. It is meant to clarify the issues and enable the parties to focus upon them as they prepare for trial. One of the problems which has dogged such pre-trial proceedings over the years, however, has been the fact that whatever is decided may be overruled by the trial judge. This knowledge has undermined the effectiveness of such hearings, and frequently it has also meant that the advocates attending the PDH have not been those who will represent the parties at trial, since, if the issues can be re-canvassed when the trial begins, there is little incentive for the trial advocates to disrupt their schedules by making themselves available for a preliminary procedural hearing of little importance. They have often succumbed to the temptation of sending someone much more junior along to 'hold the brief', secure in the knowledge that, if they do not like the outcome, they can always apply to the trial judge for a different ruling.

Obviously, this attitude resulted in a diminution of value of the PDH. Sections 39 to 43 of the Criminal Procedure and Investigations Act 1996 (CPIA) attempt to remedy the situation. The new statutory provisions apply to rulings made *before* the trial begins, i.e. before a jury is sworn or a guilty plea is accepted, or a preparatory hearing starts: s 39(3). It follows that the rulings in question may be made by someone other than the trial judge, who may not even be known at the time when they are made. Rulings may be made on any question as to the admissibility of evidence or any question of law relating to the case, either on application by a party to the case or on the judge's own motion. Once such a ruling is made, it has binding effect until the jury returns a verdict or the prosecutor decides not to proceed, unless a judge discharges or varies it. A judge may discharge or vary a ruling, either on the application of a party or on his own motion, where it appears in the interests of justice to do so. Where a party makes an application to vary an earlier ruling, he must show that there has been a material change of circumstances since the original ruling was made or (where there has been a previous application) since the last application was made (s 40).

The result is that a pre-trial ruling acquires a status which means that it is not irreversible, but neither is it subject to automatic reconsideration at any time one of the parties so desires. It can be compared in this sense to a second decision to refuse bail, which can be challenged in the magistrates' court only if there are fresh circumstances (see Paragraph 6.5.1).

There are restrictions on the reporting of pre-trial rulings and the proceedings on applications relating to them. Reports may not be published or broadcast until the conclusion of the trial. There is no exemption in respect of formal details of the accused, in contrast to the restrictions on reporting of committals and preparatory hearings. However, a party may apply to the judge presiding at the pre-trial hearing for an order lifting reporting restrictions. If the accused (or one of them) objects, then the court may lift the restrictions only if it is satisfied that it is in the interests of justice to do so (ss 41 and 42 of the CPIA).

15.3 PREPARATORY HEARINGS

Sections 28 to 38 of the CPIA contain provisions for preparatory hearings in long or complex cases. They originate from the procedure established for serious fraud cases, which came into force by virtue of the Criminal Justice Act 1987 (see the description in small type at the end of this Paragraph). The new provisions came into effect in April 1997.

The decision to hold a preparatory hearing may be made by a Crown Court judge at any time before a jury is sworn, on the application of any of the parties, or by the court of its own motion. In practice, the decision is likely to be made at the PDH (see Paragraph 15.1). The preparatory hearing is in fact a stage of the trial itself, which may be used in order to settle various issues without requiring the jury to attend (s 30). In this respect, it differs from the pre-trial rulings described in Paragraph 15.2. Since the trial begins with the preparatory hearing, the same judge must preside throughout, save for exceptional circumstances such as death or serious illness on his part (see *Southwark Crown Court ex p Commissioners for Customs and Excise* [1993] 1 WLR 764, but contrast the position as far as the PDH is concerned).

Among the powers available to the judge at a preparatory hearing is the power to order the prosecution to give the defence a case statement. This will differ from the bundle of evidence supplied at committal in that it should state the facts as the prosecution believe them to be, including, e.g., any inferences which they are asking the jury to draw from the evidence. Once the prosecution have supplied such a case statement, the judge may order the defence to supply a statement setting out in general terms the nature of the defence and the principal matters on which they take issue with the prosecution, any objections which they have to the prosecution case statement, and any points of law or admissibility which they wish to take and authorities on which they intend to rely (s 31). Although this is a form of defence disclosure, it is additional to, and may be more extensive than, the general duty of disclosure outlined in Chapter 8 (e.g., it includes notification of points of law). Adverse comments and/or inferences are the sanctions which may flow from a failure to disclose, or a departure at trial from the case disclosed at a preparatory hearing. Although the sanctions are similar to those available for a breach of the general duty of disclosure, the preparatory hearing provisions apply to the prosecution as well, and there is a specific prohibition on any mention of the defence statement without the consent of the accused (s 34).

The judge may also make rulings as to any question of law relating to the case, including questions as to the admissibility of evidence (s 31(2)), but his powers in this respect may be circumscribed by the principle in *Gunawardena* [1990] 1 WLR 703. In that case, it was held that the power to make binding rulings in a preparatory hearing in a serious fraud case was limited by implication to the purposes for which preparatory hearings may be ordered. These purposes are set out in s 29(1), and may be summarised as:

(a)   identifying material issues for the jury;
(b)   assisting them to understand those issues;
(c)   expediting proceedings before them; and
(d)   helping the judge to manage the trial.

An order or ruling is binding throughout the trial, but the judge may decide on application that the interests of justice require him to vary or discharge it. There is no restriction on applications for variation such as exists in the case of pre-trial rulings under s 40 (see Paragraph 15.2). Perhaps such a restriction was not seen as necessary in view of the fact that the same judge will act throughout, and a party is likely to expect the application to meet the same fate unless there really is a change in circumstances.

There are provisions for appealing from rulings made by the judge at a preparatory hearing to the Court of Appeal and, ultimately, the House of Lords (ss 35 and 36). Where leave to appeal has been granted, the preparatory hearing may continue, but the jury trial cannot begin until the appeal has been determined or abandoned. The provision of a system of interlocutory appeals is to ensure that issues of admissibility and law are definitively resolved *before* the jury begins to deliberate, so as to ensure that a complex and potentially lengthy trial does not prove to be abortive.

Restrictions on reporting preparatory hearings are contained in s 37, although certain formal details (e.g., the names, ages, home addresses and occupations of the accused and witnesses, and the offence(s) charged) may be published by virtue of s 37(9). The court has power to lift the restrictions (s 37(3)).

> The Criminal Justice Act 1987, enacted as a result of the 1986 report of the Roskill Committee, provides in ss 7 to 11 for special 'preparatory hearings' in cases of serious fraud. The provisions were the basis for those enacted on preparatory hearings in long or complex cases described in this Paragraph. Further, efforts have been made to ensure that the preparatory hearings regime operating for fraud cases is consistent with that for long or complex cases (see CPIA, s 72 and Sch 3).

15.4   SPECIAL MEASURES FOR CERTAIN WITNESSES

The Youth Justice and Criminal Evidence Act 1999 contains a series of special measures which the court can direct in respect of certain witnesses. Where appropriate, such measures would form the subject of pre-trial rulings as described in the preceding Paragraphs in this Chapter. The measures (which are not yet in force) are:

(a)   screening the witness from the accused (s 23);

(b)   giving evidence by live television link (s 24);

(c)   ordering the removal of wigs and gowns while the witness gives evidence (s 25);

(d)   giving evidence in private (in a sexual case, or where there is a fear that the witness might be intimidated — s 26);

(e)   video-recording of evidence-in-chief (s 27);

(f)   video-recording of cross-examination or re-examination where the evidence-in-chief of the witness has been video recorded (s 28);

(g)   examination through an intermediary in the case of a young or incapacitated witness (s 29); and

(h)   provision of aids to communication for a young or incapacitated witness (s 30).

In deciding whether to make a direction incorporating any of these special measures, the court must determine whether it will improve the quality of the witness' evidence, which is stated in s 16(5) to refer to its completeness, coherence and accuracy. In order to qualify for special measures, a witness must be eligible on grounds of youth or incapacity (s 16), or be liable to suffer from fear or distress when giving evidence (s 17). The accused is specifically excluded from eligibility for special measures (s 16(1) and 17(1)) — an exclusion which is likely to be the subject of challenge in the European Court of Human Rights as a contravention of Article 6 (see Paragraph 26.2.5).

16   Pleas

A trial on indictment begins with the arraignment, which consists of putting the counts in the indictment to the accused so that he can plead guilty or not guilty. The clerk reads the indictment, pausing after each count to ask those charged in it whether they plead guilty or not guilty. A plea must be taken on each count, unless it is in the alternative to another count to which the accused has already pleaded guilty. The consequences of the accused giving an ambiguous answer when asked to plead, or saying absolutely nothing, or being incapable of pleading rationally are discussed in Paragraphs 16.3.2, 16.7.1 and 16.7.2 respectively.

16.1   TIME-LIMITS

The trial should begin (i.e. the arraignment take place) not less than two and not more than eight weeks from the date of committal for trial: Supreme Court Act 1981, s 77 and r 24 of the Crown Court Rules 1982 (SI 1982 No 1109). However, this is an indication of what ought to happen, rather than of what actually does happen, since a judge of the Crown Court may, and normally would, give permission for the trial to start after the eight-week period. Even if no permission is expressly given, a trial commencing outside that period would not be a nullity as s 77 is directory not mandatory (see *Urbanowski* [1976] 1 WLR 445 and *Governor of Spring Hill Prison ex p Sohi* [1988] 1 WLR 596, the latter case confirming that a slight change in wording between s 77 and its predecessor in the Courts Act 1971 had not been intended to affect the merely directory nature of the provision). The facts of *ex p Sohi* indicate how little attention is in practice paid to s 77 and r 24. S was committed for trial on 17 July 1986 but arraignment did not take place until some eight months later on 2 March 1987. The prosecution failed to seek an extension of time; the defence had not apparently even noticed the irregularity, and the trial went ahead without protest. Only afterwards did it occur to defence solicitors to apply to have the whole proceedings declared a nullity because of breach of s 77. As already indicated, the application failed, but Watkins LJ did pay at least lip service to the importance of proceeding timeously by saying that, if no extension of time has been obtained when it ought to have been, the judge should be made aware of that fact before arraignment. In an extreme case of unjustified delay he might then 'take the draconian step of refusing to allow the prosecution to proceed on the existing indictment' *(Ex p Sohi,* p. 602 at D).

The date of arraignment may also be affected by regulations pursuant to s 22 of the Prosecution of Offences Act 1985, which lay down that preliminary stages of criminal proceedings (including the committal to arraignment stage) should be completed within prescribed time-limits. The Act envisages two types of time-limit implemented by regulations:

(a)   Overall time-limits, which lay down the maximum period within which a particular stage (e.g., from committal to arraignment) must be completed. If the prosecution anticipate failure to complete the stage in question within the specified time-limit, they must obtain an extension from the court prior to its expiry. If they fail to apply, or the court refuses to grant an extension, the proceedings will be stayed (s 22(4)) and can only be re-instituted by the DPP, a Chief Crown Prosecutor or equivalent senior figure (s 22B). The court should only grant an extension of time for good cause and if the prosecution have acted with all due expedition (s 22(3)). No overall time-limits have yet been prescribed.

(b)   Custody time-limits, which lay down the maximum period during which the accused may be kept in custody pending completion of a particular stage of proceedings. If a custody time-limit expires, it has important implications for the accused's right to bail. Custody time-limits are now in force throughout the country (see Paragraph 6.3.4 for details).

The procedure on arraignment is that the accused is brought into the dock. If it is anticipated that he will plead not guilty to all counts in the indictment the men and women from whom the jury will be selected (the jury in waiting) may be permitted to sit at the back of court to hear him plead. If there is any chance of his pleading guilty to one count and not guilty to another, they should be kept out of court since, were they to know that he had admitted one charge, it might prejudice their trying him fairly on the others. They should also be kept out of court if some but not all the accused joined in the indictment are expected to plead guilty.

Although there is no rigid formula for what ought to be said, the clerk putting the indictment which appears on p. 212 might say — 'David Wilson, John Burton and Paul Green, you are charged in an indictment containing three counts. The first count charges you David Wilson and you John Burton with assault occasioning actual bodily harm contrary to s 47 of the Offences Against the Person Act 1861. The particulars of that offence are that, on the 1st day of January 2002 you assaulted Barry Johnson thereby occasioning him actual bodily harm. David Wilson, do you plead guilty or not guilty? . . . John Burton, do you plead guilty or not guilty? . . . The second count charges you, Paul Green, with wounding contrary to s 20 of the Offences against the Person Act 1861. The particulars of the offence are that . . .' and so on through the indictment.

Where an indictment contains counts in the alternative which are of roughly equal gravity (e.g. theft and handling the proceeds of the theft), and the accused wishes to plead guilty to one of the counts, it is advisable to tell the court of his intentions. The count to which he is pleading guilty can then be put to him first (irrespective of whether it is first on the indictment), and the other count need not be put. Counts are in the alternative if, given the nature of the prosecution evidence, a jury could properly convict on one count or the other but not on both counts. Paragraph 16.4 deals with the procedure to be followed where alternative counts are not of equal gravity.

16.2   PLEA OF 'NOT GUILTY'

A plea of not guilty puts the entire prosecution case in issue. Essentially, therefore, the prosecution will have to prove to the requisite standard (i.e., beyond reasonable doubt) each essential element of the offence charged, as defined by the substantive law of crime. That is traditionally summarised by saying that they must establish (i) that the accused committed the *actus reus* of the crime (or aided, abetted, counselled or procured someone else in its commission), and (ii) that, at the relevant time, he had the appropriate *mens rea*. Moreover, the prosecution must be able to do this initially through evidence which they tender as part of their case. If they fail to adduce evidence on which a reasonable jury could find the accused guilty, the judge is obliged to direct the jury to acquit, and the trial never reaches the point of the defence being invited to present their case (see Paragraph 18.4 for submissions of no case to answer). If there is a case to answer, then, of course, the prosecution must convince the jury on *all* the evidence (prosecution and defence) that the accused is guilty. One consequence of the principles described above is that, if a prosecution witness fails to testify as expected so that there is inadequate evidence as to an essential element of the offence, the defence are fully entitled to submit no case to answer, even though they had privately been planning to concede the element in question and base the defence upon a quite different point.

A further consequence of a not guilty plea is that, generally speaking, it requires the prosecution to negative any defences which are open to the accused (e.g., defences such as acting under duress, or non-insane automatism, or acting in reasonable self-defence if the charge is one of assault, or provocation if the charge is murder). It is, however, for the defence to raise the issue in the first place by showing (through cross-examination of prosecution witnesses and/or the testimony of defence witnesses) that the defence might be applicable. Once the possibility of the defence applying has been fairly raised, the prosecution must show beyond reasonable doubt that the accused is not entitled to rely on it. There are exceptions to this rule. For example, the accused must prove that he was insane or suffering from diminished responsibility at the time of the offence. It is also for him to prove that he comes within the terms of any exception, proviso, exemption or excuse provided by the statute creating the offence with which he is charged. Whenever the burden of proof is placed on the defence, they discharge it on a balance of probabilities. Details of these matters should be sought in works on evidence. An illustration of the effect of a not guilty plea will be found in the portion in small print below.

If the accused pleads not guilty to some or all of the counts on the indictment, the next step, in most cases, is to empanel a jury to decide whether he is guilty or not (see Chapter 17). However, sometimes the services of a jury are not required because the prosecution do not wish to proceed with the case save on those counts, if any, to which the accused pleaded guilty. There are then two options at the disposal of prosecuting counsel. One is to tell the judge that he proposes to offer no evidence, and the judge may then order that a verdict of not guilty be recorded in respect of each offence denied by the accused, that being equivalent to an acquittal by a jury: Criminal Law Act 1977, s 17. The second option is to ask that the counts to which the accused pleaded not guilty be left on the court file, marked not to be proceeded with without leave of the court or of the Court of Appeal. Although the accused is not formally acquitted of the offences left on the file, there is only one situation in which the prosecution could realistically hope to be subsequently granted leave to proceed (see below). Offering no evidence is appropriate when the prosecution genuinely think, perhaps as a result of extra evidence discovered since the committal proceedings, that the accused ought not to be convicted. Leaving counts on the file most commonly happens when the accused pleads guilty to some but not all the counts against him. In such cases, the prosecution often elect not to proceed on the 'not guilty' counts simply because proving the case would be a waste of time and money in view of the guilty pleas which have also been entered. As they still believe the accused to be guilty as charged, the prosecution will be unwilling to offer no evidence and see him actually acquitted. Leaving the counts on the file is the obvious solution. It has the additional advantage that, should the Court of Appeal subsequently set aside the convictions on the other counts on the ground, for example, that the accused's pleas of guilty were involuntary (see Paragraph 16.3.3), their lordships can give the prosecution leave to proceed with the counts left on the file. Given the possibility (however remote) of counts left on the file being re-activated, defendants occasionally object to that course being adopted, saying that the case should either go ahead or the judge should enter an acquittal. However, it would seem that, in the last resort, the decision is one for the trial judge, and there is no avenue by which an accused can appeal against an order that a count lie on the file: *Central Criminal Court ex p Raymond* [1986] 1 WLR 710.

The plea of not guilty should be made by the accused personally, not by counsel on this behalf. However, a deviation from the correct procedure for taking not guilty pleas will not necessarily give the accused a good ground of appeal against conviction should the jury find him guilty. In *Williams* [1978] QB 373 it was thought, through an administrative muddle, that W had pleaded not guilty. In fact, he had never been arraigned, although he undoubtedly intended to deny the charge. The trial proceeded exactly as if W had been arraigned and pleaded not guilty. W, who was the only person in court who knew that he had not pleaded, failed to raise any objection. The jury convicted, and the Court of Appeal dismissed the appeal, holding that the irregularity in the proceedings had not been sufficiently material to justify quashing the conviction.

To appreciate the significance of the rule that a not guilty plea puts the whole of the prosecution case in issue, consider a prosecution for assault occasioning actual bodily harm brought against two defendants, A1 and A2. The prosecution must establish (a) that the accused applied unlawful force to the victim, and (b) that this caused the victim some actual bodily harm. A, when questioned by the police, admitted that he and A2 struck the victim, but claimed that they were acting in reasonable self-defence after the victim had threatened them with a knife. A2 said nothing to the police, but gives instructions to counsel for the defence that his co-accused's account of what happened is correct and a defence statement is submitted on his behalf to that effect. At the trial, both plead not guilty. The prosecution call the victim as a witness, but he has become confused about what occurred, and says that he can no longer be sure that A1 and A2 were involved in the attack on him. He does, however, confirm that he suffered injuries amounting to actual bodily harm, and he denies defence counsel's suggestion in cross-examination that he had been the aggressor. A police officer then gives evidence of A1's response to questioning. Assume that there is no other prosecution evidence, and that the judge decides that no inference under s 34 of the Criminal Justice and Public Order Act 1994 can be drawn from A2's silence in interview. The judge must direct the jury to acquit A2, since no evidence has been called to show that he used force against the victim. He made no admissions to the police, and what A1 said to the police on the subject cannot be used against A2 because of the rule against hearsay evidence. The fact that A2 would not in reality have disputed his involvement in the incident, and was planning to run a quite different type of defence does not release the prosecution from the obligation, imposed upon them by the not guilty plea, to establish a prima facie case against him in respect of every element of the offence. A2's defence statement cannot be used by the prosecution to establish a prima facie case (see Paragraph 8.3). However, the case against A1 may proceed because the statement he made to the police *is* evidence against him that he struck the victim. Assuming A1 testifies in his own defence that the victim threatened him with a knife, the judge, when summing-up the case to the jury, must tell them only to convict if they are sure on all the evidence that A1 was not acting in reasonable self-defence. This is because of the rule that the prosecution must not only establish the elements of the offence but (subject to certain exceptions) must negative any defence fairly raised by the accused. It may well be that A1, in his testimony, will claim that A2 was also a party to the incident. If A2 were still a defendant, the jury could use A1's evidence as a basis for convicting A2 (what an accused testifies on oath is capable of being evidence against his co-accused whereas what he says to the police out of court is only capable of being evidence against himself). However, since A2 has had to be acquitted on the judge's direction, the case against him cannot be reopened, notwithstanding that subsequent developments may strongly suggest that he was guilty.

16.3 PLEA OF 'GUILTY'

A plea of guilty must be entered by the accused personally. Counsel may not plead guilty on his behalf. If he purports to do so, the plea is a nullity, and will result in the Court of Appeal quashing the conviction entered upon the plea and ordering a retrial: *Ellis* (1973)

57 Cr App R 571. In *Williams* (see Paragraph 16.2) the Court of Appeal stated that 'no qualification of or deviation from the rule that a plea of guilty must come from him who acknowledges guilt is permissible. A departure from the rule in a criminal trial would necessarily render the whole procedure void and ineffectual'.

Following a plea of guilty there is no need to empanel a jury as the accused has convicted himself out of his own mouth. The court may proceed straight to sentence or, if it needs more information about the accused, it may adjourn for the preparation of reports. The procedure before sentence is passed is described in Chapter 20. In brief, prosecuting counsel summarises the circumstances of the offence, including the previous convictions, background, education, employment, financial circumstances etc. of the accused. Any reports on him are read. Counsel for the defence then presents his plea in mitigation, and the judge passes sentence. If the accused pleads guilty on one count and not guilty on other counts, the judge will postpone sentencing him for the offence to which he has pleaded guilty until after the trial of the pleas of 'not guilty'. Should the jury convict him, the judge can sentence him at one time for all the offences.

16.3.1 Pleas by co-accused

If two accused are charged in one indictment, and one pleads guilty and the other not guilty, the usual practice is for the judge to adjourn the case of the one who has pleaded guilty. He is remanded, either in custody or on bail, to come up for sentence at the conclusion of the trial of the accused pleading not guilty. The advantage of this course of action is that, during the trial before the jury, the judge learns from the evidence full details of the case against the accused who has denied the charge, and may also learn much that he would not otherwise have known about the case against the accused who has pleaded guilty. Should the former be convicted by the jury, the judge can sentence both accused at the same time, knowing from the evidence which, if either, of the two played the major role. Whether or not to adjourn is, however, a matter for the discretion of the judge. If he is satisfied that he has sufficient information about the accused who has pleaded guilty, he may sentence him forthwith without waiting for the other to be tried.

If the prosecution proposes to call the accused who has pleaded guilty to give evidence against his co-accused, there is a strong argument for sentencing the former before he gives his evidence. Not to do so leaves room for suspicion that, in testifying, he may have said what he thought the judge wanted him to say in order to receive a lighter sentence. Accordingly, it was at one time the invariable practice in this type of case to sentence the accused forthwith. Counsel, in mitigation, indicated the sort of evidence his client was going to give, and the judge would no doubt make an appropriate reduction in sentence. If the evidence subsequently given by the accused was not what had been anticipated the judge had no power to increase the sentence originally passed: *Stone* [1970] 1 WLR 1112. The former practice is still followed sometimes and, where that is done, *Stone* remains good authority. However, in 1977 the Court of Appeal stated that, even where the accused is going to testify for the prosecution, the judge has a discretion either to sentence him forthwith or to postpone sentence until after the trial of the other accused. Subsequently, their lordships have, in a number of cases, strongly urged judges to adopt the latter course, pointing out that not to do so can lead to embarrassing disparities in sentence should the co-accused ultimately be convicted and receive a much heavier sentence than that earlier passed on his companion in crime (see especially *Weekes* (1980) 74 Cr App R 161). Even so, it is in the end a matter for the individual judge's discretion *Palmer* (1994) 158 JP 138.

16.3.2 Ambiguous pleas

Instead of merely saying 'Guilty', an accused sometimes responds to the indictment in an ambiguous way. For example, he may answer to a count for handling by saying — 'Guilty to receiving, but I wasn't sure if the goods were stolen'. The plea is ambiguous. He may mean — 'I believed them to be stolen, although nobody told me in so many words that such was the case', or he may mean — 'I was a bit suspicious about the goods, but didn't really think they were stolen'. In the former case, he should plead guilty, but not in the latter. The judge should try to elucidate the plea by explaining to the accused the elements of the offence charged. Then the indictment can be put to him again. If the plea remains ambiguous a not guilty plea must be entered on his behalf: Criminal Law Act 1967, s 6(1). If the judge proceeds to sentence upon a plea which remains ambiguous, the Court of Appeal will set aside the conviction and sentence and order that the accused be sent back to the Crown Court to plead again to the indictment. Similar principles apply whenever the accused says something when the indictment is put but will not give a direct answer to it (e.g. in a case where the motive for the offence alleged appears to be political he might say — 'I do not recognise the authority of the court'). A plea of not guilty should be entered on his behalf, and the case proceeds as if he had actually pleaded not guilty.

16.3.3 Involuntary pleas

Not only must the plea of guilty come from the lips of the accused, but his mind must go with his plea. In other words, where a guilty plea is extracted from the accused by pressure and the circumstances are such that he cannot genuinely choose between pleading guilty and pleading not guilty, then that plea is a nullity. If he appeals, the Court of Appeal will quash the conviction and order a retrial. The pressure necessary for a plea of guilty to be rendered a nullity may come either from the judge or from counsel. An example of the former is provided by *Barnes* (1970) 55 Cr App R 100. B pleaded not guilty, but half way through the prosecution case the judge, having sent the jury to their room, said in effect that B was plainly guilty and was wasting the court's time. Even so, B refused to change his plea to guilty, but, had he done so, the plea would have been a nullity. Allowing the appeal on other grounds, the Court of Appeal stated that the judge's conduct was 'wholly improper'.

A more subtle way in which the judge might pressurise the accused is illustrated by *Turner* [1970] 2 QB 321. T pleaded not guilty to a charge of theft. After some of the prosecution witnesses had given their evidence, there was a lengthy adjournment during which T discussed the conduct of the case with his counsel and solicitor. At one stage counsel went to see the judge in his private room. On his return, counsel warned T that if he persisted in a not guilty plea and was found guilty there was a 'very real possibility' that he would receive a sentence of imprisonment, but that if he pleaded guilty he would be dealt with by a fine or other non-custodial sentence. Counsel was, in fact, expressing his personal opinion of the case, but inevitably it appeared to T that he was passing on what the judge had said. T changed his plea to guilty. The Court of Appeal (Lord Parker CJ presiding) quashed his conviction and ordered a retrial. Once T felt that the advice his counsel gave him as to sentence was 'an intimation emanating from the judge, it is really idle in the opinion of this court to think that he really had a free choice in the matter' of his plea. Lord Parker went on to say that the judge should 'never indicate the sentence which he is minded to impose', unless he can say that 'whatever happens, whether the accused pleads guilty or not guilty, the sentence will or will not take a particular form, e.g., a probation order or a fine or a custodial sentence' (see *Turner* supra at p. 327). The value of such an indication is that out of fear, let us say, of a custodial sentence, an accused may persist in a not guilty plea although he knows he is guilty and the evidence against him is overwhelming. If he can be told, on the judge's authority, that he will not go to prison, he may be willing to admit his guilt. No pressure is brought upon him to plead as the promise of a non-custodial sentence applies whether he pleads guilty or is found guilty by a jury. What the judge may not do, however, as a result of *Turner,* is to indicate expressly that a plea of guilty will be followed by a more lenient form of sentence than that which would follow a verdict of guilty by a jury. Nor may he impliedly give an indication to the same effect by saying what form the sentence will or will not take if there is a guilty plea, and leaving the accused to infer the consequences of a 'Not Guilty' plea. If the judge does, in breach of *Turner* principles, give an indication of sentence on a guilty plea only, then if the accused pleads not guilty and is convicted, the judge is bound by his indication (*Keily* [1990] Crim LR 204).

Lord Parker's judgment in *Turner* clearly governs what the judge may say about sentence in open court, in the hearing of the accused. It also governs what he may say privately to defence counsel on the matter, for one of the subsidiary points made in the case is that if there is a private discussion between the judge and counsel about sentence the latter should tell his client both that he has seen the judge and what the judge said (see Paragraph 18.1.3 for further discussion).

The second source of pressure capable of rendering a plea of guilty a nullity is that which may be exerted by the accused's own 'counsel. In the decided cases the Court of Appeal have held that the conduct complained of was not sufficient to deprive the accused of his free choice as to plea. However, advice by defence counsel along the lines that 'the prosecution case is so strong that your only possible course of action is to plead guilty whether you committed the offence charged or not' would cause any plea of guilty to be a nullity. The principles governing the advice that counsel should give the accused about his plea are discussed in *Turner* at p. 326. It is counsel's duty to give the best advice he can, if need be in 'strong terms'. That advice may include his view on the strength of the prosecution case and the difficulties thrown up by the nature of the defence (e.g., he might warn the accused that a defence involving attacks on the characters of the prosecution witnesses would lead to his being cross-examined about his previous convictions if he chose to give evidence). The accused should also be told, if he does not know already, that a conviction upon a plea of guilty is likely to attract a more lenient sentence than a conviction following a not guilty plea. Counsel can also indicate his personal view of the sentence the judge is likely to pass. The mischief in *Turner* arose not from the nature of counsel's advice on sentence, but from the implication that the 'advice' was a repetition of what the judge had said. Finally, it must be emphasised to the accused that the choice of plea is one for him, not counsel, to make, and that he should only plead guilty if he is indeed guilty. The mere fact that the accused pleads guilty reluctantly after receiving strong advice from counsel does not make the plea a nullity. It is only a nullity if, when he makes it, the accused has lost the power to make a voluntary and deliberate choice: *Peace* [1976] Crim LR 119.

Inability to make a genuine choice may very occasionally arise from something for which only the accused himself is to blame. Even then the Court of Appeal has been willing to treat his plea as a nullity. The point is illustrated by *Swain* [1986] Crim LR 480, where S changed his plea to guilty half way through the prosecution case. He gave no coherent reason to counsel, merely saying — 'Have you looked up at the sky lately? Have you seen the stars?' After he had been sentenced, it emerged through his mother that he had obtained drugs in prison, and had been under the influence of LSD at the relevant time. Psychiatric evidence was called before the Court of Appeal that LSD can put the user into a state akin to schizophrenia, where he drifts in and out of a delusional world and makes irrational decisions. That seemed to be the explanation for the change of plea, and the Court was therefore obliged to hold it a nullity and quash the conviction.

16.4 PLEA OF 'GUILTY' TO A LESSER OFFENCE

Halfway between a plea of guilty and not guilty is the plea of guilty to a lesser offence. It is a corollary of the option given to juries in certain cases by s 6 of the Criminal Law Act 1967 to return a verdict of 'not guilty as charged but guilty of some other (lesser) offence' (see Paragraph 19.4 for details). Familiar examples are that on a count for murder the jury can convict of manslaughter; on a count for burglary contrary to s 9(1)(b) of the Theft Act they can convict of theft, and on a count for wounding with intent contrary to the Offences against the Person Act 1861, s 18 they can convict of unlawful wounding contrary to s 20. Whenever a count is put to the accused on which the jury could find him guilty of a lesser offence, he may offer a plea of not guilty as charged but guilty of the lesser offence: Criminal Law Act 1967, s 6(1)(b). If the plea is accepted, he stands acquitted of the offence charged, and the court proceeds to sentence him for the lesser matter: s 6(5).

The prosecution are not, of course, obliged to accept a proffered plea of guilty of a lesser offence. The Code for Crown Prosecutors (para 9.1) stipulates that the defendant's plea to a lesser charge should be accepted only if the court will be able to pass a sentence that matches the seriousness of the offence. Crown prosecutors are told that they must not accept a guilty plea just because it is convenient.

If the prosecutor is not prepared to accept the defendant's plea of guilty of a lesser offence, he can insist on the trial proceeding. The court then enters a straightforward not guilty plea on behalf of the accused; the plea to the lesser offence is impliedly withdrawn, and a jury is empanelled. The evidence is then called in the normal way. At the end of the case, the jury can either convict as charged, convict of the lesser offence, or even simply acquit (the consequences of their doing the latter are discussed below). Even if the prosecution are willing to accept a plea of guilty to a lesser offence, the judge may indicate that it is not an appropriate course to adopt: *Soanes* [1948] 1 All ER 289. That case in fact suggests that the judge's consent to the plea is essential as a matter of law but, in the light of analogous later cases, the true position appears to be that the final decision is for the prosecution, although in practice they would rarely if ever act against the judge's expressed wishes (see Paragraph 16.6). Strictly speaking, there should be something in the evidence on the committal statements or in the general circumstances of the case to suggest that the accused may not be guilty as charged — otherwise the trial ought to proceed. In practice, however, the savings in time and money to be derived from not having to hold a jury trial may make it fairly easy to persuade both prosecution and judge that a plea of guilty to a lesser offence is appropriate.

An odd consequence of rejecting a plea of guilty to a lesser offence is illustrated by *Hazeltine* [1967] 2 QB 857. H pleaded not guilty to wounding with intent to cause grievous bodily harm but guilty of unlawful wounding. The plea was not accepted. The trial proceeded, and the jury simply acquitted H. They did not, as they were entitled to, find him not guilty as charged but guilty of unlawful wounding. The judge nevertheless proceeded to sentence H for that offence, relying on the fact that he had originally pleaded guilty to it. The Court of Appeal quashed the sentence. When the court entered on H's behalf a plea of not guilty to wounding with intent, his plea to unlawful wounding was by implication withdrawn and could not subsequently be reinstated by the judge. Nor could the prosecution prefer a fresh charge for unlawful wounding as the jury's acquittal for wounding with intent amounted impliedly to an acquittal for unlawful wounding also, and any proceedings would have been countered by the plea of autrefois acquit (see Paragraph 16.8). However, the Court of Appeal did suggest a means by which a repetition of what happened in *Hazeltine* can be avoided. Upon realising that the defence are putting forward a version of events which, if accepted, would result in a complete acquittal, prosecuting counsel should call evidence before the jury that the accused originally pleaded guilty to the lesser offence. In the absence of a convincing explanation of why, if he is completely innocent, he did not simply plead not guilty, the jury will almost certainly convict him at least of the lesser offence. But, should the prosecution not have called evidence of the original plea, the judge must not tell the jury about it in his summing-up. Nor can he direct the jury to convict of the lesser offence, as opposed to telling them that they have the option of doing so: *Lee* [1985] Crim LR 798; *Notman* [1994] Crim LR 518.

A variation on the theme of pleading guilty to a lesser offence in respect of a single count arises when there are two counts on the indictment, one more serious than the other, and the prosecution case is such that they do not seek a conviction on both counts (i.e. the counts are in the alternative). An example is an indictment containing counts against the accused for robbery and for handling all or some of the proceeds of the robbery. If he pleads guilty to handling and not guilty to robbery, but the prosecution still want to try to prove the robbery against him, there is no need for the court to withdraw his plea of guilty to handling as that is a plea entered on a quite separate count. The trial proceeds on the robbery count, and if the accused is acquitted he can then be sentenced for handling. If he is convicted of robbery, he is sentenced for that, but not for handling. Although his plea of guilty to handling remains on the court file, he does not stand convicted of handling as, technically speaking, a guilty plea does not amount to a conviction until sentence has been passed (see *Cole* [1965] 2 QB 388). It is possible that a similar procedure would have assisted the prosecution in the circumstances of *Hazeltine's* case (see above). Prosecuting counsel could have invited the judge to amend the indictment so as to have two counts; H would then have pleaded not guilty to count one (wounding with intent) but guilty to count two (unlawful wounding), and, upon the jury acquitting on count one, the judge would have sentenced H for the count two offence. The difficulty is that there would have been a contradiction between the jury's outright acquittal on count one, implying an acquittal for unlawful wounding also, and the accused's plea of guilty to unlawful wounding. That difficulty did not arise in *Cole* because a jury trying a count for robbery cannot bring in a verdict of guilty of handling.

16.5 CHANGE OF PLEA

The possibility of an accused changing his plea from not guilty to guilty has already been mentioned in Paragraph 16.3.3 (see the discussion of *Barnes* and *Turner*). This may be done at any stage of the trial. Defence counsel asks for the indictment to be put again to his client, and, upon that being done, the accused pleads guilty. Like any other plea of guilty, it must come from the accused personally, not from counsel on his behalf. In addition, the jury, empanelled as a result of the original not guilty plea, must return a formal verdict of guilty. If they fail to do so, the change of plea is ineffective, and the trial rendered a nullity: *Heyes* [1951] 1 KB 29. The judge in sentencing may give the accused some credit for having changed his plea, although it should not be as much as if he had admitted his guilt from the outset.

A change of plea from guilty to not guilty is also possible, but is subject to the judge giving his consent. The granting of consent is a matter of discretion, and is not automatically forthcoming even where the accused was unrepresented when he originally pleaded. Relevant considerations are whether he apparently understood the nature of the charge and/or genuinely intended to admit his guilt of it. If he seems merely to have changed his mind about plea out of tactical considerations (e.g., the judge's attitude when the prosecution summarised the facts makes him fear a heavier sentence than he first anticipated), the judge is fully entitled to hold him to his original admission (see, for example, *McNally* [1954] 1 WLR 933). Applications to withdraw a guilty plea may be made at any stage before sentence is passed: *S (an infant) v Recorder of Manchester* [1971] AC 481. They are often prompted by the accused using an adjournment between his plea and the date fixed for sentence to obtain legal advice for the first time, but, as already mentioned, his being unrepresented when he pleaded does not guarantee that the application will succeed.

16.6 PLEA BARGAINING

Turner [1970] 2 QB 321 was partly concerned with what Lord Parker described as the 'vexed question' of plea bargaining. The phrase is an imprecise one which may be used in at least four different senses. It can mean an agreement between the judge and the accused that if he pleads guilty to some or all of the offences charged against him the sentence will or will not take a certain form. As a consequence of *Turner* a guilty plea made in such circumstances is a nullity and the conviction is liable to be quashed on appeal (see Paragraph 16.3.3). Second, plea bargaining can mean an undertaking by the prosecution that if the accused will admit to certain charges they will refrain from putting more serious charges into the indictment or will ask the judge to impose a relatively light sentence. This form of bargaining is not possible under the English system as the indictment is drawn up quite independently of the defence, and, at the sentencing stage, the prosecution's function is merely to tell the judge the facts, not to suggest an appropriate sentence. Thirdly, plea bargaining may refer to the prosecution agreeing with the defence that if the accused pleads guilty to a lesser offence they will accept the plea (see Paragraph 16.4), and, lastly, it may refer to the prosecution agreeing not to proceed on one or more counts in the indictment against the accused if he will plead guilty to the remainder. As explained in Paragraph 16.2, the usual arrangement is for the judge to be asked to leave the counts denied by the accused on the court file, marked not to be proceeded with without leave of the court or of the Court of Appeal.

Plea bargaining in the third and fourth senses described above is a frequent occurrence, approved by the courts. It is not usually in the public interest to spend time and money proving the accused guilty precisely as charged if he is prepared to admit the bulk of the case against him, either by pleading guilty to a lesser offence or by pleading guilty to some but not all the counts. The bargain is usually struck by prosecuting and defence counsel outside court before the commencement of the trial. The question arises whether the judge must approve what is proposed. In *Coward* (1980) 70 Cr App R 70, Lawton LJ put the onus solely on prosecuting counsel, saying that it was for him to make up his mind what pleas to accept. No doubt, as a matter of courtesy, he will explain his decision to the judge and, should the latter not approve, he may say so in open court. In the light of the judge's comments counsel might well change his original decision. But, in the last resort, the judge cannot force the prosecution to proceed. In *Broad* (1979) 68 Cr App R 28, on the other hand, the prosecution had originally been prepared to offer no evidence against B if her co-accused pleaded guilty but, upon seeking the judge's views and discovering that he disapproved, decided to proceed. B was convicted. Dismissing her appeal, the Court of Appeal held that the judge was not a 'rubber stamp' to sanction whatever counsel thought appropriate. The Report of the Farquharson Committee (see Paragraph 18.1.1 and the Trinity 1986 edition of *Counsel* magazine) suggested that if prosecuting counsel expressly asks for the judge's approval before agreeing to a defence proposal, he is bound by the judge's decision whatever it may be (*Broad* above). But, where counsel chooses to act without seeking prior approval, his only obligation is to explain to the judge the reasoning behind his decision. If the judge disapproves, counsel should reconsider his position and even consult the Director of Public Prosecutions about the matter. In the final analysis, however, counsel's views must prevail. The report of the Farquharson Committee was referred to with approval in *Grafton* [1993] QB 101, which focused on a disagreement between judge and prosecuting counsel about whether the prosecution could discontinue its case once the trial had commenced (see Paragraph 18.10 for further discussion of this question).

Sometimes the defendant is willing to plead guilty on the basis of a particular version of the facts. The defence and the prosecution may therefore try to reach agreement on the factual basis upon which a plea of guilty would be accepted, e.g., the prosecution might be prepared to accept that the defendant assaulted the victim recklessly (rather than intentionally). Such an agreement is likely to have an impact on the sentencing process. The issues arose in *Beswick* [1996] 1 Cr App R (S) 343, and are dealt with in Paragraph 20.1.

The role of plea bargaining in the English criminal justice system was considered by the Royal Commission on Criminal Justice, chaired by Lord Runciman, in its report in 1993. The Commission's proposals have direct relevance to the discount which defendants receive for a plea of guilty, and are dealt with in Paragraph 21.5.2.

16.7   THE ACCUSED WHO WILL NOT OR CANNOT PLEAD

So far it has been assumed that when the accused is arraigned he says something rational in answer to the charges. What he says may fall short of a proper plea of guilty or not guilty, but, at least, his response shows that he has heard and understood the clerk's words to him. However, the accused may be unwilling to reply when the indictment is put, or he may be incapable of replying in a sensible way. The first possibility raises the question of 'mute of malice', the second the question of unfitness to plead.

16.7.1   Muteness

If the accused remains silent, this may be by choice or because he is incapable of responding to the arraignment. In the former case, he is said to be 'mute of malice'. A plea of not guilty is entered on behalf of an accused who is mute of malice, and the case then proceeds as if he had himself pleaded not guilty: Criminal Law Act 1967, s 6(1)(c). A jury must be empanelled to decide whether or not muteness is malicious, the burden of proof being on the prosecution to show beyond reasonable doubt that the accused stays silent by choice. This they might do through medical evidence or through the evidence of a witness who has recently heard the accused speak. There is nothing to stop a jury which has found an accused mute of malice also trying the substantive case against him, provided the trial commences within 24 hours of the jury having been constituted to try muteness (see Paragraph 17.4.7).

If the accused is not mute of malice, he is said to be 'mute by visitation of God'. When the jury return a verdict of mute by visitation of God, they are also asked to specify the cause of the muteness. If it arises from the accused being speech-handicapped, or deaf so that he cannot hear what the clerk says to him, the case is adjourned with a view to finding a way of communicating with him (e.g., through an expert in sign language). Should there be no way of overcoming the problem, the Attorney-General might eventually be forced to enter a *nolle prosequi* (see Paragraph 3.4). If the cause of the muteness seems to be that the accused suffers from mental problems, and so cannot reply when the indictment is put, the jury may be further asked to consider whether he is unfit to plead (see the next Paragraph).

16.7.2   Unfitness to plead

An accused is unfit to plead or stand his trial if his intellect is defective, so that he cannot comprehend the course of the proceedings so as to make a proper defence to the indictment.

Whether he can answer when arraigned is obviously one relevant factor. Other relevant factors are whether he is capable of challenging a juror to whom he might wish to object (see Chapter 17), whether he can instruct his legal representatives, and whether he would be able to follow the evidence. An accused is not unfit to plead merely because he is highly abnormal (*Berry* (1977) 66 Cr App R 157), or because he is likely to act against his own best interests (*Robertson* [1968] 1 WLR 1767), or even because he is suffering from amnesia so as not to be able to recall the alleged offence or the circumstances surrounding it: *Podola* [1960] 1 QB 325. Section 4(2) of the Criminal Procedure (Insanity) Act 1964 permits the court to postpone consideration of unfitness until any time up to the opening of the defence case. The court must be of the opinion that postponement is 'expedient' and 'in the interests of the accused'.

Where the accused may be unfit to plead, either the prosecution or the defence should, before the arraignment, bring the matter to the judge's attention. Although one would normally expect the defence to do this, the prosecution might feel it their duty to take the initiative if, for instance, the accused is unrepresented but is clearly in no fit state to understand the proceedings. A jury is empanelled to decide the issue, evidence is called, and the judge directs the jury about the meaning of 'unfitness to plead'. The burden and standard of proof depends upon who raised the issue. If it was the prosecution, they must prove unfitness beyond reasonable doubt; if it was the defence, they must do so on a balance of probabilities (see *Robertson* and *Podola* respectively).

Where the jury has determined that the accused is unfit to plead, s 4A of the Criminal Procedure (Insanity) Act 1964 applies. This provision, which was inserted in 1991, lays down that it must then be determined by a jury whether the accused 'did the act or made the omission charged against him as the offence' (s 4A(2)). If they are satisfied that he did, they must find accordingly (s 4A(3)). If they are not satisfied, they must acquit. If the question of fitness to plead was determined on arraignment, then a fresh jury must be empanelled to try the issue of whether the accused did the act or made the omission. If it was postponed under s 4(2), the jury by whom the accused was being tried should also determine whether he did the act or made the omission (s 4A(5)).

Section 4(6) of the 1964 Act (also inserted in 1991) provides that a jury may not determine the question of fitness to plead except on the evidence (written or oral) of two or more registered medical practitioners, at least one of whom must have been approved by the Secretary of State as having special experience in the diagnosis or treatment of mental disorder.

In *M* [2002] Crim LR 57, the Court of Appeal considered the above procedures in the light of the Human Rights Act 1998, and particularly in the context of Art 6 of the European Convention on Human Rights (see Paragraph 26.2.5). The court held that the criminal charge provisions of Art 6 do not apply to proceedings under ss 4 and 4A of the 1964 Act, since those proceedings cannot result in a conviction. In any event, they concluded that the procedure under ss 4 and 4A of the 1964 Act constituted a fair procedure, providing an opportunity for investigation of the facts on behalf of a disabled person, so far as possible. It fairly balanced the public interest and the interest of the person alleged to have committed the act. Therefore, if Art 6 had applied to the procedure under the 1964 Act, it would not have been infringed. In addition, their lordships stated that the defence was able to make an application to stay proceedings for abuse of process when it appeared necessary, and this could be either before arraignment or before any question of disability fell to be determined.

Under s 5 of the 1964 Act (as amended in 1991), if the accused is found unfit to plead, and the jury determines that he did the act or made the omission as charged, then the court may make:

(a)   an admission order to a hospital approved by the Secretary of State;
(b)   a guardianship order under the Mental Health Act 1983;
(c)   a supervision and treatment order; or
(d)   an order for the accused's absolute discharge.

See Paragraph 23.22 for further details.

16.8   PLEAS OF 'AUTREFOIS ACQUIT' AND 'AUTREFOIS CONVICT'

The pleas of 'autrefois acquit' and 'autrefois convict' (i.e., the accused has, on a previous occasion, been acquitted or convicted of the offence alleged in a count of the indictment) give effect to the vital constitutional principle that no one shall be prosecuted twice to acquittal or conviction for the same offence. If one or other of the pleas is raised successfully it is a bar to all further proceedings on the count concerned. These pleas, together with the plea of pardon (see Paragraph 16.9), are known as special pleas in bar. Despite the importance of the pleas being available to prevent harassment of the individual by repeated prosecutions for one crime, it is rare in practice for the defence to be forced to have recourse to them. This is because court records are available to establish clearly whether a person has previously been prosecuted for an offence, and if so, the result of that prosecution. If it ended in his being convicted or acquitted — as opposed, for example, to the jury being unable to agree on a verdict — nobody would for a moment consider prosecuting him again for the same offence. However, although infrequently pleaded autrefois acquit and convict have led to a disproportionately large body of case law as the appellate courts have been called upon to define the precise limits of the pleas. The following Paragraphs seek to describe the main applications of the pleas without delving over-deeply into the minutiae of the subject.

16.8.1   Procedure on a plea of 'autrefois acquit' or 'autrefois convict'

The plea is made in writing signed by defence counsel on behalf of the accused. The form of words suggested is — 'John Smith says thàt the Queen ought not further to prosecute the indictment against him because he has been lawfully acquitted/convicted of the offence charged therein.' However, should the accused be unrepresented, he is allowed to make the plea orally. The correct time for doing so is before arraignment but the court has a discretion to entertain the plea at any stage during the trial. Assuming the prosecution do not accept the defence contention, they join issue through a written 'replication' signed by an appropriate officer of the Crown Court. It simply says — 'David Brown joins issue on behalf of the Queen.'

Until recently, whether autrefois did or did not apply had to be decided by a jury sworn in for the purpose. That procedure was somewhat unsatisfactory since autrefois rarely involves disputes of fact although it does very often raise complex points of law. Consequently, there was a tendency to read out to the jury an agreed statement of the relevant facts, after which the judge — probably following legal argument in the jury's absence — would give them a 'robust' direction on the law, virtually telling them what their decision ought to be. The Criminal Justice Act 1988 recognised the reality of the situation and provided in s 122 that — 'Where an accused pleads autrefois acquit or autrefois convict it shall be for the judge, *without the presence of a jury* to decide the issue.' Should the plea fail, the indictment is put in the normal way, the accused's right to plead not guilty being in no way affected: Criminal Law Act 1967, s 6(1)(a).

16.8.2 Applicability of the pleas

The following propositions are based mainly upon the speech of Lord Morris of Borth-y-Gest in *Connelly v DPP* [1964] AC 1254 at pp. 1305–6. They must be read subject to the decision in *Beedie* [1997] 2 Cr App R 167 (see below), and to the provisions of the Criminal Procedure and Investigations Act 1996, relating to 'tainted acquittals' (see Paragraph 16.8.4).

(a) A man cannot be tried for a crime in respect of which he has previously been acquitted or convicted. This is the straightforward application of autrefois acquit and convict. If the accused is charged with an offence which is identical in law and on the facts to one of which he has already been acquitted or convicted, then autrefois will bar any further proceedings on that charge.

(b) A man cannot be tried for a crime in respect of which he could on some previous indictment have been convicted by way of a verdict of guilty of a lesser offence (see Paragraph 19.4). This extension of (a) is necessary because, where jurors are entitled to convict of a lesser offence but choose simply to acquit, they decide by implication that the accused was not guilty both of the offence charged and the lesser matter. Accordingly, autrefois acquit bars proceedings for both offences. Thus, an acquittal on a count for murdering X entitles the accused to raise autrefois if he is subsequently indicted for the manslaughter of X.

(c) A man cannot be tried for a crime proof of which would necessarily, as a matter of law, entail proof of another crime of which he has already been acquitted (per Lord Hodson in *Connelly* at p. 1332). Therefore, to reverse the example given in proposition (b) above, an accused who is charged with X's murder, having previously been acquitted of his manslaughter, is entitled to rely on autrefois acquit because, having regard to the legal definitions of murder and manslaughter, proof of the latter is a necessary step towards proving the former.

(d) A man cannot be tried for a crime which is in effect the same or substantially the same as one of which he has previously been acquitted or convicted (or could have been convicted through a verdict of guilty of a lesser offence). Thus, in *King* [1897] 1 QB 214, K, who had previously been convicted of obtaining credit for goods by false pretences, was held to be entitled to rely on autrefois convict when subsequently indicted for larceny of the same goods. But, the cases are markedly inconsistent as to the degree of similarity necessary before it can be said that a later charge is 'substantially' the same as an earlier offence. *King* may, for example, be contrasted with *Kendrick and Smith* (1931) 23 Cr App R 1 where a conviction for threatening to publish photographic negatives with intent to extort money did not bar a subsequent prosecution for sending letters demanding money with menaces, both prosecutions arising out of the same facts. Lord Devlin in *Connelly* suggested a means of avoiding elaborate attempts to reconcile the cases on this aspect of autrefois. He said that the pleas proper should be restricted to the circumstances set out in (a)–(c) above, but, in other analagous cases, the trial judge should use his discretionary power to halt the prosecution if letting it continue would be unfair or oppressive to the accused in the light of previous proceedings against him. So, in *Moxon-Tritsch* [1988] Crim LR 46, where M-T was privately prosecuted for causing the death of her passengers by reckless driving after the driving in question had earlier resulted in her being fined and disqualified for careless driving, the trial judge held that the proceedings were oppressive and the count should lie on the file marked not to be proceeded with. It is submitted that, with the abolition of juries for determination of issues of autrefois, the approach of Lord Devlin and the judge in *Moxon-Tritsch* is the appropriate one and will make irrelevant the old case-law on precisely when autrefois does or does not apply.

(e)   A man may not be successively prosecuted for a number of offences arising out of the same criminal conduct where the later prosecutions are for aggravated forms of an offence of which he was earlier acquitted or convicted — e.g. if he has already been convicted or acquitted of assault occasioning actual bodily harm he cannot, on the same facts, be indicted for unlawful wounding or causing grievous bodily harm (see *Elrington* (1861) 1 B & S 688). This applies whether or not the situation can be brought within (c) above. Moreover, as argued in (d), there is little point worrying whether the principle derives from autrefois proper or from the judge's discretion to halt an oppressive prosecution. However, one important qualification to the principle should be noted, namely that a conviction for an offence of violence does not protect the offender from a prosecution for homicide should the victim later die of his injuries: *Thomas* (1949) 33 Cr App R 200.

(f)   A plea of autrefois may fail even though the prosecution allege the same facts and call the same evidence as they did at an earlier trial resulting in the accused's acquittal or conviction. The point is well illustrated by the facts of *Connelly*. C and three others took part in an office robbery, during the course of which a person was killed. They were charged with murder and convicted, but C's conviction was quashed because of errors in the conduct of the trial. He was therefore treated as if he had been acquitted of murder (see below). In line with the practice then prevailing, the murder indictment had not included any counts for other offences, so upon the murder conviction being quashed the prosecution sought to proceed against C on an indictment for robbery. Following an unsuccessful plea of autrefois acquit, they called the evidence which they had already used at the murder trial, and C was again convicted. The House of Lords held that the plea of autrefois had rightly been rejected. C could not bring himself within any of the four propositions (a) to (d) above. The crimes of murder and robbery were obviously not identical (proposition (a)), nor, in view of their totally different legal characteristics, could they be regarded as substantially the same (proposition (d)). On a count for murder, a jury are not entitled to bring in a verdict of guilty of robbery (proposition (b)), and, as a matter of *law*, the prosecution did not have to prove murder in order to prove robbery (proposition (c)).

(g)   The principles of autrefois acquit and convict apply equally in summary trials, although there is no special form of plea or procedure as there is at trials on indictment — the defence raise the issue on a simple not guilty plea.

In *Beedie* [1997] 2 Cr App R 167, however, the Court of Appeal was unable to accept that Lord Morris's speech correctly represented the reasoning of the majority in the House of Lords. B was the landlord of a woman who died of carbon monoxide poisoning caused by the use of a defective gas fire at her bedsit. He was prosecuted under the Health and Safety at Work Act 1974 by the Health and Safety Executive, and was fined. He was subsequently prosecuted by the CPS for manslaughter on substantially the same facts. Rose LJ said that the principle of autrefois was confined to the situation where the second indictment charges the same offence as the first, and therefore did not operate to prevent B's prosecution for manslaughter. Judicial discretion should, however, be exercised to order a stay on the indictment in appropriate circumstances. Such a stay should have been ordered in circumstances such as those in *Beedie*. B's appeal succeeded, therefore. Although the trial judge had correctly analysed the case as falling outside the autrefois principle, he had failed properly to consider the discretion which he had to stay proceedings where the second offence arises out of substantially the same facts as the first. That discretion should be exercised in favour of the accused unless the prosecution discharges the onus of showing that there are special circumstances for not doing so. In this case, there were no special circumstances and the indictment should have been stayed.

Many of the cases on autrefois are about what amounts to an acquittal or conviction for purposes of the pleas. No distinction is drawn between acquittals or convictions on indictment and those following summary trial. However, for the pleas to apply, the court trying the case must have been acting within its jurisdiction (see *West* [1964] 1 QB 15 where a purported acquittal by magistrates on a charge which they were not entitled to try did not prevent their subsequently committing W for trial or his being convicted at quarter sessions). Discharge of the accused by the examining justices after committal proceedings is not an acquittal (*Manchester City Stipendiary Magistrate ex p Snelson* [1977] 1 WLR 911), nor is the quashing of an indictment following a motion to quash. Where, however, the Court of Appeal quashes an accused's conviction, the successful appellant is treated as if he had been acquitted by the jury that tried him. Hence, he cannot be prosecuted again for the same offence unless the Court of Appeal has exercised its discretionary power to order a retrial (see s 7 of the Criminal Appeal Act 1968 as amended and Paragraph 24.4.2).

In summary trial in the magistrates' court, there is an important distinction between the withdrawal of a summons by the prosecution and its dismissal by the justices. Where the summons is withdrawn without the justices considering the merits, there is no acquittal such as to found autrefois. On the other hand, if the accused pleads not guilty and the prosecution formally offer no evidence, so that the justices dismiss the summons, the accused is acquitted and there can be no further proceedings (see *Grays Justices ex p Low* [1990] 1 QB 54 and Paragraph 9.4). But no plea of autrefois can be founded on proceedings where the information is so faulty that the accused could never have been in jeopardy upon it (*DPP v Porthouse* (1988) 89 Cr App R 21).

To sustain a plea of autrefois convict, it is not enough that the court before which the defendant was first charged should have accepted his plea of guilty, or returned a verdict of guilty. It is necessary also that the court should have sentenced him, since the purpose of the doctrine is to avoid double punishment (*Richards v The Queen* [1993] AC 217). Civil contempt proceedings do not constitute a conviction so as to ground a plea of autrefois (*Green* [1993] Crim LR 46). A finding of 'guilt' in disciplinary proceedings followed by the imposition of a penalty is not a conviction (*Hogan and Tompkins* [1960] 2 QB 513, where prison escapees, who had been punished for the escape by the visiting committee of magistrates under the Prison Rules, could not rely on autrefois convict at a subsequent trial for the offence of escaping by force). Similarly, if a court takes another offence into consideration when sentencing an offender for an offence of which he has been convicted, there is no conviction in respect of the offence taken into consideration: *Nicholson* (1947) 32 Cr App R 98 and see Paragraph 20.5. Acquittals or convictions before foreign courts or by courts martial are in general sufficient grounds for autrefois (see, for example, *Aughet* (1919) 13 Cr App R 101). Where, however, an accused has been convicted and sentenced in his absence by a foreign court, but there is no realistic possibility of his ever returning to the country concerned to serve his sentence, autrefois convict will not apply if he is prosecuted for the same matter in England (*Thomas* [1985] QB 604).

16.8.3 Issue estoppel

Prior to 1976, it was from time to time suggested that, even if autrefois acquit did not apply, the prosecution could be estopped from re-opening a particular issue of fact which had clearly been decided in favour of the accused at an earlier trial ending in his acquittal. Opportunities to test the validity of this suggestion were rare, for nearly all criminal trials involve more than one issue, and if the jury simply find the accused not guilty it is impossible to know on what issue the prosecution failed to satisfy them. At last, however, a case arose in which the defence could plausibly point to an issue estoppel. The case was *DPP v Humphrys* [1977] AC 1. H was acquitted of driving while disqualified on a day in 1972. He admitted that he was disqualified on the relevant day, but gave evidence that he had not driven either on that day or at all in 1972. Thus, the only possible reason for the acquittal was that the jury were not satisfied that H had been driving on the relevant day. H was then prosecuted for perjury. To prove that his evidence at the driving while disqualified trial had been false, the prosecution again called the evidence they had used at that trial indicating that H had driven on the relevant day, and there was also evidence from other witnesses, not available for the first trial, that H had driven on other occasions in 1972. H was convicted and the House of Lords rejected his appeal. They held that the prosecution were entitled to re-open the issue of whether H drove on the relevant day, because the doctrine of issue estoppel has no place in criminal proceedings. Neither the prosecution nor the defence can rely on it. The decision in *Humphrys* might seem a dangerous one, allowing the prosecution in effect to challenge an acquittal by the device of prosecuting the acquitted person for perjury. However, the majority of the House of Lords emphasised that a trial judge has a discretion to prevent a prosecution continuing if it would be an abuse of the process of the court, and implied that the prosecution in *Humphrys* was only saved from being an abuse of process by the fact that the evidence of perjury related not just to H's evidence that he had not driven on the day of the driving while disqualified charge, but also to his evidence that he had not driven at all during 1972.

> As stated above, the prosecution are no more able to rely on an issue estoppel than are the defence. This means that if the accused pleads not guilty to Offence A, having previously been convicted of Offence B, the prosecution must prove *all* the elements of Offence A even if they had to prove some of those elements to secure the conviction for Offence B. Lawson J's ruling at first instance in *Hogan* [1974] QB 398 — that if, at a trial for murder, the prosecution can show that the accused has already been convicted on the same facts of causing grievous bodily harm with intent to the victim of the alleged murder, then the defence are estopped from denying all elements of the prosecution case apart from the causal link between the harm caused and the death of the victim — was held by the House of Lords in *Humphrys* to be incorrect.
>
> It appears that, notwithstanding the general rule outlined above, issue estoppel *does* have relevance in an application for habeas corpus (*Govenor of Brixton Prison ex p Osman* [1991] 1 WLR 281).

16.8.4   Tainted acquittals

Sections 54 to 57 of the Criminal Procedure and Investigations Act 1996, which relate to 'tainted acquittals', constitute a major exception to the availability of autrefois acquit. They enable the prosecution of an accused for a second time for a crime of which he has already been acquitted at trial, if the following conditions are met:

(a)   a defendant has been acquitted of an offence (s 54(1)(a)); and

(b)   a person has been convicted of an administration of justice offence involving interference with or intimidation of a juror or a witness or potential witness (s 54(1)(b)); and

(c)   the court convicting of the administration of justice offence certifies that there is a real possibility that, but for the interference or intimidation, the acquitted person would not have been acquitted, and that it would not be contrary to the interests of justice to proceed against the acquitted person (s 54(2) and (5)).

An application may then be made to the High Court for an order quashing the acquittal. The High Court must make the order if the four conditions set out in s 55 are satisfied. These are that it appears to the High Court:

(i)   likely that, but for the interference or intimidation, the acquitted person would not have been acquitted;

(ii)   that it is not contrary to the interests of justice to take proceedings against the acquitted person for the offence of which he was acquitted, e.g. because of the lapse of time;

(iii)   that the acquitted person has been given a reasonable opportunity to make written representations to the High Court; and

(iv)   that the conviction for the administration of justice offence will stand.

The provisions of ss 54 to 57 apply in relation to acquittals in respect of offences alleged to be committed on or after 15 April 1997. It should be emphasised that it is the *original* offence, i.e., the offence of which the defendant was acquitted, which must be alleged to have been committed on or after that date (s 54(7)).

16.9   OTHER POSSIBLE PLEAS

For the sake of completeness, three other pleas should be mentioned, although they are hardly ever used in practice.

(a)   *The plea of pardon.*   Pardons are granted by the Crown, upon the advice of the Home Secretary, in the exercise of the royal prerogative of mercy (see Paragraph 24.10 for further details). The effect of a pardon is that the recipient is freed from the consequences that would normally result from a crime which he allegedly committed. In previous centuries, pardons were occasionally granted prior to or during proceedings for the crime in question. The pardoned person would then plead the pardon either on being arraigned or (if it was granted after arraignment) at the first opportunity. The plea barred any further proceedings on the indictment. Thus, a properly pleaded pardon prevented an accused being convicted of his crime. In modern times, however, pardons are only granted *after* conviction and sentence. They are used in cases where the normal avenues of appeal have been exhausted or would probably prove unsuccessful, but there is good reason to doubt the correctness of the conviction. The pardon does not affect the fact of the conviction, but all adverse consequences flowing therefrom are removed (see *Foster* [1985] QB 115). Thus, if the 'pardonee' was sentenced to imprisonment he will be entitled to be released immediately, and will not be at risk of being returned to prison. In the very unlikely event of a person being reprosecuted for a crime in respect of which he has been pardoned, it would seem that he could either bar the prosecution by pleading the pardon, or, since he still stands convicted of the offence as a matter of law, he could rely on autrefois convict.

(b)   *A plea to the jurisdiction,* which must be in writing, is to the effect that the court has no jurisdiction to try the offence. It would be appropriate in the unlikely event of the indictment alleging a summary offence (other than one falling within the Criminal Justice Act 1988, s 40). It could also be relied upon where the defence argue that the offence was committed outside the territorial jurisdiction of the English courts (see Paragraph 4.4.1), although the point could equally well be taken on an ordinary not guilty plea. The Court of Appeal in *Cumberworth* (1989) 89 Cr App R 187 expressed the view that a point of territorial jurisdiction could have been raised by way of demurrer (see (c) below).

(c)   *A demurrer* which, like a plea to the jurisdiction, must be in writing, is an objection to the wording of an indictment. Any objection which could be taken on a demurrer can more conveniently be taken on a motion to quash. For that reason Lord Parker CJ expressed the wish that demurrer 'will be allowed to die naturally': *Deputy Chairman of Inner London Sessions ex p Commissioner of Metropolitan Police* [1970] 2 QB 80. In *Cumberworth,* by contrast, the Court of Appeal suggested that a challenge to the jurisdiction, raised by the defence on a not guilty plea, could have been more sensibly dealt with by way of demurrer (although a plea to the jurisdiction would seem to be at least equally appropriate).

17   The Jury

If the accused pleads not guilty then, unless the prosecution chooses to offer no evidence, a jury must be empanelled (or, more colloquially, sworn in) to try the case. The law concerning juries is contained chiefly in the Juries Act 1974, which is denoted in the remainder of this Chapter by the letters 'JA'.

17.1   ELIGIBILITY FOR JURY SERVICE

Jurors are drawn from a broad, though not complete, cross-section of the population. Subject to the exceptions mentioned below, everyone aged 18 to 70, who is registered as a parliamentary or local government elector is eligible for jury service, provided he has been ordinarily resident in the United Kingdom for any period of at least five years since attaining the age of 13: JA, s 1. If it appears to a Crown Court officer that a person attending at the court for jury service may not have a sufficient understanding of English to be able to act effectively as a juror, he may bring that person before a judge of the court for a ruling that he be discharged from jury service: JA, s 10. As to the maximum age for jury service, that was raised from 65 to 70 by the Criminal Justice Act 1988. However, those over 65 are given an automatic right to be excused from service if they so wish.

Section 1 of the JA, together with Parts I and II of Sch 1 to the Act, as amended by the Juries (Disqualification) Act 1984, exclude certain groups of the population from sitting on juries. The excluded groups are:

(a)   The judiciary, which includes all holders of high judicial office, circuit judges, recorders, lay and stipendiary magistrates and all former holders of any such office.

(b)   Others concerned in the administration of justice. These include barristers and solicitors (whether practising or not); magistrates' clerks, articled clerks and barristers' clerks; court staff involved in the day-today administration of the court; members of the Parole Board and members of local committees advising the Parole Board; probation officers, prison officers, police officers and some civilians employed for police purposes, and any person who within the last 10 years has come within any of the above groups.

(c)   The clergy, whether of the Church of England or any other religious denomination.

(d)   Persons who by reason of mental illness are resident in a hospital or regularly attend for treatment by a doctor.

(e)   Persons who at any time have received a custodial sentence of five years or more (or life). 'Custodial sentence' in this context includes not only imprisonment but also detention in a young offender institution (the sentence for under-21s introduced by the Criminal Justice Act 1988) and youth custody (the former medium-to-long term custodial sentence for young offenders abolished by the 1988 Act).

(f)   Persons who, in the past ten years, have been given a custodial sentence of less than five years. 'Custodial sentence' here includes those mentioned in (e) above, plus suspended sentences of imprisonment and detention centre orders (the short term custodial sentence for under-21s abolished by the CJA 1988).

(g)   Persons who, in the past ten years, have been ordered to perform community service.

(h)   Persons who, in the past five years, have been placed on probation.

(i)   Persons who are on bail in criminal proceedings (Criminal Justice and Public Order Act 1994, s 40).

Those in categories (a) to (e) are described as ineligible for jury service, while those in categories (f) to (i) are said to be disqualified from it. Broadly speaking, the effect of (e) and (f) is that a custodial sentence of five years or more disqualifies one from jury service for life, whereas a custodial sentence of less than five years disqualifies one for ten years.

The reasoning behind the exclusion of the above groups from jury service is fairly obvious. Judges, barristers, solicitors etc. might exert too great an influence over their lay colleagues on a jury, police officers could be suspected of bias towards the prosecution, and, conversely, probation officers could favour the defence. The exclusion of the clergy is a little surprising, and may spring from a feeling that a clergyman, by reason of his vocation, would not wish to sit in judgment on others. As to the exclusion of some convicted criminals, it was formerly the case that suspended sentences of imprisonment, community service and probation had no effect on eligibility for jury service. However, that was felt to be unsatisfactory in that too many 'villains' were sitting in the jury box with the result that some villains in the dock were being acquitted when they ought to have been convicted. Accordingly, the JA 1974 was amended by the Juries (Disqualification) Act 1984 so as to produce the present position. But, even now, an offender fined or given a conditional discharge remains entitled to serve on a jury. Since about half those convicted of indictable offences are so dealt with, it is perfectly possible for a person to be convicted by a jury one day and serve on a jury trying somebody else the next.

Notwithstanding the ineligible and excluded groups, the broad effect of s 1 and Sch 1 is that most adults are eligible for jury service. This may be contrasted with the pre-1974 position under which only householders were eligible. Juries were then criticised (or, depending on one's point of view, commended) for being 'middle-aged, middle-class and middle-income'. It would be difficult now to sustain such a criticism. Note, however, that a person's being eligible to sit on a jury does not inevitably mean that, if summoned for service, he will take his place in the jury box. The procedures for asking a juror to stand by and challenging jurors (see Paragraph 17.4) are meant to prevent unsuitable, though eligible, jurors serving on the jury in a particular case.

> A person who serves on a jury knowing that he is disqualified from or ineligible for jury service commits a summary offence punishable, in the former case, with a fine of up to £5,000 and, in the latter case, a fine of up to £1,000. Prosecutions for the offence are, however, very rare.

17.2   SUMMONING JURORS

The Lord Chancellor is responsible for summoning jurors to attend for jury service in the Crown Court: JA, s 2. He acts, of course, through officers of the Crown Court. The summons, which must be in writing, may be sent by post. It requires the juror to attend on certain days at a stated location of the Crown Court. The location should, if possible, be within reasonable daily travelling distance of the juror's home, and the average period for which a juror is asked to attend is two weeks. At some courts, such as the Central Criminal Court, which regularly deal with long cases, the period may be greater. If a lengthy case is anticipated it is normal to ask jurors whether they have any objection to being involved. Jurors are, of course, entitled to payment in respect of *inter alia* travelling and subsistence expenses and loss of earnings, but the rates of payment laid down by the Lord Chancellor may not provide full compensation for the losses incurred. The summons should be accompanied by a notice explaining the restrictions on eligibility for jury service, the penalties for non-attendance when summoned and the possibility of being excused from jury service.

The names and addresses of the persons summoned for jury service are taken at random from the names and addresses on the electoral roll. Save that the roll indicates those who are ineligible by reason of age, the summoning officer does not know and has no means of checking whether the persons he summons are entitled to sit on a jury. The courts rely on ineligible or disqualified 'jurors' reading the notice which accompanies the summons, and informing the court of their ineligibility. No doubt a High Court judge can be relied upon to do this should he be summoned, but persons who are disqualified from jury service as a result of their criminal records may sometimes conceal that fact, and therefore sit on juries.

There is a fundamental weakness in this exclusive reliance on the electoral register. Some people (about 8 per cent of those eligible according to the Home Office's 1999 research) do not register. In respect of those who do register, the electoral register becomes increasingly inaccurate until it is updated. As a result, there is a significant minority of those who should be in the 'pool' for jury service who are ignored by the system. This becomes more serious when one considers that certain sections of the community are under-represented as a result, namely those aged 20–24, ethnic minorities and those living in rented accommodation (see the Auld Report, p. 144).

The Lord Chancellor is also responsible, through the Crown Court officers, for drawing up lists (or panels) of the names, addresses and dates for attendance of those who have been summoned for jury service at the various locations of the Crown Court: JA, s 5(1). The prosecution and defence are both entitled by s 5(2) to inspect the panel from which the jurors to try their case will be, or have been, drawn. By s 5(3), this may be done in advance of or during but not after the trial. The right to inspect the jury panel before trial enables the prosecution and defence, if they so wish, to make enquiries about the potential jurors with a view to objecting to one or more of them sitting on the jury. In practice, the defence do not have the resources to conduct such inquiries. The prosecution have relatively easy access, through the police computer system, to the criminal records of potential jurors, but their use of this information is restricted by the Attorney-General's Guidelines (see Paragraphs 17.4.2 and 17.4.5).

The usual pattern is to summon many more jurors for service than are likely to be required. Should a miscalculation occur, however, so that a full jury cannot be made up from those on the jury panel, the court may summon, without written notice, any person in, or in the vicinity of, the court to complete the jury: JA, s 6. The names of persons so summoned are added to the jury panel. There is only a very remote possibility of the court actually having to make use of s 6.

A person who is eligible and summoned for jury service is under a duty to attend as required, and, unless excused from doing so, commits an offence by not attending without reasonable cause: JA s 20. The offence is punishable with a fine of up to £1,000. The matter may be tried summarily, or, more conveniently, it may be dealt with by a judge of the Crown Court as if a criminal contempt had been committed in the face of the court. This means that, if the juror does not admit the offence, the judge can hear evidence and decide if the case has been proved without the necessity of empanelling a jury. It must be shown that the summons was duly served on the juror at least 14 days before the date fixed in it for his first attendance at court. Sudden illness or bereavement would, no doubt, be a reasonable cause for not attending.

The following persons, although eligible for jury service, are entitled to be excused:

(a)   Those aged 65 or over.
(b)   Those who have attended a court for jury service within the two years preceding the service of the summons on them.
(c)   Those whom a court has excused from jury service for a period which has not yet terminated (occasionally, after a very long case, the judge will express his thanks to the jurors by saying that they are excused any further jury service).
(d)   Members of Parliament.
(e)   Full-time serving members of the armed forces.
(f)   Doctors, nurses and other members of the medical professions.
(g)   Practising members of a religious society or order whose tenents or beliefs are incompatible with jury service (a ground inserted by the Criminal Justice and Public Order Act 1994, s 42).

With the exception of members of the armed forces, persons claiming to be in the above groups must satisfy an appropriate officer of the Crown Court that they are, indeed, entitled to be excused service. In the case of members of the armed forces, the commanding officer of the person summoned certifies that the latter's absence from duty would be prejudicial to the efficiency of the service.

If the juror is not entitled to be excused but none the less thinks there is a good reason why he should not be required to attend, he may apply to the appropriate officer for discretionary excusal.

Alternatively, application may be made for deferral of service. That would be appropriate where the dates for which the juror has been summoned clash with holidays or business commitments. If the application is granted, a later date is fixed for the service to be performed.

Excusal and deferral of jury service are dealt with in ss 8, 9, 9A and 9B of the JA. Should the appropriate officer refuse an application under one or other of the sections, appeal may be made to a Crown Court judge.

Section 9B of the JA deals with the procedure where someone may be unable to act as a juror because of physical disability. It states that the judge 'shall affirm the summons unless he is of the opinion that the person will not, on account of his disability, be capable of acting effectively as a juror, in which case he shall discharge the summons'. In *Re Osman* [1996] 1 Cr App R 126, the Recorder of London held at first instance that a person summonsed to be a juror who was profoundly deaf should be excused from jury service pursuant to s 9B. In order to follow proceedings in court or in the jury room, the prospective juror needed the assistance of an interpreter in sign language. It was held to be an incurable irregularity in the proceedings for the interpreter to retire with the jury when they considered their verdict.

17.3   EMPANELLING A JURY

The next stage in the procedure is to select, from amongst the jury panel summoned to attend at a location of the Crown Court on a certain day, the twelve men and women who will form the jury to try a particular case. This is the empanelling or swearing-in of the jury.

Twenty or more members of the jury panel (known as the jury in waiting) are either in court when the accused pleads not guilty, or are brought into court by an usher immediately after the plea has been taken. The clerk of court calls the names of twelve of them, asking them to step into the jury box. He has the names of all the jurors in waiting, and must choose the ones he calls at random: JA, s 11 — 'the jury to try an issue before a court shall be selected by ballot in open court from the panel, or part of the panel, of jurors . . .'. (The importance of the random nature of the selection process was stressed in *Salt* [1996] Crim

LR 517 — a case where the son of one of the ushers at the Crown Court was called upon by his father to sit as a juror when the number available was insufficient!) The ballot is normally carried out by giving to the clerk some cards, each card having on it the name and address of a juror in waiting. He shuffles the cards, and calls the names on the top twelve.

In *Comerford* [1998] 1 Cr App R 235, the judge ordered that the names of the jurors should not be read in open court, but that they should be called by numbers allocated to them. This unusual measure was meant to allay the jurors' fears of intimidation, in view of an earlier abortive trial. Although defence counsel objected to this course, the Court of Appeal held that it did not render the trial a nullity unless it made the proceedings unfair to the defendant or otherwise violated his rights. In the present case, there was no such violation, and the appeal was dismissed. It is submitted that there would be unfairness to the defendant if his right to challenge for cause was impeded by the adoption of this process. The defendant is entitled to as much information as the law and practical considerations allow in determining whether a potential juror may be prejudiced against him. The names of the potential jurors form part of that information. As defence counsel put it, 'a name may ring a bell where a face does not'. In *Comerford*, however, there was no denial of the defence's right to see in advance the names of those on the jury panel, and a challenge could have been formulated as a result of such an inspection, but was not.

Once twelve persons are in the jury box, the clerk says to the accused — 'John Smith, the names that you are about to hear called are the names of the jurors who are to try you. If therefore you wish to object to them or to any of them, you must do so as they come to the book to be sworn, and before they are sworn, and your objection shall be heard.' This is meant to inform the accused of his right to challenge jurors (see Paragraph 17.4). Whether an unrepresented accused, unfamiliar with court procedure, would understand exactly how he should object to a juror is open to some doubt. However, the obscurity, if there be any, in what is said matters little, since most accused are legally represented in the Crown Court, and the right to challenge a juror is always exercised by counsel on behalf of his client.

Next the clerk calls individually on each person in the jury box to take the juror's oath, which is — 'I swear by almighty God that I will faithfully try the defendant[s] and give a true verdict[s] according to the evidence'. The juror reads the words of the oath from a printed card while holding in his right hand the appropriate book (New Testament for Christians, Old Testament for Jews, Koran for Moslems, etc.). If he so wishes, he may affirm. It is possible for the parties to object to a juror before he takes the oath, either by asking him to stand by (prosecution only) or by challenging for cause. The procedure and grounds for doing so are explained in the following Paragraphs. If the objection succeeds, the juror is asked to leave the box and is replaced by another juror in waiting (who could himself be the subject of objection). However, as a result of the abolition of peremptory challenges (see Paragraph 17.4.1) it is now far less likely than it used to be that a juror originally called into the box will be replaced. Once a full jury of twelve has taken the oath, the clerk formally asks them if they are all sworn and puts the accused in their charge. This is a traditional, although not strictly essential part of the procedure. The clerk says something to the effect that — 'John Smith is charged in an indictment containing *X* counts. Count One is for theft contrary to section 1 of the Theft Act 1968, the particulars being that on the 1st of January 2000 he stole £10 belonging to Jane Brown. Count Two is for . . . [and so on through the indictment]. To this indictment he has pleaded not guilty. It is your charge, having heard the evidence, to say whether he be guilty or not.' If the accused has pleaded guilty to some counts on the indictment but not guilty to others, the jury are not told about the guilty pleas. Once the accused is in the jury's charge, prosecuting counsel begins his opening speech.

17.4   CHALLENGES TO JURORS

Two contrasting views may be held on the best way to select a jury. One is that the process should be left as much as possible to chance. According to this view, certain groups (e.g., children and the mentally sick) must inevitably be excluded from jury service, but these groups should be as narrowly defined as possible. Moreover, if a person has been chosen to serve on the jury for a particular case by whatever method of random selection the judicial system in question uses, then it should not be possible to object to his presence on the jury save on the ground that he comes within one of the excluded groups. Lawton LJ in *Mason* [1981] QB 881 suggested that this approach could lead to unfairness. For example, the jury to try an accused who, while out poaching, is alleged to have unlawfully wounded a gamekeeper might include a juror with several convictions for poaching, the convictions not having resulted in a sentence which would disqualify him from jury service. The counter argument is that the jury could just as well include a gamekeeper, and, anyway, the provisions for majority verdicts (see Paragraph 19.5) prevent any one juror having a decisive influence on the case.

The second view on selecting a jury is that every effort should be made to choose jurors who have no discernible prejudices relevant to the case, whether it be a prejudice against the particular type of crime alleged, or for or against accused persons in general, or for or against the particular accused charged. This approach is adopted in some of the American states. It involves giving the parties the opportunity to examine a potential juror, call evidence about him and present argument about his suitability. The difficulty is that the process of selecting a jury can become almost as lengthy and expensive as the trial itself. It is probably no accident that the process has been developed in one of the wealthiest and most litigious societies in the world.

The approach of the English courts represents a compromise between the above views, although leaning strongly in favour of random selection. The groups not entitled to serve on juries are fairly small (see Paragraph 17.1), the names of those to be summoned for jury service are chosen at random (see Paragraph 17.2), and the selection from the jury panel of those who go into the jury box with a view to taking the oath and forming the jury is by ballot (see Paragraph 17.3). However, the random nature of the choice is qualified by the possibility that either the prosecution or defence will prevent one or more of those originally picked from sitting on the jury. The prosecution can ask a juror to 'stand by'; both prosecution and defence can challenge a juror for cause. Until 1988 it was also possible for the defence to challenge jurors without giving a reason, but this right has now been lost (see the next Paragraph). The change reinforces the random nature of jury selection.

17.4.1   Abolition of peremptory challenges

For centuries, the defence had the right to prevent a certain number of jurors sitting on the jury without giving any reason whatsoever. All defence counsel had to do was say 'Challenge' immediately before a juror in waiting would otherwise have taken the oath, and that juror then had to leave the box to be replaced by another. Such challenges were known as challenges without cause or peremptory challenges. The number allowed per defendant was progressively reduced, from 25 to 12 in 1925; from 12 to 7 in 1948, and finally from 7 to 3 in 1977. None the less, protests still arose about alleged abuse of the right of peremptory challenge, it being said that defence counsel too often challenged for frivolous or downright improper reasons. Finally, in the face of spirited resistance from the retentionists, it was decided to abolish peremptory challenges. The change was made very simply by s 118(1) of the Criminal Justice Act 1988 which provides that — 'The right to challenge jurors without cause in proceedings for the trial of a person on indictment is abolished'. Thus, in one sense, peremptory challenges are now merely a matter of legal history. However, they cannot be totally ignored, since the general development of the law on juries has been profoundly influenced by the fact that the defence until very recently had the option of removing a juror they did not like just by saying so.

17.4.2   Jurors asked to stand by

The prosecution never had a right of peremptory challenge as such. However, they did and do have a right which is in effect just the same. It is the right to stand a juror by. If prosecuting counsel does not want someone on the jury, he says 'stand by' immediately before that person would otherwise take the oath. The 'juror' then leaves the box and is replaced by another juror in waiting. Counsel does not, at the time, have to give a reason for the 'stand by'. It will only be necessary for him to give reasons in the unlikely event of the entire jury panel being exhausted without a full jury having been obtained. Since it is the practice of the courts to summon many more jurors for service than are ever likely to be needed at the same time, counsel would have to stand by an inordinately large number of potential jurors to be in danger of running through the whole panel. If, however, he were to do so, the first of those he stood by would be asked to return to the box, and would join the jury unless successfully challenged for cause (see the next Paragraph).

The position of prosecuting counsel in standing jurors by was clarified in *Mason* [1981] QB 881. The Court of Appeal (Lawton LJ giving judgment) held that the right to stand jurors by is not dependent upon counsel having a reason for so doing which would be capable of founding a successful challenge for cause. In theory, therefore, a juror can be stood by for any or no reason. But prosecuting counsel should use his power responsibly. The importance of the right of stand-by has since been vastly reduced by the *Attorney-General's Guidelines on Exercise by the Crown of its Right of Stand-by* (1989) 88 Cr App R 123. The guidelines set out the legislative background, emphasising that the primary responsibility for excluding those incompetent to serve on the jury rests with the court officer and, ultimately, the trial judge. In view of the abolition of the defence right to challenge, the Crown should only assert its right to stand-by in restricted circumstances. Paragraph 5 of the guidelines then states, in effect, that these circumstances only exist (a) in cases where national security or terrorism is involved, and the personal authority of the Attorney-General has been granted; or (b) where a juror is obviously unsuitable and the defence agree to the exercise of the right to stand-by.

The defence have no right to stand jurors by: *Chandler* [1964] 2 QB 322.

17.4.3   Challenges for cause

Both prosecution and defence are entitled to challenge as many individual jurors as they wish for cause. A considerable volume of arcane eighteenth century law categorises challenges for cause under a variety of headings such as *propter honoris respectum, propter defectum* and *propter affectum*. However, the upshot of the old cases is that a juror may be challenged *either* on the basis that he is ineligible for or disqualified from jury service, *or* on the basis that he is or may reasonably be suspected of being biased. As to bias, jurors have been successfully challenged when they were employed by or related to a party; when they had been entertained at the house of a party; when they had expressed a wish or opinion as to the outcome of the case; and when they had shown hostility to the accused (see *O'Coigley* (1798) 26 St Tr 1191 where the challenged juror, on looking at the defendants in the dock, said 'Damned rascals'). More recently, in *Kray* (1969) 53 Cr App R 412, the trial judge was prepared to exclude from the jury anyone who had read certain lurid and probably inaccurate newspaper accounts of the alleged gangland activities of the accused.

By contrast in *Pennington* [1985] Crim LR 394, the Court of Appeal implied that a juror who had worked during the miners' strike of 1984–5 was fit to serve on a jury trying P, a leading striking miner, for an offence of criminal damage allegedly committed while, on picket-line duty. The point was not, however, directly in issue as the defence did not discover the relevant facts until after the trial and so no challenge was actually made.

The procedure for making a challenge for cause is that the challenging party says 'challenge' immediately before the 'juror' takes the oath. The burden is then on him to satisfy the judge on a balance of probabilities that his objection is well founded. To discharge that burden he must normally call prima facie evidence of the juror's unsuitability — e.g. that he is disqualified on account of previous convictions, or ineligible by reason of his occupation, or biased one way or the other. Until that prima facie evidence has been led, no questions may be asked of the juror himself. In other words, the parties are not allowed to embark on a 'fishing expedition' asking each member of the jury panel about their attitudes, life-histories, etc. with a view to eliciting a possible ground for challenge. This restrictive rule has the advantage of shortening the process of jury selection. It has the disadvantage that, with jury panels at large Crown Court centres numbering several hundred, it is virtually impossible for the parties to check before trial whether the potential jurors for their case are suitable or not. Almost certainly a significant proportion of challengeable jurors go unchallenged simply because nobody has the necessary information at the relevant time. It is clear from *Morris* (1990) 93 Cr App R 102 that the right to challenge for cause is limited to the time when the jury is sworn, and cannot be exercised during the course of the trial. M was charged with stealing from a Marks and Spencer store. After the store detective had given evidence, one of the jurors said that she was a personnel assistant with a different branch of the company. The judge refused to discharge the juror, saying that the right way to deal with the matter was by a challenge for cause. The trial proceeded and M was convicted. The Court of Appeal allowed his appeal. By the time the facts about the juror had emerged, it was too late to challenge for cause, which could only be done when the jury was sworn.

Partly as a result of the procedural difficulties just described and partly because — if there was any doubt about a juror — it was far easier to use a peremptory challenge or stand him by, challenges for cause largely fell into disuse. The question for the future is whether, with the abolition of peremptory challenges, the defence in particular will resort again to challenges for cause. And will judges aid the process by allowing jurors in waiting to be questioned about their suitability *before* rather than after prima facie evidence of a ground for challenge has been led? The rule against putting preliminary questions to the whole jury in waiting is merely a judge-made one of practice and, even in the past, has been departed from in exceptional circumstances. Thus, in *Kray* (1969) 53 Cr App R 412 (see above) the judge permitted each juror to be asked whether he had read the offending newspaper articles, even though there was no reason to suppose that any individual had done so.

A challenge to the whole jury panel may be made in addition to challenges to individual jurors. This is known as a challenge to the array, and is on the ground that the Crown Court officer appointed to summon the panel was biased or otherwise acted improperly. Although challenges to the array are preserved by s 12(6) of the JA, they are virtually unknown in modern times.

17.4.4 The judge's powers

The trial judge has a residual power to stand a juror by. The commonest example is where, on a juror beginning to take the oath, it becomes apparent that he would not be sufficiently literate to understand documentary evidence that will be advanced during the course of the trial. The judge can ask the juror to step down.

Whether it would ever be appropriate for a judge to intervene more generally so as to obtain what he considers to be a properly balanced jury is an open question. It is a question which has arisen especially in the context of defendants from a racial minority who want to have representatives of their own race (or, at least, of the black community in general) on the jury. In *Binns* [1982] Crim LR 522, B and eleven others were tried (and ultimately acquitted) of offences arising out of racial disturbances in Bristol. All but one of the defendants was young and of West Indian parentage. In the absence of the jury in waiting, defence counsel asked the judge (Stocker J) to ensure that the jury was racially balanced — i.e. included members of the black community — because they could be expected to understand black youngsters and their relationships with a predominantly white police force better than white jurors. Stocker J was sympathetic to the application, and indicated that, as a last resort, he himself would stand by white jurors until a sufficient number of black jurors had been called into the jury box. He would not, however, have been prepared to discharge the jury panel and summon a fresh one if the first had been wholly white. In the event, random selection from the jury panel and judicious use of peremptory challenges resulted in a jury acceptable to the defendants without the judge's intervention. Stocker J's approach contrasted markedly with that of Judge Mander in *McCalla* [1986] Crim LR 335. The defence asked for at least two black jurors, but the judge said that granting their wish was beyond his powers since he could not properly interfere with the random selection of the jury from the jury panel, nor could he artificially enlarge the panel so as to incorporate more black people. Moreover, as a matter of principle, a defendant should not be allowed to stipulate the type of jury he wanted to try him.

The extent to which a judge may properly influence the composition of a jury is one that has assumed greater importance with the abolition of peremptory challenges. Formerly, especially in multi-defendant cases (where each accused had three challenges), the defence could often achieve a balanced jury without the judge's assistance. That will no longer be possible. In *Ford* [1989] QB 868, F appealed against his convictions for reckless driving and taking a motor vehicle without consent. It was argued on his behalf that the trial judge had wrongly refused an application for a racially balanced jury. The argument was rejected by the Court of Appeal. Any challenge to the array of jurors must be on the ground of bias or other irregularity on the part of the summoning officer. If there is a complaint of disproportion of persons of a certain ethnic group then it must be corrected by administrative (rather than judicial) intervention — unless due to bias or irregularity. As far as individual jurors are concerned, the mere fact that a juror is of a particular race or religion cannot found a challenge for cause on the ground of bias. Further, the judge may not discharge individual jurors selected in the ballot, in order to secure a jury of a particular racial mix. Insofar as the judge in *Binns* was prepared to stand jurors by for this purpose, he was in error.

The matter remained controversial, and the Royal Commission on Criminal Justice, appointed in 1991 under the chairmanship of Lord Runciman, asked those submitting evidence whether the decision in *Ford* was satisfactory. If not, they asked, 'What procedure could be devised to permit judges in exceptional cases to exercise such a power (namely, to stand jurors by)?' The Commission for Racial Equality (CRE) responded, in its evidence, by voicing concern at the low proportion of jurors from ethnic minorities. It suggested that this might in part be due to such factors as a lower propensity to register on the electoral roll, and a lower rate of eligibility because of residence requirements. The CRE also pointed out that some accused are tried away from the area of the alleged offence, e.g., many accused from South London (with a relatively high ethnic minority population) are tried in Kingston-upon-Thames (which has a virtually all-white population). The CRE proposed to the Royal Commission that it should be possible for either the prosecution or the defence to apply to the judge before the trial for the selection of a jury containing up to three people from ethnic minority communities. If the judge granted the application, it would be for the jury bailiff to continue to draw names randomly selected from the available pool until three such people were drawn. The Royal Commission, in its Report (HMSO 1993, p. 133) agreed with this proposal, provided that the prosecution or defence, as the case might be, could persuade the judge that such an approach was reasonable because of the unusual and special features of the case. The Royal Commission suggested that a black defendant charged with burglary would be unlikely to succeed in such an application. But black people accused of violence against a member of an extremist organisation whom they alleged had been making racial taunts against them might well succeed. There has been no indication that this particular proposal from the Royal Commission will find its way into the statute book.

When the Auld Report appeared in 2001, an alternative proposal was put forward (p. 159). In summary, it was proposed that the parties should be asked prior to trial whether race was likely to be an issue and, if so, whether steps should be taken to ensure ethnic minority representation on the jury. If so, a larger number of jurors would then be empanelled for that case. If those selected did not include a minimum of, say, three ethnic minority jurors, the remainder would be stood down until the minimum was reached. There has been no indication that either Lord Justice Auld's recommendation or that of the Royal Commission would find its way into the statute book.

In *Tarrant* [1998] Crim LR 342, the trial was held at Snaresbrook in the East End of London. The prosecution applied for the case to be moved from the area, because of fears that the jury might be intimidated. The judge refused to transfer the case, but ordered that a random panel of jurors be brought in from outside the area. The defendant was convicted, and appealed. The Court of Appeal emphasised that both the nomination of prospective jurors on to the panel, and the selection of jurors from the panel to try the case had to be random. Further, the process had to be carried out by the court administration, and not by the judge. Since the defendant had been deprived of a genuinely randomly selected jury, the conviction was quashed.

17.4.5 Jury vetting

A matter which has given rise to public controversy is whether the parties should be allowed to 'vet' the jury — i.e. make enquiries about the members of the jury panel with a view to exercising more effectively their rights of challenge and stand by. Jury vetting is not of itself illegal. On the contrary, it is facilitated by JA, s 5(2) which entitles the parties to inspect the jury panel prior to trial (see Paragraph 17.2). By doing so, they can discover the names and addresses of the panellists, and there is then nothing in law to prevent them investigating the backgrounds, likely attitudes, etc. of those who have been summoned for service for the dates when their case is likely to be heard. In practice, the size of the jury panel makes it impossible for the defence to do any effective 'vetting' — the legal aid fund would certainly not pay for the army of private investigators that would be needed! The prosecution (through the police) have greater resources at their disposal, but, in general, the only check which they consider it right to make is into the panellists' criminal records. If it turns out that a juror in waiting has disqualifying convictions or (although not disqualified) is none the less unsuitable by reason of a previous offence, prosecuting counsel may challenge for cause. *Mason* [1981] QB 881 (see Paragraph 17.4.2) expressly approved jury vetting in this limited sense although it must now be restricted further in practice by the *Attorney-General's Guidelines on Exercise by the Crown of its Right of Stand-by*. Shortly after the judgment in *Mason,* the Association of Chief Police Officers issued recommendations, indicating when the police would consider it appropriate to check the jury panellists for previous convictions. The recommendations are reported in (1989) 88 Cr App R 123 at p. 125. They identify three situations in which a check may be carried out. They are:

(a)   it appears that an attempt is being made to introduce disqualified persons onto a jury, or that a particular juror may be disqualified; or

(b)   it is believed that, in a previous related abortive trial, an attempt was made to interfere with jurors; or

(c)   it is thought especially important, having regard to the nature of the particular case, to ensure that no disqualified person sits on the jury.

The police will not check jurors on behalf of the defence unless specifically requested to do so by the Director of Prosecutions. Nor will they carry out checks in addition to the check on convictions unless that is authorised under the Attorney-General's guidelines (see the paragraph in small print below).

The Attorney-General's guidelines (1989) 88 Cr App R 123 state that, in two types of case, enquiries about the jurors going beyond a mere check on convictions may be justified. The types of case are — (i) those in which national security is involved and part of the evidence is likely to be heard in camera, and (ii) terrorist cases. Extra checks are said to be needed because, in such cases, a person of extreme political views might allow those views to interfere with his objective assessment of the evidence. Further, as regards security cases, it is thought essential to exclude from the jury anybody who might be tempted to divulge evidence heard in camera. Therefore, in both categories of cases, the files of the police Special Branch may be consulted; in security cases, the aid of the security services themselves may additionally be sought. However, such checks require the personal authorisation of the Attorney-General, and are consequently known as 'authorised checks'. The results of any authorised cheek are, at the discretion of the Director of Public Prosecutions, passed on to prosecuting counsel who may then — bearing in mind the risks against which the check was intended to guard — use the information to stand jurors by. Since the Attorney gives his authority only in a handful of cases, authorised checks are of little significance in the overall scheme of jury selection.

17.4.6   Jury protection

Where the judge is concerned about 'jury nobbling' (e.g. intimidation or bribery), he may make a jury protection order. In essence, this will involve the police providing protection for the members of the jury during the course of the trial, so that their deliberations can be carried out without outside interference. Usually, such an order would be considered as a result of an application by the prosecution. Generally, the judge will be reluctant to accede to such an application without substantial grounds. There is the danger that a jury subjected to the intrusive attention which protection is likely to involve will assume that the defendant is to blame for the inconvenience, and must be the object of suspicion if he has associates suspected of jury nobbling. There is also the converse danger that the less robust among the jury may fear adverse consequences if they convict, and will decide to acquit. Nevertheless, the judge has a discretion as to whether to order jury protection. The prosecution will make its application in the absence of the jury, and wherever possible in the presence of the defence. Usually, reasons will be given by the prosecution, and evidence called, the witnesses being subject to cross-examination. Occasionally, a departure from this procedure may be sanctioned by the judge, e.g., to allow the prosecution to make its application in the absence of the defence or without calling evidence. But any departure from the usual procedure should not be sanctioned unless it is necessary and does not result in unfairness to the defendant. In any event, if the judge decides to authorise protection, there is no need for the jury to be told of the reasons, as to do so may merely compound the inevitable problems which the protection order involves. Some explanation, however, is usually necessary, and it is customary for a formula to be agreed between counsel and the judge, which will stress that the jurors should not be alarmed, and must in no way be prejudiced against the defendant by reason of the precautions taken. The phenomenon of jury protection, which is increasingly common, was analysed by the Court of Appeal in *Comerford* [1998] 1 Cr App R 235, from which the above points are taken.

17.4.7 Issues triable by one jury

A jury selected by the procedures described in the preceding Paragraphs will normally be kept together to try only one issue. The issue will nearly always be whether the accused is guilty or not guilty of the charges in the indictment preferred against him, although exceptionally it might be an issue such as fitness to plead or muteness. Having brought in their verdict, the jury is disbanded and its constituent members are then available for selection for further juries. Section 11(4) of the JA does, however, provide that a jury may try more than one issue if the trial of the second (or last) issue begins within 24 hours of the time when the jury was constituted. This provision is useful in cases of muteness where the jury which found the accused mute of malice may go on to try the general issue of guilt or innocence (assuming, of course, that it took them less than a day to find that the accused was not mute by visitation of God). Furthermore, it is specifically provided in s 4(4)(b) of the Criminal Procedure (Insanity) Act 1964 that, when determination of fitness to plead is postponed until the end of the prosecution case, the jury trying the general issue may also try fitness. Similarly, where the accused is found unfit to plead, the same jury should go on to determine whether he did 'the act or made the omission which constitutes the *actus reus* of the offence (s 4A(5) of the Criminal Procedure (Insanity) Act 1964, as amended in 1991; see Paragraph 16.7.2). Outside of these situations, juries are not in practice retained to try more than one issue even if that might be technically permissible under s 11(4). Thus, if a trial on indictment takes less than a day, the jurors will simply return to the pool of jurors in waiting rather than be asked to start a second trial.

17.5   THE COMPOSITION OF THE JURY AS A GROUND OF APPEAL

It is in the public interest that the verdicts of juries should be treated with respect, and should not be overturned on appeal unless there was some significant error during the trial which preceded the verdict (e.g., the reception of inadmissible evidence or a misdirection in law during the summing-up), or the appellate court is left with a real feeling that a miscarriage of justice may have occurred (see Chapter 24 for the grounds on which the Court of Appeal upholds an appeal against conviction). If it were possible, as a matter of course, to challenge convictions by impugning the competence of individual jurors or the way they collectively came to their decision in the case, then public confidence in the jury system would be undermined, and members of the public would be reluctant to serve on juries for fear of being subsequently criticised before the Court of Appeal. So, Parliament and the Court of Appeal have combined to make it very difficult for an offender to challenge his conviction by attacking the jury.

First, the Court of Appeal has long had a settled principle that it will not investigate what occurred in the jury room, however strong the suspicion may be that there was some irregularity (see Paragraph 19.1.2 for details). Secondly, if it is discovered by the defence after the trial that one of the jurors knew facts to the accused's detriment of which he ought to have been unaware and/or was heavily biased against the accused, that is not regarded as a good ground of appeal unless the defence can discharge the near impossible burden of showing that the juror concerned had made up his mind *before* the trial to convict the accused regardless of the evidence. Thus, in *Box and Box* [1964] 1 QB 430, the convictions were upheld despite the fact that the foreman of the jury knew that the appellants were ex-burglars, villains and associates of prostitutes, and had said to an acquaintance that he 'did not need to hear the the the evidence' and 'would get them ten years'. Of course, it was quite wrong for the foreman to serve on the jury — he should have told the judge what he knew about the accused, and the judge would have released him. And, if the defence had known soon enough what the foreman knew, they would obviously have challenged him for cause, and the challenge would inevitably have succeeded. But, given that the relevant facts did not come to light until after verdict, the Court of Appeal decided that the conviction would have to be upheld, despite the doubts one may have as to whether the jury really decided the case fairly according to the evidence or were swayed by the foreman's anti-defence bias. Similarly, in *Pennington* (1985) 81 Cr App R 217 (see Paragraph 17.4.3 for the facts) the alleged bias of the non-striking miner on the jury — even if it might have been a ground for a challenge for cause had it been discovered earlier — was unhesitatingly rejected as a reason for quashing P's conviction after the event. Thirdly, the Court of Appeal's approach in cases such as *Box and Box* has been statutorily confirmed by s 18 of the JA.

Section 18 provides that a conviction may not be quashed on any of the following grounds:

(a) that the provisions of the JA about the summoning of jurors or their selection by ballot were not complied with;

(b) that a juror was not qualified to serve under s 1 of the JA;

(c) that a juror was misnamed or misdescribed (e.g., in the jury summons or on the panel);

(d) that a juror was unfit to serve.

Section 18 does not apply to breaches of the JA coming within (a) above if objection was made at the time or as soon as practicable thereafter, and nothing was done to correct the irregularity. Nor does s 18 apply to cases where a person wrongfully served on a jury by impersonating somebody else who had been properly summoned for service. But, subject to those two provisos, the section will defeat appeals based on grounds such as a juror having been ineligible for or disqualified from or otherwise unfit for jury service, even though the relevant facts were not known until after the trial. A simple illustration is provided by *Raviraj* (1987) 85 Cr App R 93 where the defence discovered post-conviction that one of the jurors had been ineligible through having served as a police officer within the preceding ten years. The appeal was dismissed because of s 18. Similarly, but more controversially, in *Chapman and Lauday* (1976) 63 Cr App R 75 the appellants failed even though a juror was deaf, and had heard only half the evidence and none of the summing-up. Clearly, a juror who has not heard the proceedings is incapable of discharging his oath to give a true verdict according to the evidence, but the deaf juror was not challenged at the time (because nobody then knew of his disability), and there was no way in which the defence could disguise the fact that their ground of appeal was simply his unfitness to be a juror. In effect, the appellants had been tried by eleven, not twelve, jurors but s 18 still applied to save the conviction. Arguably, a juror is unfit within the meaning of s 18 not only when (as in *Chapman and Lauday)* he would be physically or mentally unsuited to serve on *any* jury, but also when his knowledge about or attitude to a particular accused makes him unsuitable to try that man, although he would be acceptable on other juries. Perhaps, though, such cases are best left to the common law principles explained in *Box and Box* (see above) and should not be brought within s 18.

> In *Chapman and Lauday,* the Court of Appeal did suggest obiter dicta an alternative approach which, in different circumstances, might ameliorate the apparently harsh effects of the section. That approach is to argue that the entire circumstances of the case — including but not limited to the alleged deficiency of the juror — give rise to a turking doubt that justice was not done, and that therefore the conviction is unsafe. For example, had the verdict in *Chapman and Lauday* been by the minimum permissible majority of 10–2 rather than being unanimous, their Lordships could not have been confident about the justice of a conviction which depended for its legality upon the vote of a juror who had not heard the evidence. They would therefore have quashed the conviction, notwithstanding s 18, on the ground of unsafeness. Taking their cue from the dicta in *Chapman and Lauday,* the appellants in *Raviraj* contended that the former policeman on the jury rendered the convictions unsafe. Again, however, the argument failed on the facts since the juror concerned had left the force some nine years earlier and, anyway, had only been in it for three years. Such a weak link with the police did not suggest that he would have been so pro-prosecution as to fail to listen fairly to the evidence himself and/or exercise undue influence on his colleagues on the jury.

17.6 DISCHARGE OF JURORS OR A JURY

Once a jury has been empanelled, the normal course of events is that those twelve men and women hear the entire case and return a verdict at the end of it. However, the judge may discharge up to three jurors and allow the trial to continue with the remainder. Alternatively, he may discharge the entire jury from giving a verdict, leaving open the possibility of a fresh jury being sworn in to try the accused at a later date. Discharge of jurors or the jury is frequently connected with allegations of misconduct by them during the course of the hearing. It is therefore convenient, first, to summarise the rules on the conduct of jurors.

17.6.1 Conduct of the jury during the trial

The trial judge has a discretion to allow the jury to separate from each other at any time prior to their retiring to consider their verdict: JA, s 13. This discretion is extended by the Criminal Justice and Public Order Act 1994, s 43, to cover the time after they have retired to consider their verdict. For obvious reasons it is normal to permit such separations both during lunch adjournments and overnight. But, when they first separate, the jury should be warned by the judge not to speak about the case to anyone who is not of their number (see *Prime* (1973) 57 Cr App R 632). It is especially important that they do not speak to the parties, witnesses, counsel or anybody else actually involved in the trial. Neither, however, should they discuss the case with relatives, friends, etc. This is partly because they (and nobody else) are charged with the duty of ultimately returning a verdict, and partly because a person to whom they speak might have strong views on the issues raised by the trial and, whether by accident or design, colour the juror's attitude to the proceedings (see *Spencer* [1987] AC 128 for an extreme example of this occurring). Breach of the above rules may lead to a juror or the entire jury being discharged (see Paragraphs 17.6.2 and 19.1).

17.6.2   Discharge of individual jurors

Section 16 of the JA provides that if, during the course of a trial, a juror dies or is discharged by the judge 'whether as being through illness incapable of continuing to act or for any other reason', the remainder of the jury may complete the hearing of the case and return a verdict provided their number is not reduced below nine. Section 16 does not itself define the reasons (other than incapacitating illness) which justify discharge. At common law, however, discharge is allowed only if there is an 'evident necessity' for it (see *Hamberry* [1977] QB 924). What amounts to an evident necessity is essentially a matter for the judge's discretion, and it is not in practice particularly difficult to show it exists. Thus, in *Hamberry* a juror was discharged merely because the unexpectedly long duration of the trial meant that, had she remained on the jury, her holiday plans would have been interfered with. The Court of Appeal approved the trial judge's decision. Similarly, in *Richardson* [1979] 1 WLR 1316, their lordships had no difficulty in holding that it was right to discharge a juror whose husband had died during an overnight adjournment.

Misconduct by a juror, resulting in a suspicion of bias, may also necessitate his being discharged. The decided cases show two different strands of authority, revealing that different tests have been applied when considering questions of bias. In the leading case of *Gough* [1993] AC 646, the two competing tests were identified as:

(a)   whether there was a real danger of bias on the part of the juror concerned; and
(b)   whether a reasonable person might reasonably suspect bias on the juror's part.

The House of Lords in *Gough* confirmed that the correct test for the trial judge to apply was (a), that is, whether there was a real danger of bias affecting the mind of the individual juror. Their lordships also made it clear that the same test applied to all cases of apparent bias, whether in respect of jurors or justices. Further, the judge must not take into account irrelevant matters, e.g. the fact that there has been an earlier trial which was abortive: *Walker* [1996] Crim LR 752.

In *Sawyer* (1980) 71 Cr App R 283 three jurors had been seen talking to prosecution witnesses in the court restaurant but, when asked by the judge what the conversation had been about, they assured him that it was on neutral matters unconnected with the trial. The judge decided that there was no real danger of prejudice and refused to discharge the jurors, which decision was approved by the Court of Appeal. Similar principles apply if it is discovered during the course of the trial that a juror knows the accused and/or knows that he is of bad character; or knows a witness in the case; or has expressed an opinion about the case suggesting that he might have made his mind up in advance. If there is a real risk of prejudice, the judge must certainly discharge the juror, and he may have to consider discharging the whole jury (see *Hood* [1968] 1 WLR 773).

In *Sander v UK* [2000] Crim LR 767, the European Court of Human Rights emphasised that any allegation of bias must be looked at from an objective, as well as a subjective point of view. In other words, a finding that the jury were not in fact biased did not end the matter. There was a further question which had to be posed: were there 'sufficient guarantees to exclude any objectively justified or legitimate doubts as to the impartiality' of the jury. The decision in *Gough* should be read subject to this analysis, which would seem to indicate that both tests (a) and (b) referred to above need to be satisfied.

Discharge of a juror does not require the consent of the parties. The former rule that consent was needed in murder cases has been abolished by the Criminal Justice Act 1988. Normally, the judge would ask for representations before making any decision but even that is not essential. Indeed, the judge can exercise the power of discharge otherwise than in open court and without telling the parties what he has done (see *Richardson* (above) where the juror was told over the telephone that she was discharged, and the judge failed even to announce his decision in open court so that, on the trial resuming, counsel did not immediately realise that a juror was missing — nonetheless the conviction was upheld).

17.6.3 Discharge of the whole jury

The judge has a discretion to discharge the whole jury from giving a verdict. If he does so, the accused does not stand acquitted of the offence charged but can be retried by a different jury on the same indictment. The main situations for discharge of a jury are as follows:

(a) *Where they cannot agree upon their verdict.* This is discussed in Chapter 19.

(b) *Where inadmissible 'evidence' prejudicial to the accused has inadvertently been given.* Thus, if a witness tells the jury that the accused has previous convictions and it is not one of the exceptional cases where evidence of character is allowed, then there is a good chance that the judge will accede to a defence application to discharge the jury. But, it remains a matter for discretion, and the judge will consider especially how explicit the reference to bad character was; how far the defence were to blame for what happened through asking ill-advised questions in cross-examination; and what impact the inadmissible information is likely to have on the jury. In *Weaver* [1968] 1 QB 353, cross-examination by defence counsel of a police officer led to answers which, in effect, revealed to the jury that the accused had previous convictions. The judge refused to discharge the jury and W was convicted. The Court of Appeal dismissed the appeal. The factors weighing against discharge were (a) that defence counsel was himself responsible for inviting the answers which he then complained of; and (b) the judge's summing-up had minimised the degree of prejudice. Contrast the case of *Boyes* [1991] Crim LR 717, in which, as the judge concluded his summing-up on charges of rape and indecent assault, the complainant's mother shouted from the public gallery, 'When is it going to come out about the other five girls he has attacked?' The judge told the jury not to pay any attention to the outburst. The jury convicted. The Court of Appeal allowed the appeal. One of the bases for their decision was the judge's failure to enquire of the jury whether they had heard the outburst. If they had, one could hardly think of more damaging and prejudicial evidence being taken to the jury room. The judge should have considered a fresh trial.

In *McCann* [1991] Crim LR 136, M and others were tried for conspiracy to murder Mr King, then Secretary of State for Northern Ireland, and others. They elected not to give evidence. During the closing stages of the trial, the Home Secretary announced in the House of Commons the government's intention of changing the law on the right to silence. That night, interviews with Mr King and Lord Denning were televised, expressing in strong terms their view that in terrorist cases a failure to answer questions or give evidence was tantamount to guilt. The trial judge refused to dismiss the jury, and the defendants were convicted. The Court of Appeal allowed the appeal. There was a real risk that the jury had been influenced by the statements. The only way in which justice could be done and be obviously seen to be done was by discharging the jury and ordering a retrial.

The problems outlined in relation to the revelation of matters prejudicial to the accused may also arise where it is discovered that one of the jurors has personal knowledge of the accused, or of one of the witnesses in the case. The judge would then need to decide, on the basis of the 'real danger' test outlined in *Gough* [1993] AC 646 (see Paragraph 17.6.2), whether the individual juror, or the whole jury, should be discharged. If there is a real danger of bias on the part of the individual juror, then the suspicion must also be addressed that he will have contaminated the other members of the jury by communicating his prejudice to them. If that is the case, then the whole jury should be discharged.

(c)   *Where one or more jurors has been guilty of misconduct and/or might be prejudiced against the accused, and the matter cannot be satisfactorily dealt with by discharge of the individual jurors concerned.*   The test for whether the jury should be discharged in such cases is the one stated in *Gough* [1993] AC 646 (see Paragraph 17.6.2), namely, whether there is a real danger of bias on the part of the original jury. Again, this is essentially a matter for the judge's discretion. Therefore, the Court of Appeal will overturn a conviction only if the appellant can show that the judge's refusal to discharge was totally unreasonable and/or arrived at by applying incorrect principles. In *Spencer* [1987] AC 128, however, the House of Lords did quash S's conviction on the basis of non-discharge. The facts were that S was charged with ill-treating patients during the course of his employment as a nurse at Rampton special security mental hospital. During the trial a juror (Mr Peet) evinced signs of obvious hostility towards the accused (e.g., by showing impatience at having to listen to the cross-examination of the patients called as prosecution witnesses). On the penultimate day of the trial an usher discovered that Mr Peet's wife worked at another mental hospital and may well have heard gossip about what allegedly went on at Rampton, which she in turn could have passed on to her husband. The usher told the judge, and the judge discharged Mr Peet. However, the judge allowed him to continue his usual practice of driving three of the remaining jurors home from the Crown Court to the nearby town where they all lived. A warning was given that they should not discuss the case as Mr Peet was no longer a member of the jury, The next morning defence counsel asked for the whole jury to be discharged on the basis that, in the car rides home, Mr Peet would almost certainly have infected the other three jurors with his anti-defence bias. The judge refused the application, apparently holding that the defence had to show a 'very high risk' that Mr Peet had improperly influenced other jury-members. Both the Court of Appeal and the House of Lords affirmed that that was the wrong test — the defence merely had to show a real danger of prejudice. However, the Court of Appeal dismissed the appeal as, in their view, there was no such danger on the facts of the case. The House of Lords reversed that decision (i.e. quashed the conviction) but only because they had before them an affidavit from Mr Peet in which he admitted that he had disobeyed the judge's warning and had discussed the case with the other three jurors during the car journey home on the evening after he had been discharged. There was a real risk that — piqued by being off the jury and desperate to ensure a conviction — Mr Peet would then have imparted information derived from his wife of which neither he nor any juror should have been aware. However, the implication of the House of Lords judgments is that, on the facts known to him at the time, the trial judge was justified in refusing the application for discharge.

One difficult set of cases deals with approaches made to the jury by outsiders in an attempt to influence their decision. In *Thorpe* [1996] Crim LR 273, the Court of Appeal said that a distinction should be drawn between a case where the approach is immediately reported to the judge, and a case where the matter comes to light only after the verdict has been delivered. If the juror who has been approached reports it immediately to the judge, that will be an indication that his integrity remains intact, and the approach has not influenced him.

Where a judge does decide to discharge the jury — whether for one of the reasons summarised above or for a totally inadequate reason — and the accused is subsequently convicted at a retrial, no appeal can be brought on the basis that the first trial should have been allowed to continue: *Gorman* [1987] 1 WLR 545.

18 The Course of the Trial

18.1 COUNSEL AND THE JUDGE

The judge at a trial on indictment must be a professional judge (i.e., a High Court judge; circuit judge or deputy circuit judge; or recorder). The distribution of work between these various types of judge is described in Paragraph 13.2. The prosecution *must* be legally represented; the accused usually chooses to be so, and will probably be able to obtain representation from the Criminal Defence Service. Although some solicitors now have rights of audience in the Crown Court, legal representation for trial on indictment still usually involves instructing solicitors who in turn brief counsel (see Paragraph 13.4). The following Paragraphs deal with some aspects of the role of prosecuting and defence counsel, and their relationship with the judge. The discussion is based upon dicta in decided cases and also upon the Code of Conduct for the Bar. The Code does not have the force of law, but is of great persuasive value, and a barrister who conforms with its spirit cannot be guilty of a breach of professional discipline.

The criminal justice system in this country is essentially adversarial. It is the duty of the prosecution to present the case for the Crown; and the role of counsel for the defence is to represent the accused. It follows that the judge's interventions must be limited to providing a framework in which counsel carry out their duties efficiently and fairly. In *Whybrow* (1994) *The Times*, 14 February 1994, the appellants complained that the judge had prevented them from giving their evidence in chief properly, and had intervened with such frequency and hostility as to deny them a fair trial. The Court of Appeal quashed their convictions, and ordered a retrial. Their lordships stressed that there were occasions when the judge could, and indeed should intervene. For example, if a witness gave an ambiguous answer, the judge should have it clarified 'as briefly as possible'. If he did not hear an answer, he could have it repeated so that he could note it accurately. He should 'intervene to curb prolixity and repetition and to exclude irrelevance, discursiveness and oppression of witnesses'. In this case, however, the Court of Appeal took the view that the judge's interventions went 'far beyond the bounds of legitimate judicial conduct'. One of the cases on which their lordships relied was *Hulusi* (1973) 58 Cr App R 378, in which it was said (per Lawton LJ at p. 385):

> It is a fundamental principle of an English trial that, if an accused gives evidence, he must be allowed to do so without being badgered and interrupted. Judges should remember that most people go into the witness-box, whether they be witnesses for the Crown or the

defence, in a state of nervousness. They are anxious to do their best. They expect to receive a courteous hearing, and when they find, almost as soon as they get into the witness-box and are starting to tell their story, that the judge of all people is intervening in a hostile way, then, human nature being what it is, they are liable to become confused and not to do as well as they would have done had they not been badgered and interrupted.

In *Marsh* (1993) *The Times*, 6 July 1993, it was stressed that it was particularly unfair for the judge to interrupt a defendant when he was giving evidence.

18.1.1   The role of prosecuting counsel

Counsel for the prosecution is not in court to win the case at all costs. Of course, he should present the prosecution evidence as persuasively as possible, and cross-examine the defence witnesses with all proper vigour and guile. Nevertheless, as Avory J put it in *Banks* [1916] 2 KB 621, prosecuting counsel 'ought not to struggle for the verdict against the prisoner, but they ought to bear themselves rather in the character of ministers of justice assisting in the administration of justice'. One aspect of this role is that, should the defence suggest a plea of guilty to a lesser offence or guilty on some but not all the counts in the indictment (see Chapter 14), prosecuting counsel does not consider only whether the evidence he has available might secure a conviction on all counts as charged, but whether the proposed pleas represent a fair way of dealing with the case. If they do, and subject to any comments by the judge, he should accept the pleas, even though that means giving up the chance of 'extra' convictions. Again, if the prosecution knows that one of its witnesses has previous convictions, there is a duty to reveal to the defence the nature and occasion of those convictions, although by doing so the defence is presented with a useful line of cross-examination. Thus in *Paraskeva* (1983) 76 Cr App R 162, the Court of Appeal quashed P's conviction for assault occasioning actual bodily harm because the case against him turned upon whether the victim of the alleged offence was telling the truth or deliberately lying, and the prosecution failed to disclose that the victim had been convicted in 1975 of an offence of dishonesty. Having been informed that a prosecution witness is not of good character, the defence sometimes choose not to cross-examine him about it (e.g., because to do so would expose the accused to cross-examination about his own previous convictions). In such a case, prosecuting counsel might himself reveal his witness's character to the jury, but he is under no duty to do so. The principle is that the prosecution should be scrupulously fair to the accused, but need not be quixotically generous.

In *Gomez* [1999] All ER (D) 674, the Court of Appeal endorsed the description of prosecuting counsel as a minister of justice, stating that it was incumbent on him not to be betrayed by personal feelings, not to excite emotions or to inflame the minds of the jury and not to make comments which could reasonably be construed as racist and bigoted. He was to be clinical and dispassionate.

> In 1986, the Chairman of the Bar set up a committee to consider the role of prosecuting counsel in the light of the imminent introduction of the Crown Prosecution Service. The committee was chaired by Farquharson J and also included distinguished members of the Bar. Its report was published in the Trinity 1986 edition of *Counsel* magazine. Appropriate points have been incorporated in annexe H [now annexe F] to the Bar's Code of Conduct.
>
> The Report began by reiterating the special duty of prosecuting counsel to be fair, etc. and to conduct himself as a 'minister of justice'. This duty does entail counsel having 'greater independence

from those instructing him than enjoyed by other counsel', although on the whole differences of opinion between him and the CPS should be resolved by sensible give-and-take on both sides, not by counsel insisting upon his rights. Most *tactical* decisions concerning the conduct of a trial (e.g. whether or not to call a certain witness, or what submissions to make as to the relevant law) arise at court when counsel is probably attended only by an unqualified clerk, and in such circumstances the only practical course is for counsel to take the decision himself. If the CPS do not approve, they have the sanction available to all disappointed solicitors of not briefing that counsel again. There are also what may be described as *policy* decisions, in particular as to whether to accept proferred pleas of guilty to part of the indictment or to a lesser offence and whether to offer no evidence at all. Is counsel then entitled to act contrary to his instructions? — i.e. accept the plea even though the CPS want him to continue or vice versa. The Committee state, first, that counsel should strive to prevent such a situation arising by advising promptly before trial on the point in question. If the CPS do not like the advice, they can take a second opinion and, if need be, brief other counsel. Where, however, the question arises too close to trial for that to be a realistic option and discussions between CPS lawyers and counsel have failed to resolve the disagreement, then — as a last resort — counsel must do what he conscientiously believes to be right, even if that means acting contrary to instructions. After trial, the Attorney-General might require him to submit a written report as to why he acted as he did.

Thus, in respect of trials on indictment, counsel is the person ultimately in charge of the case for the prosecution and cannot be forced to act contrary to his views of what ought to be done. This may be contrasted with the position of solicitor or counsel acting as agent for the CPS in a magistrates' court who (at least in theory) is subject to any directions given him by a Crown Prosecutor and must obtain authorisation before, for example, offering no evidence (see Paragraph 3.2.3).

18.1.2   The role of defence counsel

Counsel for the defence is not placed under the same constraints as prosecuting counsel. He is under no duty to regard himself as a minister of justice, or to be fair to the prosecution, or to tell them that his client or one of his witnesses has previous convictions. Subject to what is said below, he may use all means at his disposal to secure an acquittal. For example, if he notices a purely technical flaw in the prosecution case, which could be easily corrected if dealt with at an early stage of the trial, he need not draw his opponent's or the court's attention to the matter before the last possible moment (see *Nelson* (1977) 65 Cr App R 119 where the Court of Appeal did not criticise N's counsel for waiting until after N had been convicted to mention that there was a defect in the indictment — his only motive for not mentioning it sooner was to make it harder to remedy the defect by amendment). Nevertheless, he has 'an overriding duty to the court to ensure in the public interest that the proper and efficient administration of justice is achieved: he must assist the court in the administration of justice and must not deceive or knowingly or recklessly mislead the court' (para 202 of the Code of Conduct). If a procedural irregularity, such as a juror leaving the jury room after they have retired to consider their verdict, comes to defence counsel's knowledge before the verdict is announced, he should inform the court as soon as he can. He should not keep silent so as to be able to raise the irregularity on appeal should there be a conviction (*Smith* [1994] Crim LR 458).

The greater latitude afforded to defence counsel should not be exaggerated. Like all counsel, he owes a duty not just to his client but to the court. It follows that he must not deliberately mislead the court, or behave unethically in any other way. While he may point out the difficulties in the defence the accused wants to put forward, he must not suggest or invent a more plausible defence. Although he need not reveal that the accused or his witness has convictions, he must not positively assert that they are of good character if he knows that to be false. He should also avoid wasting the court's time through prolixity or repetition, and should not be made the channel for allegations which are only intended to insult the persons against whom they are made without advancing the defence case.

Perhaps the clearest statement of defence counsel's role is to be found in some principles outlined by the Chairman of the Bar (see 62 Cr App R 193). The statement followed criticism by Melford Stevenson J in the case of *McFadden and Cunningham* (1976) 62 Cr App R 187, of the way in which defence counsel had presented their case and cross-examined police witnesses. The Chairman of the Bar said that defence counsel's duty is to present to the court, 'fearlessly and without regard to his personal interests', the defence of the accused. His personal opinion of the truth or falsity of the defence, or of the character of the accused, or of the nature of the charge should all be left out of account — 'that is a cardinal rule of the Bar, and it would be a grave matter in any free society were it not'. Of course, if the accused tells counsel that he is guilty, it would not be right for counsel to call evidence suggesting the opposite, as he would be deliberately misleading the court. If the accused insists on pleading not guilty despite his admission to counsel, guidance is provided by the Bar's Code of Conduct, Annexe F, paras 13.1 to 13.6. Where counsel does continue to act, he should confine himself to cross-examining the prosecution witnesses with a view to showing that their evidence does not establish guilt beyond a reasonable doubt. Provided, however, that the accused has not actually said he is guilty, counsel may, and indeed is under a duty, to put forward the defence as persuasively as possible, even though his personal opinion is that it is a tissue of lies.

Further examples of the difference between the prosecution and defence approach to a case will be found in the remainder of this Chapter. For a critical analysis of the difference, see Blake and Ashworth, 'Some Ethical Issues in Prosecuting and Defending' [1998] Crim LR 16.

18.1.3 Counsel seeing the judge in private

In appropriate circumstances, counsel should be permitted to see the judge in his private room in order to discuss with him matters relevant to the case in the absence of the parties and the public. As Lord Parker CJ put in in *Turner* [1970] 2 QB 321 (see also Paragraph 16.3.3), 'there must be freedom of access between counsel and judge'. But his Lordship went on to say:

> It is of course imperative that, as far as possible, justice must be administered in open court. Counsel should, therefore, only ask to see the judge when it is felt to be really necessary, and the judge must be careful only to treat such communications as private where, in fairness to the accused person, this is necessary.

Since *Turner* the Court of Appeal have stressed in cases such as *Coward* (1980) 70 Cr App R 70 and *Llewellyn* (1977) 67 Cr App R 149, that private access to the judge should be kept to an absolute minimum. One clear example of private access being appropriate is where defence counsel, who is to mitigate on behalf of an offender prior to sentencing, receives instructions that his client believes himself to be healthy but is in fact suffering from an incurable disease. Clearly the judge should be told of the offender's ill health, so as to avoid, if at all possible, passing a sentence which would result in his dying in prison. Equally clearly, to mention the fact in open court with the offender listening could have disastrous consequences. Private access may also be useful when counsel want to ask whether a proposed 'deal' on pleas would be acceptable to the judge, and when the judge wants to give an indication on sentence consistent with the principles in *Turner's* case. However,

Llewellyn and *Coward* (supra) suggested that even these matters are better raised in open court.

The initiative for a private meeting should in general come from counsel not the judge (see Watkins LJ's judgment in *Cullen* (1984) 81 Cr App R 17 at p. 19). Both prosecuting and defence counsel should be present, together with the defence solicitor if he wishes and somebody (e.g. the court shorthand writer) to take a note of what is said. The latter's presence is essential because otherwise embarrassing differences of recollection may arise on appeal (see *Cullen*, where the judge thought he had indicated merely that he would not pass an *immediate* custodial sentence but defence counsel told C that the judge had said there would not be a custodial sentence of any form — in the absence of any contemporaneous record, the Court of Appeal had to accept the defence version of events and quash C's suspended sentence of imprisonment on the basis that it departed from what the judge had privately indicated to counsel). Following the meeting, counsel should do what defence counsel in *Cullen* did — i.e., tell his client what took place unless there is good reason for his being kept in ignorance. Further, should the judge have said something about the sentence he has in mind, then, according to *Turner,* that must be passed on to the accused even if it will nullify any plea of guilty he subsequently enters (see Paragraph 16.3.3 for when a plea of guilty is a nullity).

The Attorney-General's Guidelines on the Acceptance of Pleas give guidance to prosecutors where there is a discussion on plea and sentence in chambers. Such discussions should only take place 'in the most exceptional circumstances'. Where they do take place, the prosecution advocate should if necessary remind the judge of the desirability of an independent record, and should himself make a full note, recording all decisions and comments. This note should be made available to the prosecuting authority. Where there is a discussion on plea and sentence and the prosecution advocate does not believe that the circumstances are exceptional, he should remind the judge of the relevant decisions of the Court of Appeal and disassociate himself from any discussion on sentence. He should not say or do anything which might be taken to agree, expressly or by implication, with a particular sentence. In cases where s 35 of the Criminal Justice Act 1988 applies, he should indicate that the Attorney-General may, if he sees fit, seek leave to refer any sentence as unduly lenient (see Paragraph 27.4.2).

18.1.4 Judge's discretion to halt prosecution

Once an indictment against the accused has been signed there is very little the defence can do to prevent the prosecution going ahead. They can move to quash the indictment, or raise a special plea in bar (autrefois acquit, autrefois convict or pardon), or plead that the Crown Court has no jurisdiction to try the case, but all these remedies are of limited scope and rarely assist in practice. If, however, defence counsel thinks that the prosecution is grossly unfair he has one further remedy at his disposal. He can ask the judge to intervene and stay the prosecution, i.e., order that it shall not proceed without leave of the court or of the Court of Appeal. It is now generally agreed that the Crown Court has inherent power to prevent its process from abuse. In *Connelly v DPP* [1964] AC 1254, for example, Lord Devlin stated at p. 1355 that, where particular criminal proceedings constitute an abuse of process, the court is empowered to refuse to allow the indictment to proceed to trial. The remarks of Lord Salmon in *DPP v Humphrys* [1977] AC 1 stress the importance of this discretion:

A judge has not and should not appear to have any responsibility for the institution of prosecutions, nor has he any power to refuse to allow a prosecution to proceed merely because he considers, as a matter of policy, it ought not to have been brought. It is only if the prosecution amounts to an abuse of the process of the court and is oppressive and vexatious that the judge has power to intervene. Fortunately such prosecutions are hardly ever brought.

Several recent cases have dealt with the issue of whether undue delay can constitute an abuse of process. There is, of course, no general time-limit upon the issue of proceedings for indictable offences (compare the six-month time-limit in respect of summary offences discussed in Paragraph 9.3). Nevertheless, in *Bell v DPP of Jamaica* [1985] AC 397, the Privy Council accepted that courts have an inherent jurisdiction to prevent a trial which would be oppressive because of unreasonable delay (see also Paragraphs 9.4 and 12.1.4 for an examination of the position as far as the magistrates' courts are concerned).

In *Central Criminal Court ex p Randle* [1991] Crim LR 551, the applicants were charged with offences arising out of the escape from custody of George Blake while he was serving a 42-year sentence for spying. They appeared before the Central Criminal Court in 1990, some 23 years after the alleged offences. They applied for proceedings to be stayed on the grounds of unreasonable delay. The judge refused, and they sought judicial review of that decision. Whilst the Divisional Court refused their application, it was accepted that delay could by itself, in appropriate circumstances, be such as to render criminal proceedings an abuse of process. In this case, however, the applicants had published a book in 1989, which had provided much of the material upon which the prosecution relied. In the light of its contents, the plea of failing memory could not be advanced, and the Divisional Court would not interfere with the judge's discretion. The trial therefore has to proceed, although the accused were in due course found not guilty by the jury.

In *Bell v DPP* the Privy Council laid down guidelines for determining whether the delay would deprive the accused of a fair trial. The relevant factors were said to be:

(a) length of delay;
(b) the prosecution's reasons to justify the delay;
(c) the accused's efforts to assert his rights; and
(d) the prejudice caused to the accused.

Clearly in *ex p Randle,* the lack of prejudice to the defendants was held to be fatal to their argument, despite a delay of 23 years. In *Buzalek* [1991] Crim LR 115, the appellants were convicted of fraudulent trading, the case having been tried some six and a half years after they had been suspended from their jobs. The alleged fraud was of a mammoth nature, requiring the inspection of a great number of documents, many of which had to be translated from German. The trial judge had held that there was no reason why they should not receive a fair trial. The Court of Appeal dismissed the appeal. The case turned largely on documents, and it was possible for the memories of witnesses to be refreshed by referring to them. The passage of time would be much more prejudicial where a case turned, for example, on what witnesses saw in an affray, an assault or a road accident.

If there has been a lengthy delay between the offences and the trial then, even if the judge does not stay the indictment on the ground of abuse of process, he should comment on any difficulties which the defence may have faced because of the age of the complaints: *Birchall* (1995) *The Times,* 23 March 1995, and *E* [1996] 1 Cr App R 88. The judge's consideration of the question of abuse of process is not confined to the question of delay. There are other factors involved, including any unconscionable behaviour by the prosecution. Similar considerations apply in the current context to those which are taken into account in the magistrates' court (see Paragraphs 9.4 (summary trial) and 12.1.4 (committal proceedings)).

In *Dobson* [2001] All ER (D) 109, the Court of Appeal considered the position where police had failed to obtain CCTV footage relating to the defendant's defence of alibi. Their lordships said that, in determining whether there was an abuse of process, it was appropriate to consider:

(a) what was the duty of the police;

(b) whether they had failed in it by not obtaining or retaining the appropriate video footage;

(c) whether there was serious prejudice which rendered a fair trial impossible; and

(d) whether the police failure was a result of bad faith or serious fault independently from the serious prejudice so that a trial would not be fair.

In the instant case, the police should have looked at the CCTV footage, and had failed in their duty to do so. However, the prejudice was not serious because it was uncertain that the footage would have assisted the defence, the defendant was in a position to understand the relevance of the footage and could have requested it and/or sought other evidence to support his alibi. There was no question of malice or intentional omission as opposed to oversight on behalf of the police. The judge was therefore right to conclude that a fair trial was possible and the conviction was upheld.

This Paragraph has dealt with the judge's very limited power to intervene in the accused's favour before the prosecution have called their evidence. Much more significant, however, is his power — indeed duty — to intervene after the prosecution evidence, and direct the jury to acquit if no case to answer is disclosed (see Paragraph 18.4).

18.2 THE PROSECUTION OPENING

After the accused has been put in the charge of the jury, prosecuting counsel opens his case. The prosecution opening gives the members of the jury an overall view of the case. Counsel will remind them of the charges against the accused, which the clerk has just read out to them, explaining any relevant points of law which may not be familiar to lay persons. Probably he will tell them that the prosecution has to prove its case so that they are sure of the accused's guilt, and, if they are not so convinced, they must acquit. Whenever counsel refer to the law it is usual to warn the jury that what they (counsel) say about the law is merely intended as a guide, and is subject to whatever the judge may rule — the jury take the law from the judge not from counsel.

After his explanation of the charges, counsel summarises the evidence he intends to call. In his brief, counsel has copies of the committal statements, i.e. the documents tendered in evidence at the committal proceedings. Basing himself on these he tells the jury the main facts which (he hopes) his various witnesses will prove, and indicates how the pieces of testimony fit together so as to show, beyond reasonable doubt, that the accused committed the offence charged. Having had a general picture of the case, the jury will be able to appreciate the significance of each witness's evidence as it is given. Three detailed points relevant to the opening are that:

(a) If counsel is told by the defence that they intend to object to certain pieces of prosecution evidence, that evidence should not be included in the prosecution's opening to the jury.

(b)   It is sometimes advisable to 'open the case low' — i.e., slightly to underplay what a witness is expected to say. If counsel puts great weight on what a witness is going to prove, and then, in the event, the evidence is not quite as strong as the jury were led to expect, they may think that the whole prosecution case has been undermined. Had less been made of the evidence in the opening, there would be no risk of their so reacting.

(c)   As part of his duty not to 'struggle after the verdict' counsel should avoid unnecessarily emotive language. Indeed, in cases where the facts alleged are likely to cause especial sympathy for the victim or repugnance towards the criminal, it is desirable for the opening to warn the jury against such natural feelings. They should return a verdict upon the evidence, not upon feelings of sympathy or horror.

18.3   THE PROSECUTION CASE

Next, the prosecution call witnesses to give oral evidence and tender in evidence written statements which are read to the jury. At this point the subjects of evidence and procedure become intertwined. This book does not attempt to deal with evidence *per se,* so reference should be made to works on the subject for information on topics such as the competence and compellability of witnesses, oaths and affirmations and unsworn evidence, the course of a witness' examination, the admissibility of similar fact evidence and character evidence, the extent to which an accused may be cross-examined about his previous convictions, the rule against hearsay, exceptions to it such as confessions, and the various exclusionary rules of evidence. However, some matters which are, in a sense, part of the law of evidence, also have important procedural aspects, and these will be considered in the succeeding Paragraphs. (For a summary of the order in which events take place at trial, see Appendix 6.)

18.3.1   The witnesses the prosecution should call

The persons who made written statements or depositions which were tendered by the prosecution at committal are known collectively as 'witnesses whose names appear on the back of the indictment'. The term derives from the old practice of literally writing the names on the reverse of the indictment. The defence naturally assume that the prosecution will call at the trial on indictment all the witnesses whose names are on the back of the indictment (or that they will read out a statement or deposition made by the witness if that is permissible by virtue of one of the provisions described in Paragraph 18.3.4). Furthermore, it would be wrong for defence solicitors to speak to a witness on the back of the indictment prior to the trial, because that could be construed as interfering with the prosecution case. However, it does not follow that because a witness is on the back of the indictment, and thus prima facie favourable to the prosecution, that the defence will necessarily be pleased if he is not called. It may be that part of the witness' anticipated evidence will support the accused's case, or that the defence hope through skilled cross-examination so to undermine the witness' testimony that doubt will be cast on the entire prosecution case. In such a case, the defence would feel aggrieved if the prosecution did not call the witness. Therefore, the rule is that prosecuting counsel must call a witness whose name is on the back of the indictment unless *either* it will be possible to read out his statement or deposition, or the witness has failed to come to court despite the prosecution having taken all reasonable steps to secure his attendance (see Paragraph 18.3.2), *or* the witness does not appear to be a credible witness worthy of belief. In the latter case the prosecution remain under a duty to secure the witness' attendance at court so that the defence can call him if they so wish.

In the normal course of events the prosecution would not, at committal proceedings, make use of evidence from a person considered to be unworthy of belief. Thus, almost by definition, a witness on the back of the indictment is a witness the prosecution regard as credible. However, it can happen that the prosecution view of a witness changes between committal proceedings and trial on indictment, and it is in that situation that prosecuting counsel might decline to call the witness. In *Oliva* [1965] 1 WLR 1028, for example, the witness (W) had been the victim of an offence of causing grievous bodily harm. He made a statement to the police naming O as the culprit, and in evidence on the first day of committal proceedings testified for the prosecution to that effect. Following an overnight adjournment, he reversed his evidence and exonerated O, but O was nevertheless committed for trial on the basis of other evidence. Since W had been called by the prosecution at committal proceedings, he was a witness whose name appeared on the back of the indictment, but the Court of Appeal held that prosecuting counsel rightly refused to call him at the trial as his sudden change of evidence at committal proceedings showed he was not worthy of belief. Had prosecuting counsel been forced to call W the jury would have been confused by a prosecution witness who flatly contradicted the prosecution case, and counsel would have found it difficult to challenge W's evidence because of the rule that one cannot cross-examine one's own witness. As it was, defence counsel was given a not unfair choice between managing without W's evidence all together and calling W himself, in which event prosecuting counsel would be able to cross-examine.

Sometimes, when the prosecution do not need a person's evidence (e.g. because several witnesses have already given the relevant evidence which he could give) but they consider him a credible witness, they 'tender him for cross-examination'. This means that they call him, establish his name and address, and then allow the defence to question him as they see fit. Where the judge considers that the prosecution are wrong not to call a witness, he may himself call the person concerned.

18.3.2   Securing the attendance of witnesses

It is the prosecution's duty to take all reasonable steps to secure the attendance at court of the witnesses whose names appear on the back of the indictment unless, in the case of any particular witness, they will be able to read his deposition or written statement to the jury under the rules described in Paragraph 18.3.4. The defence must arrange for the attendance of the witnesses they wish to call. If a witness is not at court on the day of the trial the judge has a discretion either to adjourn the case or allow it to continue, notwithstanding that the jury will possibly be deprived of useful evidence. The exercise of the judge's discretion will turn upon matters such as the importance of the evidence the witness is likely to give; the reason for his absence (sickness, disappearance, absence abroad, possible intimidation etc.), and the likelihood of his attending on the next occasion were the case to be adjourned for a short time. Where the prosecution wish the case to proceed even though one of their witnesses is absent, the judge should especially consider the extent to which the absent witness might in part support the defence case: *Cavanagh and Shaw* [1972] 1 WLR 676.

The parties may need assistance in securing the attendance of the witnesses whom they wish to call at trial. Until the changes made to committal proceedings by the Criminal Procedure and Investigations Act 1996, the long-standing practice was for the examining justices to make a witness order in respect of each witness whose evidence they received. If a witness' evidence could be read at trial, then the defence would agree to a conditional witness order. If the defence were not prepared for this to happen, then they would indicate that there should be a full witness order which, in effect, put the witness on notice of the need to attend the trial. In April 1997, this practice was abolished by the CPIA, s 68 and Sch 2. The position now is that all evidence tendered at committal 'may without further proof be read as evidence on the trial of the accused . . . unless a party to the proceedings objects'. Since only the prosecution can tender evidence at committal, the objection will in practice come from the accused (or one of them). If there is no objection from the defence, the prosecution can decide to call the witness in question, or read his statement. If the defence wishes to object, then it must give written notification to the prosecutor and the Crown Court within 14 days of committal (Magistrates' Courts Rules 1981, r 8, inserted in 1997). The defence objection will not necessarily conclude the matter, as it may be overruled by the trial judge (see Paragraph 18.3.4).

> In addition, a party wishing to secure the attendance of a witness at trial may apply to the Crown Court for a witness summons under s 2 of the Criminal Procedure (Attendance of Witnesses) Act 1965. The Crown Court must be satisfied that the witness is likely to give material evidence, or produce a document or exhibit which is likely to be material evidence; and that he will not do so voluntarily. The application must be made as soon as reasonably practicable after the committal. A witness summons is useful where the prosecution or defence wish to call a witness who was not involved at the committal proceedings. If a witness who is subject to a witness summons fails to attend before the Crown Court when required, the judge can order that a notice be served on him telling him to attend at a time specified in the notice. Alternatively, if a notice has already been served or if there are reasonable grounds for believing that the witness has failed to attend without just excuse, the judge can issue a warrant to arrest him and bring him before the court: s 4(2). He can then be remanded in custody or on bail until he gives his evidence. Failure to obey, without just excuse, a witness order or summons is a contempt of court punishable with up to three months imprisonment: s 3.
>
> The test for a 'just excuse' as laid down by the Court of Appeal in *Abdulaziz* [1989] Crim LR 717 is remarkably strict: only sheer impossibility of attendance seems to constitute a good enough reason.
>
> While the 1965 Act is a useful aid in securing the attendance of reluctant witnesses, it is worth bearing in mind that no legislation can force a witness to give the evidence desired by the party calling him. A reluctant witness may be a difficult witness, who does more harm than good to his side's case.

18.3.3 Additional evidence

A witness may be called for the prosecution at a trial on indictment even though they did not tender his statement or deposition at committal proceedings. The obvious reason for not making use of a witness' evidence at committal proceedings but calling him at the trial is that the prosecution only became aware that the witness could give relevant evidence during the period between committal and the trial's commencement. However, even where the prosecution, at the time of the committal proceedings, know of the evidence the witness is able to give and intend to call him at the Crown Court, they are under no duty to tender his statement before the examining justices: *Epping and Harlow Justices ex p Massaro* [1973] QB 433. In fact, there is little or nothing to be gained by not revealing the evidence at committal proceedings, since the prosecution at the trial on indictment are not allowed to take the defence by surprise with evidence of which they have given no prior warning. The rule is that a notice of intention to call an additional witness, together with a written account of the evidence it is proposed he should give, should be served by the prosecution on both the defence and the court. Usually they serve a copy of a statement signed by the witness and complying with the requirements of the Criminal Justice Act 1967, s 9 (see Paragraph 18.3.4). The advantage of so doing is that, if the defence do not object, the original statement can be tendered in evidence, thus avoiding the need to call the witness.

Where no notice is served, the defence should be granted an adjournment so that they can deal properly with the additional evidence.

18.3.4 Depositions and written statements as evidence

As a general rule a witness, whether for the prosecution or the defence, should give his evidence orally in court. The jury can then see him, hear him and decide how trustworthy he is, and the party against whom he is called can challenge his evidence by cross-examination. This is merely one aspect of the rule against hearsay evidence. In certain exceptional cases, however, a deposition or written statement may be read to the jury as evidence, and there is thus no need to call the maker as a witness. Although these exceptional cases form just some of the many exceptions to the rule against hearsay — and so might be regarded as part of the law of evidence — it is appropriate to describe them here because of their relevance to the question of which witnesses the parties should arrange to have at court. The exceptions are contained in Sch 2 to the Criminal Procedure and Investigations Act 1996, s 43 of the Children and Young Persons Act 1933, s 9 of the Criminal Justice Act 1967, and ss 23 to 28 of the Criminal Justice Act 1988.

(a) The Criminal Procedure and Investigations Act 1996, Sch 2, provides for the statements tendered at committal (see Paragraph 12.4.2) by the prosecution to be read in evidence at the subsequent Crown Court trial. Identical provisions apply to a deposition taken under s 97A of the Magistrates' Courts Act 1980, and tendered in evidence at committal. The defence must give written notification to the prosecutor and the Crown Court within 14 days of committal, stating that there is objection to the statement or objection being read at trial. That does not, however, conclude the matter. The objection of the defence can be overruled by the trial judge. According to para 1(4) of Sch 2 to the CPIA, 'the court of trial may order that the objection shall have no effect if the court considers it to be in the interests of justice so to order'. This power is potentially very important, since if the trial judge overrules the objection then the accused will have no opportunity to cross-examine the witness in question. In the Parliamentary debate on the subject, it was stated by the government that it was anticipated that the courts, in applying the 'interests of justice' test, would turn for guidance to s 26 of the Criminal Justice Act 1988 (Baroness Blatch, *Hansard,* Lords, 26 June 1996, cols 951–952). That section refers to the admissibility of certain hearsay statements under ss 23 and 24 of the CJA 1988 (see (d) below). In considering whether the admission of such a statement would be in the interests of justice, the court must have regard to its contents, the risk of unfairness to the accused resulting from the inability to controvert the statement, and any other circumstances which may appear to be relevant. It is submitted that the Crown Court ought to be extremely wary about overruling the objections of the defence, and thus denying the accused the right to see those who are giving evidence against him, let alone the right to cross-examine them. Any suspicion that objections were overruled for reasons which were less than compelling would be contrary to well-established principle, and would be likely to lead to the prospect of a challenge based upon Article 6(3)(d) of the European Convention on Human Rights (see Chapter 26).

(b) A deposition taken out of court under the Children and Young Persons Act 1933, s 42, from a child or young person who was the victim of one of a list of sexual or violent offences is admissible in evidence at the trial on indictment if the court is satisfied, upon medical evidence, that the attendance of the child or young person before the court would involve serious danger to his life or health (s 43 of the 1933 Act). The deposition is only admissible against the accused if he was given notice of the intention to take it and an opportunity to cross-examine the child or young person. This provision predates, and is additional to, the limited provision for video recordings of the evidence-in-chief of child witnesses (s 32A of the Criminal Justice Act 1988), for the detail of which reference should be made to works on evidence.

(c) The Criminal Justice Act 1967, s 9 provides for the admissibility of written statements in criminal proceedings other than committal proceedings. To be admissible under s 9 the statement must be signed and contain a declaration that it is true to the best of the maker's knowledge and belief etc. The party proposing to tender the statement in evidence must serve a copy of it on each of the other parties. If one of those parties, during the period of seven days from the date of the service of the copy on him, serves notice on the party wishing to use the statement that he objects to it going into evidence, the statement cannot be tendered. Thus, s 9 statements are only admissible if all the parties agree. Even where a statement is admissible under s 9 the court may require that the maker attend to give oral evidence. This would be appropriate where the defence dispute the contents of a s 9 statement but, through inadvertence, failed to serve notice objecting to it being tendered. Section 9 applies both to summary trials and to trials on indictment. At the latter, it is chiefly used where the prosecution wish to adduce evidence additional to that which they used at committal proceedings (see Paragraph 18.3.2).

(d) Sections 23–28 of the Criminal Justice Act 1988 made major inroads into the rule against hearsay in criminal proceedings. In particular, s 23 provides that a statement in a document shall be admissible as evidence of any fact of which the maker of the statement could give direct oral evidence, provided inter alia that the maker is dead or too sick to attend court, or he is outside the UK and cannot be brought back, or he cannot be traced. Admissibility is always subject to the trial judge's discretion and, where the statement was prepared for purposes of a criminal investigation, there is an initial presumption against allowing it in. The details of ss 23 to 28 are beyond the scope of this book; see Seabrooke and Sprack, *Criminal Evidence and Procedure: The Statutory Framework*, Chapter 8.

18.3.5 Defence objections to proposed prosecution evidence

Having read the committal statements, the defence may consider that some of the proposed prosecution evidence is inadmissible. It is a fundamental principle of trials on indictment that questions of law, including the admissibility of evidence, are decided by the judge not the jury. Therefore, the defence will have to ask the judge to exclude the evidence to which they object. Should the objection be upheld, it would obviously be prejudicial for the jury to hear reference to the inadmissible material. The procedure described below is designed to prevent that occurring.

Before the start of the trial, defence counsel should warn his opponent that he intends to object to certain evidence. In his opening speech counsel therefore refrains from mentioning that evidence. He then calls his remaining evidence in the normal way up to the point when the disputed material would otherwise be introduced. Then one or other counsel (probably defence) invites the judge to ask the jury to leave court, perhaps saying that a point of law has arisen which only concerns the lawyers. Once the jury have retired to their room, defence counsel makes his objection to the evidence; prosecuting counsel replies, and the judge makes his ruling. If the evidence is inadmissible, the jury hear nothing about it; if it is admissible, it is called immediately upon their returning to court; in either event, they are told nothing of what occurred in their absence. The above procedure is all that is needed where the admissibility of the evidence can be decided solely by reference to the relevant law and the evidence itself as foreshadowed in the committal statements. Sometimes, however, admissibility depends upon the circumstances in which the evidence was obtained, and those circumstances may themselves be in dispute. It is then for the judge to decide (i) the factual question of how the prosecution got the evidence, and (ii) the legal question of whether, in the light of his findings of fact, the evidence is admissible. In such cases, there has to be a *trial on the 'voir dire'*. By far the commonest example of this occurring is where the defence represent that a confession should be excluded under s 76 and/or s 78 of the Police and Criminal Evidence Act 1984. It will therefore be convenient to describe 'voir dires' through the illustration of challenges to confessions, although such challenges are not the only possible reason for adopting the procedure.

Up to the jury leaving court, the procedure is as for any other dispute on evidence — i.e. prosecuting counsel does not refer to the confession in his opening speech; the case proceeds as normal until the police officer to whom the confession was made is about to testify about it, and the jury are then sent out. Next, the officer gives evidence before the judge as to the making of the confession. He will probably say that he and a fellow officer interviewed the accused at the police station; that a contemporaneous note was taken of what was said, and that, at the end, the accused read through and signed the note. The signed note, containing damaging admissions, is then produced before the judge. Defence counsel may then cross-examine the officer. Typically it will be suggested that threats were made in order to induce the confession; or bail was promised; or the accused was held for an unacceptably long period without access to a solicitor or proper rest, refreshment, etc. The second officer who was present at the interview (and any other prosecution witnesses who can give relevant evidence) may then be called and cross-examined. After that, the accused himself is at liberty to testify and may also call witnesses (e.g. a doctor who examined him immediately after his release from the police station and saw bruises consistent with his claim that he was beaten up by the police). All these witnesses give their testimony on a special form of oath, known as the 'voir dire', the wording of which is — 'I swear by almighty God that I will true answer make to all such questions as the court shall demand of me'. The questions they are asked on the voir dire, whether in chief or cross-examination, must relate only to the admissibility or otherwise of the confession. At common law the accused could not even be asked if the confession was true (see *Wong Kam-Ming v R* [1980] AC 247). The same rule applies under s 76 of PACE, since — unless the prosecution prove that the confession was not obtained in contravention of the section — it must be excluded 'notwithstanding that it may be true' (see s 76(2)(b)). Once the evidence on the voir dire has been given, the judge listens to counsel's submissions and announces his decision, both as to the facts and their legal consequences. If the confession is held inadmissible, the jury, of course, hear nothing of it. If it is admissible, the self-same evidence and cross-examination as was advanced on the voir dire may be advanced again before the jury as part of the general prosecution and defence cases. At this stage, however, the evidence goes merely to the weight that the jury should attach to the confession, not to the question of admissibility. Should the accused choose to testify before the jury, he cannot be asked about anything he said on the voir dire, save that if he gives evidence as to how he came to confess which is inconsistent with the explanation he gave at the voir dire stage, he can be cross examined about the discrepancy (see *Wong Kam-Ming v R* supra). For obvious reasons, the above procedure is colloquially known as a 'trial within a trial'.

As already stated, trials within a trial are not by law restricted to confession cases. However, they should only be held if the decision on admissibility of evidence genuinely cannot be reached without making prior determinations of fact. Outside of inadmissible confessions, it will nearly always be possible for the judge to make his ruling simply on the basis of the committal statements without hearing evidence. Thus in *Flemming* (1987) 86 Cr App R 32 the Court of Appeal upheld the judge's decision to admit identification evidence despite a defence contention that its quality was so poor that its prejudicial effect would exceed its probative value, but criticised him for holding a full trial within a trial. The relevant considerations (i.e., the circumstances of the identification and alleged breach of the rules on holding identification parades) emerged perfectly well from the committal statements. On the other hand, the trial within a trial procedure has been commended by the Court of Appeal to judges deciding upon the admissibility of a computer printout (*Minors* [1989] 1 WLR 441).

The voir dire procedure is intended for the benefit of the defence. It follows that they should not be forced to adopt it against their will. The disadvantage that some defence advocates perceive in having a trial within a trial is that the prosecution witnesses dealing with the obtaining of the allegedly inadmissible evidence are alerted to the defence line of attack. Should the judge rule that the evidence is admissible, the witnesses will be able to counter the defence cross-examination before the jury more effectively than if they had not had, so to speak, a 'dry run' on the voir dire. Lord Bridge, giving the judgment of the Privy Council in *Ajodha v The State* [1982] AC 204, said *obiter* that, at the 'vast majority' of trials where the admissibility of a confession is to be challenged, the procedure already described will be adopted. But, as an alternative, it is open to defence counsel merely to impugn the confession before the jury during the ordinary course of cross-examination of prosecution witnesses and calling of defence evidence. At the end of the evidence, he may then ask the judge to rule the confession inadmissible as a matter of law. If the judge agrees, he will tell the jury in his summing-up to ignore the confession completely or, if there is no case to answer without it, direct them to acquit the accused. In *Airey* [1985] Crim LR 305, the Court of Appeal quashed A's conviction because the judge had not allowed the defence to follow such a course. In *Sat-Bhambra* (1988) 88 Cr App R 55, however, the Court of Appeal held that the defence could not seek a retrospective ruling on the admissibility of a confession on the basis of s 76 of PACE because of the wording of that section. It refers to a decision about evidence which has not yet been put before the court, using the formulae 'proposes to be given in evidence' and 'shall not allow the confession to be given'. The same logic would seem to apply to an objection based on s 78 of PACE, which also applies where 'the prosecution proposes to rely on evidence'. There remains a common law discretion for the judge to exclude evidence (preserved by s 82(3) of PACE), which can be exercised after a confession has been admitted in evidence (see for details, *Blackstone's Criminal Practice*, F17.14 and F17.25).

In any event, it is clear that the Court still regards a hearing on the voir dire as the normal and preferred way of dealing with objections to confessions, and their Lordships have held that — where the alternative procedure is adopted — the defence cannot ask the judge to consider the confession's admissibility at the end of the prosecution evidence but must wait until the end of *all* the evidence: *Jackson* [1985] Crim LR 444. This means that defence counsel is forced to take the vital decision on whether to call his client without knowing whether the jury will be told to ignore the confession completely or merely told to give it such weight as they think proper. It should also be noted that the judge is given a discretion by s 76(3) of PACE to raise the issue of a confession's admissibility on his own initiative, in which event a trial within a trial would presumably be held whether defence counsel wanted it or not.

According to *Hendry* (1988) 88 Cr App R 187 the judge has the power to ask the jury to retire during submissions on the admissibility of evidence, even if that is against the wishes of the defence.

A further variation on the standard procedure for objecting to evidence is that the judge can be asked to deal with the question as a preliminary issue immediately after the jury has been empanelled. This is an appropriate course to adopt when the prosecution case depends very largely on the challenged evidence, and counsel could not sensibly open his case to the jury without referring to it (see *Hammond* [1941] 3 All ER 318). If the judge rules the evidence inadmissible, counsel will probably offer no evidence; if it is admissible, counsel's potential problem with his opening speech is overcome.

18.3.6 Limits set on defence cross-examination

In general, defence counsel may ask a prosecution witness any question in cross-examination provided it is relevant, and provided the answer will not involve inadmissible material such as hearsay or non-expert opinion. A question is relevant if it concerns an issue in the case, i.e., it relates directly to whether the accused committed the offence, or it relates to a fact which increases or decreases the likelihood of his having done so. A question is also relevant if it concerns the credit of the witness, i.e., it relates to a fact from which the jury may conclude that he is not the sort of person who can be trusted to speak the truth. Thus, counsel is free, to a large extent, to cross-examine on whatever he thinks will assist his client's case. This freedom is limited by the Bar's Code of Conduct, with which barristers have a duty to comply. The following extracts from annexe F of the Code are particularly relevant (references in parentheses are to paragraphs of the annexe):

(a)   Counsel must at all times promote and protect fearlessly and by all proper and lawful means his lay client's best interests (para 5.1);

(b)   he must not make statements or ask questions which are merely scandalous, or intended or calculated only to vilify, insult or annoy the witness or some other person (para 5.10(e));

(c)   he must not in a speech impugn a witness whom he has had an opportunity to cross-examine, unless in cross-examination he gave the witness an opportunity to answer the allegation (para 5.10(g));

(d)   he must not suggest that a victim, witness or other person is guilty of crime, fraud or misconduct, or attribute to another person the crime with which his client is charged, unless such allegations go to a matter in issue (including credibility of the witness) material to his client's case, and appear to him to be supported by reasonable grounds (para 5.10(h)).

The above rules also apply where appropriate to prosecution cross-examination of defence witnesses.

18.3.7 Formal admissions

Reading a witness' deposition or written statement (see Paragraph 18.3.4) is a convenient method of proving facts which are not in dispute. Another way of proving an undisputed fact is for the party against whom evidence of the fact would otherwise be led, to admit formally that it is true. The formal admission is conclusive evidence of the fact admitted, so no evidence on the matter need be adduced. The Criminal Justice Act 1967, s 10 which applies both to summary trials and to trials on indictment, governs the making of formal admissions.

Section 10 provides that any fact of which oral evidence may be given in criminal proceedings may be formally admitted, for purposes of those proceedings, by either the prosecution or defence. The admission may be made at or before trial. Unless made in court (e.g., at the trial or at a pre-trial review), it must be in writing and signed. An admission by the defence must be made by the accused personally or by counsel or solicitor on his behalf. If the admission is made by the accused personally before trial, it must be approved by counsel or solicitor on his behalf either at the time it is made or subsequently. The admission only binds the party making it in the criminal proceedings for purposes of which it was made and in any subsequent criminal proceedings, such as a retrial or appeal, arising out of the original proceedings. Thus, if the defence at a trial on indictment for dangerous driving formally admit that on 1 January 1999 the accused was driving car number ABC 123 in Acacia Avenue, they cannot deny that fact either at the trial or on an appeal to the Court of Appeal against conviction, but if the accused is subsequently prosecuted for driving while disqualified on the same occasion or is sued in civil proceedings based on the alleged dangerous driving, he is free to deny that he was driving the car. The formal admission in the dangerous driving proceedings might be used as evidence against him in the other proceedings, but it would not be conclusive evidence. Even in the proceedings for purposes of which it was made a formal admission can be withdrawn with leave of the court: s 10(4).

Where an admission is made by counsel in argument in court but in the absence of the jury, it may be treated as an admission in terms of s 10 of the Criminal Justice Act 1967, even though it was not intended as such (*Lewis* [1989] Crim LR 61). Counsel therefore needs to be careful not to make unguarded statements during the course of an argument before the judge.

A formal admission by the defence under s 10 must not be confused with a confession by the accused in which he informally admits to the police or some other person that he committed the crime (or admits a fact which makes it more likely he committed the crime). Provided it was not obtained by oppression or as a result of words or conduct likely to render it unreliable, a confession is admissible evidence to prove the facts stated in it. Often it is very powerful evidence, but it is not conclusive evidence of the facts admitted as a formal admission is. The defence may, and often do, agree that the accused made a confession, but deny the truth of the facts confessed; if they have made a formal admission they cannot deny the fact admitted, unless the court gives leave for the admission to be withdrawn. Also, whereas a formal admission made out of court must be in writing and approved by counsel or solicitor, neither of these two conditions apply to confessions — indeed, it is hard to imagine defence counsel ever approving a confession if he could block its admissibility by withholding approval.

18.4   SUBMISSION OF NO CASE TO ANSWER

After the prosecution evidence, oral and written, has been adduced, prosecuting counsel closes his case by saying 'that is the case for the prosecution', or words to that effect. Defence counsel may then, if he so wishes, submit that there is no case to answer (see Paragraphs 9.7.3 and 12.2.3 for the equivalent submissions in summary trials and committal proceedings, respectively). If the accused is unrepresented, or even if he is but counsel apparently is not going to make a submission when one is called for, the judge can raise the matter on his own initiative. The submission may be made on all or any of the counts, or on behalf of all or any of the accused joined in the indictment. If a submission on a count succeeds the judge directs the jury to acquit on that count the accused on whose behalf the submission was made.

There is no case to answer if the prosecution have failed to adduce evidence on which a jury, properly directed by the judge in his summing-up, could properly convict: *Galbraith* [1981] 1 WLR 1039. If there is literally no evidence relating to an essential element of the offence (e.g., because a prosecution witness has failed to give the evidence expected of him), a submission of no case must clearly succeed. A submission should also succeed if the prosecution rely on circumstantial evidence to establish an element of the offence, but the inferences they ask the jury to draw from the evidence cannot reasonably be drawn. Thus, on a charge of handling stolen goods, the judge could rule no case to answer if the only evidence of guilty knowledge is that the accused bought the goods at an under-value, but the difference between the price he paid and the true value was too small to put the accused on suspicion that the goods might be stolen.

Difficult problems arise where there is some evidence that the accused committed the offence but, for one reason or another, it seems unconvincing. The basic principle is that the jury should decide whether witnesses are telling the truth or not, and the judge should not usurp their function by directing them to acquit merely because he thinks the prosecution witnesses are lying. As it was put in *Galbraith* [1981] 1 WLR 1039 (at p. 1042):

> How then should the judge approach a submission of 'no case?' (1) If there is no evidence that the crime alleged has been committed by the defendant, there is no difficulty. The judge will of course stop the case. (2) The difficulty arises where there is some evidence but it is of a tenuous character, for example because of inherent weakness or vagueness or because it is inconsistent with other evidence. (a) Where the judge comes to the conclusion that the prosecution evidence, taken at its highest, is such that a jury properly directed could not properly convict upon it, it is his duty, upon a submission being made, to stop the case. (b) Where however the prosecution evidence is such that its strength or weakness depends on the view to be taken of a witness's reliability, or other matters which are generally speaking within the province of the jury and where on one possible view of the facts there *is* evidence upon which a jury could properly come to the conclusion that the defendant is guilty, then the judge should allow the matter to be tried by the jury.

There is some room for interpretation of the judge's role as set out in *Galbraith*, however. In two more recent cases, the Court of Appeal has indicated that a judge must ensure that the case should not go to the jury if it would be unsafe to convict. In *Brown* [1998] Crim LR 196 Rose LJ said:

> It seems to us that, throughout a trial, the judge has a responsibility not to allow a jury to consider evidence on which they could not safely convict. . . . If, at the conclusion of all the evidence, a trial judge is of the view that no reasonable jury, properly directed, could safely convict, he should, generally speaking, whether a submission of no case has been made at the conclusion of the prosecution case or not, raise that view for discussion with counsel, in the absence of the jury. If, having heard submissions, he remains of that view, then he should, in our judgment, withdraw the case from the jury . . .

In *Shire* [2001] EWCA Crim 2800, the accused was charged with causing death by dangerous driving. The Court of Appeal considered the evidence of a group of his friends who appeared, according to impartial observers to be 'in high spirits' at the time of the accident, and may have been trying to get the accused's bus to stop so they could board it. There were inconsistencies in their statements, which were at odds in important respects with those of the impartial observers. Nevertheless, it could be said on one possible view of the facts' (to quote *Galbraith*) that a jury could have concluded that the accused was guilty. The Court of Appeal, however, did not seem to think that the jury could have done so 'properly', and stated that:

The inherent risk of unreliability of the evidence given by that group was such that when considered in the light of the discrepancies in the evidence, it would be necessary, before leaving it to the jury, to have some evidence independent of that evidence which could justify the jury concluding that it could be reliable evidence.

To put it another way, as Turner J did at first instance in *Shippey* [1988] Crim LR 767, the obligation to 'take the prosecution case at its highest' does not require a trial judge to 'take out the plums, leaving the duff behind'.

The procedure for a submission of no case is that the jury are asked to leave court. This is so that counsel and the judge can comment freely upon the quality and significance of the evidence without the risk of the jury being influenced by what is said. Once the jury hav gone, defence counsel makes his submission, and prosecuting counsel is given an opportunity to reply. The judge then announces his decision, and the jury are brought back into court. If the judge has decided that there is no case to answer on all counts, he explains briefly to the jury the decision he has reached. He then asks them to appoint a foreman to speak for them, and the clerk of court takes from the foreman on each count a verdict of not guilty upon the judge's direction. If the decision was that there is no case to answer on one or more counts, but there is a case to answer on other counts, the judge tells the jury that at the end of the trial he will be directing them to return a verdict of not guilty on the counts in respect of which there is no case, and so, for the remainder of the trial, they should ignore those counts. However, on the remaining counts, the case will proceed as normal. If the submission failed on all counts, the jury are told nothing of what went on in their absence.

The judge's power to direct an acquittal after a submission of no case to answer is an important one. According to statistics in the Crown Prosecution Service Report for 1998/9, 21.2 per cent of all acquittals in the Crown Court were directed by the judge at the close of the prosecution case.

In one important type of case the correct approach to submissions of no case has been explained by the Court of Appeal with some precision. Where the main issue in the case is one of mistaken identity (i.e. the case against the accused depends substantially on the correctness of one or more identifications of him which the defence allege to be mistaken), the judge should assess the quality of the identifying evidence. If it is poor, and if there is no other evidence to support the correctness of the identification, the judge should withdraw the case from the jury: *Turnbull* [1977] QB 224. Identification evidence is poor if the witnesses only saw whoever committed the offence for a short space of time, or saw him in circumstances of fear or confusion, or if the lighting conditions were bad, or if a long time elapsed between seeing the culprit and picking out the accused at an identification parade. The detailed guidance given to judges on how they should decide submissions of no case in identification cases is necessary because judicial experience has shown mistaken identifications by honest witnesses to be a prime factor in wrongful convictions.

For similar reasons, special guidance was laid down in *MacKenzie* (1992) 96 Cr App R 98, for a trial judge who is considering a submission of no case to answer in certain cases depending on a confession by the accused. The judge should withdraw the case from the jury if all the following conditions apply:

(a)   the prosecution case depended wholly upon confessions;
(b)   the defendant suffered from a significant degree of mental handicap; and
(c)   the confessions were unconvincing to a point where a jury properly directed could not properly convict upon them.

Confessions might be unconvincing, for example, because they lacked the incriminating details to be expected of a guilty and willing confessor, because they were inconsistent with other evidence, or because they were otherwise inherently improbable.

18.5 THE DEFENCE CASE

Assuming there is a prosecution case to answer, the next stage of the trial is for the defence to present their case. Since it is for the prosecution to prove each element of the offence charged beyond reasonable doubt, the defence are under no obligation to adduce any evidence whatsoever. Defence counsel can, without calling evidence of his own, submit to the jury in a closing speech that the accused should be acquitted as the prosecution evidence fails to establish their case to the requisite standard of proof. Such a strategy may be right when the prosecution's case is weak, but in general there are obvious dangers in the jury only hearing evidence favouring the prosecution. It is therefore unusual for the defence not to call evidence.

18.5.1 Defence opening speech

If defence counsel is calling evidence as to the facts of the case other than or in addition to the evidence of the accused, he has the right to make an opening speech to the jury. In that speech he may both outline his own case and criticise the evidence which has been called by the prosecution. Where the only defence evidence is from the accused, or from the accused and witnesses who speak only as to his good character, defence counsel does not have an opening speech: Criminal Evidence Act 1898, s 2.

18.5.2 Defence evidence

The accused is a competent but not compellable witness for the defence (Criminal Evidence Act 1898, s 1) — i.e., he is entitled but cannot be forced to give evidence. Irrespective of whether he goes into the witness-box, other persons may be called for the defence, and may testify about the factual issues in dispute or the character of the accused or both. The defence may also take advantage of the various statutory provisions permitting the reading of depositions and written statements (see Paragraph 18.3.4). Where defence witnesses are to be called in addition to the accused, the latter should normally be called first. This is partly because the accused is the person best able to tell the jury what the defence case is, and partly because he is allowed to be in court throughout the trial and so, if permitted to testify after his witnesses, would be able to tailor his evidence to fit in with what he has heard them say. Witnesses other than the accused, whether called for the prosecution or defence, are kept out of court until after they have testified. The judge does, however, have a discretion to let a defence witness be called before the accused: Police and Criminal Evidence Act 1984, s 79. It might be appropriate to exercise that discretion if, for example, the witness has a pressing engagement elsewhere and his evidence is unlikely to be challenged by the prosecution.

Details about the accused as a witness must be sought in the books on evidence. Very briefly, the position is that he is treated like any other witness except that:

(a) He can be asked questions which tend to incriminate him as to the offence charged, and to that extent cannot, as witnesses normally can, claim a privilege against self-incrimination: Criminal Evidence Act 1898, s 1(e). It would obviously be absurd if the accused could give evidence exonerating himself and then avoid any questions in cross-examination which might tend to show him guilty.

(b) Again unlike other witnesses, he is protected from questions in cross-examination designed to discredit him by showing that he has previous convictions or is of bad character.

He loses this protection if his defence has cast imputations on the character of a prosecution witness, or if he has given evidence of his own good character, or he gives evidence against another accused joined in the same indictment: Criminal Evidence Act 1898, s 1(f).

Nothing should be said or done to suggest to the jury that the accused, as a witness, is inferior to the other witnesses in the case. This is illustrated in a symbolic way by the fact that in the absence of compelling reasons to the contrary (e.g., the risk of violence or attempted escape), the accused should testify from the witness box not the dock (Criminal Evidence Act 1898, s 1(g) and see *Farnham Justices ex p Gibson* [1991] Crim LR 642). However, being treated essentially like the other witnesses is often a dubious advantage for the accused, as he is exposed to cross-examination by prosecuting counsel. This is particularly damaging where he is of bad character, but has lost the protection against questions about previous convictions etc. mentioned above. Until fairly recently the accused could avoid the risks inherent in cross-examination, but still tell the jury his side of the story, by making an unsworn statement while standing in the dock. He was not then subject to questioning either by his own counsel, or prosecuting counsel or anybody else. However, the right to make an unsworn statement was abolished by s 72 of the Criminal Justice Act 1982. Thus, the accused now faces a stark choice between saying nothing — which the jury will probably find suspicious — and giving evidence on oath which, of course, will be subject to cross-examination. The decision must be his. As the Bar's Code of Conduct puts it (annexe F, para 12.4):

A barrister acting for a defendant should advise his client as to whether or not to give evidence in his own defence but the decision must be taken by the client himself.

Should the decision be against going into the box, defence counsel should always record the decision and ensure that the defendant signs the record, indicating (a) that he has decided of his own accord not to give evidence and (b) that he has so decided bearing in mind the advice (regardless of what it was) given by counsel (*Bevan* (1994) 98 Cr App R 354). The usual way in which this is done is for the record to be endorsed in a note on counsel's brief.

18.5.3 Disclosure and alibi evidence

As part of their duty of disclosure (see Paragraph 8.3), the defence should have served the prosecution and the court, prior to trial, with a statement setting out the general terms of the defence, the matters on which they take issue with the prosecution case and the reasons why (Criminal Procedure and Investigations Act 1996, s 5(6)). In addition, they should have given certain particulars if the defence involves an alibi, i.e., the name and address, or other information to aid tracing, of any witness who is able to give evidence in support of alibi (s 5(7)).

The general consequences which flow from the service (or non-service) of a defence statement are dealt with in Paragraph 8.3. These consequences apply equally to a defence statement which raises alibi. The peculiar feature of alibi as a defence, however, is that it requires the accused to provide details of prospective witnesses. The definition of 'alibi' contained in s 5(8) is therefore important; 'alibi' means evidence 'tending to show that by reason of the presence of the (accused) at a particular place . . . at a particular time he was not . . . at the place where the offence is alleged to have been committed' at the relevant time. Evidence which merely indicates that the accused was not present as the place where the offence was committed is not 'evidence in support of an alibi'. To be caught by the definition in s 5(8), the evidence must be evidence that the accused was at some other place (*Johnson* [1995] 2 Cr App R 41).

The cases about alibi pre-date the CPIA, and relate to the previous, much more limited, duty of disclosure on the defence. This was imposed by the Criminal Justice Act 1967, s 11 and dealt with evidence of alibi alone. The case law on that section will remain relevant when the court decides whether to draw inferences from defence disclosure which is arguably incomplete, i.e., the prosecution is arguing that if the disclosure relates to alibi evidence, then details of the witnesses should have been disclosed.

The question of whether the defence raised was one of alibi arose, for example, in *Lewis* [1969] 2 QB 1, where the prosecution sought to support their allegation that L had dishonestly handled stolen postal orders on 14 February 1968 by evidence of L's cashing two of them on 16 February, L was under no duty to give notice of evidence he intended to call as to his whereabouts on 16 February. The offence was allegedly committed on the 14th, so evidence about the 16th could not come within the statutory definition of alibi. Further, it was stated in *Hassan* [1970] 1 QB 423 that the section appears 'to envisage an offence which necessarily involves the accused being at a particular place at a particular time'. Therefore, H, who was charged with living on the earnings of prostitution between 29 July and 21 August 1968 in Cardiff, did not have to give notice that on the morning of 20 August, he was at his brother's house, rather than being, as the prosecution alleged, at the prostitute's flat. The crime charged was 'anchored to no particular location', and so the statutory duty did not apply.

A somewhat more liberal interpretation was employed in *Fields* (1990) 155 JP 396, however (see the smaller print below for the facts).

Although defence counsel has general authority to make tactical decisions about the way a case should be run and need not obtain his client's express approval at every point, any decision not to call alibi evidence is so fundamental that it should not be taken unless there has been prior consultation at which the accused agrees (preferably in writing) that the alibi should not after all be advanced. Thus, in *Irwin* [1987] 1 WLR 902 counsel's conduct in taking a spot decision while the appellant was in the witness box not to call his wife and daughter in support of his alibi amounted to a material irregularity in the course of the trial that necessitated the quashing of the conviction. Although *Irwin* was said in *Ensor* [1989] 1 WLR 497 to be 'regarded as being confined to its own facts', it is submitted that it remains good authority in relation to a decision by counsel, without consultation, not to call an alibi witness (see further Paragraph 24.4.1).

In *Fields* (1991) 155 JP 396, F was charged, together with A, with robbery. They were identified by S, who lived near the scene of the crime. On the afternoon of the robbery, she waited for 10 minutes between 2.45 and 3.30 p.m. outside a telephone kiosk, which was occupied by a man whom she later identified in a parade as F. S returned to the kiosk at about 6 p.m. and, whilst waiting to use the kiosk again, witnessed the robbery by two men, now masked, whom she later identified in parades as A and F. In a letter from F's solicitor, it was claimed that F was in Durham (25 miles away from the scene of the crime) at around 3 p.m. and hence could not have been observed by S in the telephone kiosk. The Crown successfully sought to admit this letter at trial as a notice of alibi. On appeal F claimed that admitting the letter in evidence for the prosecution prejudiced him by forcing him to testify so as to support his alibi. He argued that the letter should not have been admitted because it was not a notice of alibi. The Court of Appeal dismissed the appeal. S's evidence on the committal papers was that the man whom she saw in the kiosk at about 3 p.m. was the same man whom she later saw taking part in the robbery. The alibi evidence would tend to show that F could not have been at the scene of the robbery when it took place. Hence the letter was a notice of alibi. It was therefore deemed to have been given with F's authority unless he proved the contrary. This flowed from s 11(5) of the Criminal Justice Act 1967 (now repealed). It is doubtful whether the same result would follow under the Criminal Procedure and Investigations Act 1996 (see Paragraph 8.3).

18.5.4 Expert evidence

The requirement to reveal to the prosecution, in advance of trial, any expert evidence which the defence propose to adduce was introduced by the Crown Court (Advance Notice of Expert Evidence) Rules (SI 1987 No 716).

In brief, the rules state that, unless he has already done so, a party to a trial on indictment who proposes to adduce expert evidence shall, as soon as possible after committal, provide the other parties with a written statement setting out his expert's finding or opinion. If the expert bases his view upon some experiment, observation, calculation or other procedure that he has carried out, the other parties are also entitled, on request, to a record of or opportunity to examine the experiment, etc. Exemption from the requirements of the rules may be sought on the ground that compliance might lead to intimidation of the expert or other interference with the course of justice. Assuming no exemption has been granted, non-compliance will mean that the expert evidence can only be adduced with leave of the court.

The sanction is therefore different in kind from that imposed in other cases of incomplete defence disclosure (see Paragraph 8.3). It applies to the prosecution also, although it is to be expected that any expert evidence for the prosecution will in any event be served at committal or thereafter by way of a notice of additional evidence.

18.5.5 More than one accused in the indictment

If two or more accused are charged in one indictment and are separately represented their cases are presented in the order in which their names appear on the indictment. Thus, if Robert Smith precedes John Brown on the indictment, counsel for Smith makes his opening speech (if he has the right to one), then calls Smith and his other witnesses. Counsel for Brown may question each witness after his evidence in chief and before cross-examination by the prosecution. Then Brown's counsel opens his case, and so forth. There is little authority on who should be named first on an indictment. It may seem strange that the order of the defence cases depends on how prosecuting counsel or an officer of the Crown Court chooses to draft the indictment.

Where two of more accused are jointly represented they are treated as, in effect, presenting a joint defence. Counsel has one opening speech on behalf of both accused, and may then call them in turn to give evidence.

18.5.6 The unrepresented accused

Although an accused at the Crown Court is encouraged to obtain legal representation, he is entitled to conduct his own defence throughout, or, indeed, to start with the benefit of legal representation and dismiss his counsel at any stage of the trial (subject to the limitation dealt with below). The judge should assist an unrepresented accused in matters such as the cross-examination of the prosecution witnesses, the giving of his own evidence, and the examination in chief of any witnesses he may choose to call. Often a judge has to explain to the accused that when he cross-examines a witness he must ask questions rather than make a speech of his own disagreeing with what the witness has said. It is particularly important that at the close of the prosecution case the accused should be told that he may give evidence himself and/or call other witnesses. The judge's failure to ask the accused if he wishes to call evidence in his defence may lead to any conviction being quashed: *Carter* (1960) 44 Cr App R 225.

The Youth Justice and Criminal Evidence Act 1999 restricts the right of the unrepresented defendant to cross-examine certain witnesses. These provisions came into force on 1 April 2000. The 1999 Act lays down that:

(a)   A defendant charged with rape or other specified sexual offences who chooses to conduct his own defence may not himself cross-examine the alleged victim of the offence. This prohibition also extends to any other offence with which the defendant is charged in the proceedings.

(b)   A defendant who is charged with an offence of violence, a specified sexual offence, kidnapping, false imprisonment or abduction may not cross-examine a child who is an alleged victim or witness to the commission of the offence.

(c)   The court is given power to prohibit unrepresented defendants from cross-examining witnesses in cases not covered by the specific prohibitions laid down in (a) and (b) if it is satisfied that the circumstances of the witness and the case merit it and that a prohibition would not be contrary to the interests of justice.

(d)   Where the accused is barred from cross-examining a witness, a representative can be appointed by him to carry out that cross-examination.

(e)   If he does not appoint a legal representative to carry out the cross-examination, the court has to consider whether it is necessary, in the interests of justice, for the witness's evidence to be tested. If it decides that it is, it will appoint a legal representative to cross-examine the witness. That representative will not, however, be instructed by the defendant, and will not be responsible to him.

18.5.7   Presence of the accused

The accused must be present at the start of a trial on indictment in order to plead. If he is not, the judge will adjourn and, unless there is some good reason for the absence such as sickness, issue a bench warrant for the accused's arrest under s 7 of the Bail Act 1976.

Having attended for the arraignment, the general rule is that the accused should be present throughout the trial. It is obviously fair that he should hear what the prosecution and their witnesses have to say against him so as to be in a position to answer their allegations. Should he, at any stage of the trial, fail or be unable to appear in court the judge will normally have to adjourn the case and, depending on the circumstances, issue a warrant for arrest. If his absence looks like being prolonged (e.g., he has contracted an illness which will last several days) the judge will consider discharging the jury from giving a verdict. The case will then re-commence before a different jury once the accused is able to attend. The principle that the accused should be present during his trial demands that he should be able to understand proceedings. It follows that the failure to ensure that an interpreter translates the evidence constitutes a substantial miscarriage of justice: *Kunnath v The State* [1993] 1 WLR 1315.

There are, however, two main situations in which the judge has a discretion to allow the trial to proceed in the accused's absence. The first is when he shouts, misbehaves or otherwise makes such a nuisance of himself that it is impracticable to continue with him present (per Lord Reading CJ in *Lee Kung* [1916] 1 KB 337). The second is if he voluntarily absents himself. In *Hayward* [2001] 3 WLR 125, the Court of Appeal considered the principles which the trial judge ought to apply when dealing with an absent defendant, and summarised them as follows:

(a) A defendant has, in general, a right to be present at his trial and a right to be legally represented.

(b) Those rights can be waived, separately or together, wholly or in part, by the defendant himself:

(i) They may be wholly waived if, knowing or having the means of knowledge as to when and where his trial is to take place, he deliberately and voluntarily absents himself and/or withdraws instructions from those representing him.

(ii) They maybe waived in part if, being present and represented at the outset, the defendant, during the course of the trial, behaves in such a way as to obstruct the proper course of the proceedings and/or withdraws his instructions from those representing him.

(c) The trial judge has a discretion as to whether a trial should take place or continue in the absence of a defendant and/or his legal representatives.

(d) That discretion must be exercised with great care and it is only in rare and exceptional cases that it should be exercised in favour of a trial taking place or continuing, particularly if the defendant is unrepresented.

(e) In exercising that discretion, fairness to the defence is of prime importance but fairness to the prosecution must also be taken into account. The judge must have regard to all the circumstances of the case including, in particular:

(i) the nature and circumstances of the behaviour in absenting himself from the trial or disrupting it, as the case may be and, in particular, whether his behaviour was deliberate, voluntary and such as plainly waived his right to appear;

(ii) whether an adjournment might result in the defendant being caught or attending voluntarily and/or not disrupting the proceedings;

(iii) the likely length of such an adjournment;

(iv) whether the defendant, though absent, is, or wishes to be, legally represented at the trial or has, by his conduct, waived his right to representation;

(v) whether an absent defendant's legal representatives are able to receive instructions from him during the trial and the extent to which they are able to present his defence;

(vi) the extent of the disadvantage to the defendant in not being able to give his account of events, having regard to the nature of the evidence against him;

(vii) the risk of the jury reaching an improper conclusion about the absence of the defendant;

(viii) the seriousness of the offence, which affects defendant, victim and public;

(ix) the general public interest and the particular interest of victims and witnesses that a trial should take place within a reasonable time of the events to which it relates;

(x) the effect of delay on the memories of witnesses;

(xi) where there is more than one defendant and not all have absconded, the undesirability of separate trials, and the prospects of a fair trial for the defendants who are present.

(f)   If the judge decides that a trial should take place or continue in the absence of an unrepresented defendant, he must ensure that the trial is as fair as the circumstances permit. He must, in particular, take reasonable steps, both during the giving of evidence and in the summing up, to expose weaknesses in the prosecution case and to make such points on behalf of the defendant as the evidence permits. In summing up he must warn the jury that absence is not an admission of guilt and adds nothing to the prosecution case.

The overall effect is to underline the need for caution before proceeding with the trial when the defendant is absent. In view of the need to ensure compliance with Art 6 of the European Convention on Human Rights, that caution is entirely proper. It is also right that the focus in determining whether to proceed should be upon the defendant's right to attend the trial and be represented at it. The notion of participation in the criminal proceedings is crucial not only from the perspective of the defendant, but also in ensuring the legitimacy of the system. It is submitted that the court ought to be particularly cautious in concluding that the defendant has waived his rights. There is considerable merit in the suggestion made by counsel for the appellant in *Hayward* that such waiver should be established to the criminal standard. Although that point was not expressly adopted by their lordships, it is submitted that it is in accordance with the spirit of the guidelines set out in the case.

18.6   COUNSEL'S CLOSING SPEECHES

After the close of the defence case (or the last of the defence cases where there are more than one accused separately represented) prosecuting counsel may sum up his case to the jury. In doing so he should continue to regard himself as a 'minister of justice', not an advocate striving at all costs for a conviction. In his speech he can for example remind the jury of the most cogent parts of the prosecution evidence, and comment upon any implausibilities in the defence case. The only situation where the prosecution does not have the right to a closing speech is where an accused is unrepresented and did not call evidence as to the facts other than his own. It does not follow, however, that whenever counsel has the right to a speech he should necessarily make one. If the defence are represented but choose not to call evidence, prosecuting counsel is still entitled to a closing speech but may well consider that he need not make one: *Bryant* [1979] QB 108. In that case it was further said by Watkin J that 'the majority of speeches by prosecuting and defence counsel should bear the becoming hallmark of brevity' — advice which perhaps is not followed on all occasions.

The last word, in a criminal trial, leaving aside the judge's summing-up, belongs to the defence. After the prosecution closing speech, defence counsel sums up his case to the jury. He has a broad discretion to say anything he considers desirable on the whole case, but he should not allege as fact matters of which no evidence has been given. As it was put in *Bateson* (1991) *The Times*, 10 April 1991, he should not 'conjure explanations out of the air', but he is entitled to suggest, for example, that there might be an innocent explanation for his client's lies, if there was evidence in the case on which to base such an explanation. The rule applies equally to prosecuting counsel, but defence counsel may be more tempted to transgress it. If there are two or more accused separately represented the speeches on their behalves are given in the order in which their names appear on the indictment. An unrepresented accused can, of course, make both a closing and, if he is entitled to one, an opening speech on his own behalf.

18.7 JURY STOPPING THE CASE

Paragraph 18.4 dealt with the judge's duty to *direct* the jury to acquit if the evidence called by the prosecution is so weak that no jury could properly convict on it. As explained in that Paragraph, the Court of Appeal's judgment in *Galbraith* [1981] 1 WLR 1039 has narrowed the circumstances in which it is right to direct an acquittal. However, it does not follow that, because a submission of no case has failed, the trial will inevitably run its full course. At any stage after the close of the prosecution case, the jury may say that they do not wish the proceedings to continue, whereupon they acquit the accused. Since few juries will be aware that they possess this power, it is open to the judge to 'remind' them of it, although he should not in so many words invite them to acquit (see *Kemp* [1995] 1 Cr App R 151 and *Falconer-Atlee* (1973) 58 Cr App R 348). The judge might remind the jury of their power to acquit forthwith if the prosecution case is a little too strong for him to direct an acquittal, but nonetheless their evidence looks feeble in the light of defence cross-examination. The jury may not, of course, convict without first listening to the entire case.

18.8 THE JUDGE'S SUMMING-UP

The final and very significant stage of a trial on indictment is the judge's summing-up. In it he directs the jury on the law and assists them in their task of deciding the facts. While it is impossible to know the reasons for a jury returning a certain verdict, a reasonable assumption is that the judge's apparent view of the case sways them considerably. Having heard persuasive and eloquent speeches from the various counsel in the case which usually arrive at directly opposite conclusions, the jurors turn with relief to the judge who can put the arguments in perspective, identify the 'red herrings' and clarify the issues. Counsel, of course, are not always as convinced of the impartiality and wisdom of the judge as the jurors may be.

The following matters are nearly always dealt with in a summing-up:

(a)   The judge explains to the jury his and their respective roles — i.e. the judge decides on the law, and they must accept whatever he says about the law; the jury decide what facts have been proved, in which task they may be helped but are in no way bound by what he says. As was said in *Wootton* [1990] Crim LR 201, this explanation of functions is no mere formality. Its omission may by itself ground a successful appeal.

(b)   The jury are told that it is for the prosecution to prove the guilt of the accused, that the accused does not have to prove anything, and that, unless they are satisfied beyond reasonable doubt on all the evidence that the accused committed the offence charged, they must acquit him. An acceptable alternative is to direct the jury that in order to find the defendant guilty they must be 'sure' or 'satisfied so that they feel sure'. An amalgam of the two alternatives, along the lines of 'You must be satisfied beyond reasonable doubt so that you feel sure of the defendant's guilt' has also been suggested (see *Ferguson v The Queen* [1979] 1 WLR 94).

(c)   The judge defines the offence charged, explaining the matters which the prosecution have to prove in order to establish guilt. If possible he keeps his statement of the law simple and basic. For example, if Smith is charged with stealing Jones' umbrella and the defence is mistaken identity, the judge might say something like — 'Members of the jury, you all know what is meant by stealing — it is taking somebody else's property dishonestly, knowing it does not belong to you, and intending that they shall not get it back again. Now,

Mr Jones has told you that at 1 p.m. he left his umbrella in the cloakroom, and that at 2 p.m. when he returned to collect it it had gone, and he did not see it again until he was shown it at the police station. That evidence was not disputed by the defence, so you may not have much difficulty in deciding — it's a matter entirely for you, ladies and gentlemen — that somebody stole the umbrella. The question is, was it this defendant? . . .' If the defence raised by Smith was mistake (he took the umbrella thinking it was his own) or an unauthorised loan (he took the umbrella for use in a heavy shower intending to return it), the judge would have to emphasise, in the one case, that the appropriation must be dishonest and, in the other, that there must be an intention permanently to deprive.

(d) Depending on the evidence called in the particular case, it may be necessary to explain some evidential points to the jury. For example, the basic direction on the burden and standard of proof is inadequate where, on an assault charge, the accused raises the defence of acting in reasonable self-defence, for the jury might be left with the impression that the accused has to show that he was so acting. The judge should therefore tell the jury expressly that it is for the prosecution to prove beyond reasonable doubt that the accused was not acting in reasonable self-defence. Similar principles apply where the defence raised is one of alibi. Conversely, if the burden of establishing a defence is, by way of exception to the general rule, upon the accused (e.g., where a defence of diminished responsibility is raised upon a charge of murder) the judge explains both that and the standard of proof required of the defence (i.e. upon a balance of probabilities). Where the defence is mistaken identity the judge should mention the special need for caution before convicting on the basis of the evidence from the identifying witnesses (see *Turnbull* [1977] QB 224 for full details of what the judge should say in mistaken identity cases). If the accused's character, good or bad, has been put into evidence, the judge should explain the bearing it has upon the case — usually the direction will be that it may help the jury in deciding what weight to attach to the accused's evidence but it does not directly go to prove that he did or did not commit the offence charged. Depending on the evidence in the particular case many other points may have to be considered in the summing-up.

(e) If two or more accused are joined in one indictment, the judge must direct the jury to consider the case of each accused separately. In particular, if evidence has been given against A which, although inadmissible against B, is prejudicial to his defence (e.g., A has made a confession in B's absence which implicates both himself and B), the jury must be told to ignore that evidence when reaching their verdict on B. Similarly, if an accused is charged in one indictment with two or more offences, the jury are warned to give separate consideration to each count. The fact that they have decided to convict or acquit the accused on count one is normally irrelevant to their decision on count two, and vice versa. Where there is a striking similarity between the offence charged in one count and that charged in a second count (see *DPP v Boardman* [1975] AC 421) the judge has the difficult task of explaining that, while the evidence in respect of each count is admissible to support the prosecution case on the other count, the jury must nonetheless reach independent verdicts on each count.

(f) The last part of the summing-up deals with the evidence in the case. Using the note of evidence which he takes during the trial, the judge reminds the jury of the evidence they have heard and comments upon it. Judges vary in the way they discharge this part of their duty. Some merely read out the significant parts of each witness' evidence, concentrating upon the evidence in chief, others seek to define the issues in the case, and relate the evidence to those issues. Some keep their own view of the case discreetly hidden, others, whether directly or indirectly, let the jury know their opinion of the facts. In *Charles* (1979)

68 Cr App R 334, Lawton LJ commented upon the desirable method of summing-up in a long case. In a trial which lasted for a total of 35 days and involved complex allegations of fraudulent business dealings, the summing-up took three days. After an introductory survey of the law and issues relevant to the case, the judge adopted the technique of reading out from his notes what each witness had said. The Court of Appeal criticised his approach because, in long fraud cases especially, it is important for the judge to 'analyse the issues' and relate the evidence to the issues' (p. 341). Merely reading a note of the evidence is unsatisfactory, not least because 'it must bore the jury to sleep' (p. 339). In general, judges 'should not indulge in long-winded summings-up which are more likely to confuse than help the jury' (p. 341). Whatever method of summing-up the judge uses, it is essential that he put the defence before the jury in a form which they can appreciate. He is entitled to express his opinion on that defence (or, indeed, on any of the facts of the case), provided that he leaves the issues of fact to the jury to determine. Thus, in *O'Donnell* (1917) 12 Cr App R 219, a conviction was upheld where the judge said that the prisoner's story was a 'remarkable' one and contrary to previous statements he had made, but in *Canny* (1945) 30 Cr App R 143 repeatedly telling the jury that the defence was 'absurd' and that there was no foundation for defence allegations amounted to a direction to find the case against the accused proved. The conviction was therefore quashed. As it was trenchantly put by Lord Lane CJ in *Marr* (1989) 90 Cr App R 154, however distasteful the crime, however repulsive the accused, however laughable the defence, he was entitled to have his case presented fairly by both counsel and judge. That especially applied when the cards seemed stacked against him. Whether a judge may ever with propriety tell the jury to convict is open to doubt. The better view seems to be that, even where his view of the law is that the defence's own version of events itself shows the accused to be guilty as charged, he should still leave the ultimate issue of guilt or innocence with the jury, albeit with the comment that the evidence all points in one direction (see *DPP v Stonehouse* [1978] AC 55 and *Thompson* [1984] 1 WLR 962).

(g) Occasionally, the question arises whether the judge is confined, when summarising the case against the defendant, to the same basis as that on which the prosecution has put its case. In *Falconer-Atlee* (1973) 58 Cr App R 348, the judge left it open to the jury to convict on a basis which had never been put forward by the prosecution. This was one of the reasons given by the Court of Appeal for quashing the conviction. But in *Japes* [1994] Crim LR 605, the Court of Appeal said that a judge was not bound by the way in which the Crown opened its case. As the evidence developed, it might become apparent that the offence may have been committed on a somewhat different factual basis, e.g., the appropriation necessary for theft may have taken place at a later stage than the prosecution originally thought. If so, the judge was not debarred from putting that basis before the jury to consider, so long as the defendant was not disadvantaged or prejudiced by this course of action.

(h) At the very end of the summing-up, the judge advises the jury to appoint one of themselves to be their foreman. The foreman will act as their spokesman and, in due course, announce their verdict. Finally, the judge tells them to retire, consider their verdict and seek to reach a unanimous decision. Where the prosecution have put their case on more than one basis it may be necessary to tell them that, in order to convict, they must be unanimous not only as to the accused being guilty but also as to the *basis* on which he is guilty: *Brown* (1984) 79 Cr App R 115. In that case, the prosecution alleged the obtaining of property by the use of two deceptions, and the Court of Appeal held that the jury should have been directed that — if not unanimous that B used both deceptions — they should at least all agree as to which one he used. If six thought he used deception *a* and the remainder thought he used deception *b*, he should not be convicted. See generally J.C. Smith, 'Satisfying the jury' [1988] Crim LR 335 and *Mitchell* [1994] Crim LR 66.

> Before he starts summing-up, the judge may ask counsel to assist him on the law and facts with which he is to deal, but he should never seek counsel's help after the jury have retired, and only in exceptional circumstances should he discuss the law with counsel after finishing his summing-up but before the jury's retirement: *Cocks* (1976) 63 Cr App R 79. Asking counsel to interrupt the summing-up in order to correct any errors as they are made is also unwise as it may disrupt the jury's train of thought and appear to undermine the judge's authority (*Charles* (supra), where counsel intervened 33 times in the course of a three-day summing-up). If, having listened to the summing-up, prosecuting counsel appreciates that there has been some misdirection of law or fact, he should raise the matter with the judge before the jury retire so that the error can be corrected. Failure to do so may expose counsel to criticism if the defence subsequently appeal (for an example, see *Donoghue* [1988] Crim LR 60). Although the point is not free from doubt, it seems that defence counsel is under no duty to mention any error he may notice. If he thinks it in the best interests of his client, he may say nothing in the hope that, should the accused be found guilty, he will be able to appeal successfully against conviction (see the comments of Robert Goff LJ in *Edwards* (1983) 77 Cr App R 5). He obviously takes a risk in doing so, even though the dismissal of an appeal based on these circumstances is not inevitable (*Holden* [1991] Crim LR 478). The position appears to be different where a procedural irregularity is in issue (see Paragraph 18.1.2 and *Smith* [1994] Crim LR 458).
> What if the judge does realise that his summing-up is in error (whether as a result of counsel's intervention or of his own accord)? He should expressly refer to the error, tell the jury to disregard it, and then give the correct direction (*Cole* [1994] Crim LR 300).
> Counsel should take a note of the summing-up. This will assist him when advising on the merits of an appeal and drafting the initial Grounds of Appeal, at which stage a transcript of the shorthand writer's note of the summing-up is unlikely to be available.

18.9   EVIDENCE GIVEN OUT OF THE NORMAL ORDER

The prosecution may not in general call evidence after they have closed their case, or even cross-examine the accused about matters which they could have proved as part of their case had they so chosen.

> The rule is illustrated by *Day* [1940] 1 All ER 402. D's conviction for forging a cheque was quashed because, after the defence had closed their case, the judge allowed the prosecution to call a handwriting expert to compare the writing on the cheque with a sample of D's writing.
> The exceptions to the general rule are as follows:
>
> (a)   If, in the course of the defence case, a matter arises *ex improviso,* which no human ingenuity can foresee, the prosecution may adduce evidence to rebut the defence evidence on the matter. In *Blick* (1966) 50 Cr App R 280, for example, B who, according to the police, was arrested following a chase and charged with robbery, testified that at the time of the chase he was in a public lavatory. The prosecution were correctly allowed to reopen their case and call evidence that at the relevant time the lavatory was closed for repairs. No human ingenuity could have foreseen that access to a public lavatory would be relevant to the case against B. *Blick* may be compared with *Day* where the prosecution should have anticipated that a handwriting expert would be needed to help establish that the writing on the cheque was D's.
> (b)   The judge has a discretion to allow the prosecution to call a witness who was not available to them before they closed their case, even though his evidence does not go to rebut a matter raised *ex improviso* by the defence. Cases where it is proper to exercise the discretion are rare. Leave to call the witness should be refused if the only reason for the prosecution not calling him before they closed their case was that they wished to 'keep him up their sleeve' or had not been sufficiently diligent in preparing the case. In *Doran* (1972) 56 Cr App R 429 prosecuting counsel was informed, after he had closed his case, that two members of the public sitting in the gallery, had realised that

they could give relevant evidence. He was allowed to call them, and the Court of Appeal confirmed the conviction because, although the case did not fall within the principle of (a) above, the prosecution could not have found out about the witnesses before closing their case.

(c)   Where the prosecution inadvertently omit to lead evidence of a purely formal nature the judge may allow them to reopen their case and repair the omission. Evidence that a steamroller is made mainly of iron or steel comes within the category of evidence of a purely formal nature (*McKenna* (1957) 40 Cr App R 65, where M was charged with exporting manufactured goods 'wholly or mainly of iron or steel'). The principle has been extended somewhat to cover cases where the prosecution by mistake fail to call evidence identifying the accused as the person who committed the *actus reus* of the offence (see, for example, *Francis* [1990] 1 WLR 1264). Even in a case where identity is not in dispute, this could hardly be said to be evidence of a purely formal nature, but it seems that the court has a discretion to let prosecuting counsel reopen his case.

(d)   The rule of evidence that a party cross-examining the other side's witness about matters going only to the witness' credibility, not the issues in the case, cannot adduce his own evidence to rebut the answer he receives in cross-examination does not apply if the witness is asked about his previous convictions, previous inconsistent statement or bias. Therefore, if prosecuting counsel asks a defence witness about, for example, his previous convictions and the witness denies having any, the prosecution can adduce evidence to prove the convictions even though their case will obviously have been closed before the defence witness was called to testify.

Where there are proper grounds for allowing the prosecution to reopen their case, their evidence may be called during or at the close of the defence case, or even after counsel's closing speeches: *Flynn* (1958) 42 Cr App R 15. The judge also has a broad discretion to allow the defence to reopen their case. In *Sanderson* [1953] 1 WLR 392, where a defence witness did not arrive until the summing-up was virtually completed, the judge rightly allowed the witness to testify at the end of the summing-up, and then delivered a supplementary summing-up dealing with his evidence.

18.10   POWER OF JUDGE TO CALL WITNESSES

The judge has a right to call a witness if, in his opinion, it is necessary for him to do so in the interests of justice.

The judge asks the witness questions, and then allows either or both counsel to cross-examine. However, the judge's power to call a witness should be exercised sparingly. In any event, the judge must not call any further prosecution witnesses in a case where the Crown has decided not to continue the prosecution. To do so would be, in effect, to take the prosecution over (*Grafton* [1993] QB 101). If the witness is likely to favour the prosecution and they have already closed their case, the judge should only call him if the circumstances are such that he could accede to a prosecution application to reopen their case were one to be made. One situation where a judge might call a witness is where the witness is named on the back of the indictment but the prosecution decline to call him (see *Oliva* [1965] 1 WLR 1028 and Paragraph 18.3.1).

The judge has a discretion to recall for further questioning witnesses who have been called by the prosecution or defence, provided this does not allow the prosecution improperly to reopen their case. The power to recall witnesses includes power to recall the accused himself if he has testified. Where assertions are made by counsel or witnesses in the course of the defence case which should have been put to a prosecution witness in the course of cross-examination, the witness can be recalled to deal with the assertions. It is wrong, however, to recall a witness merely so that his evidence can be heard twice over.

18.11   HEARING IN OPEN COURT AND PUBLICITY

It is not only the parties who have an interest in criminal proceedings — the public also are concerned that, as far as is possible, the innocent shall be acquitted, the guilty convicted and offenders properly sentenced. Therefore, it is a fundamental principle of common law that justice shall be administered in open court. The principle was re-stated by Lord Diplock in *AG v Leveller Magazine* [1980] AC 440 at p. 450A–D:

As a general rule the English system of administering justice does require that it be done in public. If the way that the courts behave cannot be hidden from the public ear and eye this provides a safeguard against judicial arbitrariness and idiosyncracy and maintains the public confidence in the administration of justice. The application of the principle of open justice has two aspects: as respects proceedings in the court itself it requires that they should be held in open court to which the press and public are admitted and that, in criminal cases at any rate, all evidence communicated to the court is communicated publicly. As respects the publication to a wider public of fair and accurate reports of proceedings that have taken place in court the principle requires that nothing should be done to discourage this.

   However, since the purpose of the general rule is to serve the ends of justice it may be necessary to depart from it where the nature or circumstances of the particular proceedings are such that the application of the general rule in its entirety would frustrate or render impracticable the administration of justice. Apart from statutory exceptions, however, where a court in the exercise of its inherent power to control the conduct of proceedings before it departs in any way from the general rule, the departure is justified to the extent and to no more than the extent that the court reasonably believes it to be necessary to serve the ends of justice.

Thus, according to Lord Diplock, the principle of open justice has two main aspects, although the first really sub-divides into two. First, hearings should be in open court, not in camera; second, evidence communicated to the court should be communicated openly; and, third, the press should be free to report all that is openly done and communicated in open court. At common law, each aspect of the principle may be departed from if, and only if, insisting on the principle in its entirely would frustrate the ends of justice in the particular case before the court. Moreover, such departure as is allowed must be no more than is strictly necessary to overcome the perceived threat to justice.

   The overwhelming trend of appellate decisions is to limit approval for derogations from the principle of open justice to very exceptional cases. Thus, sitting in camera is not justified by possible danger to an offender through mitigation (including the fact that he was a 'supergrass') being presented in open court and thereafter reported: *Reigate Justices ex p Argus Newspapers* (1983) 5 Cr App R (S) 181. Nor is it justified by a drink-driver's 'overwhelming fear' of having embarrassing details about her personal life and medical problems aired publicly (*Malvern Justices ex p Evans* [1988] QB 540), or by the supposed undesirability of the general public being entertained with salacious items of evidence (per Viscount Haldane LC in *Scott v Scott* [1913] AC 417), or even by considerations of national safety (per Lord Scarman in *AG v Leveller Magazine* supra). In fact, almost the only clear example given in the decided cases of closed hearings being appropriate is where feelings about a case are running so high that there would be a risk of 'tumult or disorder' should the public be admitted (per Lord Loreburn in *Scott v Scott* supra). There are also dicta suggesting that excluding the public is justifiable if, given the nature of the anticipated evidence and/or the occupation of the witnesses, there is no realistic prospect of their being willing to testify unless guaranteed confidentiality (see Viscount Haldane in *Scott v Scott* and Lord Scarman in *AG v Leveller Magazine,* where his Lordship implied that examining justices would have been entitled to hear the evidence of a colonel of the Defence Intelligence Staff in camera, not because of danger to the colonel or national safety per se but because the Crown might have been deterred from prosecuting in future similar cases by the knowledge that sensitive evidence could not be protected).

Sometimes the adverse consequences of an open hearing can be largely avoided by allowing a certain piece of evidence to be communicated to the court privately. By far the commonest example is where a witness is allowed to write down his name and/or address instead of giving it orally. In theory, this should happen only if the court would otherwise be entitled to sit in camera, but in practice the derogation from the principle of open justice involved is so slight that it is allowed without too much argument. Thus, in *AG v Leveller Magazine* the House of Lords was unanimous in its approval of the examining justices' decision to proceed in open court but with the intelligence officer mentioned above referred to simply as 'Colonel B'. Blackmail victims are also commonly protected by pseudonyms. However, the courts are far less willing to afford the same protection to the accused himself. In *Evesham Justices ex p McDonagh* [1988] QB 553 the High Court held that magistrates trying an information for using a car without a valid MOT test certificate should have insisted on the accused giving his address orally. His reason for wanting to write it down — namely, that he feared harassment from his ex-wife should she find out where he was living — was insufficient. According to Watkins LJ, the accused's 'comfort and feelings' cannot outweigh the public interest in knowing precisely who has been charged with or found guilty of an offence.

The strictness of the common law principle of open justice is modified by miscellaneous statutory provisions which permit restrictions either on public access to the court or on the reporting of what takes place in open court. The chief provisions are as follows:

(a) *Official Secrets Act 1920, s 8.* Where the publication of any part of proceedings for an offence under the Official Secrets Acts would be 'prejudicial to the national safety', the court may, on the prosecution's application, order that the public shall be excluded from the hearing. Sentence, however, must be passed in open court.

(b) *Children and Young Persons Act 1933, ss 36, 37 and 39.* Save when their presence is required as witnesses or defendants, children under 14 are not permitted in court during criminal proceedings (s 36). Where a juvenile is called as a witness in proceedings for an offence of indecency the court may direct that the public, but not the press, shall be excluded while the juvenile testifies (s 37). In proceedings of any description the court may direct that the media shall not publish identifying details of any juvenile involved, irrespective of whether he is the accused, a witness or concerned in some other way (s 39). There are also special statutory rules governing access to and reporting of youth court hearings (see Chapter 10).

(c) *Contempt of Court Act 1981, s 4.* At common law, any media reporting that creates a substantial risk of prejudice to the course of justice amounts to contempt of court, and is punishable even if the offender had no intention of causing such prejudice. This 'strict liability' rule is preserved by s 2 of the Contempt of Court Act 1981. The Act also preserves the major common law exception to liability, namely that fair and accurate reporting of legal proceedings held in public is not contempt, provided the report is published contemporaneously and in good faith (see s 4(1)). Far from discouraging such reporting, the courts have recognised its vital role in the administration of justice (e.g., Lord Diplock's judgment in *AG v Leveller Magazine*). However, s 4(2) creates an exception to the exception in that it empowers a court to order that publication of reports of all or part of its proceedings shall be postponed. An order may be made only if 'it appears to be necessary for avoiding a substantial risk of prejudice to the administration of justice' in the proceedings before the court or in any other 'pending or imminent proceedings'. Both in scope and duration an order must not exceed that which is strictly necessary to remove the threatened prejudice (see *Horsham Justices ex p Farquharson* [1982] QB 762). Any publication in breach of a s 4(2) order is automatically to be regarded as having been made in bad faith, and therefore those responsible cannot claim the protection of s 4(1) even if there was no actual damage to the interests of justice (per the majority in *ex p Farquharson*, Lord Denning dissenting on the point). The value and proper use of s 4(2) is illustrated by the facts of the last-mentioned case. After lifting the reporting restrictions which normally apply to committal proceedings (see Chapter 12), examining justices in effect re-imposed them by ordering that nothing should be published until the trial on indictment had commenced. The Court of Appeal held that s 4(2) did potentially apply to committals; that the trial which would, in the normal course of events, follow upon committal came within the definition of 'pending or imminent proceedings', and there was a risk of prejudice to that trial if the media reported forthwith sensational and highly prejudicial allegations to the effect that weapons the accused were charged with illegally exporting were intended for use in blowing up a mosque. But the magistrates had erred in making a blanket order covering the entire proceedings before them — it would have been sufficient to ban immediate publication of the evidence concerning the bomb plot. The matter was remitted to them for reconsideration. At Crown Court level, orders under s 4(2) are especially appropriate where the accused is to be tried within a short space of time on two separate indictments. To avoid prejudicing the jurors for the second trial, the judge at the first trial might postpone reporting until after the second's conclusion. Similarly, where the jury are excluded from a trial within a trial, the judge may postpone reporting until he has decided whether the disputed evidence is admissible (see *AG v Leveller Magazine* at p. 450). Before postponing publication in this way, however, the judge should be satisfied that postponement 'appears to be necessary for avoiding' the risk of prejudice, as s 4(2) requires (*The Telegraph* [1994] Crim LR 114). The judge should bear in mind that the jury, in a future trial will inevitably be given a direction to decide the case only on the evidence before them. It may be that such a direction will be sufficient to avoid the risk of prejudice, and a postponement order under s 4(2) will therefore not be necessary.

(d)   *Contempt of Court Act 1981, s 11.*   Where a court validly exercises its common law power to order that a name or other piece of evidence be communicated to it privately (see above), it may further impose a permanent ban on publication of that material. This is to cover against the possibility of the media discovering and reporting what the court had wanted withheld from the public. The validity of a s 11 order is, however, dependent upon the validity of the court's prior decision to have evidence communicated privately: *Evesham Justices ex p McDonagh* (supra).

(e)   *Sexual Offences (Amendment) Act 1976, s 4.*   This section, as amended, essentially prevents the media naming or giving the address of the complainant in a rape case, or publishing anything else likely to enable the public to identify her. The protection given by the section operates from the moment of the complaint being made, and lasts for the complainant's lifetime. The Crown Court has a discretion both before and at trial to order that the section shall not apply (e.g., because the accused needs publicity in order for witnesses to come forward). A parallel provision in s 6 of the 1976 Act, which used to protect the accused's identity unless and until he was convicted, was repealed by the Criminal Justice Act 1988.

The above discussion of open justice has covered both Crown Court and magistrates' courts' proceedings, since the same basic principles apply in both courts. However, special statutory rules apply both to access to youth court proceedings and reporting of committal proceedings. They are dealt with in Chapters 10 and 12 respectively.

19 The Verdict

19.1 RETIREMENT OF THE JURY

When the judge has finished his summing-up, a court usher takes an oath to keep the jury in some 'private and convenient place', to prevent anybody speaking to them without leave of the court, and not to speak to them himself 'except it be to ask them if they are agreed upon their verdict'. Having so sworn, the usher, who is referred to as the jury bailiff, leads the jury to their room and stations himself outside. During the period of their retirement the jury are kept together so that through discussion and argument they can arrive at a unanimous verdict (or, at least, at a verdict upon which ten of them are agreed: see Paragraph 19.5). As far as possible, they are kept apart from everybody else, because no outside influences should affect a jury's verdict. They and they alone must reach a decision on the guilt or innocence of the accused, and they should reach that decision solely on the basis of the evidence and speeches they have heard in court combined with their own experience of life and good sense. Three interconnected rules are designed to ensure that nothing untoward occurs while the jury are considering their verdict.

First, the jury must stay in the custody of the jury bailiff. This means that the jury bailiff must be in a position to prevent anybody speaking to the jury or any individual member of it. He should not himself go into the jury room or speak to the jurors unless the judge orders him to do so (e.g., to pass on a message from the judge or ask a question). Convictions have been quashed where either the whole jury or a juror left the jury bailiff's custody. In *Neal* [1949] 2 KB 590, the jury, with the judge's permission but after having retired to consider their verdict, left the court building to go to a restaurant for lunch. The jury bailiff did not go with them. Having lunched, they returned to court and convicted N. The conviction was quashed because they had been out of the bailiff's custody for a substantial period, during which time numerous persons could have spoken to them about the case. Similarly, in *Ketteridge* [1915] 1 KB 467, K's conviction was quashed because a member of the jury, instead of retiring with his colleagues to the jury room, by mistake left the court building and was absent for fifteen minutes before rejoining the other jurors. Just as in *Neal* there was ample opportunity for non-jury members to speak to the juror.

Second, the jury must not leave their room without the judge's permission. The commonest reason for the jury leaving their room is the judge asking them to return to court for further directions about the case or for the answer to a question they have asked. Also, in cases of 'evident necessity', the judge may let them leave not just their room but the entire court buildings: *Neal* (supra). Although the Court of Criminal Appeal in *Neal* did not find it necessary to decide whether the judge could properly have allowed the jury to go to a restaurant in the custody of the jury bailiff, the obtaining of refreshments away from the court building could hardly now amount to an 'evident necessity' as the jury may have sandwiches brought to them (they may be allowed reasonable refreshment at their own expense — Juries Act 1974, s 15). Where the jury are far from agreement and it is getting late, the judge may decide that there is an evident necessity for them to be taken to an hotel for the night, so that they can return to their room the next morning refreshed by a good sleep. This is only appropriate in very long or complex cases where it is reasonable for the jury to take a day or more to consider their verdict. Normally, if a jury have been given several hours to deliberate and are still nowhere near a verdict, the judge discharges them (see Paragraph 19.6). If the jury are kept at an hotel for the night or allowed to leave their room for any reason, they must still remain in the custody of the jury bailiff.

The third rule, which is really a corollary of the second, is that the jury must not separate, save with the permission of the judge. Until 1994, the jury had to be kept together after they had retired to consider their verdict, even if this meant that they had to stay overnight in a hotel. The position now is that the judge has a discretion to permit the jury to separate at any time during the trial, even if it is after they have retired to consider their verdict (Criminal Justice and Public Order Act 1994, s 43). It is still possible that the judge will decide against allowing the jury to separate, thus necessitating an overnight stay in a hotel, but at least there is a judicial discretion. In *Oliver* [1996] 2 Cr App R 514, the Court of Appeal said that, if the judge permitted the jury to separate during consideration of their evidence, then he should tell them:

(a)   to decide the case on the evidence and the arguments seen and heard in court, and not on anything seen or heard outside the court;

(b)   that the evidence had been completed and it would be wrong for any juror to seek or receive further evidence or information of any sort about the case;

(c)   not to talk to anyone about the case save to the other members of the jury and then only when they were deliberating in the jury room;

(d)   not to allow anyone to talk to them about the case unless that person was a juror and he or she was in the jury room deliberating about the case; and

(e)   on leaving the court, to set the case on one side until they retired to the jury room to continue the process of deliberating about their verdict.

An infringement of the rules described above, however trivial, is an irregularity in the course of the trial but it will not lead to a conviction being quashed by the Court of Appeal unless it 'goes to the root of the case'. Thus, in *Alexander* [1974] 1 WLR 422 a conviction was upheld where, after the jury had left court in the charge of the jury bailiff, one of them returned to collect an exhibit (the judge had told them that they might see any exhibit they wanted). Technically the juror had both separated himself from his colleagues and left the custody of the jury bailiff, but since the separation was for a matter of seconds only and since he had been observed by defence counsel throughout those few seconds, the irregularity did not go to the root of the case. In *Goodson* [1975] 1 WLR 549, on the other hand, the jury bailiff allowed a juror to leave the jury room to use a telephone. By chance, prosecuting counsel discovered what was happening, and took steps to prevent the juror rejoining his colleagues. The judge discharged him from the jury, and the remaining eleven convicted. The Court of Appeal held that the irregularity was such that the conviction had to be quashed. The bailiff's error, for which the court had to take ultimate responsibility, had deprived G 'of the voice of one juror in the jury room' (per James LJ at p. 552).

In a more recent case, however, the fact that a juror had communicated with the outside world by telephone was viewed as irregular, but not sufficiently material to ground a successful appeal. In

Farooq (1994) *The Times*, 12 May 1994, a juror made two telephone calls to ask about a sick child. The Court of Appeal saw no valid reason to disbelieve the juror, and was satisfied that no miscarriage of justice had occurred. It did, however, criticise the procedure which the judge had adopted to deal with the matter. When told about the telephone calls, he had asked the chief clerk to make enquiries. The clerk then told counsel informally what the juror said about the telephone calls. The judge was then told that all counsel had said they were satisfied, and the jury continued with their deliberations. The Court of Appeal said that the court should have been reconvened, the relevant facts stated in open court, and counsel given the opportunity to ask for further clarification.

19.1.1 Questions from the jury

Even though they have retired to consider their verdict, the jury may ask the judge for further explanation of matters of law arising in the case. They may also ask him to remind them of any part of the evidence. If they ask for information about a point on which no evidence has, in fact, been given the judge must tell them there is no evidence on the matter and that they must decide the case on the evidence they have heard. It is an absolute rule that no evidence shall be adduced before the jury after they have begun to consider their verdict (*Owen* [1952] 2 QB 362). They should not therefore be allowed to view the scene of the alleged crime (*Lawrence* (1968) 52 Cr App R 163). In *Stewart* (1989) 89 Cr App R 273, the Court of Appeal held that the trial judge had erred in letting the jury have a pair of scales after they had retired. The case was one in which the weight of a quantity of drugs was highly relevant. The Court of Appeal was clearly concerned that the jury had, in effect, been permitted to carry out experiments without judge, counsel or accused being present. In *Maggs* (1990) 91 Cr App R 243, on the other hand, it was stated that the supply of a tape measure or a magnifying glass would not normally raise the prospect of such experiments, and would be unobjectionable. In any event, the jury are normally entitled to take the exhibits in the case with them when they retire, including a tape of an interview which has been played to them during the trial (*Emmerson* (1990) 92 Cr App R 284). Where the tape has not been played during the trial, but the jury have been given a transcript, then if they ask after retirement to hear the tape, they are entitled to hear it. The tape is the exhibit, and the transcript is merely a convenient method of presenting it. Although it is a matter for the judge's discretion, the best course in these circumstances is to bring the jury back into court to hear the tape. Problems might arise if they are allowed free access to the tape, including the risk that they might hear matters left on it which they should not hear, e.g., evidence which is inadmissible (*Riaz* (1991) 94 Cr App R 339). In *Rawlings* [1995] 1 WLR 178, the Court of Appeal said that the jury would usually, though not always, be allowed to see an exhibit on request. This general rule would apply to a request from the jury to see a replay of a video. If the judge decided to accede to the request, it was important that the replay should be in open court, with judge, counsel and defendant present. The judge should warn the jury against giving disproportionate weight to evidence-in-chief which they were hearing for the first time, and remind them to bear in mind the other evidence in the case. To assist in maintaining a fair balance, the judge should remind the jury of the cross-examination and re-examination of the complainant, whether asked by the jury to do so or not. As far as the last point is concerned, it appears that the judge may, if asked by the jury to remind them of a witness' evidence-in-chief, use his discretion as to whether to remind them also of the cross-examination and re-examination (*Morgan* [1996] Crim LR 600). It appears that the judge will be more likely to do so where the evidence in the case is complicated, or where the jury's request entails viewing a video of evidence-in-chief by a child, as was the case in *Rawlings*.

Where the jury have a question or communication for the judge, they should write it down and give it to the jury bailiff, who passes it on to the judge. The judge then asks for counsel and the accused to return to court; the note is read out, and counsel may be invited to comment on the appropriate method of dealing with it. Next, the jury are brought back. The judge confirms with them the question they wish to raise, and the answer is given. Where the jury's note reveals something that should really be kept confidential (e.g., their provisional voting figures), the judge should summarise its contents omitting what ought not to be disclosed (see *Gorman* [1987] 1 WLR 545). Numerous cases over the years have dealt with the proper way of answering jury questions (e.g. *Furlong* [1950] 1 All ER 636; *Green* [1950] 1 All ER 38; *Lamb* (1974) 59 Cr App R 196; *Townshend* [1982] 1 All ER 509, and *Gorman* (supra)). Although they may differ on points of detail, their guiding principle is that both the question and the answer should be given publicly in open court at the time the matter is raised by the jury, and certainly before they return their verdict. Any suggestion that the judge has indulged in secret communications with the jury is likely to lead to a successful appeal, even if what he actually told them was unexceptionable. Indeed, this is one area of procedure where the *appearance* of justice is as important as its reality. Whether departure from the proper practice will necessitate the quashing of the accused's conviction does, however, depend upon the facts of the individual case, in particular the extent of the departure and the strength of the prosecution evidence.

It does seem that there is a distinction to be drawn between matters affecting the trial, and what has been termed 'domestic management'. As far as the first category is concerned, the judge should, other than in the most exceptional cases, inform counsel of the fact and general nature of the communication. In cases where the communication relates to 'domestic management', the same principle applies, but the integrity of the trial process is not harmed, and any appeal is unlikely to succeed. Although this distinction was set out by the Court of Appeal in *Conroy* [1997] 2 Cr App R 285, it is not always easy to say which category a communication falls into. In *Brown* [1998] Crim LR 505, for example, the judge was told, before he sent the jury out, that it was inconvenient for two jurors to return on the following Monday. As a result, he asked them to retire at 3.15 p.m. on Friday afternoon (rather than waiting until the Monday morning before sending them out as he might otherwise have done). This communication was treated by the judge as a matter of domestic management, and he did not adopt the procedure set out above for dealing with communications from the jury. When the matter came to the Court of Appeal, they viewed it as a matter affecting the trial, since it went to the length of time the jury might need to deliberate, and hence to possible pressure upon them if their deliberations went into another day. Nevertheless, they held that in view of the brevity of the trial, the verdict was a safe one, and they dismissed the appeal. Overall, it would seem that the safest course for the judge is to disclose all communications from the jury to counsel (with the exception of confidential matters such as provisional voting figures).

19.1.2   The privacy of the jury room

The extreme reluctance of the Court of Appeal to quash a conviction because of any inadequacy, or apparent bias, or misconduct by a juror has already been noted (see Paragraph 17.5). This reluctance is complemented by a total refusal to enquire, for purposes of an appeal, into what took place in the jury room. The general public interest requires that jurors should feel free, in the privacy of their room, to express whatever view they wish about the case, without the fear that a wrong word could be seized upon by the defence, following a conviction, and made the subject of an appeal. While the broad principle is understandable it may sometimes work apparent injustice in the case of an individual appellant. In *Thompson* [1962] 1 All ER 65 the Court of Criminal Appeal refused to hear evidence that the jury, in a case where T's character had not been revealed in evidence, were going to acquit until the foreman read to them a list of T's previous convictions which, in some unexplained way, had come into his possession. Similarly, in *Roads* [1967] 2 QB 108 evidence that one of the jurors had not agreed with the verdict of guilty was not received by the court.

The confidentiality of jury deliberations is reinforced by s 8 of the Contempt of Court Act 1981, which makes it an offence to obtain or disclose information about such deliberations. The main purpose of s 8 was apparently to prevent newspapers interviewing jurors after a particularly newsworthy trial, and publishing an account of why the jurors reached the verdict they did.

A particularly blatant example was provided by the publication in 1992 of an article in the *Mail on Sunday* which referred to accounts by three jurors of their deliberations in the Blue Arrow fraud trial. The jurors described how they reached their decisions, commented on the evidence in issue at the trial, and gave an opinion of one of the other jurors. Fines of £30,000, £20,000 and £10,000 were imposed on the publisher, editor and journalist respectively (*Attorney-General v Associated Newspapers Ltd* [1994] 2 AC 238).

The prohibition does not only apply to the media, however. In *Mickleburgh* [1995] 1 Cr App R 297, the Court of Appeal made it clear that it applies to court officials, ushers and jury bailiffs as much as to anyone else. In *McCluskey* (1993) 98 Cr App R 218, it was emphasised that any enquiries of the jury about an alleged irregularity could only be set in train with the consent of the court. Where sentence had been pronounced, the trial judge was *functus officio*, and such enquiries could only be conducted with the consent of the Court of Appeal.

Whilst there are clear reasons of public policy for preserving the privacy of the jury room from intrusion, the Contempt of Court Act 1981, s 8, does have the unfortunate effect of making unlawful an important and potentially useful field of research into the way jurors approach their task, and the factors which influence them. The Royal Commission on Criminal Justice therefore recommends in its report (HMSO, 1993, p. 2) that the Act ought to be amended to allow research into the deliberations of juries, 'so that informed debate can take place rather than argument based only on surmise and anecdote'.

The prohibition does not, in any event, extend to events happening outside the jury room, e.g., in the hotel at which the jury is accommodated overnight: *Young* [1995] QB 324. In this case, the jurors stayed overnight in an hotel, after they had retired to consider their verdict in a murder trial. Several of them got together and sought the views of the deceased as to the defendant's guilt, using a ouija board to summon up his spirit! The Court of Appeal took the view that this incident was not 'in the course of' the jury's deliberations, but during an overnight break from those deliberations. Their Lordships held, therefore, that they were entitled to enquire into the incident. Having done so, they allowed the appeal and ordered a retrial.

19.2 RETURNING THE VERDICT

At the end of his summing-up the judge directs the jury to try to reach a unanimous verdict. If they succeed in doing so, they come into court, and the clerk asks the foreman if they have reached a verdict on which they are all agreed. He answers 'yes', after which their verdict on each count is announced. The jury must return a verdict on each count, and in respect of each accused joined in a count, unless they are discharged from giving a verdict on a certain count (see Paragraph 19.3). They can, of course, find an accused guilty on some counts and not guilty on others, or they can find one accused guilty and his co-accused not guilty. They can also find the accused guilty of, for example, stealing a part but not all of the goods named in a count for theft: *Furlong* [1950] 1 All ER 636. In asking for the verdicts, the clerk says something like — 'On count one, which charges the defendant with theft, do you find the defendant guilty or not guilty? . . . On count two, which charges the defendant with going equipped to steal, do you find him guilty or not guilty?' . . . and so on, through the indictment. If there are more than one accused joined in the indictment the clerk obviously has to name the accused in respect of whom he requests a verdict, rather than just referring to the defendant. Where, after a submission of no case to answer, the judge ruled that there was no case on count one, but that the trial should proceed on count two, the clerk says — 'On count one, charging the defendant with . . . do you, upon His Honour's direction, find the defendant not guilty?' The foreman obediently replies 'Not guilty', and the verdict on count two is taken in the normal way. Unless one of them protests at the time, it is conclusively presumed that the jurors are in agreement with the verdicts returned on their behalf: *Roads* [1967] 2 QB 108.

The circumstances in which a jury may return a majority verdict and the procedure for doing so are described in Paragraph 19.5.

19.3 VERDICTS ON COUNTS IN THE ALTERNATIVE

The prosecution case on two counts is sometimes such that the accused may be found guilty on one count or the other but not on both (e.g., if the evidence is that the accused was found in possession of stolen goods shortly after they were stolen and he failed to give an explanation of how he came by the goods, then the jury can convict him of either theft or handling — see Paragraph 14.5.4 on alternative counts). If, on an indictment containing alternative counts, the jury convict on, say, count one and are discharged from giving a verdict on count two, the Court of Appeal have power to quash the conviction on count one and substitute a conviction on count two provided it appears to them that the jury must have been satisfied of facts which proved the accused guilty on that count: Criminal Appeal Act 1968, s 3. If, on the other hand, the jury convict on count one and actually acquit on count two, the Court of Appeal cannot overturn the latter verdict: *Melvin and Eden* [1953] 1 QB 481. Therefore, if the count one conviction has to be quashed, the accused will stand acquitted on both counts, even though the Court of Appeal consider that he richly deserved to be convicted on the second count. To avoid such a miscarriage of justice, the foreman of the jury should be asked, in a case where there are counts in the alternative, whether the jury find the accused guilty on either count. If the answer is 'yes', he is further asked to name the count on which they wish to convict, and the verdict is taken on that count. The judge then discharges them from giving a verdict on the other count. If the answer is 'no', the clerk confirms that the jury acquit the accused on both counts.

19.4 VERDICTS OF GUILTY OF AN ALTERNATIVE OFFENCE

Normally, when the jury are considering their verdict on a count, they have a simple choice between acquitting and convicting the accused. Sometimes, however, a third option is open to them. They can find the accused not guilty as charged in the count, but guilty of some other (lesser) indictable offence. The circumstances in which they may do this are set out in the Criminal Law Act 1967, s 6(2)–(4) and s 4(2). (For discussion of the related topic of a plea of guilty to a lesser offence, see Paragraph 16.4.)

19.4.1 The general provision

If the allegations in a count for an offence other than treason or murder 'amount to or include (expressly or by implication) an allegation of another [indictable] offence', the jury may find the accused not guilty of the offence charged but guilty of the other offence: Criminal Law Act 1967, s 6(3).

A count *expressly* includes an allegation of another offence if, having struck out from the particulars those allegations which have not or might not have been established by the evidence led before the jury, there remain valid particulars for the other offence. This is illustrated by the facts of the leading case of *Lillis* [1972] 2 QB 236. L was charged with burglary contrary to s 9(1)(b) of the Theft Act 1968 in that he had entered a building as a trespasser on a certain date and had stolen therein a lawnmower. The prosecution evidence in fact showed that he had had permission both to enter the building and to borrow the lawnmower, but he had failed to return it when he ought. The judge ruled that there was no case to answer in respect of burglary, but that the jury could convict of theft on the basis that L had appropriated the mower dishonestly by keeping it. The jury did so convict, and L argued on appeal that a count which essentially alleged that he had stolen property inside a building on a certain day should not expose him to the risk of conviction for subsequently stealing the property outside the building. The argument was rejected. The Court of Appeal held that, omitting everything in the count the prosecution could not prove (namely the entry as a trespasser and the place where the offence occurred), there was still a valid count for theft, i.e., 'L, on . . . stole a lawnmower'. Admittedly, the date alleged for the theft was incorrect, but a variation between the date laid in the indictment and the evidence as to when the offence occurred will only be a good ground of appeal if the variation prejudiced or embarrassed the accused in the presentation of his defence (see Paragraph 14.8). On the facts of *Lillis,* there was no such prejudice.

The test to apply when deciding whether a count *by implication* includes an allegation of another offence was elaborated by the House of Lords decision in *Wilson* [1984] AC 242. Lord Roskill (giving the judgment of the House) held that the previously accepted test, laid down by Sachs LJ in *Springfield* (1969) 53 Cr App R 608, was too restrictive. It is not easy to discern what test Lord Roskill wished to put in place of the *Springfield* test. What is clear is that those cases decided before *Wilson* which upheld the jury's verdict of guilty of an alternative offence are still good law, whereas those which reached the opposite conclusion may call for reconsideration. Three main propositions emerge from Lord Roskill's judgment in *Wilson:*

(a) If committing the offence alleged in a count would inevitably have involved the accused committing another offence, the jury may convict of that other offence. In other words, a verdict of guilty of an alternative offence may lawfully be returned when committing the alternative is a *necessary step* towards committing the offence charged. Thus, on a count for robbery, the jury may acquit of robbery but convict of theft. The count will merely state, for example, that 'AB, on . . . robbed CD of a wallet and £20 in cash'. Clearly, there is no express allegation of theft. But, s 8 of the Theft Act 1968 provides that a person is guilty of robbery 'if he *steals,* and in order to do so he uses force on any person or puts or seeks to put any person in fear of being then and there subjected to force'. In view of that statutory definition, it is literally impossible for a person to commit robbery without committing theft. Therefore, if the jury are not satisfied that AB used or threatened force, but they are satisfied that he stole the wallet and money, they should convict him of theft. By a similar reasoning process, it has been held that on a count for either rape or unlawful sexual intercourse with a girl under 16 the accused may be convicted of indecent assault (see *Hodgson* [1973] 1 QB 565 and *McCormack* [1969] 2 QB 442).

(b)   The *ratio* of *Springfield* was that the accused could be convicted of an alternative offence by virtue of the Criminal Law Act 1967, s 6(3), *only* when the 'necessary step' test explained in (a) was satisfied. This meant that convictions for alternative offences were often quashed because, as a matter of law, it was possible to commit the offence charged without committing the alternative, even though it was highly unlikely that anybody would do so and even though the committal statements made it clear that the prosecution were in fact alleging that the accused committed the alternative as well as the offence charged. In *Wilson* the question for the House of Lords was whether the appellants had lawfully been convicted of assault occasioning actual bodily harm on counts which charged them with (respectively) maliciously inflicting grievous bodily harm contrary to s 20 of the Offences against the Person Act 1861 and burglary by entering a building as a trespasser and inflicting grievous bodily harm on a person therein contrary to s 9(1)(b) of the Theft Act 1968. In other words, does an allegation of inflicting grievous bodily harm impliedly include an allegation of assault occasioning actual bodily harm? The House assumed in favour of the appellants that it is possible to inflict harm without assaulting the victim (e.g., by deliberately causing panic in a crowded building so that people hurt themselves in a rush for the exits). Nonetheless, it is obvious that in the vast majority of cases harm will be inflicted through an assault, so, although the 'necessary step' test was not satisfied, their Lordships upheld the convictions. It is difficult to extract any clear *ratio* from Lord Roskill's judgment. However, the thrust of it seems to be that a count for Offence A impliedly contains an allegation of Offence B not only when commission of B is in law a necessary step towards committing A but also when a person committing the one offence will, *in the normal course of events,* commit the other also.

Application of *Wilson* led the Court of Appeal to hold that, on a count for burglary contrary to s 9(1)(b) of the Theft Act, there may be a verdict of guilty of s 9(1)(a) burglary (see *Whiting* [1987] Crim LR 473, reversing the earlier decision in *Hollis* [1971] Crim LR 525). Croom-Johnson LJ conceded that the s 9(1)(b) offence of entering a building as a trespasser and then stealing does not require the offender to have formed a theftous intent at the moment of entering, whereas s 9(1)(a) (entering as a trespasser with intent to steal) clearly does. However, the alternative verdict was available since, 'in the vast majority of cases', a trespasser who steals will have had the intent to steal before he entered and thus be guilty under both limbs of s 9(1). The impact of *Wilson* has been greatest, however, in the field of offences against the person. The *Wilson* case itself restored a conviction for assault occasioning actual bodily harm contrary to s 47 of the Offences Against the Person Act 1861, where the count in the indictment alleged inflicting grievous bodily harm contrary to s 20. In *Savage* [1992] 1 AC 699, the House of Lords held that a verdict of guilty of assault contrary to s 47 is a permissible alternative verdict on a count alleging unlawful wounding contrary to s 20. In *Mandair* [1995] 1 AC 208, the House of Lords held that 'causing' grievous bodily harm contrary to s 18 was wide enough to include any action that could amount to inflicting grievous bodily harm under s 20.

(c)   In determining the questions posed by (a) and (b) above, the courts are not entitled to take into account the manner in which, according to the prosecution witnesses, the offence alleged was actually committed. Whether an alternative verdict is open to the jury is a question of law decided solely by reference to the wording of the count and the legal definitions of the offence charged and the proposed alternative. For example, if the accused is charged only with burglary in that he entered a building as a trespasser with intent to steal, he could not be convicted of criminal damage even if the prosecution case had always been that he broke a window to effect the entry. Criminal damage is not a necessary step towards burglary; nor is it even an offence which will in the normal course of events be committed by a burglar. Therefore if the accused admits that he broke the window but says that his purpose was merely to find shelter for the night, the prosecution will not be entitled to invite the jury to convict of criminal damage in the event of their believing the accused's story. Of course, if the indictment included counts for both burglary and criminal damage, the jury could convict on one or other or both. Thus, if there is any doubt as to the availability of an alternative verdict, the prosecution should have separate counts for the various alternatives (see also below).

It has been suggested that, to overcome the difficulties inherent in deciding whether a count impliedly includes an allegation of another offence, the prosecution could add to the particulars of a count allegations which they strictly do not have to prove to establish the offence charged in the count, but which are essential to the other offence (see dicta in *McCready* [1978] 1 WLR 1376). Thus, the count could say that 'AB caused CD grievous bodily harm *by assaulting* him with intent to cause grievous bodily harm, contrary to s 18 of the Offences against the Person Act 1861'. If the italicised words are omitted, the jury may not — as the law presently stands — convict either of maliciously inflicting grievous bodily harm or of assault occasioning actual bodily harm or of common assault (see (b) above). But, with the addition of those words, all three alternatives are open to them. However, deliberately inserting unnecessary allegations into a count seems to be contrary to the spirit of the Indictment Rules, and may amount to a breach of the rule against duplicity (see Paragraph 14.4). Thus, the more sensible course for the prosecution to follow in cases of doubt is to have several counts (e.g., one for causing grievous bodily harm with intent; one for inflicting grievous bodily harm, and a third for assault occasioning actual bodily harm). If the jury convict on the most serious count, they will be discharged from giving a verdict on the other counts; if they acquit on the major count, it is still open to them to convict on one or other of the less serious ones (see *Mandair* [1995] 1 AC 208).

Reference has just been made to 'the major count' and the 'less serious counts', and it is natural to think of s 6(3) of the Criminal Law Act 1967 in terms of a greater offence charged in the count and a lesser offence of which the jury may convict as an alternative. However, as was pointed out by Lord Roskill in *Wilson*, those expressions are not used in the subsection. It is therefore possible that the alternative offence will be of equivalent gravity to — or even more serious than — the count offence.

19.4.2 Specific provisions

The Criminal Law Act 1967, s 6(3), which makes general provision for verdicts of guilty of a lesser offence, is supplemented by three further subsections of the 1967 Act and s 24 of the Road Traffic Offenders Act 1988, which all deal with the verdicts which may be returned in particular types of case. If the jury find the accused not guilty of the offence charged in the count then:

(a) On a count for murder they may convict of any one of the following — manslaughter, causing grievous bodily harm with intent, infanticide, child destruction or attempt to commit any of the aforementioned: Criminal Law Act 1967, s 6(2).

(b) On a count for a completed offence the jury may convict of an attempt to commit that offence or of an attempt to commit another offence of which the accused could be convicted on the count: Criminal Law Act 1967, s 6(4). Thus, if the accused is charged with robbery, the jury could convict him of attempted robbery or attempted theft. In the converse case of the accused merely being charged with the attempt but the evidence showing that the completed offence was committed, the jury may convict of the attempt or the judge may, in his discretion, discharge them from giving a verdict so that a fresh indictment may be preferred alleging the completed offence.

(c)   On a count for an arrestable offence, if the jury are satisfied that the offence charged (or another of which they could convict on the count) was committed by someone other than the accused, they may convict the accused of assisting whoever the offender was by impeding his apprehension or prosecution: Criminal Law Act 1967, s 4(2). Thus, on a count for murder, the accused could be convicted of assisting an offender who had committed either the murder or manslaughter or any other of the offences listed in (a) above. An 'arrestable offence' means one which is punishable with five years' imprisonment or more, plus certain other specified offences such as taking a motor vehicle without lawful authority (see Police and Criminal Evidence Act 1984, s 24(1) and (2) and Chapter 2).

(d)   On a count for dangerous driving or causing death by dangerous driving the jury may convict the accused of careless driving (Road Traffic Offenders Act 1988, s 24). This is an unusual provision in that it allows a jury to convict of a summary offence (other than one specified in s 40 of the Criminal Justice Act 1988: see Paragraph 12.9.1).

19.4.3   Judge's discretion

Even when the jury could as a matter of law return a verdict of guilty of a lesser offence, the judge has a discretion not to mention that option to them in his summing-up. The existence of the discretion was emphasised by Lord Roskill in *Wilson* [1984] AC 242 to counter the argument that extending the availability of alternative verdicts by abandoning the *Springfield* test (see Paragraph 19.4.1) was unfair to the defence. His Lordship said — 'a judge must always ensure, before deciding to leave the possibility of another offence to the jury, that that course will involve no risk of injustice to the defendant'. If the alternative offence has not been the subject of argument and submission in counsel's speeches, it is certainly wrong to introduce it for the first time in the summing-up: *Hazell* [1985] Crim LR 513. Counsel should at least be warned beforehand of what the judge has in mind, and given the opportunity to make a supplementary closing speech. In *Harris* (1993) *The Times*, 22 March 1993, the introduction by the prosecution of an alternative offence after the defence case and before closing speeches was held to be prejudicial. Steyn LJ said that such a course of action was only appropriate if it caused no risk to the defendant, and he was allowed a full opportunity to deal with the altered basis of the case against him.

In appropriate cases, there is, of course, nothing to stop counsel dealing with the issue in their respective closing speeches. However, the implication of *Fairbanks* [1986] 1 WLR 1202 is that the judge still has a discretion to tell the jury that they should ignore the alternative mentioned by counsel and either convict as charged or acquit. Mustill LJ summarised the principles involved by saying (at pp. 1205H–1206E) that 'the judge is obliged to leave the lesser alternative only if this is necessary in the interests of justice'. Where the case has been presented to the court in such a way that the lesser verdict simply does not arise (e.g. the defence have agreed that somebody committed the offence charged in the count but deny that it was the accused), mentioning the possibility in the summing-up would merely confuse the jury and so be contrary to the interests of justice. Similarly, if the alternative is very trivial by comparison with the actual charge, it is best not to distract the jury 'by forcing them to consider something which is remote from the real point of the case'. Where, however, the issue of a lesser offence clearly arises on the case as presented to the jury and where directing them on that issue would not be distracting or confusing, the judge should leave the alternative to them, even if one or other counsel objects. The interests of justice 'include the interests of the public as well as those of the defendant, and if the evidence is such that he ought at least to be convicted of the lesser offence, it would be wrong for him to be acquitted altogether merely because the jury cannot be sure that he was guilty of the greater'.

In *Fairbanks* it was the defence rather than the prosecution who wanted the alternative left. F was indicted for causing death by reckless driving. The essence of the prosecution case was that he had been responsible for a fatal accident by driving at recklessly high speeds along narrow country lanes. The defence more or less conceded that he had driven too fast but challenged, with some success, the actual speeds alleged by the prosecution. In his closing speech counsel argued that the jury might be sure that F was careless but not that he was reckless. Counsel for the prosecution, on the other hand, maintained a 'neck or nothing' approach — the jury should either convict as charged or acquit. Tactically, counsel did not wish them to have the easy option of conviction merely of careless driving. After argument, the judge took the prosecution's line, telling the jury that they should put careless driving 'out of their minds altogether' and consider only whether F's conduct was reckless. The jury convicted as charged, but only after a five-hour retirement in which questions they asked indicated that a conviction for careless driving (as suggested by defence counsel) might have been attractive to them. The Court of Appeal, applying the principles summarised above, held that failure to leave the alternative in the summing-up was a material irregularity and they therefore substituted a conviction for the lesser offence.

The decision in *Fairbanks* was approved by the House of Lords in *Maxwell* [1990] 1 WLR 401. M was charged with robbery. He admitted that he would have pleaded guilty to burglary, but denied that he had intended any violence to the victims. The prosecution declined to apply to amend the indictment to include a count of burglary. A verdict of guilty of burglary was not, in law, open to the jury on the robbery count. About an hour after the jury had retired, they returned with the question: 'We would like to know if there is a lesser charge that we can bring against M . . . other than robbery?' The judge took the question as being directed to whether the jury were entitled to bring in a verdict of burglary. He directed that they could not. The jury could, of course, have been directed that they were entitled to bring in a verdict of guilty to the even lesser charge of theft. The judge did not deal with that possibility. After retiring for a further three and a half hours, the jury found M guilty of robbery. M appealed and his appeal was dismissed by the Court of Appeal. On appeal to the House of Lords, it was held that (a) the prosecution were entitled, on the evidence, to take the view that the jury should not be distracted by an inappropriate alternative count of burglary; (b) the judge had been entitled to accept that view; (c) the judge had been entitled to decline to leave the alternative of theft to the jury since it was relatively trifling, and the essential issue was: Did M intend violence to be used? Although coming to a conclusion which was different on the facts from *Fairbanks*, their lordships approved the reasoning in the latter case. Lord Ackner, with whose reasons the other Law Lords agreed, stated the test, in cases where the judge has failed to leave an alternative offence to the jury, as follows (at p. 408):

. . . the court, before interfering with the verdict, must be satisfied that the jury may have convicted out of a reluctance to see the defendant get clean away with what, on any view was disgraceful conduct. If they are so satisfied then the conviction cannot be safe or satisfactory.

19.4.4 Decision on the offence charged

Through what is probably an unintended quirk in the wording of the subsections, the power to bring in an alternative verdict under both CLA, s 6(2) (counts for murder) and s 6(3) (the general provision) only arises if the accused is found not guilty of the offence charged. In *Collison* (1980) 71 Cr App R 249 the jury sent a note to the judge saying that they were agreed that C was guilty of the alternative of unlawful wounding but could not agree that he should be acquitted of wounding with intent as alleged in the indictment. The ironic possibility therefore arose that the jury might have to be discharged from giving any verdict whatsoever as an acquittal for the greater offence appeared to be a pre-condition of a conviction for the lesser. The judge rescued the situation by allowing an amendment to the indictment so as to add a separate count for the lesser offence. The jury then convicted on the new count and were discharged from giving a verdict on the original one. The Court of Appeal approved the course of action adopted. In *Saunders* [1988] AC 148, however, the trial judge, when it became obvious that the jury could not agree to acquit of the offence charged (murder), simply discharged them from giving a verdict as to that and, with the consent of the defence, accepted a verdict of guilty of manslaughter. He failed to follow the *Collison* procedure of adding a manslaughter count. The House of Lords held that, contrary to what had been tacitly assumed in *Collison,* s 6 of the Criminal Law Act does not totally replace the former common law. At least where the jury cannot agree on their verdict for the offence in the count, the common law on alternative verdicts still survives. Since, at common law, an accused indicted for murder could be convicted of manslaughter whether or not the jury specifically found him not guilty as charged, the verdict returned against S was a valid one. The decision in *Saunders* was convenient in that S's conviction would otherwise have had to have been quashed, even though the defence at trial had virtually run the case on the basis that he must have been guilty of manslaughter and the initiative for taking a verdict on manslaughter had come from them, not the prosecution. None the less, it is submitted that it would be unfortunate to extend the decision beyond its own facts. Subsections (2) and (3) of s 6 have every appearance of being a self-contained code intended to supersede the pre-existing law, whether statutory or common. Moreover, in the highly significant area of non-fatal offences of violence, the availability of alternative verdicts has been covered by statute for over a century. Finding out what the common law is will thus turn into an exercise in legal history. The solution to the problem of the jury who obstinately refuse to acquit of the offence charged even though they are agreed on the alternative is surely best overcome by the course adopted in *Collison* rather than by resurrecting the common law.

19.5 MAJORITY VERDICTS

Until 1967 the verdict of a jury had to be unanimous. This may have helped prevent mistaken convictions, but it had the disadvantage that one obstinate or unreasonable juror could prevent his colleagues reaching a verdict when, in truth, the evidence one way or the other was absolutely clear. There was also the possibility that a juror could be threatened or bribed into refusing to agree to a conviction. The Criminal Justice Act 1967, therefore, departed from centuries of tradition by introducing majority verdicts. The present legislation is contained in the Juries Act 1974, s 17.

Section 17 provides for verdicts by a majority of 11 to 1 or 10 to 2, or, if the jury is reduced below twelve, by a majority of 10 to 1 or 9 to 1. A majority of 9 to 2 is not acceptable. If the jury is reduced to nine they must be unanimous. A jury can both acquit and convict by a majority, although if they convict the foreman must state in open court what the majority was: s 17(3). Juries empanelled to try preliminary issues such as unfitness to plead may also decide the issue by a majority. The chief restriction upon majority verdicts is that before one may be accepted by the court the jury must have had two hours, or such longer period as the judge 'thinks reasonable having regard to the nature and complexity of the case', in which to try to reach a unanimous verdict: s 17(4). It is for this reason that the judge, at the end of his summing-up, directs the jury that they must try to reach a verdict on which they are all agreed. He is entitled also, if he so wishes, to indicate that the possibility of their returning a verdict which is not the verdict of them all may arise at some future stage, in which event he will give them further directions. He should not, however, indicate precisely how long must elapse before he can give such directions: *Thomas* [1983] Crim LR 745. In *Guthrie* (1994) *The Times*, 23 February 1994, the Court of Appeal confirmed that it was desirable not to mention the time at which a majority direction could be given, but said that on the facts of the case, mentioning the time did not amount to pressure on the jury. The two-hour minimum period laid down in s 17 has, in effect, been extended slightly by *Practice Direction (Crime: Majority Verdict)* [1970] 1 WLR 916, which states that at least two hours and ten minutes must elapse between the jury leaving their box and their returning with a majority verdict. The extra ten minutes is meant to allow them time for going to their room, settling down in their room, returning to court with any questions and any other matters which reduce the period they actually spend deliberating their verdict.

The procedure for the taking of majority verdicts is set out in *Practice Direction (Crime: Majority Verdicts)* [1967] 1 WLR 1198. Should the jury come into court, apparently with a verdict, before the two hours and ten minutes or such longer period as the judge considers reasonable has elapsed, the clerk asks the foreman if they have reached a verdict on which they are all agreed (see Paragraph 19.2). If they have, the verdict is taken in the usual way; if not, the judge sends them out again with a further direction to arrive if possible at a unanimous verdict. If the jury return to court or are sent for by the judge after the two hours and ten minutes or longer period, they are again asked if they have agreed unanimously. At this stage, however, should the foreman answer 'no', the judge gives them the majority verdict direction — i.e. he tells them they should retire once more and endeavour to reach a unanimous verdict, but if they cannot he will accept a majority verdict. He then informs them what the permissible majorities are. When the jury finally return to court after the majority verdict direction, the clerk asks — 'Have at least ten [or, if the jury has only 10 members, nine] of you agreed upon your verdict?' If they have, the verdict is taken, the clerk stressing that the foreman should only answer 'Guilty' or 'Not Guilty'. This is to avoid the foreman saying 'Not Guilty by a majority', as the whole aim of the rather elaborate procedure prescribed by the Practice Direction is to prevent the public knowing, if it be the case, that the accused, although acquitted, was only acquitted by a majority. Accordingly, if the verdict is not guilty, nothing further is said. If, however, the jury convict they are asked if their decision was by a majority, and, if so, the foreman states the majority. Although a literal reading of s 17(3) of the Juries Act might lead to an opposite conclusion, it is not necessary for the foreman to state expressly both how many jurors agreed and how many disagreed — it is sufficient if he says ten or eleven, as the case may be, agreed, leaving the size of the minority to be calculated by the most elementary arithmetic: *Pigg* [1983] 1 WLR 6. On an appeal against conviction the Court of Appeal may, in a border-line case, be swayed in their decision by the fact that the verdict was only by a 10 to 2 majority.

Although the Court of Appeal have stressed the importance of the procedure in the 1967 practice direction being followed, the direction does not have the force of law and failure to comply with it will not in itself lead to a conviction being quashed (*Gilbert* (1978) 66 Cr App R 237; *Trickett* [1991] Crim LR 59). The position is different where s 17 itself is contravened through a majority verdict being returned within the two hour period or the foreman failing to say by what majority the jury decided to convict. The verdict then is not 'a proper or lawful one', so an appeal must succeed: *Barry* [1975] 1 WLR 1190. *Barry* can be contrasted with *Shields* [1997] Crim LR 758, where, although the judge gave a majority direction after an hour and 47 minutes, this was remedied by telling the jury (once the mistake was discovered) that it was too early for a majority verdict, and they must reach a unanimous verdict. The jury did not in fact return a verdict until three hours and 47 minutes after their original retirement, and the conviction by a majority of 10 to 2 was upheld by the Court of Appeal.

> The readiness of the judge to accept a majority verdict varies depending upon the gravity and complexity of the case and the views of the individual judge on the desirability of unanimity. In *Mansfield* [1977] 1 WLR 1102, for example, Cobb J twice had the jury back into court to stress the 'utter desirability' of a unanimous verdict, and delayed for over six hours before giving a majority verdict direction. Melford Stevenson J, on the other hand, in *Gilbert* (supra) told the jury that he would accept a majority verdict after only the bare statutory minimum period had elapsed. In both *Mansfield* and *Gilbert* the accused was charged with murder, although the former was admittedly the more serious case in that there were seven counts of murder and three of arson. The evidence in *Mansfield* was also more complicated than that in *Gilbert*. Even so, the reluctance in the one case and the readiness in the other to accept a majority verdict seemed to spring essentially from the attitude of the judges concerned to such verdicts. Some indication of the Court of Appeal's view on how long the jury should have to reach a unanimous verdict is derived from *Rose* [1982] 1 WLR 614. In the circumstances of that case — a complicated murder trial lasting 15 days — two hours and forty minutes after retirement was 'a little soon' for the majority verdict direction. However, in a case which is not especially serious or complicated one would expect the direction to be given soon after the two hours and ten minutes have elapsed.

19.6   DISCHARGING THE JURY FROM GIVING A VERDICT

Where a jury cannot agree upon their verdict, the judge discharges them from giving one. The procedure is that, after giving them the majority verdict direction, the judge allows them whatever time he thinks reasonable for further deliberations. If they still do not return with a verdict, he has them brought back into court and finds out from the foreman whether there is any real possibility of their arriving at a decision. Should the answer be that they are so badly split that, even given more time, they would not reach a verdict, the judge discharges them. Discharge of the jury from giving a verdict is not equivalent to an acquittal. Therefore, the accused may be tried again by a fresh jury on the same indictment, and a plea of autrefois acquit will fail. In theory, there could be an infinite number of trials for the same offence, with the jury failing to agree and being discharged on each occasion. In practice, if two juries have disagreed, the prosecution offer no evidence at the start of what would otherwise be the third trial, and the judge enters a verdict of not guilty. Occasionally the prosecution do not even insist upon a second trial (e.g., when the offence is not especially serious in itself, but the accused is a well-known public figure who has already suffered a great deal of pressure and adverse publicity as a result of the first trial). In *Henworth* [2001] Crim LR 505, it was stressed that this was a convention, rather a proposition of law. In some cases, a further trial might be proper, e.g. if a jury had been tampered with, or some cogent piece of evidence for the Crown had since been discovered. Whether it was an abuse of process for the prosecution to seek a further trial must depend on the facts, including:

(a)   the overall period of the delay and the reasons for it;

(b)   the results of the previous trials;

(c)   the seriousness of the offence; and (possibly)

(d)   the extent to which the case against the defendant had changed since previous trials.

However anxious the judge is for the jury to agree he must not pressurise them into doing so. Subject to being discharged from giving a verdict, the jury must be allowed as much time as they need to deliberate freely and reach a proper verdict. If the judge does exert undue pressure, any conviction will be quashed. An example is provided by *McKenna* [1960] 1 QB 411. At 2.40 p.m., after the jury had been considering their verdict for two and a quarter hours, the judge told them that he was leaving court within ten minutes, and if they had not by then agreed they would have to be 'kept all night'. The reason for this ultimatum was that the judge was anxious to catch a train. After six minutes the jury returned with a verdict of guilty. Describing the judge's words as a threat, and pointing out that the jury might have thought that they would be locked in their room until the next morning, the Court of Criminal Appeal quashed the conviction. As Cassels J said at p. 422 — 'It is a cardinal principle of our criminal law that in considering their verdict . . . a jury shall deliberate in complete freedom, uninfluenced by any promise, unintimidated by any threat'. The attitude of the Court of Appeal in *McKenna* is a far cry from that which prevailed a century or so earlier. Until 1860, the jury bailiff swore to keep the jury without food, water or light, which must have given them a powerful incentive to agree upon a verdict quickly!

The Court of Appeal has also disapproved of less blatant forms of pressure, e.g., telling the jury during the majority direction that if they failed to agree, another trial might have to take place (*Boyes* [1991] Crim LR 717).

Failure by the jury to agree is regrettable because a second trial involves extra public expense and inconvenience for the witnesses. To encourage awkward jurors to listen to their colleagues' arguments while not putting undue pressure on them to change their minds, judges over the years have used a form of direction first sanctioned by Lord Goddard CJ in *Walhein* (1952) 36 Cr App R 167. The so-called '*Walhein*' direction had two elements. First, the jurors were told that, in order to return a collective verdict, there necessarily had to be some give and take between them and a willingness on the part of the minority to subordinate their views to the majority, while always bearing in mind that each of them had to stay true to his juror's oath to return what he regarded as 'a true verdict according to the evidence'. Secondly, the judge could point out the inconvenience and expense caused by one or more jurors being unwilling to listen to the arguments of the rest. Quite often juries which had appeared hopelessly deadlocked returned a verdict shortly after receiving such a direction, the clinching factor probably being the reference to public expense. The introduction of majority verdicts greatly reduced the need for *Walhein* directions because one or two obstinate or unreasonable jurors could be outvoted by the others.

Because of uncertainties over the propriety of *Walhein* directions, the issue was considered by a five-judge Court of Appeal in *Watson* [1988] QB 690, judgment given by the Lord Chief Justice. The main points are that:

(i)   The original *Walhein* direction was capable of putting improper pressure on juries to agree, chiefly because of the reference to the adverse consequences of disagreements.

(ii)   But, there is no reason why juries should not be directed as follows:

Each of you has taken an oath to return to true verdict according to the evidence. No one must be false to that oath, but you have a duty not only as individuals but collectively.

That is the strength of the jury system. Each of you takes into the jury box with you your individual experience and wisdom. Your task is to pool that experience and wisdom. You do that by giving your views and listening to the views of others. There must necessarily be discussion, argument and give and take within the scope of your oath. That is the way in which agreement is reached. If, unhappily, [10 of] you cannot reach agreement you must say so.

(iii)   There will usually be no need to give such a direction. Whether to do so or not is a matter for the judge's discretion. Similarly, the stage at which it is given (whether before or after the majority verdict direction) is a matter for discretion.

As to (iii), giving the *Watson* direction before the majority verdict direction might be appropriate where the jury take the initiative by sending the judge a note to the effect that they are split in such a way that even decision by a majority will be impossible unless some of them are prepared to change their minds. More usually, the judge will consider giving the *Watson* direction after the jury has had a reasonable time to consider the majority direction. It is in any event clear from *Buono* (1992) 95 Cr App R 338, that a *Watson* direction should never be given at the same time as a majority direction. Finally, it should be stressed that a *Watson* direction is unusual, even within the strict limits laid down by the Court of Appeal. In the great majority of cases, the trial judge will, when it becomes plain that the jury cannot agree even on a majority basis, discharge them.

19.7   ACCEPTING THE VERDICT

In general, the judge has no power to reject the jury's verdict however much he may disagree with it: *Lester* (1940) 27 Cr App R 8 — for exceptions, see below. Nor should he ask the jury any questions about the verdict (e.g., the reason why they convicted of manslaughter and not murder — *Larkin* [1943] KB 174). Once the jury have completed giving their verdict they are discharged. If the accused has been acquitted on all counts, he is discharged as well. If he has been convicted on any count, the judge either proceeds to sentence him forthwith, or adjourns so that reports on him can be prepared. He may be released on bail or kept in custody for the period of the adjournment. The procedure before sentence is passed is dealt with in Chapter 20. Should the jury realise before they have dispersed that they have inadvertently announced the wrong verdict, the judge has a discretion to let them correct their error (see *Andrews* [1986] Crim LR 124, where the Court of Appeal emphasised that such a correction would not be allowed if there was any possibility of the jury having heard something after the first 'verdict' which prompted them to change their minds; see also *Froud* [1990] Crim LR 197).

In the following cases the judge is not obliged to accept the first verdict returned by the jury:

(a)   If their verdict is one which, on the indictment, they have no power to return the judge can ask them to reconsider it. An example is if the jury purport to convict of an offence not charged in the indictment which does not fall within the provisions of the Criminal Law Act 1967 on alternative verdicts.

(b)   If a verdict on a count is ambiguous the judge should not accept it in the form it is given, but should ask questions to resolve the ambiguity and, if need be, further direct the jury on the law. Usually the verdict is an unambiguous guilty, not guilty or guilty of another offence, but occasionally something more is said which raises a doubt as to what the jury's decision really is. In *Hawkes* (1931)

22 Cr App R 172 the foreman said 'Guilty' when asked the jury's verdict on a count for driving while unfit through drink, but a moment later he added 'We find the defendant guilty of being under the influence of drink'. This remark introduced an element of ambiguity into the original verdict, since it might have meant that the jury, although satisfied that H had consumed alcohol, were not satisfied that it had impaired his ability to drive. The judge failed to take steps to clear up the ambiguity, so the conviction had to be quashed.

(c) If a verdict appears, having regard to the evidence adduced at the trial, to be inconsistent with another verdict returned by the jury in the same case the judge may ask them to reconsider the verdicts. He should only do this if the verdicts genuinely cannot be reconciled. If there is a possible, though unlikely, view of the evidence on which they can be supported, the judge should accept them. In *Burrows* [1970] Crim LR 419, where the jury were trying three accused on a joint count for theft of a purse and one of the three on a second count, in the alternative, for handling the purse, the judge thought that acquittals of all three on the theft count were inconsistent with a conviction on the handling count. He asked the jury how they could convict the handler when they had found that the purse was not stolen by acquitting all the alleged thieves. The Court of Appeal held that the verdicts were not inconsistent. The jury might have been satisfied that one of the three accused had stolen the purse, but were unable to say which it was.

If the judge, in a proper case, declines to accept the jury's first verdict, and, as a result of his further directions, they alter their verdict, the second verdict is the operative one. If, despite the judge's efforts, the jury insist upon their **first** verdict it seems that it would have to be accepted although any conviction would have to be quashed on appeal.

20   Procedure before Sentencing

This chapter, and the three which follow, summarise the sentencing process, placing emphasis upon its procedural aspects. For more detail, reference should be made to *Blackstone's Criminal Practice*, part E.

Once the accused has pleaded guilty or been found guilty by the jury or magistrates, the court's task is to sentence him. Before it does so, the procedures described in this chapter must be gone through. The court may either embark on them immediately after conviction, or it may adjourn (e.g., to obtain reports on the offender, or to await the outcome of a co-accused's trial so that, in the event of his being convicted as well, they can both be sentenced together). During the period of any adjournment the offender may be remanded in custody or on bail at the court's discretion. The description that follows is mainly of procedure preparatory to sentencing in the Crown Court. Although the same basic principles apply in the magistrates' courts, what happens there tends to be less elaborate and less formal than the Crown Court equivalent. Paragraph 20.8 deals with the differences.

In the magistrates' courts the decision on what sentence to impose, like the decision as to verdict, may be taken by a majority of the magistrates. In the Crown Court, the responsibility for sentencing rests solely upon the judge and any magistrates with whom he may be sitting. The only way a jury may try to influence sentence is by adding a rider to their verdict recommending leniency. They very rarely do so. Since counsel in their speeches and the judge in his summing-up do not refer to the possibility of recommending leniency, the jurors probably do not even know that they could make such a recommendation. Moreover, in *Sahota* [1980] Crim LR 678, where the jury asked if they could recommend leniency and the judge answered 'yes', the Court of Appeal stated that he should have told them that matters of sentencing were not for their consideration.

The procedure before sentencing is divided into the presentation of the facts of the offence by the prosecution; the reading of any reports on the offender; and mitigation by the defence.

20.1   THE FACTS OF THE OFFENCE

Where the offender has pleaded not guilty and has been convicted by the jury, the Crown Court judge, having heard the evidence, knows full well the facts of the offence, and does not need to be reminded of them. If the offender pleads guilty, on the other hand, it is prosecuting counsel's duty to summarise the facts of the offence. He does this partly to assist the judge, partly to establish the prosecution version of how the offence was committed, and partly so that the public may know what occurred and form their own views on the justice of the sentence passed.

In summarising the facts, counsel makes use of copies, given to him in his brief, of the statements made by the prosecution witnesses for purposes of the committal proceedings. He explains how the offence was committed, mentioning facts especially relevant to its gravity — e.g., if it was an offence of theft, he tells the judge the value of the property stolen and the amount which has been recovered; if it was an offence of violence, he recites the injuries suffered by the victim; if it was an offence committed when in a position of trust, he describes the position held by the offender. He goes on to describe the arrest of the offender, and his reaction when asked about the offence. If the offender was immediately cooperative, admitting his guilt to the police, it is a point in his favour which may result in the sentence being lighter than it would otherwise have been. Therefore, prosecuting counsel should acknowledge, if it be the case, that the offender did frankly confess to the crime. If there was a formal interview with the offender at the police station, counsel could either read out the record of it in full, or, more usually, summarise its contents and leave the defence to refer to it in more detail if they so wish.

At the sentencing stage, the prosecution take a neutral attitude towards the case. They do not suggest any particular sentence, nor do they advocate a severe sentence. Prosecuting counsel is still to regard himself as a minister of justice (see Paragraph 18.1.1), conceding to the defence those points which can fairly be made on the offender's behalf. This general statement is subject to some qualifications. For example:

(a) Prosecuting counsel should apply for compensation, confiscation or forfeiture, backing up the application with evidence and argument if necessary (see Paragraphs 23.17 to 23.20 for details).

(b) Counsel should assist the judge by drawing attention to any limits on the court's sentencing powers, so that no unlawful sentence is passed. This duty applies also to defence counsel (*Komsta* (1990) 12 Cr App R (S) 63). Prosecuting counsel should also draw the judge's attention to guidelines cases (*Panayioutou* (1989) 11 Cr App R (S) 535; see Paragraph 22.6.3 for the role of guideline cases).

Rather more controversial is the question of the extent to which the prosecution should make reference to the impact of the offence on the victim. In *Attorney-General's Reference (No 2 of 1995)* [1996] 1 Cr App R (S) 274, the Court of Appeal said it was appropriate that a judge should receive factual information as to the impact of offending on the victim. Any such information should, however, be put in proper form, e.g. a witness statement, served on the defence in advance and forming part of the judge's papers (see *Hobstaff* (1993) 14 Cr App R (S) 632, where the point was also made that the prosecution should avoid colourful and emotive language in dealing with the impact on the victim). In *H* (1999) *The Times,* 18 March 1999, the Court of Appeal emphasised that where the prosecution does provide a statement from the victim, then the sentencer should approach it with some care. Since it was generally inappropriate for the defence to investigate such a statement, it would necessarily reflect one side of the case only.

In *Perks* [2001] 1 Cr App R (8) 66, the following guidelines were laid down for courts when taking into account what have become known as 'victim impact statements':

(a) a sentencer should not make assumptions unsupported by the evidence about the effect of an offence on the victim;

(b) if the offence had a particularly distressing or disturbing effect upon the victim, the court should be so informed and account should be taken of this fact in passing sentence;

(c)   evidence of an offence on the victim should be in the proper form as a witness statement or expert report, and be properly served on the defence prior to sentence;

(d)   evidence of the victim should be approached with care, particularly if it dealt with matters which the defence could not be expected to investigate; and

(e)   opinions of the victim's close relatives on the appropriate level of sentence should not be taken into account.

In any event, the prosecution should not accept the defence version of the offence if it does not accord with the account given by the prosecution witnesses. Hence, there is the possibility of a dispute arising about the facts of the offence, even after the offender has quite properly entered a plea of guilty. If the dispute is on a minor point, it can be glossed over because the sentence the judge passes will be the same irrespective of which of the opposing contentions he believes. But, where there is a 'substantial conflict between the two sides' involving a 'sharp divergence on questions of fact', the judge, having heard submissions from counsel, must *either:*

(a)   obtain the answer to the problem from a jury; or

(b)   accept the defence account 'as far as that is possible', *or*

(c)   give both parties the opportunity to call evidence about the disputed matters,

and then decide himself what happened 'acting so to speak as his own jury on the issue which is the root of the problem'.

What he must *not* do is to come down in favour of the prosecution version of events without hearing evidence. The benefit of any reasonable doubt should be given to the offender. The above statement of the law is based on Lord Lane CJ's judgment in the leading case of *Newton* (1982) 77 Cr App R 13, the facts of which illustrate the importance which can attach to disputes about the facts after a guilty plea. N pleaded guilty to buggery of his wife. Buggery of a female was at that time an offence punishable with life imprisonment, regardless of whether the 'victim' consented. The wife, in a complaint she made to the police, said that she had not consented, but N claimed that she had. On his own admission, he was guilty as charged, but the appropriate sentence would be significantly more severe if he acted against his wife's will. Without hearing evidence from N or from the wife, the judge announced that he was sentencing on the basis that she had not consented, and he imprisoned N for seven years. The Court of Appeal (in reducing the term of imprisonment so as to allow for N's immediate release) said that the judge should not have decided such an important issue against the defence without hearing evidence. (The substantive law has been amended by the Criminal Justice and Public Order Act 1994. Buggery of a man or woman now constitutes rape where the victim did not consent and the accused knew of that lack of consent or was reckless as to whether there was consent or not. If N was to be dealt with today, the indictment would no doubt include a count of rape, and the procedural problem would be resolved in that way.)

Uncertainty about the facts of the offence can also occur where the offender pleaded not guilty and was found guilty by the jury. For example, in *Stosiek* (1982) 4 Cr App R (S) 205, S, who had punched a plain-clothes police officer and broken his nose, was found guilty of assault occasioning actual bodily harm. Prior to the assault, the officer had touched S lightly on the arm, shown him his warrant card, and said 'I want a word with you'. The evidence was consistent either with S having realised that a policeman was trying to arrest him and committing the assault to resist arrest, or with his not noticing the warrant-card and over-reacting to what he took to be a minor assault on him by a member of the public. On either hypothesis, the jury would have to convict, but on the first-mentioned hypothesis a sentence of imprisonment was almost inevitable, whereas on the second (given that S was of previous good character) non-custodial sanctions were appropriate. The Court of Appeal held that in such cases it is for the judge to assess the evidence led before the jury, and decide on the basis thereof what the facts of the offence were. He is not obliged to accept the least serious construction of the evidence consistent with the jury's verdict (*Solomon* [1984] Crim LR 433), but he should be 'extremely astute' to give the benefit of any doubt to the offender (*Stosiek*). In passing sentence, the judge must always respect the jury's verdict, so that if the offender was found guilty merely of a lesser offence the sentence must be appropriate to that lesser offence, even if the judge thinks that the evidence showed beyond doubt that the offender was guilty as charged: *Hazelwood* [1984] Crim LR 375.

A judge must not, under guise of hearing evidence about the facts of what occurred, in effect find the accused guilty of an offence more serious than that to which he has pleaded guilty. Thus, in *Courtie* [1984] AC 463, the House of Lords held that the Crown Court judge had no jurisdiction to decide the issue of whether a 19-year-old male 'victim' of buggery had consented or not. Since there were separate offences of buggery against a male aged 16–20 inclusive who does consent and buggery against a male of that age who does not consent, and since the count to which C pleaded guilty contained no allegation that the victim did not consent, the judge should have invited the prosecution to add a count for non-consensual buggery which could then have been tried by a jury. The distinction between *Courtie* and *Newton* is that the latter case concerned buggery of a female, which was a single offence encompassing both buggery with the victim's consent and buggery against her will. Therefore, the judge in *Newton,* had he heard evidence on the issue, would have been entitled to hold that N's wife had not consented to the act of buggery.

The decision in *Nottingham Crown Court ex p Director of Public Prosecutions* [1995] Crim LR 902 would appear to run counter to the well-established principle outlined in the preceding paragraph. In that case, the prosecution charged assault by beating contrary to s 39 of the Criminal Justice Act 1988 (which requires no proof of injury), rather than assault contrary to s 47 of the Offences Against the Person Act 1861 (which does). The Divisional Court held that the sentencer should have taken into account, in passing sentence, injuries caused to the victim. It is submitted that the decision is best viewed as confined to the offence of assault by beating, and should not be extended to other offences.

A judge must also not use an inquiry into the facts of the offence as a means of deciding that the offender has committed similar offences on other occasions. This principle is important to bear in mind should the prosecution, in their summary of the facts following a guilty plea, suggest that the counts on the indictment merely represent a sample of a continuing course of conduct by the offender. If this is accepted by the defence, the judge may pass sentence on that basis. But, if the defence claim that the indictment represents the full extent of the offender's criminality, then the judge must ignore the allegations about a continuing course of conduct, leaving the prosecution to bring separate proceedings in respect of the other occasions if they have the necessary evidence. Thus, in *Huchison* [1972] 1 All ER 936, the Court of Appeal halved a four-year sentence passed on H for incest with his daughter. The indictment contained one count to which H pleaded guilty. The prosecution alleged that there had been regular intercourse over a long period, whereas the defence said it had only happened the once. Having heard evidence from both the daughter and H, the judge believed the daughter, and sentenced on the basis that the count represented but a small part of a continuing course of conduct. Their Lordships held that the judge had adopted the wrong procedure. Instead of hearing evidence himself, he should have sentenced H strictly for the one offence to which he had pleaded guilty, leaving the prosecution to commence further proceedings for the other alleged acts of incest if they so wished. Similarly, in *Burfoot* (1990) 12 Cr App R (S) 252, B pleaded guilty to six counts and was convicted of a further 19. The prosecution case, however, was that the 19 counts on which he was convicted were specimen charges, and that he had committed some 600 offences! The judge proceeded to sentence on the basis that he had committed all the offences. The Court of Appeal said that this was wrong, and reduced six years' imprisonment to four, which was said to be appropriate for those matters in respect of which he had either pleaded guilty or been convicted. The Court of Appeal endorsed this approach, and rejected authorities cited to the contrary, in *Clark* [1996] Crim LR 448. In *Canavan* [1998] 1 Cr App R 79, the Court of Appeal endorsed the approach in *Clark*, and said that the court below could not base its decision as to sentence on the commission of offences not forming part of the offence for which the offender was to be sentenced. This seems to resolve the matter authoritatively.

Since the Court of Appeal's decision in *Newton* (supra) there has been a plethora of decisions refining and expanding upon Lord Lane CJ's basic dictum that, if the prosecution and defence disagree about the facts of the offence, the judge must either proceed on the basis most favourable to the defence or himself hear evidence on the disputed issues. Among the points dealt with in the post-*Newton* cases are the following:

(a)   The Court of Appeal has stated that counsel are under a duty to make it clear when a *Newton* hearing is appropriate. In *Gardener* (1994) 15 Cr App R (S) 667, the court said that where there is a dispute about relevant facts which might affect sentence, defence counsel should make that clear to the prosecution. The court should be informed at the outset of the hearing, if not by the prosecution then by the defence. If for any reason this did not happen, defence counsel should ensure during mitigation that the judge was aware, not merely that there was a dispute, but that the defence wished to have it resolved in a *Newton* hearing. The Court of Appeal would not normally consider an argument that the sentencer had failed to order a hearing unless the possibility of such a hearing was raised unequivocally and expressly in the Crown Court (see also *Attorney-General's References (Nos 3 and 4 of 1996)* [1996] Crim LR 607). In *Tolera* [1998] Crim LR 425, the Court of Appeal said that the initiative rested with the defence to make it clear that it was asking the court to pass sentence on any basis other than that disclosed by the prosecution case. The mere fact that the defendant put forward an alternative version to the probation service, which was reflected in the pre-sentence report, was not sufficient to alert the judge to the need for a *Newton* hearing. If the defendant wanted that account to be used as the basis of sentence, he should expressly draw the relevant paragraphs of the report to the attention of the court, and ask that he be sentenced on that basis. *Tolera* seems to run counter to *Oakley* [1997] Crim LR 607, which suggested that the judge ought to take the initiative in ensuring a *Newton* hearing in these circumstances. Certainly, the defence advocate will be on safer ground in following the suggestion in *Tolera* and drawing the judge's attention to the need for a *Newton* hearing.

(b)   Some difficulty arises where the defendant changes his plea to guilty after some evidence has been given by prosecution witnesses. In *Mottram* (1981) 3 Cr App R (S) 123, it was held that the judge should then hear evidence from the defendant (and, presumably from any witnesses the defence wished to call), before deciding on the version of the facts which will form the basis for sentence. The totality of the evidence received on the point relevant to sentence can then be treated as a *Newton* hearing (see also *Archer* [1994] Crim LR 80).

(c)   A *Newton* hearing may arise by decision of the court, even where prosecution and defence are agreed on the facts on which the plea is based (*McNulty* [1994] Crim LR 385). Sometimes an agreement is reached between prosecution and defence as to the basis on which a plea of guilty will be given and accepted, e.g. the accused agrees to plead guilty to assault occasioning actual bodily harm, but only on the basis of recklessness, and the prosecution are willing to accept this. In *Beswick* [1996] 1 Cr App R (S) 343, the Court of Appeal set out principles to guide the court in such cases. It stressed that the court should sentence an offender on a basis which was true, and that the prosecution should not lend itself to any agreement with the defence based upon an unreal set of facts. If that had happened, then the judge was entitled to call for a *Newton* hearing to determine the true factual basis for sentence. The judge's decision to do so did not of itself entitle the defendant to change his plea from guilty to not guilty. Once the judge had decided to hold a *Newton* hearing, then the prosecution should no longer regard themselves as bound by the original agreement which they had made with the defence, which was conditional on the sentencer's approval. They should therefore assist the court in the conduct of the *Newton* hearing by presenting evidence and testing any evidence called by the defence.

(d)   In *Oudkerk* [1994] Crim LR 700, it was held that where the imposition of a longer than normal sentence under the Criminal Justice Act 1991, s 2(2)(b), is contemplated, the sentencing court must resolve by a *Newton* hearing any important issue relevant to the application of that provision (see Paragraph 22.6 for longer than normal sentences). In the case in question, the plea had been tendered throughout on the basis that the assaults in the indictment were the result of a lovers' tiff, rather than a random attack on a woman whom the appellant did not know. That was an issue relevant to the application of s 2(2)(b), and should have been resolved by a *Newton* hearing.

(e)   If the court decides to have a '*Newton* hearing', the same rules apply regarding burden and standard of proof as apply at the trial of a not guilty plea. In other words, the court may sentence on the prosecution version of what occurred only if satisfied beyond reasonable doubt that the defence version is wrong (see dicta in *Ahmed* (1984) 6 Cr App R (S) 391 and *Stosiek* (supra)). In *Ahmed,* the Court of Appeal also intimated that they will not interfere with the Crown Court's decision as to the facts established at a *Newton* hearing unless the appellant can show that it was totally unreasonable or arrived at by applying incorrect principles (e.g. not giving him the benefit of any doubt). For a case in which the judge's findings of fact were successfully challenged, see *Gandy* (1989) 11 Cr App R (S) 564, which makes it clear that, where there is a *Newton* hearing:

(i)   the rules of evidence should be strictly followed; and
(ii)   the judge should direct himself appropriately as the trier of fact, e.g. in accordance with the guidance in *Turnbull* [1977] QB 224 on identification evidence.

(f)   Where the differences between the prosecution and defence as to what occurred are too slight to affect sentence, the Crown Court may sentence on the basis of the facts alleged by the prosecution without hearing evidence. (In such a case, the judge will frequently indicate that he is accepting the defence version purely for the purpose of sentence. Since it will not make any difference to the outcome, there is no point giving the offender a sense of grievance by openly disbelieving what is put forward on his behalf.) Thus, in *Bent* (1986) 8 Cr App R (S) 19, the Court of Appeal dismissed B's appeal against a sentence of six months' youth custody for assaulting a store detective who tried to arrest him for shoplifting since, although the judge in passing sentence clearly accepted the prosecution case that B had used a stick in attacking the detective (whereas defence counsel had said in mitigation that his client merely *threatened* to use a stick), the gravamen of the charge was that the appellant had resisted arrest. As there was no suggestion even from the prosecution that the store detective had suffered actual harm through the assault, the question of whether the stick had lightly come into contact with his face or had merely been waved threateningly was peripheral to sentence.

(g) Sometimes it is possible to avoid a *Newton* hearing by inviting the prosecution to add a subsidiary count to the indictment which will enable a jury, in effect, to decide how the offence alleged in the primary count was committed. Thus, if the accused pleads guilty to robbery but denies the prosecution allegation that he used a firearm to commit the offence, the correct procedure is to have a second count for carrying a firearm with intent to commit an indictable offence. The accused will presumably deny that charge, and, if the jury acquit him, the sentence for robbery will have to be passed on the basis that it was committed unarmed. Lord Lane in *Newton* specifically referred to, if possible, obtaining the answer as to the facts of the offence from a jury, and only resorting to a *Newton* hearing if there is no count that can be added to the indictment which will conveniently resolve the issues in dispute. In *Gandy* (above), the Court of Appeal regretted that the Crown had not adopted this course.

The clearest statement of the priority to be given to the role of the jury was delivered in *Eubank* [2001] Crim LR 495. E was arrested following the robbery of a shop. He was identified as the robber by a shop assistant, who claimed he had threatened her with a firearm. E had no firearm on him when arrested, and none was ever recovered. The prosecution case was that he had been carrying one, but he denied it. The judge held a *Newton* hearing, determined that he had been carrying a firearm, and sentenced him on that basis. E appealed on the basis that it would have been more appropriate for the Crown to have made the issue of the firearm a separate count on the indictment, so as to leave open the option of a jury trial on the question. The appeal was allowed. The fact that a *Newton* hearing might have been more expeditious and economical could not override the right of a defendant to have the verdict of a jury on the issue. There should have been a separate count on the indictment to reflect that right. As Dr Thomas points out in the *Criminal Law Review* commentary on *Eubank*, the implication is that if an offence of robbery with a firearm is to be treated as a 'serious offence' for the purposes of Powers of Criminal Courts (Sentencing) Act 2000, s 109 so as to lead to the imposition of a mandatory life sentence (see Paragraph 22.8), there must have been a count on the indictment charging an offence under ss 16, 17 or 18 of the Firearms Act 1968 committed at the same time. Since these Firearms Act offences are themselves 'serious offences' for the purposes of s 109, s 109(5)(h), which classifies robbery with a firearm as a 'serious offence' is in effect redundant. That would indeed seem to be the inevitable implication of the decision in *Eubank*.

(h) The principles explained in *Newton* do not apply when the facts advanced by the defence in mitigation are peculiarly within the knowledge of the accused himself, so that the prosecution cannot realistically be expected either to accept or to challenge what is put forward on his behalf, for example, where the accused pleads guilty to importing cocaine but says that he thought the drug was cannabis, or where he claims to have committed an offence as a result of threats that fell short of actual duress. In such cases, which have been usefully described as 'reverse *Newton*' situations, the onus would seem to be on the defence to establish the mitigation. Whether they do so simply by counsel making assertions of fact in his speech in mitigation (see Paragraph 20.4) or by calling evidence, is a matter for their judgment. In *Guppy* (1994) 16 Cr App R (S) 25, the Court of Appeal held that where the defendant raised extraneous matters of mitigation, a burden of proof rested upon the defence, i.e., on the balance of probabilities to the civil standard. The court did state, however, that in the general run of cases the sentencer would readily accept the accuracy of defence counsel's statements. (See also *Broderick* (1993) 15 Cr App R (S) 476, in which it was held that the mitigation alleging duress went to matters outside the prosecution's knowledge, so that *Newton* principles did not apply.) In *Tolera* [1998] Crim LR 425, however, the defendant pleaded guilty to the possession of heroin with intent to supply, and claimed that he had been threatened with violence if he did not assist in the drug dealing. The Court of Appeal held that there was an onus on the prosecution to rebut an explanation of this kind, and reduced the sentence from five to four years because they had not done so. It may be that the distinction is in the last resort practical (if intellectually unsatisfactory), and depends on the answer to the question: how feasible is it for the prosecution to rebut the defendant's version? If they ought to be able to do so, then on this line of argument the case falls within the reasoning in *Tolera*; if not, then the rule in *Guppy* applies.

(i)   The judge is entitled to decide that the defence version is not capable of belief and thus does not warrant the holding of a *Newton* hearing (see, for example, *Kerr* (1980) 2 Cr App R (S) 54, *Gandhi* (1986) 8 Cr App R (S) 391). The judge's view that the defence version is manifestly absurd must, however, be in accordance with the facts. In *Costley* (1989) 11 Cr App R (S) 357, C pleaded guilty to inflicting grievous bodily harm. The prosecution alleged that C hit V about the head and body with a piece of wood, causing a fractured rib, a broken arm and extensive bruises. C claimed he struck V with his fists only, after V had made a homosexual approach and dripped blood on him, claiming that he was suffering from AIDS and would pass the condition on to C. The judge sentenced C solely on the basis of the prosecution opening and the defence speech in mitigation. He said:

> I find as a fact that the attack was totally unprovoked by anything [V] said or did . . . I reject your explanation for the use of violence as being wholly incredible.

The Court of Appeal held that it was not open to the judge to come to these conclusions, and upheld the appeal against sentence. In a case where the judge is faced with a substantial conflict on issues such as this, a *Newton* hearing should be held. In *Tolera* [1998] Crim LR 425, the Court of Appeal stressed that, while the judge was not bound to hold a *Newton* hearing where the defence version was manifestly implausible, he should indicate his view to the defendant. The defendant would then have the opportunity to convince the judge of the truth of his story.

(j)   When one accused pleads guilty and a co-accused pleads not guilty, two principles for determining the factual basis of sentence come into conflict. Should the judge hold a *Newton* hearing (which would normally be done in respect of a guilty plea)? Or should he rely on the evidence heard in the trial (as would be the usual procedure for the accused who pleaded not guilty)?

In *Smith* (1988) 87 Cr App R 393, S pleaded guilty to conspiracy to obtain property by deception, the prosecution case being that he had supplied stolen credit cards to his co-accused (cashiers at a petrol filling-station), who used them to create receipts for non-existent transactions. Two of his co-accused pleaded not guilty, and ran the defence that they acted under duress from S. They were convicted. When the judge came to sentence both S and the co-accused, he said that he was taking the preliminary view that S was the ringleader, but offered S an opportunity to testify that he was not. The invitation was declined, and S was sentenced to 21 months' imprisonment, while his co-accused were given community service. The Court of Appeal held that the judge was entitled, in sentencing S, to take into account evidence at the trial of his co-accused. There was no need to recall the witnesses for cross-examination on S's behalf, notwithstanding the fact that his counsel had had no opportunity to cross-examine them during the trial. As the judge had given S a chance to give evidence himself, he had handled the procedure impeccably, and the appeal was dismissed. The approach in *Smith,* while understandable as a pragmatic solution to a difficult problem, may lead to a sense of unfairness being felt by an offender who is sentenced on a view of the facts which he disputes and which his counsel has not been able to test in the usual way by cross-examination of the witnesses who support the prosecution case. It is worth noting that the Court of Appeal in *Smith* did stress that the sentencing judge should bear in mind that evidence at the trial had not been tested by cross-examination on behalf of the offender who had pleaded guilty (see also *Winter* [1997] Crim LR 66).

A further anomaly appears when one compares the approach outlined in *Smith* with that adopted in a case such as *Gandy* (above). In *Gandy,* G pleaded guilty to violent disorder. His co-accused were then tried. Once their trial was completed, the judge held a *Newton* hearing to determine whether G had thrown a glass, causing the loss of V's eye. The Court of Appeal held that the judge should, in the *Newton* hearing, have followed the rules which would govern the use of evidence in a jury trial. Clearly, there is no equivalent protection for the accused where the *Smith* procedure is concerned. The resultant distinction seems arbitrary and exacerbates the sense of unfairness already referred to.

(k)   If the judge, after a *Newton* hearing, decides the issue of fact against the defence, the accused may lose some of the mitigation he would otherwise receive for a guilty plea (*Stevens* (1986) 8 Cr App R (S) 291). He is nonetheless entitled to *some* credit for his plea (*Williams* (1990) 12 Cr App R (S) 415). (See Paragraph 21.5.2 for the policy of giving a discount for plea.)

(l)   In appropriate cases, the Court of Appeal can itself hold a *Newton* hearing: *Guppy* (1995) 16 Cr App R (S) 25.

20.2 ANTECEDENTS

Immediately following the committal of the case to the Crown Court, the police should prepare a document containing what are known as the Crown Court antecedents. A copy of the antecedents is given to the defence not later than the jury's retiring to consider their verdict, or, in the case of a guilty plea, the entry of the plea. A copy is also given to each member of the court and to the shorthand writer, and to prosecuting counsel in his brief.

The antecedents should contain details of the offender's age, education, past and present employment, his domestic circumstances and income, the date of his arrest, whether he has been remanded in custody or on bail, and the date of his last release from prison or other custodial institution. There should also be a summary of his previous convictions and findings of guilt. This may include findings of guilt made when the offender was under 14, despite the Children and Young Persons Act 1963, s 16(2), which provides that in proceedings against a person who has attained the age of 21 findings of guilt when under 14 shall be disregarded for the purposes of evidence relating to previous convictions. Attached to the antecedents is a form giving full details of the offender's criminal record, save that, unlike the summary, it omits mention of s 16(2) findings of guilt. As regards each conviction or finding of guilt on it, the form states the name of the convicting court, the offence dealt with, the sentence passed, and the date of release if the sentence was a custodial one. Convictions which are spent (see Paragraph 20.2.2) are included in both the summary of convictions and the previous convictions form, but they should be marked as such on the latter. The defence are entitled before or at any stage during the trial to be supplied with details of the accused's previous convictions. The judge also knows about them, in contrast to magistrates trying a case summarily who, if possible, are kept in ignorance of the accused's criminal record until after conviction. In the Crown Court, the police are expected to provide brief details of the circumstances of the last three similar convictions, and also of any other convictions likely to be of interest to the court. This information is provided separately, and attached to the antecedents.

Formal cautions (see Paragraph 4.2.1) should not appear in the list of previous convictions. But cautions issued for offences committed within three years of the current offences may be cited in court, although they should appear on a separate sheet from previous convictions (Home Office Circular 59/1990).

In the great majority of cases where the contents of the antecedents are not challenged, prosecuting counsel will summarise the information which they contain. The judge has the full list and may not want to hear the details of all of them, and so may say, for example, 'last three only', or 'starting from 1995'. Counsel will then read out the last three convictions, or those dating from 1995, as the case may be.

Practice Direction (Crime: Antecedents) (No 2) [1997] 1 WLR 1482, deals with the contents of the antecedents. Examples of antecedents and previous convictions forms will be found in Appendix 5.

After these matters have been dealt with, the prosecution case is closed.

20.2.1 Challenges to the antecedents

Where the defence challenge the prosecution version of the antecedents, it would be usual for the prosecution to call the police officer in the case. If the prosecution assertions remain in dispute, the onus remains upon them to satisfy the judge of the truth of the assertion by calling evidence of a type which would be admissible during the trial of a not guilty plea — not, for example, inadmissible hearsay or opinion. If the prosecution fail so to satisfy the judge, he should ignore the challenged assertion in passing sentence, and state that he is ignoring it: *Campbell* (1911) 6 Cr App R 131.

The prosecution should, in any event, be restrained from making generalised allegations, prejudicial to the offender, which are incapable of strict proof or disproof. In *Van Pelz* (1942) 29 Cr App R 10, where VP had been convicted of an offence of larceny, the Court of Criminal Appeal criticised the prosecution for allowing the officer giving the antecedents to say that VP had led a loose and immoral life, was very well known as a prostitute, had associated constantly with thieves, and was regarded as a very dangerous woman indeed. Even where a prejudicial allegation is specific enough for the defence, assuming it to be untrue, to challenge it effectively, the allegation should be made by an officer with first-hand knowledge of the matter, not by an officer relying upon what others have told him. In *Wilkins* (1978) 66 Cr App R 49, the Court of Appeal reduced W's sentence for living on the earnings of prostitution from three years to two years because the officer giving the antecedents evidence testified that some 82 women, who had worked for an escort agency run by W, had stated that they used the agency as a medium for prostitution. The evidence at W's trial, while satisfying the jury that he had lived on the earnings of prostitution, had not suggested that he was involved in the organisation of prostitution on such a substantial scale. Clearly, the officer in making his allegations was not speaking of matters within his first-hand knowledge — he was repeating what the prostitutes had said. In all probability he had not even interviewed the prostitutes personally, but was telling the judge what other officers had told him of the prostitutes' allegations. The Court of Appeal emphasised the irregularity in the giving of the antecedents by reducing W's sentence even though, by the time the appeal was heard, he had been released from prison — a point of principle was involved. If allegations in the antecedents are likely to be disputed it may be advisable for the prosecution to give the defence advance notice of them and of the evidence they intend to adduce: see *Robinson* (1969) 53 Cr App R 314.

If the defence challenge the correctness of the prosecution evidence about any of the previous convictions, the principles described above apply, so the prosecution must provide strict proof of the conviction. They can do this by (a) producing a certificate of conviction, signed by the clerk of the convicting court, and (b) adducing evidence that the offender who is to be sentenced is the person named in the certificate: Police and Criminal Evidence Act 1984, s 73. The evidence of identity could come from someone who was present in court on the occasion of the previous conviction. Alternatively, s 39 of the Criminal Justice Act 1948 enables the prosecution to produce further certificates, establishing that the fingerprints of the person named in the certificate of conviction are identical to the fingerprints of the offender. Although convenient, this latter procedure is obviously dependent upon the police having the necessary fingerprints available.

20.2.2 Spent convictions

The Rehabilitation of Offenders Act 1974 is meant to enable offenders to 'live down' their past. Broadly speaking, the scheme of the Act is that after the elapsing from the date of conviction of a certain period of time (known as the 'rehabilitation period'), the offender becomes a rehabilitated person and his conviction is spent. A rehabilitated person is treated 'for all purposes in law as a person who has not committed . . . or been convicted of or sentenced for the offence or offences' of which he was convicted (s 4(1) of the Act). This means, for example, that when a rehabilitated person applies for a job he does not, generally speaking, have to disclose his spent convictions, and any questions on the job application form about the applicant's criminal record are deemed not to relate to such convictions. Similarly, in most civil proceedings questions about spent convictions and evidence of the offences to which they related are inadmissible.

Section 4(1) is subject to the remainder of the Act, which contains provisions restricting the circumstances in which the subsection is to apply. Thus, a person wishing to follow certain professions or occupations designated by the Home Secretary may be asked about spent convictions by a person assessing his suitability for the profession or occupation. Not surprisingly, any would-be barristers, solicitors or judges must declare their spent convictions. More to the point as far as criminal procedure is concerned, s 7(2) provides that s 4(1) is not to apply at all to criminal proceedings — i.e., there is no statutory restriction on the evidence which may be given of, and questions which may be asked about, spent convictions that does not apply equally to convictions which are not spent. However, in the *Practice Direction (Crime: Spent Convictions)* [1975] 1 WLR 1065, Lord Widgery CJ recommended that both courts and counsel should give effect to the general intention of Parliament expressed in the debates leading up to the passing of the Act, and should not refer to a spent conviction when that can reasonably be avoided. Indeed, counsel must always obtain the judge's authority before mentioning a spent conviction, that authority only being given where the interests of justice so require. At the sentencing stage of proceedings, the record supplied to the court of the offender's convictions should mark those which are spent. In passing sentence, the judge may disclose the existence of a spent conviction only if that is necessary to explain the sentence he is passing (e.g. because it would seem unreasonably severe were it not revealed that in the relatively recent past the offender had committed an offence similar to that for which he is now being sentenced).

The period after which a conviction becomes spent (the rehabilitation period) depends upon the sentence passed for the offence. The periods are as follows:

(a) If the offender was sentenced to imprisonment for life or for a term exceeding 30 months (or to equivalent sentences of detention in a young offender institution or detention under s 53 of the Children and Young Persons Act 1933) then the conviction never becomes spent.

(b) If the sentence was one of more than six but not more than 30 months' imprisonment, the rehabilitation period is 10 years; if the sentence was six months' or less imprisonment, the period is seven years; if the sentence was suspended, the period is the same as if it had been immediate.

(c) If the sentence was one of detention in a young offender institution for a term of 30 months or less, the rehabilitation period is the same as it would be for an equivalent term of imprisonment, save that if the offender was under 18 at the date of his conviction the period is halved.

(d) If the sentence was a fine, community service order or probation order, the period is five years (two and a half years for a juvenile).

(e) If the offender was conditionally discharged or bound over to keep the peace or be of good behaviour, the period is one year or that for which the order remains in force, whichever is the longer.

(f) If the offender was given an attendance centre order or secure training order, the period ends one year after the order expires.

(g) If the offender was discharged absolutely, the period is six months.

(h) If the offender was disqualified from driving, the period is that for which he remains disqualified.

Where more than one sentence is imposed for a conviction (e.g. for a drink/driving offence the offender is sentenced to six months' imprisonment suspended for two years; is fined £100, and disqualified from driving for three years), the rehabilitation period is the longest of the relevant periods (i.e. in the example given above, seven years for the suspended prison sentence, not five years for the fine or three years for the disqualification).

A convicted person can be rehabilitated only if not reconvicted during the rehabilitation period (s 6(4)). If an offender is reconvicted of anything other than a summary offence, the rehabilitation period for the first offence continues to run until the expiry of the rehabilitation period for the second offence. This is very important in practice, since it means that persistent offenders are unlikely to have any spent convictions. The rehabilitation periods for their early convictions are extended by their later convictions. This subsequent-offence rule does not, however, apply to orders of disqualification (s 6(5)).

20.2.3 Suspended sentence etc.

If the offence of which the offender has been convicted was committed during the operational period of a suspended sentence, the Crown Court or, in certain circumstances, a magistrates' court can bring the suspended sentence into effect (see Paragraph 22.9.4). Also, if the offence was committed during the currency of a conditional discharge or probation order, the court may sentence the offender for the offence in respect of which the order was made (see Paragraphs 23.6 and 23.14). When it becomes apparent during the evidence of previous convictions that the offender is in breach of a suspended sentence, conditional discharge or probation, he should be asked whether he admits the breach. If he does, the court may deal with him for that matter when it sentences him for the present offence. If he does not, strict proof must be provided of the previous conviction and sentence (see Paragraph 20.2.1). Upon such proof, the court may deal with the breach.

20.3 REPORTS ON THE OFFENDER

After the prosecution opening, the judge reads any reports which have been prepared on the offender. The defence are given copies of the reports. Counsel may refer to their contents in mitigation, but it is not normal practice to read them out in full. Where medical or psychiatric reports are concerned, it is obviously necessary to use them with discretion for fear that the offender should learn something about his physical or mental condition which it would be better for him not to know.

The main types of reports are as follows:

(a) Pre-sentence reports (formerly called social inquiry reports) — these are prepared by probation officers if the offender is an adult. In the cases of children under 13, they are prepared by local authority social workers; for intermediate ages, the work is shared between the probation service and social workers. Probation officers are appointed by a probation committee, which consists of magistrates, together with co-opted members and perhaps a circuit judge or recorder assigned to the committee by the Lord Chancellor. There is a probation committee either for a single petty sessional division or for a combined group of petty sessional divisions, and it is the committee's duty to appoint for the area for which it has responsibility sufficient probation officers to carry out the work of the probation service in that area. That work includes befriending and helping offenders who are placed on community rehabilitation orders, organising community punishment order schemes, supervising prisoners released on licence, supervising young offenders released from detention in a young offender institution, and preparing reports either on their own initiative or after receiving a request to do so from a court. There is normally a probation officer present in court to receive any request for a report.

According to the Home Office document, *National Standards for the Supervision of Offenders in the Community* (1992), the pre-sentence report should summarise the offence 'fairly and objectively', and 'analyse the offender's behaviour and attitude to the offence'. This information must be provided 'impartially', after one or more interviews with the offender. Typically, the report should address the offender's explanation for the offence, acceptance of responsibility, feelings of remorse, motivations, character, criminal history, relationships, personal problems such as alcohol or drug misuse, difficulties with finance, housing or employment, and any medical or psychiatric information available.

The *National Standards* do not require the report writer to make a recommendation as to sentence. Nevertheless, it is customary for reports to make proposals, particularly as to any community sentence which might be suitable. If the pre-sentence report proposes a community punishment order (see Chapter 23 for details), then it must state whether it is available.

By the Powers of Criminal Courts (Sentencing) Act 2000 (PCC(S)A), ss 36 and 81, the court must obtain a pre-sentence report when it is considering passing a custodial sentence or one of the more onerous forms of community sentence. Where the offender is aged 18 or over, however, the court need not have a pre-sentence report if it is of the opinion that it is unnecessary to have one. Where the offender is aged 17 or under, the court must obtain a pre-sentence report, unless:

(i) the offence is indictable-only and the court considers it unnecessary to obtain one; or

(ii) there is a pre-existing report and the court has considered its content.

Even if there is no statutory requirement to have a report, the court may well regard it as good sentencing practice to have one, particularly if it is firmly requested by the defence. Nevertheless, even where the obtaining of a pre-sentence report is 'mandatory', the court's failure to obtain one will not of itself invalidate the sentence. If the case is appealed, however, the appellate court must obtain and consider a pre-sentence report unless that is thought to be unnecessary.

Should the court want a report but one is not available when an offender initially appears to be sentenced, there will have to be an adjournment. To avoid such unnecessary delays, the probation service often prepare reports in advance of conviction. They are generally reluctant to prepare pre-trial reports on defendants who plead not guilty, because the accused obviously cannot be asked about his or her attitude to the offence. Practice as to pre-trial reports in the adult magistrates' courts and youth courts varies too much for any helpful generalisations to be made.

A copy of the report must be given to counsel or solicitor for the offender, or, if he is unrepresented, to the offender himself. If the offender is a juvenile and unrepresented, the report may be given to his parent or guardian: PCC(S)A 2000, s 156. The prosecution are *not* given a copy of the pre-sentence report. The defence can require the probation officer who prepared the report to give evidence, so that for instance they can challenge unfavourable comment about the offender contained in the report.

(b) Medical and psychiatric reports — as already explained in Paragraph 9.8, a magistrates' court has power to remand a person (in custody or on bail) for the preparation of medical reports. The magistrates must be satisfied that the person concerned has committed the *actus reus* of an imprisonable offence, but they need not have convicted him of the offence. Following conviction on indictment or prior to sentencing on a committal for sentence, the Crown Court also may adjourn with a view to the preparation of medical reports. Again, the offender may be remanded in custody or on bail as the court sees fit. A further option — namely to remand an accused person/offender to hospital for the preparation of reports on his mental condition — has been given to the courts by s 35 of the Mental Health Act 1983 (see Paragraph 23.22).

Medical and psychiatric reports are essential if the court is to make an order under s 37 of the Mental Health Act 1983 (detention in a mental hospital), or under PCC(S)A 2000, s 42 (community rehabilitation) with a requirement that the probationer receive treatment for a mental condition). In addition the court must order a medical report to be prepared on any offender who appears to be mentally disordered before a custodial sentence (other than for murder) is passed (Criminal Justice Act 1991, s 4(1)). The court need not obtain one if it thinks it unnecessary (s 4(2)). Failure to comply does not render the sentence invalid, but places a duty to obtain one on the appellate court where the matter is appealed (s 4(4)). Where the offender is legally represented, a copy of the report must be given to his counsel or solicitor, but if he is unrepresented he is not entitled to look at the report himself although the gist of it should be disclosed to him: Mental Health Act 1983, s 54(3). The practitioner who prepared the report may be required to attend to give oral evidence, and evidence may be called on behalf of the offender to rebut that contained in the report. In practice, it is often difficult to obtain psychiatric reports through the court, and it may be necessary for defence solicitors to take the initiative and ask a consultant who has been treating their client for a mental condition to prepare a report on him. It appears to be open to the defence to choose whether to put that report in front of the sentencer. The psychiatrist, on the other hand, if he discovers that his evidence is not to be put before the judge, is free to make it available through other channels, e.g. via the prosecution (*Crozier* [1991] Crim LR 138).

(c) In the case of a juvenile, there may be reports from social workers involved with the juvenile and his family. Where the juvenile, prior to being dealt with for the offence, is remanded in the care of a local authority, detailed reports may be prepared on him covering matters such as his intelligence, behaviour in care, reaction to persons in authority and relationships with his peers. There may also be a report from his school.

The mere act of adjourning for a pre-sentence report can raise in the offender's mind an expectation that, should the report be favourable in the sense of recommending a non-custodial disposition, the court will follow the recommendation. If, notwithstanding a favourable report, he is then given a custodial sentence, he will have an understandable sense of grievance, and the Court of Appeal will feel obliged to quash the custodial sentence, even if it was perfectly justifiable in the light of the gravity of the offence and the offender's record (see *Gillam* (1980) 2 Cr App R (S) 267). To avoid such an outcome, a court adjourning for reports but wishing to leave all options open should tell the offender that there is no implied promise of a lenient sentence, and, whatever the reports say, the eventual outcome may well be imprisonment or detention. Provided the above was made clear at the time of the adjournment, there can be no objection to the court rejecting a non-custodial recommendation in a report: *Horton and Alexander* (1985) 7 Cr App R (S) 299. Moreover, the mere fact that the judge, on adjourning for reports, remains silent as to the prospect of a custodial sentence, should not be taken as an indication that a non-custodial sentence will eventually be passed (*Renan* [1994] Crim LR 379).

20.4 MITIGATION

Once the reports have been read and, if necessary, the makers of the reports called to give evidence, defence counsel presents the mitigation on behalf of the offender. Much of it may be foreshadowed in the reports, and counsel can refer the judge to passages in them which are of especial assistance to his argument. Usually, counsel deals with the immediate circumstances of the offence, stressing any factor which may lessen its gravity. If it is an offence of dishonesty, he may be able to say that it was committed on the impulse of the moment, when temptation was suddenly and unexpectedly placed in the offender's way. If it is an offence of violence, he could point to extreme provocation which led the offender to lose his temper. Counsel must be careful, however, not to put forward in mitigation anything which in fact amounts to a defence to the charge — e.g., he should not assert that an assault was committed in self-defence. Where there is nothing that can sensibly be said with a view to making the offence appear less serious, it is best to turn rapidly to the circumstances of the offender. If the offence was committed when the offender was going through a period of difficulty, financial or otherwise, that may provide some explanation for what occurred. Looking to the future, there may have been a change in the offender's circumstances which offers hope for him staying out of trouble — he may have found a good job, or been reconciled with his wife, or accepted treatment for a drink problem which contributed to his offending. Finally, a co-operative attitude with the police when arrested, and a plea of guilty in court are both good points in mitigation.

In addition to his speech in mitigation counsel may call character witnesses on behalf of the offender to say (e.g.) that the offence was completely out of character and that they are convinced nothing like it will ever happen again. Such character witnesses can be called at the beginning or end of mitigation, or in the middle. If the offender has no previous convictions it is, of course, a very strong argument in mitigation whether or not any character witnesses are called. (For further details see Paragraph 21.5.)

The Criminal Procedure and Investigations Act 1996, s 58 gives a court power to impose reporting restrictions on false or irrelevant assertions made during a speech in mitigation, where they are derogatory to a person's character. No such order can be made if the assertion has been made at an earlier stage of proceedings, e.g. at trial. Orders may be revoked at any time by the court, and if not revoked expire after a year. It is an offence to publish or broadcast in breach of such an order.

The offender may decline legal representation and put forward his mitigation in person if he so wishes. Generally speaking, however, it is of assistance to the court to have counsel or solicitor emphasise those matters which genuinely argue for a light sentence — an offender in person, through ignorance, may concentrate upon points which if anything exacerbate the offence and ignore some which are good mitigation. Legal representation for the offender is especially important where he is in danger of a first sentence of imprisonment. Except as a last resort when it is really unavoidable, the courts should try to avoid sending to prison an offender who has not previously been there, if only because having experienced prison he may become hardened to it, and not deterred by the risk of it as he was before serving his sentence. So that all possible alternatives to imprisonment can be explored, it is desirable to have a lawyer mitigate for the offender. As Lord Bridge of Harwich put it in *Re McC (A Minor)* [1985] AC 528:

> No one should be liable to a first sentence of imprisonment . . . unless he has had the opportunity of having his case in mitigation presented to the court in the best possible light. For an inarticulate defendant, such presentation may be crucial to his liberty.

Therefore, the PCC(S)A 2000, s 83 provides that a court shall not pass a sentence of imprisonment on an offender who is not legally represented, and who has not previously been so sentenced unless he has been informed of his right to apply for representation by the Criminal Defence Service and has had the opportunity to do so but has failed to make any application. Broadly speaking, the effect of s 83 is that a court considering a first sentence of imprisonment must tell an unrepresented offender that he can apply for free legal representation, and grant, say, a week's adjournment to allow him to make the application. If he makes the application and is represented at the resumed hearing, the object of the section has been achieved. If he fails to make any application and is still unrepresented, the court has done all it reasonably could to persuade him to be represented, and is at liberty to pass whatever sentence it thinks fit.

Legal representation is also important whenever a court is considering depriving a young offender of his liberty. Therefore, identical provisions apply to the passing of a sentence of a detention and training order or detention under s 91 of the PCC(S)A 2000. In the above cases, no distinction is drawn between an offender who has, and an offender who has not, previously been dealt with by means of the sentence or order in question.

A sentence of imprisonment which is suspended (see Paragraph 22.9) is nonetheless a prison sentence, and so s 83 of the PCC(S)A 2000 will apply when a court is considering suspended imprisonment just as it applies when it is considering immediate imprisonment. But the statute provides that, for purposes of deciding whether or not an offender has previously been sentenced to imprisonment, a suspended sentence which has not been brought into force shall be disregarded. Thus, before passing even a suspended sentence on an unrepresented offender whose only previous prison sentence is an unactivated suspended one, the court is obliged by s 83 to adjourn to let him apply for free legal representation.

20.5 TAKING OTHER OFFENCES INTO CONSIDERATION

A suspect who is questioned by the police about an offence and admits that he committed it may be further questioned about other crimes, as yet unsolved, which bear some similarity to the crime to which he has confessed. If the suspect is responsible for some or all of these other crimes, he might nevertheless be unwilling to acknowledge responsibility should each crime appear as a separate count on an indictment against him. A system has therefore developed which allows an offender to admit to other offences without actually being convicted of them. It is known as taking other offences into consideration when passing sentence. The procedure can be used in both the magistrates' courts and Crown Court.

The police prepare a list of the other offences which they believe or suspect the offender has also committed. The offender studies the list, and, if he so wishes, indicates that he did commit at least some of the offences. He then signs the list, those offences which he denies having been deleted. Committal proceedings will then take place in respect, probably, of the offence for which the offender was arrested and one or two of the most serious of the other offences. The indictment is drafted accordingly. At the trial, the offender pleads guilty to the counts in the indictment. During his summary of the facts, prosecuting counsel tells the judge that he understands that the offender wishes to have other offences taken into consideration. The judge, who is given the list of offences which the offender has signed, asks him whether he admits committing each of the offences and whether he wants them taken into consideration when sentence is passed. Upon the offender answering 'yes' the judge will nearly always comply with his request. Prosecuting counsel will not give full details of the way the other offences were committed, but he may tell the judge for instance the total value of the property stolen in the other offences and the amount recovered.

In passing sentence, the maximum sentence the court may impose is the maximum for the offences of which the offender has been convicted. This, in practice, is not a significant limitation on the court's powers, since maximum penalties are usually far in excess of that which the court would want to impose even for a serious instance of the offence in question. To take a typical example, an offender might plead guilty on indictment to two burglaries of dwelling-houses and to theft from a car. He might also ask for two more burglaries of dwelling-houses and three car thefts to be taken into consideration. Domestic burglary carries 14 years' imprisonment, and theft seven years. Thus, the theoretical maximum penalty for the three counts on the indictment (bearing in mind that any prison terms could be made to run consecutively) is no less than 35 years. In fact, with the extra five offences taken into consideration, the sentence is unlikely to exceed a sixth of the maximum. The magistrates' powers of sentencing are, of course, much more restricted than the Crown Court's, but, assuming the offender is aged 18 or over and has been convicted of an offence triable either way, they can commit him to the Crown Court for sentence under the PCC(S)A 2000, s 3 if the offences he wants taken into consideration make the punishment they can inflict inadequate.

The judge should not automatically take other offences into consideration merely because the prosecution and defence wish him to do so. Where the other offences are of a different type from those charged in the indictment, it may not be right to agree to the request to take them into consideration. Certainly, an offence which is punishable with endorsement of the driving licence and discretionary or obligatory disqualification from driving should not be taken into consideration when none of the offences on the indictment are so punishable: *Collins* [1947] KB 560. The reason is that, since the court's powers of sentencing are limited to those it possesses in respect of the counts in the indictment, an offender who was allowed to 't.i.c.' an endorsable offence when none of the offences on the indictment carried endorsement, would unfairly escape endorsement of his licence and possible disqualification. It is also wrong for magistrates to take into consideration offences which they have no jurisdiction to try — i.e. they should not 't.i.c.' offences triable only on indictment.

Where an offence is taken into consideration, the offender is not convicted of it and accordingly could not successfully raise the plea of autrefois convict if subsequently prosecuted for the offence:

Nicholson [1947] 2 All ER 535. In practice, the police would never consider instituting proceedings for an offence which was taken into consideration. The 't.i.c.' system helps them to reduce the list of unsolved crimes by encouraging offenders who have little option but to admit to one offence to admit, at the same time, to other offences which, in the absence of such admission, it would be difficult or impossible to prove against them. The obvious question is — why should an offender admit to and ask to have taken into consideration other offences when, if the police had had sufficient evidence against him, they would have arrested him for those other offences? The answer is that, although the judge may increase his sentence somewhat because of the 't.i.c.' offences, the increase is unlikely to be significant, and the offender has the advantage of having his 'slate wiped clean'. When he has served his sentence, he can lead an honest life without worrying about the police uncovering evidence which would enable them to prosecute him for one of his past crimes.

The above discussion of taking offences into consideration has proceeded on the assumption that the offender is pleading guilty to the counts in the indictment or the informations preferred against him. However, there is nothing to stop the police asking an accused who is pleading not guilty whether, in the event of a conviction, he would like to have other offences considered, or there may be an opportunity between conviction and sentence to raise the matter with him. In general, though, the 't.i.c.' system is geared to the offender who is pleading guilty.

20.6   VARIATION OF SENTENCE

The sentence imposed or other order made by the Crown Court when dealing with an offender may be varied or rescinded within a period of 28 days beginning with the date of sentence: PCC(S)A 2000, s 155. If two or more persons are jointly tried on an indictment, the period is 28 days from the conclusion of the joint trial or 56 days from the imposition of the sentence which is to be varied or rescinded, whichever is the shorter. The obvious use of s 155 is to correct some technical error in the original sentence, or to alter it substantially to the offender's advantage if the judge after sentencing thinks he might have been too severe. The section may, however, be used to add to a sentence (e.g., *Reilly* [1982] QB 1208 in which the Court of Appeal held that the Crown Court judge had power to add to his original sentence of three years' imprisonment a criminal bankruptcy order in the sum of £178,000). Only in the most exceptional circumstances, however, would it be right to increase the length of a custodial sentence or to replace an original non-custodial sentence with a custodial one. Thus, in *Grice* (1978) 66 Cr App R 167, where the judge had passed a suspended sentence for an offence of unlawful sexual intercourse, the Court of Appeal reversed his subsequent decision to make the sentence immediate. The reason for the variation was that the judge had suspended the sentence in return for G promising that he would not go near his adopted daughter, with whom he had committed the offence. G's breaking his promise within the 28-day period for variation was not a sufficient reason for 'unsuspending' his sentence.

Once the period specified in s 155 has elapsed the Crown Court has no power to vary or rescind its sentence. Thus, an order made outside the relevant period that the offender should forfeit money which he had been carrying in order to facilitate the commission of drugs offences, was quashed by the House of Lords because the addition of a forfeiture order amounted to a variation of sentence, and so had to be made within the statutory time limits (*Menocal* [19801 AC 598). Similarly, the period for variation cannot be extended by quashing the original sentence within 28 days, and then passing a new sentence after the expiry of 28 days (*Stilwell* (1991) 94 Cr App R 65).

A magistrates' court can also vary or rescind a sentence or other order made when dealing with an offender: Magistrates' Courts Act 1980, s 142(1). Similar provisions apply when a magistrates' court has convicted an accused, and the magistrates who made up the court have doubts about the correctness of their decision (see Paragraph 9.7.5).

20.7   DEFERRING SENTENCE

Counsel mitigating for an offender often makes optimistic or even extravagant claims on his behalf. If given a chance by the court (i.e., not sent to prison) his client will cease to commit crime; settle down in society; hold a steady job; marry his girl-friend, and make full reparation to the victims of his past offences. The court, having perhaps heard such claims on many previous occasions and not always found them borne out by subsequent events, may not be convinced by counsel's argument, but nevertheless may feel that the offender deserves a chance to prove himself. Time will show whether he can live up to the promises made on his behalf. To give him that time, the court may defer sentencing him.

Section 1 of the PCC(S)A 2000 empowers both the Crown Court and magistrates' courts to defer passing sentence on an offender for up to *six months* so that, when the court does come to determine what the sentence shall be, it may have regard to (a) the offender's conduct after conviction and (b) any change in his circumstances. Conduct after conviction is expressly stated to include making reparation for the offence where that is appropriate. Deferment under s 1 is always conditional upon the offender consenting to it and, subject to an exception explained below, is not allowed more than once per case. Moreover, it is desirable that sentence should actually be passed on the date specified by the court when it deferred sentencing. However, the court does not lose jurisdiction to sentence if it cannot deal with the offender on that date (e.g., because the judge reserved the case to himself and then is unavailable on the relevant day, or because the offender fails to appear, or because necessary reports have not been prepared) — see *Ingle* [1974] 3 All ER 811 and *Anderson* (1983) 78 Cr App R 251. In the latter case, sentence was originally deferred for five months, but A, through a chapter of accidents, was not sentenced until seven months after the deferment. Despite that being outside the statutory six-month period, the Court of Appeal held that the Crown Court's jurisdiction was unaffected, although the sentence it actually chose to pass should reflect the staleness of the offence. Following deferment, the sentencing court may deal with the offender in any way the court which deferred could have dealt with him: PCC(S)A 2000, s 2.

The approach to and procedure for deferring sentence was summarised by Lord Lane CJ in his judgment in *George* [1984] 1 WLR 1082. It is the responsibility of the deferring court to make it clear to the offender why sentence is being deferred, and what conduct is expected of him during the deferment. Obviously, he will be expected not to commit further offences, but he might also be told that he should stay in and/or make genuine efforts to find employment, or that he should accept help and advice from a probation officer, or that he should save money with a view to making reparation for the offence, or that he should cut down on his consumption of alcohol. It is not appropriate, however, to tell the offender that he must go to hospital to receive treatment for a mental condition, for such restrictions on an offender's freedom of action should be imposed by virtue of a hospital order or probation order with a requirement for treatment, not as a side wind of a deferment of sentence: *Skelton* [1983] Crim LR 686. In general, the courts should not defer sentence when the desired improvements in the offender's conduct are sufficiently precise to be included in requirements attached to a community rehabilitation order (see Paragraph 23.2.1). The court should make a note of the reasons for deferment and, ideally, give a copy to the offender. When the offender appears to be sentenced, the sentencing court may then easily ascertain, with the help of up-to-date reports, whether he has 'substantially conformed or attempted to conform with the proper expectations of the deferring court'. If he has, an immediate custodial sentence should not be imposed; if he has not, the sentencing court should state precisely in what respects there has been failure (see Lord Lane CJ's judgment in *George* at p. 1085). Commission of further offences during the deferment period is likely to result in a custodial sentence both for the subsequent offence and the deferred-sentence offence. But, merely staying out of trouble will not necessarily guarantee the offender a non-custodial sentence. Thus, in *Smith* (1977) 64 Cr App R 116 the Court of Appeal upheld a sentence of 18 months' immediate imprisonment for several burglaries, the facts being that S (with a bad record for dishonesty) had had sentence deferred to see if he would (a) work regularly and (b) cut down on his drinking. He had done neither, and his not having committed further offences was not sufficient to save him from prison. Conversely, if the offender has both 'gone straight' and done at least most of what the deferring court required of him, an immediate custodial sentence will be wrong in principle (see *Smith* (1979) 1 Cr App R (S) 339 for an example). *Aquilina* (1990) 11 Cr App R (S) 431 deals with the situation where it is alleged that the offender has committed offences during the period of deferment, but the allegations remain unresolved. It was held that they should not influence sentence in any way unless and until he has been convicted of the later alleged offences.

One of the reasons for asking courts to make a note of why they defer sentence is that the sentencing court may well not comprise the same judge or magistrates who deferred sentence. Wherever possible, though, the deferring judge or magistrates should make themselves available to pass sentence (*Gurney* [1974] Crim LR 472), and counsel who represented the offender at deferment should also do his utmost to be there for sentencing (*Ryan* [1976] Crim LR 508).

When sentence is deferred, the offender is not bailed, but is simply told that he must come to court on the appropriate day. If he fails to do so, a summons or warrant for his arrest may be issued. Conviction for a further offence during the deferment period entitles the deferring court to sentence the offender immediately upon securing his attendance before it. Alternatively, the court convicting of the subsequent offence may also sentence for the deferred-sentence offence, save that a magistrates' court may not deal with a matter in respect of which the Crown Court deferred sentence. Also, the Crown Court, when dealing with a matter in respect of which magistrates deferred, is limited to the sentencing powers which a magistrates' court dealing with the offender would have.

It was stated above that sentence may only be deferred once. There is one exception to this rule, which arises as follows. The exercise by magistrates of their power to defer sentence does not preclude them, when the offender appears to be sentenced, from committing him to the Crown Court to be dealt with. The Crown Court may then, if it chooses, also defer sentence.

20.8 SENTENCING IN MAGISTRATES' COURTS

The pre-sentencing procedure described in this Chapter is essentially applicable in both the Crown Court and magistrates' courts. Thus, Crown Court judges and justices alike must be told the facts of the offence and be informed about the offender's antecedents, after which they read reports and listen to mitigation. Similarly, specific procedures such as taking other offences into consideration and deferring sentence are the same in both the higher and lower tribunals. However, in the magistrates' courts, the whole sequence of events is swifter and less formalised than in the Crown Court. In particular, the antecedents are given simply by the prosecutor handing to the court a list of previous convictions. Furthermore, where the court is merely dealing with a road traffic matter, the practice is not to obtain a full list of previous convictions but to sentence on the basis of the endorsements shown on the motorist's licence. If there is no licence, a print out of the offender's driving record is obtained from the Drivers and Vehicles Licensing Centre in Swansea.

The justices are required to hold a *Newton* hearing in the same circumstances as a Crown Court judge. What if an offender is committed to the Crown Court for sentence (see

Chapter 11) and there is a dispute about the facts of the case upon which he has been committed? Which court ought to hold the *Newton* hearing: the Crown Court or the magistrates court? In *Munroe v Crown Prosecution Service* [1988] Crim LR 823, the Divisional Court held that:

(a)   Where the matter arises before the magistrates, they should conduct the *Newton* hearing, and, if they decide to commit, ensure that the Crown Court is informed of their findings of fact. The Crown Court should sentence on that basis, and not allow the dispute to be revived.

(b)   If the issue arises for the first time in the Crown Court, then it should conduct the *Newton* hearing.

(c)   Where there was doubt whether the issue had been raised before the magistrates, then the Crown Court could either resolve the matter itself, or remit it to the magistrates, at its discretion.

What was said in *Munroe* should now be read subject to *Warley Magistrates' Court ex p DPP* [1998] 2 Cr App R 307 (see Paragraph 11.2.1). If it appears to the magistrates that they will be committing the case to the Crown Court for sentence in any event, then they should not conduct the *Newton* hearing, but should leave it for the Crown Court to do so. If the outcome of the *Newton* hearing is crucial to their decision whether to commit for sentence, however, then the magistrates must conduct it. It may therefore still happen that the magistrates conduct a *Newton* hearing where the matter ends up in the Crown Court.

21 Determining the Sentence

Chapter 20 dealt with the procedure which the court follows prior to passing sentence. The sentencer should therefore have the information upon which to decide sentence. That decision involves a choice between a series of options. In any particular case, the range of options will be in part determined by the circumstances of the offence (e.g., whether it is imprisonable and the maximum punishment which the law lays down) and of the offender (e.g., his age). Usually, however, the sentencer has a fairly wide range of possibilities for disposing of the case. The various options for sentence are considered in detail in Chapters 22 and 23. Without any attempt to be exhaustive, such options include (in roughly increasing order of gravity):

    (a)   an absolute or conditional discharge,
    (b)   a fine,
    (c)   a supervision order,
    (d)   an attendance centre order,
    (e)   a curfew order,
    (f)   a community rehabilitation order,
    (g)   a community punishment order,
    (h)   a suspended sentence,
    (i)   an immediate custodial sentence.

As already mentioned, the nature of the offence and the characteristics of the offender impose certain limitations upon the freedom which the sentencer has to choose between the available options. In addition, a legislative framework is laid down by the Criminal Justice Act 1991, now consolidated in the Powers of Criminal Courts (Sentencing) Act 2000 (PCC(S)A), which imposes criteria for determining whether the sentencer may pass a custodial sentence, for example. This legislative framework is detailed in Paragraph 21.1.

Within that framework, the decisions of the courts provide further guidance in determining the sentence which a court is likely to impose (as distinct from the question of the sentence which it is empowered to impose). Certain points need to be borne in mind in considering the guidance available from the courts, however.

On passing sentence, judges do not always give reasons, and even if they do they need to keep the reasons short and simple so that the offender can readily understand what is being said to him. Therefore, it is from judgments of the Court of Appeal when disposing of appeals against sentence, not from the words of the sentencing judges themselves, that the principles governing the sentencing process are to be deduced.

It should, however, be emphasised that precedent plays a relatively small part in sentencing. This is for three reasons. First, the truism that every case turns upon its own facts is never truer than in the context of sentencing. No two offenders and no two offences are ever precisely the same, whatever the similarities between them. Therefore, if told about a Court of Appeal decision in a comparable case, a judge can always find a reason for distinguishing it if he so chooses. In fact, it is relatively rare for counsel to quote any cases when mitigating. He does not even suggest a precise sentence, but merely argues for a certain form of sentence. For example, he might say: 'If this offence is so serious that a prison sentence is required, then it should be suspended and not immediate', or 'In the light of my client's previous good character and regular income, the case can suitably be dealt with by means of a fine', but he would be unlikely to say that in the case of X the Court of Appeal reduced a five-year prison sentence to three years and therefore, since the present case is a little less serious than X's, the proper sentence is two years. Such an argument is more likely to be used before the Court of Appeal than in mitigation before the sentencing judge. Second, the Court of Appeal does not attempt to prescribe the one right sentence for a particular case. Instead, their lordships allow Crown Court judges a broad discretion, and, in general, only interfere to reduce a sentence if it is outside the range of sentences appropriate to the gravity of the offence when taken in conjunction with any mitigating factors. Third, until the passing of ss 35 and 36 of the Criminal Justice Act 1988, there was no procedure that was apt to allow the Court of Appeal to pronounce a sentence too light. It remains the case that, if the defence appeal, the Court of Appeal has no power to increase sentence, although their lordships do on occasion state that, if they had been sitting in the Crown Court, they would have imposed a harsher penalty.

Despite these limitations, and the growth in importance of the statutory dimension, reports of Court of Appeal decisions provide a useful guide to the way in which judges arrive, or should arrive, at their sentencing decisions. Notwithstanding the point made above about the reluctance of defence counsel to quote authority in the Crown Court, the recent trend in the Court of Appeal has been to encourage judges at first instance to make use of authorities in determining sentence (*Johnson* [1994] Crim LR 537). A number of sources are available to assist the court, and counsel appearing before it. There is a series of reports consisting entirely of sentencing appeals: *Criminal Appeal Reports (Sentencing)* cited as Cr App R (S). The *Criminal Law Review* publishes reports of sentencing decisions on a monthly basis. *Blackstone's Criminal Practice* contains a substantial section on sentencing (part E), and deals with the guideline cases, which encapsulate the Court of Appeal's views on sentencing for particular offences, under the offences in question (parts B and C). A great number of decisions of the Court of Appeal are collected together and organised according to subject-matter in the encyclopaedia, *Current Sentencing Practice*.

21.1 THRESHOLDS FOR CUSTODY AND COMMUNITY SENTENCES

The Criminal Justice Act 1991 lays down the criteria which the sentencer must consider in deciding:

(a) whether to impose a community sentence; and
(b) whether to impose a custodial sentence.

These provisions are perhaps best seen as thresholds. In other words, the sentencer must consider whether the offender has crossed the threshold for a community sentence, or, as the case may be, a custodial sentence.

Under s 35 of PCC(S)A 2000, a court shall not pass a community sentence 'unless it is of the opinion that the offence, or the combination of the offence and one or more offences associated with it, was serious enough to warrant such a sentence'.

The position as far as custodial sentences is concerned is slightly more complex, in that the court must find one of two alternative justifications for such a sentence. By s 79 such a sentence may be imposed if either:

(a)   the offence (in combination if necessary with one or more offences associated with it) was so serious that only a custodial sentence is justified; or

(b)   the offence is a violent or sexual offence, and only a custodial sentence would be adequate to protect the public from harm from the offender.

These criteria are examined in rather more detail below (see Paragraphs 21.2 and 21.3), together with the related concept of offence combination (Paragraph 21.4). The overall effect of these provisions is to create a hierarchy of sentencing bands. In the bottom band are the discharges (whether absolute or conditional). In the next band comes the fine. No specific conditions have to be met for the imposition of these relatively less severe penalties, although there are, of course, considerations which the court must bear in mind in deciding, for example, the size of the fine (see Chapter 23). The next band upward is occupied by community orders. Only if the court thinks that the offence is too serious for a financial penalty can it proceed to impose a community order. In the top band come the various forms of custodial sentence. Again, the court must decide whether the offender has passed over the custodial threshold, applying this time the alternative criteria for offence seriousness and public protection.

It is implicit in the criteria which are laid down for progression from one band to another that the primary aim of sentencing is *proportionality*. In the past, the sentencer was able to choose between a variety of sentencing aims, such as deterrence, retribution, prevention and rehabilitation. In practice, it should be said, this range was rarely stated explicitly by the courts in passing sentence, and it must be a matter of conjecture whether sentencers always bore these aims in mind when carrying out the decision-making process. In any event, the statutory provisions now, in effect, determine that the primary aim of sentencing should be to give the offender the punishment which is proportional to the offence. Nonetheless, s 79 preserves the role of prevention (in the guise of public protection) as far as sexual and violent offences are concerned. The way in which the concept of 'offence seriousness' has been interpreted by the Court of Appeal, moreover, allows the sentencer to take account of deterrence (*Cunningham* (1993) 14 Cr App R (S) 444). Further, the proportionality requirement, whilst relevant to the various community orders, does not entirely preclude a court from seeking to rehabilitate an offender. The thrust of the statutory provisions seems to be that community orders should be both proportionate to the offence (particularly in terms of the restrictions which they impose), and tailored to the individual offender. Despite these features, it is now broadly true to say that the courts are required to have proportionality as their primary aim in sentencing.

21.2   OFFENCE SERIOUSNESS

It is the seriousness of the offence which is the sole criterion in determining whether a community sentence may be passed. Further, offence seriousness is the primary criterion for a custodial sentence, although in that case the sentencer may in the case of violent or sexual offences rely upon the need to protect the public as an alternative justification for a custodial sentence. Offence seriousness is, again, the crucial factor in determining the length of a custodial sentence (see Paragraph 22.6). It also looms large in fixing the amount of a fine (see Paragraph 23.13).

The question of whether an offence is a serious one is clearly, then, a vital one for the sentencer. There are really two issues at stake:

(a)   What is the *test* to apply in determining whether an offence is serious?

(b)   What *material* ought the court to take into account in deciding whether an offence is serious?

As far as (a) is concerned, the Court of Appeal has provided some guidance as to the test to be applied. In *Cox* [1993] 1 WLR 188, it was said that what was needed to satisfy the seriousness criterion was: 'The kind of offence which . . . would make all right thinking members of the public, knowing all the facts, feel that justice had not been done by the passing of any sentence other than a custodial one'. In *Howells* [1998] Crim LR 836, it was recognised that the 'right-thinking members of the public' test was not very helpful, since there was a natural tendency for the court to assume that its own views reflected those of the members of the public in question. The Court of Appeal in *Howells* (Lord Bingham CJ) therefore identified some factors affecting offence seriousness which sentencers should bear in mind in approaching cases on or near the custody threshold, including the following:

(i)   the nature and extent of the defendant's criminal intention;

(ii)   the nature and extent of any injury or damage caused to the victim;

(iii)   whether the offence was premeditated or spontaneous;

(iv)   any provocation to which the offender was subjected;

(v)   any personal injury or mental trauma suffered by the victim, particularly if permanent (such a feature would usually make an offence more serious than one which inflicted financial loss only);

(vi)   any previous convictions of the offender and any failure to respond to previous sentences;

(vii)   whether the offence was committed on bail.

The Lord Chief Justice then went on to set out mitigating factors relating to the offender (see also Paragraph 21.5), and said that the following matters ought normally to be taken into account in deciding whether to impose a custodial sentence in borderline cases:

(i)   an offender's admission of responsibility for the offence, especially where reflected in an early plea of guilty and accompanied by hard evidence of genuine remorse (e.g., an expression of regret to the victim and an offer of compensation);

(ii)   where offending was fuelled by addiction to drink or drugs, a genuine self-motivated determination to address the addiction, demonstrated by taking practical steps to that end;

(iii)   youth and immaturity;

(iv)   previous good character;

(v)   family responsibilities;

(vi)   physical or mental disability;

(vii)   the fact that the offender had never before served a custodial sentence.

According to *Cunningham* (1993) 14 Cr App R (S) 444, in determining offence seriousness it is legitimate to take account of deterrence. Further, the prevalence of an offence is a relevant factor in deciding on the appropriate sentence though the Court of Appeal also made it clear that the statutory provisions prohibit the addition of any extra element to make an example of the offender.

In fact, the Court of Appeal has in practice set the threshold of seriousness for a custodial sentence at a remarkably low level. In *Fenton* (1994) 15 Cr App R (S) 682, a custodial sentence was held appropriate for common assault, where the offender pushed the victim in the chest in the course of a motoring dispute, because of the danger of such disputes escalating. In *McCormick* (1994) 16 Cr App R (S) 134, offences of theft and going equipped were held properly to have attracted a custodial sentence despite the low value involved (£15) because a breach of trust was involved. On the other hand, in *Tetteh* (1994) 15 Cr App R (S) 46, burglary of a spirits store was held not to be so serious that only a custodial sentence could be justified — it was a non-domestic burglary, nothing was taken, and the offence was unplanned and opportunistic. In *Bond* (1994) 15 Cr App R (S) 430, theft of gammon steaks (value £3.50) from a supermarket was held not to pass the seriousness test. Similarly, in *Elder* (1994) 15 Cr App R (S) 514, an offence of importing 200 grams of cannabis and 700 grams of herbal cannabis was held not to be so serious that only custody was justified.

When we come to issue (b) — the material which the court should consider — then the statute is directly helpful in the following respects:

(i) In certain circumstances, the court must obtain and consider a pre-sentence report (PCC(S)A, 2000, ss 36 and 81 and see Paragraph 20.3).

(ii) Whenever it is judging the seriousness of an offence, the court must take into account all information available to it about the circumstances of the offence, including any aggravating or mitigating factors (PCC(S)A 2000, s 81(4)(a)). (Note that the court is, in addition, allowed to take into account any matters which it views as relevant in *mitigation* (PCC(S)A 2000, s 158(1))). Hence it is not confined to matters relevant to the seriousness of the offence, but may take into account matters which relate to the offender, at least insofar as they go to mitigation, rather than aggravation, e.g., his efforts at reparation: for more detail see Paragraph 21.5.)

(iii) By virtue of PCC(S)A 2000, s 151(1), the court may have regard to previous convictions and the failure to respond to previous sentences in considering the seriousness of the current offence. This provision is considered further in Paragraph 21.5.4.

(iv) PCC(S)A 2000, s 151(2), states that the court shall treat the fact that an offence was committed on bail as an aggravating factor — hence increasing its seriousness. The reason would seem to be that an offender committing an offence while on bail is in breach of the trust reposed in him by the court.

21.3 PROTECTION OF THE PUBLIC

While the prime aim of the sentencer must be proportionality, the protection of the public is a crucial consideration in arriving at certain decisions. In coming to the view that a custodial sentence is justified, the court may, as an alternative ground to offence seriousness, rely upon PCC(S)A 2000, s 79(2)(b):

where the offence is a violent or sexual offence, that only such a sentence would be adequate to protect the public from him.

A similar formula is contained in s 80(2)(b), enabling the Court to take the protection of the public into account in determining the length of a custodial sentence.

It is clear from the wording which the statute adopts that the harm from which the public must be protected is harm from the offender himself ('from him'), and not harm from others who might commit similar offences unless warned by the knowledge of what happended to this offender. In other words, the public protection criterion may be used to prevent this offender from reoffending, but not to deter others (see *Jacobs* (1989) 11 Cr App R (S) 171, a case decided on the equivalent provision for young offenders in CJA 1982, which is now subsumed under the more comprehensive scheme in PCC(S)A 2000).

The offence must be 'a violent or sexual offence' for the public protection justification to become available. According to PCC(S)A 2000, s 161(1) a violent offence is one 'which leads, or is intended or likely to lead' to death or physical injury. Arson is deemed to be a violent offence, whether it falls within that definition or not. In cases other than arson, however, in order to decide whether the offence in question is a violent one, the sentencer must look at the facts. It follows that an offence of robbery may fall within s 161(1) or outside it depending on the circumstances. In *Chapman* (1994) 15 Cr App R (S) 844, the Court of Appeal unsurprisingly held that a robbery which involved the discharge of a loaded firearm was violent because it was likely to lead to physical injury. In *Bibby* (1995) 16 Cr App R (S) 127, the robber threatened building society staff with a knife, but there was no physical injury caused or intended. The Court of Appeal held that it was not a violent offence satisfying s 31(1). In *Khan* (1995) 16 Cr App R (S) 180, the carrying of an unloaded firearm in the course of a robbery was held not to amount to a violent offence. The same conclusion was reached in respect of an imitation firearm in *Palin* (1995) 16 Cr App R (S) 888.

Because the injury required for *this* part of the definition must be physical, threatening to kill was held not to come within it in *Richart* (1995) 16 Cr App R (S) 977.

Other cases have turned on the question of the degree of risk of injury. In *Cochrane* (1994) 15 Cr App R (S) 382, it was held that there must be a significant risk of physical injury for it to be likely, but this did not mean that such injury had to be a necessary or probable consequence of the offence. It is clear that the injury must be physical rather than psychological, so that shock alone is insufficient (*Robinson* (1993) 14 Cr App R (S) 448).

'Sexual offence' is defined by providing a list of the statutory offences which fall within the ambit of the definition. In sum, it includes rape, the more serious cases of buggery, incest, intercourse with under-age females, indecent assault, taking indecent photographs of children, burglary with intent to rape, and also conspiracies, attempts and incitements to commit any of these offences.

The public protection criterion can only be considered if the court is of the opinion that the offender poses a risk of 'serious harm' to the public. According to s 161, 'serious harm' consists of 'death or serious personal injury, whether physical or psychological'. What is at issue is not the seriousness of the risk that the offender will commit further offences, but the risk that if he does so the public will suffer serious harm (see *Birch* (1989) 11 Cr App R (S) 202, based on the analogous provisions of s 41 of the Mental Health Act 1983). Even if an individual or a small group of people is in need of protection, the 'public' element in the test can be satisfied (*Hashi* (1994) 16 Cr App R (S) 121). The requirement of 'serious harm' expressly encompasses psychological as well as physical injury (contrast the definition of 'violent offence' which, as explained above, excludes psychological injury). Further, in determining whether harm to the public will be 'serious', the court can have regard to the vulnerability of particular potential victims, e.g., children (*Bowler* (1994) 15 Cr App R (S) 78).

The sentencer should inform counsel when considering whether to invoke s 1(2)(b) (*Baverstock* (1992) 14 Cr App R (S) 471). If necessary a *Newton* hearing (see Paragraph 20.1) should be held to establish the necessary factual basis for sentence (*Oudkerk* [1994] Crim LR 700).

21.4   COMBINATION OF OFFENCES

How should the courts deal with cases where the offender has to be sentenced for two or more offences? The court may consider 'the offence, or the combination of the offence and one or more other offences associated with it' when determining whether the case crosses over the seriousness threshold so as to justify custody (PCC(S)A 2000, s 79(2)(a)) or a community sentence (s 35(1)).

As a result, the sentencer can lump together a series of minor offences and decide that they merit custody (or a community sentence) once viewed together. In order to do so, however, the offences must be 'associated'. Section 161 lays down that offences are associated if:

(i)   the offender is convicted of the offences in the same proceedings (a plea of guilty being equivalent to a conviction);
(ii)   the offender is sentenced for the offences at the same time; or
(iii)   the offender is convicted of one offence and asks for the other or others to be taken into consideration.

If the court has decided on a custodial sentence, can it aggregate a number of offences for the purpose of deciding on the proper length of the sentence? This time, the answer is contained in PCC(S)A 2000, s 80(2)(a), which states that the court may have regard to 'the combination of the offence and one or more offences associated with it' in determining the duration of the sentence. Again, the meaning of 'associated' offences is to be found in s 161.

There are some offences which do not fall within the scope of 'associated offences', however, e.g., an earlier offence for which a suspended sentence was imposed, of which the offender is now in breach: *Crawford* (1993) 98 Cr App R 297. Similarly, where an offender has been convicted of a number of charges described as 'sample counts', offences not on the indictment or formally taken into consideration are not associated offences: *Clark* [1996] Cr App R (S) 351.

The way in which the principle operates is illustrated by *Clugston* (1992) 13 Cr App R (S) 165. The approach in this case is consistent with the current statutory rules, although it predates them. C obtained £5,000 by deception in 100 transactions worth £50 each. The court aggregated the offences and imposed a sentence of three years' imprisonment, which was upheld on appeal. The severity of the sentence could be justified only by the process of aggregating the various offences.

Where an offender is being sentenced for several offences, there is a danger that the total sentence might be disproportionate to the overall seriousness of what the offender has done. In order to avoid such a result, the 'totality principle' has evolved. This requires a court to consider the overall sentence in relation to the totality of the offending, and in relation to sentence levels for other crimes. Hence it would be wrong just to perform the arithmetic and pass a sentence for a number of offences of theft which exceeded that for a single offence of, say, rape. This sentencing principle now finds statutory expression in the

PCC(S)A 2000, s 158(2)(b), which states that 'nothing shall prevent a court . . . in the case of an offender who is convicted of one or more other offences, from mitigating his sentence by applying any rule of law as to the totality of sentences'.

21.5 THE IMPORTANCE OF MITIGATION

Some indication of the potential effect of mitigation personal to the offender has already been indicated in this Chapter. The paragraphs which follow deal first with the statutory considerations which affect the court's consideration of mitigation (and its converse, aggravation), and then discuss four of the commonest mitigating factors.

21.5.1 The statutory framework

The PCC(S)A 2000 makes a number of references to mitigating factors, usually in conjunction with aggravating factors:

(a)   Before imposing a custodial sentence, the court must 'take into account all such information about the circumstances of the offence (including any aggravating or mitigating factors) as is available to it' (s 81(4)(a)).

(b)   There is a similar requirement in relation to any decision to impose a community sentence (s 36(1)).

(c)   The same obligations attach to the consideration of the *length* of any custodial sentence (s 81(4)(a)).

(d)   The above points need to be considered alongside s 158(1), which states that nothing in the relevant part of the Act 'shall prevent a court from mitigating an offender's sentence by taking into account any such matters as, in the opinion of the court, are relevant in mitigation'.

It seems that there is a distinction between the provisions summarised in (a), (b) and (c), on the one hand, and the way in which (d) is meant to operate. In considering the matters under (a), (b) and (c), the court is looking at the factors which affect the seriousness of the offence. It is under an obligation to consider those factors. The scope of its duty includes both mitigation (e.g., provocation, acting on impulse rather than with premeditation, peripheral role in the enterprise), and aggravation (e.g., abuse of trust, gratuitous violence, the high value of unrecovered property stolen).

Section 158(1), however, is rather different (see (d) above). It encompasses matters other than the seriousness of the offence which the court might wish to take into account in deciding whether to impose a custodial sentence, and its length, or, for that matter, a community sentence. It permits consideration of *mitigating* factors only. It gives the court a *discretion* to consider such factors if it wishes to take them into account. Notwithstanding this discretionary form, it is submitted that the courts will continue to take into account the variety of factors relating to the offender's personal circumstances which they have considered in the past. Further, failure to do so will no doubt provide good grounds of appeal in appropriate cases. The following paragraphs deal with four of the grounds most commonly relied on by the defence as good mitigation.

One general point which should be borne in mind is that, even if the offence is such that it passes the custody threshold, personal mitigation such as that set out below may pull the offender back from the threshold, so that he receives a non-custodial sentence: *Cox* [1993] 1 WLR 188.

21.5.2 Plea of guilty

A judge must not increase the sentence he passes because the accused pleaded not guilty, even if he considers that the accused, in giving evidence in his own defence, committed perjury (*Quinn* (1932) 23 Cr App R 196). Nor must he increase sentence because the nature of the defence involved grave allegations against the police officers in the case (*Skone* (1967) 51 Cr App R 165), or because, by pleading not guilty, the accused forced the prosecution to call witnesses who might well have found giving evidence particularly distressing or even harmful (e.g. child witnesses to a sexual offence). The principle is, however, slightly unreal because, provided the judge does not actually say that he has added to the sentence because of the not guilty plea, he can in fact pass a severer sentence than he would otherwise have done. Furthermore, it is a well established common law principle that a guilty plea attracts a somewhat lighter sentence than a conviction following a not guilty plea (*Cain* [1976] QB 496), and, if the accused does not know this before he decides on his plea, he should be told it by counsel. In other words, a guilty plea is an excellent reason for reducing sentence, but a not guilty plea is no justification for increasing sentence. Pragmatism is probably the major reason for treating a guilty plea as mitigation. If every defendant pleaded not guilty, the legal system could not cope with the extra work involved. If there is nothing to be gained by pleading guilty, why should any defendant give up the chance, however slight, of an acquittal? Therefore, the guilty are encouraged to plead guilty by giving them a discount in their sentence. In mitigation, counsel may say that, by pleading guilty and not wasting the court's time, the offender has shown his contrition for the past and his determination to reform in the future. The judge may suspect that the offender is only sorry about being caught, but it is still in everyone's interests to cut his sentence somewhat. This applies even when the evidence is so overwhelming that the offender would have stood virtually no chance of an acquittal had he denied the charge (see *Davis* (1980) 2 Cr App R (S) 168).

The common law principle that a discount should be given for a guilty plea is now given statutory backing by the PCC(S)A 2000, s 152. This section deals with the determination of sentence where the offender has pleaded guilty. It states that the:

court shall take into account—
    (a) the stage in the proceedings for the offence at which the offender indicated his intention to plead guilty, and
    (b) the circumstances in which this indication was given.

In *Howells* [1998] Crim LR 836, Lord Bingham CJ made it clear that a sentencer should take into account in deciding whether the custody threshold had been passed: 'An offender's admission of responsibility for the offence, particularly if reflected in a plea of guilty tendered at the earliest opportunity and accompanied by hard evidence of genuine remorse, as shown (for example) by an expression of regret to the victim and an offer of compensation.'

The principle that the discount for a guilty plea should be more generous the earlier it is tendered originated in decisions of the Court of Appeal, for example, in *Hollington* (1985) 7 Cr App R (S) 364 Lawton LJ said, at p. 367:

This court has long said that discounts on sentences are appropriate but everything depends upon the circumstances of each case. If a man is arrested and at once tells the police that he is guilty and cooperates with them in the recovery of property and the identification of others concerned in the offence, he can expect to get a substantial discount. But if a man is arrested in circumstances in which he cannot hope to put forward a defence of not guilty, he cannot expect much by way of discount. In between comes this kind of case, where the court has been put to considerable trouble as a result of a tactical plea. The sooner it is appreciated that defendants are not going to get full discount for pleas of guilty in these sort of circumstances, the better it will be for the administration of justice.

In *Rafferty* [1998] 2 Cr App R (S) 449, the Court of Appeal stressed that the earliest stage at which a defendant could plead guilty, in respect of a triable either way matter, was at the plea before venue hearing in the magistrates' court. If he did so, he would usually be entitled to a greater discount than a person who delayed until pleading to the indictment at the Crown Court, for example in the course of the plea and directions hearing.

There is no precise percentage by which the sentence should be reduced on account of a guilty plea. Court of Appeal cases suggest that up to a third off a custodial sentence is about right (see, for example, *Buffery* (1992) 14 Cr App R (S) 511). The *Sentencing Guidelines* issued by the Magistrates' Association (1997) state that 'a timely guilty plea may attract a sentencing discount of up to one third but the precise amount of discount will depend on the facts of each case and a last minute plea of guilty may attract only a minimal reduction'. According to the relevant statutory provision, the discount ought to be less where the offender indicates his intention to plead guilty at a late stage in the proceedings (s 152(1)). Other circumstances in which it is likely to be reduced include the case where the offender would only have had a very slim chance of acquittal if he had denied the charge (see *Davis* (1980) 2 Cr App R (S) 168 and *Morris* (1988) 10 Cr App R (S) 216), or if he insists on having a *Newton* hearing at which most of the prosecution evidence is called and his version of the facts of the offence is disbelieved.

Two other points should be made about the operation of s 152(1). First, the graduated discount should apply not only to shorten the length of a custodial sentence, but also in relation to non-custodial sentences, e.g., to reduce the size of a fine. Second, as the statute speaks of a punishment 'less severe' than it would otherwise have been, the credit for a timely guilty plea may result in, say, a community sentence rather than a custodial one. It should not, however, result in suspension of a sentence of imprisonment, since it is not capable of constituting the 'exceptional circumstances' which are necessary for a suspended sentence (*Okinikan* [1993] 1 WLR 173, and see Paragraph 22.9.1).

21.5.3 Co-operation with the police

Co-operation with the police, in the sense of not resisting arrest and confessing frankly to the offence at the police station, is good mitigation, although it may not add much to the effect of an early guilty plea. Co-operation in the sense of giving evidence for the prosecution against one's accomplices should lead to a substantial reduction in sentence (see Paragraph 16.3.1 for a discussion of whether the offender should be sentenced before or after he testifies for the Crown). Even greater reductions are available for the handful of offenders who give information and/or evidence which leads to the conviction of large numbers of their criminal associates. The case of *Lowe* (1977) 66 Cr App R 122 illustrates the point. L was arrested on charges of robbing a garage and having a sawn-off shotgun. He offered 'to tell the police everything', and was as good as his word. He made statements in which he admitted to 91 offences including 15 robberies (some armed), 11 conspiracies to rob and 31 burglaries. More importantly, he implicated 45 other people, many of whom were arrested and charged. The police officer in charge of the investigation told the Court of Appeal that as a result of L's information the police were in the process of clearing up most of the serious gangs of criminals throughout the East End of London. L's information also enabled the police to recover no less than £400,000 worth of stolen property. L was only indicted for a total of 12 offences, but those included the most serious of the offences in which he was concerned (robbery of over a thousand cases of whisky). The Crown Court judge sentenced him to 10 years' imprisonment for that, concurrent sentences on the other counts, and activated a suspended sentence of 18 months to run consecutively to the 10 years, making a total of $11\frac{1}{2}$ years. The Court of Appeal reduced the total sentence to five years. Only by information such as L gave could criminal gangs be broken up. It was in the public interest that criminals who have become involved in gang activities should be encouraged to assist the police. Unless credit was given to people like L when they were sentenced, others would not come forward. Accordingly, L received a sentence which was far below the tariff for the offences he had committed. The amount by which the sentence of a 'supergrass' is reduced will depend on the criminality of the admitted offences, weighed against the assistance which he has given to the police (*Rose* (1980) 71 Cr App R 296).

The above principles were restated by the Lord Chief Justice in *King* (1985) 7 Cr App R (S) 227, where he also indicated that an offender who has given really substantial help to the police, including naming names and either confronting the persons named or giving evidence against them, is entitled to as much as a half to two-thirds off the normal 'tariff' sentence. Other cases have shown that a proportionate reduction should also be made in more trivial cases where neither the crimes for which the offender is sentenced nor those about which he gives evidence or information are in the first rank of gravity (see *Wood* [1987] Crim LR 715 and *Thomas* (1985) 7 Cr App R (S) 95).

21.5.4 Good character

Traditionally, the courts have regarded the previous good character of the offender as excellent mitigation. The long-standing sentencing policy of the courts, underpinned by the decisions of the Court of Appeal, is to treat first offenders with leniency.

Many examples could be given of the leniency with which first offenders are generally treated, but three will suffice. In *Ward* (1981) 3 Cr App R (S) 350, W (aged 29, a shy and solitary character, living with parents to whom he was a great help) pleaded guilty to stealing £6,000-worth of electrical equipment which he was supposed to be guarding in the course of his employment with a security firm. Notwithstanding the aggravating feature of blatant breach of trust and the not inconsiderable amount of property involved, the Court of Appeal cut his sentence from 12 to three months. In *Czechak* [1983] Crim LR 340 an accounts officer with the National Trust stole £68,000 from his employers over a four-year period, and covered his tracks by false accounting. His original four-year sentence was halved, and half of what was left was suspended (i.e., he was left with only a year to serve immediately). Lastly, in *Haley* (1983) 5 Cr App R (S) 9, a 'mild, inoffensive and unspectacular man' became obsessed with fears that his wife was having an affair with another man. He went to the latter's house, and stabbed him four times in the back and chest. Although the victim fortunately made a complete recovery, he could very easily have been killed. The Court of Appeal decided that the right sentence was 18 months' imprisonment, of which nine were suspended. In each of these three cases the appellant had no previous convictions.

A variation on the argument that the offender has no previous convictions whatsoever is that he has no previous for the kind of offence of which he has been convicted. For example, counsel in mitigation might say that, although his client has a record for petty dishonesty, he has no history of violence so that *vis-à-vis* the assault for which he is to be sentenced he should be treated as a person of good character. Yet another argument is that there has been a substantial gap between the present offence and the last one, indicating that the offender has made a genuine effort to 'go straight'. Thus, in *Canfield* (1982) 4 Cr App R (S) 94, a nine-month prison sentence for a clumsy attempted burglary from a social club was replaced with community service. C (aged 32) had had an appalling record for burglary during the period 1967 to 1976 but, after his release from prison in 1977, he had changed his way of life, found a job and married. Apart from some road-traffic matters (which had led to loss of his job), this was the first time he had been in trouble since 1977. The five years of good behaviour saved him from going to prison again.

The common law principles set out above have been characterised as 'progressive loss of mitigation'. The offender may be thought of as starting with substantial credit for good character. That credit is progressively diminished by each offence of which he or she is convicted. If there is a break in offending, some credit accumulates again, only to be diminished with a subsequent offence.

The principles are reinforced by PCC(S)A 2000, s 151(1):

> In considering the seriousness of any offence, the court may take into account any previous convictions of the offender or any failure of his to respond to previous sentences.

As has been pointed out (see A. Ashworth and B. Gibson, 'Altering the sentencing framework' [1994] Crim LR 104), the statutory formula makes no mention of the *circumstances* of previous convictions (as opposed to the mere fact of conviction). In practice, however, the court 'should identify any convictions relevant for this purpose and then consider to what extent they affect the seriousness of the present offence' (The Magistrates' Association, *Sentencing Guidelines* (2000)). Offences of a similar nature are therefore liable to weigh more heavily against the offender than those of a different character.

Section 151 also states that the court may take into account, in calculating the seriousness of the offence, the offender's failure to respond to previous sentences. It is unclear at present how this will be interpreted. The wording ('previous sentences') does seem to imply that the offender must have been sentenced at least twice before for this provision to bite. According to s 151(3) to (6), 'sentence' includes community rehabilitation orders and absolute or conditional discharges. Clearly the court would be likely to hold against the offender, for example, the breach of a current community rehabilitation order, and s 151 entitles it to regard the seriousness of the offence as enhanced for that reason.

In *Howells* [1998] Crim LR 836, Lord Bingham CJ said that leniency would ordinarily be extended to offenders of previous good character, the more so if there was evidence of positive good character (such as a solid employment record or faithful discharge of family duties) as opposed to a mere absence of previous convictions. Such 'positive good character' was given weight, for example, in *Clark* (1999) *The Times*, 27 January 1999. The Court of Appeal were dealing with an offender who had brought up her four nephews and nieces in difficult circumstances when their mother died, and who was involved in a number of local community and charitable activities. Although she had pleaded guilty to two offences of false accounting and one of obtaining property by deception, amounting to fraud of £18,000 in total, her sentence of six months' imprisonment was reduced to seven days.

21.5.5 Youth

The youth of the offender can be a most important mitigating factor. If a young offender is given a custodial sentence, its length is likely to be shorter than the corresponding sentence of imprisonment which an offender over 21 would receive. For example, in *Storey* [1984] Crim LR 438, sentences of five years' detention passed on three 16-year-olds who had burnt down part of their school, causing £370,000-worth of damage, were reduced to three years. The Court of Appeal's reason was that, although severe sentences were called for because of the exceptional nature of the case, the term chosen should not be so long that 'to young men like this [the end would] seem completely out of sight'. Turning to a slightly older age group, cases suggest that for serious crimes an offender in his late teens or early twenties should receive about a 25% reduction on the sentence which a mature offender might expect (e.g., *Paget* (1982) 4 Cr App R (S) 399 — sentences for manslaughter of an elderly man in the course of a robbery reduced from eight to six years because the appellants were aged 19 and 20). Similarly, Lord Lane CJ in *Billam* [1986] 1 WLR 349, having given guidelines about the terms of imprisonment to be passed on offenders over the age of 21 convicted of rape, said that although a custodial sentence was also inevitable, in the case of rapists aged 17–20 it should be reduced proportionately to their age.

There is also some authority for the view that youth can be crucial, not just in reducing sentence length, but in determining the type of sentence (see, for example, *Seymour* (1983) 5 Cr App R (S) 85, where the Court of Appeal urged the use of community punishment orders rather than custody in dealing with certain categories of burglary committed by young offenders).

22 Custodial Sentences

This Chapter and the one following describe the sentencing options open to the courts. The general nature of a particular sentence, the age group for which it is intended and any restrictions on its imposition are explained. The special limitations on the powers of the magistrates' courts, and on the powers of an adult magistrates' court when dealing with a juvenile have already been explained (see Paragraphs 9.8, 10.5.2, 10.5.3 and 11.1). This Chapter concentrates upon those sentences which can be described as 'custodial'. It covers imprisonment (in the case of an adult), whether immediate or suspended and its equivalent, in the case of those under 21.

When passing sentence the court may also have power to make various ancillary financial and property orders (e.g., orders to pay costs to the prosecution, to compensate the victim of the offence or to restore stolen property to its rightful owner). These orders, with the exception of compensation orders, can only be ordered as an addition to some other form of sentence or order in lieu of sentence, so they are not independent methods of dealing with offenders. However, from the offender's point of view, the distinction between the sentence and ancillary orders probably seems academic. He will regard a fine of £300 as being just the same as a fine of £100 coupled with orders to pay £100 prosecution costs and £100 compensation. In other words, ancillary orders may be an important component in the overall treatment meted out to an offender. This point would no doubt have been endorsed by one Sinclair who, following his conviction for serious offences connected with the importation of drugs, was ordered by the trial judge to pay £1,000,000 (£1 million!) costs to the prosecution (see *Maher, Sinclair and others* [1983] QB 784 and Paragraph 27.2).

22.1 PRISONS

Prisons are classified into various types. There are open and closed prisons, and there are also local and training ones. *Closed prisons,* as the name implies, have a boundary wall or fence, and strict perimeter security. The movement of prisoners about the institution is more or less strictly controlled, and they are locked up at nights. Probably, the accommodation will consist of the traditional cell. *Open prisons* have a far more relaxed regime, depending for security on regular roll-calls rather than perimeter security and other physical controls. Only about a tenth of male prisoners (a third of females) are detained in open prisons. *Local prisons* house prisoners on remand awaiting trial or sentence; offenders who have been given a short or shortish prison term; and long-term prisoners who are awaiting allocation to a suitable training prison. Local prisons are always closed, are nearly always located near large centres of population, and, since they tend to date from the Victorian era, are often notoriously inadequate for modern needs. *Training prisons* may be either open or closed, although the majority are the latter. They are meant to provide better standards of accommodation, better work facilities and better recreational opportunities than the local prisons.

The closed training prisons subdivide into a minority of maximum-security dispersal prisons at which the most dangerous prisoners are detained, plus category B and C prisons which cater for lower-risk inmates. Where an offender serves his sentence will depend mainly on the length of the term and the security classification he is given. As already mentioned, a prisoner given a short term (say, less than six months) will probably serve the whole of it in a local prison. Category A prisoners are the most dangerous, and they are held at the dispersal prisons. Some Category B prisoners (the next security classification down) also go to dispersal prisons, although the actual regime they are subjected to there will not be as tight as that enforced in respect of Category A prisoners. The remainder are sent to the Category B non-dispersal training prisons. Category C prisoners (those who cannot be trusted in open conditions but who are reckoned incapable of making a determined escape attempt) go either to Category B or Category C training prisons. Category D prisoners are eligible for detention in open conditions, but whether they are so detained will depend amongst other things, on the availability of places in open prison. A prisoner who is initially classified as being in one of the higher-risk categories may be put into a lower group as his sentence progresses, and, often, a long-term prisoner is allowed to spend the last few months of his sentence in open conditions so as to prepare him for release. Conversely, a Category D prisoner who absconds would be reclassified in the B or C groups.

The annual reports of Her Majesty's Chief Inspector of Prisons are an interesting and often alarming guide to conditions in prisons. Over the years the reports have stressed three interlocking problems. One is the lack of space in prisons. Over a third of prisoners share (sometimes with two or three others) cells originally designed for one. Secondly, most prisons were built in the last century, and are becoming dilapidated.

Lastly, although the Prison Rules state that a prisoner serving a sentence may be required to work for a certain number of hours a week, it is often difficult to provide work, and such work as there is may be boring and repetitive. The result of prisoners not being able to work is that they are locked up in their cells not only at night, but also for much of the day. The problem is especially acute in the local prisons, where the need to employ prison officers on tasks such as escorting remand prisoners to court often means that there are no officers available to supervise working parties. In the context of a book on criminal procedure, these problems are particularly relevant for the effect they have on the attitude of courts to sentences of imprisonment. In particular, some sentencers have lost faith in prison as an instrument of reform, and will seek an alternative to custody wherever possible. Where all the alternatives are inappropriate, the term of imprisonment should be short if possible (see Paragraph 22.6.1).

22.2 MINIMUM AGE FOR IMPRISONMENT

The minimum age for a sentence of imprisonment is 21: Powers of Criminal Courts (Sentencing) Act 2000 (PCC(S)A), s 89. The relevant consideration is the offender's age when sentence is passed, not his age when the offence was committed or even his age when he was found or pleaded guilty if that and the passing of sentence occur on different days. It should be noted, however, that s 89 merely prohibits *sentences* of imprisonment in the cases of under-21s — it does not say that a young offender can never in any circumstances be detained in prison. In fact, a minority of 17–20-year-olds sentenced to detention in a young offender institution serve all or part of the term imposed in prison, but that does not alter the fact that the sentence was one of detention rather than imprisonment.

22.3 REQUIREMENTS FOR CUSTODIAL SENTENCES

When it is considering the imposition of a custodial sentence, the court has to abide by certain statutory requirements. In particular:

(a) A court shall not pass a first sentence of imprisonment upon an offender who is not legally represented, without giving him a chance to be legally represented (PCC(S)A 2000, s 83: see Paragraph 20.4 for details).

(b) Before passing a custodial sentence, the court must be satisfied that it is justified on the basis of the criteria set out in the PCC(S)A 2000, s 79(2). These criteria are discussed in Paragraph 21.2 (which deals with offence seriousness) and Paragraph 21.3 (which deals with public protection in the case of violent and sexual offences).

(c) In order to determine whether those criteria are satisfied, the court is obliged in certain circumstances to 'obtain and consider a pre-sentence report' (PCC(S)A 2000, s 81). These reports are discussed in Paragraph 22.3.1.

(d) In addition to its consideration of the pre-sentence report, the court must 'take into account all such information about the circumstances of the offence (including any aggravating or mitigating factors) as is available to it' (PCC(S)A 2000, s 81(4)(a)) discussed in Paragraph 21.5).

(e) Any court passing a custodial sentence must state its reasons (PCC(S)A 2000, s 79(4): see Paragraph 22.3.2).

22.3.1 Pre-sentence reports

As mentioned in Paragraph 20.3, reports on an offender frequently play a major role in the court's decision on sentence. When the court is deciding whether one of the grounds specified in s 79(2) of the PCC(S)A 2000 is made out, so as to justify a custodial sentence, then it must obtain and consider a pre-sentence report. It has a similar obligation when deciding upon the length of a custodial sentence (s 81(1)). The court has power, however, to dispense with a pre-sentence report, which varies according to the age of the offender:

(a) In the case of an offender aged 18 or over, the obligation to obtain a pre-sentence report when considering a custodial sentence does not apply if the court is of the opinion that a report is not necessary.

(b) Where the offender is under 18, the court may not decide that a pre-sentence report is unnecessary unless one of the offences is triable only on indictment or there exists a previous pre-sentence report which the court has regard to (PCC(S)A 2000, s 81(3)).

The overall effect is that the court has a wide discretion to dispense with a report where the offender is aged 18 or over. It will no doubt make use of its power where custody is inevitable and a report would be a waste of time. In the case of an offender aged under 18, on the other hand, the court must see a pre-sentence report unless one of the offences is triable on indictment only, and a report is regarded as unnecessary.

In any event, s 81(5) of PCC(S)A 2000 states that no sentence shall be invalidated by failure to comply with s 81(1). In the event of an appeal against a custodial sentence passed in the absence of a pre-sentence report, however, the Court of Appeal shall obtain and consider one unless the court below was justified in dispensing with one, or there is no longer any need to obtain one.

22.3.2 Giving reasons for custody

When passing a custodial sentence, any court has a duty (see PCC(S)A 2000, s 79(4)(a)) to state in open court that such a sentence is justified under either s 79(2)(a) (offence seriousness) or s 79(2)(b) (public protection in relation to sexual or violent crimes), or both. Further, it must explain why it has come to that view. In addition, the court must (by s 79(4)(b)) explain to the offender 'in open court and in ordinary language why it is passing a custodial sentence on him'. Further, in the magistrates' court, the reason must be recorded in the warrant of commitment and the court register. It would seem that failure to comply with these procedural requirements will not invalidate any custodial sentence passed (see, by analogy, *McQueen* (1989) 11 Cr App R (S) 196).

22.3.3 Explaining what the sentence will mean in practice

In the *Practice Direction (Custodial Sentences: Explanations)* [1998] 1 WLR 278, the Court of Appeal issued a requirement on sentencers in the Crown Court to explain the practical effect of any custodial sentence which is imposed. Sentencers must give the explanation in terms of their own choosing, whilst ensuring that it is clear and accurate. The *Practice Direction* (which is to be found in *Blackstone's Criminal Practice*, E1.20) sets out short statements which the sentencer can adapt, and which deal with the different principles applicable to short and long-term sentences (see Paragraph 22.10).

22.4 MAXIMUM TERMS OF IMPRISONMENT

Common law offences are prima facie punishable with imprisonment for life. In other words, the court may, at its discretion, pass a fixed term of any length or make the sentence extend to the term of the offender's life. In fact, there are very few remaining common law offences, and for most that do remain statute has altered the common law position as regards penalty. Thus, the maximum sentence for the common law offence of common assault is now a mere six months and for conspiracy to defraud it is 10 years (see CJA 1988, s 39 and CJA 1987, s 12 respectively). By contrast the penalty for murder is a mandatory life sentence (see Paragraph 22.7). Manslaughter provides the best example of a common law offence for which the penalty is simply a discretionary life sentence.

The table below indicates the maximum terms of imprisonment imposable for some common statutory offences:

Offence	*Penalty*
Child destruction, abortion, rape, intercourse with a girl under 13, causing grievous bodily harm with intent, possessing a firearm with intent to endanger life or carrying one with intent to commit an indictable offence, criminal damage committed with an intent to endanger life or by the use of fire, aggravated burglary, robbery, importing or supplying controlled drugs in Class A.	Imprisonment for life

Offence	*Penalty*
Burglary of a dwelling, handling stolen goods, blackmail, obtaining or, communicating etc. information useful to an enemy contrary to s 1 of the Official Secrets Act 1911, supplying controlled drugs in Class B.	14 years
Obtaining property by deception, burglary (other than of a dwelling), non-aggravated criminal damage, indecent assault, and forgery and counterfeiting offences where the offender's intention in making, using etc. the forgery/counterfeit was to pass it off as genuine to the prejudice of another, causing death by dangerous driving.	10 years
Theft, perjury, bigamy, living on the earnings of prostitution, and having possession of a Class A controlled drug.	7 years
Unlawful wounding, inflicting grievous bodily harm, assault occasioning actual bodily harm, obtaining services by deception, evading liability by deception, having possession of a Class B controlled drug and supplying a Class C controlled drug.	5 years
Going equipped for burglary, theft or cheat.	3 years
Dangerous driving, forgery and counterfeiting offences where there was no intention to pass off the article concerned as genuine, making off without payment, having an offensive weapon, unlawful sexual intercourse with girl aged 13, 14 or 15, and having possession of a Class C controlled drug.	2 years
Assaulting a police constable in the execution of his duty, drink/driving offences, driving while disqualified, taking a motor vehicle without the owner's consent, and using threatening behaviour with intent to put a person in fear of violence, etc.	6 months
Interfering with a motor vehicle, criminal damage dealt with as a summary offence under the special procedure in s 22 of the MCA and drink/being in charge of a motor vehicle offences.	3 months
Obstructing a police constable in the execution of his duty.	1 month

If a statute creates an indictable offence, provides that it is to be punishable with imprisonment, but fails to state what the maximum term shall be, the offence is punishable with up to two years' imprisonment upon conviction on indictment: PCC(S)A 2000, s 77. For attempts contrary to s 1 of the Criminal Attempts Act 1981 and conspiracy contrary to s 1 of the Criminal Law Act 1977, the maximum is the same as for the offence to which the attempt or conspiracy related. A magistrates' court cannot impose more than six months' imprisonment for one offence (PCC(S)A 2000, s 78 and see Paragraph 9.8).

As will be seen from the above, the maximum terms roughly, but only roughly, reflect the relative gravity of the various offences. There are apparent anomalies, such as handling stolen goods being punishable with a sentence twice as long as perjury. For many indictable offences, including burglary, handling, theft and criminal damage, the maxima are much higher than the terms which would actually be imposed save in the gravest of cases, but fixing the maximum term high allows for suitable punishment for the man who steals the Crown jewels or damages the National Gallery's most valuable painting. It should not be thought that the penalty which could theoretically be imposed plays a major part in determining the penalty which is actually imposed on a particular offender for a particular crime — i.e. a judge does not pass a sentence of three and a half years' imprisonment for an offence of theft which he regards as being of average gravity on the basis that the maximum for theft is seven years. Subject, of course, to not exceeding the lawful maximum, the sentence will reflect the character of the offender and the gravity of his conduct, not the label (robbery, burglary, theft, handling or whatever) which is attached to that conduct. For example, a person who enters a restaurant with no money, orders and consumes an expensive meal for which he never had any intention of paying, and leaves without paying when the waiter is not looking, could be convicted of obtaining property by deception (the food he has eaten) or obtaining services by deception (the services of the waiter and kitchen staff). Notwithstanding that the former offence is punishable with up to ten years' and the latter with up to five years' imprisonment, the sentence he will receive will be exactly the same whether he is convicted of either, or for that matter both, offences. However, if he were to challenge the assertion that he *never* intended to pay, and if he were to be convicted only of making off without payment, then the sentence should be rather less. This is not because the offence carries only two years' imprisonment, but because running away on impulse without paying is to some extent less reprehensible than planning all along not to pay.

22.5 CONCURRENT AND CONSECUTIVE SENTENCES

When a court deals with an offender for two or more offences by means of sentences of imprisonment it may either order that the terms of imprisonment shall run at the same time as each other, or it may order that they shall run one after the other. In the former case, the sentences of imprisonment are *concurrent;* in the latter case, they are *consecutive.* Similarly, if a court passes a sentence of imprisonment on an offender who is already serving a term of imprisonment it may order that the term it imposes shall run concurrently with or consecutively to the other term. The judge or presiding magistrate should expressly state whether prison sentences are concurrent or consecutive. If nothing is said, they are presumed to be concurrent. Where consecutive sentences are imposed for two or more offences the aggregate sentence may exceed that which could have been imposed for any one of them (see *Blake* [1962] 2 QB 377 where for five offences under the Official Secrets Act 1911, B was sentenced to a total of 42 years' imprisonment, even though 14 years is the maximum for one such offence). A magistrates' court's power to impose consecutive sentences is limited by s 133 of the Magistrates' Courts Act 1980 (see Paragraph 9.8).

Consecutive sentences are wrong in principle if they are imposed for offences which, although distinct in law, arose out of a single act so that — looking at what the offender did in a common-sense way — he really only committed one crime. Returning to the example given in Paragraph 22.4 of a man who orders a meal at a restaurant and leaves without paying, if he is convicted of obtaining property by deception, obtaining services by deception and making off without payment and the court decides to pass a prison sentence, the sentences for the three offences should be made to run concurrently. He has, effectively, committed only one criminal act. If he is spotted leaving by a waiter and assaults the waiter in an attempt to avoid apprehension, that constitutes a second distinct criminal act, and he could properly be sentenced for it to a consecutive term of imprisonment. *Hussain* [1962] Crim LR 712 illustrates the appellate court's attitude to consecutive and concurrent sentences. H, who tried unsuccessfully to smuggle Indian hemp through customs at Heathrow airport, was given three years for possessing a dangerous drug and two years to run consecutively for unloading prohibited goods from an aircraft. The Court of Criminal Appeal held that, since both offences consisted of precisely the same act (i.e., leaving the plane at Heathrow with Indian hemp in his possession), it was wrong to impose consecutive sentences. H's pleasure at a successful appeal was short-lived, because the sentence was varied to one of five years' imprisonment for each offence to run concurrently.

Where an offender is convicted of several similar offences committed at different times, he could be sentenced to consecutive terms of imprisonment. The danger with such an approach is that the individual sentences may, in themselves, be short and well justified by the criminal conduct in respect of which they are passed, but taken in the aggregate they can amount to an unreasonably severe punishment. To avoid this danger, a judge sentencing an offender for, say, five offences of burglary from dwelling-houses committed over a six-month period should first decide whether the offences together justify a custodial sentence (see Paragraph 21.4). He should then look at the totality of the offences during the period, and decide upon the appropriate sentence for that criminal conduct overall (using the criteria discussed in Paragraph 22.6). He might, as a result of this process, decide that three years' imprisonment is right. He will then pass a sentence of three years' imprisonment for the most serious of the burglaries and make the sentences for the other burglaries run concurrently with each other and with the three-year sentence.

It is often difficult to distinguish between cases such as *Hussain* and those where the offences, although arising out of a continuous course of conduct by the offender, are sufficiently distinct for consecutive terms to be justified. Thus, in *Newbury* [1975] Crim LR 295, the Court of Appeal upheld consecutive terms for taking a car without the owner's consent and then driving it recklessly. And, in *Wheatley* (1983) 5 Cr App R (S) 417 the then maximum terms of 12 months for driving while disqualified and six months consecutive for driving with excess alcohol in the blood were approved, even though both offences happened on the same occasion. The decision can be explained by saying that, although there was only one criminal act by W (the driving of the car when he should not have done so), it was criminal for two quite distinct reasons, namely his being disqualified and his having drunk too much. W's conviction for driving while disqualified in no way presupposed that he was also guilty of the drink-driving matter, whereas Hussain could not have committed the offence of unloading prohibited goods in the manner alleged against him by the prosecution without incidentally committing the offence of being in possession of dangerous drugs. However, although the sentence in *Wheatley's* case was upheld because of W's appalling record for similar offences, the normal practice where offences arise out of a continuous course of conduct is to make the sentences concurrent, even if the offences can be regarded as to some extent distinct from each other. Moreover, in the absence of exceptional factors, consecutive terms passed at first instance for offences committed on the same occasion are likely to be made concurrent by the Court of Appeal (see *Jones* (1980) 2 Cr App R (S) 152 for a statement of the general principle and *Skinner* (1986) 8 Cr App R (S) 166 for an application thereof). However, the Court of Appeal's approach lacks consistency. Thus, their lordships have said that a term of imprisonment for assaulting a police officer when escaping from the scene of a crime should be made consecutive to whatever sentence is passed for the latter matter: *Hill* (1983) 5 Cr App R (S) 214. Similarly, there is no objection in a case of armed robbery to making the terms for robbery and carrying a firearm with intent to commit an indictable offence consecutive to each other (see *Faulkner* (1972) 56 Cr App R 594 and *Bottomley* (1985) 7 Cr App R (S) 355).

22.6 LENGTH OF CUSTODIAL SENTENCE

Once it has made the decision that an offender's conduct passes the custody 'threshold' (see Paragraphs 21.2 and 21.3), so that a custodial sentence is justified, the important question remains: what should the length of the sentence be? The criteria are laid down in PCC(S)A 2000, s 80(2).

Section 80(2) states that the custodial sentence shall be:

(a) for such term (not exceeding the permitted maximum) as in the opinion of the court is commensurate with the seriousness of the offence, or the combination of the offence and other offences associated with it; or

(b) where the offence is a violent or sexual offence, for such longer term (not exceeding that maximum) as in the opinion of the court is necessary to protect the public from harm from the offender.

Any offence for which the sentence is fixed by law is, logically, excluded from the operation of these criteria (s 80(1)). This includes murder and offences under the PCC(S)A 2000, ss 109, 110 and 111 (see Paragraphs 22.7 and 22.8). Any sentence imposed must be within the permitted maximum. This means, of course, that the sentence must be within the maximum applicable to the offence in question (see Paragraph 22.4), as well as those which relate to the offender's age (see Paragraph 22.10.1) and the powers of the court (see Paragraph 9.8 for the limits on the magistrates' powers).

Looking first at the criterion embodied in s 80(2)(a), it gives primacy to the principle of proportionality — the sentence should primarily be determined by (or proportionate to) the seriousness of the offence. Clearly in considering the seriousness of the offence as the determinant of length, the court must take into account any aggravating or mitigating circumstances which have bearing upon the seriousness of the offence itself (s 81(4)(a)). It should also have regard to mitigating factors which relate to the offender himself, even if they are totally irrelevant to the seriousness of the offence(s) for which he is being sentenced, e.g., the fact that he has pleaded guilty. The court is permitted to do this by s 158(1), which states that: 'Nothing in this part shall prevent a court from mitigating an offender's sentence by taking into account any such matters as, in the opinion of the court, are relevant in mitigation of sentence'. (See Paragraphs 21.5.2 to 21.5.5 for a fuller exposition of the main factors which provide good mitigation.)

The court may conclude that a term longer than that justified by offence seriousness is called for if the criteria in s 80(2)(b) are met. To depart from the principle of proportionality in this way, the offence must be a violent or a sexual one, and the court must take the view that the sentence is necessary to protect the public from serious harm from the offender (see Paragraph 21.3 for discussion of these terms). The sentencer should alert counsel to the fact that he or she is minded to impose a longer than normal sentence under s 80(2)(b) (*Baverstock* (1992) 14 Cr App R (S) 471). The material which might lead to a decision to invoke s 80(2)(b) could include the circumstances of the offence before the court, the nature of previous offences, or medical or other evidence about the offender. A sentence under s 80(2)(b), whilst long enough to protect the public, should still bear a reasonable relationship to the offence for which it is imposed.

In any event, in making its decision on sentence length, the court must obtain and consider a pre-sentence report (s 81), subject to the discretion to dispense with a report (see Paragraph 22.3.1).

22.6.1 'Clang of the prison gates'

In interpreting the criterion of 'offence seriousness', in particular, the approach of the Court of Appeal to the length of custodial sentences in such cases as *Bibi* [1980] 1 WLR 1193 has been reinforced by the new statutory framework in CJA 1991. That case articulated the important principle that, where loss of liberty is inevitable, the sentence should be kept as short as possible. As Lord Lane CJ put it in *Bibi*:

> It is no secret that our prisons are at the moment dangerously overcrowded. So much so that sentencing courts must be particularly careful to examine each case to ensure, if an immediate custodial sentence is necessary, that the sentence is as short as possible consistent only with the duty to protect the interests of the public and to punish and deter the criminal. Many offenders can be dealt with equally justly and effectively by a sentence of six or nine months imprisonment as by one of 18 months or three years.

The Lord Chief Justice emphasised that this applied not only to first offenders (who are often given disproportionately short sentences on the basis that merely hearing the prison gates 'clang shut' behind them will be a severe punishment), but also to those with criminal records and even to those with past experience of custodial penalties. He then gave examples of situations where shorter sentences than had previously been considered appropriate would be sufficient. The examples included less serious factory or shopbreaking, minor cases of sexual indecency, petty frauds and fringe participation in serious crime.

The principle in *Bibi* was endorsed in *Ollerenshaw* [1998] Crim LR 515.

22.6.2 Reasons for sentence length

Where the court relies, in the case of a violent or sexual offence, upon the need to protect the public as the reason for imposing a longer sentence than the seriousness of the offence alone would justify, then it must explain in open court that CJA 1991, s 80(2)(b), applies, and why it has come to that view. Further, it must explain to the offender 'in open court and in ordinary language' why the sentence is for a longer term (s 80(4)). These procedural requirements are comparable to those which apply to the decision to impose any sort of custodial sentence, which are discussed in Paragraph 22.3.2.

22.6.3 Guidelines cases

From time to time in recent years, the Court of Appeal has sought to have a more direct influence upon sentencing levels at first instance by giving 'guidelines' on how certain types of offence should be dealt with.

It is beyond the scope of this work to attempt any comprehensive survey of such cases — for that the reader is referred to the specialist books on sentencing. Reference to a few of the most established of the guidelines cases, however, will help to get the feel of the concepts involved.

22.6.3.1 Breach of trust In cases of dishonesty involving a breach of trust, the guidelines case is *Barrick* (1985) 7 Cr App R (S) 142, which deals with situations where:

> a person in a position of trust, for example, an accountant, solicitor, bank employee or postman, has used that privileged and trusted position to defraud his partners or clients or employers or the general public of sizeable sums of money. He will usually, as in this

case, be a person of hitherto impeccable character. It is practically certain, again as in this case, that he will never offend again and, in the nature of things, he will never again in his life be able to secure similar employment with all that that means in the shape of disgrace for himself and hardship for himself and also his family.

The guidelines indicate that such a case will attract immediate custody, save in very exceptional circumstances or where the sum involved is small. More detailed guidance was then set out in relation to different amounts involved, and the appropriate custodial sentence for each bracket. In *Clark* [1998] 2 Cr App R (S) 95, the Court of Appeal indicated that these sentencing brackets now required revision because of the impact of inflation, changes in the system of early release, and the reduction of the maximum sentence for theft from ten to seven years. The guidelines in *Clark* state that where the amount involved was not small but was less than £17,500, terms of imprisonment from the very short up to 21 months would be appropriate. Cases involving sums between £17,500 and £100,000 would merit two to three years. Cases in the £100,000 to £250,000 bracket would merit three to four years. Those where the amount was between £250,000 and £1 million would merit five to nine years, and cases involving £1 million or more would merit ten years or more. (In the light of the maximum sentence for theft, such sentences would have to be reserved for multiple offences, or for other crimes such as obtaining property by deception.) These figures assume that the case is contested. In the event of a guilty plea, an appropriate discount should be given. Other matters to be taken into account by the court, apart from the size of the sum involved, are (a) the quality and degree of trust reposed in the offender, (b) the period over which the thefts were committed, (c) the use to which the money was put, (d) the effect upon the victim, (e) the impact on the public and public confidence, (f) effect upon fellow employees or business partners, (g) effect on the offender, (h) his own history, (i) matters of mitigation special to himself, (j) any help given by him to the police.

The Magistrates' Association Guidelines (2000) indicate that the guideline sentence for these offences is custody, and list five factors which might reduce seriousness, viz. impulsive action, unsupported junior, single item, low value, and previous inconsistent attitude by employer.

22.6.3.2 Rape As far as the offence of rape is concerned, the guidelines case is *Billam* [1986] 1 WLR 349. Lord Lane CJ said, at pp. 350–2:

> This court emphasised in *Roberts* [1982] 1 WLR 133, that rape is always a serious crime which calls for an immediate custodial sentence other than in wholly exceptional circumstances. . . .
>
> The variable factors in cases of rape are so numerous that it is difficult to lay down guidelines as to the proper length of sentence in terms of years. That aspect of the problem was not considered in *Roberts,* There are however many reported decisions of the court which give an indication of what current practice ought to be and it may be useful to summarise their general effect.
>
> For rape committed by an adult without any aggravating or mitigating features, a figure of five years should be taken as the starting-point in a contested case. Where a rape is committed by two or more men acting together, or by a man who has broken into or otherwise gained access to a place where the victim is living, or by a person who is in a position of responsibility towards the victim, or by a person who abducts the victim and holds her captive, the starting-point should be eight years.

At the top of the scale comes the defendant who has carried out what might be described as a campaign of rape, committing the crime upon a number of different women or girls. He represents a more than ordinary danger and a sentence of 15 years or more may be appropriate.

Where the defendant's behaviour has manifested perverted or psychopathic tendencies or gross personality disorder, and where he is likely, if at large, to remain a danger to women for an indefinite time, a life sentence will not be inappropriate.

The crime should in any event be treated as aggravated by any of the following factors: (1) violence is used over and above the force necessary to commit the rape; (2) a weapon is used to frighten or wound the victim; (3) the rape is repeated; (4) the rape has been carefully planned; (5) the defendant has previous convictions for rape or other serious offences of a violent or sexual kind; (6) the victim is subjected to further sexual indignities or perversions; (7) the victim is either very old or very young; (8) the effect upon the victim, whether physical or mental, is of special seriousness. Where any one or more of these aggravating features are present, the sentence should be substantially higher than the figure suggested as the starting-point.

The extra distress which giving evidence can cause to a victim means that a plea of guilty, perhaps more so than in other cases, should normally result in some reduction from what would otherwise be the appropriate sentence. The amount of such reduction will of course depend on all the circumstances, including the likelihood of a finding of not guilty had the matter been contested.

The fact that the victim may be considered to have exposed herself to danger by acting imprudently (as for instance by accepting a lift in a car from a stranger) is not a mitigating factor; and the victim's previous sexual experience is equally irrelevant. But if the victim has behaved in a manner which was calculated to lead the defendant to believe that she would consent to sexual intercourse, then there should be some mitigation of the sentence. Previous good character is of only minor relevance.

The starting-point for attempted rape should normally be less than for the completed offence, especially if it is desisted at a comparatively early stage. But . . . attempted rape may be made by aggravating features into an offence even more serious than some examples of the full offence.

The Lord Chief Justice went on to deal with those offenders who are under the age of 21. He indicated that 'in the ordinary case' a custodial sentence would be appropriate:

. . . following the term suggested as terms of imprisonment for adults, but making some reduction to reflect the youth of the offender. A man of 20 will accordingly not receive much less than a man of 22, but a youth of 17 or 18 may well receive less.

In the case of a juvenile, the court will in most cases exercise the power to order detention under [s 91 of the PCC(S)A 2000]. In view of the procedural limitations to which the power is subject, it is important that a magistrates' court dealing with a juvenile charged with rape should *never* accept jurisdiction to deal with the case itself, but should invariably commit the case to the Crown Court for trial to ensure that the power is available.

22.6.3.3 Drugs For drugs offences, the guidelines case is *Aramah* (1982) 4 Cr App R (S) 407, as modified by *Bilinski* (1987) 9 Cr App R (S) 360, *Singh* (1988) 10 Cr App R (S) 402 and *Aroyewumi* (1994) 16 Cr App R (S) 211. Minor modifications from later cases have been incorporated in the following quotation from *Aramah,* at pp. 408–10:

Class A drugs and particularly heroin and morphine: It is common knowledge that these are the most dangerous of all the addictive drugs for a number of reasons: first of all, they are easy to handle. Small parcels can be made up into huge numbers of doses. Secondly, the profits are so enormous that they attract the worst type of criminal. Many of such criminals may think, and indeed do think, that it is less dangerous and more profitable to traffic in heroin or morphine than it is to rob a bank. It does not require much imagination to realise the consequential evils of corruption and bribery which the huge profits are likely to produce. This factor is also important when considering the advisability of granting bail. Sums which to the ordinary person, and indeed the ordinary defendant, might seem enormous are often trivial for the trafficker in drugs.

The two main sources of supply are South East Asia and South West Asia. These two sources are in competition, one with the other, and with the stakes so high, this may be a fruitful source of violence and internecine strife. Fourthly, the heroin taker, once addicted (and it takes very little experimentation with the drug to produce addiction), has to obtain supplies of the drug to satisfy the terrible craving. It may take anything up to hundreds of pounds a week to buy enough heroin to satisfy the craving, depending on the degree of addiction of the person involved. The only way, it is obvious, in which sums of this order can be obtained is by resorting to crime. This in its turn may be trafficking in the drug itself and disseminating accordingly its use still further.

Fifthly, and lastly, and we have purposely left it for the last, because it is the most horrifying aspect, comes the degradation and suffering and not infrequently the death which the drug brings to the addict. It is not difficult to understand why in some parts of the world traffickers in heroin in any substantial quantity are sentenced to death and executed.

Consequently anything which the courts of this country can do by way of deterrent sentences on those found guilty of crimes involving these Class A drugs should be done.

Then I turn to the importation of heroin, morphine and so on: Large scale importation, that is where the [weight of the drugs at 100 per cent purity is of the order of 500 grammes] or more, sentences of [10 years] and upwards are appropriate. There will be cases where the [weight at 100 per cent purity is of the order of 5 kilogrammes] or more, in which case the offence should be visited by sentences of [14 years and upwards]. It will be seldom that an importer of any appreciable amount of the drug will deserve less than four years.

This, however, is one area in which it is particularly important that offenders should be encouraged to give information to the police, and a confession of guilt, coupled with considerable assistance to the police can properly be marked by a substantial reduction in what would otherwise be the proper sentence.

Next, supplying heroin, morphine etc.: It goes without saying that the sentence will largely depend on the degree of involvement, the amount of trafficking and the value of the drug handled. It is seldom that a sentence of less than [five] years will be justified and the nearer the source of supply the defendant is shown to be, the heavier will be the sentence. There may well be cases where sentences similar to those appropriate to large-scale importers may be necessary. It is however unhappily all too seldom that those big fish amongst the suppliers get caught.

Possession of heroin, morphine etc. (simple possession): It is at this level that the circumstances of the individual offender become of much greater importance. Indeed the possible variety of considerations is so wide, including often those of a medical nature, that we feel it impossible to lay down any practical guidelines. On the other hand the maximum penalty for simple possession of Class A drugs is seven years' imprisonment and/or a fine, and there will be very many cases where deprivation of liberty is both proper and expedient.

Class B Drugs, particularly cannabis: We select this from among the Class B drugs as being the drug most likely to be exercising the minds of the courts.

Importation of cannabis: Importation of very small amounts for personal use can be dealt with as if it were simple possession, with which we will deal later. Otherwise importations of amounts up to about 20 kg of herbal cannabis, or the equivalent in cannabis resin or cannabis oil, will, save in the most exceptional circumstances, attract sentences of between 18 months and three years, with the lowest ranges reserved for pleas of guilty where there has been small profit to the offender. The good character of the courier (as he usually is) is of less importance than the good character of the defendant in other cases. The reason for this is, it is well known that the large-scale operator looks for couriers of good character and for people of a sort which are likely to exercise the sympathy of the court if they are detected and arrested. Consequently one will frequently find that students and sick and elderly people are used as couriers for two reasons: first of all they are vulnerable to suggestion and vulnerable to the offer of quick profit, and secondly it is felt that the courts may be moved to misplaced sympathy in their case. There are few, if any, occasions when anything other than an immediate custodial sentence is proper in this type of importation.

Medium quantities over 20 kg will attract sentences of three to six years' imprisonment, depending upon the amount involved, and all the other circumstances of the case.

Large-scale or wholesale importation of massive quantities will justify sentences in the region of 10 years' imprisonment for those playing other than a subordinate role.

Supply of cannabis: Here again the supply of massive quantities will justify sentences in the region of 10 years for those playing anything more than a subordinate role. Otherwise the bracket should be between one to four years' imprisonment, depending on the scale of the operation. Supplying a number of small sellers — wholesaling if you like — comes at the top of the bracket. At the lower end will be the retailer of a small amount to a consumer. Where there is no commercial motive (for example, where cannabis is supplied at a party) the offence may well be serious enough to justify a custodial sentence.

Possession of cannabis: When only small amounts are involved being for personal use, the offence can often be met by a fine. If the history shows however a persisting flouting of the law, imprisonment may become necessary.

In *Martinez* (1984) 6 Cr App R (S) 364 at 365, Lord Lane CJ confirmed that the guidelines in *Aramah* on Class A drugs are not aimed at heroin alone:

The fact that in the decision to which I have referred, namely *Aramah,* particular mention was made of heroin was because at that time, in terms of availability, heroin presented the greatest threat to the community. The same considerations as applied to heroin apply equally to other Class A drugs. Any idea that those who import or deal in cocaine or LSD, as it is known, should be treated more leniently is entirely wrong.

In *Scaramonie* (1992) 13 Cr App R (S) 702, attention was focused on the bracket where the street value exceeded £1 million. It was said in *Aramah* that this category should attract sentences of '14 years and upwards', but that left open what should be understood by the phrase 'and upwards'. A sentence of 20 years was upheld in *Scaramonie*, even after a plea of guilty and assistance to the authorities. A sentence of 25 years would have been appropriate without those features.

In *Aroyewumi* (1994) 16 Cr App R (S) 211, the Court of Appeal said that sentencing for an importation should be related to the weight of the pure drug in the consignment, rather than its street value.

22.6.3.4 Status of guideline cases In relation to these and the other guidelines cases, it is worth bearing in mind that they provide guidance only, and do not lay down a strict set of criteria. In *Nicholas* (1986) *The Times,* 23 April 1986, Lord Lane CJ emphasised that the guidelines were only guidelines, and were not intended to be applied rigidly in every case. They were meant to provide assistance, and were not to be used as rules which must never be departed from.

At the other extreme, the sentencer is not free to ignore the guidelines given by the Court of Appeal. In *Johnson* (1994) 15 Cr App R (S) 827, the judge stated that the Court of Appeal had been reducing sentences in similar cases (it was the street robbery of a postal worker), but he did not agree with the principles on which the court acted, and would not act on them. The Court of Appeal said that its decisions were no more than guidelines for Crown Court judges, who should take many factors into account in arriving at a proper sentence e.g., the prevalence of a particular crime in the area, the especially distressing effect on the victim, or the fact that the offender had behaved in a particularly vicious manner. But the judge must pay attention to the guidance given by the Court of Appeal, and sentences should be broadly in line with guideline cases, unless there were factors applicable to the instant case which required or enabled the judge to depart from the normal level of sentence. The Court of Appeal reduced the total sentence from seven years to five because of the judge's 'unfortunate' sentencing remarks, and made it plain that, but for these remarks, the sentence would have been upheld as severe but not excessive.

22.7 LIFE IMPRISONMENT

An offender aged 21 or over who has been convicted of murder *must* be sentenced to life imprisonment (Murder (Abolition of Death Penalty) Act 1965, s 1(1)). When he passes sentence, the judge may make a recommendation about the minimum term the offender should serve in prison before being paroled. The Court of Appeal has advised against minimum-term recommendations of less than 12 years — if the judge would be content to see the offender at liberty in under 12 years, he should make no recommendation and the Home Secretary would then probably consider release after around 10 years (see dicta in *Fleming* [1973] 2 All ER 401). Although obviously highly significant, a minimum-term recommendation is not binding on the Home Secretary, and does not rank as an order of the court. Accordingly, there cannot be an appeal against a recommendation (*Aitken* [1966] 1 WLR 1076).

In addition to this formal power, the judge is expected to indicate the 'tariff' period, necessary to meet the requirement of retribution and deterrence. This indication is sent in a report to the Lord Chief Justice, who adds his view. It is then forwarded to the Home Secretary, who may set a higher or lower tariff than the judges.

The sentence for murder is also mandatory in the cases of offenders under 21. It is either custody for life or detention during Her Majesty's pleasure, depending on the offender's age at the date of the crime (see Paragraph 22.10.3). The only other offences for which the sentence is mandatory are high treason and piracy with violence, for both of which the death penalty is retained. When statute empowers the courts to pass a certain sentence or make a certain order, it normally uses a formula such as 'except when the sentence is fixed by law' to indicate that the provision should not be interpreted as entitling the courts to depart from the mandatory sentence for murder etc. In the remainder of the discussion on sentencing powers, any reference to a sentence etc. being available 'when an offender is convicted of an offence/imprisonable offence' should be understood as not applying to offenders convicted of murder (or high treason or piracy with violence if there were ever to be a prosecution for those offences).

As explained in Paragraph 22.4, common law offences (unless there is a statutory provision to the contrary) and some very serious statutory offences carry a maximum penalty of life imprisonment. Contrary to what one might imagine, life sentences for crimes such as manslaughter, rape, causing grievous bodily harm with intent and robbery are not necessarily reserved for the most serious instances of the offence in question. Of course, it would be wrong to resort to life imprisonment for, e.g., a minor robbery, but, leaving aside murder cases, the sentence has most often been used where the offender is (a) mentally unstable to such a degree that, if at liberty, he would probably re-offend and be a grave danger to the public, and (b) he will remain unstable and dangerous for a long and/or uncertain period of time. Provided the offence is punishable with life imprisonment, it has not had to be in absolutely the first rank of gravity (see *Ashdown* [1974] Crim LR 131, where life was upheld for offences which, the Court of Appeal said, were only intrinsically serious enough to merit about five years). Hospital orders under s 37 of the Mental Health Act 1983 (see Paragraph 23.22) are sometimes a possible alternative to life imprisonment for the disturbed offender, but often the strict medical preconditions for such an order are not fulfilled or there is simply not a place available at a secure mental hospital.

As indicated in Paragraph 22.6, the court must comply with PCC(S)A 2000, s 80(2), when determining the length of any custodial sentence. Clearly, this includes the decision to impose a discretionary life sentence. Hence such a sentence must be justified either on the ground of offence seriousness (s 80(2)(a)) or public protection (s 80(2)(b)). In most cases it is likely that the relevant ground will be public protection. This ground can only be used in the case of a violent or sexual offence (for the definition of 'violent' and 'sexual' see PCC(S)A 2000, s 161, and Paragraph 21.3).

Where the court imposes a discretionary life sentence based upon s 80(2)(b), s 82A, becomes relevant. This enables the sentencer to lay down what portion of the discretionary life sentence must expire before the offender's release on licence is considered by the Parole Board (see Paragraph 22.11).

After release, whether the life sentence was mandatory or discretionary, the ex-prisoner is on licence for the rest of his life. In that sense, a life sentence is just that.

An example of the way in which the Court of Appeal views the use of the discretionary life sentence is provided by *Chapman* [1994] Crim LR 609. C pleaded guilty to a robbery from a security guard in which a gun was fired twice and subsequently found in C's possession. He had previous convictions for serious robberies for which he had received sentences of 6, 10 and 12 years. The judge imposed a life sentence, with a period of 15 years specified under CJA 1991, s 34. The Court of Appeal held that a life sentence should be passed only where the offender was in a *mental state* which made him dangerous to members of the public. C was not in that category, so a life sentence was inappropriate. But he was very dangerous indeed, and the court imposed an enhanced sentence under what is now s 80(2)(b) of PCC(S)A 2000 of 20 years.

22.8 MANDATORY MINIMUM SENTENCES

The PCC(S)A 2000, ss 109 to 111 set out mandatory minimum sentences for certain specified offences. This was something of an innovation in this jurisdiction, although their introduction had become increasingly widespread in the United States. The new sentences attracted fierce controversy, since their inevitable effect is to fetter the judge who is passing sentence, and eliminate the possibility of taking the circumstances of the offence or the offender into account, other than within the constraints of the statutory minimum. Nevertheless, such sentences are now part of the sentencing landscape, and there is no suggestion of any domestic initiative to remove them, although the impact of the European Convention on Human Rights (ECHR) has yet to be tested in this field.

Section 109 imposes a mandatory life sentence for any offender, aged 18 or over, convicted of a second serious offence. Serious offences are defined for this purpose as including:

(a) attempted murder;

(b) conspiracy, incitement or solicitation to murder;

(c) manslaughter;

(d) wounding with intent or causing grievous bodily harm with intent (contrary to s 18 of the Offences Against the Person Act 1861);

(e) rape or attempted rape;

(f) unlawful sexual intercourse with a girl under 13;

(g) robbery with a firearm or imitation firearm; and

(h) offences under ss 16, 17 or 18 of the Firearms Act 1968.

Where the offender is convicted of a second such serious offence, no matter how long the interval between the two, the court is obliged to impose a sentence of life imprisonment, unless there are 'exceptional circumstances'. The meaning of that phrase was considered in *Kelly* [1999] Crim LR 240. The Court of Appeal held that, even if the sentencer was of the view that the imposition of a life sentence was unjust, that did not by itself constitute 'exceptional circumstances'. In *Offen (No 2)* [2001] 1 WLR 253, the Court of Appeal heard argument about the scope of 'exceptional circumstances' based upon Arts 3 and 5 of the European Convention on Human Rights. Lord Woolf CJ delivered the judgment of the court that it was inconsistent with those Convention rights (for detail see Paragraph 26.2.5) to sentence an offender to life imprisonment unless he constituted a significant risk to the public. Hence the PCC(S)A 2000, s 109 had to be interpreted in such a way that a court should hold that there are 'exceptional circumstances' for not imposing an automatic life sentence unless there is a significant risk to the public.

Section 110 applies to any person aged 18 or over who is convicted of a Class A drug trafficking offence, and who has previously been convicted on two separate occasions of such offences. Such an offender must receive a minimum of seven years' imprisonment. There is a discretion available to the court, however. The court need not impose the minimum term if it is of the opinion that there are specific circumstances which (a) relate to any of the offences or to the offender; and (b) would make the prescribed minimum sentence unjust in all the circumstances.

Section 111 deals with repeat offences of burglary. It lays down a minimum sentence of three years' imprisonment for the third conviction of burglary of a dwelling. The court is given the same discretion as applies to s 110.

A concession to the rigidity of the minimum sentence which must be imposed by ss 110 and 111 is laid down in s 152(3) of the Criminal Justice and Public Order Act 1994, which allows the court to give a discount for a guilty plea by reducing the actual sentence passed to 80 per cent of the statutory minimum. Even this falls somewhat short of the recognised reduction of up to one-third for an early guilty plea (see Paragraph 21.5.2).

22.9 SUSPENDED SENTENCES

In the case of an offender over the age of 21, the court may suspend certain sentences of imprisonment. It is crucial to note that a custodial sentence upon someone under 21 cannot be suspended.

The provisions in PCC(S)A, ss 79 to 81, relating to the passing of a custodial sentence (in relation to justifying its imposition, determining its length, pre-sentence reports, stating reasons etc.: see Paragraphs 22.3, 22.3.1, 22.3.2, 22.6.1 and 22.6.2) apply equally to the passing of a suspended sentence. The court must, in particular, be clear that it would have passed a sentence of immediate imprisonment if it did not have the power to suspend.

22.9.1 Passing a suspended sentence

The term of a suspended sentence must not exceed two years, and must not exceed the maximum which the court could have imposed as a sentence of immediate imprisonment (s 118). When a court passes sentences of imprisonment for two or more offences, it is the *aggregate* term which must not exceed two years (see s 152). In other words, sentences of two years for each of several offences may be suspended if the terms are made to run concurrently, but not if they are made consecutive.

The operational period of a suspended sentence is the period during which commission of an imprisonable offence carries with it the risk of the sentence being activated. The period runs from the date of the sentence, and is fixed by the court when it passes the sentence, within the statutory limits of not less than one and not more than two years. The court must explain to the offender in ordinary language the consequences of committing an imprisonable offence during the operational period.

A suspended sentence may not be passed unless, in the absence of a power to suspend, a sentence of immediate imprisonment would be appropriate.

In addition, the court shall not pass a suspended sentence unless it is of the opinion 'that the exercise of that power can be justified by the exceptional circumstances of the case'.

In *Okinikan* [1993] 1 WLR 173, Lord Taylor of Gosforth CJ said that 'taken on their own or in combination, good character, youth and an early plea' were not exceptional circumstances such as to justify a suspended sentence, since they were common features of many cases and could not be characterised as exceptional. In *Ullah Khan* (1994) 15 Cr App R (S) 320, on the other hand, the defendant's mental condition was held to fall within the definition of 'exceptional circumstances'. He was a solicitor convicted of mortgage fraud, and there was evidence that he was suffering from a paranoid psychosis which would have affected his concentration and judgement. In *French* (1994) 15 Cr App R (S) 194, the defendant's depressive illness was held to constitute 'exceptional circumstances', but in *Bradley* (1994) 15 Cr App R (S) 597 it did not. In *Kondal* (1995) 16 Cr App R (S) 845, the defendant was a sub-postmistress. She pleaded guilty to charges of theft and false accounting. She was sentenced to 18 months' immediate custody, but the Court of Appeal reduced this to 12 months suspended, holding that there were exceptional circumstances. In particular, she had the intention and reasonable expectation of repaying in a short time sums taken from the Post Office, and she had admitted the deficits in her accounts at the outset.

22.9.2 Combining a suspended sentence with other orders

A court which passes a suspended sentence is required by s 118 to consider whether the circumstances are such as to warrant in addition the imposition of a fine or the making of a compensation order. A common sentencing practice is to add a financial order to the suspended sentence so that the offender and the public do not see the court's overall disposition as a 'let-off'.

A suspended sentence may not be combined with probation even if the offender is being dealt with for two or more matters on one occasion (i.e., he cannot be put on probation for one offence and given a suspended sentence for a second offence). However, the Crown Court has power to make a suspended sentence supervision order, the effect of which is very similar to a suspended sentence plus probation (see Paragraph 22.9.5).

If an offender is currently serving a sentence of imprisonment, it is wrong in principle to pass a suspended sentence (*Baker* (1971) 55 Cr App R 182). Similarly, an offender should not on one occasion be sentenced to immediate imprisonment (say six months for one offence) and suspended imprisonment (say two years suspended for two years for a second offence). According to *Sapiano* (1968) 52 Cr App R 674, suspended sentences and sentences of immediate imprisonment fall into different categories and should not be combined.

22.9.3 Breach of a suspended sentence

If an offender is convicted of an imprisonable offence (summary or indictable) committed during the operational period of a suspended sentence, a court having power to deal with the matter (see Paragraph 22.9.4) may either:

(a) bring the suspended sentence into effect with its term unaltered; or
(b) bring it into effect with a shorter term substituted for the original term; or
(c) vary the length of the operational period so that it lasts until a date not more than two years from the date of variation; or
(d) make no order in respect of the suspended sentence.

The above options are set out in s 119 of the PCC(S)A, 2000, which goes on to provide that the court *must* make an order as in (a) unless it would be unjust to do so in all the circumstances. 'All the circumstances' include both the facts of the offence for which the suspended sentence was passed (the 'original offence') and the facts of the offence which has put the offender in breach of the suspended sentence (the 'subsequent offence'). When the court does not follow course (a) (i.e., refrains from activating the suspended sentence with its term unaltered), it must state its reasons for believing that that would have been unjust. In many cases, however, the court will both activate the suspended sentence and pass a sentence of immediate imprisonment for the subsequent offence. It should then, generally speaking, make the two terms run consecutively: *Ithell* [1969] 1 WLR 272.

Guidance on the correct approach to dealing with breaches of suspended sentence has been given by the Court of Appeal. The fact that the original offence and the subsequent offence differ in type does not of itself make it unjust to bring the whole suspended term into effect (per Lord Parker CJ in *Saunders* (1970) 54 Cr App R 247, where S failed in his appeal against activation of a six-month suspended sentence passed for petty theft consecutive to 12 months for subsequent offences of driving while disqualified, reckless driving and assault on a police officer). Where, however, the subsequent offence is both trivial and different in type from the original offence the court should either not activate the suspended term at all or substantially reduce its length. Thus, in *Moylan* [1970] 1 QB 143 an appeal against four months for criminal damage with an 18-months suspended sentence brought into effect to run consecutively was upheld, because the original offence had been theft of a television set and the subsequent offence consisted merely of breaking a window at a bus station when the worse for drink. M did not escape imprisonment completely, since the Court of Appeal confirmed the immediate term for the subsequent offence and did no more than cut the suspended term to six months. Bearing in mind M's apparent drink problem and the extreme triviality of the matter which actually brought him before the court, the judge might have decided that the circumstances were so exceptional that the subsequent offence could be dealt with by a non-custodial sentence (e.g., probation). Had he taken that view, it would have been wrong in principle to activate the suspended sentence even with a reduced term, since the result would have been an unsatisfactory mixing of custodial and non-custodial methods of dealing with an offender (see *Seymour* [1983] Crim LR 410 and *McElthorne* (1983) 5 Cr App R (S) 53 where the Court of Appeal quashed the activating of suspended sentences on the ground that the subsequent offences had been dealt with by community service orders). A final argument for not activating a suspended sentence (or activating it with a reduced term) is that the subsequent offence was committed at the very end of the operational period (*Wilson* [1980] 1 WLR 376 where 22 months of the two-year operational period had elapsed before W's fall from grace).

Although the general tenor of the Court of Appeal's approach to suspended sentences may seem harsh, it should not be thought that Crown Court judges and magistrates will inevitably activate terms when, according to a strict interpretation of cases such as *Saunders,* they really ought to do so. A lenient judge, on facts such as those in *Saunders,* might find in the difference between driving offences and dishonesty a reason for not implementing the suspended sentence, at least if the offender also has powerful mitigation relating to his personal circumstances. Since the CJA 1991 was passed, there is an additional factor for the sentencer to take into consideration in deciding whether a suspended sentence should be activated. What if the latest offence is not so serious that only a custodial sentence can be justified for it? Can the suspended sentence be activated, notwithstanding the inability of the court to impose a custodial sentence for the latest offence? It will usually be inappropriate to activate the suspended sentence in such a case (*Burnard* (1994) 15 Cr App R (S) 218). There is, however, no absolute prohibition on doing so (see *McQuillan* [1993] Crim LR 894, for example).

22.9.4   Powers to deal with breach of a suspended sentence

The Crown Court, when sentencing an offender who turns out to be in breach of a suspended sentence, has power to deal with the breach irrespective of whether the sentence was passed by the Crown Court or by a magistrates' court: PCC(S)A 2000, s 120. A magistrates' court has power to deal with a breach only if the suspended sentence was passed by itself or another magistrates' court. Should a summary conviction put an offender in breach of a Crown Court suspended sentence, s 120 places two options at the disposal of the magistrates. They may either commit the offender to the Crown Court to be dealt with for the breach, or they can decline to commit but give notice of the conviction to the Crown

Court. In the latter event, the Crown Court may (but need not) issue a summons or warrant for arrest to secure the offender's attendance before it, with a view to activating the suspended sentence if it sees fit: s 121.

A committal to the Crown Court to be dealt with for breach of a suspended sentence may be in custody or on bail. At the same time as they commit for the breach, the magistrates commit the offender to be sentenced for the offence of which they have just convicted him, so that one court can deal with both matters. The latter committal may be under s 6 (see Paragraph 11.3) or, if the offence of which the offender has been convicted is triable either way, under s 3 or 4 (see Paragraph 11.2).

If the magistrates choose merely to notify the Crown Court of the breach, they sentence the offender for the subsequent offence. By not committing him, they obviously indicate their view that the subsequent offence does not require activation of the suspended sentence, but the decision is one for the Crown Court not them. Therefore, they should not deal with the subsequent offence in a way which would make it impossible for the Crown Court to bring the suspended sentence into effect. Since a conviction which results in the offender being discharged conditionally or absolutely is deemed not to be a conviction, magistrates should not use this method when sentencing an offender in breach of a Crown Court suspended sentence: *Tarry* [1970] 2 QB 561. It is also undesirable for the magistrates to impose a community sentence for the subsequent offence, since that will render the task of the Crown Court in dealing with the suspended sentence much more difficult (*Stewart* (1984) 6 Cr App R (S) 166). If they think that a discharge, or a community sentence is appropriate they should commit the offender to the Crown Court under s 120 (for breach of the suspended sentence) and under s 6, for the subsequent offence, and hope that the Crown Court judge will share their view of the case.

22.9.5 Suspended sentence supervision orders

Although an offender may not, on one occasion, be given a suspended sentence and put on probation (see Paragraph 22.9.2), the Crown Court can achieve a similar result by passing a suspended sentence and ordering that for a period, not exceeding the operational period of the suspended sentence, the offender shall be placed under the supervision of a probation officer: PCC(S)A 2000, s 122. This is known as a suspended sentence supervision order. If the offender fails to keep in touch with the probation officer, he can be fined up to £1,000 by the magistrates' court for the area in which he resides: s 123. However, the imposition of such a fine has no effect on the continuance of the supervision order, nor is there any question of the suspended sentence itself being brought into effect. On the other hand, should the offender be convicted of an imprisonable offence committed during the operational period, s 119 (see Paragraph 22.9.3) will apply as it applies to breaches of ordinary suspended sentences, and if the sentence is brought into effect the supervision order automatically terminates: s 124.

Two further points should be noted. First, a supervision order can be added to a suspended sentence only if a term of more than six months is passed (and suspended) in respect of one offence. The significance of this is that a magistrates' court cannot make a suspended sentence supervision order, as it cannot pass a sentence of more than six months' imprisonment for any one offence. Secondly, a suspended sentence supervision order merely puts upon the offender an obligation to stay in touch with the probation officer. That is the basic effect of a probation order as well, but other more onerous requirements may be included in a probation order (see Paragraph 23.2.1) which may not be included in a s 122 order.

22.10   CUSTODY FOR OFFENDERS UNDER 21

An offender under the age of 21 may not be sentenced to imprisonment. Instead, there are four custodial sentences that, depending on his precise age, may be applicable to such an offender. They are:

(a)   detention in a young offender institution;
(b)   detention under s 91 of the PCC(S)A 2000;
(c)   custody for life;
(d)   a detention and training order.

It will be convenient to refer to the totality of offenders under 21 by the phrase 'young offenders', although that term is not used in legislation.

As was described in Paragraphs 22.3 to 22.3.2, there is now a statutory scheme which lays down the criteria and procedure for custodial sentences generally. It applies to young offenders just as it does to adults.

In sentencing young offenders, it is necessary to know the relevant date for determining age, so that the sentences available can be ascertained, as well as the length of any custodial sentence. In *Starkey* [1994] Crim LR 380, the offender turned 18 between being committed for sentence by the magistrates and his appearance for sentence in the Crown Court. He was 18 when the court sentenced him to one year and six weeks, and the question arose whether this sentence was lawful, the statutory maximum at that time for a juvenile of 17 being 12 months. It was held by the Court of Appeal that the relevant date was the date of conviction, when he was 17, with the result that the sentence had to be reduced to 12 months.

22.10.1   Sentence of detention in a young offender institution

Detention in a young offender institution is restricted to offenders aged 18, 19 and 20. As far as juveniles are concerned, it has been replaced by the detention and training order (see Paragraph 22.10.5). The term of a sentence of detention in a young offender institution may never exceed the maximum term of imprisonment that could be imposed for the offence if the offender were 21 or over. The minimum term is 21 days.

22.10.2   Sentences of detention under s 91 of the Powers of Criminal Courts (Sentencing) Act 2000

Where the offence is such that it merits a longer custodial sentence than that described in the preceding Paragraph, the court may consider a sentence under s 91. Such sentences, although not as uncommon as they used to be, remain very few in proportion to the number of juveniles sentenced for offences that theoretically could have been dealt with in that way. The qualifying conditions for a s 91 sentence are that the offender must be a person aged from 10 to 17 inclusive who is *convicted on indictment* of:

(a)   an offence punishable in the case of an adult with at least 14 years' imprisonment; or
(b)   indecent assault on a woman (contrary to the Sexual Offences Act 1956 s 14); or
(c)   (where the offender is aged from 14 to 17 inclusive) causing death by dangerous driving (under the Road Traffic Act 1988, s 1) or causing death by careless driving while under the influence of drink or drugs (under the Road Traffic Act 1988, s 3A).

The court must be of the opinion that none of the other methods of dealing with the juvenile (including a detention and training order) is appropriate. The term of the sentence ay be anything up to the maximum prison sentence imposable for the offence. While serving the sentence, the offender is held in accordance with the Home Secretary's directions. That will probably mean that he is kept in a young offender institution, but, depending on his age and needs, the Home Secretary might direct that he go to a mental hospital or even allow him to live in a community home. A s 91 detainee may be released at any stage of his sentence by the Home Secretary acting on a recommendation from the Parole Board. He then remains on licence for the remainder of the term passed by the court. Both the provisions about service of s 91 sentences and the release provisions mean that the sentence is much more flexible than a sentence of detention in a young offender institution. The appellate courts have issued guidance as to the cases where a sentence under s 91 should be imposed (see Paragraph 10.1).

Note that time spent in custody (or local authority secure accommodation) on remand counts towards a sentence imposed under s 91, just as it does for other custodial sentences.

The crucial limitation on the implementation of s 91 is the fact that the subsection requires the offender to have been convicted on indictment. As explained in Paragraph 10.1, youth courts tend almost automatically to proceed to the summary trial of a juvenile without considering whether he should be committed for trial so as to leave open the option of a more severe sentence than they can impose. In fixing the term of a sentence under s 91, the court must abide by the provisions of the PCC(S)A 2000, s 80 (see Paragraph 22.6). Offence seriousness and (for sexual or violent offences) protection of the public will therefore determine the length of sentence. Moreover the judge should realise that a term of, say, five years will seem like an eternity to a youngster. Therefore, it may well be proper to make the term much less than would have been appropriate in the case of an older offender convicted of a similar crime (see *Storey* [1984] Crim LR 438).

An offender convicted of murder, who was under 18 when he committed the offence, must be sentenced to be detained during Her Majesty's pleasure: PCC(S)A 2000, s 90. To all intents and purposes, the effect of the sentence is precisely the same as a sentence of detention for life under s 91. One oddity of the subsection is that the relevant consideration is the offender's age when he committed the offence, not his age at the date of sentence. The reason for the apparent anomaly is that, in the days of capital punishment, the rule was that only those over 18 when they killed were liable to be hanged, and detention during Her Majesty's pleasure was made the alternative for younger murderers.

22.10.3 Custody for life

This is the equivalent for 18–20-year-olds of life imprisonment for older offenders. Section 94 of the PCC(S)A 2000 provides that an offender who has attained the age of 18 but is not yet 21 may be sentenced to custody for life if the offence of which he has been convicted carries life imprisonment. As explained in Paragraph 22.7, life sentences are used not so much as the appropriate term for absolutely the most serious crimes, but as a way of dealing with offenders who, by reason of mental instability, would be a danger to the public if at large. In the absence of evidence of personality disorder, mental illness or the like, the court should pass a fixed term appropriate to the gravity of his offence, not life. The same principles apply to custody for life as apply to imprisonment (see *Turton* (1986) 8 Cr App R (S) 174). For murder, there is a *mandatory* sentence of custody for life if the offender is under 21, unless he was under 18 when he committed the offence, in which case the sentence is detention during Her Majesty's pleasure (s 94).

An offender sentenced to custody for life must be detained in a young offender institution unless the Home Secretary directs otherwise.

22.10.4   Detention and training order

The detention and training order is now the standard form of custodial sentence for young offenders. Its availability extends down to those as young as 10. It is a custodial sentence for the purposes of ss 79 to 81 of the PCC(S)A 2000, and the court must be satisfied that the custody threshold has been reached before imposing such an order (see Paragraph 21.1). In addition, in the case of an offender under the age of 15 at the time of conviction, the court may not make a detention and training order unless it is satisfied that he is 'a persistent offender'. Further, where the offender is under the age of 12 at the time of conviction, the court may only pass such an order if satisfied that 'only a custodial sentence would be adequate to protect the public from further offending from him'. (The power to pass a detention and training order in respect of an offender aged 10 or 11 will in any event be dependent upon a further order from the Secretary of State.)

As far as the length of the order is concerned, that is governed by s 101, which states that it shall be for 4, 6, 8, 10, 12, 18 or 24 months. It appears that any of the periods specified in s 101 can be imposed by the youth court (as well as the Crown Court), up to a maximum of 24 months: *Medway Crown Court ex p A* (1999) *The Times*, 30 June 1999. That case concerned a secure training order, but the Divisional Court made it clear that the same reasoning would apply to a detention and training order.

Half of whatever period imposed is to be spent in custody, in detention and training. When that portion is complete, a period of supervision under the auspices of a probation officer, social worker or member of a youth sentencing team commences, and continues until the end of the sentence.

22.11   RELEASE FROM CUSTODY

If an offender sentenced to imprisonment was held in custody for the whole or part of the period during which he was awaiting his trial or sentence, the time he so spent in custody counts towards service of the prison sentence unless he would have been in custody anyway as a result, for example, of an earlier prison sentence (Criminal Justice Act 1967, s 67).

This rule governs, then, the effective date of commencement of the offender's term of custody. The length of the term which he has to serve has, in recent history, been subject to a series of rules embodying the related but distinct concepts of 'remission', 'parole', 'licence' and 'early release'. In other words, the sentence pronounced in court is not the last word on how long the offender will be detained. That is determined by the rules relating to early release, by whatever name it is called.

Prior to CJA 1991, the crucial factors determining the length of sentence served were (a) remission and (b) parole. Every offender sentenced to 12 months or less received one half remission; and every offender sentenced to more than 12 months received one third remission. Remission could only be taken away for offences against prison discipline. Parole, on the other hand, was entirely discretionary, being granted only after consideration by the Parole Board, subject to the final decision of the Home Secretary. Parole was a possibility after an offender had served six months or one third of his sentence, whichever came later. Once released on parole, a prisoner was subject to the conditions specified in his licence, which included supervision by a probation officer. The offender's licence was liable to revocation by the Crown Court if he was convicted of an imprisonable offence, or by the Home Secretary in the event of breach of licence conditions.

This system of parole and remission was repealed by Criminal Justice Act 1991 which sets up a unified system of 'early release' for all prisoners, normally on licence.

The rules are now set out in the PCC(S)A 2000, which in summary states:

(a) Prisoners with sentences under 12 months serve half their sentence. They are then released 'unconditionally' (but see Paragraph 22.11.1 for the condition which is in practice imposed by s 116(2) of the PCC(S)A 2000).

(b) ·Those with sentences of 12 months or more but less than four years also serve half their sentence. They will then be released on licence, subject to supervision by the probation service. The licence and the supervision will expire at the three-quarter point of the sentence (but, again, see Paragraph 22.11.1 for the effect of s 116(2)).

(c) Long-term prisoners, with sentences of four years or more, must serve between half and two-thirds of their sentence, depending on whether the Parole Board recommends release on licence to the Home Secretary. At whatever point such a prisoner is released, his licence will continue in force and he will be supervised by the probation service until the three-quarter point (as with those in category (b)), and he will remain at risk under s 116(2), thereafter (see Paragraph 22.11.1).

(d) The release date of discretionary life prisoners (i.e., in effect, those whose life sentence was for a crime other than murder) is considered by the Parole Board after the expiry of such part of their sentence as the sentencing court determined, taking into account, in particular, the seriousness of the offence. The Parole Board may decide to release such a prisoner after the date specified by the court is reached, if satisfied that his confinement is no longer necessary to protect the public. If he is released, it will be on licence, for the rest of his life subject to probation service supervision.

(e) In the case of mandatory life prisoners (i.e., those convicted of murder), the Home Secretary has a discretion as to when to release the prisoner on licence and under supervision, after he has received a recommendation to that effect from the Parole Board. Although he must consult with the Lord Chief Justice, and the trial judge (if available), the Home Secretary has the final decision.

22.11.1 Subsequent conviction or breach of licence

A released prisoner, whether short or long-term, is subject to the operation of PCC(S)A 2000, s 116(2). If he commits an offence punishable with imprisonment 'before the date on which he would (but for his release) have served his sentence in full', then the court sentencing him may order him to return to prison to serve the remainder of his sentence. That order may be in addition to any sentence passed on him for the further offence. He is in jeopardy of such an order even if his licence has expired. In other words, s 116(2) continues to bite until the very end of the sentence which was pronounced in court for the original offence.

22.11.2 Sexual offenders

Sexual offenders are subject to potentially broader provisions in relation to supervision. When the court so directs, they will be subject to supervision right up to the end of the sentence, and not just up to the three-quarter point (PCC(S)A 2000, s 117). In addition, where the offender is recalled to prison for breach of his licence conditions, he is liable to remain there until the end of his sentence, rather than to the three-quarter point.

22.11.3 Time served on remand

In many cases, the prisoner will have been in custody on remand prior to sentence. By Criminal Justice Act 1967, s 67, such periods are deducted from the sentence to be served. Such remand time counts towards the calculation of whether a half, two-thirds or three-quarters of the sentence imposed has been served.

23 Sentences other than Custody

Chapter 22 dealt with the range of custodial penalties at the court's disposal. The great majority of offenders, however, are dealt with by some means other than custody, and this chapter is concerned with the non-custodial options.

This Chapter begins with some general points about community sentences (Paragraph 23.1), and then goes on to deal with the various community sentences in more detail, followed by financial penalties and the range of other orders which the court may make.

23.1 COMMUNITY SENTENCES

A community sentence consists of one or more community orders. Community orders are listed in s 33(1), PCC(S)A 2000:

(a) a community rehabilitation order,
(b) a community punishment order,
(c) a community punishment and rehabilitation order,
(d) a curfew order,
(e) a supervision order,
(f) an attendance centre order,
(g) a drug treatment and testing order,
(h) an action plan order,
(i) a drug abstinence order.

23.1.1 Justifying community sentences

There is a threshold requirement for the imposition of a community sentence, in the same way as there is for a custodial sentence. Unlike a decision to impose custody, however (which can be based on the need for public protection: see Paragraph 21.3), a community sentence can only be justified on the basis of offence seriousness (PCC(S)A 2000, s 35(1)). The court must consider the seriousness of 'the offence, or the combination of the offence and one or more offences associated with it', which is the same formulation as is contained in s 79(2)(a) in relation to custody: see Paragraph 21.4.

23.1.2   Objectives for community sentences

Once the court has decided that the offence (together with any associated offences) passes the community sentence threshold then PCC(S)A 2000, s 35(3), comes into play. It requires that the court must, in choosing the appropriate community order(s) achieve two objectives. First, the restrictions on liberty imposed by the order(s) must be 'commensurate with the seriousness of the offence'. Secondly, the sentence must be 'the most suitable for the offender'.

23.1.3   Pre-sentence reports

Pre-sentence reports replace social inquiry reports. According to PCC(S)A 2000, s 36(5), such a report is mandatory whenever a court is considering the imposition of:

(a)   a community rehabilitation order where it includes additional requirements authorised under the PCC(S)A 2000, Sch 2,
(b)   a community punishment order,
(c)   a community punishment and rehabilitation order, or
(d)   a supervision order containing requirements imposed under Sch 6, PCC(S)A 2000.

However the sentencing court may dispense with a pre-sentence report if it regards it as 'unnecessary', and the offender is aged 18 or over (s 81(2)). For offenders under the age of 18, on the other hand, the court is required to have sight of a pre-sentence report unless one of the offences is triable only on indictment and the court thinks it unnecessary.

In any event, the court is required, prior to deciding whether a community sentence is justified, and which one to impose, to 'take into account all such information about the circumstances of the offence (including any aggravating or mitigating factors) as is available to it' (this provision again mirrors that relating to custodial sentences). In carrying out this duty, the court would no doubt frequently obtain a pre-sentence report, even if it is not statutorily obliged to do so.

23.1.4   Consent to certain community sentences

Until 1997, the consent of the offender was required before the court could impose certain community sentences. The position was altered by the Crime (Sentences) Act 1997, which did away with the requirement of consent to a community sentence, except where the court imposes:

(a)   a requirement of treatment for alcohol or drug dependency as part of a probation order; or
(b)   a requirement of treatment for a mental condition in a probation order or a supervision order where the offender is aged 14 or over.

Where the offender refuses to consent, the court may impose a custodial sentence. Its decision to do so need not be justified on the usual bases of offence seriousness or public protection, since the imposition of a custodial sentence in these circumstances constitutes an exception to the usual need to find justification on one of these two grounds (PCC(S)A 2000, s 79(3)).

23.1.5 Combining community sentences

The courts may combine any two of the community orders, and may add a fine or compensation order. This more flexible approach was introduced by CJA 1991. Prior to its introduction, there were various prohibitions on the combining of different orders.

23.2 COMMUNITY REHABILITATION ORDERS

The main statutory provision relating to the community rehabilitation order is s 80 of the PCC(S)A 2000. It is restricted to offenders aged 16 and over. Subject to the threshold and procedural constraints outlined above, the court may place such an offender on a community rehabilitation order for a period of between six months and three years. The effect is that the offender must accept the supervision of, and keep in touch with, his probation officer.

The purposes of a community rehabilitation order are (according to the PCC(S)A 2000, s 41):

(a) the rehabilitation of the offender, or

(b) protecting the public from him or preventing the commission by him of further offences.

23.2.1 Requirements of a community rehabilitation order

Inherent in the order is a requirement that the offender submit to being supervised by a probation officer, whom he must visit at times fixed by the officer. The officer assigned to look after him will be one of those appointed for or attached to the petty sessional area in which he resides, and the magistrates' court for that area — which has certain responsibilities in connection with the enforcement of the order — is known as the 'supervising court'.

There are standard conditions inserted in community rehabilitation order. They require that the offender:

(a) be of good behaviour and lead an industrious life;

(b) inform the probation officer immediately of any change of address or employment;

(c) comply with the probation officer's instructions about reporting to the officer and receiving visits from the officer at home.

The above standard conditions are non-statutory. In addition, the court may impose one or more of the following additional requirements. (PCC(S)A 2000, Sch 2):

(a) *A residence requirement.*   Having considered the offender's home surroundings, the court may require him to reside with a certain person or at a certain address. A particularly useful form of residential requirement is one which sends the offender to a hostel, approved by the Home Secretary, where the environment and support available should help him to stay out of trouble. The period for which a offender must reside at a hostel should be specified in the order.

(b) *A treatment requirement.*   Upon being satisfied by the evidence (written or oral) of a duly qualified medical practitioner that the offender is suffering from a mental condition which needs treatment but which is not such as to warrant a hospital order (see Paragraph 23.22), the court may require him to submit to appropriate treatment either as an in-patient at a hospital or mental nursing home, or as an out-patient at an institution named in the order, or as the patient of a duly qualified doctor or chartered psychologist. The period for which he is to receive treatment is specified in the order, and must not exceed the period of the order itself.

There is also a statutory framework for the insertion into community rehabilitation orders of conditions requiring the offender to undergo treatment for drug or alcohol dependency. The court must be satisfied that the dependency caused or contributed to the offence in question. Further, the dependency must be such as requires and is susceptible to treatment. As with a requirement for treatment of a mental condition, the court must ensure that arrangements have been made for the offender to be received at the place where the treatment is to be carried out. The place and period of treatment must be specified. The period may be for the whole or part of the period of the order.

(c) *A probation centre requirement.* Probation centres are non-residential premises at which there are facilities to assist in the rehabilitation of offenders. Those facilities have to be approved by the Secretary of State. Having consulted a probation officer and been satisfied that arrangements can be made for the offender to attend at a particular centre, the court may require him to attend at that centre in accordance with his probation officer's instructions. The number of days on which the offender must go to the centre, and the dates on which he must go, are determined by the probation officer not the court, but the number must not exceed 60 and the dates must all be within the period of the order. As far as possible, attendance at a centre should not clash with school or working hours.

Where an offender has been convicted of a sexual offence, the usual 60-day limit in relation to attendance at a probation centre does not apply. This requirement may extend, in such cases, for the duration of the order, but the court must specify the number of days' attendance required.

(d) *An activity requirement.* Having consulted a probation officer, the court may require the offender to present himself to specified persons at a specified place and/or participate in specified activities. 'Specified' means specified in the order. As with a requirement to attend a probation centre, the days on which the offender must 'present himself or 'participate' as the case may be are determined by the probation officer up to a maximum of 60. Again, a condition in the case of an offender who has committed a sexual offence is not subject to the 60-day limit.

(e) *Negative requirements.* The court may require the offender to refrain from participating in specified activities either for the whole period of the order, or for part of it, or on specified days during it.

23.3 COMMUNITY PUNISHMENT ORDERS

A court dealing with an offender aged 16 or over for an imprisonable offence may make in his case a community punishment order, i.e., an order that he perform, without pay, work of value to the community. The order fixes the number of hours to be worked within a minimum of 40 and a maximum of 240 hours.

For a court to have power to make a community punishment order, five conditions must be satisfied (in addition to the requirements for all community sentences; see Paragraph 23.1):

(a) the offender must have been convicted of an imprisonable offence;
(b) he must have attained the age of 16;

(c) the court must be satisfied, in the light of a probation officer's or social worker's report, that the offender is a suitable person for a community punishment order;

(d) the court must be satisfied that arrangements can be made for him to perform the work ordered in the petty sessions area in which he resides.

Subject to not going outside the statutory limits of 40–240 hours, the court has total discretion in fixing the hours of service to be performed. The work is performed under the instructions of a probation officer for the area in which the offender resides. Normally, it should be completed within 12 months at times which do not clash with the offender's school or working hours.

A court dealing with an offender for two or more offences may make a community punishment order in respect of each offence. It may further order that the hours specified in each order be worked concurrently with or consecutively to each other, but in the latter case the aggregate number of hours must not exceed 240 (s 46(8)).

The attraction of a community punishment order as a 'last resort' alternative to custody is that it genuinely punishes the offender in that he loses his leisure time doing work for which he is not paid. On the other hand, if he cooperates in doing the work, the contact with those running the scheme can be genuinely constructive and rewarding. Certainly, the sentence is said to be successful in the sense that most offenders do the work they are ordered to do and do not have to come back before the court to be fined or even sentenced for the original offence.

23.4 COMMUNITY PUNISHMENT AND REHABILITATION ORDERS

In effect, this order is a mixture of the community rehabilitation and community punishment orders. It was introduced by the CJA 1991, the government's aim being to provide the courts with a sentencing option which 'should be particularly suitable for some persistent property offenders' (White Paper, *Crime, Justice and Protecting the Public* (Cm 965) (London: HMSO, 1990)).

The community rehabilitation element in the combination must be for a minimum of 12 months (whereas the usual minimum is six months). The maximum is three years. As far as the community punishment element is concerned, that must be for between 40 and 100 hours (compare the usual maximum of 240 hours). Other points worth bearing in mind about such orders are:

(a) The court must obtain and consider a pre-sentence report before imposing such an order (PCC(S)A 2000, s 36(4)) subject to the qualifications set out in Paragraph 23.1.3.

(b) The offender must be over the age of 16.

(c) The offence must be punishable with imprisonment.

(d) The court must be satisfied, before making the order, that it is desirable in the interests of securing the offender's rehabilitation, or protecting the public from harm from him or preventing the commission by him of further offences (as for a community rehabilitation order: see Paragraph 23.2.1)

(e) The court can insert any of the additional requirements which it could have inserted into a community rehabilitation order, provided that they do not prevent the fulfilment of the community punishment element of the order.

(f) The community punishment element must be completed within 12 months of the making of the order.

A community rehabilitation order and a community punishment order cannot be imposed on the same occasion, even for separate offences, except in the form of a community punishment and rehabilitation order (s 35(2) of the PCC(S)A 2000).

23.5   CURFEW ORDERS

The curfew order requires the offender to remain at a particular place (e.g., at home) for between two and 12 hours on any days, over a period which must not exceed six months from the date when the order is made. In the White Paper *Crime, Justice and Protecting the Public* (Cm 965) (London: HMSO, 1990), the government stated that:

> Curfews could be helpful in reducing some forms of crime, thefts of and from cars, pub brawls and other types of disorder. A curfew order could be used to keep people away from particular places, such as shopping centres or pubs, or to keep them at home in the evenings or at weekends.

As the White Paper pointed out, the imposition of a curfew order would not prevent the offender from working, attending a training course or a probation centre, or receiving treatment for, say, drug abuse.

Provided that it is within the limits indicated above, the curfew order may specify different places or periods of curfew in respect of different days. The order must name the person who is to be responsible for monitoring the offender's whereabouts during curfew periods. A pre-sentence report must be obtained and considered before a curfew order is imposed (subject to the qualifications set out in Paragraph 23.1.3). The court must have information about the place to which the offender is to be restricted, including information about the attitude of any persons likely to be affected by his enforced presence there (s 12(6)).

A curfew order may include requirements for electronic monitoring, so as to keep a check upon the offender's whereabouts during the curfew (s 13). Such a requirement can only be imposed where an electronic monitoring scheme is in operation in the area in question.

23.6   BREACH, REVOCATION AND AMENDMENT OF COMMUNITY SENTENCES

The breach, revocation and amendment of community rehabilitation orders, community punishment orders, curfew orders and community rehabilitation and punishment orders are dealt with in Sch 3 to the PCC(S)A 2000 (for the position in relation to supervision and attendance centre orders, see Paragraphs 23.7 and 23.8).

If there has been a breach of one of these orders (i.e., a failure to comply with the terms of the order rather than the commission of a further offence) the offender is brought before the magistrates' court for the area. The question which the court must then consider is: has he failed without reasonable excuse to comply with the requirements of the order? If he has, then the magistrates can adopt one of the following courses of action:

(a)   Impose a fine up to a maximum of £1,000.
(b)   Impose a community punishment order up to a maximum of 60 hours.
(c)   If the offender is in breach of a community rehabilitation order, make an attendance centre order.

(d) If the original order was imposed by the Crown Court, commit him to the Crown Court in custody or on bail.

(e) If the original order was imposed by a magistrates' court, revoke the order and deal with him in respect of the original offence, in any way in which they could deal with him if he had just been convicted by them.

If the decision which the magistrates make is (a), (b) or (c), then the order may continue in force. If the course decided upon is (d), then the fate of the original order awaits the Crown Court's disposition. If the option which the magistrates choose is (e), then the order ceases to have effect, and the court re-sentences. In doing so, it must take into effect the extent that the offender has complied with the original order. For example, if he has performed 50 hours of a community service order then the new sentence must give him credit for that. It is in any event likely (though not certain) that the court will be considering a custodial sentence since it has decided that the breach is sufficiently serious to revoke and re-sentence. It is entitled (but not obliged) to assume that the offender has refused consent to a community sentence requiring that consent — thus paving the way for the passing of a custodial sentence under PCC(S)A 2000, s 79(3).

Assume, on the other hand, that the magistrates decide upon option (d). In that case, the matter will in due course come before the Crown Court. The Crown Court can for its part decide on any of the options (a) to (c). Alternatively, it, too, may revoke the order and deal with the offender in any manner in which the Crown Court could deal with him if he had just been convicted by it of the offence.

Revocation is to be distinguished from breach. A community order may be revoked because it has been breached (as in (e) above). More generally, however, the court may revoke the order if it is in the interests of justice to do so. This may be either a simple revocation (e.g., because of the offender's good progress) or revocation coupled with re-sentencing for the original offence. The commission of a further offence would be likely, but not certain, to trigger off revocation and re-sentencing in this way.

If they do revoke and re-sentence, the court must again give credit to the offender for the extent to which he has complied with the original order. If that order was made by the Crown Court, the magistrates should commit any offender who falls to be re-sentenced to the Crown Court, on bail or in custody. If the magistrates re-sentence, they are confined to dealing with him as if he had just been convicted by them of the offence. The Crown Court can, if re-sentencing him, deal with him as if he had just been convicted by it of the offence.

Any of the community sentences can be amended. This might be done to take account of a change in the offender's circumstances, e.g., his area of residence, the success of treatment, ill-health.

23.7 SUPERVISION ORDERS

The Crown Court or a youth court, when dealing with a young person for an offence, may make a supervision order (PCC(S)A 2000, s 63). There is power to make a supervision order even if the offence concerned is non-imprisonable. Subject to earlier discharge, the order lasts for three years or such shorter period as the court may specify (s 63(7)). The supervisor is designated in the order, and is usually the local authority in whose area the offender resides, although it may be a probation officer (s 63). It is the duty of the supervisor to 'advise, assist and befriend' the supervisee (s 64). Where the local authority is the supervisor it discharges that duty through social workers. The order may contain appropriate provisions to help the supervisor carry out his functions (e.g., a provision that the supervisee visit the supervisor when told to do so). In addition, the court may include in a supervision order one or more of a wide range of requirements. Some of these requirements (e.g., to reside with a named individual or to submit to treatment for a mental condition) are analogous to requirements which can be inserted in a probation order (see Paragraph 23.2.1). Others are peculiar to supervision orders. In particular, the court may impose a requirement for intermediate treatment, the effect of which is that for up to 90 days the supervisor may, at his discretion, direct the supervisee to participate in specified activities and/or report to a named person at a certain place and/or live at a specified place. Thus, the supervisee could be sent away from home for up to 90 days (e.g., to a community home or on an adventure holiday or on a useful course of training). A supervision order with a requirement for intermediate treatment is thus halfway between an ordinary supervision order and a care order.

Supervision orders are clearly comparable to community rehabilitation orders, although they are applicable to a younger age group (the supervision order being available for an offender under 18, the community rehabilitation order if he is over 16).

The sanctions for breach of a supervision order are:

(a)   payment of a fine not exceeding £1,000;

(b)   a curfew order;

(c)   an attendance centre order;

(d)   if the supervision order was made by a relevant court, it may discharge the order and deal with the offender, for the offence in respect of which the order was made, in any manner in which he could have been dealt with for that offence by the court which made the order if the order had not been made;

(e)   if the supervision order was made by the Crown Court, the relevant court may commit the offender in custody or release him on bail to appear before the Crown Court.

Whether or not there has been a breach of supervision requirements, the court has a wide discretion to discharge the order, or to discharge it and replace it with a care order, or to vary or add to the requirements originally included. Thus, if the supervisee has made good progress the court could simply discharge the order ahead of its expiry date, or, in the opposite case, it could strengthen the order by, for example, including a requirement for intermediate treatment, or even discharge the order and put the ex-supervisee into care. The above provisions are contained in Sch 7 to the PCC(S)A 2000.

It is primarily the supervisor's responsibility to apply to the court for the discharge or variation of an order or its replacement by a care order, although the supervisee also has the right to apply. Enforcement of a supervision order by bringing any breach of requirement to the court's attention is entirely a matter for the supervisor. The court to which application must be made is a youth court in the case of a supervisee who is under 18 and an adult magistrates' court in other cases.

Requirements relating to the following matters may be included in a supervision order (see PCC(S)A 2000, Sch 6):

(a)   *Residence.*   The supervisee may be required to live with a named individual who agrees to the proposed requirement. Alternatively, he may be required to live in local authority accommodation.

(b) *Mental treatment.* The supervisee may be required to submit to treatment for a mental condition which is not such as to warrant the making of a hospital order.

(c) *Intermediate treatment.* The supervisee may be required to comply with directions given by his supervisor to the effect that he live at a certain place and/or report to a named person at a certain place and/or participate in specified activities. What, if any, directions are given is in the discretion of the supervisor, but the directions may not relate to a total of more than 90 days (or such lesser number of days as may be specified in the supervision order).

(d) *Court-nominated intermediate treatment.* The court may itself nominate and include as requirement/s of the supervision order any direction that the supervisor could give pursuant to a requirement under (c) above. Thus, the court can specify where the supervisee shall live or what activities he shall participate in. Subject to (e) below, the directions may relate to a total of up to 90 days. Where the court includes requirements under as an alternative to passing a custodial sentence, it should state in open court that that is the case, and should certify the same in the supervision order itself. If the supervisee breaches any of the requirements, he may, even if he is still under 18, be sentenced for the original offence.

(e) *Night restrictions.* For specified periods between 6 p.m. and 6 a.m. the supervisee may be required to remain at a place specified in the supervision order, or at one of several places so specified. One of the specified places must be his home. A night restriction must not require the supervisee to remain at a place for more than 10 hours on any one night; nor may it relate to more than 30 nights in all, and nor may it relate to a night more than three months after the supervision order was made. If the court imposes requirements under (d) above and a night restriction, the total number of days affected by the requirements must not exceed 90. During the operation of a night restriction the supervisee may leave the specified place only if accompanied by his parents, his supervisor or another person named in the order.

(f) *Educational requirements.* While he remains of compulsory school age, the supervisee may be required to comply with arrangements for his education made by his parents. The arrangements must be approved by the local education authority, which must be consulted by the court before inclusion of the requirement.

(g) *Negative requirements.* The supervisee may be required *not* to participate in activities specified in the supervision order either for the whole period of the order, or for part of that period, or for specified days within the period.

The requirements described in (d), (e) and (f) above may not be combined with an ordinary intermediate treatment requirement. Also, they can only be included in an order if the court first consults the supervisor, and is satisfied both that the requirements are necessary to prevent the offender re-offending and that it is feasible to secure his compliance with them.

23.8 ATTENDANCE CENTRE ORDERS

Magistrates' courts have been able to make attendance centre orders since 1948. The present legislation on the subject is contained in ss 60 and 62 of the PCC(S)A 2000. Section 62(2) defines an attendance centre as a place where offenders under 21 'may be required to attend and be given under supervision appropriate occupation or instruction'. Most centres open on Saturday afternoons, and are run by police officers in their spare time at premises such as schools or youth clubs. Typically, an offender might be required to attend at a centre for six two-hour sessions, during which he will be kept under firm discipline and will engage in activities such as physical training and handicrafts. The aim is not only to punish an offender by depriving him of his leisure time, but also to encourage him to use his leisure more constructively once it is restored to him. Most attendance centres are for boys under 17, but in recent years efforts have been made to provide more centres for males aged 17 to 20 and girls.

A court dealing with an offender under the age of 21 for an imprisonable offence may make an attendance centre order provided that the court has been notified that there is a suitable centre available for him to attend. This constitutes a significant restriction on the making of attendance centre orders because the centre to be attended, which must be specified in the order, should be reasonably accessible to the offender, and there may not be a centre for persons of his or her age and sex near where he or she lives.

Attendance centre orders are equally at the disposal of the Crown Court, youth court and adult magistrates' court, save that the last-mentioned may not make an order in respect of a juvenile.

The number of hours for which the offender must attend is fixed in the order. It must be at least 12, save that in the case of a child under 14 the court may order less if 12 hours' attendance would be excessive (s 60(3)). It must not be more than 12 unless, in all the circumstances, the court thinks that 12 hours is inadequate, in which case the maximum is 24 hours where the offender is under 16 and 36 hours where the offender is aged 16 to 20 (s 60(4)). When a court deals with an offender for two or more offences by means of attendance centre orders it is the *aggregate* number of hours fixed in the orders which must not be less than the minimum or more than the maximum. The order specifies when the offender must first attend the centre, but subsequent times are fixed by the person in charge of it. An offender cannot be required to attend more than once a day or for more than three hours on any one occasion (s 60(10)). Failure to attend in accordance with an order may result in its being revoked and the offender being dealt with for the offence in respect of which it was made in any way the court which made it could have dealt with him (Sch 5). The same applies if the offender attends the centre but misbehaves. In dealing with the offender for the original offence, the court must take into account the extent to which he has complied with the attendance centre order.

As an alternative to discharging the attendance centre order, the court can decide that the order should continue, but impose a fine not exceeding £1,000.

> Attendance centre orders may be made not only when sentencing for an offence but also when dealing with a person under 21 for default in paying a fine or breach of requirements in a probation or supervision order (see PCC(S)A 2000, s 60(1)(b) and Sch 7, para 4).

23.9 DRUG TREATMENT AND TESTING ORDERS AND DRUG ABSTINENCE ORDERS

A court dealing with an offender aged 16 or over can impose a drug treatment and testing order (PCC(S)A 2000, ss 52 to 55). Before making a drug treatment and testing order, the court must be satisfied that the offender is dependent on, or has a propensity to misuse drugs, and that the dependency requires and may be susceptible to treatment. As is implied by the name, the order has elements of treatment (to eliminate the dependency or propensity) and testing (to ascertain whether the offender has any drugs in his body). There is provision for review of the offender's progress at monthly intervals, and the order as a whole must last for a period of between six months and three years. It is a community sentence, and is subject to the general provisions relating to such sentences, e.g., as to the threshold for imposition, penalties for breach (see Paragraph 23.1).

Under the PCC(S)A 2000, s 58A, the court can impose a 'drug abstinence order' on certain offenders aged 18 or over. The order requires the offender to abstain from using Class A drugs, and to provide when required by the responsible officer a sample to determine whether he has any such drug in his body. The order can only be made if, in the opinion of the court, the offender is 'dependent on, or has a propensity to misuse' specified Class A drugs. Further, the offence for which the offender is being sentenced must be one of a list, which includes most of the major offences of dishonesty, and those related to the possession and supply of drugs. The order may be for a period of between six months and three years. Again, the drug abstinence order is a community sentence, and is subject to the provisions applicable to such sentences.

23.10   ACTION PLAN ORDER

This is a community sentence, and is subject to the general provisions for such sentences set out in Paragraph 23.1. It is available in the case of a juvenile who is convicted of any offence by the youth court or the Crown Court. It requires him to comply for a period of three months with an action plan which lays down certain requirements about his actions and whereabouts. For the period of the order, the offender is put under the supervision of a probation officer. The order is dealt within ss 69 to 71, PCC(S)A 2000.

23.11   REPARATION ORDER

A reparation order requires the offender to make reparation to the victim or someone 'otherwise affected' by the offence. It is not a community sentence, and is not subject to the general provisions relating to such sentences, e.g., as to threshold. The reparations in question consist of a certain amount of work up to a maximum of 24 hours (for details, see PCC(S)A 2000, ss 73 and 74).

23.12   PARENTING ORDER

The Crown Court and the youth court have the power to impose these orders upon the parent or guardian of a juvenile offender where he has been convicted of any offence. The order may be for a period up to 12 months, and may impose certain requirements upon the parent in question during that period, e.g., to ensure that the child is accompanied to and from school each day, and is kept within the home from a certain hour each evening. In any event, the order must include a requirement that the parent attends specified counselling or guidance sessions. This order was introduced by ss 8 to 10 of the Crime and Disorder Act 1998.

23.13   FINES

The fine is by far the commonest penalty imposed for summary offences. In addition, it is also the most frequent penalty for offences which are triable either way. The Paragraphs which follow deal first with the maximum fines which can be imposed by the different courts in respect of different offences and offenders (Paragraph 23.13.1); then with the way in which the court should decide how much to fine an individual offender (Paragraph 23.13.2); then the practicalities of recovering fines are described, including imprisonment in default (Paragraphs 23.13.3 to 5); and finally, the question of combining a fine with another form of penalty is considered (Paragraph 23.13.6).

From the point of view of the offender, fines are not the only financial orders which may be imposed. An order to pay compensation to the victim, or an order for restitution, confiscation or forfeiture will have similar effects (see Paragraphs 23.18 to 23.20).

23.13.1   Maximum fines

There is no statutory limit on the size of the fine which the Crown Court may impose on an offender who has been convicted on indictment or committed for sentence under s 3 of the PCC(S)A 2000. Following summary conviction for an offence triable either way, the magistrates may, generally speaking, impose a fine of up to £5,000 (see Paragraph 11.1 for further details). For summary offences, the maximum fines imposable are fixed by reference to a *standard scale of fines*. The vast majority of summary offences have been classified as either a level 1 offence, or a level 2 offence, and so on up to level 5. For each level, the standard scale specifies the maximum fine which the magistrates may order the offender to pay. However, there is nothing to stop Parliament ignoring the standard scale and fixing the fine in direct monetary terms (e.g., if it wants the magistrates to have power to impose a substantial penalty, well in excess of the maximum sum on the standard scale). The advantage of using the standard scale is that the Home Secretary is able to vary by statutory instrument the amounts specified in the scale in line with changes in the value of money. There is no need for amending legislation to be put through Parliament. Formerly, there was a recurring problem of the maximum fines laid down by the vast number of statutes creating summary offences becoming unrealistically low as inflation raged and Parliament did not have the time to amend each provision so as to restore the maximum fine to what, in real terms, it had originally been.

The relevant maxima are set out below.

Level on the scale	Amount of fine
1	£200
2	£500
3	£1,000
4	£2,500
5	£5,000

At present the highest sum on the standard scale corresponds with the 'prescribed sum' (i.e., the maximum fine, again variable by the Home Secretary, which can be imposed by the magistrates following conviction for an either-way offence listed in Sch 1 to the Magistrates' Courts Act 1980). There is no reason why the prescribed sum should always be the same as the sum at level 5 on the standard scale. However, if Parliament wishes a maximum fine imposable on summary conviction (either for a summary offence or for an either-way offence not listed in Sch 1) to be the same as whatever the prescribed sum shall from time to time be, it simply provides that the fine shall not exceed the '*statutory maximum*'.

Where an offender under the age of 18 is fined in the magistrates' or youth court, the maximum is £1,000. The limit for those under 14 is £250. There is no statutory limit on the fine which the Crown Court may impose upon a juvenile.

23.13.2   Determining the size of a fine

The court needs to take a series of steps in deciding the size of the fine to impose. The first step is to determine what fine would reflect the seriousness of the offence (PCC(S)A 2000, s 128), including any aggravating or mitigating factors which relate to the offence itself. Secondly, any mitigation personal to the offender should be taken into account (s 158). Then the court should turn to the financial circumstances of the offender, and make any appropriate adjustments (s 128(3)). This must be done whether it increases or reduces the amount of the fine (s 128(4)). This latter statutory provision has the effect of changing quite radically the law as it stood prior to the introduction of the CJA 1991, when the position was that a fine should be decreased if the offender was impecunious, but should not be increased for a wealthy defendant (*Fairbairn* (1980) 2 Cr App R (S) 315).

In the Magistrates' Association's *Sentencing Guidelines* (2000), guideline fines are set out in relation to some of the common offences which are likely to be dealt with by way of fine. Hence, guideline fines are set out for theft (but not for burglary) and for possession of a drug of Class B (but not Class A). The decision-making sequence suggested in the *Sentencing Guidelines* is as follows. Magistrates are advised to consider first the seriousness of the offence, then to look at aggravating and mitigating factors, and mitigation appropriate to the offender. They are told to consider their sentence at that stage, and compare it with the suggested guidelines. They should reconsider their reasons carefully if they have chosen a sentence at a different level. A discount should be considered for a timely guilty plea. They should then decide their sentence. The Guidelines set out indicative fines, based upon weekly income net of tax and national insurance, and taking into account other relevant outgoings. There are three levels of guideline fine, A, B and C, which represent one half of weekly income, weekly income, and one and a half times weekly income respectively.

Although the *Sentencing Guidelines* apply to the magistrates' court, the essentials of the decision-making process are the same in the Crown Court.

23.13.3 Time to pay

A court imposing a fine is usually under a duty to give the offender time to pay. Even when it is not under a duty to do so, the court always has a discretion to allow time. The only occasions on which a court may refuse an offender time to pay are when:

(a) the offence is imprisonable, and he appears to have the money to pay forthwith; or
(b) he is of no fixed abode or is likely to leave the United Kingdom; or
(c) he is already serving a custodial sentence, or is given a custodial sentence by the court at the same time as it imposes the fine (Magistrates' Courts Act 1980, s 82).

The court may order the offender to be searched, so that money found on him can be used to pay the fine (PCC(S)A 2000, s 80(1)). When a court grants time to pay it either fixes a period within which the entire sum must be paid, or it orders that the sum be paid by fixed instalments. In *Olliver* (1989) 11 Cr App R (S) 10 the Court of Appeal said that a period of two years would seldom be too long, and three years might be acceptable in an appropriate case. The Magistrates' Association *Sentencing Guidelines* (2000) state, however, that 'The fine is payable on the day and the defendant should always be asked for immediate payment. If periodic payments are allowed, the fine should normally be payable within a maximum of 12 months.'

If the court refuses time to pay, and the offender does not produce the money forthwith, he is committed to prison until either he does pay or he has served the term in default. Part-payment results in a proportionate reduction of the term (see Paragraph 23.13.4). If time to pay is granted, enforcement is the responsibility of a magistrates' court. Where the fine was imposed by the Crown Court, the enforcing magistrates' court is either named in the fine order or is the court which committed the offender for trial or sentence; where the fine was imposed by a magistrates' court, that court is the enforcing court; in either case, the initial enforcing court can transfer its responsibilities to the court for the area in which the offender resides. If the offender realises that he will have difficulty in paying, he may apply to the enforcing court for more time to pay. Should he fail to pay (either within the time originally ordered or within any extension of time he may have obtained), the enforcing court summons him to appear before a *means inquiry* and orders him, for purposes of that inquiry, to provide a statement of his means. Following the inquiry, the magistrates may, if changes in circumstances since the fine was imposed make it just to do so, remit part or all of the fine. If the fine was imposed by the Crown Court, they need that court's consent. Where, on the other hand, the magistrates consider that the defaulter is to blame for his failure to pay and that other methods of enforcement would not work, they may issue a warrant committing him to prison for, in the case of a Crown Court fine, the term in default fixed by the Crown Court judge, or, in the case of a magistrates' court fine, a term not exceeding the maximum allowed by Sch 4 to the Magistrates' Courts Act 1980 for the size of the fine in question. If part-payment has already been made, the term fixed by the Crown Court judge or maximum term allowed by Sch 4 is reduced proportionately. As an alternative to sending the defaulter to prison forthwith, the magistrates may suspend issue of the warrant upon condition that he comply with stated terms as to payment. If he subsequently fails to comply, the warrant may be issued and the defaulter consequently committed to prison without a further court hearing.

The law on enforcement of fines is contained in the Magistrates' Courts Act 1980, ss 75 to 91 and the Powers of Criminal Courts Act 1973, s 32. There are several variations on the basic system of enforcement described above. For example, the enforcing court may issue a warrant of distress under which the offender's goods are seized and sold to raise money for the fine, or it may make an attachment of earnings order requiring his employer to deduct the money from his wages and pay it to the court. There is also power to order the offender to pay the fine under the supervision of a probation officer or other suitable person.

23.13.4   Imprisonment in default

At the same time as it imposes a fine, the Crown Court must fix a term of imprisonment to be served in default of payment. The maximum terms which may be fixed in default are prescribed by a table contained in PCC(S)A 2000, s 139(4). At the bottom end of the scale, the term in default for a fine of £200 or less must not exceed seven days; at the very top of the scale, the term for a fine exceeding £1 million (!) must not exceed 10 years. Needless to say, fines of the latter amount are very rare indeed. In *Szrajber* [1994] Crim LR 543, it was made clear that the default term in relation to each band of fines was a *maximum*. In fixing the period to be served in default, the court had a discretion and would normally decide on a term between the maximum for the band applicable and the maximum of the band below, in line with the circumstances of the case. It should be noted, however, that, where an offender is fined for several offences, the Crown Court fixes a term in default for each fine and may order that those terms shall be served consecutively, even if the aggregate term exceeds that which could have been fixed for any of the fines taken individually (see *Savundranayagan* [1968] 1 WLR 1761). The court may also order that a term in default shall be served consecutively to any custodial sentence that it imposes or another court imposed, on the offender. In the cases of offenders over 18 but under 21, the court does not fix a term of imprisonment in default, but fixes a term of detention in a young offender institution.

When a magistrates' court fines an offender, it has no power to fix a term in default unless the circumstances are such that it need not grant time to pay (Magistrates' Courts Act 1980, s 82(2)). As explained above, it is only in exceptional cases that time to pay can be refused. If, however, the court *could* order immediate payment, it may fix a default term whether or not it in fact grants time. A table in Sch 4 to the Magistrates' Courts Act 1980 prescribes the maximum terms that may be fixed.

23.13.5 Recovery of fines from income support

Regulations drawn up under s 24 of the Criminal Justice Act 1991 allow for the deduction of fines imposed by the magistrates' court (but not by the Crown Court) from an offender's income support.

23.13.6 Combining a fine with another penalty

As a result of the changes brought about by the Criminal Justice Act 1991, it is possible for the courts to combine a financial penalty with any of the community sentences. In addition, the courts continue to be able to combine a fine or compensation order with a custodial sentence, whether immediate or suspended, provided that the custodial sentence is justified by the seriousness of the offence, and proper regard is had to the offender's means of fixing the fine. As far as a suspended sentence is concerned, the court is positively required to consider, when imposing the suspended sentence, whether the circumstances of the case are such as to warrant in addition the imposition of a fine or the making of a compensation order (PCC(S)A 2000, s 118(5)). The combination of a suspended sentence with a financial penalty may therefore be regarded as a 'favoured mix' — the aim apparently being to avoid any perception that the offender has been let off lightly.

23.14 CONDITIONAL AND ABSOLUTE DISCHARGES

When a court dealing with an offender for an offence considers that it is inexpedient to inflict punishment it may make an order discharging him either absolutely or on condition that, during a period specified in the order, he commits no offence. The specified period runs from the date of the order, and must not exceed three years. The law relating to discharges is contained in ss 12 to 15 of the PCC(S)A 2000.

A court may discharge an offender whatever his age and whatever offence he has been convicted of (provided, of course, the sentence is not fixed by law). A discharge for an offence may be combined with an ancillary order, but not with any other sentence, although if an offender is dealt with for more than one offence he may be discharged for one and otherwise dealt with for the remainder. It is, in fact, quite common for an offender to be given a substantial sentence for the most serious offence of which he has been convicted, and to be conditionally discharged for other less serious ones.

An absolute discharge has no adverse effects at all on the offender — it is a complete 'let-off'. Thus, it is appropriate in those cases where the offender is technically guilty of an offence, but no blame whatsoever attaches to him. If an offender is conditionally discharged, and does not commit an offence during the period of the discharge, he is never sentenced for the offence for which he was discharged (the 'original offence'). Where an offence is committed while subject to a conditional discharge, the offender may be sentenced for the original offence as well as for the subsequent offence, in which case the discharge ceases to have effect, or the courts may choose not to sentence him for the original offence, in which case he will still be subject to the discharge. When making a conditional discharge, the court should explain its effect to the offender.

A conditional discharge has something in common with a suspended sentence in that, if the offender does not commit an offence during the period of the discharge, no actual penalty is inflicted on him, just as an offender who avoids committing an imprisonable offence during the operational period of a suspended sentence never serves the term of imprisonment. However, the two ways of dealing with offenders are markedly different in other respects. In particular, a court dealing with an offender for breach of a suspended sentence cannot itself choose how to sentence him for the offence for which he was given the sentence — essentially, the court either does or does not activate the sentence of imprisonment which the court on the previous occasion saw fit to suspend. On the other hand, conviction for an offence committed during a conditional discharge entitles the appropriate court to sentence the offender for the original offence as if he had just been convicted of it, and so the court has a full range of sentencing options at its disposal. Also, breach of a suspended sentence normally results in the term of imprisonment being brought into effect, whereas it is commonplace for the courts to overlook a breach of conditional discharge in the sense that the offender is merely sentenced for the subsequent offence with the conditional discharge being allowed to continue in force.

23.15 BINDING OVER

Two other methods of dealing with offenders — namely binding over to keep the peace and binding over to come up for judgment — may conveniently be described at this point.

First, if there is material before a court leading it to fear that, unless steps are taken to prevent it, there might be a breach of the peace, it may order a person to be bound over to keep the peace and be of good behaviour. The person concerned must then enter into an undertaking (or recognisance) that he will keep the peace for a certain period upon pain of forfeiting a certain sum of money if he fails to do so. Both the period and the sum are fixed by the court when it orders the bind-over. If the person refuses to enter into the undertaking, he can be sent to prison for contempt of court. If he enters into the undertaking and breaks it, e.g., by committing an offence such as common assault during the relevant period, the court which bound him over can order him to forfeit part or all of the sum specified. Binding over is essentially a measure of preventive justice, designed to avoid future breaches of the peace. It is not appropriate where an offender has been convicted of an offence such as theft, repetition of which is most unlikely to involve violence or public disturbance. It is appropriate — and common — in cases of petty violence, especially in disputes between neighbours where Smith alleges that he was assaulted by Jones and Jones alleges that he was assaulted by Smith, and the magistrates metaphorically knock their heads together by ordering that they both be bound over to keep the peace for a year. A bind-over may be ordered in addition to another penalty for an offence, or instead of any other penalty, or even where the person concerned has not been convicted of an offence. Thus, in the example of Smith and Jones, the magistrates could acquit either or both of them and still order them both to be bound over. Another common occurrence is for an accused charged with a minor public order offence (e.g. threatening behaviour likely to cause alarm, harassment or distress) to plead not guilty but agree to be bound over on the prosecution undertaking to offer no evidence against him. Again, the bind-over will specify a sum of money to be forfeited in the event of breach. Even where a person appears before a court solely in the capacity of a witness (e.g. a hunt saboteur allegedly assaulted by a member of the hunt), a bind-over is possible. The power of magistrates to bind a person over to keep the peace is contained in the Magistrates' Courts Act 1980, s 115 and the Justices of the Peace Act 1361. The power of the Crown Court to do so is confirmed by the Justices of the Peace Act 1968, s 1(7).

Secondly, provided he consents, the Crown Court (but not a magistrates' court) has power at common law to bind an offender over to come up for judgment — i.e., he is released without being sentenced but enters into an undertaking that he will appear before the court to be sentenced on a certain day or on a day to be notified to him, upon pain of forfeiting a specified sum of money if he fails to do so. If the court merely wishes to adjourn before sentencing an offender, it is much more convenient to remand him on bail rather than binding him over. Similarly, if the court wants to defer sentence there is power to do so under s 1 of the PCC(S)A 2000 (see Paragraph 20.7). The real value of a bind-over to come up for judgment lies in the conditions which may be attached to it, and often the hope is that, if the offender abides by these conditions there will be no need to sentence him at all.

In *Hashman v UK* [2000] Crim LR 185, the European Court of Human Rights dealt with a complaint by two applicants who disturbed a fox hunt by blowing a horn and shouting at the hounds. They were bound over to keep the peace and be of good behaviour. On appeal to the Crown Court, it was decided that there had been no breach of the peace, but they were nevertheless bound over to be of good behaviour for a year. The European Court found that there had been a violation of Article 10 of the ECHR, which guarantees freedom of expression. The non-violent protest conducted by the applicants was an exercise of their right to freedom of expression. It would be legitimate to restrict this right if Article 10(2) applied, but that paragraph requires any interference with freedom of expression to be 'prescribed by law'. The law that is relied upon must be 'certain' in the sense that it must be 'formulated with sufficient precision to enable the citizen to regulate his conduct'. The phrase 'to be of good behaviour' (which English law defines as 'behaviour which is wrong rather than right in the judgment of the majority of contemporary fellow citizens') was too imprecise, and did not give the applicants sufficiently clear guidance on how they should behave in future. It appears, therefore, that the bindover 'to be of good behaviour' is contary to the Convention, unless the good behaviour in question is defined with some particularity. The decision does not, however, affect the power to bind over to keep the peace.

23.16   ENDORSEMENT AND DISQUALIFICATION FROM DRIVING

Most road traffic offences are endorsable, i.e., in the absence of special reasons for not doing so, the court must order that particulars of a conviction for the offence be endorsed on the offender's driving licence. Unless the offender is disqualified from driving on the occasion when endorsement is ordered, the number of penalty points appropriate to the offence are also endorsed on the licence. Drink/driving offences and causing death by dangerous driving carry obligatory disqualification from driving for a period of at least a year (two years in the latter case) unless there are special reasons for not disqualifying (or for disqualifying for less than a year). Other endorsable offences carry disqualification at the discretion of the court. If the offender has been convicted of an endorsable offence, and the penalty points for that offence added to any other points endorsed on the licence total 12 or more, then — provided the offences concerned were all committed within a three year period — he must be disqualified for at least six months unless, having regard to all the circumstances, the court thinks fit not to disqualify him (or to disqualify him for less than six months).

The law on endorsement and disqualification is detailed and in parts complex, so within the scope of this book it is only possible to summarise the relevant provisions. Of greatest importance are ss 34 and 35 of the Road Traffic Offenders Act 1988 and Sch 2 to that Act.

23.16.1   Endorsement of an offender's driving licence

Offences carrying endorsement are listed in Sch 2 to the Road Traffic Offenders Act 1988. There are over 30 of them, but by no means all offences connected with motor vehicles are endorsable. For example, failing to stop one's vehicle when required by a police constable to do so, not having an MOT test certificate and most offences connected with the condition of one's vehicle are non-endorsable. Each endorsable offence carries a certain number of penalty points, the number being prescribed by Sch 2 to the Road Traffic Offenders Act 1988. Below is a table setting out the commonest endorsable offences and their penalty points:

Offence	Statute creating the offence	Penalty points
Driving when unfit through drink or drugs	RTA 1988, s 4(1)	3–11
Driving with excess alcohol in the breath, blood or urine	RTA 1988, s 5(1)(a)	3–11
Being in charge of motor vehicle when unfit or with excess alcohol	RTA 1988, s 4(2) and 5(1)(b)	10
Causing death by dangerous driving	RTA 1988, s 1	3–11
Dangerous driving	RTA 1988, s 2	3–11
Careless driving	RTA 1988, s 3	3–9
Failing to stop after accident or give particulars or report an accident	RTA 1988, s 170	5–10
Speeding	Road Traffic Regulation Act 1984, s 89	3–6
Disobeying traffic lights	RTA 1988, s 36	3
Driving while disqualified	RTA 1988, s 103(1)(b)	6
Using uninsured motor vehicle	RTA 1988, s 143	6–8

Unless there are special reasons for not doing so, a court dealing with an offender for an endorsable offence *must* order that particulars of the conviction (i.e., the date of the conviction, the convicting court, the offence committed and the penalty imposed) be endorsed on the offender's licence (Road Traffic Offenders Act 1988, s 44). Since any special reasons for not endorsing must be connected with the circumstances of the offence not the offender, and since such reasons are very narrowly defined, a conviction for an endorsable offence almost always results in endorsement. If the offender is disqualified on the occasion of an endorsement, particulars of the disqualification are also endorsed but there are no penalty points — the disqualification is considered a sufficient penalty without putting the offender on the path to a further disqualification under the 'totting-up' provisions (see Paragraph 23.16.4). If the offender is not disqualified, the appropriate number of penalty points are endorsed. Where Sch 2 to the Road Traffic Offenders Act 1988 prescribes a range of penalty points (e.g. for careless driving and using a motor vehicle without insurance), the court fixes the number to be endorsed within the prescribed range. Where an offender is convicted of two or more endorsable offences committed on the same occasion, points are usually endorsed only in respect of the offence carrying the highest number (or, if they all carry the same number, in respect of one of the offences). Thus, an offender who on one occasion commits offences of taking a motor vehicle (8 points), dangerous driving (3–11 points) and using a motor vehicle without insurance (6–8 points) will normally acquire only 11 penalty points, not 17–27 points. However, the court may, under s 28(5) of the Road

Traffic Offenders Act 1988, order endorsement with penalty points for more than one offence committed on the same occasion.

> An offender charged with an endorsable offence must deliver or post his licence to the court prior to the hearing, or have it with him at the hearing (Road Traffic Offenders Act 1988, s 27). If he is convicted, the licence is shown to the court, and any endorsements on it are taken into account when passing sentence. Failure to produce one's licence is a summary offence, but it is a defence to establish that one has applied for a new licence and not received it. After the elapse of a prescribed period a person who has had his licence endorsed can apply for the issue of a new licence free of the endorsement (Road Traffic Offenders Act 1988, s 45(5)). The period is 11 years if the endorsement was for a drink/driving offence involving obligatory disqualification (see the next Paragraph), and four years in other cases. The period runs from the date of commission of the offence if the offender was not disqualified, and from the date of the conviction if he was. Where a court orders endorsement in the case of an offender who does not have a licence, the effect is that any licence he may obtain within the four or 11 year period must be appropriately endorsed (s 45(2)).

23.16.2 Obligatory disqualification

The following offences carry obligatory disqualification:

(a) causing death by dangerous driving, contrary to RTA 1988, s 1;

(b) dangerous driving, contrary to RTA 1988, s 2;

(c) driving or attempting to drive when unfit through drink or drugs, contrary to RTA 1988, s 4(1);

(d) driving or attempting to drive with excess alcohol in breath, blood or urine, contrary to RTA 1988, s 5(1)(a); and

(e) failing to provide a specimen required to ascertain one's ability to drive or the proportion of alcohol in one's system at the time of driving or attempting to drive, contrary to RTA 1988, s 7(6).

A court dealing with an offender for an offence carrying obligatory disqualification *must* disqualify him for at least 12 months (two years in the case of causing death by dangerous driving) unless there are special reasons (Road Traffic Offenders Act 1988, s 36). If an offender is convicted of a drink/driving offence carrying obligatory disqualification and it was committed within 10 years of a previous conviction for such an offence, the minimum period of disqualification is increased to three years. Where a court has power to disqualify, there is no statutory limit on the period for which it may order disqualification, and therefore it is always open to the court to disqualify for more than the obligatory minimum. It might well do so, for example, in a case where the proportion of alcohol in a drunken driver's breath was more than twice the legal maximum.

Any special reasons put forward for not disqualifying (or for disqualifying for less than the normal minimum) must relate to the circumstances of the offence itself, not the circumstances of the offender, and the courts are usually very reluctant to find that special reasons have been established. Thus, in *Jackson* [1970] 1 QB 647, the Court of Appeal held that a medical condition of which the offender was unaware and which caused him to retain alcohol for an unusually long time, was not a sufficient reason for shorter or non-disqualification. Exceptional hardship which the offender will suffer through disqualification (e.g., losing his employment) is incapable of being a special reason (contrast the position where a conviction for an offence carrying discretionary disqualification makes the offender liable to a 'totting-up' disqualification). Reasons which might justify non-disqualification are that the offender's non-alcoholic drink was 'laced' without his knowledge thus putting his alcohol level just above the legal limit, or that he killed a person by reckless driving when trying to reach hospital as quickly as possible with a third person who required urgent treatment.

Chatters and Burke [1986] 1 WLR 1321 lists the following factors which the court ought to consider in deciding whether there are special reasons:

(a)   how far the vehicle was driven,
(b)   in what manner it was driven,
(c)   what was the state of the vehicle,
(d)   whether it was the driver's intention to drive any further,
(e)   the prevailing conditions with regard to the road and traffic on it,
(f)   whether there was any possibility of danger by contact with other road users,
(g)   what was the reason for the vehicle being driven at all.

Offences involving obligatory disqualification carry only three penalty points, whereas there are other less serious offences carrying anything up to 10 points (see the table in Paragraph 23.16.1). This apparent anomaly is explained by the fact that when an offender is disqualified no points are endorsed on the licence, whatever the nature of the offence of which he has been convicted. If an offender is not disqualified for an offence involving obligatory disqualification, it means that there must have been something quite exceptional about the circumstances rendering the offence much less serious than an offence of that type is normally considered to be. Therefore, it is understandable that the penalty points are kept low.

23.16.3   Discretionary disqualification

A court dealing with an offender for an offence carrying discretionary disqualification may, but need not, disqualify him: Road Traffic Offenders Act 1988, s 34(2). There is no limit on the period of disqualification which may be imposed, but the trend is against overlong disqualifications because they merely invite further offending in the shape of driving while disqualified. Indeed, it is unusual for an offender to be disqualified at all for an offence merely carrying discretionary disqualification unless the offence makes him liable to a 'totting-up' disqualification (see Paragraph 23.16.4). Offences such as careless driving, speeding, going through a red traffic light, failing to stop after an accident and even not having insurance are mostly dealt with by means of a fine and endorsement, without disqualification. A bad case of careless driving would probably attract disqualification. Speeds of 100 mph plus on the motorway also tend to result in disqualification, although the period may be as short as a fortnight.

A disqualification commences immediately upon its being ordered. It follows that a court has no power to make a disqualification consecutive to another disqualification which it imposes on the same occasion, or which another court has imposed on a previous occasion. However, this is not a significant limitation on judicial power because, as already stated, there are no statutory restrictions on the length of a disqualification, so a court which wants to further disqualify an offender already subject to disqualification simply makes its disqualification long enough to continue running after the existing disqualification will have expired.

Section 42 of the Road Traffic Offenders Act 1988 allows an offender who has been disqualified by a court for more than two years to apply to the court which disqualified him for early removal of the disqualification — the period the offender must wait before being able to apply varies depending upon the length of the disqualification.

23.16.4 Disqualification under the penalty points procedure

Section 35 of the Road Traffic Offenders Act 1988 deals with what are colloquially known as 'totting-up' disqualifications. The procedure came into force in 1982 by the Transport Act 1981. It replaced the former 'totting-up' system, which depended simply on the number and dates of the endorsements on an offender's licence, with a system which depends on the number of penalty points the offender has acquired.

Essentially, the section provides that where an offender is being dealt with for an endorsable offence (the 'present offence'), and the penalty points to be taken into consideration under the section (the 'relevant points') total 12 or more, then the offender *must* be disqualified for at least six months unless there are special grounds for not doing so. The relevant points are those which will be endorsed for the present offence if the offender is not disqualified, and those already endorsed on the licence in respect of offences committed in the three years preceding commission of the present offence. This is subject to the major qualification that, if the offender has been disqualified since the date on which points were ordered to be endorsed, those points are left out of the reckoning — in other words, a disqualification 'wipes the slate clean' as far as liability to a penalty points disqualification is concerned.

An offender who has acquired 12 or more relevant points need not be disqualified, or may be disqualified for less than the full six months, if the court is satisfied that 'there are grounds for mitigating the normal consequences of the conviction. Whereas special reasons for not disqualifying for an offence involving obligatory disqualification must be connected with the offence itself (see Paragraph 23.16.2), there is no such restriction on the grounds which are capable of justifying non-disqualification of a 'totter' — subject to s 35(4) (see below), the court may have regard to 'all the circumstances', including those personal to the offender. Thus, it is much easier to avoid a six-month 'totting-up' disqualification than it is to avoid the obligatory 12 months for an offence such as driving with excess alcohol in the blood. Most 'totters' rely on the hardship which disqualification would cause them. However, s 35(4)(b) provides that the court may only take into account 'exceptional hardship'. Parliament was apparently concerned that offenders were avoiding disqualification by advancing the flimsiest suggestion of hardship, but there is no attempt in the Act to define 'exceptional hardship'. Loss of one's job, either because it involves driving or because it is virtually impossible to reach the place of work by public transport, is likely to constitute exceptional hardship (see *Owen v Jones* (1989) 9 Cr App R (S) 34). Less extreme consequences of disqualification (e.g., inconvenience in getting to work by public transport) might be 'hardship' but fall short of being 'exceptional hardship', and so would not be grounds for non-disqualification. Section 35(4) also provides (in subsection (a)) that the triviality of the present offence is not a ground for non-disqualification, while the House of Lords has indicated that the triviality of the previous offences for which penalty points were endorsed is of, at most, marginal significance (see *Woodage v Lambie* [1971] 1 WLR 754). The reasoning behind s 35(4)(a) and *Woodage v Lambie* is that the 'totting-up' provisions are intended to deter the offender who frequently commits minor road-traffic offences, and so it would defeat the object of the legislation if an offender could save his licence by saying that he was only just over the speed limit or that the lights had turned to red the moment before he went through them. Lastly, s 35(4)(c) applies to a 'totter' who has, in the three years preceding his present court appearance, been excused a 'totting-up' disqualification because there were special grounds. He is not allowed, on the present occasion, to rely on any circumstances which the court took into account on the previous occasion. Thus, for example, somebody who earns his living by driving cannot repeatedly avoid disqualification by arguing that loss of his licence would involve loss of his job.

Where a court decides that s 35 obliges it to disqualify for, say, six months that is, of course, a minimum period, and the actual disqualification will be for whatever period the court considers appropriate having regard to the gravity of the offence, the offender's previous record and any other relevant circumstances. If an offender is convicted on one occasion of two or more endorsable offences which each render him liable to a s 35 disqualification, the length of the disqualification should reflect the fact that there were several offences. Only one disqualification is imposed, but for purposes of any appeal against sentence that disqualification is deemed to have been ordered in respect of each of the offences.

The following additional points about 'totting-up' disqualifications should be noted:

(a) Courts do not always dispose of a person's alleged offences in chronological order, so it occasionally happens that the present offence was committed before an offence of which the offender has already been convicted, penalty points for which have been endorsed on the licence. In such a case, the relevant points are those for the present offence, those for the most recent endorsed offence, and those for any other endorsed offence committed within the three years preceding commission of the most recent endorsed offence (not the three years preceding commission of the present offence).

(b) If, within the three years preceding the commission of the present offence (or most recent endorsed offence if that was committed after the present offence), the offender has been disqualified once, then the normal minimum period for a 'totting-up' disqualification is increased from six months to one year. If he has been disqualified more than once, then it is increased to two years.

(c) It is for the offender to establish, on a balance of probabilities, that there are grounds for mitigating the normal consequences of acquiring 12 penalty points. This will normally involve him going into the witness box to give evidence, contrary to the general practice which is that, at the sentencing stage of proceedings, the offender stays silent in the dock while his advocate mitigates on his behalf. Similarly, an offender convicted of an offence involving obligatory disqualification who wishes to argue special reasons for not disqualifying must testify about the special reasons.

23.16.5 Disqualification, endorsement and other penalties

A disqualification is valid even if no other penalty is imposed for the offence (*Bignell* (1968) 52 Cr App R 10), but orders for endorsement and disqualification are almost invariably combined with some other sentence or order in lieu of sentence. Minor endorsable offences are normally dealt with by a fine or conditional discharge plus endorsement. Disqualification is unlikely except where the 'totting-up' provisions apply. More serious endorsable offences (e.g. taking a motor vehicle without consent, causing death by dangerous driving, possibly drink/driving offences) could well involve a custodial sentence plus endorsement and disqualification.

23.16.6 Disqualification under s 147 of the Powers of Criminal Courts (Sentencing) Act 2000

Where an offender is convicted on indictment of an offence carrying two years or more imprisonment, or is committed for sentence under s 38 of the Magistrates' Courts Act 1980 to be sentenced for such an offence, the Crown Court may disqualify him for such period as it thinks fit if satisfied that a motor vehicle was used in committing the offence: Powers of Criminal Courts Act, s 44. This applies even if the offence is not endorsable, and even if the offender disqualified did not himself use the vehicle (i.e. it was used by an accomplice).

23.17 FORFEITURE ORDERS

A court (Crown Court or magistrates' court) dealing with an offender for an offence of any description may order the forfeiture of any property which was in his possession or under his control at the time of his apprehension (or, if he was proceeded against by way of summons without being arrested, in his possession or control at the time of the issue of the summons), provided the court is satisfied that the property has been used to commit or facilitate the commission of an offence or was intended by him to be used for that purpose (PCC(S)A 2000, s 143).

Forfeiture orders are used as ancillaries to a primary sentence such as imprisonment, fine or community service. But, unlike other ancillary orders, they are regarded by the courts as essentially punitive — not compensatory — in purpose. Thus, the Court of Appeal held in *Lidster* [1976] Crim LR 80 that it was wrong in principle to deal with one offence by a combination of conditional discharge plus forfeiture order, since the former order implies that the court considers it 'inexpedient to inflict punishment' and so is inconsistent with the simultaneous imposition of a punitive ancillary order. The actual effect of the decision in *Lidster* has been reversed by statute. However, the case still illustrates the general attitude of the courts to such orders. An order may be made irrespective of the offence of which the offender has been convicted. Property in his possession at the time of the issue of a summons may be forfeited.

Provided the offender *intended* the relevant property to be used to commit/facilitate the commission of an offence, a forfeiture order may be made even though neither he — nor, indeed, anybody else — actually did use the property for that purpose. 'Facilitating the commission of an offence' includes taking steps after its commission to avoid arrest or detection, or to dispose of any property to which it related. In decided cases, forfeiture orders have been made to deprive a handler of the car he had used to transport stolen goods at the request of the thieves; to deprive burglars of a motor-caravan in which they had driven to the scene of the crime and had intended to make their 'getaway' afterwards, and to deprive a petrol thief of a specially adapted pump by which he had siphoned off petrol from the tanks of numerous cars. The court should, however, have regard to the value of the property that it is considering forfeiting and to the likely financial effect on the offender of the making of the order, taken in conjunction with any other penalty (financial or otherwise) which may be imposed (see s 143(5) of the PCC(S)A 2000). In other words, the forfeiture order must be treated as part of the global penalty for the offence, and must not be allowed to make that penalty out of proportion to the gravity of what the offender did (see *Scully* (1985) 7 Cr App R (S) 119).

The effect of a s 143 order is to deprive the offender of his rights, if any, in the property concerned. The property is taken into the possession of the police. If a person other than the offender claims to be entitled to the property, he has six months in which to apply to a magistrates' court for an order that it be returned to him. To succeed, he must not only satisfy the magistrates of his right to the property, but must also show that he either did not consent to the offender having the property or did not know the purpose for which it was to be used.

In addition to the general power of the PCC(S)A 2000, s 143, certain statutes contain their own specific forfeiture provisions, e.g., the Misuse of Drugs Act 1971, and the Prevention of Crime Act 1953 (in relation to offensive weapons). See also Paragraph 23.20, which deals with confiscation orders.

23.18 COMPENSATION ORDERS

The power to order an offender to pay compensation to the victim of his offence was introduced by the Criminal Justice Act 1972, and is now contained in the PCC(S)A 2000, s 130. The propositions below summarise the position the law has now reached as a result of the amendments to the original legislation and judical interpretation:

(i)   A court dealing with an offender for an offence (whether summary or indictable, imprisonable or non-imprisonable) may make an order requiring him to pay compensation for any 'personal injury, loss or damage resulting from that offence' or any other offence taken into consideration (s 130(1)(a)). Where the offence results in a death (other than death in a road traffic accident), the court may further order that the offender make payments for funeral expenses and/or bereavement (s 130(1)(b)). Bereavement payments may be ordered only in favour of a person who could claim damages for bereavement under s 1A of the Fatal Accidents Act 1976 (i.e. a surviving spouse or the parents of a deceased child under 18). Similarly, the sum awarded must not exceed that which would be recoverable under the 1976 Act (s 130(9) and (10)).

(ii)   A compensation order may be made instead of or in addition to dealing with the offender in any other way for the offence (s 130(1)). Thus, an order may be combined with non-punitive sentences, such as a community rehabilitation order or conditional discharge. It may even be employed as a sentence in its own right — i.e. as the only order made by a court when dealing with an offender.

(iii)   If a court, having power to make a compensation order, chooses not to do so, it must give its reasons (s 130(3)). The requirement for reasons for not making an order reflects the Government's apparent anxiety, expressed in numerous speeches by Home Office ministers, that the courts should use their powers to order compensation to the full.

(iv)   Where, as a result of an offence under the Theft Act 1968, the owner of property is temporarily deprived thereof but it is subsequently restored to him, any damage to the property occurring while it was out of his possession is conclusively presumed to have resulted from the offence, regardless of how it actually occurred (s 130(5)). The offender is therefore liable to pay compensation even if he was not directly to blame for the damage.

(v)   As regards loss arising from road traffic accidents, the general policy is that the victim should recover from the offender's insurers rather than direct from the offender himself. Thus, s 130(6) provides that compensation may not be ordered in respect of injury, loss or damage 'due to an accident arising out of the presence of a motor vehicle on a road', unless *either* the loss is attributed to the offender by virtue of s 130(5) (damage caused while stolen property was out of the owner's possession conclusively presumed to have been caused by the thief), *or* the offender was uninsured and the victim cannot claim under the Motor Insurers' Bureau Scheme.

(vi)   In deciding the amount of compensation that is appropriate, the court shall have regard to any evidence and to any 'representations' made by or on behalf of the accused or the prosecution (s 130(4)).

(vii)   The imposition of a compensation order is given statutory priority over a fine (s 130(12)). In effect, this means that a fine should be reduced or, if necessary, dispensed with altogether to enable compensation to be paid.

(viii) Where a juvenile is convicted of an offence and the court orders compensation, it should normally order the juvenile's parent or guardian to pay the compensation order (s 137).

In the magistrates' court, the maximum compensation order which can be imposed in respect of any offence is £5,000 (s 131). There is no statutory limit on the compensation which the Crown Court can order.

Numerous Court of Appeal decisions have outlined the correct judicial approach to the making of compensation orders. They are not intended as punitive orders *per se,* nor even as a means of depriving the offender of the proceeds of his crime. They are, rather, meant to provide the victim with a 'convenient and rapid means of avoiding the expense of resorting to civil litigation when the criminal clearly has means which would enable the compensation to be paid' (see *Inwood* (1975) 60 Cr App R 70). In other words, the victim obtains quickly and without expense through the criminal courts a remedy which he could otherwise have obtained through civil proceedings. However, it is undesirable that the criminal courts should become embroiled in complicated questions of civil law. Therefore, compensation orders are appropriate only where there is no real doubt about the offender's liability to compensate (see *Vivian* [1979] 1 WLR 291). Thus, in *Kneeshaw* [1975] QB 57 the Court of Appeal quashed an order that K pay £114 compensation in respect of four rings stolen in the course of a burglary since, although K pleaded guilty on the basis that he stole the bulk of the items listed in the count, he had made it clear through counsel in mitigation that he did not accept that he stole the rings. In the absence of an acceptance by the defence that compensation was payable for the rings, or overwhelming evidence that K had taken them, the Crown Court should have left the victim to seek his remedy in the county court. In *Amey* [1983] 1 WLR 346, similar principles were applied where the dispute related not to whether the offender had stolen an article for which compensation was claimed, but to its value. A pleaded guilty to theft of a vintage three-wheeler Morgan sports car, which the owner said was worth £3,000. Apart from the owner's claim, the only evidence of value came from A himself, who said that he had sold the car to a dealer for £600. The Crown Court judge plucked out of the air a compromise figure of £1,000, but the Court of Appeal reduced it to the £600 which had been agreed by the defence.

Where the offender is convicted on a specimen count or counts, it is unlawful to base the value of the compensation order on losses alleged to result from offences which were neither charged nor taken into consideration (*Crutchley* (1994) 15 Cr App R (S) 627).

Section 130(4), which was originally inserted into the Powers of Criminal Courts Act 1973 by the CJA 1982, on the face of it was intended to reduce the rigour of decisions such as those quoted above by allowing the courts to act not only on 'evidence' as to the liability to compensate but also on the 'representations' of the parties. However, it appears to have made little difference in practice. Indeed, in *Swann* [1984] Crim LR 300, the Court of Appeal stated that the added subsection only 'slightly reduced' the obligation on the sentencer to satisfy himself that — in the absence of an admission from the defence — there was clear evidence of the offender's liability to pay the sum claimed. The above approach has especially inhibited the willingness of the courts to order compensation for personal injury, since assessing the 'value' of a cut eye or a broken jaw or whatever other injury was suffered by the victim, is notoriously difficult. The sentencer may, however, properly obtain guidance on appropriate compensation from the amounts paid by the Criminal Injuries Compensation Board in comparable cases (see dicta in *Broughton* (1986) 8 Cr App R (S) 380).

The Magistrates' Association *Sentencing Guidelines* (2000) set out guidance, for example:

Type of injury		*Guideline*
Graze	Some pain for a few days and depending on size	up to £75
Bruise	Depending on size	up to £100
Black eye		£125
Cut (no permanent scarring)	Depending on size and whether stitched	£100–500
Sprain	Depending on loss of mobility	£100–1,000
Loss of tooth	Depending on position of tooth and age of victim	£500–1,500

These figures are not to be regarded as a fixed tariff, but only as a guide. They reflect the element which relates to general damages (pain, suffering, loss of facility) and should be added to special damages for financial loss sustained (e.g., loss of earnings, dental expenses etc.).

Even where the offender's liability to make compensation is admitted or incontrovertibly established, the court should only make such order as is reasonably within his ability to pay. An order which is beyond his means is likely to be quashed or reduced on appeal. Because of the tendency of offenders to make extravagant claims as to their ability to compensate in the hope of thereby avoiding or reducing a custodial sentence, counsel and solicitors for the defence are under a duty to investigate any proposals for compensation, and should put them before the court only if satisfied that the information provided by the offender as to his means is correct (see *Huish* (1985) 7 Cr App R (S) 272). Although *Huish* has been confirmed by several subsequent cases (e.g. *Roberts* [1987] Crim LR 712), the concept of defence lawyers making themselves responsible for the accuracy of certain matters presented to the sentencer in mitigation contradicts the general principle that counsel acts on his instructions whether he personally thinks them to be true or not. In any event, if an offender misleads the court into believing he can pay compensation, his subsequent appeal against the compensation order will not succeed: *Dando* [1996] 1 Cr App R (S) 155. He must pay the compensation, or serve the appropriate term in default of payment.

Of course, compensation is not usually ordered to be paid forthwith but may be made payable by instalments. The factors to be considered in relation to length of payment are similar to those in the case of a fine. An order for compensation should normally be payable within 12 months, but this can be exceeded up to a three year limit where the circumstances justify it (see *Olliver* (1989) 11 Cr App R (S) 10 and Paragraph 23.13.3 for the analogous position relating to a fine). Any other financial orders the court may make will obviously affect the ability to make compensation. However, it is specifically provided by s 130(12) that, if a sentencer is considering both compensation and a fine, but the offender would not have the means to pay both, priority should be given to the compensation.

As to the procedure for obtaining a compensation order, it is not necessary for the victim to attend court and make an application in person. Usually, he will indicate on his statement to the police the extent of his loss and his desire for compensation. In addition, the CPS file may include a form specifying the amount claimed and the name and address of the claimant, which form can be handed in to the court. Receipts, etc. confirming the claim are also of value. Armed with this material, the prosecutor will ask for compensation in the appropriate sum at the end of his summary of the facts (assuming it is a guilty plea). If the plea is not guilty, evidence relevant to compensation will no doubt emerge during the course of the trial. As already explained, an order will be made only if the compensation is admitted or the material before the court makes it abundantly clear that it should be paid. In most cases where the plea is guilty, the defence will also admit the liability to compensate, and the argument will centre on the offender's ability to pay. If the criminal court refuses to make a compensation order (or makes an order for less than the full amount of the loss), the victim's civil rights are not, of course, affected, and he may commence proceedings in the county court or High Court for the amount by which his true loss exceeds the amount of the compensation order.

23.19 RESTITUTION ORDERS

Section 148 of the PCC(S)A 2000 provides that, where goods have been stolen and an offender is convicted of an offence with reference to the theft (or has such an offence taken into consideration), the court may order anyone having possession or control of the goods to restore them to any person entitled to recover them from him. 'Stolen goods' include goods obtained by deception or through blackmail, and 'an offence with reference to theft' includes handling stolen goods and, possibly, conspiracy to steal or assisting a thief. Persons other than the offender may be ordered to restore goods under s 148, but the court would only make an order against a third party in the clearest of cases. The obvious application of s 148 is where a convicted thief or handler was caught in possession of the stolen goods. If there is no doubt as to the true owner, the court can, at the conclusion of the trial, order that the goods be restored to him.

There is also power under s 148 to order that goods in the offender's possession which directly or indirectly represent the stolen goods be transferred to the person entitled to the stolen goods (e.g. if O steals A's television set and exchanges it for a video recorder, O could be ordered to transfer the video recorder to A). Lastly, the court may order that, out of money taken from the offender's possession on his arrest, the person entitled to the stolen goods shall be paid a sum not exceeding their value. In view of the wide powers the courts now have to order compensation under the PCC(S)A 2000, s 130, orders for payment of money under s 148 seem to be of limited value.

23.20 CONFISCATION ORDERS

Part VI of the Criminal Justice Act 1988 (ss 71–102) introduced an ancillary order, known as a 'confiscation order'. It replaced criminal bankruptcy orders, which were formerly a means by which major criminals could be deprived of the proceeds of their crimes. The new legislation is extremely detailed and complex, and only a bare outline of the provisions will be attempted.

The usual confiscation procedure is laid down in s 71 of the CJA 1988. It applies to the Crown Court and (in respect of certain listed summary offences) to the magistrates' court. It can be invoked by the prosecution or by the court of its own motion. The court must determine whether the offender has benefited from the offence(s) of which he has been convicted or which he has asked the court to take into consideration. If he has benefited, the court must determine the amount of the benefit and order the offender to pay it. The amount of the benefit is equal to the value of any property or pecuniary advantage obtained. The amount of the confiscation order is whichever is the *less* of the benefit received by the offender and the amount which may be realised by selling his assets (s 71(6)). The standard of proof applicable is the civil one.

There is also a much more complex procedure which is contained in s 72AA of the CJA 1988. It allows the court to confiscate the proceeds of offences with which the defendant has not been charged (see *Blackstone's Criminal Practice*, E21.9 for the statutory provisions and commentary). Part VI of the CJA does not extend to drug-trafficking crimes because a separate analogous scheme is already in operation under the Drug Trafficking Act 1994 (for an outline of these provisions, see *Blackstone's Criminal Practice*, E21.2).

23.21   RECOMMENDATIONS FOR DEPORTATION

Where a non-British citizen, who has attained the age of 17, is convicted of an imprisonable offence, the court dealing with him for the offence may recommend that he be deported.

Recommendations for deportation are dealt with in s 3 of the Immigration Act 1971, as amended by the British Nationality Act 1981. Such recommendations may be made by both the Crown Court and magistrates' courts. The recommendation is made to the Home Secretary, who, in deciding whether to act upon it, may take into account matters which could not properly be considered by the court (e.g., the possibility of the offender being persecuted if returned to his own country). A recommendation for deportation may be made in addition to any other penalty (custodial or otherwise) imposed for the offence. Even if no custodial sentence is passed the offender may be detained pending the Home Secretary's decision. The court may not recommend deportation unless the offender has been given notice in writing explaining that British citizens are not liable to deportation, and describing the persons who fall within that category. The notice must be given at least seven days before the recommendation is made.

A full enquiry into the circumstances of the case should be made before deportation is recommended, and reasons for a recommendation should be given. If considering making a recommendation, it is advisable for a judge to ask counsel for the offender to address him on the matter. The court must consider whether the offender's continued presence in the United Kingdom would be to the country's detriment (*Caird* (1970) 54 Cr App R 499), but the fact that he has a criminal record is not in itself a sufficient reason for deporting him. The question is whether, in the light of the present offence and his previous record, he is likely to re-offend. If he is, that would be a good ground for recommending his deportation. If, on the other hand, he is likely to be completely rehabilitated after serving whatever sentence is imposed, he should be allowed to stay in the country. The principles in *Caird* have been restated in *Secretary of State for the Home Department ex p Santillo* [1981] QB 778 and *Nazari* (1980) 71 Cr App R 87. Where the offender is an EC national the court should also bear in mind the guidance given by the European Court of Justice in *Bouchereau* (reported at (1978) 66 Cr App R 202), although that guidance is very vaguely worded and appears to add little to what is contained in the cases already mentioned (see *Compassi* (1987) 9 Cr App R (S) 270).

23.22   HOSPITAL ORDERS

Upon receiving appropriate medical evidence, a court dealing with an offender for an imprisonable offence may order that he be admitted to and detained in a hospital where he will receive treatment for a mental disorder. Such an order is known as a 'hospital order'. When the Crown Court makes a hospital order it may add to it a 'restriction order', the effect of which is that the offender may only be discharged from hospital upon the direction of either the Home Secretary or a Mental Health Review Tribunal (Mental Health Act 1983, ss 37 to 43).

Hospital orders and imprisonment have this in common — they are the only two forms of sentence which entail the compulsory detention of offenders who have attained the age of 21. In other respects they are totally dissimilar. A hospital order is intended to assist and cure the offender, not to punish or deter him, and once he is in hospital he is subject to essentially the same regime as applies to non-offender compulsory patients. For these reasons it is better to think of a hospital order as being in lieu of sentence, rather than as a sentence in the strict sense of the word. The law on the subject is now contained in the Mental Health Act 1983 which consolidated earlier legislation.

Irrespective of the age of the offender, both the Crown Court and magistrates' courts have power to make a hospital order. The preconditions for the making of an order, set out in s 37(1) and (2) of the Mental Health Act 1983, are that:

(a)   The court must be dealing with the offender for an imprisonable offence.

(b)   The court must be satisfied that:

(i)   the offender is suffering from mental illness, psychopathic disorder, mental impairment or severe mental impairment; and

(ii)   the mental illness etc. is of a nature which makes it appropriate for the offender to be detained in hospital for medical treatment; and

(iii)   in the case of psychopathic disorder or mental impairment, the treatment is likely to alleviate or prevent a deterioration in his condition; or

(iv)   in the case of an offender who has attained the age of 16 years, the mental disorder is of a nature or degree which warrants his reception into guardianship under the Act.

(c)   The court must be satisfied that arrangements have been made for the offender's admission to the hospital which it is proposed to name in the order.

(d)   Having regard to matters such as the nature of the offence and the antecedents of the offender, the court must be of the opinion that a hospital order is the most suitable method of dealing with the case.

As to the matters mentioned in (b) above, the court must have evidence (written or oral) from two registered medical practitioners, one of whom must be a specialist in the diagnosis or treatment of mental illness. The significance of (d) above is that if the court considers that, notwithstanding his mental problems, the offender ought to be punished for what he has done, it may choose a sentence of imprisonment in preference to a hospital order (see *Gunnell* (1966) 50 Cr App R 242, a case decided under equivalent provisions in the Mental Health Act 1959).

Broadly speaking, the effect of a hospital order is to authorise the offender's conveyance to hospital and his detention there for an initial period of six months. Even during the six months, the doctor in charge of the offender's treatment may discharge him from hospital. Conversely, after the six months, the doctor may authorise detention for a further six months, and thereafter he may authorise further detention at yearly intervals. If the offender is dissatisfied with the doctor's decision to authorise further detention, he may apply to a Mental Health Review Tribunal (MHRT), which may direct that he be discharged. A Mental Health Review Tribunal consists of a legally qualified chairman, a psychiatrist and a layman who, in deciding whether or not to direct discharge, consider whether the offender is still suffering from mental disorder; whether, if he is, his health or safety or the protection of others require that he should continue to receive treatment, and whether he would be able to look after himself properly out of hospital. Precisely the same considerations govern the discharge of non-offender patients.

The system of discharge described above is satisfactory in the cases of mentally disordered offenders who present little or no danger to the public. However, where the offender has committed or might in the future commit serious offences, especially offences of violence, it is thought unwise to leave the date of his discharge from hospital in the hands initially of the doctor in charge of his treatment. Accordingly, s 41 of the Mental Health Act 1983 provides that when the Crown Court makes a hospital order it may add to it a '*restriction order*' if it considers that such an order is necessary to protect the public from serious harm. (See *Birch* (1989) 11 Cr App R (S) 202 for the way in which the court should approach such cases.) In deciding whether a restriction order is necessary the Crown Court must have regard to the nature of the offender's offence, his antecedents and the likelihood of his committing further offences if set at large. A restriction order may be for a fixed term or without a time limit. Its effect is that, for its duration, the offender can be discharged from hospital only on the direction of the Home Secretary or an MHRT. The offender may make yearly applications to the MHRT for discharge, and, if no application is made for three years, the Home Secretary is under a duty to refer the case to them for consideration. It is noteworthy that the MHRT can now order discharge against the wishes of the Home Secretary — prior to 1983, the Home Secretary would ask for advice on discharge of offenders subject to restriction orders, but the final decision was always his. As an alternative to unconditional discharge, the MHRT may allow release from hospital on terms that, until the expiry of the restriction order, the offender shall be liable to recall for treatment at the discretion of the Home Secretary.

It has been held to be contrary to Article 5 of the European Convention on Human Rights (see Paragraph 26.2) to continue a restriction order if the patient's mental condition does not justify it. Danger to the public alone cannot be sufficient grounds for continuing detention under a restriction order: *X v UK* (1981) 4 EHRR 188.

A magistrates' court has no power to make a restriction order. However, where magistrates have convicted an offender aged 14 or over of an imprisonable offence and they consider that a hospital order with restriction order is called for, they may commit the offender to the Crown Court: Mental Health Act 1983, s 43. The Crown Court may then make a hospital order (with or without a restriction order), or deal with the offender in any way the magistrates could have dealt with him. While awaiting sentence at the Crown Court, the offender is either kept in custody or detained in a suitable hospital: s 44.

As an alternative to making a hospital order, the Crown Court or a magistrates' court may, in appropriate cases, make a guardianship order. The effect of such an order is that the offender is placed under the guardianship of a local social services authority or a person approved by the authority. The guardian may *inter alia* require the offender to reside at a certain address, and require him to attend places for treatment, training or education.

There are various other ways in which the process of criminal justice can result in a person being detained in a mental hospital:

(a) Upon a finding of not guilty by reason of insanity or unfitness to plead, the court may order that the accused be admitted to a hospital specified by the Home Secretary: Criminal Procedure (Insanity) Act 1964, s 5 (see Paragraph 16.7.2).

(b) Magistrates may make a hospital order under s 37(3) of the Mental Health Act 1983 without convicting the accused (see Paragraph 9.8).

(c) The Home Secretary may, upon receiving appropriate medical evidence, order that a person serving a prison sentence be transferred from prison to a mental hospital: Mental Health Act 1983, s 47.

Finally, it is necessary to summarise three powers given to the courts by ss 35, 36 and 38 of the Mental Health Act 1983, the broad aim of which is to facilitate the making of hospital orders. Section 35 provides that, where medical evidence suggests that an accused may be suffering from one of the forms of mental disorder which would justify the making of a hospital order, the court may remand him *to a hospital* for full reports on his condition. Magistrates may exercise this power in respect of somebody they have convicted of an imprisonable offence, or in respect of somebody charged with such an offence who either consents to the remand or who has been shown to the magistrates' satisfaction to have committed *the actus reus* of the offence. The Crown Court may exercise the power in respect of somebody who is awaiting trial on indictment, who is being tried on indictment or who has been convicted on indictment but not yet sentenced. A remand under s 35 must not be for more than 28 days. Although there may be further remands after the initial one, the total period must not exceed 12 weeks. If a person remanded under s 35 absconds from hospital, he may be arrested without warrant and brought before the court which remanded him. The court could then replace the s 35 remand with an ordinary remand in custody. The advantage of s 35 remands is that the court does not take the chance of allowing the accused to remain at liberty, but it avoids sending a disturbed person to prison or remand centre. Section 35 is complemented by s 36, which allows the Crown Court (but not magistrates) to remand an accused to hospital for treatment for mental illness or severe mental impairment. The power may be used only in respect of persons committed for trial in custody or remanded in custody during the course of the Crown Court proceedings. In effect, it is a means of transferring an accused from prison to hospital. The maximum period for s 36 remands is the same as for s 35 ones. Section 38, unlike ss 35 and 36, only applies after conviction. If there is medical evidence showing that the offender is suffering from a mental disorder which would permit the making of a hospital order, the court (magistrates' or Crown) may make an interim hospital order with a view to seeing whether a full hospital order will ultimately be appropriate. An interim order may authorise the offender's detention in hospital for a period of up to 12 weeks, and may be renewed for periods not exceeding 28 days at a time up to a total period of 6 months. The making of an interim hospital order in no way obliges the court to eventually deal with the offender by means of a full hospital order, but the former can be converted into the latter without the need for the offender to be brought before the court, provided he is legally represented.

23.23 BINDING OVER OF PARENTS

A court dealing with a young person for an offence may order his parent or guardian to enter into a recognisance to take proper care of him and exercise proper control over him (PCC(S)A 2000, s 150). Such an order may be made by the Crown Court, adult magistrates' court or youth court. The court is under a duty to do so in the case of the parents of a young offender who is under 16, if it is satisfied that it is desirable in order to prevent further offences by the young offender. If the court is not so satisfied, it should state its reasons in open court. The offence concerned need not be imprisonable. Further, whenever the court has passed a community order in respect of an offender under the age of 16, it may include in the recognisance a provision that the offender's parent or guardian must ensure that the offender complies with the requirements of the sentence. The effect of an order is that the parent or guardian has to undertake to take care of and exercise control over the juvenile, upon pain of forfeiting a certain sum of money should he fail to do so. The sum to be forfeited and the period for which the undertaking is to last are fixed by the court within maxima of £1,000 and three years respectively. Of course, no money is handed to the court when the undertaking is entered into — the liability to pay only arises should the undertaking be breached.

24   Appeals from the Crown Court

Appeals against conviction on indictment, against sentence following conviction on indictment, and against sentence passed following committal to the Crown Court for sentence, are all heard in the Criminal Division of the Court of Appeal. Decisions of the Crown Court in matters not relating to trial on indictment (e.g., in disposing of appeals from magistrates' courts) may be challenged by appealing by way of case stated to a Divisional Court of the Queen's Bench Division, or by applying for judicial review. Since appeals by case stated and applications for judicial review are chiefly used to correct errors made by magistrates, they are described in Chapter 25. The structure of the criminal appeal system is summarised in Figure 24.1.

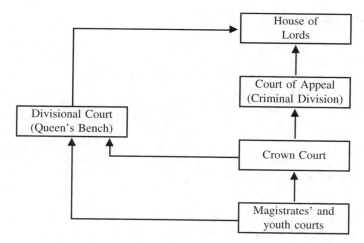

Figure 24.1   Structure of the criminal appeal system

24.1   THE CRIMINAL DIVISION OF THE COURT OF APPEAL

Prior to 1907, a person convicted on indictment had no general right of appeal, but the trial judge might in his discretion reserve a point of law for consideration by the Court of Crown

Cases Reserved. The Criminal Appeal Act of 1907 created the Court of Criminal Appeal, which replaced the Court of Crown Cases Reserved. It had a much wider jurisdiction than the latter court, being able to hear appeals against conviction based on grounds of fact or mixed law and fact, and appeals against sentence where the appellant argued that his sentence, although lawful, was too severe. The Court of Criminal Appeal was in its turn abolished by the Criminal Appeal Act 1966, which transferred its jurisdiction to the Criminal Division of the Court of Appeal. The powers of the Criminal Division are only slightly different from those of the old Court of Criminal Appeal save that its primary function of hearing appeals by the defence against the accused's conviction or sentence has been supplemented by a power to increase an over-lenient sentence upon its being referred to the Court by the Attorney-General (see the Criminal Justice Act 1988, ss 35 and 36, and Paragraph 24.7.2). There is also power to give an opinion on a point of law arising during a trial which ended in the accused's acquittal, but the acquittal itself may never be overturned (see Paragraph 24.7.1). The present legislation on the membership of the Criminal Division and its composition for particular types of hearing is contained in the Supreme Court Act 1981. The jurisdiction, powers and procedure of the Division are principally governed by the Criminal Appeal Act 1968 and the Criminal Appeal Rules 1968 made thereunder (SI 1968 No 1262). In this Chapter the Criminal Appeal Act and the Criminal Appeal Rules are denoted by the letters 'CAA' and 'CAR' respectively.

The Court of Appeal consists of up to 32 Lords Justices of Appeal and certain ex officio judges, in particular the Lord Chief Justice: Supreme Court Act 1981, s 2(2). Any member of the Court of Appeal is equally entitled to sit in the Criminal and Civil Divisions of the Court, but in practice the Lords Justices who exercise the jurisdiction of the Criminal Division are likely to have had experience as advocates or judges in the Crown Court. The Lord Chief Justice is president of the Criminal Division: Supreme Court Act 1981, s 3(2). He may request any High Court or circuit judge to act as a judge of the Division: s 9(1). A request under s 9(1) is more in the nature of a command, because it is the judge's duty to comply with it: s 9(3).

Any number of courts of the Criminal Division may sit simultaneously: Supreme Court Act 1981, s 3(5). When determining an appeal against conviction a court must consist of at least three judges: s 55(2). The same applies when there is an application for leave to appeal from the Court of Appeal to the House of Lords and when a person is appealing against a finding that he was unfit to plead or a verdict of not guilty by reason of insanity. Appeals against sentence may be determined by a two judge court. This was a change introduced by the Supreme Court Act 1981 — until the Act appeals against sentence, like appeals against conviction, required three judges. There is nothing to stop a court comprising more than three judges, provided the number is uneven. In fact, five judge courts are a rarity, confined to cases of exceptional importance or difficulty, e.g., *Turnbull* [1977] QB 224 where the Court of Appeal gave guidance to Crown Court judges on how they should deal with identification evidence.

Many applications incidental to the conduct of an appeal are decided not by a court but by a single judge. The judge does not usually hear argument from the parties, but merely reads through the papers in the case. Matters commonly dealt with by a single judge are applications for leave to appeal, for bail pending determination of the appeal, or for an order that a witness attend court with a view to giving evidence at the hearing of the appeal. If the single judge decides against the appellant, he may renew the application before a court, which need only consist of two judges. It is also possible to make an incidental application direct to a court, without first going to a single judge. Whether the court should then consist of two or three judges depends on the nature of the application. This topic is dealt with in detail in Paragraph 24.6.4.

The decision of a court of the Criminal Division may be taken by a majority of its members. If a two judge court is divided on what its decision should be, the matter should be re-argued before a three judge court: Supreme Court Act 1981, s 55(5). Even where the judges are not unanimous, the usual rule is that only one judgment is pronounced: s 59. However, the judge presiding in the court (i.e., the Lord Chief Justice if he is sitting, otherwise the most senior Lord Justice) may allow separate judgments if he considers that the question raised is one of law and that more than one judgment would be convenient. If there is only one judgment, the presiding judge either pronounces it himself or asks one of the other members of the court to undertake the task. A single judgment in a case makes for certainty in the law, and certainty in the criminal law is even more important than it is in the civil law.

In order to carry out its work, the Criminal Division needs administrative support. This is provided by the Registrar of Criminal Appeals and his staff. The Registrar is a barrister or solicitor of at least ten years standing, appointed by the Lord Chancellor: Supreme Court Act 1981, s 89(1). Notices of appeal and notices of application for leave to appeal (see Paragraph 24.6.1) are sent to the Registrar by the Crown Court officer on whom they were initially served. The Registrar's responsibilities then include obtaining any necessary transcript of the note taken by the shorthand writer of the Crown Court proceedings, obtaining from the Crown Court any exhibits or information it has relevant to the appeal, instructing counsel to represent an appellant who does not have a solicitor, and giving notice of the time fixed for the hearing of the appeal.

As already mentioned, Queen's Bench Division judges may be, and often are, asked to sit in the Criminal Division. The single judge who decides incidental applications is also usually a QBD judge. Queen's Bench Division judges also sit as Crown Court judges (see Paragraph 13.1.1) and circuit judges may also be asked to sit in the Court of Appeal (though not as a single judge). Therefore, the possibility arises of a judge hearing an appeal against his own decision. To avoid this happening, s 56(2) of the Supreme Court Act 1981 provides that a judge must not sit in the Criminal Division for the hearing of, or make any incidental decision connected with, an appeal against conviction or sentence if he was the judge in the lower court.

24.2 THE RIGHT OF APPEAL AGAINST CONVICTION

Subject to obtaining leave to appeal when that is necessary, a person convicted on indictment may appeal to the Court of Appeal against his conviction: CAA, s 1(1). Leave to appeal is granted by the court itself, usually acting through a single judge.

24.2.1 Appeals based on trial judge's certificate

No leave to appeal against conviction is required if the trial judge from the Crown Court has granted a certificate that the case is fit for appeal: CAA, s 1(2)(a). In all other cases, leave must be obtained.

A certificate of fitness for appeal may mention a ground of fact, mixed law and fact or pure law. It is very rare for the trial judge to grant a certificate. It will not be granted merely because the judge is uneasy about the verdict. There must be a particular and cogent ground of appeal with a substantial chance of success (*Parkin* (1928) 20 Cr App R 173, and *Practice Direction* (*Crown Court: Bail Pending Appeal*) [1983] 1 WLR 1292, para 3).

24.2.2 Appeals with leave

The power to grant leave to appeal is one of the powers of the Court of Appeal which may be — and most frequently is — exercised not by a court, but by a single judge. The procedure is described in more detail in Paragraph 24.6.4, but, in essence, it involves the papers in the case being handed to the single judge for his consideration. The papers will include the appellant's 'Notice of Application for Leave to Appeal' and 'Grounds of Appeal', often together with an Advice on Appeal. They may also include a transcript of the trial judge's summing-up and possibly, depending on the nature of the points raised in the Grounds of Appeal, a transcript of part of the evidence. The judge reads through the papers privately. He could, but hardly ever does, call on counsel for the appellant to present argument. Having read the papers, he decides whether to grant leave or not. If leave is refused, the appellant has the right to have the application decided by a court of the Criminal Division. The risk, from his point of view, in exercising that right is that if the court, like the single judge, refuses leave, it may well order that time he has spent in custody since the commencement of the appeal shall not count as part of any custodial sentence imposed upon him (see CAA, s 29 and Paragraph 24.6.6 on directions for loss of time). Most appellants who are refused leave to appeal by a single judge do not renew the application before the court.

In granting or refusing leave to appeal the single judge acts as a kind of filter, ensuring that cases do not go before a court for a full hearing unless there is an arguable point.

24.2.3 Appeal against conviction following guilty plea

In entitling persons convicted on indictment to appeal against conviction, s 1 of the CAA does not distinguish between those who pleaded guilty and those who denied the charge. On the face of it, the former have as much right to appeal as the latter. But, for obvious reasons, the Court of Appeal is most reluctant to grant leave to appeal against conviction if the appellant admitted his guilt in the Crown Court. The classic passage on the matter comes from Avory J in *Forde* [1923] 2 KB 400, although it has since been stressed that it should not be construed as a comprehensive statement of all the situations in which an appeal may be heard despite there having been a guilty plea. Avory J said:

> A plea of guilty having been recorded, this court can only entertain an appeal against conviction if it appears (1) that the appellant did not appreciate the nature of the charge or did not intend to admit he was guilty of it, or (2) that upon the admitted facts he could not in law have been convicted of the offence charged.

The first of the two situations mentioned by his lordship covers *inter alia* cases where a purported plea of guilty is said to have been a nullity because of pressure brought to bear on the accused by the judge and/or counsel (see *Turner* [1970] 2 QB 321 and Paragraph 16.3.3). The second situation does not often arise in practice, since it presupposes that both the prosecution and the defence at the Crown Court were mistaken about the essential elements which the prosecution had to prove to establish the offence charged — if the defence had not been mistaken as well as the prosecution, they ought not to have allowed the case to proceed on a guilty plea.

In addition to cases which can clearly be brought within the terms of Avory J's proposition, appeals are heard where a plea of guilty is induced by the trial judge's wrong ruling in law. Thus, in *Clarke* [1972] 1 All ER 219, C successfully appealed against a conviction for shoplifting, the facts being that she abandoned her original plea of not guilty after the judge decided that her defence (that she put the goods into her bag in a moment of absent-mindedness and then forgot to pay) amounted to a plea of not guilty by reason of insanity. Not surprisingly, C preferred to plead guilty rather than be found not guilty and made the subject of a hospital order. In the circumstances, her change of plea did not preclude her appealing. Finally, there will be occasional cases which are not covered by any of the headings described above, but where the interests of justice demand that the appeal be allowed to proceed. An excellent example is *Lee* [1984] 1 WLR 578. Although fit to plead, L was of very low intelligence. He was charged with numerous offences of arson and manslaughter. The case against him consisted entirely of confessions which he had made to the police, but, notwithstanding the confessions, he instructed his legal representatives until shortly before the trial that he intended to plead not guilty. He then changed his mind and pleaded guilty to all counts. He subsequently attributed this volte-face to his having been told that a place had been found for him at a special mental hospital, so that if he pleaded guilty he would leave prison (where he had been for several months on remand) and be sent to hospital under a hospital order. That was in fact what happened. There was no question of L being pressured by counsel or judge into pleading guilty — on the contrary counsel told the judge privately that he was most unhappy about what L was doing, not least because a public inquiry into the cause of one fire which L now admitted to starting had concluded that it began by accident. Subsequent investigations by the *Sunday Times* cast more doubt on the correctness of L's convictions, and suggested that for at least some of the offences he had convincing alibis. Thus encouraged, L applied for leave to appeal out of time. The defence attributed his confessions to his low intelligence, a desire for 'notoriety and publicity' and the remorseless nature of the police interrogation. In the highly unusual circumstances of the case, L was given leave to appeal. As Ackner LJ said:

> The fact that the appellant was fit to plead; knew what he was doing; intended to make the pleas he did; pleaded guilty without equivocation after receiving expert advice, although factors highly relevant to [whether the appeal should ultimately succeed] cannot of themselves deprive the court of the jurisdiction to hear [the appeal].

In *Chalkley* [1998] 2 Cr App R 79, the Court of Appeal distinguished:

(a)   cases where an incorrect ruling of law on admitted facts left a defendant with no legal escape from a verdict guilty on those facts; and
(b)   cases where an accused was influenced to change his plea to guilty because he recognised that as a result of a ruling to admit strong evidence against him, his case was hopeless.

It was held that a conviction under category (a) was unsafe, whereas a conviction under category (b) was not.

In *Togher* [2001] 3 All ER 463, the Court of Appeal stated that the effect on an appeal against conviction of a plea of guilty following a judge's ruling depended on a choice between:

(a)   a 'narrow' approach, that an appeal could be entertained only where the ruling left no legal basis for a plea of not guilty; and

(b) a 'wide' approach, that a plea of guilty following a material irregularity could also found an appeal.

The Court of Appeal adopted the wide approach in preference to the narrower approach adopted in *Chalkley* [1998] 2 Cr App R 79. In particular, the word 'unsafe' should be applied in a way compatible with the European Convention on Human Rights. Fairness of trial and safety of conviction went together. If a defendant were denied a fair trial it was almost inevitable that the conviction would be unsafe. Also, if he pleaded guilty in ignorance of matters which might amount to abuse of process and justify a stay of the prosecution, such conviction might properly be set aside.

24.3 APPEAL AGAINST SENTENCE

Appellants to the Court of Appeal against sentence fall into two categories — those who were sentenced for an offence following conviction on indictment, and those who were sentenced for an offence following summary conviction and committal to the Crown Court for sentence. Leave to appeal is always required, unless the judge who passed sentence grants a certificate that the case is fit for appeal.

24.3.1 Sentence following conviction on indictment

A person convicted on indictment of an offence other than murder may appeal to the Court of Appeal against any sentence passed on him by the Crown Court for the offence: CAA, s 9. For purposes of the CAA, 'sentence' has a wide meaning. It includes 'any order made by a court when dealing with an offender': CAA, s 50. Thus, an offender may appeal not only against an order which is obviously a punishment (e.g., imprisonment, detention in a young offender institution, a fine or a community service order), but also against non-punitive orders such as probation, conditional discharge or even an absolute discharge. Section 50 specifically provides that hospital orders and recommendations for deportation are 'sentences'. Even orders which are normally regarded as ancillary to the sentence proper (e.g., costs for the prosecution or compensation for the victim) are orders made 'when dealing with an offender', and so fall within the s 50 definition.

> There is no appeal against the sentence for murder because it is mandatory. Neither can a murderer appeal against any recommendation the judge makes as to the minimum term he should serve in prison before being released on parole. This is because minimum-term recommendations are not binding on the Home Secretary, and so cannot be regarded as orders of the court within the meaning of s 50.

24.3.2 Sentence following summary conviction

Section 10 of the Criminal Appeal Act 1968 provides that a person sentenced by the Crown Court for an offence following summary conviction and committal for sentence (see Chapter 11) may appeal against his sentence if:

(a) for the offence (or for that offence and others for which sentence was passed on the same occasion) he was sentenced to imprisonment or detention in a young offender institution for a term of six months or more; or

(b)   the sentence for the offence was one which the magistrates could not have passed (e.g. four months' imprisonment for an offence triable either way when the statute creating the offence provides that the maximum penalty upon summary conviction shall be three months); or

(c)   in dealing with him for the offence, the Crown Court disqualified him from driving, recommended that he be deported or brought into effect a suspended sentence of which the offence put him in breach.

The effect of the section is that an appeal by an offender dealt with on a committal for sentence is usually restricted to cases where the Crown Court's sentence was as severe or more severe than the greatest sentence the magistrates could have imposed had they not committed. The justification for so restricting the right of appeal is that the magistrates would not have committed unless they felt the offender deserved a sentence in excess of six months' imprisonment or detention. By imposing less than that term, the Crown Court implicitly takes a less serious view of the case than the lower court did. It is therefore unnecessary to let the offender go to the Court of Appeal when he has had a 'good result' in the Crown Court.

> Section 10 also gives a right of appeal to an offender who, following a summary conviction which puts him in breach of probation or a conditional discharge, is dealt with by the Crown Court for the original offence. The appeal lies in the same circumstances as does an appeal following committal for sentence (i.e., essentially, the offender must have been given six months or more either for the original offence alone or for that and other offences dealt with on the same occasion by the Crown Court). To illustrate the working of s 10, consider a case where O is summarily convicted of an offence committed during the period of a community rehabilitation order made by the Crown Court. If the sequence of events is that (a) the magistrates pass a sentence of three months' imprisonment for the subsequent offence, and (b) the Crown Court later has the offender brought before it and sentences him to three months consecutive for the original offence, then there is no appeal to the Court of Appeal against the latter sentence because it is for less than six months. If, on the other hand, the magistrates commit O to the Crown Court to be dealt with both for the subsequent offence and the breach of probation and the Crown Court imposes two three-month terms to run consecutively, then there is a right of appeal because the total sentence passed on the one occasion is six months. Where the Crown Court activates a suspended sentence of which the offender was put in breach by a summary conviction, there is a right of appeal against the activation regardless of whether the term activated is more or less than six months and regardless of whether the Crown Court is also dealing with O for the subsequent offence.

24.3.3   Leave to appeal against sentence

Unless the Crown Court judge certifies that the case is fit for appeal, an appeal against sentence lies only with leave: CAA, s 11(1). This applies whether the appeal is brought under s 9 or s 10 of the CAA, and whether it is on a point of law or otherwise. The power to grant a certificate that a sentence is fit for appeal was introduced in 1982, as a result of amendments to the CAA made by the Criminal Justice Act of that year. The Court of Appeal has, however, discouraged Crown Court judges from exercising the power (see, for example, *Grant* (1990) 12 Cr App R (S) 441). Indeed it is hard to see why a judge should readily declare that a sentence he has just passed is appealable — if he thought the sentence was too severe, he presumably would not have passed it. As a result, virtually all offenders seeking a reduction in their sentence require leave. The procedure for obtaining leave is the same as for obtaining leave to appeal against conviction (see Paragraph 24.2.2).

24.4 DETERMINATION OF APPEALS AGAINST CONVICTION

Section 2(1) of the CAA 1968 provides the statutory framework for the determination of appeals against conviction. It states that the Court of Appeal 'shall allow an appeal against conviction if they think that the conviction is unsafe; and . . . shall dismiss an appeal in any other case'. This new simplified test was introduced by the Criminal Appeal Act 1995. Before that, the Court of Appeal had to consider whether the conviction was unsafe or unsatisfactory, whether the judge had made a wrong decision on a question of law, or whether there had been a material irregularity in the course of the trial. If they decided that one of these conditions was met, the Court of Appeal had then to proceed to determine whether a miscarriage of justice had actually occurred. The test is now greatly simplified, but the historical position should be borne in mind in studying cases decided before s 2 of the CAA 1968 was amended by the 1995 Act.

In any event, it is clear that the intention of Parliament was that there should be no change in effect despite the simplified wording. In moving the Second Reading of the Criminal Appeal Bill, the then Home Secretary said: 'In substance it restates the existing practice of the Court of Appeal.' It was made clear that this statement followed upon consultation with the Lord Chief Justice (*Hansard*, vol. 256, para 24, 6 March 1995; and see also Standing Committee B, 21 March 1995, col. 26). The fact that there is no difference in practice between the old and the new tests is illustrated by the case of *Mullen* [1999] Crim LR 561, where an appeal was based upon the circumstances in which the appellant was brought to trial. The English prosecuting authorities, in collusion with Zimbabwean authorities, had procured his deportation from Zimbabwe to England in circumstances which amounted to an abuse of process. The Court of Appeal described the conduct of the British authorities as so unworthy or shameful that it was an affront to the public conscience to allow the prosecution to succeed. Nevertheless, the conduct of the trial itself was not challenged. The real question was whether it was fair to try the accused in view of the way in which he had been brought before the court. In applying the statutory test relating to appeals, did this mean that the conviction was unsafe? The Court of Appeal had recourse to *Hansard*, from which it was apparent that the new form of s 2 of the CAA was intended to re-state the existing practice of the Court of Appeal. That practice allowed abuse of process to be a ground for quashing a conviction. Furthermore, for a conviction to be safe, it must be lawful. If the trial should never have taken place, then the conviction could not be regarded as safe.

Another illustration of the way in which the test (safety of the conviction) is applied is provided by the case of *Smith* (1999) *The Times*, 31 May 1999. Here the ground of appeal was the wrongful rejection of a submission of no case to answer. After the submission had been rejected, the defendant gave evidence and in cross-examination admitted his guilt! Before the unified test for appeals was introduced, the authorities favoured the view that in such a case the appeal should succeed since the accused had been deprived, by the wrong ruling, of the absolute certainty of an acquittal upon the judge's direction (*Cockley* (1984) 79 Cr App R 181). Since the accused had admitted his guilt in court, however, how accurate was it to say, under the new test, that the conviction was 'unsafe'? In *Smith*, the Court of Appeal had no hesitation in doing so. Even in an extreme case, such as this one, the wrongful rejection of a submission of no case to answer meant that the appeal must succeed. Again, it would appear that the change in wording in s 2 of the CAA had had no practical effect.

It is becoming increasingly clear that the new test is meant to reflect the practice adopted by the Court of Appeal in interpreting the old one. The restrictive reading of the word 'unsafe' anticipated by some commentators has not generally found favour in practice, despite dicta to the contrary, e.g., in *Chalkley* [1998] 3 WLR 146.

In *Condron v UK* [2000] Crim LR 679, the European Court of Human Rights emphasised the need for the Court of Appeal to focus upon the fairness of the trial, rather than the safety of the conviction, in deciding whether to uphold an appeal from the Crown Court. In para 65 of their judgment, the Court said:

The question whether or not the rights of the defence guaranteed to an accused under Art 6 of the Convention were secured in any given case cannot be assimilated to a finding that his conviction was safe in the absence of any enquiry into the issue of fairness.

In *Togher* [2001] 3 All ER 463, the Court of Appeal considered the relationship between the requirement for a fair trial and the safety of any conviction which resulted. Lord Woolf CJ said that if the accused had been denied a fair trial, it was almost inevitable that his conviction would be regarded as unsafe, now that the Convention had been incorporated into domestic law.

In their grounds of appeal, many appellants refer first to specific legal or procedural errors which arose at their trial, and then supplement these specific grounds with a general claim that the conviction was therefore unsafe. There is a school of thought that all misdirections in the summing-up should be classified as factors rendering the conviction unsafe rather than as wrong decisions of law or material irregularities. But, nothing in s 2(1) of the CAA expressly limits appeals based on the unsafe nature of the conviction to cases where the appellant can point to some specific mistake in the conduct of his trial. As a matter of pure statutory construction, he may legitimately argue that the evidence against him (although just sufficient to establish a prima facie case) was so weak that the jury's verdict should not stand. However, in practice it is very difficult to raise a doubt in their lordships' minds about the safety of a conviction merely by attacking the quality of the evidence given at trial. They take the view that the jury saw and heard the witnesses (unlike themselves who rarely have more than a transcript of the summing-up). What seems a thin case on paper may have been totally convincing 'in the flesh'. Therefore, 'if all the material was before the jury and the summing-up was impeccable . . . the court shall not lightly interfere' (per Lord Widgery CJ in *Cooper* [1969] 1 QB 267). In other words, assuming the trial to have been legally error-free, the appellant will only succeed if he can point to something exceptional in the overall circumstances which absolutely drives the court to the conclusion that an injustice may have been done. In *Cooper* itself the special factors which led to C's conviction for assault being quashed were that the case against him rested on a somewhat dubious identification by the victim, and there was evidence that X (who closely resembled C and had a record for violence) had privately confessed to the crime. C had been able to call the third person to whom X had made his confession, but for obvious reasons he was unable to call X himself. Similarly, in *Pattinson* (1974) 58 Cr App R 417, P's appeal against a conviction for robbery succeeded because the prosection's only evidence was a confession which P had allegedly made at the police station, and the circumstances of that confession were too bizarre for the police to be believed (after he had been charged — and so could not be further questioned — P, according to the police, had talked to himself when he thought he was not being overheard and had obligingly admitted his involvement in the robbery). But, it is well established that convictions can be sustained even though the only evidence against the appellant was an oral confession to the police for which there is no independent (i.e. non-police) corroboration (see *Mallinson* [1977] Crim LR 161 — the problem in *Pattinson* was the improbable form the confession took, not the lack of other independent evidence).

24.4.1 Errors in the trial as grounds of appeal

As indicated in the previous Paragraph, the Court of Appeal will be most reluctant to uphold a conviction where the trial was legally error-free. Such errors therefore form the grounds on which most appeals are argued. Among the commonest grounds of appeal put forward are errors in the judge's summing-up, e.g., wrongly defining the elements of the offence, failing to leave to the jury a defence for which a foundation has been laid by the evidence, failing to give an adequate direction on the burden and/or standard of proof. Other grounds frequently relied on amount to procedural errors in the course of the trial, e.g., allowing the prosecution to amend the indictment when that involved the risk of injustice, allowing evidence to be admitted when it should have been excluded, failing to deal properly with a note from the jury, failing to comply with the statutory limitations on majority verdicts. All of these are common examples from an endless list of potential errors in a trial. In the end, however, the crucial question (however many errors there were) is: was the conviction safe?

Sometimes an appellant relies on alleged errors by counsel defending him at the Crown Court as a basis for appeal. Traditionally the Court of Appeal has been very reluctant to accept such arguments. In *Clinton* [1993] 1 WLR 1181, their lordships said it was rare for a verdict to be quashed because of defence counsel's conduct of the trial. The correct approach was whether the conviction was unsafe or unsatisfactory under all the circumstances. In *Clinton*, C had been charged with kidnapping and indecent assault. The complainant described her attacker in terms sharply at variance with the appearance of C (including a history of tattoos and scars). C did not give or call evidence at the trial. He was convicted, the case being almost entirely based on the complainant's evidence. The Court of Appeal, in allowing the appeal, said that C should have been strongly advised to give evidence to underline the discrepancies. His counsel had not in fact tried to wean him from his reluctance to testify, and that was a grave error. Exceptionally, where a tactical decision (such as not calling the defendant) was taken without proper instructions or against the promptings of good sense, the Court of Appeal could set aside the verdict.

Prior to *Clinton*, there was a line of cases, culminating in *Ensor* [1989] 1 WLR 497, in which the Court of Appeal concentrated its attention on the extent of counsel's alleged ineptitude. In *Ensor* E was charged with two counts of rape. He told his counsel that he wanted them severed, and it was common ground at appeal that an application to sever, if made, should have succeeded. For tactical reasons, E's counsel decided not to apply to sever. He did not inform E of his decision. E was convicted on both counts, and appealed on the basis of his counsel's conduct. The Court of Appeal stated that a conviction could not be set aside on the ground that counsel's action was mistaken or unwise, even if it was also contrary to the accused's wishes. There was an exception in the case of 'flagrantly incompetent advocacy'. Here counsel's actions, even if erroneous, were not incompetent, let alone flagrantly so. In another decision, the Court of Appeal held that failure by counsel to discuss with his client whether or not to call alibi witnesses could afford a ground of appeal (see *Irwin* [1987] 2 All ER 1085, which, however, was said in *Ensor* ought to be regarded as confined to its own facts).

Clinton, it is submitted, puts the consideration of alleged errors by counsel in a proper perspective. It must surely be better to concentrate on the way in which the trial was affected, rather than the standard of advocacy. The proper question is, therefore, that posed by the statute: was the conviction unsafe?

In *Ullah* [2000] Crim LR 108, the Court of Appeal emphasised that in a case of this kind, the crucial question was whether the conviction was safe, but ineptitude on the part of counsel was a necessary pre-requisite. In considering whether counsel had been incompetent, their Lordships suggest that the test might be whether his conduct was based on such fundamentally flawed reasons that it might properly be regarded as *Wednesbury* unreasonable (applying the criteria in *Associated Picture Houses Ltd v Wednesbury Corporation* [1948] 1 KB 223).

In *Nangle* [2001] Crim LR 506, the Court of Appeal stated that 'flagrant incompetence' might not now be the appropriate measure to apply in deciding whether to quash a conviction. In the light of the Human Rights Act 1998 and Art 6 of the European Convention on Human Rights, what was required was that the hearing of the charges against the defendant should be fair. If the conduct of his legal advisers was such that this objective had not been met, then the Court of Appeal might be compelled to intervene. The issue was considered by the European Court of Human Rights in *Daud v Portugal* [1999] EHRLR 634, where the defence lawyer had only three days to prepare for a complex fraud trial which resulted in a nine-year prison sentence. It was held that the defendant's right under Art 6(3)(c) had been violated, since he had not had the benefit of a practical and effective defence. The time given was too short for a serious and complex case. As is stated in Professor Ashworth's commentary on *Nangle*, this suggests that a test less demanding than 'flagrant incompetence' may now be appropriate. In any event, it seems increasingly clear that the focus is upon the impact of the lawyer's errors, rather than their extent.

24.4.2   The effect of a successful appeal

If the Court of Appeal finds that the conviction is unsafe it must allow the appeal and quash the appellant's conviction (CAA, s 2(2)). Unless the Court also orders that the appellant be re-tried, the effect of quashing a conviction is that the Crown Court is directed to record an acquittal instead of a conviction, and the appellant is treated just as if the jury had found him not guilty: s 2(3). Consequently, any attempt by the prosecution to re-prosecute him for the same offence would be barred by the plea of autrefois acquit.

Section 7 of the CAA deals with ordering retrials. Until it was amended by the Criminal Justice Act 1988, s 7 applied only when the Court allowed an appeal on the basis of fresh evidence which it had heard. Such cases, as explained in Paragraph 24.6.9, account for only a tiny fraction of the Court's workload. Therefore, retrials on the direction of the Court of Appeal were very rare. That position has been transformed by the amendments, passed in 1988, the effect of which is that, whenever they allow an appeal, their lordships have a discretion to order a retrial should they consider that the interests of justice so require. Thus, if an appeal succeeds the appellant will not enjoy complete immunity from the possibility of further proceedings for the offence in question. Instead, the Court will look at the circumstances and decide in their discretion whether or not to order that he be retried. The Court of Appeal has indicated that the period which elapsed since the original trial, whether or not the appellant had been in custody for that period, and the apparent strength of the case against him were factors they would take into account in deciding where the interests of justice lay (see *Saunders* (1973) 58 Cr App R 248 and *Flower* (1965) 50 Cr App R 22).

One issue which must sometimes be considered in deciding whether a retrial should be held is the publicity surrounding the original trial and the appeal, in view of the potential impact on any future jury. In *Taylor* (1994) 98 Cr App R 361, the Court of Appeal, having upheld an appeal against conviction for murder in part because of the sensational and inaccurate publicity surrounding the trial, went on to say:

Moreover, by reason of the view we take of the way in which this case was reported, we do not think that a fair trial could now take place. Hence we do not order a retrial.

In *Stone* [2001] Crim LR 465, the Court of Appeal considered whether exceptional publicity surrounding both the original trial for murder and the successful appeal of the appellant precluded a retrial. Although the publicity was sensational and possibly inaccurate in parts, the court was not satisfied on the balance of probabilities that it was such as to make a retrial oppressive or unfair or make a verdict in the retrial unsafe. A retrial was ordered.

Section 8, as amended, deals with the procedure when a retrial is ordered. A fresh indictment is preferred. Normally that will be for the self-same offence as was alleged in the original indictment, but the Court may order that the appellant be retried for an offence of which he could have been convicted at the first trial by way of alternative verdict, or an offence alleged in an alternative count in respect of which the jury were discharged from giving a verdict because they convicted on the other count (see s 7(2)(b) and (c)). The new indictment should be preferred promptly since an arraignment more than two months after the order for retrial will require leave from the Court: s 8(1A). Moreover, once the two-month period has elapsed, the appellant himself is entitled to apply to have the order for a retrial set aside. On a prosecution application to arraign out of time or on a defence application to set aside an order for a retrial, their Lordships must decide in favour of the appellant unless satisfied that the prosecution acted 'with all due expedition' and that there are still sufficient grounds for a retrial despite the lapse of time which precipitated the application: s 8(1B). Pending a retrial, the appellant is remanded in custody or on bail at the discretion of the Court of Appeal. Should he again be convicted, the sentence passed must not be more severe than that imposed after the first trial, although it may, of course, be more lenient (see Sch 2 to the CAA).

24.4.3 A writ of venire de novo

In the vast majority of cases coming before it, the Court of Appeal will rely on the powers given it by s 2 of the CAA in order to quash or, as the case may be, uphold a conviction. However, the Court also has a power, independent of statute and inherited from the old Court of Crown Cases Reserved, to quash a conviction and issue a writ of venire de novo. The effect of issuing the writ is virtually the same as ordering a retrial.

The somewhat arcane law on the subject is summarised in the propositions below which are based on dicta from Lord Diplock's judgment in *Rose* [1982] AC 822) and Watkins LJ's in *Newland* [1988] QB 402.

(i) The power to issue a writ of venire de novo arises only when a procedural irregularity occurred before or at the outset of the Crown Court proceedings which was of such a fundamental nature as to render the appellant's so-called 'trial' a total mistrial, with the consequence that he was never at any stage of the hearing before the jury in danger of a valid conviction. Examples are where the committal proceedings purporting to justify the preferment of a bill of indictment were invalid, where a jury were asked to try two separate indictments simultaneously, where the defence were prevented from challenging jurors, where joinder of two counts in a single indictment was wrong in law as contravening r 9 of the Indictment Rules, and where the accused was improperly pressured into pleading guilty. Venire de novo is not, however, appropriate when the appellant complains of an irregularity occurring during a validly commenced trial, even if it is the type of error that seems to go to the root of the jury's power to return a verdict (e.g. suggestions that the jury separated after they had retired to consider their verdict, or that a question they asked the judge was not dealt with by the correct procedure, or that they returned a majority verdict when the provisions of s 17 of the Juries Act were not complied with). In such cases, the appellant must simply rely on the grounds of appeal specified in s 2(1) of the CAA (see especially *Rose* [1982] AC 822 at p. 831–3).

(ii)   If the Court does have power to issue venire de novo, it may, at its discretion, simply quash the conviction and do no more — i.e. it is not obliged to order that the successful appellant be retried.

(iii)   As issue of venire de novo presupposes that the appellant's trial was a total nullity, whereas the ground for allowing an appeal set out in s 2(1) of the CAA presupposes the opposite, there will never be circumstances in which the Court can choose to quash a conviction either by virtue of its inherent common law power or by virtue of its statutory powers. In other words, if the point raised by the appellant arguably entitles him to a venire de novo, it will not be a case for quashing the conviction under s 2(1) on the basis that there was a procedural irregularity in the course of his trial, and similarly vice versa (see especially *Rose* at p. 833; *Newland* at p. 408).

(iv)   Now that the Court of Appeal has a discretion to order a retrial whenever it allows an appeal under s 2(1) and not just in fresh evidence cases, much of the point of distinguishing between venire de novo situations and 'ordinary' appeals has been lost.

24.4.4   Partially successful appeals

If an appellant was convicted at the Crown Court on two or more counts, and appeals against all those convictions, the Court of Appeal may, of course, allow the appeal on some but not all the counts. Further, where the indictment against the appellant was such that the jury could have convicted him on it of an offence other than the one of which they did convict him, the Court may substitute for the jury's verdict a verdict of guilty of that other offence: CAA, s 3. The Court of Appeal must take the view that the jury must have been satisfied of the facts proving the appellant guilty of the other offence. Section 3 may apply in two situations. First, if the jury, on a count in the indictment, convicted the appellant as charged, but could have returned a verdict of not guilty as charged but guilty of a lesser offence, the Court of Appeal can substitute for their verdict a conviction for the lesser offence. Secondly, if the jury convicted of one of two counts on the indictment in the alternative, and were discharged from giving a verdict on the other count, the Court of Appeal can reverse the verdicts (i.e., quash the conviction and enter a verdict of guilty of the offence in respect of which the jury were discharged from giving a verdict) (see Paragraph 19.3). In *Worton* (1990) 154 JP 201, for example, W was one of several charged with violent disorder under s 2 of the Public Order Act 1986. The trial judge failed to direct the jury correctly as to the effect on the case against W of his co-accused being acquitted (i.e., it might reduce the number participating to under three and therefore make the only possible verdict affray rather than violent disorder). The Court of Appeal quashed the conviction, then substituted a conviction for affray. In *Horsman* (1997) *The Times*, 3 July 1997, the Court of Appeal made it clear that s 3 gave them no power to substitute a verdict of guilty of an alternative offence where the defendant had pleaded guilty prior to being put in the charge of the jury.

24.4.5   Single right of appeal

Once an appeal has been dealt with, the appellant is debarred from bringing a second appeal in the matter (*Pinfold* [1988] QB 462). This is the case even if the point to be raised at the second appeal is entirely different from that which was dealt with at the first. In *Pinfold*, P's original appeal was on the basis of a misdirection in the summing-up. His proposed second appeal would have relied on fresh evidence. It was held that the court had no jurisdiction to determine a second appeal in the light of the dismissal of the earlier one.

The rule restricting the appellant to a single appeal can create a strange anomaly where there are several grounds of appeal, and the Court of Appeal indicates that it will allow the appeal on one ground, without hearing argument on the others, in order to save time. It may then be open to the Crown to appeal to the House of Lords against the Court of Appeal's decision to allow the appeal (see Paragraph 24.9). If the Crown is successful in the House of Lords, the appellant will be unable to revive those grounds which were never considered by the Court of Appeal. The problem can be avoided if the Crown indicates to the Court of Appeal, immediately an appeal is allowed on one of several grounds, that it is likely to take the matter to the House of Lords. The Court of Appeal can then decide whether to consider the other grounds of appeal (see *Berry* [1994] Crim LR 276, where this procedure was commended as a way out of the dilemma). Another possibility is for the House of Lords to exercise the powers of the Court of Appeal in relation to any grounds not disposed of by the latter court (*Mandair* [1995] 1 AC 208).

24.5 DETERMINATION OF APPEALS AGAINST SENTENCE

On an appeal against sentence, the Court of Appeal may quash any sentence or order which is the subject of the appeal, and replace it with the sentence or order it considers appropriate provided:

(a)   the sentence it passes or order it makes is one which the Crown Court could have passed or made, and

(b)   taking the case as a whole, the appellant is not more severely dealt with on appeal than he was by the Crown Court: CAA, s 11(3).

Unlike the old Court of Criminal Appeal, the Court of Appeal does not have the power to increase sentence in cases where the appeal is brought by the sentenced offender. Where, however, the Court allows an appeal in respect of one count but confirms the conviction in respect of another count, it may increase the sentence for the count on which the appellant still stands convicted, provided it does not make the sentence more severe than the total sentence passed by the Crown Court on both counts: s 4. If the Court of Appeal substitutes for the jury's verdict a verdict of guilty of a lesser offence (see Paragraph 24.4.4) it may pass a sentence for the lesser offence which again must not be more severe than the Crown Court sentence: s 3(2). Despite the prohibition on increasing sentence, an appellant serving a custodial sentence may find that his sentence has in effect been increased through the court directing that the time he has spent in custody pending determination of his appeal shall not count as part of his sentence. Section 11 (no increase in sentence) should therefore be considered in conjunction with s 29 (directions for loss of time: see Paragraph 24.6.6). It should also be borne in mind that the Attorney-General may refer a sentence to the Court of Appeal if he considers it too lenient, and their Lordships may then deal with the offender more severely than the Crown Court judge did (see Paragraph 24.7.2). Attorney-General's sentencing references are, however, quite distinct from appeals by the offender, where the basic rule is still that the Court cannot increase sentence.

Apart from ruling out any increase in the appellant's sentence, s 11(3) of the CAA places no restriction on the Court of Appeal's approach to determining appeals. There is no statutory bar on the Court habitually substituting its own view of what the sentence should have been for the sentence actually passed, even if the reduction in sentence is very slight. However, their Lordships have always recognised that views on sentencing legitimately vary from judge to judge — some are bound to be on the severe side, others on the lenient side, and the individual sentencer is entitled to a measure of discretion in performing his task.

Thus, there is no one right sentence for a particular case but rather an acceptable range within which the sentence actually imposed should fall. Provided the appellant's sentence was within the acceptable range, it is unlikely to be reduced on appeal, even if it was at the top end of the range and greater than the individual members of the Court of Appeal would have imposed had they been the judges at first instance. As Lord Hewart CJ expressed it in *Gumbs* (1926) 19 Cr App R 74:

> This court never interferes with the discretion of the court below merely on the ground that this court might have passed a somewhat different sentence; for this court to revise a sentence there must be some error in principle.

The principal situations in which an appeal is likely to succeed are as follows:

(a) *Sentence wrong in law.* If the Crown Court judge's sentence was one which he was not in law entitled to pass, the Court of Appeal will obviously have to replace it with a lawful sentence.

(b) *Sentence wrong in principle or manifestly excessive.* This is by far the commonest basis for a successful appeal. As explained above, the appellant must do more than show that his sentence was 'on the severe side'. He must show that it was outside the commonly accepted range of penalties for his type of case. 'Wrong in principle' is a phrase particularly apt to cover cases where the judge chose completely the wrong type of sentence — e.g., passed a custodial sentence when the offence did not pass the 'custody threshold' as laid down in the Criminal Justice Act 1991, s 1(2). Wrong in principle also covers mistakes in combining different forms of sentence (e.g., passing a sentence of imprisonment at the same time as imposing a community rehabilitation order). 'Manifestly excessive' applies when the right form of sentence is chosen, but it is simply much too severe, or, to use the terminology explained in Paragraph 22.6, the sentence is clearly disproportionate to the offence.

(c) *Wrong approach to sentencing.* If it is apparent from the judge's remarks when he passed sentence that he dealt with the offender more severely than he would otherwise have done on account of a factor which he ought to have left out of consideration, the sentence will probably be reduced. Examples are when the judge says that he is increasing sentence because the offender pleaded not guilty and/or ran a defence in which imputations were cast on the conduct or veracity of the prosecution witnesses (*Skone* (1967) 51 Cr App R 165).

(d) *Wrong procedure prior to sentence.* Several cases were described in Chapter 20 where faulty procedures were adopted in the Crown Court between conviction and sentence to the potential detriment of the offender (e.g., *Newton* (1982) 77 Cr App R 13 where the judge accepted the prosecution version of the facts of the offence without hearing evidence, and *Wilkins* (1978) 66 Cr App R 49 where antecedents evidence prejudicial to the offender was tendered by an officer without first-hand knowledge of the matters about which he testified). The Court of Appeal will usually mark their disapproval of such irregularities by reducing the sentence. However, they sometimes say that the sentence itself was the correct one despite the procedural lapse, and therefore uphold it.

(e) *Disparity.* A marked difference in the treatment handed out to co-offenders, when that cannot be justified either by their differing degrees of involvement in the offence or the differing amounts of mitigation at their disposal, is sometimes put forward by the one more severely dealt with as a ground for reducing his sentence. The Court of Appeal's attitude to such arguments has been very inconsistent. One approach is to allow the appeal if the disparity is so marked that (even though the sentence received by the appellant was not wrong in principle or manifestly excessive) he would be left with a burning and understandable sense of grievance as he contemplated the more lenient penalty with which his equally culpable co-offender escaped (see *Dickinson* [1977] Crim LR 303). The alternative approach is to say that 'two wrongs do not make a right'. The fact that O1 was given too lenient a sentence is no justification for reducing the sentence of his accomplice, O2, assuming that O2's sentence would not otherwise be open to criticism. As it was put in *Stroud* (1977) 65 Cr App R 150: 'The appellant's proposition is that where you have one wrong sentence and one right sentence, this Court should produce two wrong sentences. That is a submission which this Court cannot accept.' According to *Stroud,* disparity should never be regarded as a good ground for appealing a sentence. However, there have certainly been cases since *Stroud* where it has seemed to be the major if not the only argument relied on by a successful appellant (see, for example, *Wood* (1983) 5 Cr App R (S) 381). Perhaps the true position is that disparity of sentence between co-offenders is a factor which the Court of Appeal ought to take into consideration when the more heavily sentenced offender appeals, but if the sentence was well within the accepted norms the appeal will probably fail. If, however, the sentence (even viewed in isolation) was on the severe side, the added consideration of disparity and the appearance of unfairness in the original treatment of the appellant will tip the scales in favour of reducing the sentence. It may also be easier to succeed on the ground of disparity when the co-offenders were sentenced by the same judge on the same occasion.

24.6 PROCEDURE FOR APPEALING

In outline, the standard procedure for appealing against conviction or sentence is as follows:

(a) Within 28 days of conviction or sentence, depending on which the appeal is against, the appellant serves on the Crown Court a notice of application for leave to appeal. The notice must be accompanied by grounds of appeal. If counsel has advised the appeal, he settles and signs the grounds. Otherwise, the appellant does the drafting himself. It is regarded as good practice, where counsel advises on appeal, that the advice should be sent to the solicitor within 14 days of conviction and that the solicitor should ensure that the lay client receives it within a further seven days. If the appellant was legally aided for the proceedings in the Crown Court, that legal aid covers advice on the merits of an appeal and, if so advised, the serving of notice and drafting of grounds of appeal. Having received the notice and grounds, the Crown Court forwards them to the Registrar of Criminal Appeals.

(b) Where the appeal is against conviction, the drafting of grounds of appeal nearly always falls into two stages. The grounds submitted with the notice of application for leave to appeal (the 'initial grounds') are based on counsel's longhand note of what happened at the Crown Court. Inevitably, the note will be incomplete and partially inaccurate. However, a shorthand writer takes a full note of Crown Court proceedings, and counsel asks the registrar to obtain a transcript of as much of the note as he (counsel) considers is needed for the proper presentation of the appeal. Unless the registrar thinks that counsel is making unjustified demands, he does as requested, and delivers a copy of the transcript to counsel. A transcript of the judge's summing-up is hardly ever refused. A transcript of at least part of the evidence may also be necessary, depending on the nature of the initial grounds. Having read the transcript, counsel may advise that the appeal be abandoned. This, of course, does not prevent the appellant continuing the appeal without legal assistance, but if he does so he runs the risk of a direction for loss of time (see Paragraph 24.6.6). On the other hand, if counsel continues to think that the appellant has a reasonably arguable case, he *perfects* his initial grounds of appeal — i.e., he amends them in the light of and with cross-references to the transcript. For what the perfected grounds should contain, see Paragraph 24.6.2.

(c) The papers in the case are put before a single judge. The papers will include the perfected grounds of appeal, the transcript and any other relevant documents (e.g. documentary exhibits adduced in evidence at the Crown Court, or a statement from a witness who has just come forward and whom the appellant wishes to call at the hearing of the appeal). In the light of these documents, the single judge decides whether to grant leave to appeal. If he does so, he might also *inter alia* grant the appellant an order for legal representation at the hearing, grant him bail pending determination of the appeal, or order that a potential witness attend for examination.

(d) The appellant is notified of the single judge's decision. If it is unfavourable, he has 14 days in which to notify the registrar that he wishes to renew the application before a court of the Criminal Division (see Paragraph 24.6.4). Assuming leave to appeal is granted (whether by the single judge or a court on a renewed application), the registrar and his staff check that the papers are all in order, prepare a summary of the case and fix a hearing date. The summary is read by the judges who are to hear the appeal, and is available to counsel in the case. It is a purely factual document, which does not contain any views on the merits of the case.

(e) At the hearing, counsel for the appellant presents argument. If the appeal is against conviction, the Crown will almost certainly be represented, and may be called upon in reply to the appellant's case. Occasionally witnesses are called by the appellant (e.g. an alibi witness whose identity could not have been known at the time of the trial on indictment), but usually the appeal will involve only consideration of the transcript and of counsel's arguments. At an appeal against sentence only, the Crown is unlikely to be represented, as it is not the prosecution's task, either at the Crown Court or on appeal, to argue for a high sentence.

There are two main variations on the above standard procedure. First, of course, the appellant may have received a certificate from the trial judge (see Paragraph 24.2.1). In that event, he gives notice of appeal (not notice of application for leave to appeal), and the registrar simply lists the case for full hearing by a court. The second possibility is that the registrar, looking at the grounds of appeal served on behalf of an appellant who does need leave, sees that the appeal prima facie has a good chance of success. The registrar might then bypass the single judge procedure through listing the application for leave to appeal for hearing by a court. He also grants the appellant legal aid, and asks the prosecution to arrange to be represented. The court can then grant leave to appeal and proceed forthwith to determine the appeal.

In the Paragraphs which follow, some of the matters touched upon in the above outline of appeal procedure are explained in more detail. The reader may also wish to refer to a booklet issued by the registrar in 1983 (and updated in 1997) which has the approval of the Lord Chief Justice and which is entitled 'A Guide to Proceedings in the Court of Appeal Criminal Division'.

24.6.1 Notice of application for leave to appeal

The appellant's notice of application for leave to appeal must be given on a standard form provided by the Criminal Appeal Office: CAR, r 2. An example of a notice is printed at page 440. As will be seen, it contains the essential details about the appeal, including the name of the appellant, his address or, if he is in custody, the address of the prison etc. where he is detained, the name of the court at which and the judge before whom he was tried, the offences of which he was convicted and the sentences for those offences, and whether he is appealing against conviction or sentence or both. The form may also be used to inform the court that the appellant is applying for legal aid, or for bail pending the hearing of the appeal, or for leave to be present at or call witnesses at the hearing. The form must be signed by the appellant or by solicitors on his behalf. If the appellant does not need leave to appeal, he simply gives notice of appeal. Where an appellant who does not need leave gives notice of application for leave, it is treated as a notice of appeal, and vice versa.

The notice should be served within 28 days of conviction or sentence (whichever is appealed against): CAA, s 18. Notice and grounds are sent to the location of the Crown Court where the appellant's case was heard. An officer of the Crown Court will then forward the document to the Court of Appeal. The Court has a discretion to give the appellant leave to apply for leave to appeal out of time, but there must be good reasons for the failure to serve the notice within the statutory period.

> The fact that the appellant absconded before the conclusion of his trial on indictment and was not recaptured until more than 28 days had elapsed from the date the jury convicted him in his absence, is not a sufficient reason for extending time for appealing, even though the appellant had indicated before his disappearance that if convicted he wanted to appeal: *Jones (No 2)* [1972] 1 WLR 887. Even if a decision of the Court of Appeal made in another case soon after the appellant's time for giving notice expired indicates that there was an error of law in the conduct of the appellant's trial, the court need not necessarily grant him leave to appeal against conviction out of time: *Ramsden* [1972] Crim LR 547. However, in *Mitchell* [1977] 1 WLR 753 the Court's discretion was exercised in M's favour because he had, within time, appealed against sentence, and not to have granted him leave to appeal against conviction would have placed their Lordships in the position of determining an appeal against sentence, knowing that, in the light of their decision in a case subsequent to his trial, M's conviction ought to be quashed.
>
> The fairly strict enforcement of the 28-day limit for giving notice ought not to lead to injustice. If the appellant is legally represented at the Crown Court, counsel or a representative of the solicitors will normally see him after the verdict and sentence, and advise informally on whether there are grounds for appeal. Most defendants at the Crown Court are legally aided, and that legal aid covers a written advice from counsel on the merits of an appeal and, if so advised, the drafting of grounds of appeal. Having received the grounds from counsel the solicitors obtain a notice form from the Criminal Appeal Office or the Crown Court, complete it on behalf of the appellant, and serve it, together with the grounds, on the Crown Court. If the appellant is unrepresented, or his representatives advise against an appeal, he may complete the forms himself. If he is in custody, the forms are available at the prison etc. where he is detained.

24.6.2 Grounds of appeal

In preparing his grounds of appeal, which should accompany the notice, the appellant must again make use of a standard form from the Criminal Appeal Office. The grounds form asks for many of the details already included in the notice form. In addition, at the bottom of the form, is a space in which the appellant may write out his grounds. However, if counsel settles and signs the grounds they are typed on a separate sheet, which is served together with the notice and grounds forms. As already explained, the grounds as initially settled may not be fit to go before the single judge. Once perfected, they should enable the single judge or court to identify the particular matters put forward by the appellant for their consideration (see para 2.2 of the registrar's Guide). It is not enough to state in general terms that 'the conviction is unsafe or unsatisfactory' or 'the sentence was too severe in all the circumstances of the case' without giving reasons for those assertions. No particular formality is required in the phrasing of the grounds, provided the point or points the appellant wishes to raise are made clear. A convenient method of drafting is to deal with the errors of which complaint is made in chronological order — e.g., ground one might deal with the trial judge failing to sever the indictment, ground two with his failing to uphold a submission of no case to answer, ground three with his wrongly allowing the appellant to be cross-examined about his previous convictions, and ground four with various misdirections in the summing-up. The grounds should refer by page number and letter to relevant passages in the transcript, and should cite authorities on which counsel intends to rely (para 4.4 of the Guide). Where the appellant wishes to call a witness at the hearing of the appeal, the reasons for doing so should be fully developed. If counsel settles grounds, he should only include those which are reasonable, have some real prospect of success and are such that he is prepared to argue them before the court (see para 2.4 of the registrar's Guide). If no such grounds exist, the appellant must be left to pursue his appeal in person if he so wishes. An example of grounds of appeal appears on pages 442–43.

> Sometimes counsel later supplements his grounds with a skeleton argument which their Lordships can read prior to the hearing of the appeal. In complicated cases, this may save some time which would otherwise be wasted in orally laying the groundwork of the appellant's argument. Skeleton arguments are not covered by the Criminal Appeal Rules, but the registrar's Guide states that 'in appropriate conviction appeals counsel should submit a typed note tabulating the propositions on which it is sought to rely' (para 10.7).
>
> A *Practice Note* [1999] 1 All ER 669 lays down the requirements for skeleton arguments in appeals against conviction. The advocate for the appellant must lodge a skeleton argument with the registrar, and serve it on the prosecuting authority, within 14 days of receipt by the advocate of leave to appeal against conviction (unless a longer period is directed). The prosecutor should lodge a skeleton argument within 14 days of receipt of the appellant's skeleton (unless directed otherwise).

24.6.3 Transcripts

A shorthand writer takes a note of any proceedings in the Crown Court upon which an appeal may lie to the Court of Appeal. The registrar and any 'interested party' has a right to be supplied with a transcript of the note, but only upon payment of a fixed charge: CAR, r 19. The cost of a transcript would inhibit most appellants from obtaining one, but the registrar has a discretion to order a transcript and supply a copy free of charge to any legally aided appellant. Virtually all appellants are legally aided, so, essentially, the supplying of transcripts depends on the registrar's discretion. In his initial grounds of appeal, counsel specifies those parts of the transcript which he needs providing names of witnesses, dates and times where necessary (para 3.2 of the Guide). If it is an appeal against conviction, he will almost certainly ask for and be given a transcript of the summing-up. It is also reasonable to have a transcript of any evidence said to be inadmissible. However, counsel should not request a transcript of *all* the evidence unless that really is essential to the determination of the appeal, since obtaining it will be both time-consuming and expensive (see *Flemming* (1987) 86 Cr App R 32 at p. 39, where Woolf LJ criticised counsel for ordering six bundles of transcript and then only referring to two at the hearing of the appeal). For an appeal against sentence, a transcript of the antecedents evidence, counsel's mitigation and any remarks the judge made when passing sentence may be of value. If the appellant pleaded guilty, the prosecution's summary of the facts could also be included. The registrar may decline to order some or all of the transcript which counsel requests. If dissatisfied with the registrar's decision, counsel may have the question referred to a single judge.

24.6.4 Applications to a single judge: Criminal Appeal Act 1968, s 31

The following ancillary powers of the Court of Appeal may be, and most frequently are, exercised by a single judge (i.e., a Lord Justice of Appeal or a High Court judge whom the Lord Chief Justice has asked to assist in the work of the Criminal Division):

    (a)   granting leave to appeal;

    (b)   granting leave to commence an appeal or to apply for leave to appeal out of time;

    (c)   allowing an appellant to be present at proceedings connected with his appeal when he is in custody and has no right to attend;

    (d)   ordering a witness, whose evidence the appellant wishes to adduce before the court, to attend for examination;

    (e)   granting bail to the appellant;

    (f)   granting an order for legal representation; and

    (g)   making a direction for loss of time.

Most of these powers have already been referred to; those which have not are described in the succeeding Paragraphs. By far the most significant of the single judge's powers is that of granting leave to appeal. As already explained, he normally considers the application privately, without counsel attending. His decision is based upon a reading of the papers in the case, in particular the transcript and counsel's grounds of appeal. This is one reason why the grounds should clearly identify the nature of the appellant's complaint(s) and should quote authority. If he gives leave to appeal, the single judge will also (when appropriate) consider the granting of bail and/or legal aid and the ordering of witnesses to attend for examination. He might also make observations to be brought to counsel's attention (e.g., as to a possible extra ground of appeal), or give administrative directions (e.g., to order extra transcript, or to obtain up-to-date reports on an appellant against sentence, or to expedite the appeal so as to avoid the risk of the appellant having served the whole of a short custodial sentence before his case is heard). If he refuses leave, the judge may also consider a direction for loss of time (see Paragraph 24.6.6).

Notification of the single judge's decision is given to the appellant. If the application is refused (whether it be an application for leave to appeal or an application for any other of the single judge's powers to be exercised in his favour), the appellant has a right to renew the application before a court: CAA, s 31(3). He must, however, serve the appropriate notice on the registrar within 14 days of being told of the single judge's adverse decision: CAR, r 12. Although there is power to extend the period for giving notice, this is only done if the appellant had good reason for not acting within time — if he merely changed his mind after the 14-day period had elapsed, he will not be able to have the matter determined by a court: *Sullivan* (1972) 56 Cr App R 541. To assist the appellant in deciding whether to renew the application, brief written reasons why he rejected it may be given by the single judge. Even on a renewed application for leave to appeal, the parties are unlikely to present argument — the prosecution have no need to at such a preliminary stage of the proceedings, and the appellant will be deterred from having representation for the purpose by the fact that the costs thereof will not normally be covered by legal aid. The court will, however, announce its decision in open court with reasons given.

Although the standard procedure is to make an ancillary application first to the single judge and then, perhaps, to a court if the single judge proves adverse, there is nothing to stop the application being made direct to a court. Sometimes this may expedite the proceedings, as when the registrar spots that an appellant needing leave to appeal has a strong prima facie case and so refers the application for leave straight to a court, with a view to their granting it and then going on to consider the appeal on its merits forthwith. For the purposes both of applications initially made to a court and of applications renewed before a court after being turned down by the single judge, the court need only consist of two judges. The one exception to this is that a two-judge court cannot refuse (although it can grant) an application for leave to appeal against conviction made to it without prior unsuccessful application to a single judge.

24.6.5   Applications to the Registrar

The Registrar of the Court of Appeal is given certain powers by s 31A(2) of the CAA 1968:

   (a) to extend the time within which notice of appeal or application for leave to appeal may be given;
   (b) to order a witness to attend for examination; and
   (c) to vary an appellant's conditions of bail.

As far as (c) is concerned, the registrar may vary conditions only if the respondent does not object. In relation to any of the powers, if the registrar refuses an application by the appellant, the appellant is entitled to have it determined by the single judge.

24.6.6   Directions concerning loss of time: Criminal Appeal Act 1968, s 29

Unless a direction to the contrary is given, the time that the appellant spends in custody between commencing his appeal and its being determined counts as part of any custodial sentence which he is serving, whether the sentence was imposed in the Crown Court proceedings which are the subject of the appeal or on some previous occasion. A direction to the contrary (i.e. a direction for loss of time) may be given by the single judge on refusing an application for leave to appeal, or by the court on an unsuccessful renewal of an application for leave to appeal, or by the court when dismissing an appeal on a ground of pure law. Directions for loss of time are a means of penalising an appellant for commencing a meritless appeal which wastes the time of the court.

It should be stressed that the Court of Appeal has no power to increase an appellant's sentence, in the strict sense.

In *Practice Direction (Crime: Sentence: Loss of Time)* [1980] 1 WLR 270, the Lord Chief Justice indicated when directions are likely to be made. Where counsel has settled and signed the grounds of appeal and supported them with a written opinion, the single judge will not order loss of time because it would be unfair to blame an appellant for pursuing an appeal advised by his legal representatives. If, however, counsel has not advised an appeal, and the single judge refuses the application for leave to appeal, he will give 'especial consideration' to making a direction, and 'it may be expected that such a direction will normally be made'. Similarly, when an application for leave is unsuccessfully renewed before the court, a direction will probably be made. At that stage, the appellant is not even protected by counsel having settled the grounds of appeal and advised the further application to the court, a point reiterated by Kennedy J when giving the court's judgment in *Gayle* (1986) *The Times,* 28 May 1986.

A direction for loss of time may relate to part only of the time the appellant has been in custody since commencing his appeal. Thus, in a case where grounds have not been settled by counsel, the single judge could order that the appellant lose, say, a month's time, and, if he were unwise enough to renew the application, the court could order that he lose a further two months.

Whether the Court of Appeal should have power to make directions for loss of time is an arguable point. Certainly, the knowledge that his custodial sentence might, in effect, be increased if he is thought to be wasting the court's time, will discourage a frivolous appeal. Time-wasting applications for leave to appeal need to be discouraged because they delay the consideration of applications which have merit. The counter-argument is that fear of a direction for loss of time might discourage not only the worthless but some worthwhile appeals. It may also seem unfair that those who have not received custodial sentences may appeal with impunity, whereas those who are serving custodial sentences and, prima facie, have more urgent reasons for appealing, are liable to possible sanctions if they do so.

In practice, directions for loss of time have thus far been very rare. In written evidence to the Royal Commission on Criminal Justice, the Lord Chancellor's Department stated that, in the period October 1990 to July 1991, only five time-loss orders were made, each for 28 days. When an order is made, in practice the maximum period ordered to be lost is 28 days (Report of the Royal Commission on Criminal Justice (London: HMSO, 1993), p. 165).

24.6.7 Bail pending hearing of the appeal: Criminal Appeal Act 1968, s 19

The Court of Appeal's power to grant bail to an appellant, pending determination of his appeal, is exercisable by a single judge. The procedure is to indicate on the notice of application for leave to appeal form that the appellant is also applying for bail. In addition, a form giving details of the application must be served on the registrar. Bail is rarely granted as, in the event of the appeal failing, the appellant will suffer the trauma of being returned to prison. The question is — 'Are there exceptional circumstances which would drive the court to the conclusion that justice can only be done by the granting of bail?': *Watton* (1979) 68 Cr App R 293. The fact that the single judge has granted leave to appeal against conviction does not in itself justify bail, but the appellant might be bailed where either the appeal seems likely to succeed, or he is serving a short custodial sentence which, in the absence of bail, is likely to be completed before the appeal is heard. The seriousness of the offence and the likelihood or otherwise of a retrial being ordered will no doubt also enter into consideration in deciding on bail.

At one time only the Court of Appeal had jurisdiction to grant bail to a person appealing to it. However, amendments made to s 81 of the Supreme Court Act 1981 by the Criminal Justice Act 1982 have given a concurrent, though more limited, jurisdiction to Crown Court judges. If, and only if, he has certified that the case is fit for appeal, the appropriate Crown Court judge may bail an appellant pending determination of the appeal. If the appeal is against conviction or against sentence following conviction on indictment, the appropriate judge is the judge at the trial on indictment; if the appeal is against sentence following a committal for sentence, the appropriate judge is the judge who passed sentence. The power to grant bail must be exercised within 28 days of conviction or sentence depending on what the appeal is against, and the power is lost if the appellant chooses to apply for bail to the Court of Appeal itself. The Court of Appeal can always revoke bail granted by the Crown

Court judge or vary the conditions on which he granted it. If bail is granted before the 'appellant' has served a notice of appeal or a notice of application for leave to appeal, the serving of notice is made a condition of bail.

> The Court of Appeal has indicated that the power should be used sparingly. In *Grant* (1990) 12 Cr App R (S) 441, their lordships stated that, if the sentencer is persuaded that he has made the wrong decision, he should use his own powers to vary sentence within 28 days (Supreme Court Act 1981, s 47(2) — see Paragraph 20.6), or allow the case to take the normal route through the appeal system. The powers to certify as fit for appeal and to grant bail should be reserved for cases where there is a 'particular and cogent ground of appeal'.
>
> A relevant factor in connection with both directions for loss of time and bail pending determination of the appeal is the period which may be expected to elapse between giving notice of application for leave to appeal and the appeal being determined. Unfortunately, the length of that period varies so much depending on the nature and complexity of the case that it is difficult to indicate how long it is likely to be. The time between giving notice and the single judge granting leave to appeal is measured in months rather than weeks, but will turn upon (e.g.) how much transcript is required and whether the grounds of appeal have to be returned to counsel to be perfected. From obtaining leave to having the appeal heard might take several months, but in difficult cases, requiring extra preparation, the delay will be longer. In the cases of young appellants and those serving short custodial sentences every effort is made to expedite the appeal.

24.6.8   Presence at the appeal: Criminal Appeal Act 1968, s 22

An appellant need not be present at the hearing of his appeal but, subject to what is mentioned below, he is entitled to attend if he so wishes. This applies both to the actual determination of the appeal and to ancillary applications. However, by way of exception to the general rule, an appellant who is in custody requires leave from a single judge if he is to attend either ancillary applications or, if the appeal is on a ground of law alone, the hearing proper. Also, whether he is in custody or not, an appellant obviously cannot attend when the single judge decides an incidental application through a private reading of the papers in the case, since there is then no hearing to be present at.

24.6.9   Evidence called before the Court of Appeal: Criminal Appeal Act 1968, s 23

The Court of Appeal has a discretionary power to receive evidence under s 23 of the Criminal Appeals Act 1968. This power is unfettered, but the factors which the Court ought to take into account are those listed in s 23(2), which states that their lordships should, in considering whether to receive any evidence, have regard in particular to whether:

(a)   it appears credible;
(b)   it appears that it may afford any ground for allowing the appeal;
(c)   it would have been admissible at trial; and
(d)   there is a reasonable explanation for the failure to adduce the evidence at trial.

It is clear that points (a) to (d) are not conditions which must be satisfied before the evidence can be heard. They are factors for the Court of Appeal to take into account in exercising its discretion.

To decide whether proposed evidence is likely to be credible (see point (a) above) the judges in the Court of Appeal consider the testimony it is anticipated the witness will give in the context of the case as a whole: *Parks* [1961] 1 WLR 1484. Relevant factors are whether the witness' proof of evidence is intrinsically credible, and whether it fits in with at least some of the other evidence in the case. As to factor (d) any explanation for not adducing the evidence at the Crown Court is closely examined by the court. The general principle is that all the relevant evidence should be put before the jury so that they can make a once and for all decision on the issues of fact. As Edmund Davies LJ expressed it in *Stafford and Luvaglio* (1969) 53 Cr App R 1 at p. 3:

> public mischief would ensue and legal process could become indefinitely prolonged were it the case that evidence produced at any time will generally be admitted when verdicts are being reviewed.

In a sample of 102 appeals which were successful in 1992, only four were allowed on the grounds of fresh evidence (Research Study No 17 for the Royal Commission on Criminal Justice by Kate Malleson (London: HMSO, 1993)). The reason often given is that explained above — the jury, not the Court of Appeal, are the tribunal of fact, and all the relevant evidence should be put before them. Where, however, the evidence the appellant wishes to adduce appears exceptionally cogent the court will, in the interests of justice to the individual, hear it. Such a case was *Lattimore* (1976) 62 Cr App R 53. L and his two co-accused were convicted of the murder of C. The prosecution case rested largely upon confessions to the police in which the defendants admitted strangling C, leaving his body in his house, and setting fire to the house so as to destroy the evidence of the murder. According to the confessions, the arson of the house took place immediately after the murder. The Court of Appeal received medical and scientific evidence which showed that at least three hours had elapsed between the two crimes. That in turn showed that the confessions were unreliable since the true murderer must have known that the arson did not follow straight after the murder, and, having decided to confess, he would have had no reason to tell lies on the point. The doubt cast upon the confessions rendered the convictions unsafe, and they were accordingly quashed. All the evidence heard by the Court of Appeal could have been adduced by the defence at the trial on indictment. Indeed, some of the witnesses before the Court of Appeal also testified at the trial, but the significance of the evidence they could give was not at that time appreciated. Because their evidence was so vital to the appellants' case, it was received by their lordships under s 23.

Having heard evidence, the members of the court ask themselves whether in the light of that evidence and all the circumstances of the case the conviction is unsafe. In *Pendleton* [2002] Crim LR 398, the House of Lords considered the approach which the Court of Appeal ought to adopt in determining the safety of the conviction where they had decided to admit fresh evidence. Lord Bingham said it was important that 'the Court of Appeal bears very clearly in mind that the question for its consideration is whether the conviction is safe and not whether the accused is guilty'. He stated:

> . . . it will usually be wise for the Court of Appeal, in a case of any difficulty, to test their own provisional view by asking whether the evidence, if given at the trial, might reasonably have affected the decision of the trial jury to convict. If it might, the conviction must be thought to be unsafe.

Should they allow the appeal, their lordships will have to consider whether or not to order a re-trial. Past practice[1] suggests that they would certainly not so order if the fresh evidence

---

[1] Fresh evidence cases were the one type of appeal in which, even prior to the amendments made to the CAA by the Criminal Justice Act 1988, the Court could order a retrial.

points very strongly to the appellant being innocent, and they will in any event bear in mind the period of time that will have elapsed from the date of the alleged offence to the date when the retrial is likely to commence. The longer that period, the less probable it is that they would order a retrial.

What if the fresh evidence which the appellant wants considered promotes a line of defence not raised at trial? That was the position in *Ahluwahlia* [1992] 4 All ER 889. A killed her husband 'after enduring many years of violence and humiliation' from him, by throwing petrol into his bedroom and setting it alight. She was tried for murder. Her case was that she did not intend to kill him or cause him really serious harm. Provocation was her secondary line of defence. The jury rejected both lines of defence and convicted her of murder. She appealed on three grounds. The first two related to the trial judge's directions on provocation and were dismissed. The third ground was that she relied on evidence of diminished responsibility, which had not been raised as a defence at trial. A number of psychiatric reports were put before the Court of Appeal, expressing the opinion that A's responsibility was diminished at the time that she killed her husband. Their lordships decided to admit the reports as fresh evidence. They concluded that there may well have been an arguable defence which was not put forward at trial, for reasons which were unexplained. They upheld the appeal on the basis that the verdict was 'unsafe and unsatisfactory', and ordered a retrial.

An appellant who wishes to adduce evidence before the court should indicate on his notice of application for leave to appeal form that he is also asking for leave to call a witness. A form should be served on the registrar giving details of the application. If the appellant fears that the witness will not attend voluntarily to testify, and he would have been a compellable (not merely a competent) witness at the trial on indictment, the single judge may order him to attend for the hearing of the appeal. Although the single judge can order a witness to attend, only the court itself can give the appellant leave to call him. Counsel for the appellant, at the hearing of the appeal, must therefore seek to persuade the court either that they are under a duty to receive the witness' evidence or that they should, in their discretion, receive it. The court will be aware of the nature of the proposed evidence because the appellant's solicitors should have sent to the registrar either an affidavit sworn by the witness or a statement from him complying with s 9 of the Criminal Justice Act 1967 (see Paragraph 18.3.4). If a witness is unwilling to cooperate in making an affidavit or statement, or if it is desirable for any other reason, a single judge can order him to attend court prior to the hearing of the appeal so that an officer appointed by the Court of Appeal can take a deposition from him: CAR, r 9.

Where the court does decide to receive the evidence, and the witness would have been compellable at the trial on indictment, he may be called by the court, rather than by one of the parties, examined in chief by a member of the court, and then tendered to both parties for cross-examination. If the court does not call the witness but gives leave for one of the parties to call him, the normal procedure for examining witnesses applies — the party calling him examines him in chief, the other party cross-examines and the court may ask any questions it thinks fit. Normally it will be the appellant who wishes the court to receive evidence, but the prosecution may seek to call a witness to rebut the evidence the court has heard on behalf of the appellant.

When determining appeals against sentence, the Court of Appeal often has the benefit of pre-sentence, medical, psychiatric and other reports. Up to date reports of the progress the appellant is making in the prison or young offender institution are also of value. When an appeal against conviction involves an allegation of an irregularity in the course of the trial, such as the judge constantly interrupting the defence or bringing improper pressure to bear on the accused to persuade him to plead guilty, the court may accept informal 'evidence' of what occurred in the shape of statements by counsel or a note from the judge.

24.6.10 Publicly-funded representation and costs

A person wishing to appeal to the Court of Appeal (Criminal Division) may be granted an order for legal representation for that purpose. The order may only be made by the Criminal

Division itself, not by the Crown Court: Criminal Defence Service (General) (No 2) Regulations 2001 (SI 2001 No 1437), reg 10. The Division may exercise its powers through a single judge or through the registrar. For the initial stages of the appeal procedure, an appellant who had a representation order for the Crown Court proceedings will not need to have any further order made in his favour, since the Crown Court order will cover advice on the merits of an appeal and — if so advised — the service of notice and drafting of grounds of appeal. Assuming the single judge grants leave to appeal, he will almost certainly make an order to cover representation at the hearing. Unless a lot of paperwork still needs to be done, the order will be 'for counsel only', rather than for 'counsel and solicitor'. In the former case, counsel is assigned by the registrar. Save that the registrar then provides him with a brief and the papers, he does not act as counsel's solicitor. Where leave to appeal is refused, the Crown Court order will pay for advice on whether it is worth renewing the application before a court, but will not pay for representation at the renewed hearing (see *Gibson* [1983] 1 WLR 1038 and *Kearney* [1983] 1 WLR 1046). If the appellant was not publicly funded in the Crown Court, he may apply to the registrar for the grant of an order which will at least cover initial advice on and preparation for appeal.

A successful appellant against conviction may be awarded his costs out of central (i.e., government) funds: Prosecution of Offences Act 1985, s 16(4). This is known as a 'defendant's costs order' (see Chapter 27 for general consideration of costs). Costs awarded under s 16(4) may include costs incurred in the Crown Court proceedings. The prosecution cannot recover costs out of central funds unless it is a private prosecution, in which case an order may be made in their favour regardless of the outcome of the appeal: POA 1985, s 17(1) and (2). If the appeal fails, the appellant may be ordered to pay to the prosecution (or any other person named by the Court of Appeal, such as the provider of the transcript of the Crown Court proceedings) whatever costs the Court considers 'just and reasonable': POA 1985, s 18(2).

24.7 OTHER WAYS IN WHICH MATTERS COME BEFORE THE COURT OF APPEAL

The main function of the Court of Appeal (Criminal Division) is to quash convictions or reduce sentences upon an appeal brought by the defendant in Crown Court proceedings. Until recently that was virtually its only function, and the prosecution had no right of redress if it considered that the accused had been wrongly acquitted or sentenced too leniently. It is still true that an accused acquitted on indictment can never have the verdict in his favour overturned. There is, however, a procedure by which the prosecution can test the correctness of a ruling on law given by the Crown Court judge during the course of the trial which culminated in an acquittal, although the accused himself remains acquitted come what may. That procedure was introduced in 1972. More recently, the Criminal Justice Act 1988 has empowered the Court of Appeal actually to increase an offender's sentence. In both types of case, the matter has to be referred to the Court by the Attorney-General.

Paragraphs 24.7.1 and 24.7.2 deal with Attorney-General's references on points of law and sentencing respectively. Paragraph 24.7.3 deals with appeals against a verdict of 'not guilty by reason of insanity'.

24.7.1 Reference by the Attorney-General: Criminal Justice Act 1972, s 36

Until 1972, no procedure existed for testing the correctness of a decision or statement of law made by a judge during the course of a trial on indictment which ended in the acquittal of the accused. This was because the prosecution could not, and still cannot, appeal against an acquittal on indictment. The absence of any method of appeal left open the possibility that a ruling by a Crown Court judge which was unduly favourable to the accused might be reported, and become accepted as representing the law, when it was, in fact, mistaken. To avoid this happening, s 36 of the Criminal Justice Act 1972 provides that where a person has been tried on indictment and acquitted (whether on the whole indictment or some counts only), the Attorney-General may refer to the Court of Appeal for their opinion any point of law which arose in the case. Before giving their opinion on the point referred, the Court must hear argument by or on behalf of the Attorney-General. The person acquitted also has the right to have counsel present argument on his behalf. However, despite his right to be represented at the hearing, the person acquitted is not put in peril by the proceedings. Whatever the opinion expressed by the Court of Appeal — even if they decide that the trial judge was wrong and the facts of the case were such that the accused clearly ought to have been convicted — the acquittal is unaffected: s 36(7). By making a reference, the Attorney-General may obtain a ruling which will assist the prosecution in future cases against other suspects, but he cannot set aside the acquittal of the particular accused whose case gave rise to the reference. In this respect, Attorney's references under the CJA 1972 differ from references under ss 35 and 36 of the CJA 1988 which may result in an offender's sentence actually being increased (see the next Paragraph).

In *Attorney-General's Reference (No 1 of 1975)* [1975] QB 733, Lord Widgery CJ stated that references by the Attorney-General should not be confined to cases where 'very heavy questions of law arise', but should also be made when 'short but important points require a quick ruling of [the Court of Appeal] before a potentially false decision of law has too wide a circulation in the courts'. The usefulness of Attorney-General's references is illustrated by *Attorney-General's References (Nos 1 and 2 of 1979)* [1979] 3 All ER 143, where 'burglars' surprised when committing the offence, had been acquitted following rulings that, although there was evidence of entering a building with intent to steal anything of value which might be found therein, s 9(1)(a) of the Theft Act 1968 required an intent to steal a specific item within the building entered, and the prosecution were unable to prove such an intent. The rulings could be interpreted as a 'burglar's charter', but the Attorney-General was able to refer the point of law to the Court of Appeal which quickly clarified the position — on a charge of burglary with intent to steal, the accused is guilty even if he intended to steal only if he found something in the building worth stealing. Had the Attorney-General not made the reference, the mistaken view of the law expressed by the Crown Court judges might have taken hold, with amending legislation the only way of remedying the situation.

24.7.2 Sentencing references: Criminal Justice Act 1988, ss 35 and 36

These are dealt with in ss 35–36 of the Criminal Justice Act 1988. Where an offender has been sentenced in the Crown Court for either (i) an offence triable only on indictment, or (ii) an offence triable either way which is amongst those specified in an order made by the Home Secretary by statutory instrument, and the Attorney-General considers that the offender was dealt with unduly leniently, he may refer the sentence to the Court of Appeal for them to review: s 36(1). On such a review, their Lordships may quash the sentence and replace it with the sentence they consider appropriate. The substituted sentence may be *more severe* than that imposed at first instance, although it must, of course, be one that the Crown Court could lawfully have passed. The bringing of the reference is subject to the Court of Appeal granting leave (contrast the Attorney's references on points of law arising in a trial that ended in acquittal which lie without leave).

In 1994, the power to refer indictable-only offences was supplemented by the Criminal Justice Act 1988 (Reviews of Sentencing) Order 1994 (SI 1994 No 119) which extended that power to the following triable-either-way offences: indecent assault on a woman or a man, threats to kill, cruelty to a person under 16, attempt or incitement to commit any of these offences. It was further extended in 2000 to cover serious fraud cases (i.e. those tried under the notice of transfer provisions in the Criminal Justice Act 1987) and certain smuggling and drug offences. Where an offender has been sentenced in the same proceedings for one offence in respect of which a reference is permissible and for a second in respect of which a reference could not otherwise be made, the Attorney-General may refer the sentencing for both matters to the Court of Appeal, which may consequently increase the sentence for both.

In *Attorney-General's Reference (No 4 of 1989)* [1990] 1 WLR 41 at pp. 45–6, the Court of Appeal set out their approach in these terms:

> The first thing to be observed is that it is implicit in the section that this court may only increase sentences which it concludes were *unduly* lenient. It cannot, we are confident, have been the intention of Parliament to subject defendants to the risk of having their sentences increased — with all the anxiety that this naturally gives rise to — merely because in the opinion of this court the sentence was less than this court would have imposed. A sentence is unduly lenient, we would hold, where it falls outside the range of sentences which the judge, applying his mind to all the relevant factors, could reasonably consider appropriate. In that connection regard must of course be had to reported cases, and in particular to the guidance given by this court from time to time in the so-called guideline cases. However it must always be remembered that sentencing is an art rather than a science; that the trial judge is particularly well placed to assess the weight to be given to various competing considerations; and that leniency is not in itself a vice. That mercy should season justice is a proposition as soundly based in law as it is in literature.
>
> The second thing to be observed about the section is that, even where it considers that the sentence was unduly lenient, this court has a discretion as to whether to exercise its powers. Without attempting an exhaustive definition of the circumstances in which this court might refuse to increase an unduly lenient sentence, we mention one obvious instance; where in the light of events since the trial it appears either that the sentence can be justified or that to increase it would be unfair to the offender or detrimental to others for whose well-being the court ought to be concerned.
>
> Finally, we point to the fact that, where this court grants leave for a reference, its powers are not confined to increasing the sentence.

In the case under consideration, their lordships quashed a suspended sentence, and replaced it with a three-year probation order. Hence, a sentence referred on the basis that it was too lenient can be replaced (albeit exceptionally) with one which is more lenient.

More generally, the Court of Appeal has said that it will not intervene unless there was some error of principle in the Crown Court sentence, so that public confidence would be damaged if the sentence were not altered (*Attorney-General's Reference (No 5 of 1989)* (1990) 90 Cr App R 358).

The Court of Appeal has also made it plain that, in suitable circumstances, the increased sentence which it has to pass will be mitigated by the fact that the offender has had to face the prospect of being sentenced twice over. Thus, in *Attorney-General's Reference (No 1 of 1991)* [1991] Crim LR 725, the trial judge had imposed a sentence of five years. In the view of the Court of Appeal, a minimum of eight years would have been appropriate. As the offender had the added anxiety of waiting for the outcome of the reference, some allowance would be made, and a sentence of seven years substituted.

In answer to a question in the House of Commons (17 March 1997), the Attorney-General stated that, during 1996, 70 sentences were referred to the Court of Appeal on grounds of undue leniency; 62 had been heard, and an increased sentence resulted in 46 of them (74 per cent).

24.7.3 Appeal against verdict of 'Not guilty by reason of insanity': Criminal Appeal Act 1968, ss 12–14

A person who is found not guilty by reason of insanity may appeal to the Court of Appeal against the verdict. The provisions as to leave to appeal and determination of the appeal parallel those which apply to appeals against conviction. If the appeal is allowed on a ground relating to the finding that the appellant was insane, the Court of Appeal may substitute a verdict of guilty of the offence charged (or guilty of a lesser offence) for the verdict of the jury. The appellant may then be sentenced for the offence. If the appeal is allowed on other grounds (i.e. even in the absence of a finding of insanity, a conviction could not have been sustained), the Court of Appeal replaces the jury's verdict with a straightforward acquittal. It may, however, order that the appellant be admitted to a mental hospital specified by the Home Secretary.

A person who has been found unfit to plead may appeal against the finding: s 15. If the issue of fitness to plead was determined after arraignment, and the Court of Appeal thinks that before it was determined the appellant should have been acquitted, the court may quash the finding of unfitness and substitute a verdict of acquittal. In other cases where the appeal is allowed, the court makes such orders as are necessary to secure the appellant's attendance at the Crown Court to be tried.

An appellant against conviction may argue that he should have been found unfit to plead or not guilty by reason of insanity instead of being convicted.

The Court of Appeal decides whether it agrees with him, on the basis of two registered medical practitioners, at least one of whom is approved by the Secretary of State was having special experience in the diagnosis or treatment of mental disorder. If it does agree, then it must make one of the orders which the Crown Court could have made in such circumstances, i.e.:

(a) admission to a mental hospital with a restriction order (this is the only available order in a case of murder),
(b) a guardianship order under the Mental Health Act 1983,
(c) a supervision and treatment order under Sch 2 to the Criminal Procedure (Insanity and Unfitness to Plead) Act 1991,
(d) an absolute discharge.

24.8 THE CRIMINAL CASES REVIEW COMMISSION

In response to the recommendation of the Royal Commission on Criminal Justice in 1993 that a new body was needed to investigate and process allegations of miscarriages of justice, the Criminal Appeal Act 1995 set up the Criminal Cases Review Commission. It began to receive cases in April 1997, and early indications were that its workload would be substantial. By August 1998, it had taken on a total of 2,763 cases. Of those, 1,124 had been reviewed, 445 were still under review, and 1,194 were awaiting review. There was major concern about the increasing backlog of applications which had been declared eligible for review, but where the review had not taken place. Unless the Commission receives the increase in staffing which it has repeatedly requested, waiting time for a review is likely to be between three and four years.

The Commission took over the functions of the Home Secretary to refer cases to the Court of Appeal. Its remit is actually wider than that which the Home Secretary formerly possessed, since it covers not only convictions after trial on indictment, but referrals in respect of sentence, and it has power to deal with cases decided in the magistrates' courts as well as in the Crown Court.

Matters may be referred to the Commission by the Court of Appeal, which may direct it to investigate a particular matter in such manner as it thinks fit. The Commission must report to the Court of Appeal once it has investigated. In addition, the Secretary of State may seek assistance in relation to the prerogative of mercy.

Primarily, however, the machinery is intended to operate in such a way that the Commission refers cases to the Court of Appeal. The test which it must apply in deciding whether to do so is laid down by s 13 of the CAA 1995. It should not refer a case unless it considers that there is a real possibility that the conviction, verdict, finding or sentence would not be upheld were the reference to be made. In the case of a conviction, the 'real possibility' must be judged, save in exceptional circumstances, on the strength of an argument or evidence not raised at trial or on appeal or on an application for leave to appeal. In the case of a sentence, the Commission must be able to identify a legal argument, or information, which was not raised at trial or in the course of an appeal. Any decision to refer a case to the Court of Appeal can only be made by a committee of at least three of the 14 Commissioners.

Once the Commission decides to refer a case which was dealt with in the Crown Court, it is treated as an appeal for the purposes of the CAA 1968. Similarly, if the case was originally dealt with in the magistrates' court, following a referral by the Commission it will be dealt with by the Crown Court. Once the case has been referred, the appeal may be on any ground relating to the conviction or sentence, whether or not the ground is related to the reason given by the Commission for making the reference.

24.9 THE SENTENCING ADVISORY PANEL

This Panel was established under ss 80 and 81 of the Crime and Disorder Act 1998. It is an independent, advisory and consultative public body, sponsored by the Home Office and the Lord Chancellor's Department. Its Chairman is Professor Martin Wasik, author of *Emmins on Sentencing* and editor of the Sentencing section of *Blackstone's Criminal Practice*. There are some 12 other members including academics and practitioners involved in the criminal justice system. The Act empowers the Panel to make proposals to the Court of Appeal of its own motion, and to respond to reference from that Court or directions from the Home Secretary. Its proposals and responses are supposed to be in relation to 'a particular category of offence'. When the Court of Appeal frames or revises sentencing guidelines (see Paragraph 22.6.3), it is required to have regard, among other matters, to the Panel's views. Any resultant guidelines may then be reflected in a judgment of the Court in a case under appeal.

24.10 APPEALS TO THE HOUSE OF LORDS: CRIMINAL APPEAL ACT 1968, s 33

Either the prosecution or defence may appeal to the House of Lords from a decision of the Criminal Division of the Court of Appeal, but the appeal is subject to:

(a)   the Court of Appeal certifying that the decision which it is sought to appeal involves a point of law of general public importance, and

(b)   either the Court of Appeal or the House of Lords giving leave to appeal because it appears to them that the point of law is one which ought to be considered by the House.

An application to the Court of Appeal for leave to appeal to the House of Lords should either be made orally immediately after the court's decision, or it should be made within 14 days of the decision, notice of the application being served on the registrar in the prescribed form. There is no appeal against a refusal by the Court of Appeal to certify that a point of law of general public importance is involved (*Gelberg v Miller* [1961] 1 WLR 459); nor is it the practice of the court to give reasons for such a refusal: *Cooper and McMahon* (1975) 61 Cr App R 215. If the Court of Appeal is willing to certify that a point of law of general public importance is involved, but nevertheless refuses leave to appeal, an application may be made to the House of Lords within 14 days of the Court of Appeal's refusal. Such applications are referred to an appeal committee consisting of three Lords of Appeal. If leave to appeal is granted, at least three Law Lords must be present for the hearing (s 35) but it is usual to have five deciding the case. In disposing of the appeal, the House of Lords may exercise any powers of the Court of Appeal or remit the case to it: s 35(3).

The Court of Appeal may grant an appellant bail pending determination of his appeal to the House of Lords: s 36. If the prosecution are appealing to the House of Lords against the Court of Appeal's decision to allow an appeal and, but for his successful appeal, the appellant in the Court of Appeal would be liable to be detained in pursuance of a custodial sentence, the Court of Appeal may order that he be detained until the appeal is decided: s 37. Should the prosecution's appeal succeed and the conviction be reinstated, no problems arise about returning him to prison. Alternatively, the Court of Appeal may order that he be released on bail instead of being released unconditionally, which would, of course, be the normal consequence of his having his conviction quashed. If the court chooses neither to order continued detention nor to release on bail but allows unconditional release, the appellant is not liable to serve the remainder of his custodial sentence even if the House of Lords restores the conviction.

24.11   FREE PARDONS

Pardons have already been considered in Paragraph 16.9 from the angle of a plea of pardon. As explained there, the modern practice is to grant pardons after conviction and sentence when it becomes tolerably plain that the convicted person was in fact innocent. The pardon is granted by the Crown, on the advice of the Home Secretary, in exercise of the royal prerogative of mercy. However, the effect of the pardon is *not* to quash the conviction or even expressly to acknowledge that the pardonee did not commit the crime. It merely, to use the words of the pardon itself, releases the recipient from 'all pains, penalties and punishments whatsoever that from the said conviction may ensue'. Since he still stands convicted, it is open to a pardoned offender to appeal to the Court of Appeal to have the conviction quashed: *Foster* [1985] QB 115. Indeed, in the eyes of the law, the pardonee's name is not cleared until that has happened.

In cases where the Home Secretary is not prepared to recommend a pardon, but the doubts about a prisoner's conviction are too great for his continued detention to be justified, the intermediate solution of remitting the remainder of his sentence may be adopted.

24.12   EXAMPLE OF APPEAL

QUEEN

and

THOMAS JONES

The contents of a Notice of Application for Leave to Appeal and the drafting of Grounds of Appeal may be illustrated by the case of *Thomas Jones*. Jones, aged 18, was found guilty by a jury following his plea of not guilty to a charge of robbing Roger Thwackum of a brief-case, a wallet and £25 in cash. The case against him rested upon the evidence of the victim and P.C. Blifil. Mr Thwackum, the headmaster of a secondary school, stated in evidence that he was walking home at about 10.30 p.m. on the night of January 26th 1999 after attending a parents' association meeting at his school. He was carrying a brief-case which happened to be empty — he had used it for taking exercise books to school in the morning. Going along a quiet residential street, he heard rapid footsteps behind him, then felt a sudden pull on his brief-case and, as he refused to let go, was pulled to the pavement, suffering scratches and bruising but no serious injury. His assailant bent over him on the pavement, and removed his wallet from his inside jacket pocket. Then the assailant ran off. Although the road was dimly lit, the incident happened near a street lamp, and Mr Thwackum said that the 'mugger' reminded him of a pupil who had left his school some two years earlier, and whom he had often had cause to chastise. That pupil was Thomas Jones. Mr Thwackum went to the police, who arrested Jones and put him on an identification parade. Mr Thwackum picked him out as the person who had robbed him.

Jones was then interviewed under caution by P.C. Blifil and another officer. According to the officers, Jones said: 'I suppose I might as well tell you what happened. I was hard up because I was out of work, and I saw this old geezer with a brief-case walking ahead of me. Well, I thought there might be something in the case, and the temptation was just too much for me. I grabbed the case, and when the bloke was on the ground took his wallet from his pocket. I'm sorry now for what I did. It was just my bad luck to pick on somebody who knew me. Mind you it makes up a bit for all those canings.' Jones refused to sign the contemporaneous record of the interview claiming that it did not correctly represent what he had said.

The Court of Appeal Criminal Division

Form **NG**
(Forms 2 & 3)

NOTICE and GROUNDS of appeal or application for leave to appeal
(Criminal Appeal Act 1968)   CAO No.   /   /

● Please read the notes for guidance overleaf. Write in BLACK INK and USE BLOCK CAPITALS

ON COMPLETION PLEASE SEND THIS FORM TO THE CROWN COURT WHERE TRIED OR SENTENCED

The appellant		
give full name	Surname ___JONES___	Prison index no. 3 6 4 1 5 0
If in custody give Prison Index Number and address where detained	Forenames ___THOMAS___	
	Address ___H.M. YOUTH CUSTODY CENTRE___	
	___at LITTLE FIELDING___	
	Post code _____ Date of birth ___3.10 79___	

The Court where tried or sentenced

Give details if the case was transferred from another court — The Crown Court at ___FIELDING TOWN___

Name of Judge ___HIS HONOUR JUDGE ALLWORTHY___

Underline the dates of conviction and sentence — Dates of appearance in the Crown Court ___26.10.99 and 9.11.99 (sentence)___

Total period of remand in custody prior to sentence ___14 days___

The conviction(s) and sentence(s)

The full Crown Court case number(s) must be given, and particulars of ALL counts, offences and sentences included.

Crown Court case number(s)	Count or charge no.	Offence	Sentence
99/3180	1	ROBBERY	(2 MONTHS DETENTION IN A YOUNG OFFENDER'S INSTITUTION (YOI)
	2	ASSAULT OCCASIONING ABH (originally conditionally discharged. Sentenced for offence because Offence I was committed during period of discharge)	
Number of offences taken into consideration	NONE		Total sentence 12 month detention YOI

Applications   SEE NOTE 5

The appellant is applying for: Please tick as appropriate

☐	Extension of time in which to apply for leave to appeal against conviction and/or sentence	☑	Legal aid
☑	Leave to appeal against conviction	☑	Bail
☑	Leave to appeal against sentence	☑	Leave to call a witness

I understand that if I am in custody, and the single judge and/or the court is of the opinion that the appeal is plainly without merit, an order may be made that time spent in custody as an appellant shall not count towards sentence.
I also understand that whether or not I am in custody the court may make an order for payment of costs against me, including the cost of any transcript obtained.

This form should be signed by the appellant but may be signed by his/her legal representative *provided* the WARNING set out above has been explained to him, and he is sent a copy of this form.

Signature of appellant   Details of any person signing on *behalf* of the appellant:

Name _____

Solicitor/Counsel*

Date _____   Address _____

*Delete as appropriate

At the trial Jones gave evidence in his own defence, and stated that at the relevant time he was at a discotheque about a mile from the scene of the robbery. He had gone with a friend who had left earlier, but at around 10.30 he was dancing with a girl named Sophia, whom he had met at the disco. He took her telephone number with a view to meeting her again, but unfortunately he lost the piece of paper on which he had written it down and, as far as he could recall, she had not mentioned her surname. He had made efforts to trace her, but without success. Therefore, Jones had no witnesses to support his alibi. As to the interview with P.C. Blifil, Jones denied saying that he had grabbed the case and taken the wallet. He had said, in response to the officer's questions, that he was hard up and that, if he had seen an old man with a brief-case walking by himself, he might have been tempted to commit an offence, but he also said that nothing of the sort had in fact happened. He said that he was sorry that Mr Thwackum had apparently been hurt by somebody. He also said, jokingly, that it made up a bit for all the times Thwackum had caned him. Prosecuting counsel in cross-examination asked Jones whether he was alleging that P.C. Blifil was deliberately lying. Jones said: 'I don't know about that, but he has certainly got what I did say all twisted up.' His Honour Judge Allworthy, trying the case, ruled that Jones' evidence amounted to an assertion that Blifil had deliberately fabricated his evidence. He therefore allowed Jones to be cross-examined about his two previous convictions, which had both been in 1992 and were for assault occasioning actual bodily harm and robbery. Jones was also asked about the way in which he had committed the previous offence of robbery, and the jury learnt that he had snatched a handbag from a woman walking by herself late at night.

In his summing-up Judge Allworthy said:

> Members of the jury, you must approach the evidence of Mr Thwackum with special care. He picked out the defendant on an identification parade as the person who had taken his brief-case and wallet, but I must warn you that mistakes can easily be made when this type of evidence is given. Many people are prone to over-estimate the accuracy of their memory and powers of observation. So you must ask yourselves — could Mr Thwackum be making a mistake? Well, ladies and gentlemen, it is a matter for you, but remember that this is not a case where a witness has picked out a complete stranger on an identification parade. There is certainly ample room for mistake in that type of case, but this is a case where Mr Thwackum has told you that at the time of the attack he recognised his attacker as a former pupil, and then later he picked him out on a parade as well. You may feel — it's a matter for you, of course — that the chance of a mistake is considerably reduced. And remember that the whole incident happened near a street lamp, and that Mr Thwackum's attacker, whoever he was, must have bent over Mr Thwackum to take his wallet from his pocket. Well, there it is. Perhaps these comments will help you decide where the truth lies in this case.

After the jury's verdict, antecedents evidence revealed that for his offence of assault Jones had been given a conditional discharge for two years of which he was in breach, and that for the robbery he had been sent to detention in a young offender institution for three months. Judge Allworthy adjourned for a pre-sentence report. He later passed a sentence of 12 months' detention in a young offender institution. He said:

> You are a young man who already has convictions for assault and robbery. Now you have injured and robbed an elderly, defenceless man. The streets must be made safe for decent,

law-abiding people. I have come to the conclusion that this offence is so serious that a custodial sentence is the only answer. The sentence is therefore one of 12 months detention in a young offender institution. For the offence of assault occasioning actual bodily harm, for which you were originally conditionally discharged, I now sentence you to one month's detention in a young offender institution, to be served concurrently to the sentence for robbery.

A week after Jones' conviction, a Miss Sophia Western contacted his solicitors, stating that she had read a report of the case in the local paper, and had realised that she was the girl Jones had been with at the discotheque. She could confirm everything that he had said, and remembered the date because it was the day before her birthday. She had been disappointed when Jones did not telephone her as promised, but now everything was explained.

The perfected Grounds of Appeal in Jones' case might read as follows:

THE QUEEN

V

THOMAS JONES

GROUNDS OF APPEAL AGAINST CONVICTION

Application is made for leave to appeal upon the ground that the conviction is unsafe for any or all of the following reasons, namely that the learned judge:

1. wrongly allowed Jones to be cross-examined about his previous convictions, whereas the Appellant retained the protection of s 1(f) of the Criminal Evidence Act 1898, since he had merely asserted his innocence of the charge;

2. wrongly failed to exercise his discretion to refuse to allow the prosecution leave to cross-examine the Appellant about his previous convictions, since the Appellant only challenged a small part of P.C. Blifil's evidence and did not suggest that the officer had been guilty of extensive fabrication;

3. wrongly allowed the cross-examination of the defendant about the way in which he committed the offence of robbery of which he had previously been convicted (p. 28A–C);

4. misdirected the jury in that:

   (i) He reminded them of certain matters which tended to confirm the correctness of Roger Thwackum's identification of the appellant as the person who robbed him, but failed to remind them of other matters which cast doubt upon the identification. In particular, he failed to remind them that Roger Thwackum saw the person who robbed him at night, in a dimly lit road, for only a short time, in circumstances likely to occasion confusion and fear (p. 40A–C).

(ii)   He told them that Roger Thwackum 'recognised his attacker as a former pupil' whereas his evidence was that his attacker 'reminded' him of a former pupil (pp. 10D and 40B).

(iii)   He exaggerated the extent to which an identification of a person previously known to the witness is more likely to be reliable than an identification of a stranger, and thus he undermined the effectiveness of the warning he had earlier given about the dangers of identification evidence (p. 40B).

Further, the appellant wishes to call one Sophia Western to give evidence before this Honourable Court that at the time the offence occurred she was with the appellant at a distance of approximately one mile from the scene of the offence. The witness did not come forward until after the appellant's conviction. Her name and address could not with reasonable diligence have been discovered by the defence in time for her to be called at the trial.

GROUNDS OF APPEAL
AGAINST SENTENCE

Having regard to s 79 of the Powers of Criminal Courts (Sentencing) Act 2000, the appellant should have been dealt with by non-custodial means. Contrary to the view expressed by the learned judge in passing sentence, the Appellant's offence was not so serious that only a custodial sentence could be justified for it; nor was it the case that such a sentence was required to protect the public from serious harm from the Appellant.

W. Partridge
Counsel for the Appellant

These Grounds of Appeal would be accompanied by an Advice on Appeal, the contents of which are beyond the scope of this work (for examples, see the Inns of Court School of Law, *Drafting Manual*, published by Blackstone Press annually).

25 Appeals from the Magistrates' Courts

A decision by a magistrates' court can be challenged by:

   (a)   appeal to the Crown Court, or
   (b)   appeal to the High Court by way of a case stated by the magistrates for the High Court's opinion, or
   (c)   application to the High Court for judicial review of the magistrates' decision.

Appeal to the Crown Court is only by a person convicted. The other two procedures are available to any person aggrieved by a magistrates' court decision, which includes both a convicted accused and an unsuccessful prosecutor. Decisions of the Crown Court, not made in connection with its jurisdiction over trials on indictment, may also be challenged through a case stated for the opinion of the High Court or an application for review. The jurisdiction of the High Court in these matters is exercised by the Administrative Court (see *Practice Direction: the Administrative Court*, 19 July 2000). Therefore, one may refer with equal correctness either to appeals and applications to the High Court or to appeals and applications to the Adminstrative Court.

25.1 APPEALS TO THE CROWN COURT

Appeals to the Crown Court from a magistrates' court are governed by the Magistrates' Courts Act 1980, ss 108 to 110, and rr 6 to 11 of the Crown Court Rules 1982 (SI 1982 No 1109).

25.1.1 The right of appeal

A person convicted by a magistrates' court following a plea of not guilty may appeal to the Crown Court against his conviction and/or his sentence. A person sentenced by the magistrates following a guilty plea may only appeal against his sentence: MCA, s 108(1).

   An appeal to the Crown Court against sentence may be brought in respect of 'any order made on conviction by a magistrates' court': MCA, s 108(3). This is subject to an express prohibition on appealing an order to pay costs to the prosecution. Otherwise 'order made on conviction' appears to have the same wide meaning as order made when dealing with an offender', which is the phrase used in s 50 of the Criminal Appeal Act 1968 to define 'sentence' in the context of appeals from the Crown Court to the Court of Appeal (see Paragraph 24.3.1). Thus, there is a right of appeal to the Crown Court against *inter alia* a magistrates' court's decision to conditionally or absolutely discharge an offender, to disqualify him from driving, to recommend him for deportation, or to make a hospital or compensation order. However, an order to contribute to one's own legal representation costs would seem to be unappealable for the same reasons as make such an order unappealable if made by the Crown Court.

Although a plea of guilty in the magistrates' court is generally a bar to appealing to the Crown Court against conviction, it is sometimes possible to argue that it should not have that consequence because it was not a genuine admission of guilt. If the Crown Court agrees, it remits the case to the magistrates with a direction that a not guilty plea be entered. Non-genuine pleas of guilty before the magistrates are usually referred to as 'equivocal pleas', but there is room for debate over the correct use of the terminology. Three main situations may be distinguished in which the Crown Court will remit for hearing on a not guilty plea following a guilty plea before the magistrates:

(a) *Pleas equivocal when made.* If the accused says 'Guilty' when the information is put to him but he immediately adds words which show that he might have a defence, the plea is clearly equivocal. An example is the accused charged with assault who pleads, 'Guilty, but I only did it to defend myself'. The magistrates should explain to him the relevant law (i.e., that if he was acting in reasonable self-defence he is not guilty of the charge) and then ask the clerk to put the information again. If the accused then unambiguously pleads guilty, the magistrates will properly proceed to sentence, but if the plea remains equivocal they should enter a not guilty plea on the accused's behalf. Failure to do so (i.e., sentencing on a plea which remains equivocal) will, in the event of an appeal, lead to the case being remitted by the Crown Court for hearing on a not guilty plea.

(b) *Pleas subsequently shown to be equivocal* A plea which is unequivocally one of guilty when made may be rendered equivocal by information given to the magistrates before they pass sentence. In *Durham Quarter Sessions ex p Virgo* [1952] 2 QB 1, for example, V, who was unrepresented, simply answered 'Guilty', when an information for stealing a motor cycle was put to him, but, when later asked if he had anything to say in mitigation, told the magistrates that he had taken the cycle by mistake believing that it was his friend's cycle and that the friend had given him permission to use it. Thus, his mitigation was inconsistent with the guilty plea. Similarly, in *Blandford Justices ex p G* [1967] 1 QB 82, the prosecution brought to the juvenile court's attention, as part of their summary of the facts following G's plea of guilty to stealing jewellery from her employer, a statement to the police made by G in which she claimed that she had merely borrowed the jewellery intending to return it. Neither Virgo nor G were invited to change their pleas. In both cases, the High Court treated the matters subsequently put before the magistrates (Virgo's mitigation and G's written statement) as if they formed part of the plea to the respective informations. Their lordships therefore held that the Crown Court should have remitted the cases to the magistrates for trial since the pleas, although unequivocal when made, were rendered equivocal by the subsequent developments. However, it is important to note that, if a would-be appellant merely tells the Crown Court that he was mistaken as to the law when he entered his guilty plea but nothing emerged during the sentencing procedure that could have alerted the magistrates to his error, then he is bound by his plea and cannot have his conviction set aside.

An alternative analysis of the situations in *Ex p Virgo* and *Ex p G* is to say that the term 'equivocal plea' should be reserved for cases falling within (a) above. If something prior to the passing of sentence throws doubt on a plea of guilty which was unequivocal when made, the question is not strictly one of whether the plea should be treated as equivocal but whether the magistrates properly exercised the discretion which they undoubtedly have to allow a change of plea. If they failed to consider exercising their discretion or exercised it in a way which no reasonable tribunal would have done, the case should be remitted to them, but otherwise the accused is bound by his guilty plea. This analysis was adopted in *P. Foster (Haulage) Ltd v Roberts* [1978] 2 All ER 751. See *Bristol Justices ex p Sawyers* [1988] Crim LR 754 and Paragraph 9.7.1.

(c) *Pleas entered under duress.*   Even if a plea of guilty was unequivocal when made and not put in doubt by any developments prior to the passing of sentence, the accused is not debarred from appealing his conviction to the Crown Court if the plea was entered under duress: *Huntingdon Crown Court ex p Jordan* [1981] QB 857. *Ex p Jordan* concerned a wife, jointly charged with her husband with shoplifting. The defence she would have run had she dared was that her husband forced her to commit the offences by threats of violence. Similar threats (so she alleged) prevented her from pleading not guilty. The High Court held that the Crown Court had jurisdiction to *remit* to the magistrates for hearing on a not guilty plea. Presumably the same would apply if a plea of guilty in the magistrates' court was induced by any of the forms of pressure which will lead the Court of Appeal to treat a plea of guilty entered on an indictment as a nullity (see Paragraph 16.3.3).

Despite the exceptional situations just described, the general rule is still that pleading guilty before the magistrates prevents one appealing against conviction to the Crown Court. If a plea was unequivocal when made, was not put into doubt by any subsequent developments prior to sentence and was not entered under duress or oppression, then MCA, s 108 permits an appeal against sentence but nothing more. There is no jurisdiction to set aside the conviction or remit to the magistrates simply on the basis that the accused now regrets pleading guilty and thinks that he might have an arguable defence (*Birmingham Crown Court ex p Sharma* [1988] Crim LR 741). By contrast, if the accused pleaded guilty and was then committed for sentence, the Crown Court has a general discretion to remit to the lower court whenever that appears just (see *Camberwell Green Justices ex p Sloper* (1978) 69 Cr App R 1). The reason for this prima facie anomalous distinction is that committing for sentence does not render the magistrates *functus officio,* whereas convicting and sentencing the accused does. In the former situation, therefore, the accused is not appealing against conviction but merely asking the Crown Court to refrain from sentencing him until proceedings have been properly completed in the lower court.

Crown Court directions that magistrates re-hear a case on a not guilty plea can lead to unbecoming inter-court disputes, with the lower court indignantly protesting that the accused's plea was totally unequivocal and therefore refusing to comply with the Crown Court's wishes. Following some contradictory earlier decisions by the High Court, the rights and duties of the respective courts were finally established by Watkin LJ's judgment in *Plymouth Justices ex p Hart* [1986] QB 950. Assuming that it conducted a proper inquiry into whether the accused's plea was equivocal and had sufficient evidence before it to come to the conclusion that it was, the Crown Court's direction that a not guilty plea be entered and a summary trial take place is binding on the magistrates and must be obeyed. Furthermore, the magistrates should assist the Crown Court in its inquiry into the equivocality of the plea by supplying affidavits (e.g. from the clerk in court or the chairman of the bench) dealing with what happened when the appellant appeared before them: *Rochdale Justices ex p Wallwork* [1981] 3 All ER 434, confirmed in *ex p Hart*. The only situation in which magistrates might be entitled to ignore a direction for a not guilty hearing is if the Crown Court appears to have given the direction without first making proper inquiries. Should the two courts not then be able to resolve their disagreement sensibly and amicably, there would have to be an application to the High Court for judicial review which could then either quash the Crown Court's direction or order the magistrates to comply with it.

25.1.2 Procedure on appeal

Notice of appeal must be given in writing to the clerk of the relevant magistrates' court and to the prosecutor within 21 days of sentence being passed: Crown Court Rules 1982, r 7. The appellant has 21 days from the date of sentence or other disposal (e.g., committal for sentence) even if that is after the date of conviction and he is only appealing against conviction. No particular form is prescribed for the notice but it must state whether the appeal is against conviction or sentence or both. The grounds of appeal need not be given, although the appellant may choose to state in very general terms why he considers the magistrates' decision was wrong. Provided notice is given within time, no leave to appeal is required. The Crown Court has a discretion to extend the time for giving notice, i.e. to give leave to appeal out of time: r 7(5).

If notice of appeal is given by an appellant upon whom the magistrates have passed an immediate custodial sentence, they may bail him to appear at the Crown Court at the time fixed for the hearing of the appeal: MCA, s 113(1). If the magistrates refuse to grant bail, application may be made to the Crown Court under the Supreme Court Act 1981, s 81(1)(b), or to a High Court judge in chambers. Bail pending the appeal is particularly important because any custodial sentence imposed by a magistrates' court is necessarily short, so if not granted bail the appellant may have served much of his sentence by the time the appeal is heard.

An appeal is listed for hearing by a circuit judge or recorder who must normally sit with two lay magistrates (*Practice Direction (Crown Court Business: Classification)* [1987] 1 WLR 1671 and Supreme Court Act 1981, s 74). Prior to the hearing, the defence may request a copy of the clerk's notes of evidence of the summary trial. Any such request for a copy should be 'viewed sympathetically' (per Lord Lane CJ in *Clerk to the Highbury Corner Justices ex p Hussein* [1986] 1 WLR 1266). The appeal itself takes the form of a re-hearing, exactly the same steps being gone through as were gone through at the summary trial. Thus, at an appeal against conviction, counsel for the respondent (i.e. the prosecution) makes an opening speech and calls his evidence, after which counsel for the appellant (i.e. the defence) may make a submission of no case to answer. If that fails, defence evidence is called, counsel makes a closing speech, and the court announces its decision. The parties are not limited to the evidence called at the summary trial, but may rely on material which has only become available to them since then, or which they simply chose not to use on the earlier occasion. The Crown Court itself, however, may neither amend the information on which the appellant was convicted (*Garfield v Maddocks* [1974] QB 7 and see *Swansea Crown Court ex p Stacey* [1990] RTR 183) nor strike out an amendment made by the magistrates: *Fairgrieve v Newman* [1986] Crim LR 47. At an appeal against sentence, the prosecution simply outline the facts and call antecedents evidence, reports (if any) on the appellant are read, and defence counsel mitigates.

25.1.3 Powers of the Crown Court

The decision of the Crown Court is announced by the judge, who should give reasons. These should be sufficient to demonstrate that the court has identified the main contentious issues in the case, and how it has resolved each of them. Failure to do so might amount to a denial of natural justice (*Harrow Crown Court ex p Dave* [1994] 1 WLR 98).

The powers of the Crown Court when disposing of an appeal are set out in s 48 of the Supreme Court Act 1981 as amended. Those powers are extensive. It may confirm, reverse or vary any part of the decision appealed against, it may remit the matter to the magistrates with its opinion thereon (e.g., where it considers the plea to be equivocal), or it may make such other order in the matter as it thinks just (e.g., in the case of a successful appeal, an order that the costs of the defence in the magistrates' court be paid by the prosecution or out of central funds). Varying the decision appealed against includes increasing the sentence imposed by the magistrates even in a case where the appeal is only against conviction, but the Crown Court sentence must not exceed that which the magistrates could have passed: s 48(4). In fact, it is unusual for the Crown Court to increase sentence, but the reason it, unlike the Court of Appeal on appeals from the Crown Court, has retained the power to do so may be that leave is never required for appeals to the Crown Court unless they are out of time. The possibility of an increase in sentence may therefore inhibit unmeritorious appeals. Furthermore, whenever an appeal fails, the appellant may be ordered to pay the prosecution's costs: Prosecution of Offences Act 1985, s 18(1)(b) and see also r 12 of the Crown Court Rules which gives the Crown Court a general discretion to make such order for costs between the parties as appears just. A successful appellant may be awarded his costs out of central funds (i.e. out of government money): POA, s 16(3). This is known as a 'defendant's costs order' and it may include the appellant's costs in the magistrates' court. A publicly funded prosecutor cannot be awarded costs out of central funds, but private prosecutors may have such an order made in their favour whether or not the appeal succeeds, provided it concerned an indictable offence: POA, s 17(1) and (2). For general discussion of costs, see Paragraph 27.2.

Section 48 now enables the Crown Court to vary (e.g. by increasing sentence) *any part* of the magistrates' decision, even if the appellant chose not to appeal against that part. Until an amendment made to the Supreme Court Act 1981 by the Criminal Justice Act 1988, s 48 had merely said that the Crown Court could vary 'the decision' appealed against. That wording gave rise to difficult problems of statutory interpretation in *Dutta v Westcott* [1987] QB 291, where D successfully appealed against a conviction for driving without insurance for which he had been disqualified, and then claimed that the Crown Court was not empowered to order that penalty points should be endorsed on his licence for other lesser offences of which the magistrates had convicted him on the same occasion as they convicted of no insurance but for which they did not order points because of the rule that no points shall be endorsed if the offender is disqualified. By a very strained interpretation of the original s 48, the High Court was able to hold that the Crown Court had had power to do what it did — indeed, it would have been absurd if D had been able to escape penalty points for offences that would normally incur them simply by getting his conviction and disqualification for something else set aside. The amendment to s 48 has given the Crown Court the statutory power to do what it did in *Dutta v Westcott*. It also would seem to give the Crown Court power when a person appeals against his summary conviction for offence A to quash it and substitute a conviction for offence B of which the magistrates acquitted on the same occasion, since the acquittal is part of the decision against which the appellant is appealing. In theory, indeed, the Crown Court could even dismiss the appeal against conviction for offence A and add a conviction for offence B. To avoid injustice to appellants, the Crown Court should, it is submitted, use its increased powers under s 48 sparingly.

The appellant may abandon his appeal by giving notice in writing to that effect to the clerk of the magistrates' court, to the appropriate officer of the Crown Court and to the prosecution: Crown Court Rules 1982, r 11. The notice should be given at least three days before the hearing of the appeal. If notice to abandon an appeal is duly given, the Crown Court is thereby deprived of its power to order the appellant to pay costs but the magistrates may make an order in respect of expenses properly incurred by the prosecutor before he received the notice: MCA, s 109.

25.2 APPEALS TO THE HIGH COURT BY CASE STATED

An appeal by way of case stated is an appeal on a point or points of law, which are identified in a document (the case) drawn up by the clerk of the magistrates' court in conjunction with the magistrates whose decision is being questioned. The appeal is to the High Court which exercises its jurisdiction through the Administrative Court.

Appeals by case stated are governed by the Magistrates' Courts Act 1980, s 111, rr 76 to 81 of the Magistrates' Courts Rules 1981 (SI 1981 No 552), and Order 56 of the Rules of the Supreme Court 1965.

25.2.1 The right of appeal

Section 111(1) of the MCA provides that '*any* person who was a party to any proceeding before a magistrates' court or is aggrieved by the conviction, order, determination or other proceeding of the court may question the proceeding on the ground that is *wrong in law* or *in excess of jurisdiction* by applying to the [magistrates] to state a case for the opinion of the High Court on the question of law or jurisdiction involved'. The subsection is not as happily worded as it might be since it thrice includes the word 'proceeding', and seems to use it in a slightly different sense on each occasion. Taking the appearances of the word in sequence, it would seem to mean (a) the entire proceedings before the magistrates; (b) a particular decision taken by the magistrates during the course of or in ultimately disposing of those proceedings, and (c) an amalgam of the first two meanings. However, whatever the difficulties raised by a close analysis of s 111(1), its broad effect is clear. The following are the chief points to note:

(a) Appeal by case stated is at the disposal of both the prosecution and the defence. Indeed, it is also at the disposal of parties to civil proceedings before the magistrates, but that is irrelevant for the purposes of this book which will discuss s 111(1) solely in the context of appeals arising out of criminal cases.

(b) The appeal must be on one or other of the two grounds mentioned in s 111(1), namely that the decision complained of was wrong in law or in excess of jurisdiction. In his initial application to the magistrates to state a case a would-be appellant must specify the question of law or jurisdiction on which the High Court's opinion is sought, and if his application mentions only a question of fact the request for a case would be refused (see Paragraph 25.2.2). The kind of issues which may properly be raised for the High Court's consideration are whether the information was bad for duplicity, whether the magistrates had power to try it, whether they were right to find that there was or (as the case may be) was not a case to answer, whether inadmissible evidence was received or admissible evidence excluded, and whether their verdict was the correct one in the light of the facts they found proved by the evidence. This last is perhaps the commonest argument put forward on a case stated. Either the prosecution says that the accused's acquittal should be reversed because on their stated view of the facts the magistrates clearly ought to have convicted, or the defence contend that the facts proved to the magistrates' satisfaction did not amount to the offence charged and so the conviction should be set aside. However, the lower court's decision as to what facts were established by the evidence cannot be appealed by case stated, save that a finding of fact which is totally unsupported by evidence or at which no reasonable tribunal properly directing itself could have arrived is treated as revealing an error of law and so may be taken to the High Court: *Bracegirdle v Oxley* [1947] KB 349. If the defence consider that the magistrates' decision on the facts was merely against the weight of the evidence, their only remedy is to go to the Crown Court for a rehearing of the evidence.

(c) Most appeals by way of case stated are aimed at overturning either a summary conviction or a summary acquittal. They are not aimed at reducing or increasing a sentence passed after summary conviction, simply because it is rare for magistrates to pass a sentence which is wrong in law or in excess of jurisdiction. However, if they should happen to do so, the aggrieved party can ask them to state a case. Thus, on a number of occasions, the prosecution have obtained a ruling that magistrates sentencing for a drink/driving offence should have disqualified the offender, since the grounds he advanced for not being disqualified were incapable of being special reasons within the meaning of the Road Traffic Offenders Act 1988 (see *Haime v Walklett* (1983) 5 Cr App R (S) 165 for an example). In truly exceptional cases, the defence on an appeal by case stated may obtain a reduction in sentence by arguing that, although it was within the magistrates' statutory powers of punishment, it was outside the normal discretionary limits. (The approach is essentially the same as in appeals against sentence by way of judicial review: see Paragraph 25.3.1.) The High Court will then presume that the magistrates in passing the sentence must have made some error in law, otherwise they would not have arrived at a decision so grossly out of line with good sentencing practice (see *Universal Salvage Ltd v Boothby* (1983) 5 Cr App R (S) 428 and Paragraph 25.3.1 for discussion of the point in the context of applications for a quashing order).

(d) On a correct interpretation of s 111(1), the right to ask the magistrates to state a case does not arise unless and until the proceedings in their court have resulted in a final determination of the would-be appellant's case (see dicta in *Atkinson v USA Government* [1971] AC 197). In the context of criminal proceedings, a final determination would be an acquittal, conviction or passing of sentence. It follows that neither errors of law during committal proceedings nor a decision to commit which was unjustified by the evidence can be challenged by case stated since a committal is not a final determination of a case: *Dewing v Cummings* [1972] Crim LR 38. The same reasoning would apply to a decision to commit for sentence, although the conviction which preceded the decision to commit could be appealed. The need for there to have been a final determination also means that if, during the course of a summary trial, the prosecution or defence consider that the magistrates have made a wrong decision in law, they must wait until the verdict has been pronounced before asking for a case to be stated — they may not seek an adjournment immediately after the decision complained of with a view to getting a ruling on the matter from the High Court during the period of the adjournment: *Streames v Copping* [1985] QB 920. Hence, in *Loade v DPP* [1990] 1 QB 1052, the High Court was asked to rule upon the validity of an information, referred to it by way of case stated from the Crown Court on appeal from the magistrates. Their lordships declined to answer the question formally, since there had been no final determination, but gave an informal indication that they would have rejected the appellant's argument if they had been in a position to do so.

25.2.2 Procedure on appeal

An application for the magistrates to state a case must be made within 21 days of acquittal or conviction, or, if the magistrates convicted an accused and adjourned before sentencing him, within 21 days of sentence: MCA, s 111(2) and (3). The application, which must be in writing, should identify the question of law or jurisdiction on which the High Court's opinion is sought: Magistrates' Courts Rules 1981, r 76. If it is suggested that there was no evidence on which the magistrates could reasonably have come to a particular finding of fact, the fact in question should be specified. The application is sent to the clerk of the relevant magistrates' court. Where the magistrates consider that an application to state a case is frivolous they may refuse to comply with the application, but must give the applicant a certificate stating that his application has been refused: s 111(5). The applicant may then apply to the High Court for an order compelling the magistrates to state a case. Even if the application cannot be classed as frivolous, the magistrates may still doubt whether the applicant genuinely intends to go through with the appeal. To discourage money and time being wasted over appeals which are started and then abandoned, they may make their agreement to state a case conditional upon the applicant entering into a recognisance that he will 'prosecute the appeal without delay' and pay any costs which are ultimately awarded against him by the High Court: MCA, s 114.

A statement of case should set out the facts as found by the magistrates, but not the evidence which led them to those findings of fact (*Turtington v United Co-operatives Ltd* [1993] Crim LR 376). The only exception to the rule arises when the appellant contends that there was no evidence on which the magistrates could reasonably have reached a finding of fact, in which case a short statement of the relevant evidence must be included. The case also sets out the charge or charges heard by the magistrates, the contentions of the parties on the questions of law or jurisdiction raised, any authorities cited, the magistrates' decision, and the question for the High Court. The clerk to the magistrates is principally responsible for drafting the case. He consults with the magistrates, and takes into account any representations by the parties. After any necessary alterations have been made to the case as initially drafted by the clerk, it is signed by at least two of the magistrates whose decision is being appealed, or by the clerk on their behalf. It is then sent to the appellant or his solicitor (Magistrates' Courts Rules 1981, r 78), who, within ten days of receiving it, must lodge it in (i.e. deliver it to) the Administrative Court Office at the Royal Courts of Justice: Rules of the Supreme Court 1965, Ord. 56, r 6. Unless time for lodging the case is extended by the High Court, failure to lodge it within the ten days will lead to the appeal being struck out. The appellant must also serve on the respondent to the appeal a notice of entry of the appeal and a copy of the case. This is done within four days of the case being lodged. The appeal is not normally heard until at least eight clear days after the service of the notice.

Where magistrates have passed on an appellant an immediate custodial sentence, they may grant him bail pending the hearing of his appeal: MCA, s 113. The terms of bail are that, unless the appeal succeeds, he must appear at the magistrates' court within ten days of the High Court's judgment being given, the precise date being fixed by the magistrates after the appeal. If the magistrates refuse bail, an application for bail may be made to a High Court judge in chambers.

An example of a case stated is shown on pages 455–56. Below are more details of the rather elaborate procedure for drawing up a case.

After an application for the magistrates to state a case has been received, the clerk immediately prepares a draft case. If necessary he consults with the magistrates and he can also discuss the application informally with either or both the parties so as to elucidate the issues. Occasionally, the appellant himself might be allowed to prepare the draft, or, if the hearing was before a district judge, he might wish to undertake the task. Within 21 days of receiving the application, the clerk sends the draft case to the appellant and respondent or their respective solicitors. They then have 21 days from when they receive the draft case to make representations about it, pointing out any apparent inaccuracies or suggesting improvements. In the light of any representations received the magistrates and clerk agree upon the final form of the case, which is then signed. This must be done within 21 days of the last day on which representations about the draft case could have been made. The signed case is sent forthwith to the appellant or his solicitor. The above procedure is set out in rr 77 and 78 of the Magistrates' Courts Rules 1981.

The time-limits mentioned in rr 77 and 78 can all be extended where necessary, but the 21 day period within which the initial application to the magistrates to state a case must be made is prescribed by statute, and cannot be varied even by the High Court: *Michael v Gowland* [1977] 1 WLR 296. Where an application is made within time but it does not comply with r 76 in that it fails to identify the question of law or jurisdiction on which the High Court's opinion is sought, the High Court will still accept jurisdiction if the defect is subsequently remedied, even if that is done out of time (see *Parsons v F W Woolworth and Co. Ltd* [1980] 1 WLR 1472 and *Croydon Justices ex p Lefore Holdings* [1980] 1 WLR 1465 where, by slightly different reasoning, differently constituted courts arrived at substantially the same conclusions).

Case stated (M.C. Act 1980, s 111; M.C. Rules 1981, rr 78, 81)
In the High Court of Justice
  Queen's Bench Division

    Between   Mohammed KHAN   Appellant
               and
               Peter CONSTABLE   Respondent

Case stated by the justices for the county of Loamshire, acting in and for the Petty Sessional Division of Loamtown in respect of their adjudication as a Magistrates' Court sitting at 1, High Street, Loamtown.

CASE

1. On the 25th day of July 2001 an information was preferred by the Respondent against the Appellant that he on the 11th day of July 2001 had with him in a public place namely Clay Road, Loamtown, an offensive weapon, namely a knuckleduster, without lawful authority or reasonable excuse, contrary to s 1(1) of the Prevention of Crime Act 1953.

2. We heard the information on the 5th day of September 2001. The appellant elected summary trial, and we found the following facts proved:

(a) On the 11th day of July 2001 the Respondent, who is a police officer, observed the Appellant and a white youth fighting in Clay Road, Loamtown. The Appellant is aged 19 and is of Asian origin. The white youth ran away, but the Respondent was able to arrest the Appellant on suspicion of having committed an offence contrary to s 4 of the Public Order Act 1986. The Respondent searched the Appellant, and found in his trouser pocket a knuckleduster. The knuckleduster was made for use for causing injury to the person.

(b) Clay Road, Loamtown is a public highway to which the public have access at all times.

(c) During a period of roughly a month before the day in question three Asian youths walking at night in the Clay Road area of Loamtown had, in separate incidents, been assaulted by white youths referred to as 'skinheads'. The last attack occurred on the 30th day of June 2001. The Appellant had never himself been assaulted prior to July 11th. He claimed that the white youth he was fighting when seen by the Respondent attacked him without cause. We made no finding on the point as the information we were trying did not directly concern the said fight.

(d) On Mondays and Wednesdays the Appellant attended evening classes which finished at approximately 10.00 p.m. His journey home necessitated his walking through the Clay Road area. After the first attack on an Asian youth he began to carry on the evenings when he attended evening classes the knuckleduster which the

Respondent found in his possession. His reason for doing so was to protect himself should he be attacked, but he did not in fact use it during the fight on July 11th.

3.   It was contended by the Appellant that he had a reasonable excuse for having a knuckleduster with him because, as a result of the attacks on Asian youths which had taken place, he was in immediate fear of attack on the occasions when he walked through the Clay Road area.

4.   It was contended by the Respondent that the permanent carrying of weapons is prohibited by the Prevention of Crime Act 1953, and that, in the absence of any very recent attack upon the Appellant personally, he had no reasonable excuse for having a knuckleduster. Recent attacks upon persons belonging to the ethnic group to which the Appellant belongs could not be a reasonable excuse for the Appellant carrying an offensive weapon.

5.   We were referred to the following cases —

Evan v Hughes [1972] 3 All ER 412
Peacock [1973] Crim LR 639
Bradley v Moss [1974] Crim LR 430
Pittard v Mahoney [1977] Crim LR 169
Southwell v Chadwick (1986) 85 Cr App R 235
Malnik v DPP [1989] Crim LR 451

6.   We were of the opinion that the Appellant had the burden of proving that he had a reasonable excuse for having the knuckleduster with him in a public place. This he failed to do because he had never himself been attacked or put in fear of attack, and furthermore ten days had elapsed since the last attack on an Asian youth in the Clay Road area. Accordingly we convicted the appellant and conditionally discharged him for 12 months.

QUESTION

7.   The question for the opinion of the High Court is whether we were right in holding, as a point of law, that the Appellant's explanation for carrying the knuckleduster could not be a reasonable excuse within the meaning of s 1(1) of the Prevention of Crime Act 1953. If we were incorrect in so holding the Court is respectfully requested to reverse or amend our decision or remit the matter to us with the opinion of the Court thereon.

Dated the 2nd day of December 2001

J. Smith
R. Brown
Justices of the Peace for Loamshire on behalf
of all the Justices adjudicating.

25.2.3   Hearing of the appeal

The appeal is heard by the Administrative Court, as part of the High Court. The court consists of at least two High Court judges (Supreme Court Act 1981, s 66(3)), but sometimes three judges sit. The Lord Chancellor may request any Lord Justice of Appeal to sit in such a court. If a two-judge court is equally divided, the opinion of the judge agreeing with the court below prevails and the appeal therefore fails: per Scrutton LJ at p. 107 in *Flannagan v Shaw* [1920] 3 KB 96. No evidence is called before the court. The appeal takes the form of legal argument for the appellant and respondent, based solely upon the facts stated in the case. If those facts give rise to a point of law not taken before the magistrates which might, if it had been taken, have provided the appellant with a good defence to the charge against him, the High Court will consider the point, so long as it does not depend upon any further findings of fact: *Whitehead v Haines* [1965] 1 QB 200. In disposing of the appeal, the High Court can 'reverse, affirm or amend' the magistrates' decision, or remit the matter to the magistrates with its opinion thereon, or make any other order it thinks fit in respect of the matter, including an order as to costs: Supreme Court Act 1981, s 28A. The powers of the High Court thus include both substituting for an appellant's conviction an acquittal, and, where the prosecution appeal following an acquittal, remitting the case to the magistrates with a direction that they convict and proceed to sentence. Alternatively, where it is plain what the sentence should be, the High Court may simply replace the acquittal with a conviction and impose the appropriate penalty themselves. If the appeal concerns a sentence which was allegedly beyond the magistrates' powers or 'harsh and oppressive', the Court on allowing the appeal may pass the sentence it considers right. Costs may be awarded to the accused out of central funds: Prosecution of Offences Act 1985, s 16(5). There is also power to order the unsuccessful party to pay his opponent's costs, but there is no power to grant the prosecution their costs out of central funds unless it is a private prosecution: Prosecution of Offences Act 1985, s 17(2).

It had been thought that, despite the wide powers given to the High Court by s 6 of the Summary Jurisdiction Act 1857 (now the Supreme Court Act 1981, s 28A), their lordships were not permitted to order a retrial. Remitting to the magistrates covers sending a case back with a direction to convict if it is plain on the facts stated that that is the correct verdict. It also covers setting an acquittal aside and telling the magistrates to continue with the hearing if the acquittal followed the erroneous upholding of a submission of no case to answer at the end of the prosecution evidence. But, 'there is no power to order a retrial in the ordinary sense of the expression' (per Lord Goddard CJ in *Rigby v Woodward* [1957] 1 WLR 250). In that case, the magistrates refused to allow counsel for R to cross-examine a co-accused who had given evidence in his own defence which implicated R. This decision was plainly wrong in law, and the High Court quashed the conviction. The prosecution asked them to remit for a rehearing, since it was more than likely that the verdict would have been the same even if R's counsel had been able to cross-examine the co-accused. The Court refused, and Lord Goddard made the general statement about not ordering retrials which has already been quoted. However, the dictum was justified by reference to the particular circumstances of R's case (a retrial would have been unfair because R would not have been able to insist on the prosecution's calling the co-accused, but if he called him himself he would have been disadvantaged by the rule that one cannot cross-examine one's own witness). Thus, it seems that *Rigby v Woodward* was merely saying that retrials should not be directed where the successful appellant by case stated would be in a worse position at the retrial than he was at the original trial.

In *Griffith v Jenkins* [1992] 2 AC 76, however, the House of Lords held that the High Court *did* have power to order a rehearing, before the same or a different bench. In that case, the justices had dismissed charges of unlawful fishing and theft, acting of their own motion and without inviting representations from the parties. The prosecution appealed, and the High Court held that the justices had erred. Since two of the bench had retired, they could not remit to the same bench. Further, their lordships took the view they had no power under s 6 of the Summary Jurisdiction Act 1857 to remit the case for rehearing before a different bench. The House of Lords held that there was always power in the High Court, on hearing an appeal by case stated under s 6, to order a rehearing before the same or a different bench. A rehearing would only be ordered in circumstances where a fair trial was still possible. It was not appropriate to order a rehearing in the present case.

In *Farrand v Galland* [1989] Crim LR 573, the accused were charged with offering to supply a car with a false odometer reading, contrary to the Trade Descriptions Act 1968. The prosecution sought to introduce as evidence, by s 68(2) of the Police and Criminal Evidence Act 1984, a card and a mileage slip. The justices ruled that the exhibits were inadmissible, as not all the conditions in s 68 were satisfied. The prosecution then closed their case. Inevitably, given the gaps in the evidence, the accused were acquitted. On appeal by way of case stated, the High Court held that s 68(2)(a)(iii) was satisfied, since the persons supplying the information on the card and the mileage slip could not reasonably be expected to recollect the matters in question. This was sufficient to make the evidence admissible. The case was remitted to the justices so they could admit the documentary evidence. They would also be expected to exercise their discretion to allow the prosecution to call the extra evidence which they would have called had the documentary evidence been admitted at the original hearing.

25.2.4 Appeal by case stated from the Crown Court

Appeal by way of case stated may be used not only to question the decisions of magistrates, but also to question the Crown Court's decisions in matters not relating to trial on indictment: Supreme Court Act 1981, s 28. The precise dividing line between decisions which do and those which do not relate to a trial on indictment is not easy to draw. Since the problem of drawing that line more commonly arises in the context of whether a Crown Court decision is subject to judicial review, detailed consideration of the question will be postponed until Paragraph 25.3.3 (judicial review of Crown Court decisions). However, it is plain that the allowing or dismissal of an appeal from a magistrates' court is a decision totally unconnected with trial on indictment. Therefore, the unsuccessful party in the Crown Court (whether it be the prosecution who have seen a summary conviction overturned or the defence who have had the same result before the Crown Court as they had in the magistrates' court) may further appeal by case stated to the High Court. Of course, just as with an appeal direct from the magistrates to the High Court, the Crown Court decision may only be questioned on the ground that it was wrong in law or in excess of jurisdiction, not on the ground that it was against the weight of the evidence.

An application to the Crown Court to state a case should be made to the appropriate officer of the court within 21 days of the decision challenged being made: Crown Court Rules 1982, r 26(1). The Crown Court Rules 1982 make provision for this and other time limits for an appeal by way of case stated against a decision by the Crown Court to be extended, before or after expiry (r 26(14)). In this respect, the position differs from appeal from the magistrates, where the time limit is a statutory one, and cannot be extended (see Paragraph 25.2.2). In *DPP v Coleman* [1998] 2 Cr App R 7, it was held that:

(a) the decision whether to extend may be taken by the Crown Court judge alone;

(b) in a case where the prosecution applied for the extension of time, the defendant must be given the right to make representations;

(c) the application would normally be considered on the basis of written representations, without the need for an oral hearing.

The main difference between the procedure for magistrates stating a case and the procedure for the Crown Court doing so is that an appellant from the Crown Court has the responsibility for drawing up an initial draft case which is put before the judge who presided at the proceedings in which the disputed decision was made: r 26(8). The respondent to the appeal is also at liberty to submit a draft case to the judge. Having read the draft(s), the judge states and signs a case: r 26(12). It is sent to the appellant, who lodges it in the Crown

Office, together with copies of the judgments or orders made both in the Crown Court and the magistrates' court: Rules of the Supreme Court, Ord. 56, r 1. The appeal should normally be entered for hearing within six months of the Crown Court decision. Pending hearing of the appeal, the appellant may be granted bail by either the Crown Court or a High Court judge in chambers: Supreme Court Act 1981, s 81(1)(d), and Criminal Justice Act 1948, s 37. On disposing of the appeal, the High Court's powers are identical to those it possesses in disposing of an appeal from the magistrates.

Upon an application being made to magistrates to state a case for the opinion of the High Court, the applicant loses any right he had to appeal to the Crown Court: MCA, s 111(4). Therefore, if a person convicted by magistrates is dissatisfied both with the view of the facts they apparently took, and with their ruling on any question of law which arose, he is well advised to appeal to the Crown Court against conviction and refrain from asking the magistrates to state a case. At the rehearing in the Crown Court, the evidence is again called, and all questions of both fact and law may be fully ventilated. If the appeal fails, the appellant still has the right to ask the Crown Court to state a case for the High Court's opinion on the question of law. Had he appealed on the law direct from the magistrates' court to the High Court, he would have lost the chance of having the evidence reheard in the Crown Court.

25.3 APPLICATION FOR JUDICIAL REVIEW

One of the High Court's tasks is to supervise the work of inferior tribunals. The principal way in which it does this is through issuing one or more of the three prerogative orders:

(a) the quashing order (known until *Practice Direction: the Administrative Court,* 19 July 2000 as *certiorari*), which quashes the decision of an inferior tribunal;

(b) the mandatory order (formerly *mandamus*), which compels an inferior tribunal to carry out its duties; and

(c) the prohibiting order (formerly the order for prohibition), which prevents an inferior tribunal acting unlawfully or in excess of jurisdiction.

The prerogative orders are only issued upon an application being made to the High Court for judicial review of the inferior tribunal's decision. In the field of administrative law, judicial review is of great importance, being used to control the way in which a wide variety of tribunals and other persons under a duty to act judicially exercise their powers. It is also available in respect of decisions by magistrates (whether those decisions were made in the exercise of their civil or criminal jurisdiction), and in respect of decisions by the Crown Court when it is not exercising its jurisdiction in matters relating to trial on indictment: Supreme Court Act 1981, s 29(3). It is a useful supplement to appeal by case stated in that a person aggrieved by a decision of a magistrates' court or by a decision of the Crown Court on an appeal from the magistrates may sometimes be able to obtain judicial review when he could not have asked the magistrates or the Crown Court to state a case (see Paragraph 25.3.4 for a comparison of the two remedies).

An applicant for judicial review must have a sufficient interest in questioning the decision which it is sought to review. Whatever may be the precise meaning of 'sufficient interest' — and the concept has caused considerable difficulty in cases where the High Court has been asked to review the decision of an inferior tribunal in a civil matter — it is clear that the prosecution and defence each have a sufficient interest to apply for judicial review both of a magistrates' court's decision in a criminal case and of a Crown Court decision upon appeal from the magistrates. The application is made to the Administrative Court (as part of the High Court). The procedure is governed by ss 29–31 of the Supreme Court Act 1981 and Ord. 53 of the Rules of the Supreme Court 1965 (as amended).

25.3.1 Scope of the orders

Broadly speaking, the purpose of judicial review is to prevent magistrates' courts and other inferior tribunals exceeding their jurisdiction; to compel them to exercise the jurisdiction which is rightfully theirs, and to control the way they exercise that jurisdiction in the sense of correcting fundamental irregularities in their procedures. Errors of law made by magistrates when exercising their proper jurisdiction in the proper manner should be questioned by appealing by case stated, not by applying for judicial review.

The effect of a quashing order is to quash the inferior tribunal's decision. Until 2000, it was known as *certiorari*. When it grants the remedy, the High Court also has the supplementary powers of (a) remitting the case to the inferior tribunal with a direction to reconsider it and reach a decision in accordance with its (the High Court's) findings, and (b) replacing an unlawful sentence which it has quashed with the sentence it considers fit: Supreme Court Act 1981, ss 31(5) and 43. The grounds on which the remedy is commonly granted are described below. As regards criminal proceedings, its commonest use is to quash a summary conviction. It is also potentially available to quash any of the other orders or decisions which magistrates take in connection with the course of a prosecution, such as a decision to commit for trial or sentence, or to withhold representation by the Criminal Defence Service, or to refuse an application to withdraw an election for summary trial. However, the rule against double jeopardy (i.e., an acquitted accused should not be reprosecuted for the same offence) means that the order is rarely granted to quash an acquittal. If the magistrates pronounced their verdict after a genuine trial at which the accused was at risk of a valid conviction, the acquittal will not be reviewed, even if the prosecution were prejudiced by a gross breach of proper trial procedures which (had it happened in reverse) would have necessitated the quashing of a conviction. Although they thought it anomalous in view of the fact that summary acquittals can be reversed through appeal by case stated, this general principle was confirmed by the House of Lords in *Dorking Justices ex p Harrington* [1984] AC 743. At the same time, they gave a generous interpretation to an exception to the principle. The exception is that, if magistrates purport to acquit when they have no jurisdiction to do so, the trial is treated as a nullity, the accused is regarded as not having been in genuine jeopardy, and a quashing order may be issued. Thus, a summary acquittal in respect of an offence triable on indictment only is quashable (*West* [1964] 1 QB 15), as is an acquittal for an offence triable either way if the correct procedures for determining mode of trial were not complied with: *Cardiff Magistrates' Court ex p Cardiff City Council* (1987) *The Times*, 24 February 1987. Moreover, if magistrates pronounce an acquittal without listening to any prosecution evidence and without having good reason for refusing to hear witnesses whom the prosecution have available at court the verdict is similarly liable to be set aside (see *Hendon Justices ex p DPP* [1994] QB 167). If a conviction is the subject of a quashing order, it would seem that the rule against double jeopardy does not prevent the accused later being reprosecuted for the same offence (*Kent Justices ex p Machin* [1952] 2 QB 355), but that is most unlikely to happen in practice.

Subject to the restrictions on quashing an acquittal, a quashing order is issued in three main situations.

First, the order is made when the inferior tribunal acts in excess of jurisdiction. *Ex p Machin* (supra) provides an example. The magistrates tried M for offences triable either way without first explaining to him the possibility of being committed to Quarter Sessions for sentence. Since the procedure set out in the relevant statute, which alone could give them jurisdiction to try an indictable offence, had not been followed, the magistrates acted in excess of their powers in trying M, and accordingly issued an order to quash his convictions. A sentence passed by magistrates may also be in excess of jurisdiction. In *Llandrindod Wells Justices ex p Gibson* [1968] 1 WLR 598 for example, G's disqualification from driving was quashed because, having pleaded guilty by post, he was disqualified in his absence without the magistrates first adjourning and notifying him of the reason for the adjournment. In those circumstances, the court had no power to disqualify him (see MCA, s 11(4) and Paragraph 9.5.3). In *St Albans Crown Court ex p Cinnamond* [1981] QB 480 the concept of a sentence in excess of jurisdiction was extended to cover a sentence which was so harsh and oppressive that no reasonable tribunal, properly understanding its powers, could have passed it. It would seem that the test which the High Court applies in appeals against sentence by way of judicial review is the same as that which is appropriate to such appeals which proceed by way of case stated (see Paragraph 25.2.1(c)). The test suggested in *Tucker v DPP* [1992] 4 All ER 901 at 903 was: 'Is the sentence by any acceptable standard truly astonishing?' But in *Truro Crown Court ex p Adair* [1997] COD 296, Lord Bingham CJ suggested that such a test was too subjective, and said that it would be more helpful to ask whether the sentence fell clearly outside the broad area of the lower court's sentencing discretion. However, the High Court clearly does not intend that an application for a quashing order should become a regular alternative to appealing against sentence to the Crown Court. An offender who feels that his sentence in the magistrates' court was harsh and oppressive should appeal in the normal way to the Crown Court, and only if that court refuses to reduce the sentence should he apply to the High Court for a quashing order: *Battle Justices ex p Shepherd and another* (1983) 5 Cr App R (S) 124. *Ex p Cinnamond* was a case where the Crown Court, far from reducing sentence, had unreasonably increased it to 18 months' disqualification for an offence of careless driving, so C's only possible remedy was to go to the High Court.

Secondly, a quashing order will be issued where the inferior tribunal acted in breach of the rules of natural justice. The modern approach to alleged breaches of the rules of natural justice is to state, simply but vaguely, that a tribunal must act fairly having regard to the nature of the inquiry on which it is engaged. Traditionally, the rules of natural justice have been defined with a little more precision, and are said to involve two main principles — no man may be a judge in his own cause, and the tribunal must hear both sides of the case. Breaches of both so-called rules have led to convictions in the magistrates' courts being quashed. Numerous cases have concerned alleged breaches of the first rule through a magistrate or a clerk taking part in a case when he has a pecuniary interest in its outcome, or a non-pecuniary interest which is such as to give rise to a reasonable suspicion of bias (see Paragraph 9.2). The second rule may be invoked where procedural irregularities have occurred which possibly prejudiced the applicant. Failure to give the accused reasonable time to prepare his defence (*Thames Magistrates' Court ex p Polemis* [1974] 1 WLR 1371) refusing to issue witness warrants (*Bradford Justices ex p Wilkinson* [1990] 1 WLR 692), failing to allow the defendant an adjournment where one of his witnesses was unavailable, (*Bracknell Justices ex p Hughes* [1990] Crim LR 266), announcing a verdict of guilty before hearing a closing speech by counsel on behalf of the accused (*Marylebone Justices ex p Farrag* [1981] Crim LR 182), and not notifying the defence of witnesses who could support their case (*Leyland Justices ex p Hawthorn* [1979] QB 283) have all been held to be breaches of the rules of natural justice. The last case is particularly interesting because a quashing order was issued even though the responsibility for not giving the defence the necessary information lay with the police not the court. Relying on that authority, the High Court has since been prepared to grant an order to quash whenever an error by the prosecution seems seriously to have prejudiced the presentation of the defence case. Thus, in *Knightsbridge Crown Court ex p Goonatilleke* [1986] QB 1 G's conviction for shoplifting was quashed because the store detective (who was treated by the High Court as being in effect the prosecutor) failed to tell the defence that he had a conviction for wasting police time arising out of his falsely informing the police while a serving officer that his warrant card had been stolen. The information would have been particularly useful as G's defence was that the store detective had 'planted' on him the items allegedly stolen so as to impress his superiors by the number of arrests he was making. Similarly, in *Liverpool Crown Court ex p Roberts* [1986] Crim LR 622 failure to tell the defence that a police officer, the alleged victim of an assault by R, had made a statement to a superior officer soon after the event which suggested the incident might have amounted only to an accidental clash of heads was fatal to the conviction. However, in the absence of default by the prosecution, a conviction will not be quashed merely because fresh evidence favourable to the defence has come to light since the summary trial, unless the appellant can achieve the very difficult task of convincing the High Court that — in the light of the additional evidence — all the crucial evidence on which the magistrates convicted must have been perjured. In *Ex p Roberts,* the police officer's failure to carry out his duty was regarded as a failure on the part of 'the total apparatus of the prosecution' (per Glidewell LJ). A similar view was taken in *Bolton Justices ex p Scally* [1991] 1 QB 537. The applicants had pleaded guilty to excess alcohol offences. The level of alcohol in their samples of breath had been within the range giving them the right to have samples of blood tested, and they had all exercised that right. Unknown to all concerned, when the blood samples were taken, medical kits were used which included skin cleansing swabs containing alcohol. The analysis of samples might therefore have produced an artifically high blood/alcohol reading. Charges pending against other defendants in similar circumstances had not been proceeded with when the contamination was discovered. The convictions were quashed. The High Court held (a) the police were responsible for issuing the kit and the associated lack of ordinary care, and they were part of the prosecution process, notwithstanding the Prosecution of Offences Act 1985; (b) although there was no dishonesty, the prosecutor (a combination of police and CPS) had corrupted the process leading to conviction in a manner which was unfair, since it gave a defendant no proper opportunity to decide whether to plead guilty or not guilty; (c) the power to quash is not limited to proceedings vitiated by fraud, and grounds analogous to fraud, collusion or perjury could be relied upon, as in the instant case — the overriding principle must be that justice should be done.

The third situation in which a quashing order will be granted is where there is an error of law apparent on the face of the record of the inferior tribunal's proceedings — i.e. just by reading the record, and without receiving evidence on affidavit or otherwise as to what occurred in the court below, the High Court can tell that a mistake has been made. Historically, the quashing order was developed to correct such patent errors, the effect of the order (or writ as it then was) being to remove the record into the King's Bench where it would be rectified. Today, appeal by way of case stated provides a remedy for errors of law much broader in scope than the remedy provided by the quashing order. The problem in relying on judicial review when one wishes to have a magistrates' court decision quashed is that magistrates never give written reasons for their decisions, and such oral reasons as they may choose to give are usually of the briefest. If the magistrates do give oral reasons, it has been held that they may be incorporated into the record of the court's proceedings (*Chertsey Justices ex p Franks* [1961] 2 QB 152), but in the absence of such reasons the record will consist only of the charges against the accused, his pleas, the verdict and the sentence passed. The only errors likely to be revealed by such basic information are jurisdictional errors such as those already discussed (e.g. passing a sentence in excess of the statutory maximum for the offence of which, according to the record, the accused was convicted). One device by which the record can be augmented is illustrated by the case of *Southampton Justices ex p Green* [1976] QB 11. G applied to the High Court to quash a decision by magistrates that she should forfeit the sum of £3,000, that being the amount in which she had stood surety for her husband who had 'jumped bail'. The record of the magistrates' court proceedings simply showed that they had made the order complained of. Since that order was undoubtedly within their powers, no error appeared, and the application for a quashing order failed. G appealed to the Court of Appeal against the High Court's decision. The Court of Appeal had before it affidavits sworn by the chairman of the magistrates and the clerk. They showed that the bench had approached its decision on whether to estreat the recognisance on a basis which was wrong in law. The affidavits were treated as part of the record (see Browne LJ's judgment at p. 22), and therefore an error appeared on the face of the record, which enabled the Court of Appeal to issue a quashing order. However, there is no obligation on magistrates to make affidavits explaining the reasoning behind their decisions, and, if they do not, the problem remains that any errors of law they may have made are unlikely to be patent on the face of the record.

A mandatory order is used to compel an inferior tribunal to carry out its duties. Until 2000, it was known as *mandamus*. Thus, in *Brown* (1857) 7 E & B 757 magistrates who had refused to try an information on the plainly inadequate ground that, in their view, other persons should have been charged with the offence as well as the accused, were ordered to hear the case. Similarly, magistrates may be ordered to state a case for the opinion of the High Court if one has been properly requested under s 111 of the MCA and there are no reasons for regarding the application as frivolous. The scope of the mandatory order is, however, fairly limited. It is appropriate where jurisdiction is wrongly refused, but not where the inferior tribunal accepts jurisdiction and then allegedly makes a mistake in the exercise of that jurisdiction. It follows that if, during the course of a summary trial or committal proceedings, magistrates come to a seemingly erroneous decision (e.g., to exclude certain evidence or disallow a line of cross-examination), the aggrieved party may not there and then obtain an adjournment and go to the High Court for a mandatory order to compel reversal of the decision. All he can do is wait until the conclusion of the hearing, and then — if the ultimate decision goes against him — challenge that by appeal by case stated or an application for a quashing order as appropriate (see *Rochford Justices ex p Buck* (1978) 68 Cr App R 114 and *Wells Street Stipendiary Magistrate ex p Seillon* [1978] 1 WLR 1002). Broadly similar principles apply when (otherwise than in the actual course of a hearing) magistrates fail or refuse to exercise a discretionary power in favour of a party to criminal proceedings (e.g., they refuse to grant representation by the Criminal Defence Service or to allow a change of plea). If they overlooked the fact that they had the power or applied the wrong principles in deciding whether or not to exercise it, the High Court will grant a mandatory order to compel them to consider or reconsider the matter, applying the correct principles as stated by their lordships (see *Highgate Justices ex p Lewis* [1977] Crim LR 611). However, the magistrates will not be ordered to exercise the power in a certain way, unless it is an 'open-and-shut case' where there is only one conclusion to which a reasonable tribunal properly understanding the law could come. In brief, a mandatory order may be used to compel proper consideration of whether to exercise a discretionary power, but not, generally speaking, to compel the actual exercise of it.

The prohibiting order is the reverse of the mandatory order. It prevents an inferior tribunal acting or continuing to act in excess of jurisdiction. Until 2000, it was known as an order for prohibition. It is, of course, unlikely that a magistrates' court would deliberately want to exceed its jurisdiction and act unlawfully, but occasionally there is genuine doubt about the limits of its powers. In that situation it is convenient to adjourn before the possibly *ultra vires* act is done, thus enabling the party who considers that what the magistrates propose is unlawful to apply to the High Court for a prohibiting order. One example of this happening is *Hatfield Justices ex p Castle* [1981] 1 WLR 217, where the magistrates had announced their intention of holding committal proceedings in respect of a charge of criminal damage to a value of £23, believing that the special procedure whereby small-value criminal damage charges *must* be tried summarily did not apply. The High Court held that the magistrates' understanding of the law was wrong (i.e. the special procedure did apply), and they therefore granted a prohibiting order to prevent the committal proceedings taking place.

Finally, it is important to notice that quashing, mandatory and prohibiting orders are always discretionary. In cases where it is in law open to the High Court to grant the remedy, their lordships may nonetheless refuse it in the broader interests of fairness and the due administration of justice. Thus, in *Battle Justices ex p Shepherd* (1983) 5 Cr App R (S) 124, an order to quash a sentence was refused because the applicant had ignored the more obvious and convenient remedy of appealing the magistrates' court's sentence to the Crown Court. Similarly, in *Birmingham Justices ex p Lamb* [1983] 1 WLR 339 (see Paragraph 9.4 for details) an application for a mandatory order to compel magistrates to try an information which they had wrongly dismissed without hearing any evidence failed on account of the undesirability of having the case heard long after the events in question, albeit that the delay was caused mainly by the prosecution having to make the application for judicial review to correct the magistrates' erroneous original decision. In *Bradford Justices ex p Wilkinson* [1990] 1 WLR 692, on the other hand, Mann LJ said: 'I believe that a defendant is entitled to have a proper trial and a proper appeal. If he does not have a proper trial, he may . . . come to this court'. *Ex p Wilkinson* was not followed in *Peterborough Justices ex p Dowler* [1996] 2 Cr App R 561. In that case, the High Court took the view that a procedurally unfair conviction before the magistrates (which had been flawed by failure to disclose a potentially helpful witness statement to the defence) might be cured by a fair trial on appeal to the Crown Court. Judicial review, as a discretionary remedy, was refused to the applicant, who had an appeal pending before the Crown Court. Exceptional cases, where the court considered that judicial review should be granted since it might be determinative of the case as a whole, could still be heard by the High Court.

Ex p Dowler was considered by the High Court in *Hereford Magistrates' Court ex p Rowlands* [1998] QB 110, and was said not to be authority for the proposition that leave to apply for judicial review should be denied where there was a plausible complaint of procedural irregularity or unfairness. It was stressed that the defendant had the right to a proper trial before the magistrates, with a right of appeal to the Crown Court.

25.3.2 Procedure for an application

The procedure for applying for judicial review is contained in s 31 of the Supreme Court Act 1981 and Ord. 53 of the Rules of the Supreme Court 1965. It falls into two main stages.

First, the applicant must obtain leave to apply for review. The application for leave is usually determined by a single judge on the basis of a private perusal of the grounds for review set out in a written statement filed by the applicant at the commencement of the proceedings. If leave to apply is granted, the application itself — the second stage in the procedure — is determined by the High Court, which will hear argument from the applicant and anybody else who appears to have a sufficient interest in the outcome. Evidence may be received by the Court, but is usually in affidavit form, not oral. Details of the procedure are set out in the smaller print below.

(a) Notice of application is given by filing in the Administrative Court Office a statement setting out the applicant's name and description, the relief sought and the grounds upon which it is sought, the name and address of the applicant's solicitors, and his address for service. An affidavit expanding upon the grounds of the application and verifying the facts relied upon to establish those grounds must also be filed. The applicant is not limited to asking for just one of the prerogative orders, but can ask for two or more of them cumulatively or in the alternative (e.g. he might seek an order to quash proceedings in excess of jurisdiction which have already taken place and a prohibiting order to prevent any resumption of them, or he might seek an order to quash a refusal to make an order in his favour and a mandatory order to compel reconsideration of the matter applying the correct principles). Notice of application should normally be given within three months of the grounds for the application arising.

(b) The application for leave to apply is made ex p (i.e. without notice being given to the other interested parties who therefore do not attend court). It is made to a High Court judge who may determine it without a hearing unless a request for one is made by the applicant. If a hearing is requested, it need not take place in open court. If there is no hearing the judge considers the applicant's statement and supporting affidavit privately, and decides whether they establish a prima facie case for judicial review which should go before the High Court. The system thus resembles that for obtaining leave to appeal to the Court of Appeal from a single judge.

(c) A copy of the judge's order is sent from the Adminstrative Court Office to the applicant. If leave to apply is refused, the applicant may renew his application before the High Court. In order to do so he must, within 10 days of being served with notice of the judge's refusal, lodge in the Administrative Court Office a notice of intention to renew the application. The application may be renewed whether or not the judge's refusal followed a hearing. The court has inherent jurisdiction in criminal matters, just as in civil, to set aside leave granted *ex p* (*Secretary of State ex p Chinoy* (1991) *The Times*, 16 April 1991).

(d) If leave to apply is granted, the application itself is made by originating motion to the High Court. Notice of motion must be served on all persons who will be directly affected by the court's decision. In the context of applications arising out of criminal matters, this simply means that where the prosecution are applying for review they must serve notice on the defence and vice versa. Notice must also be served on the clerk of the court below. The notice should be accompanied by a copy of the statement comprising the initial application for leave to apply for review (see (a) above).

(e) Evidence at the hearing before the High Court, whether it be for the applicant or the respondent, is normally in the form of affidavits. Evidence might be required to show for example that a member of the court below was biased or that, through not complying with the proper procedure, the court below was acting in excess of jurisdiction. A party proposing to use an affidavit must, on demand, supply a copy to any other party. Any party may apply by summons to a master for an order that the maker of an affidavit attend at the hearing for cross-examination, or for orders for discovery or interrogatories. Such orders are more likely to be of value where the application for review arises out of civil proceedings than when it arises from a criminal matter.

(f) The High Court hears argument for the applicant. Unless given leave to amend, he is limited to seeking the relief mentioned in his initial statement. The grounds he relies upon should also be those foreshadowed in the statement. In opposition to the application, the court hears any person who appears to it to be a proper person to be heard. At an application relating to a criminal matter, the only persons likely to wish to be heard are the prosecutor and the accused and, perhaps, the magistrates or judge in the court below.

(g) The court reaches its decision. Their lordships may make any one or more of the orders sought by the applicant, and also have power when granting a quashing order to remit the matter to the lower court for reconsideration (whether or not the applicant expressly asked for that to be done). As already mentioned, the granting of a remedy is always discretionary.

Bail pending the hearing of an application for judicial review may be granted by a judge in chambers or, if the application is in respect of one of its decisions, by the Crown Court. Magistrates do not have power to grant bail to a person who is challenging their decision by judicial review, although they do have power to bail somebody who is appealing against their decision by way of case stated (see Paragraph 25.2.2).

25.3.3 Judicial review of Crown Court decisions

Section 29(3) of the Supreme Court Act 1981 allows a decision of the Crown Court to be challenged through an application for judicial review, provided it was not a decision 'relating to a trial on indictment'. Precisely the same rule applies to appeals by way of case stated from the Crown Court (see Paragraph 25.2.4). In *Re Smalley* [1985] AC 622 the House of Lords (leading judgment given by Lord Bridge) considered what was meant by the phrase 'relating to a trial on indictment'. While not attempting a full definition, his lordship said that it extended beyond decisions taken during the actual course of a trial on indictment and covered all decisions 'affecting the conduct of the trial', even if taken at a pre-trial stage. Applying the guidance, it has been held (or suggested *obiter dicta*) that:

(a)   forfeiting the recognisance of a person who stood surety for an accused who absconded;

(b)   ordering the forfeiture of property belonging to a third party that had been used by an offender in connection with an offence of which he had been convicted;

(c)   binding over an acquitted accused to keep the peace as a measure of preventative justice; and

(d)   discharging a restriction on the publication of details which might lead to the identification of a juvenile,

could all have no bearing on the actual conduct of the accused's trial, and so were open to judicial review (see *Re Smalley* supra, *Maidstone Crown Court ex p Gill* [1986] 1 WLR 1405, *Inner London Crown Court ex p Benjamin* (1986) 85 Cr App R 267 and *Leicester Crown Court ex p S* (1990) 94 Cr App R 153 respectively). On the other hand, the following have been held to relate to trial on indictment, with the result that they are not susceptible to judicial review:

(a)   an order that counts should lie on the file marked not to be proceeded with without leave (*Central Criminal Court ex p Raymond* [1986] 1 WLR 710);

(b)   an order that police should reveal to the defence the previous convictions of the members of the jury panel (*Sheffield Crown Court ex p Brownlow* [1980] QB 530);

(c)   the decision by the trial judge whether or not the Crown Court has jurisdiction to try an indictment (*Manchester Crown Court ex p DPP* (1993) *The Times*, 26 November 1993);

(d)   the decision by the Crown Court judge that all or part of an indictment should be stayed as an abuse of process (*Re Ashton* [1994] 1 AC 9);

(e)   an order from the trial judge that statements should be disclosed to the defence, despite the claim of the prosecution that they attracted public interest immunity (*Chelmsford Crown Court ex p Chief Constable of Essex* [1994] 1 WLR 359);

(f)   the decision by the Crown Court judge whether to hold a trial as to the defendant's fitness to plead (*Bradford Crown Court ex p Bottomley* [1994] Crim LR 753).

The question of whether the decision of the Director of Public Prosecutions to consent to a prosecution is susceptible to judicial review arose in *DPP ex p Kebilene* (1999) *The Times*, 2 November 1999. The *ratio decidendi* of the House of Lords in that case seems to be that, in the absence of dishonesty or mala fides or an exceptional circumstance, the DPP's decision to consent cannot be judicially reviewed.

25.3.4   A comparison of judicial review and appeal by case stated

The functions of mandatory and prohibiting orders on the one hand, and appeal by case stated on the other are quite distinct. The appellant by case stated argues that the magistrates have made a mistake in exercising jurisdiction. The applicant for a mandatory prohibiting order argues either that the magistrates have failed to exercise their jurisdiction or that they should be prevented from exercising a jurisdiction which they do not lawfully have. The quashing order and appeal by case stated, on the other hand, serve similar purposes. The effect of both remedies is to set aside the decision of the court below, and counsel advising a person aggrieved by a decision of a magistrates' court or of the Crown Court on appeal from the magistrates may find the choice between the remedies difficult. Most of the points relevant to that choice have already been touched upon, but, in summary, the position is that:

(a)   Where the magistrates or Crown Court have acted in excess of jurisdiction both a quashing order and appeal by case stated are available.

(b)   Where an error of law has been made, but the inferior tribunal was acting within its jurisdiction, appeal by case stated is the obvious remedy. If the error of law is patent on the face of the record of the inferior tribunal's proceedings, a quashing order could also be used, but, as explained in Paragraph 25.3.1, most errors of law are latent rather than patent. Only through the statement of case will the latent error be revealed.

(c)   If the rules of natural justice have been broken, the appropriate remedy is a quashing order. This is because the procedural irregularities which typically form the basis of an alleged breach of natural justice (e.g., a magistrate had an interest in the outcome of the proceedings or the defence was not given the opportunity to present its case properly) would not emerge from a case stated, which deals essentially with the facts the magistrates found proved and the legal issues arising from those facts.

(d)   A quashing order is again the only remedy where the defence wish to quash a committal for trial or sentence. Appeal by case stated will not lie because there has not been a final determination in the case (see Paragraph 25.2.1). In fact, an application for an order to quash a committal for trial is almost certain to fail (see Paragraph 12.5), but it is at least theoretically available. Applications to quash a committal for sentence on the basis that it was in excess of jurisdiction have a better chance of success (see Paragraph 11.2).

(e)   Where both a quashing order and appeal by case stated are available the latter is preferable because it enables the facts as found by the magistrates or the Crown Court to be placed clearly before the High Court, rather than relying on devices such as an affidavit from the chairman of the bench to supplement the court record (see *Ipswich Crown Court ex p Baldwin* [1981] 1 All ER 596 where McNeill J said of a case which 'bristled with factual difficulties' that the only 'convenient and proper way' to have brought it before the High Court would have been to have appealed by case stated — B was criticised for applying for judicial review; see also *Morpeth Ward Justices ex p Ward* (1992) 95 Cr App R 215).

25.4 APPEAL FROM THE HIGH COURT TO THE HOUSE OF LORDS

The decision of the High Court in a criminal cause or matter may be appealed to the House of Lords: Administration of Justice Act 1960, s 1(1)(a). The circumstances in which the appeal will lie are analogous to those in which an appeal lies from the Criminal Division of the Court of Appeal to the House of Lords — i.e., the High Court must certify that there is a point of law of general public importance involved, and either the High Court or the House of Lords must grant leave to appeal.

By contrast with the rule governing appeals against their civil decisions, the decision of the High Court in a criminal case may only be appealed to the House of Lords — there is no intermediate right of appeal to the Court of Appeal: Supreme Court Act 1981, s 18(1). However, some decisions which are incidentally connected with criminal proceedings are nonetheless classified as being civil in nature so that s 18(1) does not apply. Thus, in *Southampton Justices ex p Green* [1976] QB 11 the Court of Appeal held that it had jurisdiction to entertain an appeal against the High Court's refusal to quash an order by magistrates forfeiting a surety's recognisance. Although the order against G would not have been made if there had not been criminal proceedings against the person for whom she was a surety, the order in itself did not and could not result in her being prosecuted for a criminal offence. Therefore, any decisions by the High Court relating to that order were not in a criminal cause. For further discussion, see below.

> Where a lower court's order was connected with but not actually made in the course of a criminal trial, it is sometimes difficult to know whether the High Court's decision to grant or not to grant judicial review of that order should be regarded as a decision in a criminal cause or matter (appeal only to the House of Lords) or a 'non-criminal' decision (appeal initially to the Court of Appeal). In *Ex p Green (supra)*, Lord Denning gave a narrow interpretation of 'criminal decision', restricting the phrase to decisions where the order under review might have led to the prosecution and punishment of the subject thereof. While the actual decision in *Green* is accepted as being correct, Lord Denning's definition is almost certainly too narrow. Thus, in *Secretary of State for the Home Department ex p Dannenberg* [1984] QB 766, the Court of Appeal held that appeal against the High Court's refusal to quash by *certiorari* a recommendation for deportation made by magistrates when dealing with D for offences of theft and fraud lay only to the House of Lords, even though the recommendation could not have entailed the prosecution of D for any offence and so (according to Lord Denning) he should have been able to take the matter to the Court of Appeal. An earlier definition of criminal decision, to which the courts now seem to be reverting, was given by Lord Wright in *Amand v Home Secretary* [1943] AC 147. His Lordship said that the High Court's decision is in a criminal cause or matter if the order to which the decision relates was made in the course of criminal proceedings, irrespective of whether it might have entailed criminal sanctions for its subject. In line with this definition, it was held in *Carr v Atkins* [1987] QB 963 that refusal of an order to quash an order for production of special procedure material (see Paragraph 2.6.2) was a decision in a criminal cause since the original Crown Court order was 'made in a criminal context', albeit that no criminal proceedings were in existence when the order was made and disobedience to the order could only have involved civil proceedings for contempt not criminal sanctions.

25.5 THE CRIMINAL CASES REVIEW COMMISSION

The Criminal Cases Review Commission (see Paragraph 24.8) has power to refer cases dealt with in a magistrates' court to the Crown Court. The Crown Court may not, on a reference, impose any punishment more severe than that imposed by the court whose decision is being referred (Criminal Appeal Act 1995, ss 11 and 12).

26 *The European Dimension*

So far, we have concentrated almost entirely on English law as it affects criminal procedure. Increasingly, however, there is a European dimension to the way in which the courts interpret our law. There are two main ways in which European jurisprudence affects the criminal courts. First, the United Kingdom, as a member of the European Union, is bound by the Treaty of Rome. In effect, our domestic law is subject to the law of the European Union, as interpreted by the European Court of Justice. This aspect of the European dimension is dealt with in Paragraph 26.1. Secondly, as a member of the Council of Europe and a signatory of the European Convention on Human Rights (ECHR), the United Kingdom has undertaken to implement the rights contained in that Convention. These rights have acquired added significance since the Human Rights Act 1998 (HRA) came into effect in October 2000. The ECHR is dealt with in Paragraph 26.2.

26.1 REFERENCES TO THE EUROPEAN COURT OF JUSTICE

Any English court, civil or criminal, may request a preliminary ruling on a point of European Community law which arises before it. The point is then referred to the European Court of Justice for a preliminary ruling under Art 234 (ex 177) of the EEC Treaty. Article 234 makes it clear that the only court which is *obliged* to make such a reference in a criminal matter is the House of Lords. Other courts have a *discretion* to make a reference.

In *Plymouth Justices ex p Rogers* [1982] QB 863 (a case concerned with whether a fishing net contravened EEC regulations) it was confirmed that magistrates have such a discretion, and that the Divisional Court will not interfere with it unless the magistrates misdirect themselves or act unreasonably. The Divisional Court said, however, that ordinarily:

> . . . justices should exercise considerable caution before referring [a case to the European Court] even after they have heard all the evidence. If they come to a wrong decision on Community law, a higher court can make the reference and frequently the higher court would be the more suitable forum to do so. The higher court is as a rule in a better position to assess whether any reference is desirable. On references the form of the question referred is of importance and the higher court will normally be in a better position to assess the appropriateness of the question and to assist in formulating it clearly. Leaving it to the higher court will often also avoid delay.

Henn v DPP [1981] AC 850 examined the exercise of the same discretion by the Crown Court. Lord Diplock warned against any tendency to rush to Europe for a preliminary ruling:

... in a criminal trial upon indictment it can seldom be a proper exercise of the presiding judge's discretion to seek a preliminary ruling before the facts of the alleged offence have been ascertained, with the result that the proceedings will be held up for nine months or more in order that at the end of the trial he may give to the jury an accurate instruction as to the relevant law, if the evidence turns out in the event to be as was anticipated at the time the reference was made — which may not always be the case. It is generally better, as the judge himself put it, that the question be decided by him in the first instance and reviewed thereafter if necessary through the hierarchy of the national courts.

As to the procedure for a preliminary ruling:

(a) the national court makes the reference;
(b) pending the ruling from the ECJ, the national proceedings are suspended;
(c) after the ruling has been made, the national court applies it to the case and continues to judgment.

26.2 EUROPEAN CONVENTION ON HUMAN RIGHTS

The European Convention on Human Rights (ECHR) was signed in 1950, and came into force in 1953. It was produced by the Council of Europe, of which the United Kingdom was one of the original ten members (now considerably expanded), in the aftermath of the Second World War and the Nuremberg Trials. There is of course no direct connection between the Council of Europe and the European Community. Like the European Union, the Council of Europe has a Commission and a Court, which are based in Strasbourg. The European Court of Justice (see Paragraph 26.1) has at times relied on the ECHR as an influence on the general principles of EU law, but the Convention has no formal role in determining EU law.

26.2.1 The legal status of the ECHR

The ECHR is an international treaty to which the United Kingdom is a signatory, and it is binding on all its signatories in international law. In most member countries of the Council of Europe, the ECHR has been made a directly enforceable part of the domestic legal system. Until the passage of the Human Rights Act 1998 (the HRA), the United Kingdom remained one of the few signatory countries which did not incorporate the Convention into its law in this way. Since the HRA was implemented in October 2000, however, the status of the ECHR in English courts has changed radically.

26.2.2 Position after incorporation by the Human Rights Act 1998

The HRA 1998 aims to integrate the ECHR into our legal system, so that all courts have an obligation to consider arguments founded upon its provisions, and to act upon the rights which formerly could only be enforced in Strasbourg. The HRA came fully into force in October 2000. Section 2 places a duty upon any court, from the magistrates' court upwards, to take into account the decisions of the European Court of Human Rights, and the other bodies in Strasbourg which have interpreted the provisions of the ECHR. Section 3 lays down that primary and secondary legislation must be interpreted in a way consistent with Convention rights if that is possible. If it is impossible, the legislation will be valid and enforceable, but the higher courts (including the House of Lords, the Court of Appeal and the High Court — but not the Crown Court) may make a declaration of incompatibility (s 4). Section 6 makes it unlawful for a public authority (including a court) to act in a way which is incompatible with a Convention right, unless required to do so by provisions contained in, or made under, primary legislation. Where a court has declared that a statutory provision is incompatible with a Convention right, s 10 sets out a 'fast-track' procedure. This enables the government to produce legislation to remove the incompatibility speedily, using the affirmative resolution procedure.

26.2.3 Procedure of the European Court of Human Rights

Where an individual considers that the domestic courts have failed to protect a right enshrined in the ECHR, then the right of petition to Strasbourg remains available after incorporation, just as it was prior to the implementation of the HRA 1998.

The aggrieved party sends a complaint to the Secretary to the Court of Human Rights at the Council of Europe in Strasbourg. The Secretary then forwards it to the Court for a decision on admissibility. Since November 1998, this preliminary issue has been considered by the Court itself. Prior to that date, admissibility was adjudicated upon by the Commission. The decision on whether the case should pass this first hurdle is an important one, and over 90 per cent of applications are rejected upon one of the bases set out in Art 35, which states that an application is inadmissible if:

(a) it is anonymous;

(b) it concerns a matter already dealt with by the Court;

(c) it is incompatible with the ECHR, e.g., it deals with a right not contained in the ECHR;

(d) domestic remedies have not been exhausted (but there is no obligation to pursue remedies which offer no chance of success, e.g., because there is a binding domestic precedent);

(e) it was not made within six months of the date on which the decision allegedly in violation of the ECHR was made (but where the breach of the ECHR is a continuing one, time will not begin to run until the continuing state of affairs ceases to exist: *Temple v UK* (1985) 8 EHRR 319);

(f) the applicant was not a 'victim' in terms of Art 34, i.e. someone who has been, or will be, personally affected (if claiming on the basis of national law or policy, the applicant must show that he is affected to a greater extent than others);

(g) it is an abuse of the right of petition; or

(h) it is manifestly ill-founded. (This final condition is, in effect, a leave requirement which is based on a preliminary assessment of the merits.)

The decision that an application is inadmissible may be taken by a unanimous vote of a committee of three judges, acting under Art 28. If no decision is taken under Art 28, a chamber (usually consisting of seven judges) will decide on admissibility (Art 29). The Court will give its decision on admissibility in writing. There is no appeal against a decision that a case is inadmissible, and such a decision precludes any further application based upon the same facts. If the Court decides that the application is admissible, it will try to reach a 'friendly settlement' (negotiated agreement) between the parties. This may involve the payment of compensation and/or a change in the law or administrative practice upon which the complaint is founded.

If there is no settlement, the parties (and individuals, organisations amid other governments with the court's leave) may make further written and oral submissions. The oral hearing itself is very short, usually lasting a couple of hours, with speeches submitted in advance to allow for simultaneous translation to be as accurate as possible. The chamber at the oral hearing usually consists of seven judges, although in exceptional cases the more important issues will be decided by a grand chamber of 17 judges, provided that the parties consent.

If the Court considers that there has been a violation, it may also award 'just satisfaction' — damages and legal costs (Art 41). Each government is committed, as a signatory to the ECHR, to implementing the judgments of the Court, which includes amending the legislation or decision upon which the violation is based.

There is the prospect of an appeal to the grand chamber of 17 judges (Art 43). The parties have three months to seek leave for such an appeal from a panel of five judges, who must grant leave if 'the case raises a serious question affecting the interpretation or application of the ECHR or the protocols thereto, or a serious issue of general importance'. There is, however, no right of appeal against a decision that an application is inadmissible.

26.2.4 Principles operated by the European Court of Human Rights

There are certain features of the approach taken by the Court in Strasbourg which need emphasis for those accustomed to the practice of the courts in England and Wales:

(a) Its approach is *purposive*. The court searches for the aims underlying the broad statements of principle enshrined in the ECHR. Its purpose is to protect individual human rights (*Soering v UK* (1989) 11 EHRR 439), and is based upon the pluralism and tolerance contained in the preamble to the ECHR (*Handyside v UK* (1976) 1 EHRR 737).

(b) Its approach is *evolutionary*, aiming at the adaptation of the ECHR in the light of the current social climate. In *Tyrer v UK* (1978) 2 EHRR 1, in holding that the use of corporal punishment as part of the criminal justice system on the Isle of Man was contrary to Art 3, the Court stated that 'the Convention is a living instrument which . . . must be interpreted in the light of present day conditions'.

(c) It produces decisions *based on specific sets of facts*, rather than laying down propositions of general applicability. Thus it is not really appropriate to suggest, for example, that 'the Court is likely to find that s 11 of the Criminal Procedure and Investigations Act 1996 is compatible with (or in violation of) Art 6 of the ECHR'. All that might be said is that a particular statutory provision will make it more (or less) likely that the rights of a defendant were violated in a particular case.

(d) It bases itself upon the *'margin of appreciation'*. Each country is permitted a certain tolerance in determining its own public policy, within the framework of review by the Court. The objective is to ensure that the political and cultural traditions of the signatory States are respected — they are given a 'margin of appreciation'.

Some of the rights in the ECHR are absolute, e.g., Art 3 prohibiting torture and inhuman or degrading treatment. Most of the rights, however, are subject to limitations. When the Court considers whether such qualifications constitute a violation, it will particularly look at:

(a) Whether the interference with the right is *prescribed by law*. If it is not, there will be a violation of the ECHR.

(b)   Whether the limitation serves a *legitimate purpose*, e.g., national security, public safety.

(c)   Whether it is necessary in a democratic society. This is sometimes framed in terms of a principle of *proportionality*. The interference will be 'disproportionate' if it is not necessary in a democratic society. Implicit in this test is the notion of balance. 'Inherent in the whole of the Convention is a search for the fair balance between the demands of the general interest of the Community and the requirements of the protection of the individual's human rights': *Soering v UK* (1989) 11 EHRR 439.

26.2.5   The rights contained in the ECHR

The content of the ECHR is largely concerned with basic personal freedoms. Cases in which the UK has been involved in alleged breaches of this and other Articles of the ECHR relevant to criminal practice are detailed in specialist works on the ECHR, to which further reference should be made (see, for example, Wadham and Mountfield, *Human Rights Act 1998* (Blackstone Press/OUP, 1999); Emmerson and Ashworth, *Human Rights and Criminal Justice* (Sweet & Maxwell 2001)). Three of the most important Articles of the ECHR are set out below, with a short commentary on each.

Article 3

No one shall be subjected to torture or to inhuman or degrading treatment or punishment.

Article 3 is one of the few articles in the ECHR where the right is guaranteed under all circumstances (the others are Arts 2, 4 and 7). In respect of the remaining articles, the governments which have ratified the ECHR have the right of derogation, i.e., to take measures required by war or other public emergencies (see Arts 15 and 16). No such right exists, however, in relation to the prohibition on torture and inhuman or degrading treatment.

Cases involving the United Kingdom in alleged violations of Art 3 have included:

(a)   the use of corporal punishment as a criminal sanction (*Tyrer v UK* (1978) 2 EHRR 1);

(b)   the treatment of terrorist suspects (*Republic of Ireland v UK* (1978) 2 EHRR 25);

(c)   extradition, possibly to face the death penalty in the United States (*Soering v UK* (1989) 11 EHRR 439).

Article 5

(1)   Everyone has the right to liberty and security of person. No one shall be deprived of his liberty save in the following cases and in accordance with a procedure prescribed by law:

(a)   the lawful detention of a person after conviction by a competent court;

(b)   the lawful arrest or detention of a person for non-compliance with the lawful order of a court or in order to secure the fulfilment of any obligation prescribed by law;

(c)   the lawful arrest or detention of a person effected for the purpose of bringing him before the competent legal authority on reasonable suspicion of having committed an offence or when it is reasonably considered necessary to prevent his committing an offence or fleeing after having done so;

(d)   the detention of a minor by lawful order for the purpose of educational supervision or his lawful detention for the purpose of bringing him before the competent legal authority;

    (e)   the lawful detention of persons for the prevention of the spreading of infectious diseases, of persons of unsound mind, alcoholics or drug addicts or vagrants;

    (f)   the lawful arrest or detention of a person to prevent his effecting an unauthorised entry into the country or of a person against whom action is being taken with a view to deportation or extradition.

    (2)   Everyone who is arrested shall be informed promptly, in a language which he understands, of the reasons for his arrest and of any charge against him.

    (3)   Everyone arrested or detained in accordance with the provisions of paragraph (1) (c) of this article shall be brought promptly before a judge or other officer authorised by law to exercise judicial power and shall be entitled to trial within a reasonable time or to release pending trial. Release may be conditioned by guarantees to appear for trial.

    (4)   Everyone who is deprived of his liberty by arrest or detention shall be entitled to take proceedings by which the lawfulness of his detention shall be decided speedily by a court and his release ordered if the detention is not lawful.

    (5)   Everyone who has been the victim of arrest or detention in contravention of the provisions of this article shall have an enforceable right to compensation.

As can be seen from the text of Art 5, it has considerable relevance to criminal practice. It prohibits deprivation of liberty, save in the circumstances described in exceptions (1)(a) to (1)(f) (although, in common with most articles, Art 5 is subject to the right of derogation laid down in Arts 15 and 16). The exceptions outlined in (a) to (f) cover, respectively, restrictions imposed as a result of:

(a)   sentence after conviction;
(b)   committal for contempt;
(c)   remand in custody;
(d)   the care of minors in specified circumstances;
(e)   infectious illness, mental illness, and addiction;
(f)   illegal immigrants.

There have been a number of cases brought against the UK, based upon Art 5, which involve the detention of suspected terrorists in the context of the situation in Northern Ireland (see, for example, *Brannigan and McBride v UK* (1993) 17 EHRR 539). Another issue which has arisen under Art 5 has been the direction for loss of time where the Court of Appeal believes that an appeal is totally without merit (see Paragraph 24.6.6): *Monnell and Morris v UK* (1987) 7 EHRR 557. In an appropriate case, the refusal of bail by a domestic court could be challenged as contrary to Art 5(3). In *Wemhoff v FRG* (1968) 1 EHRR 55, it was stated that the government must show that there are 'relevant and sufficient' reasons to justify the applicant's continued detention. In a series of decisions, the European Court has upheld grounds for refusing bail which are similar to those in Sch 1 to the Bail Act 1976, i.e. the risk of the accused failing to surrender to custody, committing further offences or interfering with the course of justice (see Chapter 6 for the law on bail). This would not necessarily preclude the issue being canvassed in Strasbourg in appropriate circumstances, however, e.g. where the refusal of bail stemmed from a statutory prohibition upon grounds other than those which the European Court of Human Rights is prepared to hold acceptable.

    Section 25 of the Criminal Justice and Public Order Act 1994, placed an absolute prohibition on bail for anyone awaiting trial for murder, attempted murder, manslaughter, rape or attempted rape if he had a previous conviction for one of those offences (see

Paragraph 6.3). Its terms made the UK government vulnerable to complaints under Art 5, and a number of cases were pending when the statute was amended by s 56 of the Crime and Disorder Act 1998. This replaced the absolute prohibition with a presumption against bail which can be rebutted only if the court considers that there are exceptional circumstances justifying the grant of bail. The European Court of Human Rights has since indicated that a strong presumption against granting bail to those charged with very serious offences is not compatible with Art 5(3) or the presumption of innocence: *Iljikov v Bulgaria*, 26 July 2001, unreported; *Caballero v UK* [2000] Crim LR 587.

Article 6

(1) In the determination of his civil rights and obligations or of any criminal charge against him, everyone is entitled to a fair and public hearing within a reasonable time by an independent and impartial tribunal established by law. Judgment shall be pronounced publicly but the press and public may be excluded from all or part of the trial in the interests of morals, public order or national security in a democratic society, where the interests of juveniles or the protection of the private life of the parties so require, or to the extent strictly necessary in the opinion of the court in special circumstances where publicity would prejudice the interests of justice.

(2) Everyone charged with a criminal offence shall be presumed innocent until proved guilty according to law.

(3) Everyone charged with a criminal offence has the following minimum rights:

(a) to be informed promptly, in a language which he understands and in detail, of the nature and cause of the accusation against him;

(b) to have adequate time and facilities for the preparation of his defence;

(c) to defend himself in person or through legal assistance of his own choosing or, if he has not sufficient means to pay for legal assistance, to be given it free when the interests of justice so require;

(d) to examine or have examined witnesses against him and to obtain the attendance and examination of witnesses on his behalf under the same conditions as witnesses against him;

(e) to have the free assistance of an interpreter if he cannot understand or speak the language used in court.

Article 6 is the most important for criminal practice. Article 6(1) deals with the general right to a fair trial in respect of both civil and criminal cases. It covers the principle of open justice, and the protection of the privacy of the parties, especially juveniles, in certain circumstances. It should be given a broad and purposive interpretation: *Moreiva de Azvedo v Portugal* (1990) 13 EHRR 721. It encompasses the principle of 'equality of arms', which is based on the right of the accused to procedural equality with the prosecution. To put it another way, the accused must have 'a reasonable opportunity of presenting his case to the court under conditions which do not place him at a substantial disadvantage *vis-a-vis* his opponent': *Kaufman v Belgium* (1986) 50 DR 98 at p. 115. There are, however, limits to the reach of Art 6(1). The European Court of Human Rights will avoid substituting its view of the facts for that of the national court, unless the latter court has drawn unfair conclusions. In an exceptional case, however, they will be prepared to assess the evidence with which the domestic court was presented: *Barbera v Spain* (1988) 11 EHRR 360.

A violation of Art 6(1) was alleged in the case of *Saunders v UK* (1996) *The Times*, 18 December 1996. The applicant was the Chief Executive Officer of Guinness Plc, whose operations in the course of a take-over battle were investigated by the Department of Trade and Industry. S was interviewed by DTI inspectors on nine occasions, and required by law to answer the questions put to him, failing which he could face a prison sentence for contempt. The DTI transcripts and documents obtained as a result of interviews were passed to the Crown Prosecution Service. S was prosecuted for false accounting and theft. At the trial, the prosecution relied on the transcripts, which were read out to the jury. S was convicted, and appealed to the Court of Appeal. Although his sentence was reduced from five years to two and a half, and the appeal against conviction was upheld on one count, he was refused leave to appeal to the House of Lords against the remaining convictions. In due course, he appealed to the European Court of Human Rights, which held that S's right not to incriminate himself had been infringed, and there had consequently been a breach of Art 6(1) of the Convention. The right against self-incrimination was stated to have close links with the presumption of innocence contained in Art 6(2).

Another case brought against the United Kingdom under Art 6 was *Murray v UK* (1996) 22 EHRR 29. The government was alleged to have violated Art 6 in two ways:

(a)   by denying M access to legal advice for the first 48 hours of detention; and

(b)   by allowing inferences to be drawn from his silence (under the Northern Ireland predecessor of the provisions in ss 34 and 35 of the Criminal Justice and Public Order Act 1994).

The European Court of Human Rights upheld the complaint as far as (a) was concerned, but not with regard to (b). They emphasised that the other evidence of guilt was strong, and laid some store by the fact that the adverse inferences had been drawn by an experienced judge, sitting without a jury (a situation which differs from that in which ss 34 and 35 of the 1994 Act operate). In the circumstances, they refused to hold that the drawing of inferences from M's behaviour shifted the burden of proof from prosecution to defence so as to infringe the principle of the presumption of innocence. M had, however, also been denied access to a lawyer during the first 48 hours of his police detention. This was particularly important in view of the significance attached to his silence. It was therefore incompatible with the accused's rights under Art 6(1), taken in conjunction with Art 6(3)(c).

The failure on the part of the prosecution to disclose material relevant to credibility may constitute a violation of Art 6(3)(d): *Edwards v UK* (1993) 96 Cr App R 1 (see also Field and Young, 'Disclosure, Appeals and Procedural Traditions: *Edwards v United Kingdom* [1994] Crim LR 264). In *Edwards*, material was discovered in time for the appeal, so that the Court of Appeal could assess its effect on the conviction's safety, and that was held by the European Court of Human Rights to have compensated for the defect in the original trial.

In *Rowe and Davis v UK* (2000) 30 EHRR 1, the European Court of Human Rights examined the issue of the prosecution duty of disclosure, in particular as it relates to material for which immunity is claimed on the basis of sensitivity (for a description of the procedure, see Paragraph 8.7). At the time of the trial of the applicants, the Criminal Procedure and Investigations Act 1996 was not yet in force, and the common law on disclosure was in a process of rapid development. The case does, however, have wider implications for the way in which the statutory procedure for disclosure (described in Chapter 8) is likely to be measured against the ECHR.

The Applicants, Rowe and Davis, were convicted (together with Johnson) in February 1990 of murder, assault occasioning grievous bodily harm and three counts of robbery. Their appeal came before the Court of Appeal in October 1992. At the first hearing, counsel for the prosecution handed a document to the court, which was not shown to defence counsel, seeking a ruling on disclosure. He informed the court that the contents were sensitive, and that he should either be heard *ex p* or if *inter partes*, only on an undertaking by defence counsel not to disclose what took place to their solicitors or clients. At that hearing, defence counsel indicated that they could not conscientiously give such an undertaking, and the prosecution in effect argued *ex p* for non-disclosure. The Court of Appeal in its judgment:

(a)   stated that the procedure relating to material in the prosecution's possession which they sought to avoid disclosing had been changed by *Ward* [1993] 1 WLR 619. It was now for the court, not the prosecution, to decide whether disclosure should be made;

(b)   set out a series of procedural guidelines to be followed in such cases (summarised in Paragraph 8.7); and

(c)   refused to order disclosure.

At the hearing of the substantive appeal, the convictions of Rowe and Davis, and their co-defendant Johnson, were upheld.

In due course, the case was referred to the Criminal Cases Review Commission (see Paragraph 24.8), which investigated the case in the period 1997–99. The investigation revealed that one of the leading prosecution witnesses was a long-standing police informant, who had approached the police and told them that the applicants Rowe and Davis were responsible for the crimes in question. He had received a reward of £10,300 and immunity from prosecution in relation to his admitted participation in the offences. He had never identified Johnson as one of the offenders. These facts had not previously been disclosed to the defence on grounds of public interest immunity. The CCRC commented that 'if the jury had been aware of this then the credibility of [the prosecution witnesses] might have been assessed in a more critical manner'. The case of the Applicants and Johnson was referred back to the Court of Appeal, which in due course upheld their appeal: *Davis* (2000) *The Times*, 25 July 2000.

Meanwhile, the Applicants sought a ruling from the European Court of Human Rights that their trial violated Art 6(1) and (3)(a) and (b). The Applicants argued that the procedure at their trial, whereby the prosecution withheld evidence from the defence without consulting the judge, violated Article 6 of the ECHR. This defect was not rectified by the *ex p* procedure before the Court of Appeal, which gave the defence no opportunity to put forward arguments on disclosure. It was argued on behalf of the Applicants that the exclusion of the accused from this procedure should have been counterbalanced by the introduction of a special independent counsel who could argue the relevance of the undisclosed evidence, test the strength of the prosecution claim to public interest immunity, and safeguard against the risk of judicial error or bias. A special counsel procedure has now been introduced in this country in respect of fair employment cases in Northern Ireland, certain immigration appeals, complaints relating to the interception of electronic communications, and cases where the trial judge prohibits an accused from cross-examining in person the complainant in a sexual offence.

The following points emerged from the decision of the full European Court of Human Rights:

(a)   The right to a fair trial means that the prosecution authorities should disclose to the defence all material evidence in their possession for and against the accused.

(b) That duty of disclosure is not absolute, and 'in any criminal proceedings there may be competing interests, such as national security or the need to protect witnesses at risk of reprisals or keep secret police methods of investigation which must be weighed against the rights of the accused'.

(c) Only such measures restricting the rights of the defence to disclosure as are strictly necessary are permissible under Art 6(1).

(d) Any difficulties caused to the defence by a limitation on its rights must be sufficiently counterbalanced by the procedure followed by the court.

(e) The procedure prior to the case of *Ward* [1993] 1 WLR 619, whereby the prosecution could decide to withhold relevant evidence without notifying the judge, was in violation of Art 6(1).

(f) The procedure adopted by the Court of Appeal at the appeal of the Applicants in relation to disclosure did not remedy the unfair procedure adopted at trial. It was *ex p* and the Court of Appeal was therefore reliant upon prosecution counsel and transcripts of the trial for an understanding of the possible relevance of the undisclosed material. In any event, if the trial judge had received the material, he could have monitored the importance of the undisclosed evidence at a stage when it could have affected the course of the trial. Further, the Court of Appeal, in considering the evidence *ex post facto* may have been unconsciously influenced by the jury's verdict of guilty into underestimating the significance of the undisclosed evidence.

The Applicants, therefore, did not get a fair trial. The case could be contrasted with that of *Edwards*. In that case, appeal proceedings were able to remedy defects in the trial because, by the time of the appeal the defence had received most of the missing information, and was able to argue in detail about the impact of the new material upon the tests for disclosure. It is worth noting, however, that the reasoning of the Court in Strasbourg on (a) and (c) above indicates the wider test of materiality under *Keane* [1994] 1 WLR 747, rather than the more limited duties under the 1996 Act. Further, the requirement as far as secondary disclosure under the 1996 Act is concerned, that it is confined to previously undisclosed prosecution material 'which might be reasonably expected to assist the accused's defence as disclosed by the defence statement' (s 7(2)(a) CPIA 1996) does not sit easily with point (c).

The European Court's decision cast doubt upon the ability of the Court of Appeal to remedy defective disclosure at trial. What it did not do, however, is to give a clear indication as to the fairness of *ex p* procedure, insofar as that procedure is adopted at first instance (now embodied in the Crown Court (Criminal Procedure and Investigations Act 1996) (Disclosure) Rules 1997). It would seem that the special independent counsel procedure which was put forward in argument for the Applicants is likely to be canvassed again in this context, given its adoption in a number of other areas, and the reasoning of the Court in point (d) above.

In *V v UK* [2000] Crim LR 187, the European Court of Human Rights scrutinised England's procedure adopted for the trial of juveniles in the Crown Court. T and V (both aged 10 at the time) abducted the two-year-old Jamie Bulger from a shopping precinct, took him on a two-mile journey, battered him to death and left him on a railway line to be run over. The trial took place over a three-week period in November 1993, in public, at the Crown Court in Preston. It was preceded and accompanied by massive publicity. Throughout the proceedings, the arrival of the defendants was greeted by a hostile crowd. On occasion, attempts were made to attack the vehicles bringing the defendants to court. In the courtroom, the press benches and public gallery were full. At the opening of the trial, the judge made an order under s 39 CYPA 1933 that there should be no publication of the names, addresses or other identifying details of the Applicant (aged 11 at the time of trial) or V, or publication of their photographs. Nevertheless, the trial took place in the full glare of national and international publicity. At the end of the trial, the defendants were found guilty, and the judge modified the order under s 39 to allow publication of the names of T and V, but no other details. In due course, T appealed to the European Court of Human Rights, on the grounds *inter alia* that:

- his trial in the Crown Court amounted to inhuman and degrading treatment within the meaning of Art 3 of the ECHR;
- he had been denied a fair trial under Art 6(1).

The Court held (by 12 votes to five) that the applicant's trial did not amount to inhuman and degrading treatment contrary to Art 3. It did, however, violate his right to a fair trial under Art 6(1) (decision reached by 16 votes to one). The Court stated that it is essential that a young child charged with a grave offence attracting high levels of media interest should be tried in such a way as to reduce as far as possible any feelings of intimidation. It considered that the formality and ritual of the Crown Court must at times have seemed incomprehensible and intimidating for a child of 11. It noted that less serious crimes in England and Wales were dealt with in the youth courts, from which the general public is excluded and there are automatic reporting restrictions. It laid emphasis upon the blaze of publicity surrounding the trial, and the judge's comments on the effect which this must have had on witnesses. The implication was that this must have been even more traumatic for the defendants. There was evidence that certain of the modifications to the courtroom, in particular the raised dock which was designed to enable the defendants to see what was going on, had the effect of increasing the applicant's sense of discomfort during the trial, since he felt exposed to the scrutiny of the press and public. Further, there was evidence that the post-traumatic stress disorder suffered by the applicant, combined with the lack of any therapeutic work since the offence, had limited his ability to instruct his lawyers or testify in his own defence. He was unable to follow the trial or take decisions in his own best interests. He was unable to participate effectively in the criminal proceedings against him and was, in consequence, denied a fair hearing in breach of Art 6(1).

The decision was in the context of a particularly harrowing crime, and an unprecedented degree of media attention. In addition, the defendant was at the lower end of the range of criminal responsibility. Nevertheless, the remarks of the European Court of Human Rights about the effects of publicity upon a child defendant and the need to ensure that all defendants must be able to participate fully in the proceedings against them will undoubtedly have far-reaching implications for the trial of juveniles in the Crown Court (see Paragraph 10.1).

One of the immediate results of the European Court's decision was the *Practice Direction (Crown Court: Trial of children and young persons)* (2000) *The Times* 17 February 2000. It stressed that the trial process should not itself expose the young defendant to avoidable intimidation, humiliation or distress, and pointed out that all possible steps should be taken to assist him to understand and participate in the proceedings. Regard should be had to the welfare of the juvenile, as required by CYPA 1933, s 44. Where a juvenile was indicted jointly with an adult, the court should ordinarily order that the juvenile should be tried on his own unless a joint trial would be in the interests of justice and would not be unduly prejudicial to the welfare of the juvenile.

If a case against a juvenile might attract widespread public interest, the assistance of the police should be enlisted to ensure that the juvenile is not exposed to intimidation or abuse when attending for trial. The judge should be ready to impose such reporting restrictions as are within his powers.

The trial of a juvenile should, if practicable, be held in a courtroom in which all the participants are on the same, or almost the same, level. The juvenile should be free to sit with members of his family, in a placed which permits easy, informal communication with his lawyers and others with whom he needs to communicate. Steps should be taken to ensure that each step of the trial is explained to him, and conducted in language which he can understand. Frequent and regular breaks would often be appropriate. Generally, robes and wigs should not be worn. Attendance at the trial should be restricted to a small number, perhaps limited to those with an immediate interest in its outcome. There should be no recognisable police presence in the courtroom save for good reason. The number of reporters might be restricted, subject to the public's right to be informed of the administration of justice in the Crown Court. If access by reporters is restricted, arrangements should be made for proceedings to be relayed to another room in the court complex if there is the need.

27 Ancillary Financial Matters

This Chapter deals with two ancillary financial matters which are of relevance to criminal proceedings: public funding and costs.

27.1 PUBLIC FUNDING

The law on public funding in criminal matters is dealt with in the Access to Justice Act 1999 (AJA), which replaced the Legal Aid Act 1988, and put into place the new Criminal Defence Service. The AJA 1999 is supplemented by various regulations. The most important are:

    (a)   the Criminal Defence Service (General) (No 2) Regulations 2001 (SI 2001 No 1437);

    (b)   the Criminal Defence Service (Representation Order Appeals) Regulations 2001 (SI 2001 No 1168); and

    (c)   the Criminal Defence Service (Recovery of Defence Costs Orders) Regulations 2001 (SI 2001 No 856).

The Criminal Defence Service (CDS) is the body which provides funding for defendants in criminal proceedings — the system formerly known as legal aid. It began its operations in April 2001. It functions under the aegis of the Legal Services Commission, which also oversees funding for civil cases. The purpose of the CDS is 'securing that individuals involved in criminal investigations or criminal proceedings have access to such advice, assistance and representation as the interests of justice require' (s 12(1) of the AJA 1999).

The CDS relies largely upon a system of contracting, based upon the 'General Criminal Contract', which solicitors in private practice are required to obtain if they wish to carry out publicly-funded criminal defence work. Once such a contract has been awarded, the firm is monitored to ensure that it meets the necessary standards.

In addition, the Legal Services Commission is engaged in a pilot scheme involving its own defender service. The pilot began in 2001, and its success will be evaluated at the conclusion of a four-year period in 2005. The pilot comprises six defender offices, which are staffed by employees of the CDS.

27.1.1 The granting of representation

The granting of representation by the CDS is dealt with in the Criminal Defence Service (General) (No 2) Regulations 2001, regs 6 to 10. In summary, these provide that:

(a)   an application for representation in respect of proceedings in a magistrates' court may be made orally or in writing to the court, or in writing to the justices' clerk;

(b)   an application in respect of Crown Court proceedings may be made orally or in writing to the court or the court manager, or to the magistrates' court (where the case is due to proceed to the Crown Court, e.g. having been committed for trial or sentence);

(c)   an application in respect of proceedings in the Court of Appeal or the House of Lords may be made orally to the Court of Appeal, or a judge of that court, or in writing to the Court of Appeal, a judge of that court, or the registrar.

As to the criteria on which the grant of a representation order is considered, these are set out in para 5 of Sch 3 to the AJA 1999. The overall decision is 'to be determined in accordance with the interests of justice'. There is no longer any means test for proceedings in the magistrates' court or Crown Court. The criteria for determining the interests of justice are:

(a)   whether, in the event of conviction, it is likely that the court would impose a sentence which would either deprive the accused of his liberty, or lead to loss of his livelihood, or seriously damage his reputation;

(b)   whether the case may involve consideration of a substantial question of law;

(c)   whether the accused may be unable to understand the proceedings or state his own case;

(d)   whether the nature of the defence is such as to involve the tracing and interviewing of potential defence witnesses or expert cross-examination of the prosecution witnesses; and

(e)   whether it is in the interests of a person other than the accused that the accused should be represented.

Some charges are so grave that, even though a grant of representation is not mandatory, it would in practice always be granted. Thus, no court would refuse one (except on grounds of means) to a person charged with for example, manslaughter or causing grievous bodily harm with intent, or rape, or robbery. Other charges may or may not justify an order depending on the facts of the particular case. Thus, although the offence of assault occasioning actual bodily harm carries five years' imprisonment, magistrates are not obliged to make an order if the allegations against the accused are in fact of a trivial nature. They should consider how serious the charge really is, and, if they have done that and decide that an order is unnecessary, the High Court will not interfere with their decision unless it is plainly unreasonable: *Highgate Justices ex p Lewis* [1977] Crim LR 611. The factors in para 5 illustrate how sometimes the granting of an order is as much an assistance to the court as it is to the accused. Where the accused would not be able to present his case adequately much time is saved by providing him with a lawyer. Similarly, where cross-examination of a witness by the accused personally would cause distress, the public interest is served by having the cross-examination carried out by a professional. But, however desirable it is that the accused be legally represented, he cannot be forced to have a lawyer — the court can do no more than offer him representation, it cannot make him accept. (There is something of an exception in respect of those cases where an unrepresented defendant is prohibited from cross-examining a particular witness by the provisions of the Youth Justice and Criminal Evidence Act 1999: see Paragraph 18.5.6.)

27.1.2 Appeals against refusal of representation

An accused who is refused the grant of a representation order is entitled to appeal by way of a renewed application to the body which refused the application. The procedure is set out in the Criminal Defence Service (Representation Order Appeals) Regulations 2001.

27.1.3 Recovery of defence costs orders

Section 17 of the AJA 1999 lays down that, where the defence is paid for by the Criminal Defence Service, there is no means test and no payment is required from the person granted representation. This is in contrast to the old legal aid system, which was means tested and subject to contribution orders. A court other than a magistrates' court, however, may make an order that an individual repay some or all of the cost of any such representation. Such an order is known as a Recovery of Defence Costs Order (RDCO). The procedure relating to the RDCO is set out in the Criminal Defence Service (Recovery of Defence Costs Orders) Regulations 2001. The judge may not make an RDCO against a defendant who has appeared in the magistrates' court only, is committed for sentence to the Crown Court or appeals against sentence to the Crown Court. Nor may a judge make an RDCO against a defendant who has been acquitted, other than in exceptional circumstances (reg 4(2)).

27.2 COSTS

Depending on the precise nature and result of the proceedings, the court before which a case or appeal is concluded may make an order *either* that the loser pay the successful party his costs, *or* that costs be paid out of central funds (i.e. out of taxpayers' money). On the whole, the party in whose favour costs are to be ordered would prefer payment out of central funds as he is then sure of his money, whereas an order for inter partes costs may be difficult to enforce, especially if it is against the accused or an impecunious private prosecutor. The law on ordering costs is now contained in ss 16–21 of the Prosecution of Offences Act 1985 (POA). The main points are as follows:

(i)   A *'defendant's costs order'* may be made by magistrates in favour of the accused if either they have found him not guilty following a summary trial, or they have discharged him following committal proceedings at which the prosecution were unable to establish a case to answer: POA 1985, s 16(1). The Crown Court may make a defendant's costs order whenever the accused in acquitted following a trial on indictment, even if he is acquitted on only one of several counts: s 16(2). It may also make such an order where it allows an appeal (whether against conviction or sentence) from the magistrates. The effect of an order is that the costs reasonably incurred by the accused in defending the proceedings are paid out of central funds. Provided the figure is agreed by the defence, the court may specify the amount the accused is to receive when it makes the order: s 16(9)(a). Otherwise, the costs are determined later by court officers in accordance with regulations made by the Lord Chancellor: s 16(9)(b). Where there are circumstances which make it inappropriate for the accused to receive his full costs, the court may assess what in its opinion would be 'just and reasonable' and specify that sum in the order, whether or not the accused agrees it: s 16(7).

(ii)   The court may order that the prosecution receive out of central funds the costs they incurred in connection with proceedings for an indictable offence: s 17(1). This applies even if the accused is acquitted, but is subject to the massive exception that a prosecuting authority which is publicly financed cannot have an order made in its favour: s 17(2) and (6). Thus, neither the police, the Crown Prosecution Service, government departments nor local authorities can apply for an order under s 17(1). In practice, therefore, orders for prosecution costs out of central funds are rare. The reason why an order may not be made in favour of the CPS, etc. is that it would effectively result in the government paying its 'own' money to an organisation which it has to finance in any event.

(iii)   Where the accused is convicted, he may be ordered to pay the prosecution such costs as the court considers 'just and reasonable': s 18(1). This applies both to trials on indictment and to summary trials, regardless of whether the offence charged is summary or triable either way. The amount to be paid must be specified in the order: s 18(3). Costs ordered against a juvenile may not exceed the amount of any fine imposed on him: s 18(5).

(iv)   Regardless of the nature of the offence charged or the result of the proceedings, the court may make an order that costs incurred by one party as a result of 'an unnecessary or improper act or omission' by another party shall be paid by that other party: s 19(1) and reg 3 of the Costs in Criminal Cases (General) Regulations 1986. Thus, if the prosecution were at fault in not having their witnesses at court on the day the case should have been tried, but the court none the less granted an adjournment, they may be ordered to pay the accused's costs of the day, even if he is ultimately convicted. In other words, the prosecution may be ordered to pay the costs which they have caused the defence to throw away and vice versa.

An order under s 19 is appropriate only where the default which caused costs to be thrown away is that of the accused or prosecutor personally.

(v)   Where the fault for the wasted costs lies with the legal representatives, then the court can order them to pay personally. The Courts and Legal Services Act 1990 inserted a new s 19A into the POA 1985. It gives the court power to order a solicitor or barrister to meet the whole or part of costs wasted 'as a result of any improper, unreasonable or negligent act or omission' by the representative or his staff.

(vi)   The 'proceedings' in respect of which costs may be ordered are defined so as to include proceedings in any court below the court which makes the order (see s 21). This means, *inter alia,* that when the Crown Court, following a trial on indictment, makes an order in favour of the accused, he will be entitled to his costs both of the Crown Court trial and of the committal proceedings. Similarly, if a conviction is set aside on appeal, the appellate court may extend its order for costs to cover the proceedings in which the appellant was convicted. As to the costs of appeals, see Paragraphs 24.6.10 (appeals to Court of Appeal), 25.1.3 (appeals to the Crown Court), and 25.2.3 (appeals to the High Court by case stated).

The making of an order for costs is always discretionary. However, the approach the courts should adopt — especially in respect of awards in favour of an acquitted accused — was set out in the *Practice Direction (Crime: Costs)* [1991] 1 WLR 498, which stated that the normal consequence of an acquittal, whether in the magistrates' court or on indictment, should be the making of a defendant's costs order. A similar result should follow in the event of a discharge following committal proceedings. The court should deny the defendant his costs, in whole or in part, only if there were positive reasons for doing so, as where, for example:

(i)   he was at fault in bringing suspicion on himself and misleading the prosecution into thinking that the case against him was stronger than it actually was; or

(ii)   he was acquitted on a technicality but there was ample evidence to support a conviction.

This was amended by the *Practice Direction (Crime. Costs in Criminal Proceedings) (No 2)* (1999) *The Times*, 6 October 1999, so as to delete (ii), on the basis that it was inconsistent with the European Convention of Human Rights. 'Acquittal on a technicality' is therefore no longer a good reason for denying a defendant his costs. It is submitted that this must be right. Technicalities are there for good reason, and if not, there are procedures for ensuring that they are removed either by Parliament or by the processes of the common law. Until they are, a defendant is innocent until proved guilty and is entitled to his costs if he has to undergo a trial which results in acquittal (with a valid exception, in the case of misleading behaviour such as is described in (i)).

As regards ordering an offender to pay prosecution costs, this is entirely discretionary and no guidelines have been given. Usually the costs are considerably less than the actual costs of the proceedings, since the court has to take into account the means of the offender and the effect of any other financial orders it is making (e.g. a fine or compensation order). A Crown Court judge should not use a high costs order as a means of 'punishing' an offender for electing trial on indictment in respect of a charge that could have been appropriately dealt with at the magistrates' court, but, on the other hand, any order made will inevitably reflect the fact that the defence did choose the more expensive mode of trial (see *Bushell* (1980) 2 Cr App R (S) 77).

Where a minor case is in the Crown Court through the prosecution's choice, by contrast, they cannot expect to recover their full costs from the accused. In *Hall* [1989] Crim LR 228, H was willing to plead guilty to careless driving. The case went to the Crown Court because the prosecution insisted on a charge of reckless driving. In the Crown Court, H pleaded guilty to careless driving, and the Crown offered no evidence on the reckless driving charge. H was conditionally discharged and ordered to pay £372 prosecution costs. On appeal, the order was reduced to £25 (the amount appropriate to a guilty plea in the magistrates' court).

The defendant may appeal against a prosecution costs order made by the Crown Court, to the Court of Appeal. There is, however, no appeal to the Crown Court against an order made by a magistrates' court against a defendant to pay prosecution costs, and the defendant's remedy in such a case is to appeal to the Divisional Court by way of case stated or judicial review as appropriate. In *Northallerton Magistrates' Court ex p Dove* [1999] Crim LR 760, the Divisional Court said that the costs which the defendant was ordered to pay by the justices should not be grossly disproportionate to any fine imposed. They quashed an order that the defendant should pay costs four and a half times the amount of the fine, and remitted the matter to the magistrates for them to reconsider what costs if any should be paid to the prosecution.

In *Associated Octel Ltd* [1997] Crim LR 144, the Court of Appeal considered whether the defendant can be ordered to pay costs incurred in the course of the investigation of the offence, as well as legal costs, and held that he could. The prosecution in this case, however, was the same as the investigatory body (the Health and Safety Executive acted in both capacities). It is submitted that the position would be different where the two functions are carried out by two distinct bodies. In such a case, it would not seem 'just and reasonable' (POA 1985, s 18(1)) for the judge or magistrates to order the defendant to pay to the CPS (for example) costs incurred by another body (the police).

Even where the court does not make a general order for payment of a party's costs, it may order that a witness called by that party shall be paid out of central funds such sum as is necessary to compensate him for the 'expense, trouble or loss of time properly incurred by him' through his attending court: POA, s 19(3). Furthermore, the Costs in Criminal Cases (General) Regulations 1986 state that defence witnesses and witnesses called by private prosecutors *shall* be allowed their expenses out of central funds, unless the court states to the contrary (reg 16). The regulations then specify how the expenses are to be calculated, breaking the sum up into a subsistence allowance, a loss of earnings allowance and travelling expenses. Special rules govern payments to interpreters, medical witnesses and other expert witnesses. The accused may claim a subsistence allowance and travelling expenses, but cannot recover for loss of earnings — see regs 17–23 for details.

Appendix 1 Offences against the Person Charging Standard

1 Charging Standard — purpose

1.1 The purpose of joint charging standards is to make sure that the most appropriate charge is selected at the earliest opportunity. This will help the police and Crown Prosecutors in preparing the case. Adoption of this joint standard should lead to a reduction in the number of times charges have to be amended which in turn should lead to an increase in efficiency and a reduction in avoidable extra work for the police and the Crown Prosecution Service.

1.2 This joint Charging Standard offers guidance to police officers who have responsibility for charging and to Crown Prosecutors on the most appropriate charge to be preferred in cases relating to offences against the person. The guidance:

- **should not be used** in the determination of any **pre-charge** decision, such as the decision to arrest;
- **does not** override any guidance issued on the use of appropriate alternative forms of disposal **short of charge**, such as cautioning;
- **does not** override the principles set out in the Code for Crown Prosecutors;
- **does not** override the need for consideration to be given in every case as to whether a charge/prosecution is in the public interest;
- **does not** remove the need for each case to be considered on its individual merits or fetter the discretion of the police to charge and the CPS to prosecute the most appropriate offence depending on the particular facts of the case in question.

2 Introduction

2.1 Offences against the person are intended to penalise those who commit assault and acts of violence. The principal offences are contained in the Offences Against the Person Act 1861 ('the Act'). This joint standard gives guidance about the charge which should be preferred if the criteria set out in the Code for Crown Prosecutors are met.

2.2 This standard covers the following offences:

- common assault, contrary to section 39 Criminal Justice Act 1988;
- assault upon a constable in the execution of his duty, contrary to section [89(1)] Police Act [1996];
- assault with intent to resist arrest, contrary to section 38 of the Act;
- assault occasioning actual bodily harm, contrary to section 47 of the Act;
- unlawful wounding/inflicting grievous bodily harm, contrary to section 20 of the Act;
- wounding/causing grievous bodily harm with intent, contrary to section 18 of the Act;
- attempted murder, contrary to section 1(1) Criminal Attempts Act 1981.

3 General principles: charging practice

3.1 You should always have in mind the following general principles when selecting the appropriate charge(s):

(i) the charge(s) should accurately reflect the extent of the defendant's alleged involvement and responsibility, thereby allowing the Courts the discretion to sentence appropriately;

(ii) the choice of charges should ensure the clear and simple presentation of the case, particularly where there is more than one defendant;

(iii) it is wrong to encourage a defendant to plead guilty to a few charges by selecting more charges than are necessary;

(iv) it is wrong to select a more serious charge which is not supported by the evidence in order to encourage a plea of guilty to a lesser allegation.

4 Common assault, contrary to section 39 Criminal Justice Act 1988

4.1 An offence of common assault is committed when a person either assaults or inflicts a battery upon another person.

4.2 An assault is committed when a person intentionally or recklessly causes another to apprehend the immediate infliction of unlawful force.

4.3 A battery is committed when a person intentionally or recklessly inflicts unlawful force upon another.

4.4 It is a summary only offence which carries a maximum penalty of six months' imprisonment and/or a fine not exceeding the statutory maximum.

4.5 Where there is a battery the defendant should be charged with 'assault by beating': *DPP v Little* [1992] 1 All ER 299.

4.6 The only factor which distinguishes common assault from assault occasioning actual bodily harm, contrary to section 47 of the Offences Against the Person Act 1861, is the degree of injury which results. Normally, aggravating factors which may be relevant to sentence and to mode of trial decisions are irrelevant when deciding whether the degree of injury justifies a charge under section 47.

4.7   Where battery results in injury, a choice of charge is available. The Code for Crown Prosecutors recognises that there will be factors which may properly lead to a decision not to prefer or continue with the gravest possible charge. Thus, although any injury can be classified as actual bodily harm, the appropriate charge will be contrary to section 39 where injuries amount to no more than the following:

- grazes;
- scratches;
- abrasions;
- minor bruising;
- swellings;
- reddening of the skin;
- superficial cuts;
- a 'black eye'.

4.8   You should always consider the injuries first and in most cases the degree of injury will determine whether the appropriate charge is section 39 or section 47. There will be borderline cases, such as where an undisplaced broken nose has resulted. When the injuries amount to no more than those described at paragraph 4.7 above, any decision to charge an offence contrary to section 47 would only be justified in the most exceptional circumstances, or where the maximum available sentence in the Magistrates' Court would be inadequate.

4.9   As common assault is not an alternative verdict to more serious offences of assault, a jury may only convict of common assault if the count has been preferred in the circumstances set out in section 40 Criminal Justice Act 1988 (see paragraph 11.6 below).

4.10   Where a charge contrary to section 47 has been preferred, the acceptance of a plea of guilty to an added count for common assault will rarely be justified in the absence of a significant change in circumstances that could not have been foreseen at the time of review.

5   Assault on a Constable in the execution of his/her duty, contrary to section [89(1)] Police Act [1996]

5.1   The offence is committed when a person assaults either:

- a constable acting in the execution of his or her duty; or
- a person assisting a constable in the execution of his/her duty.

5.2   It is a summary only offence which carries a maximum penalty of six months' imprisonment and/or a fine not exceeding the statutory maximum.

5.3   If an assault on a constable results in injury of the type described at paragraph 4.7 above, a prosecution under section [89(1)] Police Act [1996] will be appropriate, provided that the officer is acting in the execution of his/her duty.

5.4   Where the evidence that the officer was acting in the execution of his/her duty is insufficient, but proceedings for an assault are nevertheless warranted, the appropriate charge will be under section 39.

5.5   The fact that the victim is a police officer is not, in itself, an exceptional reason for charging an offence contrary to section 47 when the injuries are minor. When the injuries are such that an offence contrary to section 47 would be charged in relation to an assault on a member of the public, section 47 will be the appropriate charge for an assault on a constable.

6   Assault with intent to resist arrest, contrary to section 38 of the Act

6.1   The offence is committed when a person assaults another person with the intent to resist or prevent the lawful apprehension or detainer of himself or another for any offence.

6.2   It is an either way offence which carries a maximum penalty on indictment of two years' imprisonment and/or an unlimited fine. Summarily, the maximum penalty is six months' imprisonment and/or a fine not exceeding the statutory maximum.

6.3   A charge contrary to section 38 may properly be used for assaults on persons other than police officers, for example store detectives, who may be trying to apprehend or detain an offender.

6.4   When a police officer is assaulted, a charge under section [89(1)] will often be more appropriate unless there is clear evidence of an intent to resist apprehension or prevent detainer. Unlike section [89(1)], a charge under section 38 is triable on indictment and may therefore be coupled with other offences to be tried on indictment.

6.5   It is not bad for duplicity to charge 'resist or prevent the lawful apprehension or detainer' etc. in the one count: Rule 7 of the Indictments Rules 1971.

7   Assault occasioning actual bodily harm, contrary to section 47 of the Act

7.1   The offence is committed when a person assaults another, thereby causing actual bodily harm to that other person.

7.2   It is an either way offence which carries a maximum penalty on indictment of five years' imprisonment and/or an unlimited fine. Summarily, the maximum penalty is six months' imprisonment and/or a fine not exceeding the statutory maximum.

7.3   As is made clear in paragraph 4.6 above, the only factor in law which distinguishes a charge under section 39 from a charge under section 47 is the degree of injury. By way of example, the following injuries should normally be prosecuted under section 47:

- loss or breaking of a tooth or teeth;
- temporary loss of sensory functions (which may include loss of consciousness);
- extensive or multiple bruising;

- displaced broken nose;
- minor fractures;
- minor, but not merely superficial, cuts of a sort probably requiring medical treatment (e.g. stitches);
- psychiatric injury which is more than fear, distress or panic. (Such injury will be proved by appropriate expert evidence.)

7.4   Section 47 will also be the appropriate charge in the exceptional circumstances referred to in paragraph 4.8 above.

7.5   A verdict of assault occasioning actual bodily harm may be returned on proof of an assault together with proof of the fact that actual bodily harm was occasioned by the assault. The prosecution are not obliged to prove that the defendant intended to cause some actual bodily harm or was reckless as to whether harm would be caused: *Savage, Parmenter* [1991] 4 All ER 698.

8   Unlawful wounding/inflicting grievous bodily harm, contrary to section 20 of the Act.

8.1   The offence is committed when a person unlawfully and maliciously, either:

- wounds another person; or
- inflicts grievous bodily harm upon another person.

8.2   It is an either way offence which carries a maximum penalty on indictment of five years' imprisonment and/or an unlimited fine. Summarily, the maximum penalty is six months' imprisonment and/or a fine not exceeding the statutory maximum.

8.3   Wounding means the breaking of the continuity of the whole of the outer skin, or the inner skin within the cheek or lip. It does not include the rupturing of internal blood vessels.

8.4   The definition of wounding may encompass injuries which are relatively minor in nature, for example a small cut or laceration. An assault resulting in such minor injuries should more appropriately be charged contrary to section 47. An offence contrary to section 20 should be reserved for those wounds considered to be serious (thus equating the offence with the infliction of grievous, or serious, bodily harm under the other part of the section).

8.5   Grievous bodily harm means serious bodily harm. Examples of this are:

- injury resulting in permanent disability or permanent loss of sensory function;
- injury which results in more than minor permanent, visible disfigurement;
- broken or displaced limbs or bones, including fractured skull; compound fractures, broken cheek bone, jaw, ribs, etc;
- injuries which cause substantial loss of blood, usually necessitating a transfusion;
- injuries resulting in lengthy treatment or incapacity. (When psychiatric injury is alleged appropriate expert evidence is essential to prove the injury.)

8.6   In accordance with the recommendation in *McCready* [1978] 1 WLR 1376, if there is any reliable evidence that a sufficiently serious **wound** has been inflicted, then the charge under section 20 should be of unlawful wounding, rather than of inflicting grievous bodily harm. Where both a wound and grievous bodily harm have been inflicted, discretion should be used in choosing which part of section 20 more appropriately reflects the true nature of the offence.

8.7   The prosecution must prove under section 20 that either the defendant intended, or actually foresaw, that the act would cause some harm. It is not necessary to prove that the defendant either intended or foresaw that the unlawful act might cause physical harm of the gravity described in section 20. It is enough that the defendant foresaw that some physical harm to some person, albeit of a minor character, might result: *Savage, Parmenter* (supra).

9   Wounding/causing grievous bodily harm with intent, contrary to section 18 of the Act

9.1   The offence is committed when a person unlawfully and maliciously, with intent to do some grievous bodily harm, or with intent to resist or prevent the lawful apprehension or detainer of any person, either:

- wounds another person; or
- causes grievous bodily harm to another person.

9.2   It is an indictable only offence which carries a maximum penalty of imprisonment for life.

9.3   For the definition of wounding and grievous bodily harm, see paragraph 8 above.

9.4   The distinction between charges under section 18 and section 20 is one of intent.

9.5   The gravity of the injury resulting is not the determining factor although it may provide some evidence of intent.

9.6   When charging an offence involving grievous bodily harm, consideration should be given to the fact that a section 20 offence requires the **infliction** of harm, whereas a section 18 offence requires the **causing** of harm. This is especially significant when considering alternative verdicts (see paragraph 11 below).

9.7   Factors which may indicate the specific intent include:—

- a repeated or planned attack;
- deliberate selection of a weapon or adaptation of an article to cause injury, such as breaking a glass before an attack;
- making prior threats;
- using an offensive weapon against, or kicking, the victim's head;

9.8   The evidence of intent required is different if the offence alleged is a wounding or the causing of grievous bodily harm with intent to resist or prevent the lawful apprehension or detainer of any person. This part of section 18 is of assistance in more serious assaults upon police officers, where the evidence of an intention to prevent arrest is clear, but the evidence of an intent to cause grievous bodily harm is in doubt.

9.9   It is not bad for duplicity to indict for wounding with intent to cause grievous bodily harm or to resist lawful apprehension in one count, although it is best practice to include the allegations in separate counts. This will enable a jury to consider the different intents and the court to sentence on a clear basis of the jury's finding.

10   Attempted murder, contrary to section 1(1) Criminal Attempts Act 1981

10.1   The offence is committed when a person does an act which is more than merely preparatory to the commission of an offence of murder, and at the time the person has the intention to kill.

10.2   It is an indictable only offence which carries a maximum penalty of imprisonment for life.

10.3   Unlike murder, which requires an intention to kill or cause grievous bodily harm, **attempted murder requires evidence of an intention to kill alone**. This makes it a difficult allegation to sustain and careful consideration must be given to whether the more appropriate charge is under section 18.

10.4   The Courts will pay particular attention to counts of attempted murder and justifiably will be highly critical of any such count unless there is clear evidence of an intention to kill.

10.5   It should be borne in mind that the actions of the defendant must be more than preparatory and although words and threats may provide prima facie evidence of an intention to kill, there may be doubt as to whether they were uttered seriously or were mere bravado.

10.6   Evidence of the following factors may assist in proving the intention to kill:

- calculated planning;
- selection and use of a deadly weapon;
- threats (subject to paragraph 10.5) above;
- severity or duration of attack;
- relevant admissions in interview.

11   Alternative verdicts

11.1   In certain circumstances, it is possible for a jury to find the accused not guilty of the offence charged, but guilty of some other alternative offence. The general provisions are contained in section 6(3), Criminal Law Act 1967, and are supplemented by other provisions which relate to specific offences.

11.2   For offences against the person, the following alternatives may be found by a jury:

causing grievous bodily harm with intent, contrary to section 18 of the Act

- attempting to cause grievous bodily harm with intent;
- inflicting grievous bodily harm, contrary to section 20 of the Act;
- unlawful wounding, contrary to section 20 of the Act.

wounding with intent, contrary to section 18 of the Act

- attempting wounding with intent;
- unlawful wounding, contrary to section 20 of the Act;
- assault occasioning actual bodily harm, contrary to section 47 of the Act.

inflicting grievous bodily harm, contrary to section 20 of the Act

- assault occasioning actual bodily harm, contrary to section 47 of the Act.

unlawful wounding, contrary to section 20 of the Act

- assault occasioning actual bodily harm, contrary to section 47 of the Act.

11.3   It is essential, however, that the charge which most suits the circumstances of the case is always preferred. It will never be appropriate to charge a more serious offence in order to obtain a conviction (whether by plea or verdict) to a lesser offence.

11.4   There is authority to support the proposition that a jury may convict of wounding, contrary to section 20 of the Act, as an alternative to a count of causing grievous bodily harm with intent, contrary to section 18 of the Act: *Wilson, Jenkins & Jenkins* (1983) 77 Cr App R 319 HL, *Mandair* [1994] 2 WLR 1376 HL.

11.5   Notwithstanding that authority, prosecutors should nevertheless include a separate count on the indictment alleging wounding, contrary to section 20, where there is a realistic likelihood that the jury will convict the defendant of the lesser offence.

11.6   Common assault is not available as an alternative to any offence contrary to sections 18, 20 or 47 of the Act. A specific count alleging common assault must be included on the indictment pursuant to the provisions of section 40, Criminal Justice Act 1988.

12   Defences to assaults

12.1   Police officers and prosecutors must consider all assaults in the context in which they are allegedly committed. There will be cases in which the surrounding circumstances will be of help in deciding whether to bring criminal proceedings.

12.2   Particular care must be taken in dealing with cases of assault where the allegation is made by a 'victim' who was, at the time, engaged in criminal activity himself. For instance, a burglar who claims to have been assaulted by the occupier of the premises concerned.

12.3   It is lawful for an individual to use reasonable force in the following circumstances:

- in self-defence; or
- to defend another; or
- to defend property; or
- to prevent crime; or
- to lawfully arrest.

12.4   Where the use of force in any of these circumstances is reasonable, the 'assailant' has an absolute defence and charges relating to the assault should not be brought.

12.5   In assessing the reasonableness of the force used, two questions should be asked:

- was the use of force justified in the circumstances? (i.e. was there a need for any force at all?); and

- was the force used excessive in the circumstances?

The courts have indicated that both questions are to be answered on the basis of the facts as the accused *honestly believed* them to be. To that extent it is a *subjective* test. There is, however, an *objective* element to the test, as the court must then go on to ask whether, on the basis of the facts as the accused believed them to be, a reasonable person would regard the force used as reasonable or excessive.

12.6   There can be a fine line, however, between what constitutes reasonable and unreasonable force. When considering whether the force used was reasonable or excessive, it is important to consider the words of Lord Morris in *Palmer v R* [1971] AC 814 which emphasise the difficulties often facing someone confronted by an intruder or defending himself against attack:

> If there has been an attack so that defence is reasonably necessary, it will be recognised that a person defending himself cannot weigh to a nicety the exact measure of his defensive action. If the jury thought that in a moment of unexpected anguish a person attacked had only done what he honestly and instinctively thought necessary, that would be the most potent evidence that only reasonable defensive action had been taken . . .

12.7   Where the police are in doubt about whether a charge should be brought in cases such as these, they should seek the advice of the CPS before charging the defendant.

Appendix 2 National Mode of Trial Guidelines

The purpose of these guidelines is to help magistrates decide whether or not to commit 'either way' offences for trial in the Crown Court. Their object is to provide guidance not direction. They are not intended to impinge upon a magistrate's duty to consider each case individually and on its own particular facts.

These guidelines apply to all defendants aged 18 and above.

General mode of trial considerations

Section 19 of the Magistrates' Courts Act 1980 requires magistrates to have regard to the following matters in deciding whether an offence is more suitable for summary trial or trial on indictment: (1) the nature of the case; (2) whether the circumstances make the offence one of a serious character; (3) whether the punishment which a magistrates' court would have power to inflict for it would be adequate; (4) any other circumstances which appear to the court to make it more suitable for the offence to be tried in one way rather than the other; (5) any representations made by the prosecution or the defence.

Certain general observations can be made: (a) the court should never make its decision on the grounds of convenience or expedition; (b) the court should assume for the purpose of deciding mode of trial that the prosecution version of the facts is correct; (c) the fact that the offences are alleged to be specimens is a relevant consideration; the fact that the defendant will be asking for other offences to be taken into consideration, if convicted, is not; (d) where cases involve complex questions of fact or difficult questions of law, the court should consider committal for trial; (e) where two or more defendants are jointly charged with an offence each has an individual right to elect his mode of trial; (f) in general, except where otherwise stated, either-way offences should be tried summarily unless the court considers that the particular case has one or more of the features set out in the following pages *and* that its sentencing powers are insufficient; (g) the court should also consider its powers to commit an offender for sentence, under section 38 of the Magistrates' Courts Act 1980, as amended by section 25 of the Criminal Justice Act 1991, if information emerges during the course of the hearing which leads them to conclude that the offence is so serious, or the offender such a risk to the public, that their powers to sentence him are inadequate. This amendment means that committal for sentence is no longer determined by reference to the character or antecedents of the defendant.

Features relevant to the individual offences

Note: Where reference is made in these guidelines to property or damage of 'high value' it means a figure equal to at least twice the amount of the limit (currently £5,000) imposed by statute on a magistrates' court when making a compensation order.

[*Note*: Each of the guidelines in respect of the individual offences set out below (except those relating to drugs offences) are prefaced by a reminder in the following terms 'Cases should be tried summarily unless the court considers that one or more of the following features is present in the case *and* that its sentencing powers are insufficient. Magistrates should take account of their powers under s 25 of the Criminal Justice Act 1991 to commit for *sentence*'.]

Burglary
1. *Dwelling-house*
    (1) Entry in the daytime when the occupier (or another) is present.
    (2) Entry at night of a house which is normally occupied, whether or not the occupier (or another) is present.
    (3) The offence is alleged to be one of a series of similar offences.
    (4) When soiling, ransacking, damage or vandalism occurs.
    (5) The offence has professional hallmarks.
    (6) The unrecovered property is of high value [see above for definition of 'high value'].

Note: Attention is drawn to para 28(c) of schedule 1 to the Magistrates' Courts Act 1980, by which offences of burglary in a dwelling *cannot* be tried summarily if any person in the dwelling was subjected to violence or the threat of violence.

2. *Non-dwellings*
    (1) Entry of a pharmacy or doctor's surgery.
    (2) Fear is caused or violence is done to anyone lawfully on the premises (e.g., nightwatchman; security guard).
    (3) The offence has professional hallmarks.
    (4) Vandalism on a substantial scale.
    (5) The unrecovered property is of high value [see above for definition of 'high value'].

Theft and fraud
    (1) Breach of trust by a person in a position of substantial authority, or in whom a high degree of trust is placed.
    (2) Theft or fraud which has been committed or disguised in a sophisticated manner.
    (3) Theft or fraud committed by an organised gang.
    (4) The victim is particularly vulnerable to theft or fraud (e.g., the elderly or infirm).
    (5) The unrecovered property is of high value [see above for definition of 'high value'].

Handling
    (1) Dishonest handling of stolen property by a receiver who has commissioned the theft.
    (2) The offence has professional hallmarks.
    (3) The property is of high value [see above for definition of 'high value'].

Social security frauds
    (1)   Organised fraud on a large scale.
    (2)   The frauds are substantial and carried out over a long period of time.

Violence (sections 20 and 47 of the Offences against the Person Act 1861)
    (1)   The use of a weapon of a kind likely to cause serious injury.
    (2)   A weapon is used and serious injury is caused.
    (3)   More than minor injury is caused by kicking, head-butting or similar forms of assault.
    (4)   Serious violence is caused to those whose work has to be done in contact with the public or who are likely to face violence in the course of their work.
    (5)   Violence to vulnerable people (e.g., the elderly and infirm).
    (6)   The offence has clear racial motivation.

Note: The same considerations apply to cases of domestic violence.

Public Order Act offences
1.   Cases of violent disorder should generally be committed for trial.
2.   Affray.
    (1)   Organised violence or use of weapons.
    (2)   Significant injury or substantial damage.
    (3)   The offence has clear racial motiviation.
    (4)   An attack upon police officers, prison officers, ambulancemen, firemen and the like.

Violence to and neglect of children
    (1)   Substantial injury.
    (2)   Repeated violence or serious neglect, even if the physical harm is slight.
    (3)   Sadistic violence (e.g., deliberate burning or scalding).

Indecent assault
    (1)   Substantial disparity in age between victim and defendant, and the assault is more than trivial.
    (2)   Violence or threats of violence.
    (3)   Relationship of trust or responsibility between defendant and victim.
    (4)   Several similar offences, and the assaults are more than trivial.
    (5)   The victim is particularly vulnerable.
    (6)   Serious nature of the assault.

Unlawful sexual intercourse
    (1)   Wide disparity of age.
    (2)   Breach of position of trust.
    (3)   The victim is particularly vulnerable.

Note: Unlawful sexual intercourse with a girl under 13 is triable only on indictment.

Drugs
1.   Class A
    (a)   Supply; possession with intent to supply: these cases should be committed for trial.

(b)   Possession: should be committed for trial unless the amount is consistent only with personal use.

2.   Class B

(a)   Supply; possession with intent to supply: should be committed for trial unless there is only small scale supply for no payment.

(b)   Possession: should be committed for trial when the quantity is substantial and not consistent only with personal use.

Dangerous driving
   (1)   Alcohol or drugs contributing to dangerousness.
   (2)   Grossly excessive speed.
   (3)   Racing.
   (4)   Prolonged course of dangerous driving.
   (5)   Degree of injury or damage sustained.
   (6)   Other related offences.

Criminal damage
   (1)   Deliberate fire-raising.
   (2)   Committed by a group.
   (3)   Damage of a high value [see above for definition of 'high value'].
   (4)   The offence has clear racial motivation.

Note: Offences set out in Schedule 2 to the Magistrates' Courts Act 1980 (which includes offences of criminal damage which do not amount to arson) *must* be tried summarily if the value of the property damaged or destroyed is £5,000 or less.

Appendix 3   Code of Practice on Disclosure

CRIMINAL PROCEDURE AND INVESTIGATIONS ACT 1996
CODE OF PRACTICE UNDER PART II

Introduction

1.1   This code of practice is issued under Part II of the Criminal Procedure and Investigations Act 1996 ('the Act'). It applies in respect of criminal investigations conducted by police officers which begin on or after the day on which this code comes into effect. Persons other than police officers who are charged with the duty of conducting an investigation as defined in the Act are to have regard to the relevant provisions of the code, and should take these into account in applying their own operating procedures.

1.2   This code does not apply to persons who are not charged with the duty of conducting an investigation as defined in the Act.

1.3   Nothing in this code applies to material intercepted in obedience to a warrant issued under section 2 of the Interception of Communications Act 1985, or to any copy of that material as defined in section 10 of that Act.

1.4   This code extends only to England and Wales.

Definitions

2.1   In this code:
—   a *criminal investigation* is an investigation conducted by police officers with a view to it being ascertained whether a person should be charged with an offence, or whether a person charged with an offence is guilty of it. This will include:
    —   investigations into crimes that have been committed;
    —   investigations whose purpose is to ascertain whether a crime has been committed, with a view to the possible institution of criminal proceedings; and
    —   investigations which begin in the belief that a crime may be committed, for example when the police keep premises or individuals under observation for a period of time, with a view to the possible institution of criminal proceedings;
—   charging a person with an offence includes prosecution by way of summons;
—   an *investigator* is any police officer involved in the conduct of a criminal investigation. All investigators have a responsibility for carrying out the duties imposed on them under this code, including in particular recording information, and retaining records of information and other material;

— the *officer in charge of an investigation* is the police officer responsible for directing a criminal investigation. He is also responsible for ensuring that proper procedures are in place for recording information, and retaining records of information and other material, in the investigation;

— the *disclosure officer* is the person responsible for examining material retained by the police during the investigation; revealing material to the prosecutor during the investigation and any criminal proceedings resulting from it, and certifying that he has done this; and disclosing material to the accused at the request of the prosecutor;

— the *prosecutor* is the authority responsible for the conduct of criminal proceedings on behalf of the Crown. Particular duties may in practice fall to individuals acting on behalf of the prosecuting authority;

— *material* is material of any kind, including information and objects, which is obtained in the course of a criminal investigation and which may be relevant to the investigation;

— material may be *relevant to an investigation* if it appears to an investigator, or to the officer in charge of an investigation, or to the disclosure officer, that it has some bearing on any offence under investigation or any person being investigated, or on the surrounding circumstances of the case, unless it is incapable of having any impact on the case;

— *sensitive material* is material which the disclosure officer believes, after consulting the officer in charge of the investigation, it is not in the public interest to disclose;

— references to *primary prosecution disclosure* are to the duty of the prosecutor under section 3 of the Act to disclose material which is in his possession or which he has inspected in pursuance of this code, and which in his opinion might undermine the case against the accused;

— references to *secondary prosecution disclosure* are to the duty of the prosecutor under section 7 of the Act to disclose material which is in his possession or which he has inspected in pursuance of this code, and which might reasonably be expected to assist the defence disclosed by the accused in a defence statement given under the Act;

— references to the disclosure of material to a person accused of an offence include references to the disclosure of material to his legal representative;

— references to police officers and to the chief officer of police include those employed in a police force as defined in section 3(3) of the Prosecution of Offences Act 1985.

General responsibilities

3.1   The functions of the investigator, the officer in charge of an investigation and the disclosure officer are separate. Whether they are undertaken by one, two or more persons will depend on the complexity of the case and the administrative arrangements within each police force. Where they are undertaken by more than one person, close consultation between them is essential to the effective performance of the duties imposed by this code.

3.2   The chief officer of police for each police force is responsible for putting in place arrangements to ensure that in every investigation the identity of the officer in charge of an investigation and the disclosure officer is recorded.

3.3   The officer in charge of an investigation may delegate tasks to another investigator or to civilians employed by the police force, but he remains responsible for ensuring that these have been carried out and for accounting for any general policies followed in the investigation. In particular, it is an essential part of his duties to ensure that all material which may be relevant to an investigation is retained, and either made available to the disclosure officer or (in exceptional circumstances) revealed directly to the prosecutor.

3.4   In conducting an investigation, the investigator should pursue all reasonable lines of inquiry, whether these point towards or away from the suspect. What is reasonable in each case will depend on the particular circumstances.

3.5   If the officer in charge of an investigation believes that other persons may be in possession of material that may be relevant to the investigation, and if this has not been obtained under paragraph 3.4 above, he should ask the disclosure officer to inform them of the existence of the investigation and to invite them to retain the material in case they receive a request for its disclosure. The disclosure officer should inform the prosecutor that they may have such material. However, the officer in charge of an investigation is not required to make speculative enquiries of other persons: there must be some reason to believe that they may have relevant material. That reason may come from information provided to the police by the accused or from other inquiries made or from some other source.

3.6   If, during a criminal investigation, the officer in charge of an investigation or disclosure officer for any reason no longer has responsibility for the functions falling to him, either his supervisor or the police officer in charge of criminal investigations for the police force concerned must assign someone else to assume that responsibility. That person's identity must be recorded, as with those initially responsible for these functions in each investigation.

Recording of information

4.1   If material which may be relevant to the investigation consists of information which is not recorded in any form, the officer in charge of an investigation must ensure that it is recorded in a durable or retrievable form (whether in writing, on video or audio tape, or on computer disk).

4.2   Where it is not practicable to retain the initial record of information because it forms part of a larger record which is to be destroyed, its contents should be transferred as a true record to a durable and more easily-stored form before that happens.

4.3   Negative information is often relevant to an investigation. If it may be relevant it must be recorded. An example might be a number of people present in a particular place at a particular time who state that they saw nothing unusual.

4.4   Where information which may be relevant is obtained, it must be recorded at the time it is obtained or as soon as practicable after that time. This includes, for example, information obtained in house-to-house enquiries, although the requirement to record information promptly does not require an investigator to take a statement from a potential witness where it would not otherwise be taken.

Retention of material

(a)   Duty to retain material

5.1   The investigator must retain material obtained in a criminal investigation which may be relevant to the investigation. This includes not only material coming into the possession of the investigator (such as documents seized in the course of searching premises) but also material generated by him (such as interview records). Material may be photographed, or retained in the form of a copy rather than the original, if the original is perishable, or was supplied to the investigator rather than generated by him and is to be returned to its owner.

5.2 Where material has been seized in the exercise of the powers of seizure conferred by the Police and Criminal Evidence Act 1984, the duty to retain it under this code is subject to the provisions on the retention of seized material in section 22 of that Act.

5.3 If the officer in charge of an investigation becomes aware as a result of developments in the case that material previously examined but not retained (because it was not thought to be relevant) may now be relevant to the investigation, he should, wherever practicable, take steps to obtain it or ensure that it is retained for further inspection or for production in court if required.

5.4 The duty to retain material includes in particular the duty to retain material falling into the following categories, where it may be relevant to the investigation:

— crime reports (including crime report forms, relevant parts of incident report books or police officers' notebooks);

— custody records;

— records which are derived from tapes of telephone messages (for example, 999 calls) containing descriptions of an alleged offence or offender;

— final versions of witness statements (and draft versions where their content differs from the final version), including any exhibits mentioned (unless these have been returned to their owner on the understanding that they will be produced in court if required);

— interview records (written records, or audio or video tapes, of interviews with actual or potential witnesses or suspects);

— communications between the police and experts such as forensic scientists, reports of work carried out by experts, and schedules of scientific material prepared by the expert for the investigator, for the purposes of criminal proceedings;

— any material casting doubt on the reliability of a confession;

— any material casting doubt on the reliability of a witness;

— any other material which may fall within the test for primary prosecution disclosure in the Act.

5.5 The duty to retain material falling into these categories does not extend to items which are purely ancillary to such material and possess no independent significance (for example, duplicate copies of records or reports).

(b) Length of time for which material is to be retained

5.6 All material which may be relevant to the investigation must be retained until a decision is taken whether to institute proceedings against a person for an offence.

5.7 If a criminal investigation results in proceedings being instituted, all material which may be relevant must be retained at least until the accused is acquitted or convicted or the prosecutor decides not to proceed with the case.

5.8 Where the accused is convicted, all material which may be relevant must be retained at least until:

— the convicted person is released from custody, or discharged from hospital, in cases where the court imposes a custodial sentence or a hospital order;

— six months from the date of conviction, in all other cases.

If the court imposes a custodial sentence or hospital order and the convicted person is released from custody or discharged from hospital earlier than six months from the date of conviction, all material which may be relevant must be retained at least until six months from the date of conviction.

5.9 If an appeal against conviction is in progress when the release or discharge occurs, or at the end of the period of six months specified in paragraph 5.8, all material which may be relevant must be retained until the appeal is determined. Similarly, if the Criminal Cases Review Commission is considering an application at that point in time, all material which may be relevant must be retained at least until the Commission decides not to refer the case to the Court of Appeal, or until the Court determines the appeal resulting from the reference by the Commission.

5.10 Material need not be retained by the police as required in paragraph 5.8 if it was seized and is to be returned to its owner.

Preparation of material for prosecutor

(a) Introduction

6.1 The officer in charge of the investigation, the disclosure officer or an investigator may seek advice from the prosecutor about whether any particular item of material may be relevant to the investigation.

6.2 Material which may be relevant to an investigation, which has been retained in accordance with this code, and which the disclosure officer believes will not form part of the prosecution case, must be listed on a schedule.

6.3 Material which the disclosure officer does not believe is sensitive must be listed on a schedule of non-sensitive material. The schedule must include a statement that the disclosure officer does not believe the material is sensitive.

6.4 Any material which is believed to be sensitive must be either listed on a schedule of sensitive material or, in exceptional circumstances, revealed to the prosecutor separately.

6.5 Paragraphs 6.6 to 6.11 below apply to both sensitive and non-sensitive material. Paragraphs 6.12 to 6.14 apply to sensitive material only.

(b) Circumstances in which a schedule is to be prepared

6.6 The disclosure officer must ensure that a schedule is prepared in the following circumstances:
— the accused is charged with an offence which is triable only on indictment;
— the accused is charged with an offence which is triable either way, and it is considered either that the case is likely to be tried on indictment or that the accused is likely to plead not guilty at a summary trial;
— the accused is charged with a summary offence, and it is considered that he is likely to plead not guilty.

6.7 In respect of either way and summary offences, a schedule may not be needed if a person has admitted the offence, or if a police officer witnessed the offence and that person has not denied it.

6.8 If it is believed that the accused is likely to plead guilty at a summary trial, it is not necessary to prepare a schedule in advance. If, contrary to this belief, the accused pleads not guilty at a summary trial, or the offence is to be tried on indictment, the disclosure officer must ensure that a schedule is prepared as soon as is reasonably practicable after that happens.

(c) Way in which material is to be listed on schedule

6.9 The disclosure officer should ensure that each item of material is listed separately on the schedule, and is numbered consecutively. The description of each item should make clear the nature of the item and should contain sufficient detail to enable the prosecutor to decide whether he needs to inspect the material before deciding whether or not it should be disclosed.

6.10   In some enquiries it may not be practicable to list each item of material separately. For example, there may be many items of a similar or repetitive nature. These may be listed in a block and described by quantity and generic title.

6.11   Even if some material is listed in a block, the disclosure officer must ensure that any items among that material which might meet the test for primary prosecution disclosure are listed and described individually.

(d)   Treatment of sensitive material

6.12   Subject to paragraph 6.13 below, the disclosure officer must list on a sensitive schedule any material which he believes it is not in the public interest to disclose, and the reason for that belief. The schedule must include a statement that the disclosure officer believes the material is sensitive. Depending on the circumstances, examples of such material may include the following among others:

—   material relating to national security;
—   material received from the intelligence and security agencies;
—   material relating to intelligence from foreign sources which reveals sensitive intelligence gathering methods;
—   material given in confidence;
—   material which relates to the use of a telephone system and which is supplied to an investigator for intelligence purposes only;
—   material relating to the identity or activities of informants, or under-cover police officers, or other persons supplying information to the police who may be in danger if their identities are revealed;
—   material revealing the location of any premises or other place used for police surveillance, or the identity of any person allowing a police officer to use them for surveillance;
—   material revealing, either directly or indirectly, techniques and methods relied upon by a police officer in the course of a criminal investigation, for example covert surveillance techniques, or other methods of detecting crime;
—   material whose disclosure might facilitate the commission of other offences or hinder the prevention and detection of crime;
—   internal police communications such as management minutes;
—   material upon the strength of which search warrants were obtained;
—   material containing details of persons taking part in identification parades;
—   material supplied to an investigator during a criminal investigation which has been generated by an official of a body concerned with the regulation or supervision of bodies corporate or of persons engaged in financial activities, or which has been generated by a person retained by such a body;
—   material supplied to an investigator during a criminal investigation which relates to a child or young person and which has been generated by a local authority social services department, an Area Child Protection Committee or other party contacted by an investigator during the investigation.

6.13   In exceptional circumstances, where an investigator considers that material is so sensitive that its revelation to the prosecutor by means of an entry on the sensitive schedule is inappropriate, the existence of the material must be revealed to the prosecutor separately. This will apply where compromising the material would be likely to lead directly to the loss of life, or directly threaten national security.

6.14   In such circumstances, the responsibility for informing the prosecutor lies with the investigator who knows the detail of the sensitive material. The investigator should act as soon as is reasonably practicable after the file containing the prosecution case is sent to the prosecutor. The investigator must also ensure that the prosecutor is able to inspect the material so that he can assess whether it needs to be brought before a court for a ruling on disclosure.

Revelation of material to prosecutor

7.1   The disclosure officer must give the schedules to the prosecutor. Wherever practicable this should be at the same time as he gives him the file containing the material for the prosecution case (or as soon as is reasonably practicable after the decision on mode of trial or the plea, in cases to which paragraph 6.8 applies).

7.2   The disclosure officer should draw the attention of the prosecutor to any material an investigator has retained (whether or not listed on a schedule) which may fall within the test for primary prosecution disclosure in the Act, and should explain why he has come to that view.

7.3   At the same time as complying with the duties in paragraphs 7.1 and 7.2, the disclosure officer must give the prosecutor a copy of any material which falls into the following categories (unless such material has already been given to the prosecutor as part of the file containing the material for the prosecution case):

— records of the first description of a suspect given to the police by a potential witness, whether or not the description differs from that of the alleged offender;

— information provided by an accused person which indicates an explanation for the offence with which he has been charged;

— any material casting doubt on the reliability of a confession;

— any material casting doubt on the reliability of a witness;

— any other material which the investigator believes may fall within the test for primary prosecution disclosure in the Act.

7.4   If the prosecutor asks to inspect material which has not already been copied to him, the disclosure officer must allow him to inspect it. If the prosecutor asks for a copy of material which has not already been copied to him, the disclosure officer must give him a copy. However, this does not apply where the disclosure officer believes, having consulted the officer in charge of the investigation, that the material is too sensitive to be copied and can only be inspected.

7.5   If material consists of information which is recorded other than in writing, whether it should be given to the prosecutor in its original form as a whole, or by way of relevant extracts recorded in the same form, or in the form of a transcript, is a matter for agreement between the disclosure officer and the prosecutor.

Subsequent action by disclosure officer

8.1   At the time a schedule of non-sensitive material is prepared, the disclosure officer may not know exactly what material will form the case against the accused, and the prosecutor may not have given advice about the likely relevance of particular items of material. Once these matters have been determined, the disclosure officer must give the prosecutor, where necessary, an amended schedule listing any additional material:

— which may be relevant to the investigation,
— which does not form part of the case against the accused,
— which is not already listed on the schedule, and
— which he believes is not sensitive,

unless he is informed in writing by the prosecutor that the prosecutor intends to disclose the material to the defence.

8.2   After a defence statement has been given, the disclosure officer must look again at the material which has been retained and must draw the attention of the prosecutor to any material which might reasonably be expected to assist the defence disclosed by the accused; and he must reveal it to him in accordance with paragraphs 7.4 and 7.5 above.

8.3   Section 9 of the Act imposes a continuing duty on the prosecutor, for the duration of criminal proceedings against the accused, to disclose material which meets the tests for disclosure (subject to public interest considerations). To enable him to do this, any new material coming to light should be treated in the same way as the earlier material.

Certification by disclosure officer

9.1   The disclosure officer must certify to the prosecutor that, to the best of his knowledge and belief, all material which has been retained and made available to him has been revealed to the prosecutor in accordance with this code. He must sign and date the certificate. It will be necessary to certify not only at the time when the schedule and accompanying material is submitted to the prosecutor, but also when material which has been retained is reconsidered after the accused has given a defence statement.

Disclosure of material to accused

10.1   If material has not already been copied to the prosecutor, and he requests its disclosure to the accused on the ground that:
— it falls within the test for primary or secondary prosecution disclosure, or
— the court has ordered its disclosure after considering an application from the accused,

the disclosure officer must disclose it to the accused.

10.2   If material has been copied to the prosecutor, and it is to be disclosed, whether it is disclosed by the prosecutor or the disclosure officer is a matter for agreement between the two of them.

10.3   The disclosure officer must disclose material to the accused either by giving him a copy or by allowing him to inspect it. If the accused person asks for a copy of any material which he has been allowed to inspect, the disclosure officer must give it to him, unless in the opinion of the disclosure officer that is either not practicable (for example because the material consists of an object which cannot be copied, or because the volume of material is so great), or not desirable (for example because the material is a statement by a child witness in relation to a sexual offence).

10.4   If material which the accused has been allowed to inspect consists of information which is recorded other than in writing, whether it should be given to the accused in its original form or in the form of a transcript is a matter for the discretion of the disclosure officer. If the material is transcribed, the disclosure officer must ensure that the transcript is certified to the accused as a true record of the material which has been transcribed.

10.5   If a court concludes that it is in the public interest that an item of sensitive material must be disclosed to the accused, it will be necessary to disclose the material if the case is to proceed. This does not mean that sensitive documents must always be disclosed in their original form: for example, the court may agree that sensitive details still requiring protection should be blocked out, or that documents may be summarised, or that the prosecutor may make an admission about the substance of the material under section 10 of the Criminal Justice Act 1967.

Appendix 4   Plea and Directions Hearing: Judge's Questionnaire

Plea and Directions Hearing	The Crown Court at
Judge's Questionnaire (In accordance with the practice rules issued by the Lord Chief Justice)	Case No T PTI URN R v
	Date of PDH
A copy of this questionnaire, completed as far as possible with the agreement of both advocates, is to be handed in to the court prior to the commencement of the Plea and Directions Hearing.	Name of Prosecution Advocate at PDH Name of Defence Advocate at PDH
1 a Are the actual/proposed not guilty pleas definitely to be maintained through to a jury trial?	Yes ☐ No ☐
b Has the defence advocate advised his client of section 48 of CJPOA 1994? (*Reductions in sentence for guilty pleas*)	Yes ☐ No ☐
c Will the prosecution accept part guilty or alternative pleas?	Yes ☐ No ☐

2	How long is the trial likely to take?	
3	What are the issues in the case?	
4	Issues as to the mental or medical condition of any defendant or witness.	
5	Prosecution witnesses whose evidence will be given. Can any statement be read instead of calling the witnesses?	To be read (number) [ ] To be called (number) [ ] Names:
6 a	Number of Defence witnesses whose evidence will be placed before the Court.	Defendant + [ ]
b	Any whose statements have been served which can be agreed and accepted in writing.	
7	Is the prosecution intending to serve any further evidence? If **Yes**, what area(s) will it cover? What are the witnesses' names?	Yes [ ] No [ ]

8	Facts which are admitted and can be reduced into writing. (s 10(2)(b) CJA 1967)	
9	Exhibits and schedules which are to be admitted.	
10	Is the order and pagination of the prosecution papers agreed?	
11	Any alibi which should have been disclosed in accordance with CJA 1967?	Yes ☐ No ☐
12 a	Any points of law likely to arise at trial?	
b	Any questions of admissibility of evidence together with any authorities it is intended to rely upon.	
13 a	Has the defence notified the prosecution of any issue arising out of the record of interview? (*Practice Direction (Crime: Tape Recording of Police Interview)* [1989] 1 WLR 631)	Yes ☐ No ☐
b	What efforts have been made to agree verbatim records or summaries and have they been successful?	

14	Any applications granted/pending for:	
	(i) evidence to be given through live television links?	Yes ☐ No ☐
	(ii) evidence to be given by pre-recorded video interviews with children?	Yes ☐ No ☐
	(iii) screens?	Yes ☐ No ☐
	(iv) the use of video equipment during the trial?	Yes ☐ No ☐
	(v) use of tape playback equipment?	Yes ☐ No ☐
15	Any other significant matter which might affect the proper and convenient trial of the case? (e.g. expert witnesses or other cases outstanding against the defendant)	
16	Any other work which needs to be done. Orders of the Court with time limits should be noted on page 4.	Prosecution
		Defence
17 a	Witness availability and approximate length of witness evidence.	Prosecution
		Defence
b	Can any witness attendance be staggered?	Yes ☐ No ☐
c	If Yes, have any arrangements been agreed?	Yes ☐ No ☐
18	Advocates' availability?	Prosecution
		Defence

Case listing arrangements

Name of Trial Judge:

Custody Cases *Fixed or warned list within 16 weeks of committal*

Fixed for trial on

Place in a warned list for trial   for week beginning

Further directions fixed for

Not fixed or put in warned list within
16 weeks because:

Bail Cases

Further directions fixed for

Fixed for trial on

Fixed as a floater/backer on

Place in a reserve/warned list   for week beginning
for trial

List officer to allocate   ☐ within   [   ] days/weeks

                                    ☐ before

Sentence

Adjourned for sentence on

(to follow trial of R v

Other directions, orders, comments

Signed: *Judge*   Date:

Appendix 5   *Imaginary Brief*

John Michael Smith has been charged with burglary from a sweet shop and, in the alternative, handling part of the proceeds of the burglary. He is to stand trial at Barchester Crown Court. The following pages represent the brief which might be sent to counsel instructed to defend Smith. The brief contains illustrations of some of the documents which have been referred to in the course of this book. In particular, it contains an indictment, statements tendered at commital proceedings under s 5B of the Magistrates' Courts Act 1980, a notice of particulars of alibi and a proof of evidence from the defendant.

IN THE BARCHESTER CROWN COURT

BETWEEN

REGINA

and

John Michael SMITH

BRIEF TO COUNSEL TO APPEAR
ON BEHALF OF THE DEFENDANT

In this matter Instructing Solicitors act on behalf of the Defendant who was committed for trial from the Barchester Magistrates' Court on July 9th 1999 on charges of burglary of a sweet shop situate at 123, High Street, Barchester, and in the alternative, handling 5 boxes of chocolates, part of the proceeds of the burglary. He will plead not guilty to both charges.

Basically the prosecution will allege that the Defendant, together with two persons unknown, went to the aforesaid premises, broke in through a back door, and stole a quantity of sweets and cigarettes. The Defendant's van, according to the prosecution, was used in committing the burglary, and they will call a Mr Charles Watchman to state that he saw the burglars making their 'getaway' in a van number XYZ 999Y. That is the number of the Defendant's van. The Defendant will state that he was not involved in any way in the burglary. Either the witness made a mistake about the number of the van he saw, or the burglars, whoever they were, took the van without the Defendant's consent and returned it to where it had been parked, so that the Defendant did not know it had been taken. Unfortunately, the Defendant signed notes taken of an interview at the police station in which he admitted driving two persons, whom he does not name, to 123 High Street. These two persons broke into the shop, according to the Defendant, while he drove around in the van. At a pre-arranged time the Defendant drove back to the rear entrance of the shop, where the van was loaded with the stolen goods and then driven away. The Defendant will say that he only made these admissions because the police said he would not get bail unless he did so, and he was anxious about his wife, who was expecting a baby at the time.

As to the chocolates, these were found in the Defendant's sideboard. Apparently chocolates of this brand were stolen in the course of the burglary. The Defendant states that he bought the chocolates on the Saturday before the alleged offence. He bought them from a stall-holder in Barchester Market who was selling them cheaply. Counsel is asked to consider whether there is a case to answer as regards handling the chocolates, as there does not seem to be any evidence that they were stolen. The prosecution may try to rely on *Fuschillo* [1940] 2 All ER 489, but instructing solicitors suggest that the Defendant's case is clearly distinguishable from that of *Fuschillo*.

At the time of the alleged burglary, the Defendant was in bed with his wife.

Counsel is asked to advise generally, in conference if so desired, to draft a Defence Statement and thereafter appear on behalf of the Defendant.

No 99/1123

INDICTMENT

The Crown Court at BARCHESTER
THE QUEEN v JOHN MICHAEL SMITH

JOHN MICHAEL SMITH is CHARGED AS FOLLOWS:—

Count 1

Statement of Offence
Burglary contrary to section 9(1)(b) of the Theft Act 1968.

Particulars of Offence
JOHN MICHAEL SMITH, on the 9th day of July 1999,
having entered as a trespasser a building known as 123 High
Street, Barchester, stole therein 100 packets of Coffanchoke
cigarettes, 100 packets of Coolsmoke cigarettes, 30 boxes of
chocolates and 20 boxes of chocolate liqueurs.

Count 2

Statement of Offence
Handling stolen goods, contrary to section 22(1) of the Theft
Act 1968.

Particulars of Offence
JOHN MICHAEL SMITH, on the 9th day of July 1999,
dishonestly received stolen goods, namely 5 boxes of chocolates belonging to Stewart Sweetman, knowing or believing
the same to be stolen goods.

A. N. Other

Date: 6 August 1999

Officer of the Crown Court

STATEMENT OF WITNESS
(C.J. Act 1967 s 9; M.C. Act 1980 ss 5A(3)(a) and 5B; M.C. Rules 1981 r 70)

Statement of: Stewart SWEETMAN
Age of Witness: Over 18
Occupation of Witness: Shop-owner

This statement consisting of 1 page, signed by me, is true to the best of my knowledge and belief and I make it knowing that, if it is tendered in evidence, I shall be liable to prosecution if I have wilfully stated in it anything which I know to be false or do not believe to be true.

Dated the 15th day of July 1999

Signed: S. Sweetman
Signature witnessed by: G. Regan

I am the owner of 'Sweet-tooth's', a tobacconist's and confectioner's of 123 High Street, Barchester. Last week, on the 8th July I think it was, I locked and made secure the premises of my shop before going home at about 6 p.m. The next morning, at about 8 a.m., I opened up the shop. As I went in I noticed the burglar alarm lying on the floor. There were no other signs of an intruder in the shop itself, but when I went through to my stockroom at the rear of the shop I noticed that the door to the yard was open and the lock had apparently been forced. I checked on my stock, and found that these items had been stolen

1 carton containing 100 packets of 'Coffanchoke' cigarettes, valued at £120 — I produce the invoice No 2468, Exhibit SS/1

1 carton containing 100 packets of 'Coolsmoke' filter cigarettes, valued at £130 — invoice No 987, Exhibit SS/2

1 case containing 30 boxes of 'Naughty but Nice' chocolates, valued at £60 — invoice No 2992, Exhibit SS/3

1 case containing 20 boxes of 'Flavourful' chocolate liqueurs, valued at £50 — invoice No 5665, Exhibit SS/4

I have been shown 5 boxes of 'Naughty but Nice' chocolates (Exhibit No GR/1). They are like the chocolates which were stolen from my shop but I cannot positively identify them. I can say that my shop is the only one in Barchester which sells this brand of chocolates. I cannot remember selling 5 boxes to any one customer — if I had done I would remember.

I did not give anyone permission to enter my shop or take any property. I am willing to attend court and give evidence. I wish to claim compensation for all the property stolen from me, and also for the cost of repairing the alarm and the back door, which I estimate will come to £100.

Signed: S. Sweetman   Signature witnessed by: G. Regan

STATEMENT OF WITNESS
(C.J. Act 1967 s 9; M.C. Act 1980 ss 5A(3)(a) and 5B; M.C. Rules 1981 r 70)

Statement of: Charles WATCHMAN
Age of Witness: Over 18
Occupation of Witness: Fireman

This statement consisting of 1 page signed by me, is true to the best of my knowledge and belief and I make it knowing that, if it is tendered in evidence, I shall be liable to prosecution if I have wilfully stated in it anything which I know to be false or do not believe to be true.

Dated the 15th day of July 1999

Signed: C. Watchman
Signature witnessed by: G. Regan

I live at the above address. Opposite my house are the back entrances of a row of shops which face on to the High Street. One of the shops is a sweet shop called 'Sweet-tooth's'. About a week ago I remember getting up at about 1.30 in the morning. I had to get up at that time as I am a fireman, and that week I was on the early morning shift, so I had to be at the fire-station at 2 a.m. As I was getting dressed I noticed the sound of an alarm coming from across the road. I did not worry about it as the alarms are always going off for no reason, but I thought it went on for rather a long time. Then it stopped, and I forgot about it. I had a cup of tea, and left the house at roughly 1.45. As I opened the front gate I noticed a small, dark coloured van parked about 20 yards down the road on the opposite side. It was parked just by the back entrance to 'Sweet-tooth's'. Two men seemed to be lifting something into the back of the van. Then one of the men climbed into the back of the van and the other got into the front passenger seat, and the van drove quickly off. When I first saw the van, I remembered the burglar alarm which had gone off earlier and that made me suspicious of what the men were doing. Just before the van drove off I was able to see clearly, in the light of a street lamp, what the number was. It was XYZ 999Y. I wrote the number down on the back of an envelope which I had in my pocket. I still have the envelope. Then I went back to my house and telephoned the police.

I am willing to attend court and give evidence.

The two men I saw seemed to be fairly young and above average height, but I would not be able to recognise them if I saw them again. It was dark and they had their backs to me.

Signed: C. Watchman   Signature witnessed by: G. Regan

STATEMENT OF WITNESS
(C.J. Act 1967 s 9; M.C. Act 1980 ss 5A(3)(a) and 5B; M.C. Rules 1981 r 70)

Statement of: Brian BEATMAN
Age of Witness: (Date of Birth) Over 18
Occupation of Witness: Police Constable

This statement, consisting of 1 page signed by me, is true to the best of my knowledge and belief and I make it knowing that, if it is tendered in evidence, I shall be liable to prosecution if I have wilfully stated in it anything which I know to be false or do not believe to be true.

Dated the 9th day of July 1999

Signed: B. Beatman
Signature witnessed by: J. Carter

On 9th July 1999 at 9 a.m. I attended at Barchester Fire Station where I saw a Mr Watchman who lives at 10, Cathedral Street. As a result of what he told me I wrote an index mark, XYZ 999Y, on a piece of paper. I later transferred this number to crime sheet 1234. I did a vehicle check, and the vehicle owner came back as a Mr John Michael SMITH of 50 Fiddlers Lane, Barchester.

Signed: B. Beatman   Signature witnessed by: J. Carter

STATEMENT OF WITNESS
(C.J. Act 1967 s 9; M.C. Act 1980 ss 5A(3)(a) and 5B; M.C. Rules 1981 r 70)

Statement of: George REGAN
Age of Witness: (Date of Birth) Over 18
Occupation of Witness: Detective Sergeant
Address and Telephone Number: Barchester Police Station
                                        1, Copper Street,
                                        Barchester

This statement, consisting of 2 pages, each signed by me, is true to the best of my knowledge and belief and I make it knowing that, if it is tendered in evidence, I shall be liable to prosecution if I have wilfully stated in it anything which I know to be false or do not believe to be true.

Dated the 9th day of July 1999

                               Signed: G. Regan
                               Signature witnessed by: J. Carter

On 9th July 1999 at about 10.30 a.m., in company with D.C. CARTER, I went to 50, Fiddlers Lane, Barchester where I saw John Michael SMITH. I told him we were police officers and showed him my warrant card. He invited us into his flat.

I said to him, 'I'm making enquiries into a burglary at a sweet shop and tobacconist's called ''Sweet-tooth's'' at 123, High Street, Barchester, which occurred last night. I believe you can help me with these enquiries.'

He said, 'I don't know what you're talking about.'

I said, 'Are you the owner of a van number XYZ 999Y?'

He said, 'Why are you asking?'

I said, 'Just answer the question please.'

He said, 'Well, I used to own it, but I sold it about a month ago, and I forgot to register the change of ownership.'

I said, 'Who did you sell it to?'

Before he could answer, the street door bell rang, and a woman I now know to be Mrs Janet SMITH walked into the room. In the presence and hearing of SMITH, I said to Mrs Smith, 'Does your husband own a van number XYZ 999Y?'

She said, 'Yes, I'm sure that's the number.'

I said, 'So he hasn't sold it recently.'

She said, 'No, of course not.'

Then SMITH said, 'All right, then, I do still own the van but I had nothing to do with the burglary you're asking about.'

Signed: G. Regan   Signature witnessed by: J. Carter

I said, 'That van was used in commission of the burglary, and I am arresting you on suspicion of being involved in the offence.' I cautioned him and he said 'It's got nothing to do with me.'

I said, 'Before we go to the police station, I am going to search the flat for any proceeds of the burglary.' In the sideboard in the back room I found 5 boxes of 'Naughty but Nice' chocolates (Exhibit GR/1). I said to SMITH, 'Where did you get these chocolates from? Chocolates like these were stolen in the burglary.'

He said, 'I'm not saying nothing until I've seen a solicitor. I know my rights.'

He was then taken to Barchester Police Station.

Later I interviewed SMITH at the police station in company with D.C. CARTER. D.C. CARTER made a contemporaneous note of the interview. At the conclusion of the interview the record of the interview was read through to SMITH by D.C. CARTER, and SMITH signed each page as being a correct record. The interview commenced at 1 p.m. and concluded at 1.30 p.m. It was tape recorded.

On 9th July 1999 at 2 p.m., SMITH was charged, the charge read over and cautioned and he made no reply.

Signed: G. Regan   **Signature witnessed by:** J. Carter

[There is also a statement from D.C. CARTER (not reproduced here) which is identical in all material respects to D.S. REGAN'S statement. As CARTER recorded the interview with SMITH it is he who formally produces the record of interview as exhibit 'JC/1' and a summary of it as 'JC/2'.]

BARSETSHIRE CONSTABULARY
RECORD OF TAPE RECORDED INTERVIEW

Person interviewed	John Michael SMITH		
Place of interview	Barchester Police Station		
Date of interview	9.7.99		
Time commenced	1300 hrs	**Time concluded**	1330 hours
Duration of interview	30 mins	**Tape Reference No**	12980
Interviewing Officer	DS Regan (J543)		
Other persons present	DC Carter (J876)		

Tape counter times	Person speaking	Text
001		INTRODUCTION TO INTERVIEW. CAUTION. OPTIONS UNDER PACE 1984 EXPLAINED
025		SMITH confirms he is willing to be interviewed without a solicitor.
0100	REGAN	I am going to ask you questions about your involvement in a burglary which occurred in the early hours of this morning at a shop called 'Sweet-tooth's' in Barchester High Street. Do you own a van number XYZ 999Y?
0175	SMITH	Yes.
	REGAN	Why did you say, when I asked you at your home, that you had sold the van?
	SMITH	Because you said that I was suspected of burglary.
0215	REGAN	But I had not said that the van was anything to do with the burglary. What made you think that the van might have been used in the burglary if you had nothing to do with it?
	SMITH	Well, I just sort of guessed. The van must have been used else you wouldn't have asked about it.
0280	REGAN	So, where was your van last night.
	SMITH	Parked outside my house.
	REGAN	But I have a witness who lives at the back of 'Sweet-tooth's' who says that he saw your van at 1.30 this morning being loaded up with packages by two men and then driven away by a third man from Sweet-tooth's'. What do you say to that?

Tape counter times	Person speaking	Text
0360	SMITH	He must have made a mistake with the number, or perhaps somebody nicked the van.
	REGAN	When you went to the van this morning, had it been moved?
	SMITH	Not that I could see.
0400	REGAN	So, if it had been taken without your knowledge, the thieves had obligingly put it back in precisely the position it had been taken from. Did you leave the van locked last night?
	SMITH	I think so.
	REGAN	Was there any sign this morning that it had been broken into?
0450	SMITH	I didn't notice anything.
	REGAN	So there is no reason whatsoever to think that the van was taken without your knowledge?
		No answer
	REGAN	What about the 5 boxes of chocolates we found at your house? Boxes like those were stolen in the burglary at 'Sweet-tooth's'.
	SMITH	So what, I expect you can buy them in lots of places.
0500	REGAN	Where do you say you got them from?
	SMITH	[After a pause] Off a stall down Barchester market last Saturday.
	REGAN	Why did you want 5 boxes? That's a lot to buy isn't it?
	SMITH	They were cheap. Why shouldn't I buy 5 boxes?
0575	REGAN	So what you are saying, John, is that either a mistake was made about the number of the van (even though the number the witness got matches the type of vehicle he described), or somebody unknown nicked your van and used it to commit a burglary without your knowledge. Then you tell us a lie about having sold the van, even though we hadn't even told you that the van was used in the burglary. And when we search your flat we find that chocolates like those stolen in the burglary are in your sideboard, but you say you bought them. If you weren't the driver of the van used in the burglary then a lot of strange coincidences link you to the crime. Why don't you think it over for a moment or two? [SMITH was silent for about a minute]

Tape counter times	Person speaking	Text
0715	SMITH	All right, I may as well tell you the truth. Last night I saw two mates in the pub. They said that there was a shop they could break into easy as falling off a log but they needed wheels to take the stuff away. I said, 'Why not nick a car?' They said they did not want to take the risk, and nobody would see my van so long as we were quick. They kept on pestering me, and eventually I said that I would drive for them. So, soon after midnight last night, I drove them to the back of this shop in the High Street and left them there. I then drove around for about ten minutes — I was nothing to do with the actual break in. Then I came back, sat in the van while they loaded it up with what they had nicked, and drove us away. We unloaded the cigarettes and sweets and stuff at a lock up garage. They said I would get my share once they had sold the goods. I asked if I could have some of the chocolates as they looked nice and I could give them to people for birthday presents. They said all right, which is how you came to find them in the sideboard.
0920	REGAN	So who are the two men you say you met in the pub?
	SMITH	I'm no grass. I've told you my part in it but you aren't getting any names out of me.
	REGAN	Is there anything else you want to say about this matter?
	SMITH	No, that's about everything.

INTERVIEW CONCLUDED 1330 HOURS

JOHN MICHAEL SMITH
50, Fiddlers Lane,
Barchester.   d.o.b. 1 May 1973

will say[1]
I have been charged with burglary and handling stolen goods and intend to plead not guilty to both charges.
The facts of the matter are as follows.

On July 8th 1999 I came home from work at about 6pm, and parked my van outside my flat as I usually do. I then had my dinner, and spent the evening watching television with my wife — I remember that the tennis was on in the early part of the evening. We went to bed at about 11pm, and got up at about 9am the next morning, which was a Wednesday. At no time during the night did I leave the house. My wife can confirm this because if I had done so I would have woken her up. I know nothing about the burglary.

Turning to the statements of the prosecution witnesses. It is true that when D.S. Regan asked me if I owned the van, I panicked, and said that I had sold it. It was a stupid thing to do, but I thought that he would never believe me if I just said I had nothing to do with the burglary. About the chocolates, I bought them from a stall in Barchester Market on the Saturday before all this happened. The man was selling them cheaply, and that is why I bought five boxes. I told the police that when they found the chocolates. It is not true that I said 'I'm not saying nothing until I've seen my solicitor'.

At the police station I was left for about an hour in a cell. I was getting very worried about my wife, because she was pregnant, and I knew she would be anxious about me. When the police questioned me in the interview room, I asked them when I could go home because I had to see my wife. They said I could go as soon as I told them everything that had happened. I thought that things looked so bad anyway that I might as well say anything they wanted me to say. The admissions I made at the end of my interview were not true. I only made them so as to get bail.

I work on the production line at 'Wellmade Engineering Works'. My normal take-home pay is about £160 per week, but I am presently on short time, so I only take home £95. I have several previous convictions, but since marrying in December last year I have settled down and gone straight. Two weeks ago my wife gave birth to a baby boy.

Signed: John Smith

---

[1] Note that John's Smith's proof of evidence will be in the possession of the defence, but not the court or the prosecution.

PREVIOUS CONVICTIONS

Convictions Recorded Against: John Michael SMITH   C.R.O. No 98765/89
Charged in name of   John Michael SMITH

DATE	COURT	OFFENCES	SENTENCE	DATE OF RELEASE
8.10.89	Barchester Juvenile Court	Theft of a pedal cycle, value £30	Conditional discharge for 12 months	
25.11.89	Barchester Juvenile Court	(1) Burglary, (2) Criminal Damage (two cases t.i.c.)	Supervision Order for 2 years	
7.6.91	Fulchester Magistrates' Court	(1) and (2) Taking away m/v without lawful authority (3) and (4) Driving under age	3 months' detention in young offender institution (YO1)	2.8.91
1.12.92	Casterbridge Crown Court	(1) Robbery (2) Taking away m/v without lawful authority (3) No insurance (4 cases t.i.c.)	12 months' detention in Y01 On (2) and (3) l/e disqual. from driving for 12 months	1.7.93
24.12.95	Barchester Crown Court	(1) Assault occasioning ABH (2) Criminal Damage	2 years' probation on each	
15.10.97	Barchester Crown Court	(1) Burglary (2) Handling stolen goods	(1) 12 months' imprisonment (2) 6 months concurrent with (1) 6 months' imprisonment for concurrent ABH and criminal damage [the original offences for which SMITH was put on probation on 24.12.95].	15.4.98

NOTE ON CONTENTS OF THE BRIEF

In addition to the documents contained in this imaginary brief, there would, in real life, be a further witness statement from D.C. Carter, who accompanied D.S. Regan throughout his investigations. For all practical purposes, D.C. Carter's statement will be identical to Regan's. This is because both officers will have prepared their statements from notes written in their note-books soon after the conclusion of the interview with Smith. It is normal police practice for officers to confer together when writing their notes, and arrive at an agreed version of what took place. Since the statements repeat what is in the notes, they, like the notes, will be identical.

Defence solicitors, in addition to taking a statement from the accused, will have taken a statement from Mrs Smith confirming that on the night in question her husband did not leave the house. They may also have made efforts to trace the person who sold the accused the five boxes of chocolates.

Appendix 6   Trial Procedure in Outline

This Appendix sets out, in list form, the usual sequence of events which occur during a trial first in the magistrates' and then in the Crown Court. It is intended as an instant guide to and reminder of what has been described at length in the preceding pages.

A   SUMMARY TRIAL FOR AN OFFENCE TRIABLE EITHER WAY

1   The charge is read to the accused.

2   The clerk explains that the accused may indicate whether he would plead guilty if the case proceeded to trial. The clerk should further explain that, if the accused pleads guilty, the proceedings will be treated as a summary trial at which a guilty plea has been tendered. The clerk must also explain that the accused will be committed to the Crown Court for sentence if the magistrates regard their powers of punishment as inadequate.

3   The clerk asks the accused if he pleads guilty or not guilty.

4   If the accused has indicated a plea of guilty, then the court proceeds to sentence as if he had pleaded guilty at summary trial. If, on the other hand, the accused indicated a plea of not guilty, then the court proceeds to determine the mode of trial, as follows.

5   The prosecution and defence are asked if they have any representations to make as to the more appropriate method of trial.

6   The magistrates decide which, in their view, is the more appropriate method. If they are in favour of summary trial, the clerk warns the accused of the possibility of being summarily convicted and committed for sentence, and then asks him where he wants to be tried. If the accused agrees to summary trial, the case proceeds as in *7*. If the accused does not consent to summary trial (or the magistrates thought that trial on indictment was more appropriate) the case will be set down for committal to the Crown Court.

7   The clerk puts the information to the accused. If he pleads guilty, the prosecutor summarises the facts of the offence, and then the case proceeds as at *13* below.

8   If the accused pleads not guilty, the prosecutor makes an opening speech.

9   The prosecutor calls his witnesses to give oral evidence and/or reads out written statements copies of which were served on the defence under Criminal Justice Act 1967, s 9, and not objected to within seven days.

10   Defence counsel may, if he wishes, submit that there is no case to answer. The prosecutor replies. If the submission succeeds, the accused is acquitted.

11   Whether or not he made a submission of no case, defence counsel may, if he wishes, call evidence from the accused and/or witnesses on his behalf. He may also read out written statements by virtue of s 9 of the Criminal Justice Act 1967 (see *9*).

12   Defence counsel makes a closing speech.

13   The magistrates consider their verdict. If they convict the accused, they hear about his antecedents and character from the CPS representative. They may then adjourn for reports under MCA, s 10(3) (general power to adjourn for reports prior to sentencing), or under MCA, s 30 (power to adjourn for medical reports). The maximum period of the adjournment is three weeks in custody, four weeks on bail.

14   The magistrates read any reports on the accused, and defence counsel presents mitigation. If he wishes, he may call character evidence prior to mitigating.

15   The magistrates pass sentence (or commit for sentence under MCA, s 38).

Notes

(a)   If the offence charged is one of criminal damage, the magistrates assess the value of the property involved in the offence before asking for representations as to the more appropriate method of trial. If the value involved is clearly £5,000 or less they proceed as if the offence were triable only summarily (see Paragraph 7.4).

(b)   The defence need not be represented at a summary trial. If they are represented, either counsel or solicitor may appear. If the accused is unrepresented he may conduct cross-examination, make speeches etc. on his own behalf.

(c)   The court may give either party leave to make a second speech, but if a second speech is granted to one party it must be granted to the other as well. A second speech for the prosecution is made before the second speech for the defence.

B   TRIAL ON INDICTMENT

1   The clerk puts the indictment to the accused. If he pleads guilty, prosecuting counsel summarises the facts of the offence, and then the case proceeds as at *14* below.

2   If the accused pleads not guilty, the prosecution may offer no evidence (in which case the judge directs a verdict of not guilty to be recorded), or ask the judge to leave the indictment on the court file marked not to be proceeded with without leave. Otherwise the case proceeds as in *3* below.

3   A jury is empanelled.

4   The clerk puts the accused into the jury's charge.

5   Prosecuting counsel makes his opening speech to the jury.

6   Prosecuting counsel calls his witnesses to give oral evidence and/or reads written statements as evidence.

7   Defence counsel may, in the absence of the jury, submit to the judge that there is no case to answer. If the submission succeeds, the judge directs the jury to acquit.

8   Defence counsel makes his opening speech to the jury (but only if he is calling evidence as to the facts of the alleged offence apart from the evidence of the accused).

9   Defence counsel may, if he wishes, call the accused as a witness.

10   Whether or not he called the accused, defence counsel may call other witnesses to testify about the facts of the alleged offence and/or the character of the accused.

11   Prosecuting counsel makes his closing speech to the jury.

12   Defence counsel makes his closing speech.

13   The judge sums up the case to the jury, and tells them to retire and seek to reach a unanimous verdict. If a period of at least 2 hours and 10 minutes has elapsed since the jury retired to consider their verdict, the judge may direct them that he will accept a majority verdict.

14 If the jury find the accused guilty (whether unanimously or by a majority) a police officer gives character and antecedents evidence about him. If necessary, the judge adjourns for reports, and remands the accused in custody or on bail for the period of the adjournment.
15 The judge reads the reports on the accused, listens to any character witnesses defence counsel wishes to call, listens to defence counsel's mitigation, and passes sentence.

Notes

(a) The accused need not be legally represented. If he is not, he conducts the cross-examination, makes speeches etc. on his own behalf. If he does not have the right to make an opening speech (and he is unrepresented) prosecuting counsel loses the right to make a closing speech.

(b) If the defendant is represented, the prosecution has a statutory right to make a closing speech, but in practice should not exercise it if the defendant does not give or call evidence.

(c) If there are two or more accused separately represented, and each pleads not guilty, their defences are presented in the order in which their names appear on the indictment, i.e. A1's counsel makes an opening speech to the jury, calls A1 and calls X on behalf of A1; A2's counsel makes an opening speech to the jury, calls A2 and calls Y on behalf of A2, and so forth. If A1 and A2 are jointly represented, counsel makes a single opening speech, calls A1, calls A2 and then calls their witnesses.

(d) Where there are two or more defendants separately represented, each may cross-examine prosecution witnesses, in the order in which they appear on the indictment. When it comes to the defence case, A1's witness is cross-examined by A2 first, and then by the prosecution; A2's witness is cross-examined by A1 first, and then by the prosecution, and so on.

(e) If there are two accused, and one pleads guilty and the other not guilty, the probability is that the former will not be sentenced until after the end of the trial of the latter.

(f) Where there is a submission of no case to answer, the judge, before upholding it, would call on prosecuting counsel to present his counter-arguments, as with submissions of no case at committal proceedings and at summary trial.

Appendix 7   Internet Sites

There are many sites which provide information for practitioners and students on various aspects of criminal procedure and sentencing. The short list which follows is a selection of those available. These sites were last accessed on 1 August 2002.

Butterworths Direct

www.butterworths.co.uk

This subscription service includes Crime Online, with commentaries on recent cases by the authors of *Blackstone's Criminal Practice*. It also provides access to All England (Direct) Reports, which carry up-to-the-minute reports of criminal cases.

Criminal Cases Review Commission

www.ccrc.gov.uk

This site gives information on the work carried out by this increasingly important body.

Crown Prosecution Service

www.cps.gov.uk

Provides free access to research material, including reports of the Crown Prosecution Service (a valuable source of statistics).

Delia Venables Legal Resources Pages

www.venables.co.uk/

A comprehensive free site providing links to many sites in this country, and worldwide.

European Court of Human Rights

www.echr.coe.int/

This free site contains general information, judgments, lists of pending cases, rules of procedure, and provides a link to **HUDOC**, the searchable data-base for Strasbourg case law at www.echr.coe.int/hudoc.htm. This allows searches to be made through name, application number, Article, country, key words and manner of disposal.

HMSO

www.hmso.gov.uk/

Free access to the texts of statutes after 1996, available within 24 hours of publication in paper form. Note that what you will see is the original text of the Act in question, without any amendments passed subsequent to its passage. It also carries statutory instruments since 1997. Some explanatory notes are also available.

Home Office

www.homeoffice.gov.uk

This free site includes the text of publications, research material, and useful introductory guides to recent and pending legislation.

Law Commission

www.lawcom.gov.uk

This includes free details of proposed reforms, law currently under review, and the text of recent publications.

Lawlinks

www.ukc.ac.uk/library/lawlinks/default.htm

A comprehensive site providing free links to many sites in this country and internationally.

Lord Chancellor's Department

www.lcd.gov.uk

Free access to consultation papers and documents relating to legal aid, the operation of the criminal courts and human rights.

Official Documents

www.official-documents.co.uk

Free access to the text of selected White Papers, Green Papers and House of Commons Papers.

The Times

www.timesonline.co.uk/

If you know the date of a Times law report, you can obtain access to it from this site. Click on **Law** and then click on **Law Reports**.

UK Parliament

www.parliament.uk/

This free site includes the House of Commons Hansard from October 1996, the House of Lords Hansard from June 1996 and the text of Bills currently before Parliament.

Appendix 8 Review of the Criminal Courts of England and Wales (The Auld Report)

SUMMARY AND RECOMMENDATIONS
(EDITED EXTRACTS)

. . .

The criminal justice system

2. The criminal law should be codified under the general oversight of a new **Criminal Justice Council** and by or with the support as necessary of the Law Commission. There should be codes of offences, procedure, evidence and sentencing . . .

3. A national **Criminal Justice Board** should replace all the existing national planning and 'operational' bodies, including the Strategic Planning Group, and the Trial Issues Group. The new Board should be the means by which the criminal justice departments and agencies provide over-all direction of the criminal justice system. It should have an independent chairman and include senior departmental representatives and chief executives of the main criminal justice agencies (including the Youth Justice Board) and a small number of non-executive members. At local level, **Local Criminal Justice Boards** should be responsible for giving effect to the national Board's directions and objectives and for management of the criminal justice system in their areas. Both the national and local Boards should be supported by a centrally managed secretariat and should consult regularly with the judiciary. The national Board should be responsible for introducing an integrated technology system for the whole of the criminal justice system based upon a common language and common electronic case files, the implementation and maintenance of which should be the task of a **Criminal Case Management Agency** accountable to the Board.

4. A **Criminal Justice Council**, chaired by the Lord Chief Justice or senior Lord Justice of Appeal, should be established to replace existing advisory and consultative bodies, including the Criminal Justice Consultative Council and the Area Strategy Committees. It should have a statutory power and duty to keep the criminal justice system under review, to advise the Government on all proposed reforms, to make proposals for reform and to exercise general oversight of codification of the criminal law. The Council should be supported by a properly resourced secretariat and research staff.

A unified Criminal Court

5.   The Crown Court and magistrates' courts should be replaced by a unified Criminal Court consisting of three Divisions: the Crown Division, constituted as the Crown Court now is, to exercise jurisdiction over all indictable-only matters and the more serious 'either-way' offences allocated to it; the District Division, constituted by a judge, normally a District Judge or Recorder, and at least two magistrates, to exercise jurisdiction over a mid range of 'either-way' matters of sufficient seriousness to merit up to two years' custody; and the Magistrates' Division, constituted by a District Judge or magistrates, as magistrates' courts now are, to exercise their present jurisdiction over all summary matters and the less serious 'either-way' cases allocated to them. The courts, that is those of the Magistrates' Division, would allocate all 'either-way' cases according to the seriousness of the alleged offence and the circumstances of the defendant, looking at the possible outcome of the case at its worst from the point of view of the defendant and bearing in mind the jurisdiction of each division. In the event of a dispute as to venue, a District Judge would determine the matter after hearing representations from the prosecution and the defendant. The defendant would have no right of election to be tried in any division. (In the event of the present court structure continuing, the defendant should lose his present elective right to trial by jury in 'either-way' cases; see paragraph 10 below.)

6.   Whether or not the Crown Court and magistrates' courts are replaced with a unified Criminal Court, there should be a single centrally funded executive agency as part of the Lord Chancellor's Department responsible for the administration of all courts, civil, criminal and family (save for the Appellate Committee of the House of Lords), replacing the present Court Service and the Magistrates' Courts' Committees. For the foreseeable future, circuit boundaries and administrations should remain broadly as they are and the courts should be locally managed within the circuits and the 42 criminal justice areas. Justices' clerks and legal advisers responsible to them should continue to be responsible for the legal advice provided to magistrates.

Magistrates

7.   Magistrates and District Judges should continue to exercise their established summary jurisdiction and the work should continue to be allocated between them much as at present. If my recommendation for the establishment of a new unified Criminal Court with a District Division is adopted, they should also sit together in that division exercising its higher jurisdiction. I do not recommend any further extension of justices' clerks' case management jurisdiction. Steps should be taken to provide benches of magistrates that more broadly reflect the communities they serve. In order to strengthen the training of magistrates, the Judicial Studies Board should be made responsible, and be adequately resourced, for devising and securing the content and manner of their training.

Juries

8.   Jurors should be more widely representative than they are of the national and local communities from which they are drawn. Qualification for jury service should remain the same, save that entitlement to, rather than actual, entry on an electoral roll should be a criterion. Potential jurors should be identified from a combination of a number of public

registers and lists. While those with criminal convictions and mental disorder should continue to be disqualified from service, no one in future should be ineligible for or excusable as of right from it. Any claimed inability to serve should be a matter for discretionary deferral or excusal. Provision should be made to enable ethnic minority representation on juries where race is likely to be relevant to an important issue in the case.

9.   The law should not be amended to permit more intrusive research than is already possible into the workings of juries, though in appropriate cases trial judges and/or the Court of Appeal should be entitled to examine alleged improprieties in the jury room. The law should be declared, by statute if need be, that juries have no right to acquit defendants in defiance of the law or in disregard of the evidence.

10.   The defendant should no longer have an elective right to trial by judge and jury in 'either-way' cases. The allocation should be the responsibility of the magistrates' court alone and exercisable where there is an issue as to venue by a District Judge. The procedures of committal for trial and for sentence in 'either-way' cases should be abolished. Under my recommendation for a unified Criminal Court with three divisions, matters too serious for the Magistrates' Division would go direct either to the District or Crown Division depending on their seriousness In the meantime 'either-way' cases for the Crown Court should be 'sent' there in the same way as indictable-only cases. Trial by judge and jury should remain the main form of trial of the more serious offences triable on indictment, that is, those that would go to the Crown Division, subject to four exceptions. First, defendants in the Crown Court or, if my recommendation for a unified Court with three divisions is accepted, in the Crown and District Divisions, should be entitled with the court's consent to opt for trial by judge alone. Second, in serious and complex frauds the nominated trial judge should have the power to direct trial by himself and two lay members drawn from a panel established by the Lord Chancellor for the purpose (or, if the defendant requests, by himself alone). Third, a youth court, constituted by a judge of an appropriate level and at least two experienced youth panel magistrates, should be given jurisdiction to hear all grave cases against young defendants unless the charges are inseparably linked to those against adults. Fourth, legislation should be introduced to require a judge, not a jury, to determine the issue of fitness to plead.

The Judiciary

11.   The current hierarchy of judges and their jurisdictions should continue, subject to my recommendations for the establishment of a District Division of a new unified Criminal Court and extension of the powers of District Judges and magistrates when sitting in it. Systems of judicial management and deployment should he strengthened and also made more flexible to enable a better match of High Court and Circuit Judges to criminal cases, proper regard also being given to the arrangements for civil and family justice. In particular, there should be a significant shift in heavy work from High Court Judges to the Circuit Bench, coupled with greater flexibility in the system for allocating work between them. Save in the case of Circuit Presiding Judges, the present rigid circuiteering pattern of High Court Judges should be replaced by one in which they travel out to hear only the most serious of cases. In implementing the recent recommendations for reforms in the system of appointing judges, the Lord Chancellor's Department should exercise vigilance to root out any indirect discrimination, hurry forward the substitution of assessment exercises for short interviews

and establish and publish a clear policy for the appointment of disabled persons to judicial office. There should be a strengthening in the training provided to judges, appropriately enlarging the Judicial Studies Board's role for the purpose. There should be a system of appraisal for all part-time judges, and consideration should be given to the appraisal of full-time judges.

Decriminalisation and alternatives to conventional trial

12. I have found little scope or justification for decriminalisation of conduct that Parliament has made subject to penal sanctions. There should, however, be greater use of a system of fixed penalty notices subject to a right of challenge in court, for example for television licence evasion and the existing provisions for road traffic offences. There is no compelling case at present for the creation of any specialist courts, in particular, drugs or domestic violence courts. Consideration should be given to the wider use of conditional cautioning or 'caution-plus' alongside existing and future restorative justice schemes, for which a national strategy should be devised. Once the Financial Services Authority has assumed full responsibility for supervision in the financial services field, consideration should be given to transferring appropriate financial and market infringements from the criminal justice process to the Authority's regulatory and disciplinary control. Consideration should also be given in this field for combining parallel criminal and regulatory proceedings. Preparatory work should be undertaken with a view to removal of all civil debt enforcement from courts exercising a criminal jurisdiction.

Preparing for trial

13. The key to better preparation for, and efficient and effective disposal of, criminal cases is early identification of the issues. Four essentials are: strong and independent prosecutors; efficient and properly paid defence lawyers; ready access by defence lawyers to their clients in custody; and a modern communications system. All public prosecutions should take the form of a charge, issued without reference to the courts but for which the prosecutor in all but minor, routine or urgent cases, would have initial responsibility. It should remain the basis of the case against a defendant regardless of the court which ultimately deals with his case, thus replacing the present mix of charges, summonses and indictments. A graduated scheme of sentencing discounts should be introduced so that the earlier the plea of guilty the higher the discount for it. This should he coupled with a system of advance indication of sentence for a defendant considering pleading guilty.

14. The scheme of mutual disclosure established by the Criminal Procedure and Investigations Act 1996 should remain, but subject to the following reforms: its expression in a single and simply expressed instrument; a single and simple test of materiality for both stages of prosecution disclosure; automatic prosecution disclosure of certain documents; removal from the police to the prosecutor of such responsibility as the police have for identifying all potentially disclosable material; and encouragement, through professional conduct rules and otherwise, of the provision of adequate defence statements. There should be a new statutory scheme for third party disclosure and for instruction by the court of special independent counsel in public interest immunity cases where the court considers prosecution applications in the absence of the defendant.

15. In the preparation for trial in all criminal courts, there should be a move away from plea and directions hearings and other forms of pre-trial hearings to cooperation between the parties according to standard time-tables, wherever necessary, seeking written directions from the court. In the Crown and District Divisions and, where necessary, in the Magistrates' Division, there should then be a written or electronic 'pre-trial assessment' by the court of the parties' readiness for trial. Only if the court or the parties are unable to resolve all matters in this way should there be a pre-trial hearing before or at the stage of the pre-trial assessment. The courts should have a general power to give binding directions and rulings either in writing or at pre-trial hearings. In the Crown and District Divisions and, where necessary, in the Magistrates' Division, following the pre-trial assessment and in good time before hearing, the parties should prepare, for the approval of the judge and use by him, them, and the jury in the hearing, a written case and issues summary setting out in brief the substances of charge(s) and the issues to be resolved by the court.

The trial: procedures and evidence

16. In trials by judge and jury, the judge, by reference to the case and issues summary, copies of which should be provided to the jury, should give them a fuller introduction to the case than is now conventional. The trial should broadly take the same form as at present, though with greater use of electronic aids in appropriate cases. The judge should sum up and direct the jury, making reference as appropriate to the case and issues summary. So far as possible, he should 'filter out' the law and fashion factual questions to the issues and the law as he knows it to be. Where he considers it appropriate, he should require the jury publicly to answer each of the questions and to declare a verdict in accordance with those answers.

17. In trials by judge and magistrates in the District Division, the judge should be the sole judge of law, but he and the magistrates should together be the judges of fact, each having an equal vote. The order of proceedings would be broadly the same as, in the Crown Division. The judge should rule on matters of law, procedure and inadmissibility of evidence in the absence of the magistrates where it would be potentially unfair to the defendant to do so in their presence. The judge should not sum up the case to the magistrates, but should retire with them to consider the court's decision, which he would give and publicly reason as a judgment of the court. The judge should be solely responsible for sentence.

18. There should be a comprehensive review of the law of criminal evidence to identify and establish over-all and coherent principles and to make it an efficient and simple agent for securing justice. Subject to such review, I consider that the law should, in general, move away from technical rules of inadmissibility to trusting judicial and lay fact finders to give relevant evidence the weight it deserves. In particular, consideration should be given to the reform of the rules as to refreshing memory, the use of witness statements, hearsay, unfair evidence, previous misconduct of the defendant, similar fact evidence and the evidence of children. There should be reforms to strengthen the quality and objectivity of expert evidence and improve the manner of its presentation both from the point of view of the court and experts, following in some respects reforms made in the civil sphere by the Civil Procedure Rules. Urgent steps should be taken to increase the numbers and strengthen the quality of interpreters serving the criminal courts and to improve their working conditions. There are a number of ways in which the facilities and procedures of the courts should or

could be modernised and better serve the public. The criminal courts should be equipped with an on-line sentencing information system.

Appeals

19.   There should be the same tests for appeal against conviction and sentence respectively at all levels of appeal, namely those applicable for appeal to the Court of Appeal. There should be a single line of appeal from the Magistrates' Division (Magistrates' Courts) and above to the Court of Appeal in all criminal matters. This would involve: 1) abolition of appeal from magistrates' courts to the Crown Court by way of rehearing and its replacement by an appeal to the Crown Division (Crown Court) constituted by a judge alone; and 2) abolition of appeal from magistrates' courts and/or the Crown Court to the High Court by way of a case stated or claim for judicial review and their replacement by appeal to the Court of Appeal under its general appellate jurisdiction enlarged if and to the extent necessary.

20.   I support the general thrust of the Law Commission's recommendations for the introduction of statutory exceptions to the double jeopardy rule, save that a prosecutor's right of appeal against acquittal should not be limited to cases of murder and allied offences, but should extend to other grave offences punishable with life or long terms of imprisonment. There should be provision for appeal by the defence or the prosecution against a special verdict of a jury which on its terms is perverse; see para 16 above.

21.   The Court of Appeal should be reconstituted and its procedures should be improved to enable it to deal more efficiently with, on the one hand appeals involving matters of general public importance or of particular complexity and, on the other, with 'straightforward' appeals. The law should be amended: to widen the remit of the Sentencing Advisory Panel to include general principles of sentencing, regardless of the category of offence; and to enable the Court of Appeal to issue guidelines without having to tie them to a specific appeal before it.

Index